C000242057

THE
STOCK
MARKET

50 Years of
Capitalism at Work

✳

JOHN LITTLEWOOD

FINANCIAL TIMES
PITMAN PUBLISHING

FINANCIAL TIMES
MANAGEMENT

LONDON · SAN FRANCISCO
KUALA LUMPUR · JOHANNESBURG

*Financial Times Management delivers the knowledge,
skills and understanding that enable students,
managers and organisations to achieve their ambitions,
whatever their needs, wherever they are.*

London Office:
128 Long Acre, London WC2E 9AN
Tel: +44 (0)171 447 2000
Fax: +44 (0)171 240 5771
Website: www.ftmanagement.com

A Division of Financial Times Professional Limited

First published in Great Britain 1998

ISBN 0 273 63872 6

British Library Cataloguing in Publication Data
A CIP catalogue record for this book can be obtained
from the British Library.

1 3 5 7 9 10 8 6 4 2

Typeset by M Rules
Printed and bound in Great Britain by Biddles Ltd, Guildford & King's Lynn

*The Publishers' policy is to use paper manufactured
from sustainable forests.*

ABOUT THE AUTHOR

In 1959, John Littlewood joined a medium-sized firm of stockbrokers, Read Hurst-Brown, as a graduate trainee from New College, Oxford, where he read law. He trained as an investment analyst in a specialised sector of the market and became a partner in 1964.

In 1975, Read Hurst-Brown merged into Rowe & Pitman where his partnership responsibilities widened to research overall. In 1981, after 22 years as an investment analyst and institutional stockbroker, he assumed responsibility for the internal management of the firm as Administration Partner.

Throughout his stockbroking career he was closely involved with the Society of Investment Analysts where he was a Council Member for several years. He was later elected a Fellow of the Society, now known as the Institute of Investment Management and Reasearch (IIMR).

In 1985, as part of Big Bang, Rowe & Pitman merged with Mercury Securities, Ackroyd & Smithers and Mullens, to form S. G. Warburg Group, where he was appointed a Group Director and Member of the Chairman's Committee until his retirement in 1991.

His City career has involved investment analysis, combined with active participation at a senior level in one of the leading firms of stockbrokers and one of the leading investment banks. He has drawn upon that experience in writing this book.

To the memory of
Denis 'Ham' Martin

CONTENTS

....

Part I
THE STOCK MARKET IN 1945 AND THE
ATTLEE LABOUR GOVERNMENT
1945–51

Part II
THIRTEEN CONSERVATIVE YEARS
1951–64

Part III
INFLATIONARY YEARS
1964–79

Part IV
THE THATCHER YEARS
1979–90

FOREWORD

....

John Littlewood has written a remarkable book. It is a historical and analyti-
cal account of the London stock market since the war, and is the first
comprehensive book on the subject. It runs from 1945 to 1990, thus covering all
the large number of very important changes that have taken place in almost half
a century. However, towards the end Littlewood also deals with the most recent
past, bringing the story up to 1998 and thus making it as up to date as it is possible to be.

The book is remarkable in a number of other respects. First, it is comprehensive, detailed and meticulously researched. Second, it not only covers a gap in the
conventional sense of the word, but is a major contribution to the literature of
financial developments in the United Kingdom and by the same token, as it does
not neglect the world setting, serves as a comparison with what has been happening elsewhere.

The book is not merely an objective and, therefore, reliable account of what
has happened. Littlewood skilfully weaves the history of the stock market into
the main phases of political and, therefore, also economic development in the
decades since the end of the war. He divides this period into four phases, characterised largely by the alternation of Conservative and Labour governments and
by more or less marked economico-political trends associated with this alternation. This enables him to broaden the analysis, thus not merely covering the
actual evolution of the practices of the stock market, but also their relationship
to the wider economic and political developments in the country. Broadly speaking, this leads him to divide the period into lean years and fat years as far as the
interests of the investor are concerned.

This treatment makes not only for lively reading but also makes it possible for
the reader to discern possible differing interpretations of the role of the stock
market as a most important economic instrument within the framework of varying political and economic philosophies.

It is difficult to think of a book on a subject of this kind with the kind of scope
this volume has that serves so many different purposes and interests. It will be
invaluable to the student of financial history no less than to the practitioner in
financial markets.

Lord Roll of Ipsden

PREFACE

....

The purpose of this book is to provide a narrative of events and analysis of themes in the history of the London stock market over the 50 years since the war, and to act as a source of reference. I hope it will be of interest to all kinds of readers, ranging from the enthusiastic graduate or professional trainee about to embark on a career in the stock market and wishing to learn more about it, to those who have worked or are working in the market, and to lay readers who may be interested in the stock market because they are investors or work in quoted companies.

In writing this history, I have drawn from my own experience of a lifetime stockbroking career. My professional experience has been as an investment analyst and, for a brief interlude, as a fund manager, and this book is written from the perspective of a practitioner. Thus, it may be that some arguments are not always supported by the depth of reasoning or development of theory that an academic historian or professional economist would consider necessary, and where this is so, I apologise.

The narrative chapters in this book are defined by the movements of successive bull and bear markets. These fall naturally into place entirely with the benefit of hindsight, and I would not wish readers to conclude that calling the turn of a bull or bear market is a simple matter. It is, in fact, infernally difficult.

For those readers expecting to gain a better understanding of the stock market, may I preface your hopes by offering the wise advice of Lewis Whyte, an eminent investment manager whose career features in this book. In 1957 he wrote in the *Investors Chronicle* that:

> The ancient Greeks, when consulting the Delphic oracle, were confronted with the inscription 'know thyself'. The modern investor when consulting financial oracles should likewise always bear in mind this precept. He should know his powers and foibles.

Several years later, an American under the pseudonym of Adam Smith wrote a famous book about investment entitled *The Money Game* (Michael Joseph, 1968). He gave the same advice in one laconic sentence: 'If you don't know who you are, the stock market is an expensive place to find out.'

ACKNOWLEDGEMENTS

....

This book is dedicated to the memory of Denis 'Ham' Martin. He was a respected partner in a medium-sized firm of stockbrokers, Read Hurst-Brown, and a former England international amateur golfer. It was my good fortune to find myself playing golf for Oxford University against him and a fellow partner and former international, Edward Bromley-Davenport, in a foursomes match at the Berkshire Golf Club in February 1959. Before the round was complete I had been invited to visit the firm, which I did, whereupon I quickly agreed to join as a graduate trainee. I owe so much to Ham Martin, who recruited me into a world of which I knew nothing, conducted my training and taught me the importance of logical presentation and mathematical accuracy.

I owe thanks to many other people in the writing of this book. I thank my wife, Rosemary, for her encouragement, and for her patience in discovering that there is a difference between leisurely retirement and writing a book. I thank my sons, William and Richard, for their interest and many helpful comments.

In particular, I would like to thank two friends, Michael Attenborough and James D'Albiac. Michael has been a long-standing golfing friend from university days, and his guidance and advice about the processes of the publishing world has been invaluable. His suggestion after reading the first part of this book that it might be of wider general interest than I had supposed was a source of much encouragement.

I first met James when Read Hurst-Brown merged into Rowe & Pitman in 1975. His interest in and enthusiasm for this history has been a constant support to me, and I particularly thank him for reading through the manuscript and commenting so constructively.

Many others have helped and encouraged me on my way. In particular, I would like to thank Douglas Aldrich-Blake, Bill Benton, Chris Bull, Stephen Carr, John Chiene, Professor Roderick Floud, Sir Nicholas Goodison, Henry Grunfeld, Peter Hardy, Ian Harwood, Sir Christopher Hogg, Alan Hurst-Brown, Leonard Licht, Brian Medhurst, Norman Pilkington, Lord Roll of Ipsden, Sir David Scholey, John Stancliffe, Peter Stormonth Darling, Stuart Stradling, Denis Weaver and Peter Wilmot-Sitwell. I especially thank Eric Roll, whose experience uniquely spans so many aspects covered in this book, for his generous Foreword.

Various organisations have provided statistical information that I have either quoted or used for background comment. May I thank *Acquisitions Monthly*, Association of Unit Trusts, BZW, Datastream, London Stock Exchange,

NatWest Securities, Office for National Statistics, SBC Warburg Dillon Read, and The WM Company. The *Financial Times* newspaper has been my prime source of factual information, joined also by *The Economist*.

I would like to thank the members of staff of the libraries where most of the research was conducted, namely the Guildhall Library in the City, the Library of the University of Surrey in Guildford and the Bank of England Library. Finally, I thank Alison Stainistreet for typing the early part of the manuscript and Tony Lennard for guiding me through the intricacies of the personal computer.

INTRODUCTION

....

The stock market is the expression of capitalism at work. 'Capital' is owned by those who accumulate, inherit or save, and used by those who invest, speculate or spend. In the United Kingdom, the two are brought together by the capitalist system as it is known today. The equations are simple: savings are harnessed for investment, investment is a home for savings. One provides capital, the other uses capital, and together they create capitalism.

Capital was once supplied only by private individuals, but today it is provided mostly by the collective savings of the people in the form of pension funds, life assurance companies and unit trusts – commonly known as the institutions. Those who issue securities to attract these savings are mainly companies in the private sector, and governments and their agencies in the public sector. New issues are described as the 'primary' market. Created originally for those who wished to sell these securities is a 'secondary' market in the Stock Exchange, where buyers and sellers are brought together.

Investors are dominated today by the fund managers of the institutions, issuers are advised by merchant banks or investment banks, and practitioners in the Stock Exchange act as intermediaries. All will respond to the least sign of any opportunity for capital to be raised or investments to change hands, and the competitiveness of this process usually ensures the prices of transactions will fairly reflect the situation at any given time.

The stock market is the sum total of all this activity, and this book chronicles its history in London since 1945. The story of most activities over these 50 years will tell of rapid change, and so it has been in the stock market. Two changes stand out. First, this period of 50 years has witnessed a dramatic rise in the power of the equity shareholder within the capitalist system from neglected outsider to dominant owner.

Second, the power of technology has transformed the stock market. It has moved from the confines of domestic boundaries to become part of a global village with hardly any boundaries. Information is transmitted and capital transferred in seconds at the press of a button. The noisy, crowded Stock Exchange floor has been replaced by banks of screens in huge dealing rooms, and transactions once agreed face to face with but a pencilled note and settled with a hand-written cheque have been replaced by Reuters' terminals, anonymous voices and electronic money transfer.

In some respects, nothing has changed. The stock market remains the best short-term indicator of the state of the economy, a barometer whose reading represents an immediate sampling of the real beliefs and actions of large numbers of people. The psychology of the investor remains constant. Prices will be still be driven by the extremes of fear and greed. The same person will tend to respond to a given set of circumstances in much the same way each time and the stock market will be made up of winners and losers.

It is this home truth that has prompted some to dismiss the stock market as little more than a casino. The stock market may be the expression of the capitalist system at work, but in Britain there has always been an undercurrent of opinion that has questioned whether capitalism was working properly or would ever work or should be allowed to work at all. There has always been some suspicion of those principles of capitalism laid down by Adam Smith in his definitive work *The Wealth of Nations*, published in 1776. The British have never been quite sure about his 'hidden hand' in the marketplace that channels available resources to meet the needs of the people in the most efficient possible way.

Capitalism has not been adopted in Britain with the naked enthusiasm of the United States, but as pioneers of the Industrial Revolution and with Adam Smith writing the book, Britain might have become the natural home of capitalism. However, the nation has never been comfortable with its baggage of great personal fortunes, privately owned power and occasional financial scandals, and, combined with the mystique of the stock market, 'the City' has become an emotive phrase. On a world stage, the City has achieved success and influence far in excess of the size of the country, but at home it has failed to attract little more than grudging respect.

This ambivalence has continued through the post-war years for good reasons. In the style of a Mensa question, consider the sequence 6 .. 13 .. 6 .. 4 .. 5 .. What is the next number? The mathematician will search in vain, but the lateral thinker with a nose for politics will see the answer.

The missing number in the sequence is eighteen – these being the numbers of years in office of six alternating Labour and Conservative governments since 1945. For some this displays political maturity, but for the management of the economy it has been a disruptive cycle. Political differences have been very wide, bringing with them the confusion of diametrically opposed policies on nationalisation, taxation, controls and intervention. The economy has far too often become the battleground for political dogma.

As a result, politics and economics in the post-war years have been more intrusive in the London stock market than in comparable countries. Britain may be perceived to enjoy political stability, but it has not enjoyed the benefits of continuity given to the United States, where there is a common acceptance of capitalism by both parties. Britain has suffered since 1945 from the change and uncertainty of the policies of successive Labour and Conservative governments.

The influence of economics over the stock market is that it provides some undeniable common denominators. The economy of every country has a rate of growth, rate of inflation, rate of interest, level of unemployment, external exchange rate, balance of payments and level of government income and expenditure. Any of these indicators might be of particular significance at any time, but two of the most critical for the stock market are the rate of growth and the rate of inflation. In the 1960s and 1970s, the rate of growth of the UK economy lagged behind comparable countries, and the rate of inflation was consistently higher.

Britain has suffered badly from inflation. It is one of those precise mathematical quirks that the Retail Price Index for January 1995 stood at 146.0 and its adjusted equivalent for January 1945 was 7.3, an exact increase of 20 times over 50 years. The large, crisp and neatly scripted white £5 note of 1945 would need today a note of £100 to provide the same purchasing power, and the engraved, ornate £1 note of 1945 is today worth less than 5p. The effect of inflation on this scale has been to distort the meaning of actual figures from earlier years, and its consequences have been a long-term deterioration in the value of the pound and a regime of high interest rates.

This book is a history of the stock market in its broadest sense, covering the linkage from issuer to investor through the intermediaries in the Stock Exchange. It is not a history of the Stock Exchange as an institution. The strong influence of politics over the post-war years has created a natural division into four political eras, each of which has been reflected in an equally distinctive outcome in the performance of the stock market. These are:

- **1945–51:** the Labour Government under Attlee was characterised by nationalisation and the imposition of controls – a negative period for investors;
- **1951–64:** 13 Conservative years were characterised by economic growth and freedom from controls, but also by 'stop–go' policies and complacency – a positive if erratic period for equity investors;
- **1964–79:** these years featured a return to controls and income policies, and suffered the ravages of inflation under both Labour and Conservative governments – a long, consistently negative period for investors;
- **1979–90:** the Thatcher years, characterised by privatisation, deregulation and Big Bang – a strong period for investors and its positive influence has continued through to 1998.

The book thus falls quite naturally into four parts, and the individual chapters within these four sections have been determined by the natural flow of ten bull and ten bear markets between 1945 and 1990. These provide the source of narrative events, but, in addition, each of the four parts concludes with a review of themes and issues emerging during that period, together with a summary of 'key events'. Nationalisation, privatisation and Big Bang are the subjects of individual chapters. The closing review for 1979 to 1998 extends the discussion of some significant trends through to 1998. All important stock market events are precisely dated and discussed, and set against relevant prices or stock market indices.

The rise in the power of the equity shareholder is a continuing theme through this history. This power has accelerated in Britain since 1979, when the open, deregulated 'Anglo-Saxon' form of capitalism prevailing in the United States was embraced by the Thatcher Government, as opposed to the 'stakeholder' or 'social market' form adopted by France, Germany and Japan. Since 1990, the balance has swung towards the Anglo-Saxon form and many of its themes have been adopted by countries of every political colour. Private enterprise is currently fashionable, State ownership is being dismantled, and stock exchanges are opening in the most unlikely places. The shareholder is king.

In simple terms, the post-war era in the London stock market has been a story of discovery. The stock market discovered dividends in the 1950s, earnings in the 1960s, inflation in the 1970s, growth in the 1980s and shareholder value in the 1990s. History shows that it enjoyed the 1950s, paused in the 1960s, hated the 1970s and has thrived ever since, but as each decade passed so the valuation of equities has become ever more stretched.

PART I

THE STOCK MARKET IN 1945 AND THE ATTLEE LABOUR GOVERNMENT

1945–51

Chapter 1

THE STOCK MARKET IN 1945

The declaration of a landslide election victory for the Labour party on 27 July 1945 came as a shock to the people of the country, world opinion and the stock market. It came as a personal shock to Winston Churchill who retired hurt to Chartwell to seek the comfort of pen and paintbrush. The Financial Times (FT) Index fell by 4% on the day and 10% within a week.

Two months before the election, it had all seemed so different. The country celebrated VE Day for victory in Europe with a two-day public holiday on 8 and 9 May. The National Government had served the country well through the crisis of war and Churchill personally wished it to continue until after the defeat of Japan – then a more distant prospect than it was to prove to be. However, the general understanding had been that victory over Germany would mark the end of the coalition and political strains had become increasingly apparent as the prospect of victory came closer.

Within days of these celebrations – and prompted by an imminent annual Labour party conference due to start on 20 May – Churchill wrote to the leaders of the coalition parties suggesting either the continuation of the coalition until the defeat of Japan or dissolution and an immediate election in July. The Labour party rejected the proposal to continue and Clement Attlee replied within three days on 21 May to ask for an autumn election. This was disregarded by Churchill, who dissolved Parliament on 23 May and called an election for 5 July 1945. The result was not to be announced until Thursday 26 July because, in many constituencies in the north-west and in Scotland, polling day was deferred because it coincided with traditional industry holidays.

The result came as one of the biggest shocks then ever known to that normally sensitive barometer, the stock market, which, on this occasion, gave a very faulty reading. During the election campaign and the three weeks of waiting, the FT Index (then known as the Financial News Index) made good progress, rising from 110.4 on 24 June to 118.4 on 25 July – an increase of more than 7%.

It is difficult to say whether optimistic newspaper comments encouraged the stock market or the strength of the stock market encouraged optimistic editorials, but, apart from a lone warning in *The Economist* that 'it begins to look as if it may be a very near thing' after reporting less confidence at Conservative headquarters following the collection of poll cards, the presumption of a Conservative victory was universal. Another indicator came from the stock market practice of quoting prices in majorities, a jobbing practice that the Stock

Exchange had fruitlessly tried to ban. On the eve of the declaration, the lowest price to be found was for a Conservative majority of 80.

Against these perceptions, an overall Labour majority of 146 came as a profound shock and the main leader of the *Financial Times* on 27 July began with the words, 'The City, with the nation, was shocked by the political landslide revealed yesterday'. The FT Index fell in one day from 118.4 to 113.7, and within a week it had fallen just over 10% to 105.9 – one of the biggest falls recorded in so short a period.

This massive error of public perception should not be judged harshly by the standards of today; it was a most unusual election. The previous election had been ten years earlier in 1935. The parties to the wartime coalition had agreed since 1940 not to contest any by-election arising from within their ranks; 7,000,000 new voters had come on to registers that were, in any case, out of date and badly distorted by wartime mobility; and there was a large overseas services vote of 2,900,000, of whom 1,700,000 voted.

The campaign was altogether different from today. Information was elusive and restricted, newspapers were reduced in size to four or six pages and television was not in operation. The only visual exposure of politicians was from rather solemn black and white photographs or snippets in a cinema newsreel, except for those voters lucky enough to attend a speech given to one of the huge political rallies that were then still a feature of election campaigns. The closest rapport was created via party political broadcasts on the wireless, which, it is believed, were heard on at least one occasion by 40% of the population. Conservative and Labour each had 10 broadcasts of 20 minutes or so after the 9 o'clock news.

Today, all this has been replaced by television and newspaper exposure in abundance, endless professional comment and opinion polls. What is extraordinary about the 1945 election is that evidence was available of the kind that would now move markets by the day, but either nobody read it or nobody believed it. Opinion polls were then in their infancy, but the *News Chronicle* published the Gallup Poll. On 18 June, voting intentions were published at Labour 45% and Conservative 37%. On 4 July, one day before the election, a second Gallup Poll reported voting intentions of Labour 47% and Conservatives 41%. Both polls indicated a strong Labour majority, but why was the message never received?

At that time, newspapers rarely reported news from one another, and the *News Chronicle* was a Liberal supporter with a narrow readership. The public was not familiar with opinion polls, and the last election had been so long ago that the electoral structure was not well understood. Political continuity had been interrupted by a strenuous and tiring war.

The election campaign had stirred political memories from the 1930s of unemployment and poverty amid privilege and prosperity, and all this was now remembered as being the legacy of Conservative rule. Churchill himself was in a difficult position. He had only assumed the leadership of the Conservative party because he became Prime Minister of a wartime coalition by acclamation. This task he had performed magnificently and his instincts were to continue the coalition. He was not at his best during the campaign as a mere party leader of Conservative colleagues with whom he had never worked in peacetime, whereas a Labour party released from coalition had strong motivation to win power and a leadership of familiar political figures who had participated successfully in the wartime Government.

The issues in the election were simple. After years of deprivation, the needs of the people were peace, jobs, food and housing. In this humbler light, the drama and brilliance of Churchill's wartime leadership was suddenly made less relevant and memories of the 1930s raised doubts as to which party would best deliver these basic needs. Attlee posed the question in his quiet, succinct way in news-reel broadcasts, neatly illustrating the divide between the parties.

The man in the street followed his instincts and voted for a fairer deal from the unassuming Attlee whose strength lay in having such a variety of colleagues with whom the voters were able to identify. Two natural friends of the working class, if not of each other, were Ernest Bevin and Herbert Morrison. Bevin had been a giant of the trade union movement as former General Secretary of the Transport and General Workers Union and Morrison had been the architect of the London County Council. At the other extreme of this extraordinary political party stood the flamboyant Etonian economist, Hugh Dalton, and the austere Wykehamist intellectual, Sir Stafford Cripps, both offering role models for many a middle-class voter.

This election was one of those intense battles for power that occur when a major political sea-change is in the offing, and behind the benign challenge of returning people to a normal family life lay a very deep clash of political dogma. The two parties were bitterly and diametrically opposed behind the irreconcil-able pillars of capitalism and socialism. The war had suppressed these instinctive differences, and many hoped they had been buried for ever, but such beliefs allowed little room for compromise and they quickly resurfaced.

The election of Labour in 1945 set the country on a path of confrontational politics that plagued the country for decades. Like a slow-moving pendulum, democracy has given each party three turns in nearly 50 years, and for many of those years the climate has been dominated by clouds of doubt, uncertainty and disruption. The consequences have been destructive for the economy and, at times, traumatic for the stock market. The political consensus of the United States and Germany – where it is understood that some form of capitalism is best – has been noticeably absent.

The election result brought to an end a five-year bull market in equities. In June 1940 – when the country's fortunes were at their lowest point after Dunkirk and just before the Battle of Britain – the FT Index had fallen 61% below its pre-war high to 40.4. Thereafter, it rose every year for five years. This particular bull market was little reported because of unease about rising share values at times of suffering and deprivation. Resentment surfaced towards the end of the war in a *Sunday Express* article (17 June 1945) by campaigning journalist John Gordon, who was angry that a fortune of £440m had been made 'at the expense of the success of our fighting men'. This figure was the increase in the value of the commercial and industrial sector of the market from March 1939 to March 1944.

After the sharp fall from 118.4 to 105.9 in the week after the election, the FT Index recovered to 112 in mid-August, and then entered a long period of stagnation. The investing public was bewildered about the future and numbed into inactivity by the arrival of the Labour Government. Indices would barely change for weeks at a time. For example, over 10 working days from 19 September to 2 October, the range of the Index was 114.0 to 114.2. From the middle of August 1945 to April 1946, covering the King's Speech, an interim Budget and up to the annual Budget, the FT Index remained within a 4% trading range of 112.1 and 117.0 for 8 months.

Long desultory periods of inactivity were to be characteristic of the Stock Exchange under this Labour Government. In this and other ways, the stock market of the late 1940s bears little resemblance to the stock market of today. Very different investors invested in very different investments. The shareholders' registers were dominated by private individuals who owned 60–70% of all equities. The 2 largest British companies were ICI with 125,000 shareholders and Imperial Tobacco with 95,000. Midland Bank had 78,000 shareholders, of whom 40,000 owned 100 shares or fewer and, when they were nationalised, the railway companies had 1,100,000 shareholdings across all the classes of security. The benefits of the wartime bull market were largely reaped by private investors rather than faceless institutions, and capitalism was still closely identified with private wealth.

The emphasis has since changed decisively. Today, there are four domestic drivers of institutional investment – life assurance companies, pension funds, unit trusts and investment trusts. In 1945, the life assurance industry and the investment trust movement had long-established histories, but pension funds and unit trusts were in their infancy, and the powerful collective influence of overseas investors – a feature since the 1980s – was wholly absent.

The typical life assurance fund was invested almost entirely in fixed interest investments, with some 10% of its assets in equities. From the investor's point of view, this reflected the actuarial certainty of interest payments and redemption of government stock and company debentures, and, from the issuer's point of view, this was the way capital was largely raised. Investment in equities ranged from Sun Life with 'no less than 98% of the assets' invested in redeemable fixed interest investments, to UK Provident, which reported that 'one-seventh of our assets' were in equities thus ensuring an 'appropriate share in the prosperity of the country'.

The life assurance industry was well documented, and official Board of Trade aggregate figures show the distribution of assets, at book value, as at December 1945, as shown in Table 1.1.

Table 1.1
The distribution of assets in life assurance funds, December 1945

Assets	(£m)	Percentage
British government securities	983.5	41.4
Debentures	252.4	10.6
Other fixed interest	507.9	21.4
Preference shares	169.9	7.2
Ordinary shares	205.5	8.7
Miscellaneous	255.0	10.7
Total assets	2,374.2	

The Prudential was the largest life company in 1945, with assets of £440m, and has led the field ever since. It is a measure of the growth and scale of competing institutional investors that Prudential's dominance over all institutions seems less marked today than it did in the 1940s and 1950s.

The investment trust movement in 1945 was one of the largest sectors of the equity market. It was created originally to harness capital for collective individual investment in overseas markets, but by 1945 it invested in widely diversified portfolios that were ideal for private individuals and also used extensively by insurance companies. Investment trusts were a separately quoted sector of the stock market with a market capitalisation of £310m, or 5% of the total market – a percentage that today has fallen below 3%.

Little was known about the pension fund movement. An estimate in 1949 suggested that the Association of Superannuation Funds had a membership of 1,000 funds with total investments of £440m. Unit trusts were struggling in friendless isolation to achieve recognition, and the prices of their units were barely reported at all. Total unit trust funds were less than £100m.

There was a diversity of investments available to the investor, dominated by fixed interest. It is difficult today to comprehend the extent to which capital was raised in this way and how equities were regarded as second-class investments. The only information provided by the Stock Exchange about the market was an annual aggregation of the market value and nominal value of all quoted securities. Table 1.2 for 3 April 1945, is drawn from the last annual figures published by the Stock Exchange before nationalisation became a factor.

Two figures attracting attention are the dominance of government securities and the disastrous extent to which foreign stocks had fallen below their nominal values. The table also gives an indication of the relative size of the sectors of the market that would, in due course, be nationalised compared with the remaining industrial, commercial and financial sectors. However, these industrial sectors are confusing because of the Stock Exchange practice of including under 'companies' all quoted securities, whether debentures, preference shares or ordinary shares.

Table 1.2
Aggregation of the nominal and market values of quoted securities, 3 April 1945

Category	Nominal (£m)	Market value (£m)
Fixed Interest		
Government securities	11,863,915,985	12,167,954,807
Corporation stocks	813,183,747	833,129,458
Commonwealth stocks	1,007,928,803	989,812,996
Foreign		
Foreign stocks and bonds	983,910,493	280,676,880
Railways – American and foreign	805,550,435	202,787,660
Companies		
Commercial and industrial	1,283,552,546	3,150,677,961
Banks, finance and insurance	445,436,936	1,077,110,091
Breweries and distilleries	211,056,183	500,951,980
Oil	160,342,949	568,545,572
Investment trusts	279,540,071	307,177,230
Other companies	156,215,808	178,158,916
Railways	1,147,577,802	863,130,377
Iron, coal and steel	252,676,202	385,304,038
Electrical lighting and power	220,666,404	331,730,920
Gas	132,385,229	141,927,619
Other utilities and infrastructure	166,084,306	361,825,735
Commodities	109,472,926	212,367,325
Total	20,039,496,825	22,553,269,565

In prime place in the fixed interest market stood British government stocks, or gilts. Kings, queens and governments have, throughout history, borrowed money to fight wars, and the two world wars of this century were no exception. The national debt rose tenfold between 1914 and 1920, from £700m to £7,900m and more than doubled from £9,100m in 1940 to £22,400m in 1945.

During the war, the national debt was financed more from personal savings than by the issue of gilts, but the amount of British and Commonwealth government stock in issue still rose from £8,400m in 1939 to £13,000m in 1945. At the same time, the rest of the market – foreign bonds, debentures, preference shares and ordinary shares – fell in value from £9,500m to £7,900m. In 1945, gilts and corporation stocks represented 60% of the total market value of all quoted Stock Exchange investments.

Investors in 1945 could choose from a wide range of debentures and preference shares issued by commercial, industrial and financial companies. Many companies had layers of preference shares in issue and for statistical purposes the Stock Exchange lumped them together with ordinary shares, leaving behind a legacy of misinformation.

Preference shares became inefficient for corporate tax purposes and are now almost unknown, but in the immediate post-war period, they formed an integral part of the corporate balance sheet. An aggregated table published in *The Economist* in 1945 showed post-tax company profits allocated in the proportions of 8% for debenture interest, 21% for preference share dividends and 45% for ordinary share dividends. A typical industry example was the issued capital in the 1948 balance sheet of Associated Portland Cement – known today as Blue Circle Industries – which showed total capital of £8.9m divided between debentures of £2.4m, preference shares of £2.5m and ordinary shares of £4m.

These examples suggest that a fifth of the aggregate nominal value of shares in issue for companies was made up of preference shares, together with a further tranche for debentures. Both have now almost disappeared, and the total in issue today is equal to less than 2% of the market value of equities. However, their disappearance has not affected corporate gearing because they have been replaced by bank borrowing and other new sources of finance.

The market for capital is the same as any other market whereby supply and demand are satisfied by product and price. In the late 1940s, fixed interest securities best suited both issuer and investor, whether they were British government stocks, Commonwealth stocks, foreign bonds, corporation stocks, debentures or preference shares. To the investor of that time, from the private individual to the life assurance company, the freedom to choose between Savings 3%, Australia 5%, Argentine 3½%, Middlesex 3½%, or new issues in 1946 like Dunlop 3½% Debentures and English Electric 3¾% preference shares was just as important a portfolio choice as the geographical and sector options of equity markets today.

Despite the inflationary pressures of the war, fixed interest investments remained the investment vehicle that best satisfied the needs of both issuer and investor. Memories of the Wall Street crash of 1929 and the worldwide slump that followed still inhibited investors. The 1930s became a decade of deflation of such severity that the British Government was able to issue a Treasury 1% stock. Apart from a brief upward blip at the beginning of the war, Bank rate had stayed at 2% since 1932, and was to remain at 2% until 1951. Against this background of interest rate stability, the investor could measure his choice of yields between a typical 3% on gilts, 3¼% on corporation stocks, 3¾% on industrial debentures and 4¼% on preference shares.

Attitudes to ordinary shares were altogether different from today. The *Financial Times* referred in a leader on 1 May 1945 to yields of 4.33% on industrial equities and 3% on Consols: 'It cannot be said that 1.33% gross is sufficient margin for the difference in risk between gilt-edged stocks and a commercial venture'.

It was natural to assume that equities should yield 1% to 1½% more than gilts because of their inherent risk; and with little or no inflation and little experience of growth, many a company would pay the same dividend year after year. Conventional advice presumed in favour of fixed interest investment and the legal strictures of the Trustee Act imposed this on trust funds and many of the early pension funds. The classic board game of Monopoly, invented in the 1930s, does not mention ordinary shares at all, but it does mirror the financial markets of the day with its 'Community Chest' card instructing lucky players to receive £25 from their '7% Preference Shares'. While the manufacturers may wish to leave prices unadjusted for inflation, they might consider adjusting the mathematical impossibility of this instruction to pay £25 on a holding of 7% Preference Shares.

Just as investors and their investments were different in 1945, so also were the practitioners in the stock market. As in any other service business or professional activity, employment in the Stock Exchange shrunk dramatically during the war as mobilisation into the armed forces and the direction of labour into industries for the war effort took effect. The scale of disruption to the economy is difficult to imagine today. In 1939, the total workforce was just under 20 million people. By 1945, numbers in the armed forces had risen from 600,000 to 5.2 million and numbers in the war industries from 1.4 to 5.0 million. The total number of people directed into the war effort was 8.2 million or more than 40% of the working population. In the Stock Exchange, the number of active members and clerks fell from 6,100 in 1939 to 2,700 in 1945.

Turnover in the market during the war was low. Settlement for cash was imposed on all transactions, dealing became a matter of negotiation and new issues were non-existent. Company profits became meaningless as the excess profits tax of 100% was imposed on profits above agreed benchmarks. Stockbroking firms depended for their existence on older or retired members of staff, many of whom coped almost single-handedly, and despite inactivity most survived because their cost structure was so low.

The typical senior partner of the day hailed from that upper-class background where an instinctive caution lies close to the surface. Cheap labour was available to work in offices with cheap rentals. Information technology was not included in the vocabulary of the day. The result was a low cost base designed to cope with the bad years and produce those huge and highly geared rewards in the good years that contributed to the popular image of the stockbroker. Innate caution was to remain at the heart of the management of Stock Exchange firms for many years to come, driven only partly by the fear of unlimited liability.

In the late 1940s and early 1950s the staff were known as clerks and the gap between them and the partners was enormous. Recruitment was by a combination of introductions and nepotism for the partners, and paternalism and a degree of nepotism for the staff. Prospective partners would be recruited from the personable and probably less bright sons of relations, friends and clients, almost universally educated at public school. University was probably a disadvantage. The young trainee would later boast of his early years starting at the bottom as a clerk with the messengers or in the transfer department, although he would never have remained a clerk for more than a year or two.

The style of the firm reflected the marketplace of the time, where the majority of investors were wealthy private individuals. It was a market of gossip, tips and rumours, and picking a share in a company was a matter of knowing somebody on the Board or somebody who knew somebody on the Board, rather like dancing with a man who danced with a girl who danced with the Prince of Wales. Scrutiny of a company's business was superficial and the accounts were no help at all. Stockbroking was a matter of who you knew and what you heard.

Stockbrokers communicated with the public, acting as agents to carry out buying and selling transactions with the jobbers who worked on the floor of the Stock Exchange. Making markets in stocks and shares, and dependent on their trading skills to make a profit, the jobbers were more individual and drawn from both ends of the social spectrum. There were more than 250 firms of jobbers, with half of them having only 1 or 2 partners. It was from among the more successful of their employees that the philosophy and the image of the East End barrow-boy trading on the Stock Exchange floor emerged.

On demobilisation, members and clerks returned to the City and the Stock Exchange after absences of many years. They were to find large areas to the north and west of the City devastated by fire and bombing from many a blitz between November 1940 and May 1941. Large areas had lain waste in rubble for five years, where 'nothing flourishes but a lush crop of spendthrift willow herb', its colour purple set amid the grime and dirt of ruined buildings. Later analysis was to show that a third of the area of the City had been devastated, although the financial and banking quarter of the City survived better than did the textile and industrial areas around where the Barbican is now and the commodities area to the East. Nevertheless, many a damaged roof or broken window forced workers to sit huddled in overcoats and mittens to keep warm at their desks.

The Stock Exchange provided a helpful booklet – 'Since 1939' – to returning members: 'Physically you will not find the Stock Exchange changed very much – a little older, a little more drab', began an early comforting paragraph. However, the reality of war was spelled out in a section dealing with settlement problems created by 'war conditions, with attendant complications of bombed offices and burnt ledgers'. The publication brought members up to date with changes imposed or introduced since the beginning of the war, such as cash settlement, guaranteed minimum prices for gilts, a ban on options and restrictions on new issues. At least it had not been as bad as in August 1914 when the Stock Exchange was closed for four months.

Through the war years, good order had prevailed in the Stock Exchange. In March 1945, the Constitution of the Stock Exchange was changed, with the creation of a single 'Council of the Stock Exchange' under one Chairman, thus replacing the two separate bodies that previously represented the proprietors and the members. The Stock Exchange Council was to survive broadly in this form until 1992, part of the aftermath of Big Bang.

In its understated way, the Stock Exchange was a constructive influence. A particular strength was the rigour applied to prospectuses for new issues and quotations, where Stock Exchange requirements were more demanding than any legal requirement. For example, a condition of a new issue was that consolidated accounts should be published, putting the Stock Exchange on the progressive side of this particular accounting debate.

The disclosure of information in company accounts is governed by Companies Acts, of which the last had been enacted in 1929 following the Hatry scandal. In one of those decisions which was surprising because it was taken in the middle of a war, the government appointed Mr Justice Cohen in June 1943 to lead a committee to look at the existing Companies Acts and make recommendations. The Cohen Report was published on 18 July 1945 – during the election hiatus between voting and counting – and it begins with a ringing declaration of support for the capitalist system: 'the system of limited liability companies is so beneficial and essential to our prosperity'.

One recommendation in particular was to have far-reaching effects on the stock market. This required a parent company to consolidate the accounts of all its subsidiaries, thus removing the inconsistencies of unconsolidated accounts that so many companies sheltered behind to avoid giving information to their shareholders. Other recommendations included a 5-year rather than 3-year profits record in prospectuses, and that company directors should retire at 70, unless re-elected each year by special resolution.

In due course, the Cohen Report was taken forward with barely a change to become the basis of the 1948 Companies Act. This introduced consolidated company accounts – an accounting landmark in the history of the stock market. It was the first step towards the better understanding of equity investment and a foundation stone of the cult of the equity. From the long-term perspective, it marked the first perceptible shift in the struggle for power between the company and the issuer on the one hand, and the shareholder on the other. Until this moment, power had been firmly locked in the hands of the company and the issuer, but, from 1948 onwards, the pendulum would slowly but relentlessly swing towards the shareholder.

While the Stock Exchange may have been progressive in seeking more disclosure of information from the companies whose shares it quoted and traded, its record for disclosing information about its own marketplace activities was lamentable and was to remain so for many years.

The Stock Exchange published a daily 'Official List' that printed for all shares the different prices at which bargains had been struck during the previous business day. There were glaring weaknesses in this system. The process of marking bargains was voluntary, with no apparent sanction for brokers who did not comply. The result was that information was incomplete, to an unknown extent. No information was given about how many bargains had been struck at each price or how many shares had been traded, with the result that nothing was known about the aggregate turnover of the market, either by number of shares or value, whether for the market, its sectors or for individual stocks and shares.

This is not a judgement of hindsight, but was a matter for debate at the time. A leading article in the *Financial Times* in September 1946 asked why marking bargains should not be compulsory, and why the total number of shares should not be reported. Despite its good record in persuading companies to disclose information, it was not until 1964 that the Stock Exchange would publish the monthly aggregate of equity turnover by number of bargains and value, and until 1986 that the daily aggregate turnover in individual stocks would be published. The contrast between constructive efforts to seek greater disclosure from quoted public companies and a myopic reluctance to provide information about its own activities could hardly be greater.

In 1945, the financial pages show a number of companies the names of which have remained unchanged to this day – Barclays Bank, Legal & General and Prudential remain stalwarts in the banking and insurance sectors. Rolls-Royce and Vickers emerged strongly from the war, and the diverse names of Courtaulds, Marks & Spencer, Shell and Tate & Lyle continue to appear. Traditional prefixes such as 'Associated', 'Imperial' and 'United' have been replaced by the modern suffixes of 'Group', 'Industries' or 'International'. However, the prefix of British remains firmly in favour, particularly after privatisation in the 1980s, although, more recently, the fetish to reduce names to initials has often turned 'British' into 'B', and other fine names to have succumbed to abbreviation include GEC, GKN, ICI and T&N. As though imitating art, the barriers in corporate naming are being pushed ever forward, and are currently straying into the abstract with computerised names such as Centrica, Diageo, Rexam and Zeneca.

In 1945, investors could choose from railways and coal mines or gas and electric utilities, and the names of Bolsover Colliery and Great Western Railway stir memories. If the phrase 'growth stocks' had then been invented, they would have sprung from oil, aircraft, motors, radio, cinema and cigarettes, and the cycle industry was highlighted in the *Financial Times* on 1 September 1945 as the 'cheapest form of transport which promises greatly to expand in future years'. These were the choices available to the investor, but they typically took second place to the main helping of gilts, debentures and preference shares.

Nevertheless, investors made their selections from what shares were available and, as often as not, they would look to the largest companies as offering the safest haven. It is intriguing to compare the post-war menu of the ten largest companies measured by equity market capitalisation. Table 1.3 shows prices as at 31 December 1947 – a middling moment in the late 1940s when the FT Index stood at 128.3, and precisely 50 years later, on 31 December 1997.

Table 1.3
A comparison between the ten largest companies in 1947 and 1997

31 December 1947	Market Capitalisation (£m)	31 December 1997	Market Capitalisation (£m)
Imperial Tobacco	258	Glaxo Wellcome	50,700
ICI	198	British Petroleum	44,400
Anglo-Iranian Oil (*BP*)	170	Shell	43,800
Shell	160	Lloyds TSB	42,200
British-American Tobacco	154	HSBC	40,600
Woolworth	141	SmithKline Beecham	34,400
Distillers	120	BT	30,100
Royal Insurance	68	Barclays Bank	24,600
Guinness	58	Diageo	22,500
Courtaulds	55	Zeneca	20,200

But for the merger to create Diageo, smoking and drinking would have disappeared without trace, and, apart from BP and Shell, the lists of companies in both tables have changed out of all recognition, due to mergers, acquisitions and rights issues. However, if one were to choose a company to personify unchanging excellence over 50 years, it would be Marks & Spencer, where the comparable figures are £32m and a largely undiluted £16,900m.

The *Financial Times* assisted with daily bid and offer prices and changes on the day for some 600 UK equities, but it would be several years before figures for yields, dividends and highs and lows were available. The priorities of the day were strange when, in comparison with the number of domestic equities quoted, readers were provided with the daily publication of the prices of 230 mining shares, 140 rubber and 140 tea plantation shares.

Indices to measure the market's progress were few. The FT Index of 30 industrial ordinary shares is the only UK index to survive in more or less unchanged form today, although in 1945 it was known as the Financial News Index. The two financial newspapers – the *Financial News* and the *Financial Times* – merged in October 1945 under the name and distinctive pink colour of the *Financial Times*, but largely with the content and journalism of the *Financial News*. Their separate industrial ordinary share indices continued to be published until 1 January 1947 when the Financial News Index was renamed the Financial Times (FT) Index. Its long-term weakness has been that it started as an index of industrial shares and the oil and financial sectors were only included many decades later.

Investors, brokers and jobbers returned from the war to a familiar system that would barely change for many years to come. In contrast, the merchant banks were taking the first steps in establishing their post-war influence over financial markets. Merchant banks are peculiar to London and have no exact parallel in other financial communities. Their names were usually taken from the founding individual, and Barings, Hambros and Rothschilds have been managed by members of the original families through seven or eight generations. The founding families were mostly immigrants and often Jewish, and many were attracted here during the time of the Industrial Revolution, between 1770 and 1840.

The designation of 'merchant banks' is derived from their origins as merchants and traders in produce who came to realise that financing the trade of others was more profitable than carrying the risk and rigour of the trade itself. Their financing of trade developed into the financing of sovereign states and cities, and, in the nineteenth century, London was the prime source of capital for the rest of the world.

Their history of successful opportunism reached a peak at the turn of the century and rather faded between the wars in the 1920s and 1930s when many new companies were brought to the market. Only Helbert Wagg – itself a firm of stockbrokers turned merchant bank – played any significant part in a field dominated by Cazenove and other stockbrokers. However, their confidence returned when the combination of economic growth and inflation in the post-war era created the cult of the equity. This presented new business opportunities – first, in corporate finance and, later, in fund management – that were seized with the same alacrity and vigour that characterised earlier generations of merchant bankers in the nineteenth century.

The merchant banks made an early challenge in January 1946 when the then recently formed Issuing Houses Association published a statement about its membership and functions. The membership list was interesting for the inclusion of the new name of S. G. Warburg & Co., previously known as the New Trading Company, and the exclusion of any stockbrokers, but the statement was provocative. It claimed that new issues carried out by Stock Exchange firms were to be discouraged, controversially adding that the involvement of stockbrokers was not liked 'by higher authority'.

This last point was received with indignation by many Stock Exchange members, some of whom believed that the only contribution made by the merchant banks was to add an unnecessary layer of expense. In the event, the merchant banks flexed their muscles and the Stock Exchange firms capitulated, abandoning much of their previous role in new issues. This happened for two reasons. Stockbroking was very fragmented and lacked the capital resources of the merchant banks, which, in turn, were important customers to be cultivated rather than offended. The post-war deference of the stockbroker to the merchant banker began with the statement by the Issuing Houses Association in January 1946.

It has been seen that, after the election, the market fell sharply and was then becalmed. Investors had good reasons for indecision and bewilderment. The reality was a Labour government with a decisive mandate to carry out its manifesto and an unassailable majority that looked good for ten years. This was quickly understood when the King's Speech was read on 17 August 1945 within three weeks of taking office. Despite urgent short-term problems on a scale that would have tested the skill and ingenuity of any government, Labour immediately began to introduce legislation on its long-term policies for taking control of the economy and bringing about that irreversible change of which Labour politicians are so fond.

Chapter 2

LABOUR BULL MARKET
August 1945–January 1947

FT 30 Index	2 August 1945	105.9	
	17 January 1947	140.6	Up 32.8%

The financial community was dismayed by the election result and panic selling drove the market down by over 10% in the week following the election, taking the FT Index from 118.4 to 105.9 (see Figure 2.1). The market recovered a little, but, for many months, investors were plagued by indecision, not knowing what to make of this most unwelcome visitor – a Labour government.

In the King's Speech in August 1945, the Government made clear its intention to begin its programme of nationalisation by taking over the Bank of England and the coal industry, and the new Chancellor, Hugh Dalton, announced there would be an interim budget on 23 October. The Chancellor planned to build a ring fence around the economy by imposing financial controls. He proposed three specific measures – the nationalisation of the Bank of England, the control of the issue of capital for investment and the control of currency and exchange. The last two were already in place on a wartime footing and he merely announced future legislation to consolidate these controls rather than abandon them.

In the interim Budget in October, he continued the wartime policy of cheap interest rates and signalled a regime of high personal taxation. The standard rate of income tax was reduced from 10/- to 9/- (50% to 45%) but the maximum rate of surtax was raised from 9/6d to 10/6d (47½% to 52½%), so maintaining the maximum rate of tax at the infamous 19/6d in the pound (97½%) that had been imposed during the war in 1941. Of particular interest to the stock market was his decision to reduce the wartime excess profits tax from 100% to 60%, but his antagonism to shareholders' dividends – a constant feature of this Labour Government – was marked by the statement, 'I hope that the increase in the net profits of companies will be spent on new and up-to-date plant and will not go straight into shareholders' pockets. In the national interest capital development must stand in front of higher dividends'.

This was the first of many negative comments on dividends from different Labour chancellors, but the market reacted cheerfully with the FT Index rising from 115.5 to 117.6, because the measures could have been worse and dividends

Figure 2.1
FT INDEX 1945–51

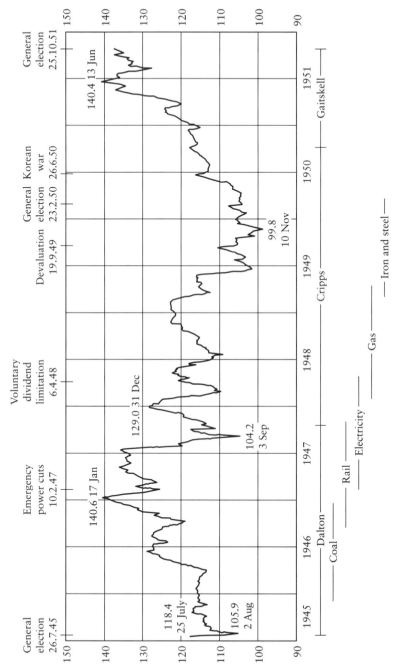

Source: Financial Times

should now increase after six years of wartime controls. The market had also been encouraged by the simplicity and fairness of the terms for the nationalisation of the Bank of England, announced two weeks before the Budget.

Nevertheless the stock market was bemused through the early months by the Labour Government pressing forward at great speed with the immediate nationalisation of the Bank of England and the coal industry. The Government was convinced that the most beneficial way to run the economy was by centralised planning and the use of controls. This was an instinctive belief on their part as socialist politicians, but participation in the wartime coalition had also convinced them that the extensive use of controls and planning involved in the successful prosecution of the war could be successfully transferred to the management of the peacetime economy.

Furthermore, they believed the spirit of cooperation displayed by people at all levels throughout the war would continue quite naturally under their administration and could be captured for the benefit of the peacetime economy. Putting all this into practice was easy because the Government had only to leave in place a whole battery of controls built up through many years of war. Nationalisation was a logical extension of this policy.

The Labour Government faced great economic problems. Fighting the war for six years had brought the country financially to its knees. When the power of the British Empire was at its height at the turn of the century, a huge portfolio of long-term foreign investments had been accumulated and, ever since, the income from these investments had financed a large deficit between imports and exports. In 1938, the last full year before the war, and a fairly normal year for the economy, the figures show imports of £920m were matched by exports of £470m, earnings from shipping of £105m and investment income of £203m. A further £44m of other invisible exports still left an overall deficit on trade of nearly £100m.

This picture accurately reflected our traditional role of importing primary products of food, tobacco, oil and other raw materials from the Empire and the United States, and exporting manufactured goods, in the main, back to the Empire, safe in the knowledge that invisible exports and investment income would make good the deficit on visible trade.

The value of long-term foreign investments was estimated in 1939 to be around £4,000m. Even allowing for the wartime generosity of the American lend–lease system, involvement in the war on so many fronts for so many years had led to the accumulation of debts of a matching amount of £4,000m. Essential imports were still needed, but exports were largely denied. To meet debts in the United States and Canada, assets to the value of £1,100m had already been subject to a forced sale on onerous terms that caused some resentment. The remaining £2,900m of assets were now balanced almost exactly by accumulated debt and, in effect, the easy affluence of income flowing from foreign investments was suddenly replaced by a chronic balance of payments deficit.

In medieval times, the problem would have been dealt with by plunder and looting, but its modern day equivalent of reparations had been discredited by the economic chaos caused by their heavy imposition on Germany after the Great War. Another solution might have been to recognise that the United Kingdom had carried a greater burden than other countries in fighting a lone battle against Germany for the first two years of the war and in many parts of the Far East to help contain Japan.

In that event, many of the sterling debts incurred in countries such as India and Egypt could have been written down, and compensation obtained from those countries in Europe rescued from German occupation. In fact, it was to prove to be a weakness of the Labour Government that it allowed countries to claim sterling debts when there was a strong case for either writing them off or negotiating them to lower levels.

In the absence of reparations or reduction of debt, only two alternatives remained. These were to resort to further borrowing or to bring the trade deficit into balance by greatly increasing exports and reducing imports. In the event, both avenues were pursued with the negotiation of large dollar loans from the United States and Canada and a trade policy of curbing imports and increasing exports. The Labour Government pursued the latter from the outset by a centrally driven 'export or die' campaign and the strict rationing of food, tobacco and raw materials.

If Churchill had remained in power, it is more than just idle speculation to consider whether or not he would have been more successful in dealing with the wartime legacy of financial problems. Would he, for example, have been able to win the case for a reduction in our debts by applying his oratorical powers to a picture of Britain standing alone against Hitler in 1940 and 1941? Would the United States' Government have turned off the tap of lend–lease aid quite so abruptly and coldly at the very hour that the war against Japan was over?

These are hypothetical questions, but there is every probability that, under Churchill's leadership, the United Kingdom would have achieved better terms for the loans from the United States and Canada in 1946 than those negotiated by the Labour Government. However, as it was, the death of President Roosevelt in April 1945 and the defeat of Churchill in the election three months later severed the links of an understanding partnership.

The famous economist Maynard Keynes went to the United States late in 1945 as representative of the British Government to negotiate financial aid, hoping for £1,500m as a gift or, at worst, an interest-free loan. He was met with a cool reception and negotiations were difficult. Some Americans resented being asked for aid to pay off debts to prop up the British Empire, others were reluctant to prop up a socialist government.

Many underestimated the scale of the financial problems facing Britain, the symbolic influence of which was far greater then than it is today. Any hopes of aid in the form of a gift were quickly dashed and eventually, on 6 December 1945, a loan of £1,100m was announced at a rate of interest of 2%, repayable over 50 years, commencing from December 1951. An interest-free period of six years was the only concession made by the Americans, but there was an understanding that debts in the sterling area would be negotiated down.

A term of the loan that sterling convertibility should be reintroduced one year after the loan came into effect caused much concern in Britain and was later to prove disastrous. On 7 March 1946, three months after the agreement of the American loan, it was announced that Canada would lend £280m to the United Kingdom on terms identical to those of the US loan.

The reception given in Britain to news of the loan from the United States was muted and there was a belief, perhaps not widely stated, that the terms were very tough and did not recognise the sacrifice Britain had made when fighting the war alone from 1940 to 1942. An instinctive antipathy on the part of the Americans towards socialism had not made the task of a team negotiating on behalf of a government proudly intent on introducing socialism into Britain any easier, and it is possible that a more generous outcome might have been negotiated by a Conservative government.

Nevertheless, the loan appeared to provide a valuable breathing space for a few years and allow time to change the balance of imports and exports. The figures already shown for 1938 – the last sensible year for any calculation – illustrated the scale of the problem, when imports stood at £920m and exports at £470m with a further benefit of £105m generated by shipping revenues as the import and export values were both calculated at the dockside in the United Kingdom. Reducing an adverse visible trade balance of some £450m was always going to be a formidable task.

In 1939, exports were dominated by manufactured goods where Britain had a market share of some 20% of world trade, but much of it was with captive Commonwealth markets where the market share was far higher. After the war it was calculated that an export target of between 150% and 175% of pre-war levels was required to correct the trade balance, suggesting a 30–35% share of the market for manufactured goods – a hopelessly unrealistic target. Such volumes might be achieved against a background of significant growth in world trade, but then it would be difficult to hold imports to pre-war levels.

British exports in 1938 were roughly made up of 60% manufactured goods, 20% textiles and 20% food, coal and raw materials. In effect the manufactured goods and textiles accounting for 80% of exports would have to double in value and, as more than half of these were exported to markets already dominated by Britain in the British Empire, and another quarter to devastated countries in Europe, the prospects were bleak. Furthermore, there was the danger of too great a dependence on the mature textile and clothing industries for a fifth of exports.

In round terms, imports were made up of 50% for food, drink and tobacco, 25% raw materials and 25% for manufactures of various kinds and other miscellaneous items. The traditional role of countries within the Empire exporting their primary products of food, tobacco and raw materials to Britain in exchange for importing back manufactured goods would no longer be sufficient.

The new Labour Government quickly identified the need for more exports and fewer imports. A campaign was mounted with all the necessary political enthusiasm, but it was born out of a bureaucratic stranglehold rather than a free-wheeling crusade. It led to a raft of controls to ration raw materials to the 'correct' exporting industries; to the inefficiencies of bulk buying of raw materials, where civil servants were expected to understand commodity prices better than commodity dealers; to the continuing closure of the Metal Exchange and the Cotton Exchange, thus denying foreign trading revenues; to peacetime rationing for many years; to the denial of consumer products to a home market long deprived by the war but with accumulated wealth to spend on products to make home life more enjoyable; above all, it led to the diversion of labour into an expanding civil service bureaucracy when every productive hand was needed to rebuild the economy. The headlong rush into nationalisation kept socialist spirits high, but was depressing to private enterprise, the efforts of which alone would make the export drive succeed.

During the Government's first nine months in power through to the annual Budget in April 1946, share prices remained stagnant. In his second Budget on 10 April, the Chancellor abolished the excess profits tax, which he had reduced to 60% in the previous November, but suggested that an alternative tax might be introduced to replace it at a future date. In addition to excess profits tax, there had also been a further tax called the national defence contribution at a rate of 5% which the Chancellor decided to retain under the new name of 'profits tax'. He announced his intention to retain purchase tax and make it permanent. He also raised the maximum rate of estate duty for death duty purposes from 65% to 75%.

The market reacted positively to the abolition of the excess profits tax and continued to move ahead through the summer of 1946, taking the FT Index to new all-time highs in May and June. Many companies were now paying increased dividends or, in some cases, special bonus dividends to compensate for the wartime standstill. In July, the US dollar loan was ratified and came into effect, but the severe spirit of the detail was illustrated by a charge against it of £162m for the settlement of lease–lend since the end of the war with Japan, leaving £938m as a future line of credit.

In the latter part of 1946, nationalisation emerged as a factor to drive share prices higher. The nationalisation of the Bank of England had handed £56m to shareholders, but the nationalisation of coal and Cable & Wireless only laid down general principles for negotiation of the detailed terms of compensation, negotiations that, in the case of coal, were still not completed by the time the Government was defeated in 1951. However, the King's Speech on 12 November 1946 specifically promised the nationalisation of transport and electricity supply.

Within a few days of the speech, the Minister of Transport announced the nationalisation of the railways based on market prices at a total cost of £1,023m in government stock. The controversy surrounding this decision is described in Chapter 5, Nationalisation, but the consequential effect on the stock market was dramatic. Within 2 days, equities had risen by some 3% to take the Index to a new all-time high of 130.5 on 20 November, encouraged also by high daily bargain volumes of around 12,000.

Two new factors were at work:

- the existing holders of securities in rail stocks were faced with a severe drop in income from the prospective issue of government stock at an interest rate of around 3%; and
- nationalisation was now perceived to be sharply reducing the available pool of equity stock.

Two months after rail nationalisation, it was announced on 10 January 1947 that the electricity supply industry was also to be nationalised on terms based on market prices. It was now apparent that nationalisation had already taken out, or would be taking out over the next year or so, around £1,700m of debenture, preference and ordinary shares and, in almost all cases, this would involve a fall in income.

The total market capitalisation of the debenture, preference and equity sectors of the market was around £9,500m, of which nearly 20% was being removed in return for compensation likely to be reinvested in an ever-diminishing supply, driven particularly by the need to replace lost income. Very high bargain volumes built up in December 1946 and January 1947 as private shareholders sold their rail and electricity supply stocks to reinvest in other ordinary and preference shares. Reduced supply and rising demand on this scale inevitably drove share prices higher and the FT Index ended the year on 31 December at an all-time high of 135.3.

The market continued in buoyant mood in the new year, receiving another boost from the announcement on 10 January 1947 of the terms of the nationalisation of the electricity supply companies. On each day of the following week, the FT Index reached a new high, taking it to 140.6 on Friday, 17 January with bargain levels consistently at more than 15,000 a day. By this time, the impetus of reinvestment had run its course. On Monday 20 January, bargain numbers reached a record of 19,438, but the sellers won the day and the Index fell by one point.

The reversal of a strongly established trend combined with very high volumes is often a strong indicator of a turning point in stock markets, at both its peaks and troughs. On this occasion, in January 1947, it was to prove to be not only the peak of this particular bull market, but also the peak for the whole of the remaining four and a half years of the Labour Government. While the single factor of reinvestment was driving prices higher, the market was choosing to ignore bearish factors that were there to be seen. Over the next three years, the economy was about to endure crisis after crisis, punitive measures would be specifically aimed at shareholders and the FT Index would fall to 99.8 in November 1949. This would prove to be one of the longest and most depressing of bear markets.

Chapter 3

DEVALUATION

January 1947–November 1949

FT Index   17 January 1947   140.6
                    10 November 1949   99.8   Down 29.0%

The Minister for Fuel and Power, Emanuel Shinwell, opened the debate in the House of Commons on the nationalisation of the electricity supply industry on 4 February 1947. With fine rhetoric he claimed that 'too long has the electricity consumer been made the victim of financial speculation'. What he actually meant was that here was another profitable industry owned by private shareholders and, therefore, by definition exploiting its customers for the benefit of a lot of speculators. As was pointed out by the *Financial Times* on the following day, he overlooked that unit prices of electricity had been falling steadily since 1930 and by some 40% in real terms.

Three days later, as dusk was gathering on a Friday afternoon, the same Emanuel Shinwell imposed on electricity consumers – those 'victims of financial speculation' – some of the most onerous power cuts ever known, effective from the following Monday morning. There would be widespread power cuts on a rota basis throughout industry and no weekday domestic power at all for three hours in the mornings and two hours in the afternoons.

These power cuts were blithely announced without warning, prompted by the onset of one of the most bitterly cold winters on record with a deep cover of snow followed by weeks of biting, freezing winds. As the roads became impassable and the railways closed down, coal could not be moved from pit head to power station. The utter dependence of the economy in the 1940s on the supply of coal is difficult to appreciate today but it also makes the occurrence of the crisis less excusable.

Several times during the previous autumn a potentially serious shortfall of production of coal had been flagged. Estimates were made that the demand for coal in 1947 would be 203,000,000 tons, but that domestic supply would be only 193,000,000 tons. Despite much prompting, no action was taken on these warnings. No attempt was made to import coal, recruit more miners or put in hand any emergency planning to build up stockpiles of coal at power stations. Shinwell gambled on a mild winter and was caught out. His combination of bluster and complacency made him deeply unpopular and reflected badly on the competence of a government that believed central planning was more efficient than private enterprise.

The announcement of the emergency power cuts led to one of the single biggest one-day falls in the FT Index during the life of the Government, when, on Monday 10 February 1947, the Index fell by 3.3% from 131.9 to 127.5. Within a few days, industry was reduced to a two- or three-day week and an estimated five million workers were made idle across the country. A ban was specifically imposed on various activities, including greyhound racing and the publication of periodicals. *The Economist* and the *Investors Chronicle* were given space in the *Financial Times* on Fridays for their regular weekly editorial columns. The situation became so serious that the Prime Minister took over personal responsibility for the problems of the supply of coal during this period, but his action highlighted failure rather than inspired confidence.

If investors are classically advised never to sell on a strike, because all strikes come to an end, so they should never sell on bad weather, for it is bound to turn for the better. So the market began to recover its nerve and awaited the Budget on 15 April 1947. In the event, the Budget was a particularly nasty one for the Stock Exchange, the activities of which Hugh Dalton had always regarded with contempt.

Since becoming Chancellor, he had followed a policy of exhorting companies to show restraint over dividend declarations. He now introduced a measure designed specifically to discourage dividend payments by separating the existing profits tax of 5% into two tiers. The rate of 5% would remain unchanged for undistributed profits, but a new rate of 12½% would apply to distributed profits.

In further measures specifically aimed at the stock market, he introduced a 10% tax on the value of scrip issues, and doubled the rate of stamp duty on the purchase of shares from 1% to 2%. It seems that he believed a scrip issue to be a free gift to shareholders, and was concerned that the public might be deceived if a scrip issue led to the declaration of a lower percentage rate of dividend. His profits tax legislation was designed to encourage retentions, but his tax on scrip issues would stop a company from making a scrip issue to bring the nominal capital more closely into line with the reserves created by those same retentions. The doubling of stamp duty was petty and its long-term result was to weaken the trading strength of the London market in foreign securities, thus forfeiting much-needed foreign revenues.

The stock market usually recovered after budgets under this Labour Government, because, however damaging the contents, the market had always feared worse. It did so briefly on this occasion before being caught in one of those long periods of lethargy seen frequently in the late 1940s. Over 8 business days from 25 April, the FT Index moved only between 134.3 and 134.6 (broadly the equivalent of 12 points in the FTSE Index today) and, over the next 2 months, the Index idled within a range from 134 to 137.

The February power cuts raised doubts about the Government's competence, and the relentless pursuit of nationalisation led to questioning of its priorities in the face of other looming problems. Most serious of all was the balance of payments. Earlier in the year, the publication of trade figures for 1946 showed imports of £1,247m and exports of £912m, a trend that would exhaust reserves before too long. The Government was still using wartime measures to solve peacetime problems. Ministers genuinely believed that civil service planning, careful rationing and cooperation of the kind that worked during the war would solve any problem, but they had now been in office long enough for the wisdom of their policies to come under increasing attack.

In a Commons debate in June 1947, Oliver Lyttelton, a leading Conservative front-bench spokesman and one of the few members of Parliament with genuine industrial experience, stated that 'Nationalisation is delaying the national recovery'. He urged the Government to break out of its barriers of controls and allow a much greater flow of consumer goods into the domestic market. This would encourage greater production in industry, which in turn would lead to more exports and bigger markets.

He quoted the example of Belgium where, two years after the war, rationing had largely disappeared as a result of the virtuous circle of allowing the domestic market to expand at its own speed by promoting prosperity. In contrast, he claimed, Britain suffered from a *vicious* circle. Too many controls and too many officials caused production to suffer, whereupon more controls were introduced to deal with shortfalls, requiring yet more officials. Round and round went this depressing circle, removing incentives to work, manufacture and expand because of the bureaucratic approvals that had to be sought from people with little or no experience or understanding of industry.

Lyttelton wanted the Government to free the marketplace, remove the emphasis on exporting and make consumer goods widely available to mop up the spending power that had built up both during and after the war. In his view, this would encourage the market to grow, supplies to expand and, from greater and more efficient production, exports would inevitably follow.

Freedom of this kind was evident in other European countries, and nowhere more so than in the newly emerging West Germany, where the freedom of the marketplace was in striking contrast to the stranglehold of Communism imposed on East Germany. The industrial and economic policies pursued in the United Kingdom in the late 1940s appeared, absurdly, to have more in common with those of East Germany than of the nascent West Germany Britain was helping to administer.

The same theme had been expressed earlier in a letter to the *Financial Times* on 15 October 1946 from Sir Miles Thomas, Deputy Chairman of Morris Motors, and later to be Chairman of BOAC. He addressed the Government's policies of allocating steel output in the face of much higher demand and wrote that, 'When industry faces excessive demand over supply, the instinct is to raise and expand supply. The instinct of the bureaucrat and the planner is to ration demand and discover priorities and in so doing introduce yet another level of form filling'.

Through the summer of 1947, concerns were growing about the chronic nature of problems with the balance of trade and the inadequacy of reserves to meet trade deficits. Of course this was not just a problem for Britain – it was shared, to some extent, by every European country involved in the war. Industrial nations such as Britain, France and Italy had been seriously weakened, and two of the great industrial nations of the world – Germany and Japan – had been devastated.

The United States alone had an economy untouched by war. It had, in any case, been the leading industrial nation of the world before the war and its huge productive capacity now dominated the world as leading or sole supplier of many goods. In early 1946, it ran a balance of payments surplus of $9,000m (£2,250m) compared with a UK trade deficit of £330m. In early 1947, the surplus was running at a rate approaching $20,000m. This was an incredible situation for the US economy, except for the problem that it was actually itself financing more than half the surplus in the form of aid, gifts or loans, and the rest of the world was rapidly running out of resources to finance the other half. Thus, an industrial boom of quite extraordinary proportions was in danger of collapsing under the weight of its own success.

This problem was identified by George Marshall, US Secretary of State, who detailed the scale of aid required by Europe to sustain trade in a famous speech at Harvard on 5 June 1947. Europe would need aid of some $6,000m a year to pay for goods needed from the United States for the next 3 to 5 years. He successfully persuaded his people of their economic interest in helping to bring about a recovery in the economies of Europe, but he was also sensitive to the political interest in strengthening Europe to provide a bulwark against the spread of Communism, even though his early thoughts involved giving aid to Russia and its East European satellites.

'A Magnificent Gesture' was the heading of the leader in the *Financial Times* on the following morning, and a few days later the same newspaper lamented that, in another time, it would have been welcomed with a 'flood of Churchillian eloquence' rather than the apparently lukewarm response so far given by the Government to this initiative. The next day, Foreign Secretary Ernest Bevin rather belatedly commented that Marshall's speech 'may well rank as one of the greatest speeches in the world's history'.

Further need for US aid surprised many in Britain because, less than a year earlier, loans of £1,380m had been negotiated with the United States and Canada to finance dollar imports over the next 3 or 4 years. One of the terms of the US loan was that sterling convertibility should be reintroduced one year after the loan came into effect. This proved to be disastrous. When sterling became freely convertible on 15 July 1947, the Government was inundated with demands from countries in the British Commonwealth and elsewhere to convert their sterling balances into dollars. These demands were partly driven by a genuine need for dollars, but perhaps more by a perception that sterling was overvalued at $4.03 to the pound. The run on sterling proved so severe that, on 21 August 1947, convertibility of the pound into dollars had to be suspended indefinitely.

Panic spread rapidly through the stock market as the seriousness of the situation unfolded, inducing a 20% fall in the FT Index in 5 weeks from 130.0 on 25 July to 104.2 on 3 September – a speed and scale of decline associated more with modern markets than with those sedate days of the 1940s and 1950s. There was a sequence from 14 August to 3 September when the FT Index fell on 14 consecutive days.

In a radio broadcast on 1 September, the noted economist Roy Harrod suggested that only half of the US loan of £1,100m had been used to finance trade, whereas half had been used up to meet claims from countries such as India, Pakistan, Ceylon, Egypt and Iraq for the settlement of debts built up during the war, and from other countries taking advantage of the window of opportunity to convert sterling into dollars. With hindsight, the Government was either too generous in acknowledging these sterling debts or did not fully understand their significance, but, whatever the reason, the word was beginning to get around that this huge dollar loan was all but exhausted within a year.

Winston Churchill was largely an absentee leader of the Conservatives in opposition in Parliament, and he preferred to attack Labour in a major speech at Blenheim Palace on 4 August 1947 for their failure to act as the dollar crisis was looming:

> The Government had the knowledge but they neither had the sense nor the decision to act. They were too busy planning and making their brave new world of controls and queues, of hordes of officials, and multitudes of regulations. They exhausted what energies they had in choking the House of Commons with partisan legislation, in disturbing, discouraging and even paralysing business enterprise by nationalisation schemes of no productive value.

Now that the crisis had surfaced, the Government responded with a flurry of activity reminiscent of its reaction to the coal crisis in February. With barely £100m remaining from the US loan and a looming trade gap for the year of more than £300m, it announced on 27 August a series of emergency measures planned to reduce imports by £228m. Draconian measures were proposed. The meat ration was cut by twopence to 1/- per week; points for food rationing were reduced by more than 10%; the basic petrol ration for private motoring was abolished; no travel was allowed outside the sterling area for holidays and within the sterling area the allowance was more than halved; and stringent controls were imposed on hotels and restaurants.

Exhilarated by gloom, and with that utter belief that a central plan will resolve any problem, Sir Stafford Cripps, President of the Board of Trade, announced on 12 September that every industry in Britain would receive an 'export target' from a committee formed under the chairmanship of Harold Wilson, and the flow of new equipment, machinery and other resources would be directed to those industries with export potential, at the expense of those without. It would certainly ensure the creation of further regiments of officials to administer more controls.

Cripps was a rising influence in the Government and, on 30 September, it was announced that he was to become the newly created Minister for Economic Affairs, with Harold Wilson replacing him as President of the Board of Trade. The Government believed difficult problems could only be resolved by planning and more planning and a return to the wartime spirit and as he announced these changes the Prime Minister lamented that, 'we have got to get something other than the profit motive. I cannot see why the motive of service to the community should not operate in peace as it did in war'. Fewer words show less understanding of how a trading and manufacturing nation functions than this denial of the profit motive, but from Attlee it was a regular theme.

The run on the pound during those few weeks of sterling convertibility in July and August unhinged the equity market and prompted whispers about devaluation. It was never discussed publicly by politicians and rarely raised in press articles, but many believed devaluation would be a partial solution to the economy's structural problems. The *Financial Times* made no specific proposals, but published a letter on 6 September 1947 from a reader, stating that 'the plain fact is that the pegged rate of $4.03 is artificial and cannot long be maintained'. He further argued that a rate of $3 to the pound would reduce the insatiable demand for dollars.

This opinion was about to be justified in a practical way following the Exchange Control Act, which came into force on 1 October 1947. The relevance of this Act for the stock market was that it permitted owners of US stocks to sell and reinvest in other dollar stocks without having to return the dollars to the Treasury. However, if sellers did not wish to reinvest, they were free to sell these 'investment' dollars to other investors in a market based on supply and demand. This became known as the dollar premium and it was to survive until 1979. Expectations in London were that the premium would start at around 10%, but within a week it reached 20%, illustrating the price investors were willing to pay to switch away from the pound. The same reasons lay behind the strength of gold shares during this period.

Devaluation was a taboo subject for discussion in 1947 because sterling was second only to the dollar in being widely used by many countries as their reserve currency and for the settlement of trade. A psychological comfort for both the Government and the stock market was an awareness that the Marshall Aid proposals were working their way through the political system in the United States, and although at this stage the extent to which Britain would participate was not known, at least something was expected to take the place of the nearly exhausted 1946 dollar loan. In the event, the struggle to defend the pound would continue for another two years before devaluation in September 1949.

After its 20% slide in the space of a few weeks, the market gradually began to recover its poise and, by early October, the FT Index had risen from a low of 104.2 on 3 September to around 117. The good news was that the Marshall Aid discussions were moving rapidly to a successful conclusion, but with puritanical frankness Cripps warned that survival was only possible with dollar aid or a further drastic cut in imports. The situation was exacerbated by a decision of the United States to freeze the last remaining £100m of the 1946 dollar loan during the Marshall Aid discussions, and morale was dampened by rumours of large transfers of gold bullion on board the Queen Elizabeth from London to New York.

At the same time, the Chancellor announced in his annual Mansion House speech the probability of a further budget in the autumn. Meanwhile, the hapless Emmanuel Shinwell was quietly transferred from the Ministry of Fuel and Power and dropped from the Cabinet. He had recently been heard to say that he would like to have completed the 'trilogy' of coal, electricity and gas, but feared that he would be moved from office. 'Men and Matters' in the *Financial Times* on 29 September – then a more political column and sometimes mouthpiece for the views of Brendan Bracken, Editor and Conservative MP – pointed out that a trilogy means 'a group of three tragedies'. With a succession of new appointments for Cripps, Gaitskell and Wilson, the same column later observed on 13 October that 'industry is now in the hands of a bevy of socialist intellectuals'.

The market remained extremely nervous in advance of Hugh Dalton's fourth Budget in just over two years on 12 November. He again admonished companies for raising dividends: 'I have noticed with regret the continuing custom on the part of many companies of declaring increased dividends'. To deal with this, and as part of a deflationary budget to curb spending, he doubled the 2 rates of profits tax, from 5% to 10% on undistributed profits and from 12½% to 25% on distributed profits. He also sharply increased the four rates of purchase tax.

However, this Budget will always be remembered not for its measures, but for the shock of his resignation on the following day, 14 November, because of a careless conversation with a journalist just prior to his rising to speak. His fate received little sympathy in the City where he was neither liked nor respected because in both word and deed he was frivolous, hostile and distrustful. The immediate appointment of Sir Stafford Cripps as Chancellor of the Exchequer was generally welcomed out of respect for his intellectual honesty.

The year closed with a new Chancellor, the prospect of Marshall Aid, and the forthcoming issue on 1 January 1948 of more than £1,000m of government stock as compensation for the railways. This was much the biggest of all the nationalisation issues and there was much selling by the private investor, reinvestment in other equities and heavy buying of a prospective gilt stock by insurance companies and pension funds. The FT Index closed the year at 128.3, a recovery of nearly a quarter from the low point of 3 September, but well below the January peak of 140.6. However, it had been a busy and prosperous year for the Stock Exchange with average daily bargains running at more than 10,000 for much of the year.

Nationalisation continued apace in 1948, with vesting date for the newly created British Transport Commission on 1 January and British Electricity Authority on 1 April. Between these two dates, on 23 January, the Bill for the nationalisation of the gas industry was presented to Parliament. On 1 March there was news that the 1946 US loan of £1,100m was now exhausted after 20 months. However, discussions on Marshall Aid were well advanced and, in April, it was announced that the UK would receive £331m in its first year – the largest allocation out of a total for the year of £1,325m.

By comparison, France was allocated £283m, Italy £175m and the western zones of Germany some £110m. The aid was to be in the form of imports from the United States, mainly by way of gift, but, in some cases, as a loan with repayment. The purpose of the aid was to enable the economies of western Europe to build up their productive capacity and develop trade volumes sufficient to sustain future US imports. In the case of the United Kingdom, the loan did little more than close the existing dollar import gap and, in the event, would come to be used largely to cover the purchase of grain, oil, chemicals, cotton and tobacco.

Marshall Aid was formally defined as the 'European Recovery Programme', but some of its terms were vague. It appeared that around 80% of the cost of the programme would be given in the form of aid, with those countries less affected by the war taking it in the form of loan and those on the brink of collapse taking it in full as a gift. For the UK, it was understood that a quarter of the total would be taken in the form of a loan and the balance as a gift. It was a condition of the programme that each government would set aside a counter-party fund from proceeds of any imports resold to help build productive capacity. In the UK, this fund was used to reduce the national debt on the basis that this would curb inflation. Other countries made more productive use of this counter-party fund for the purchase of machinery and capital goods, but it was anathema to the Labour Government that help of this kind should go directly to the private sector. It is a sombre thought that Marshall Aid is popularly believed to have equipped West Germany for its economic miracle, but it was made available to Britain in much greater amount.

Marshall Aid satisfied two strong instincts of the American people – self-interest and generosity. The programme was created out of the fear that a European economic collapse would open the door to Communism and induce a slump in the United States. The solution was generous and magnanimous, but for Britain it served more to relax than to stimulate. It allowed ministers to continue to govern from hand to mouth for another year or so before facing the inevitability of devaluation late in 1949. The idea that it was designed to build up the productive capacity of the private sector of the economy did not register with the Attlee Government.

On 1 January 1948, the Government issued £1,023m of British Transport 3% 1978/88 at par as compensation for the holders of rail stocks. This brought to a close a large traditional sector of the market known as 'home rails' with origins stretching back to the railway boom of the 1840s. In their place was this single issue of a long-dated stock with a life of 40 years, later to become well known as 'long transport' and widely used by high taxpayers in the 1960s and 1970s because of its low interest yield but high redemption yield.

On the first day of dealing, there was a huge turnover, with long queues of brokers trying to sell stock at a discount of around 2½% on the issue price. An unprecedented number of 2,036 bargains were marked in gilts that day. The FT Index was steady throughout January at around 125, with the prospect of more switching into equities as vesting date for the electricity industry approached on 1 April 1948 when some £350m of stock would be issued, and the announcement on 23 January of proposed compensation of £200m for the gas companies.

On 8 February, further help arrived in the form of the proposal of the Government of Argentina to buy out the shareholders of the Argentine Rail Companies for payment of around £150m. This provided a welcome boost to the prices of Argentine stocks, but the consideration of £150m was well short of the original nominal issued value of £250m. The stock market was still learning after more than a hundred years that foreign loans to the less developed world usually means foreign *losses*, a learning curve that was later to be experienced in the 1980s by the clearing banks in lending to the Third World.

Despite a favourable technical background from reinvestment, it all went wrong in February when the market suffered another of those alarming sell-offs that can be so bewildering to the outside investor. In the space of 3 weeks, the FT Index fell 13% from 125.3 on 3 February to 109.5 on 26 February. It was largely due to Sir Stafford Cripps, who, more than any minister before or since, believed in discussing problems in the starkest detail, seemingly unaware that people can be frightened by frank diagnosis. Two White Papers were issued on successive days in February 1948 – one on personal incomes, costs and prices and the other on the balance of payments.

It was a particular sentence in the first White Paper – 'there is no justification at the present time for any rise in incomes from profits, rents, or other like sources' – that sent shivers through the stock market. The White Paper proposed a general price freeze and some individual price cuts to be implemented immediately. Within two weeks, the Board of Trade published a series of absurdly overdetailed price standstill orders, ranging from walking sticks to shove ha'penny boards which were clearly unenforceable without further layers of bureaucracy. They were damned in a *Financial Times* leader on 25 February as the 'crowning absurdity of government by petty detailed regulation', but in reality, they were the political price paid to encourage the TUC to agree to a wages policy.

The TUC had already, in a statement on 18 February, indicated its acceptance provided that government policy was 'not only to stabilise but also to reduce profits and prices'. Many in the Government were convinced that rising profits and the payment of higher dividends were prime contributors to inflation. In fact, the effects of inflation were deliberately hidden from large parts of the population. On the one hand, subsidies were used to keep food prices down, and, on the other, strong trade unions exploited the commitment to full employment by the widespread use of restrictive practices to keep wage increases ahead of price increases. Food subsidies were costing the Exchequer around £320m a year – the equivalent of 3s 3d in the pound on income tax in 1947 – and without these subsidies the prices of basic foods would have been 30% higher.

The Chancellor continued his negotiations in advance of the 1948 Budget and was unexpectedly helped by the Federation of British Industries, the predecessor of the CBI, which responded to the White Paper by proposing for its members a voluntary policy of dividend limitation at current levels. On 15 March, the Chancellor said that he would 'gladly accept' the offer from the FBI of voluntary dividend restraint, and, on 24 March, the TUC announced its agreement with the Government on a policy of wage restraint.

Within six weeks of the publication of the original White Paper, the Chancellor had secured agreement on prices, wages and dividends, and his Budget was still two weeks away. It was a remarkable political achievement that reflected well on the honesty and integrity of the Chancellor, but dividend limitation was bad news for the stock market.

With these policies in place, the Chancellor was left with only a few details to include in his Budget on 6 April 1948. One detail owed much to prejudice when he discriminated against the owners of stocks and shares by imposing a 'once for all' levy on investment income, starting at 10% on the first £500 and rising to 50% on investment income over £5,000. It was a clumsy substitute for a wealth tax, and described by the Chancellor as a special levy intended to be 'largely payable out of capital'. Its yield of £105m in a full year would fall on relatively few shoulders.

His obsession with wealth was reflected in another measure that reduced the amount of capital allowed to be taken by persons emigrating outside the sterling area from £5,000 to £1,000. However, for the stock market, these two measures were relative irritants compared with the seriousness of dividend limitation, which, although voluntary, could at any time be enforced by statutory legislation. This period of voluntary dividend limitation was to last for two and a half years and would prove damaging to the valuation of equity shares.

One immediate effect was a reduction in activity in the Stock Exchange and the last 9 months of 1948 proved to be one of the dullest ever periods with rarely more than 5,000 or 6,000 bargains a day. On the day of the Budget on 6 April 1948, the FT Index stood at 119.1 and it ended the year at 121.3 It drifted a shade lower during the summer and at times became so becalmed that opening the market for an hour a day would have been sufficient. For example, there was a sequence of 17 successive business days from 9 September when the FT Index stayed within a range of 115.1 and 115.8.

Stockbrokers dependent on either private clients or on equity business were hit hard and there were mergers among the smaller firms. However, times were prosperous for stockbrokers in other areas of the market, particularly those involved in gilts (still much the biggest segment of the market) and new issues. In July, ICI announced that it was to raise £20.4m via a 1 for 5 rights issue at 40/6d. This was one of the largest ever rights issues, equivalent to some £400m today, and the first time ICI had raised equity capital since its formation in the 1920s. The leading new issue broker of the day was Cazenove, but the names of the four brokers to the ICI issue, Hoare & Co., Panmure Gordon, Rowe & Pitman and J. & A. Scrimgeour, give a flavour of which firms were active in new issues in this post-war period. The success of a new issue would vitally depend on the support of Leslie Brown, Investment Manager of the Prudential – one of the most influential investors of his time. His was the signature of the lead underwriter in the 1940s and 1950s.

Despite inertia in the stock market, 1948 was a year of landmark events. In West Germany, the Deutschemark came into being on 20 June 1948, to replace the Reichsmark. It started life at 13 to the pound – it is around 3 today. It was the year when Truman won the US Presidential election against all the odds on 4 November and the Dow Jones Index fell by just under 4% on the day, following a result that was just as great a shock to the Republican party and its Wall Street supporters as had been the defeat of Churchill in 1945.

However, a more important date for the stock market was 1 July 1948 as that was when the new Companies Act came into force. Companies Acts are reviewed and enacted from time to time, but the only previous Acts of any significance in this century had been in 1908 and 1929. The new Act was based almost entirely on the report by Mr Justice Cohen, commissioned during the war and published in 1945. Its landmark reform was to require companies to publish accounts consolidating the results of all their subsidiaries, whereas existing law allowed the publication of the accounts of the parent company with the subsidiaries only reflected to the extent of any dividends paid to the parent. Until this much-needed reform, the performance of subsidiaries could be hidden from the shareholder, be they highly profitable or loss-making.

The same Act allowed some concessions to secrecy to continue. Banks, insurance companies and shipping companies were permitted to make undisclosed transfers to their inner reserves before publishing a profits figure. This concession to banks and insurance companies had been an original proposal of the Cohen Report to smooth cyclical results that might otherwise have caused loss of public confidence, but for less obvious reasons pressure from the shipping companies persuaded the Government that they, too, should be allowed this concession.

Consolidated accounts made it possible for the first time for investors to assess the proper value revealed by the balance sheets and profit and loss accounts of quoted companies, and to make meaningful comparisons between companies. The disappointment of this Act was its failure to require sales figures to be published in the profit and loss account. The publication of sales, or turnover, was common practice in the United States, but it was too soon to challenge the cultural secrecy of those running British industry, who pleaded confidentiality against giving information to competitors, but as likely meant they disliked unwelcome intrusion by outsiders.

The 1948 Companies Act thus provided new ingredients for statistical analysis, and from this was born the profession of investment analysis, or research as it is popularly known. The reforms of this Act played an important role in the emergence of the cult of the equity in the 1950s.

The stock market was dormant at the turn of the year and in January and February 1949 it became completely becalmed. There was a period of four consecutive weeks when the FT Index never moved outside the range of 122.0 and 122.8. In February, the FBI agreed to a second year of voluntary dividend restraint, although feebly asked that it be linked to control over wages and salaries and reductions in the Government's expenditure. The Budget on 6 April was marginally helpful with the repeal of the 10% tax on bonus issues, and a doubling of the first year depreciation allowance on new plant from 20% to 40%, but there was little incentive to buy shares with dividends so tightly controlled.

The morale of the stock market was not helped in April when the National Executive of the Labour party proposed that the next election manifesto should include the nationalisation of industrial life assurance, cement, sugar and possibly the chemical industry. Tate & Lyle, Prudential and the cement manufacturers condemned these proposals as an unnecessary attack on efficient and profitable industries – and planned their defences, which would later include the 'Mr Cube' advertising campaign to save the sugar industry.

The Stock Exchange announced measures to encourage more business by reinstating dealing practices that had been suspended since 1939. Free closing was reintroduced so that no commission was charged on the sale or repurchase of a holding bought or sold earlier in the same fortnightly account. Also, 'contangos' were brought back, whereby settlement could be deferred from one account to the next for a small fee.

In August 1949, the Stock Exchange introduced Rule 163i(e), allowing jobbers to quote prices in the London Market in any security that 'has been granted a quotation on a Dominion, Colonial or Foreign Stock Exchange'. This rule sustained the reputation of London as the most international of all Stock Exchanges, although it was a hollow gesture compared with the burden of the 2% stamp duty that was prompting a migration of the markets in mining shares and international stocks from London to New York and Paris, where no such duty existed. A further reform introduced by the Stock Exchange in March was the principle of charging companies for the listing of their securities.

These practical measures had little effect while investors remained so numbed by the dismal economic and financial background. All prospective members of the Stock Exchange were required to purchase a 'nomination', or share, in the Stock Exchange. These were bought and sold in the open market and in August 1949 the price fell to £10, believed to be its lowest ever price. Just a year earlier, the price had been £200, and the highest ever known was 2,000 guineas. It may be an anachronism, but the price of a nomination in London, or the price of a seat in other Stock Exchanges, is always a good indicator of business levels and immediate prospects.

The economic prospects were indeed grim. The gold and dollar reserves were fast vanishing, despite the inflow of Marshall Aid. Devaluation was now openly discussed, but constantly denied. Wage increases were creeping through, despite the policy of restraint, and, although raw material prices were falling in the rest of the world, they were still rising for industry at home because of clumsy central bulk buying at earlier higher levels. Losses in the newly nationalised coal and rail industries were passed on to industrial consumers in price increases, the only way they knew how to reduce deficits. It was politically easier to pass higher prices on to industry than to individuals, who were sheltered in so many ways from the reality of the situation.

In a debate on the economic situation, the Chancellor announced on 14 July 1949 a 25% cut in dollar imports of tobacco, sugar, timber, paper and base metals, some to be replaced by imports from within the sterling area. A Toronto newspaper, the *Financial Post*, on 15 July, diagnosed the problems quite differently as 'Britain's fundamental difficulty today is, in the simplest and starkest form, the unwillingness of her people to work hard enough'. The need to impose yet further controls on imports was depressing for everybody and, a few days later, Sir Stafford Cripps was rushed to hospital in Switzerland for six weeks for the treatment of a digestive ailment. His responsibilities were taken over by the Prime Minister, assisted by Harold Wilson and Hugh Gaitskell.

Cripps returned from Switzerland in time to fly directly to Washington for previously arranged talks between the United States, Canada, and the UK about the sterling crisis. Amid worldwide rumours of devaluation he returned to London to broadcast to the nation on the evening of Sunday 18 September 1949. Cripps announced a 30% devaluation, from $4.03 to $2.80 – more than had been anticipated, although the investment dollar premium at around 35% had for some time been indicating a prospective rate of under $3.

The Stock Exchange was closed on Monday 19 September and a large and active pavement market developed outside in Throgmorton Street. Enough business was transacted to allow the calculation of a rise in the FT Index from 108.2 to 110.1. Gold shares were remarkably strong and the FT Gold Index rose by nearly 20%. Although it was an entirely logical reaction to devaluation, the rise in the price of gold shares on the pavement market on the Monday was later to attract the scorn of an outraged Aneurin Bevan in a House of Commons debate on 29 September that, 'we have asked the miners, the steel men and the railway men not to imitate the obscene plundering that went on on the Monday in Throgmorton Street'.

While the initial reaction in the stock market had been phlegmatic, prices fell away quickly, not helped by a decision of the Chancellor during a devaluation debate on 27 September to increase distributed profits tax from 25% to 30%, as a measure of 'rough justice' to even out the burden of devaluation. It was also a reminder that any further failure of voluntary dividend limitation would lead to legislation in the next Finance Bill. He had been provoked to make this comment by a recent decision of Associated Portland Cement to ignore dividend restraint with a 15% increase, because it felt powerless to achieve fair value for its shareholders in any other way under the threat of nationalisation.

The news of devaluation reverberated around the world because the sterling area was significantly larger than any currency area outside the dollar and this role of sterling made devaluation more traumatic than it would be today. Reuters estimated that 15 countries followed the devaluation exactly within a matter of hours, but others varied, with France devaluing by 20%, Belgium by 12% and Canada by 10%. Switzerland, host to the Chancellor during his recuperation, decided after a week's thought that no devaluation of their legendary Swiss franc was necessary.

Cripps returned from Switzerland to argue the case for devaluation with all the fervour and intellect of the brilliant barrister he once had been. With time to think, he had become convinced of its need, and almost with relish he explained the benefits for the country flowing from this new policy. In fact, there was relief in many countries in Europe, already convinced that an unrealistic level of the pound was holding up recovery by putting a constraint on their own currencies. Before too long, the strain on his health was to cost Cripps his life, but his reputation survives because of his honesty and openness in dealing with this and other problems. He was a rare example in Britain of a minister who regularly held press conferences to encourage open policy discussion. Nevertheless, an impression remains that each and every problem was just another brief for a brilliant lawyer, intent on a solution, but blind to the part his own Government's policies may have played in causing the problem.

The Government was now well into its fifth year of office and interest was turning to the forthcoming general election. To dispel rumours, the Prime Minister announced in October 1949 that he would not be holding an election until the following year. The highly controversial Iron and Steel Nationalisation Bill completed its passage through Parliament in November, but, at the insistence of the House of Lords, a clause was inserted to postpone the planned vesting date from 1 May 1950 to 1 January 1951 to allow for the judgement of the electorate in the forthcoming general election.

In the autumn of 1949, the country remained in a state of perpetual crisis. There was talk of an increase in Bank rate, and Consols 2½% – still a benchmark for the gilt-edged market – touched a yield of 4% for the first time in the life of this Government, the price having fallen by 40% from 100 in the early Dalton days to 60. Equities fared no better and within weeks of the devaluation on 10 November 1949, the FT Index fell below 100 for a single day, when it closed at 99.8. With hindsight, this was to prove to be the turning point and a long bear market – lasting nearly three years – had come to an end.

Chapter 4

SCENT OF VICTORY
November 1949–October 1951

FT Index	10 November 1949	99.8	
	25 October 1951	138.3	Up 38.6%

The FT Index crept slowly up from its November 1949 low to 106.4 at the year's end. The yield on equities was 5.25% compared with 3.5% on gilts, but with dividend limitation for the last two years and the FBI recommending its continuation for a third year, ordinary shares had become little more than fixed interest investments. However, there were some encouraging straws in the political wind, with the defeat of the Labour Government in Australia in December 1949, and the publication in January 1950 of two opinion polls showing Conservative leads of 10% and 14% over Labour. There was surprise on 10 January when Clement Attlee suddenly dissolved Parliament and called a general election for 23 February 1950. His overall majority of 146 seats in the 1945 election had been whittled down by by-elections to 128, but it was still a formidable majority.

For the stock market, the campaign was extraordinarily muted. The FT Index had closed at 105.3 just before the announcement of the election, and over the next month, from 11 January to 13 February, there was barely a flicker in the market, with the FT Index set between 103.4 and 104.8 throughout. For eight successive days in the middle of the campaign, it stood at 104.2 or 104.3. It was only with a week to go that share prices began to rise with growing optimism about the chances of a Conservative victory, and, on the day of the election, the Index reached 108.0, with the politically sensitive cement and life assurance shares particularly strong.

The Conservative party manifesto was a mix of specific policies and motherhood statements, but 'This is the Road' offered a different future from the socialism of the last five years. Specific measures included pledges to reduce direct taxation, remove many of the controls on industry, stop the nationalisation of iron and steel, restore road haulage to the private sector and end bulk buying. More general statements referred to the maintenance of a policy of full employment, the promotion of thrift, the re-establishment of confidence in sterling, encouragement to house building and the production of more food. The Labour party manifesto reiterated its existing policies, particularly in the field of social security, and included specific proposals for the nationalisation of sugar, cement and industrial life assurance.

There was a sharply worded debate about the stock market between Herbert Morrison and Mr J. B. Braithwaite, Chairman of the Stock Exchange. As the campaign was closing, cement and insurance shares were particularly strong because their nationalisation seemed less likely. On 19 February, with four days to go, Morrison described these movements in Stock Exchange prices during an election as 'irresponsible and flippant' and he compared stockbrokers to bookmakers. In a stern reply, the Chairman of the Stock Exchange issued a statement that:

> what Mr Morrison seems not to understand is that movements of prices are not made by the whims or wishes of members of the Stock Exchange but represent the tides of business influenced by economic and political conditions. The Stock Exchange can no more influence those tides than could King Canute order the tides of the sea.

true today?

Hostility towards the Stock Exchange was a deeply rooted instinct of the Labour party.

The election result was close to stalemate, with the overall Labour majority reduced from 128 to 6. The FT Index fell from 108.0 to 105.6 and stayed within that range for the next 3 months. The Government controversially announced its intention to implement the nationalisation of iron and steel, but the general belief in the market was that the very low majority of six would inhibit any further proposals for nationalisation or, indeed, extreme measures of any kind.

There was little in the Budget on 18 April 1950 to stimulate the market either way. There were reductions in two of the lower rates of income tax, and petrol tax was doubled from 9d to 1/6d per gallon, but this had little adverse effect on the average motorist, whose petrol ration was raised from 90 to 180 miles per month. The policy of wage restraint and voluntary dividend limitation was to continue for another year without legislation.

The stock market began to move ahead towards the end of May. The Government now understood some of the reasons for its unpopularity – particularly its reputation for rationing and controls. As a result, the rationing of petrol was ended in May and of soap in September. Steel rationing for industry was largely ended in May. The President of the Board of Trade, Harold Wilson, was later to refer to making a 'bonfire of controls' during his period in office, but the reality of this was not particularly apparent at the time.

The recovery was brought to a halt by the news on 26 June 1950 that South Korea had been invaded by North Korea. President Truman reacted fiercely and promptly and, within four weeks, was asking Congress for expenditure of $10,000m for a rearmament programme and the stockpiling of commodities. Attlee supported this initiative and, a week later, announced the provision of an extra £100m for the UK defence budget of £780m.

The stock market settled down and, for the remainder of the year, the FT Index never strayed far from around 115, holding steady because of an increasing awareness that both the balance of payments and company profitability were benefiting from devaluation. The gold and dollar reserves of the sterling area were growing, still underpinned by Marshall Aid, but helped by the US rearmament programme pushing up the prices of commodities produced in the sterling area, such as tin and rubber.

Another boost to the market came from a vote at the TUC Conference in September 1950 to end the policy of wage restraint, thereby loosening the foundations of voluntary dividend limitation. The Government's policy of wage restraint was now falling apart in the face of militant demands from the transport workers and the railwaymen. In the midst of these problems, ill health forced Sir Stafford Cripps to resign as Chancellor on 19 October. He was succeeded by Hugh Gaitskell, whose short-lived Ministry for Economic Affairs was abandoned and replaced by a Financial Secretary and an Economic Secretary to the Treasury.

The FT Index ended the year at 115.7 and markets started the new year in buoyant mood. Devaluation had been of great benefit to exports with the result that there was a balance of payments surplus of more than £200m in 1950, and such was the strength of the gold and dollar reserves that Marshall Aid was suspended for the United Kingdom from 1 January 1951. The recently introduced *Financial Times* monthly aggregate of company profits showed a 12% increase in earnings from the total of more than 3,500 companies reporting in 1950, and with wage restraint breaking down, companies began to abandon the policy of voluntary dividend limitation. The final impetus to the market came from the reinvestment of the proceeds of iron and steel nationalisation, for which vesting date had been set for 15 February 1951, when it was expected that some £200m of steel stock would be taken out of the market.

The market gathered speed in January and February 1951, with bargains frequently touching 10,000 to 12,000 a day, and a total of 16,454 bargains on 5 February was the busiest day since the market reached its peak in January 1947. On this particular day, the market was inspired by the possibility that the Government would not survive a censure debate on the Iron and Steel Act later in the week, although, ironically, it was switching from iron and steel compensation stock that was pushing the market to higher levels.

On 23 February 1951, the rail unions settled for a 7½% wages increase after repeated threats of a rail strike. It removed any pretence of a wages policy and the market, now believing voluntary dividend controls would rapidly break down, awaited Hugh Gaitskell's first Budget on 10 April 1951 with some trepidation. The Chancellor's comment on substantial dividend rises was to say 'we cannot afford that' and he abruptly raised distributed profits tax from 30% to 50% whilst leaving the undistributed profits tax unchanged at 10%. Profits tax started in April 1946 as a level tax of 5% before moving into separate distributed and undistributed bands a year later. While the latter had only changed once to its existing level of 10% in November 1947, the distributed tax had been successively increased from 5% to 12½% to 30% and now to 50%.

In this Budget, the Government had to face a dramatic increase in annual defence expenditure from £800m to £1,490m in response to the Korean war. The apparent orchestration of this war by Russia and China raised fears in the Western world about the long-term motives of these Communist empires. Following the example of the United States, a major three-year rearmament programme was launched in Britain that put an increasing burden on the economy, although some superbly designed military aircraft were successfully developed. The programme was financed partly by an increase in the standard rate of income tax from 9/- to 9/6d (45% to 47½%), with a reduction in the top rate of surtax from 10/6d to 10/- to contain the top rate at 97½%.

The stock market ignored the increase in profits tax, preferring to note the opportunities for dividend increases from the high dividend cover built up over two years of limitation. The FT Index rose from 122.6 on Budget day to 131.8 at the end of the following week.

This was to be a fateful moment for the Government. It had already been weakened by the loss of Chancellor Sir Stafford Cripps in October 1950 and Foreign Secretary Ernest Bevin in March 1951, both brought down by ill health. The Prime Minister was not in good health himself and the party was about to tear itself to pieces. On Sunday 22 April 1951, Aneurin Bevan, Minister of Labour, resigned from the Cabinet in protest against the imposition of charges in the Budget to raise £25m for dentures and spectacles in the National Health Service. He was its prime architect and Bevan will always be remembered as Minister of Health, but during his periods of office as Minister of Housing and Minister of Labour he was ineffective

He remained a wonderful orator and embodied the spirit of the left wing of the Labour party. In his resignation speech in the House of Commons on 23 April he was to show, yet again, his extraordinary sensitivity to activities in the City, and he was provoked by an onerous Budget being so well received by the stock market. He protested that 'the Budget was hailed with pleasure in the City. It is a remarkable Budget. It united the City, satisfied the Opposition and disunited the Labour party'.

Two days after his resignation, Bevan was joined on the back benches by the President of the Board of Trade, Harold Wilson, who, together with three future Labour ministers – Barbara Castle, Richard Crossman and Michael Foot – formed a small group of 'Bevanites'. With a majority of only five, the Labour party was now internally split and mortally wounded.

While these events were unfolding in Westminster, the party of nationalisation was given a taste of its own medicine. On 9 March 1951, the Parliament of

Persia had approved the nationalisation of the foreign-owned oil industry, dominated by the British-owned Anglo-Iranian Oil Company, shares in which fell by ⅜ to £5⅜, their lowest price since 1946. The Anglo-Iranian Oil Company – later to be better known as British Petroleum, or BP – was one of the largest companies quoted on the Stock Exchange. The Government had owned a controlling interest of 55.8% of its 20.1m shares since 1914, and Burmah Oil owned a further 26.5%. This dispute rumbled along through the summer, involving negotiations by British and international diplomats with Dr Mossadeq, the fiery Persian Prime Minister, and led to the closure of the Abadan refinery. However, this episode was more damaging to British pride than to the stock market.

After the resignation of Bevan and Wilson, the market roared ahead and, on 13 June 1950, the FT Index reached 140.4 – a whisker below its all-time high in January 1947. Devaluation benefits and higher depreciation allowances were now driving profits forward and the *Financial Times* table of aggregate company profits for the first six months of 1951 showed earnings rising by 18% and dividends by 10%. Ministers were making threatening noises about the level of dividend increases, but nobody was prepared for the severity of the measure suddenly proposed by the Chancellor in the economic debate on 26 July.

Gaitskell proposed to introduce legislation in the autumn to control dividends for three years, with a limit set at the average of the dividends paid in the last two accounting periods. The three-year timescale was designed to cover the period of the rearmament programme, but the calculation of the limit was onerous because any company that had increased its dividend in its latest financial year would have its norm set at a lower level because of the two-year average.

'Nothing like the proposed Dividend Control Bill has ever been seen before in British financial history', wrote Lex in the *Financial Times* on 27 July, 'It is much worse than the market had feared. It must shake investment confidence.' It did exactly that. On the following day, the FT Index fell by 3½% from 132.9 to 128.3, equal to a 200-point fall in the FTSE today. It was an occasion to revive political memories and in the debate on 30 July former Chancellor Hugh Dalton, relishing the situation, said 'My friend Mr Gaitskell's speech, whatever else it has done, has thrown the Stock Exchange into complete disorder and that is good fun, anyhow'.

On reflection, the market decided that Gaitskell's dividend controls would either be weakened by the time they were enacted or would be overtaken by an inevitable general election. Prices recovered during the traditionally quiet summer months until suddenly, without warning, Clement Attlee, in an evening broadcast on 19 September 1951, called a general election on 25 October 1951. On the following day, the FT Index bounded up from 135.3 to 138.6, strong in the belief that there would be a Conservative victory. In the event, this was the highest level reached by the Index in the course of the campaign. Despite nervousness as the early Conservative opinion poll lead of 8 points began to narrow, markets remained firm and, in the week of the election, there was persistent demand for good-class equities, amidst buoyant bargain levels regularly over 10,000 a day.

The Labour Government was now a tired team struggling in extra time. Its manifesto made no reference to nationalisation, but promised dividend controls and measures to prevent large capital gains. The Conservative party manifesto caught the public imagination, largely because of its promise to build 300,000 houses and to denationalise iron and steel.

The Conservatives, also, rather surprisingly, proposed an excess profits tax to fund the three-year rearmament programme. Years later, it would emerge from the memoirs of Harold Macmillan that Churchill had been so concerned about the Stock Exchange boom being exploited against the Conservatives as the party of business and profit, that he suggested something should be done to counter this. Of such moments are taxes born.

In the event, the result was to show that the opinion polls had correctly narrowed in the course of the campaign and the Conservatives found it as difficult to make progress in Scotland, the North and the Midlands as did Labour decades later in the South. These areas still had bitter memories of the 1930s and they had done relatively well out of socialism. The result was to turn a Labour majority of 5 into a Conservative majority of 18, and Winston Churchill was to return to Downing Street to form the new Government.

Chapter 5

NATIONALISATION

The stock market is remembered in terms of the ebb and flow of bull and bear markets. Indeed, many practitioners and investors can only recall stock market events and their outside political and economic influences by reference to the course of a bull or bear market. However, quite apart from the tides of bull and bear markets, there are some themes running over a longer course that require separate analysis. A major theme running through the Attlee Government was nationalisation – a cornerstone of Labour policy, just as its reversal four decades later by privatisation would be the cornerstone of another government equally driven by the politics of conviction.

Nationalisation had a direct impact on the stock market. For stockbrokers, there was the excitement of occasional bursts of high turnover when measures were announced or vesting dates approached. The private client takes his cash early at a discount and sells to the institutional investment manager who indirectly buys his gilts early at a discount. Never underestimate the volumes of business generated for small margins by these technicalities. The investment manager looks at a guaranteed profit quite forgetful of the juicy equity commission he pays the broker for, in effect, a gilt-edged stock. The private client takes his cash and looks for another opportunity, helped along by his broker who happily takes two nice commissions. At times like these, even stockbrokers came to believe that Labour was the market's best friend.

Behind these moments of euphoria lay an anxiety that the market was shrinking. Whole industries were being taken out by a Labour Government fully capable of mounting a sustained attack to plan the Stock Exchange out of existence, believing it to be the repository of all the worthless aspects of capitalism. The irony of nationalisation was that it represented the only takeover activity of any significance in the course of these six years, involving the acquisition of major companies by the British Government, with the consideration paid in fixed interest gilt-edged stock. The acquisitions of the 1940s were to become the issues of the 1980s.

In the 1945 election manifesto 'Let us Face the Future', the Labour party had promised to nationalise the commanding heights of the economy – the fuel and power, transport and steel industries. No sooner were they elected than they set forth on a policy of nationalisation at breakneck speed, despite the critical financial problems left behind by the war. The King's Speech on 16 August 1945 announced that the coal industry and the Bank of England would be nationalised in Labour's first year of office.

Many Labour politicians believed that State ownership was fundamental to the solution of the post-war problems facing the country. The spirit of togetherness displayed during the course of the war would be harnessed under State ownership. With no more conflicts between capital and labour, highly efficient services would benefit all the people. These beliefs inspired the Government to give a priority to nationalisation that was far higher than was ever justified in the context of the problems caused by the war.

Peace, jobs, food and housing were at the forefront of the thoughts of the average voter after a long war, and there was little evidence to show that the Labour Government won any electoral support because of its nationalisation policies. Nevertheless they were clearly set out and electoral victory was enough to claim a 'mandate' for nationalisation, though it owed more to political dogma than to reason.

This point is illustrated by a selection of comments from Labour Ministers at the time. Emanuel Shinwell, in the throes of nationalising the coal industry, lamented that the party had spent forty years talking about the politics of nationalisation without giving any practical thought about how to do it. Herbert Morrison claimed in debate that the justification for nationalising each industry had to be clearly reasoned, but it never was. Clement Attlee in a speech to the House on 28 April 1946 said that 'the success of these great schemes of public ownership will depend largely on the degree to which the people everywhere put into the operation of them the same sense of urgency and enthusiasm which was put into industrial activity during the war'. These were moments of candour, bluster and naivety about a party political venture, described by the *Financial Times* in a leader on 6 June 1945 just before the election as a 'fundamental cleavage of opinion over the means to be adopted to achieve social and economic ends'.

The Bank of England was the first candidate and a relatively easy target as a single freestanding company. The Treasury bought out the shareholders at a total cost of £58.2m by issuing £4 of Government 3% stock 1966 for each share. These terms broadly maintained shareholders' income and offered a small premium over the existing share price of around 76/-. The shares of the Bank of England had long been an anomaly. The dividend of 12% had never varied since being fixed in 1923, and the shares were quoted among government stocks. The acquisition was announced on 10 October 1945 and quickly completed on 1 March 1946, the vesting date. This is the day when ownership is legally transferred from shareholder to State, the vehicle or agency of government ownership is created, and the detail of government stock forming the compensation is announced.

The terms were widely praised for their fairness, and the shares of other nationalisation candidates responded with useful rises. They also became a topic in a wider discussion about the principles involved in nationalisation, particularly regarding compensation. Before the election, Attlee had proposed that the terms should be 'fair and reasonable but not excessive', and the TUC advocated that terms should be based on a number of years' purchase of 'reasonable net maintainable revenue'. However, the simplicity of acquiring the Bank of England gave false comfort and was no guide for the next candidate – the coal industry. This was far more complicated, with the acquisition of more than 900 collieries employing 700,000 miners and the merging of them into one huge National Coal Board. Many were quoted companies with different classes of capital, among the best-known ones were Bolsover Colliery Company and Powell Duffryn.

Before the publication of the Coal Industry Nationalisation Bill in December, the Government slipped in two other measures that had not been mentioned in either the King's Speech or the election manifesto. On 1 November 1945, the Chancellor of the Exchequer announced that the telecommunication services to and from the Empire operated by Cable & Wireless, a subsidiary of the quoted holding company, would be transferred to public ownership. On the same day, the Minister for Civil Aviation announced the nationalisation of the civil aviation industry, with BOAC being taken over and two new airlines, BEAC and BSAAC, to be formed to cover Europe and South America respectively. These measures were announced without warning and showed, very early in the Parliament, how the Government's intent to nationalise would not easily be deflected.

The coal industry brought into the open the difficult and contentious subject of compensation – in particular, how it was to be calculated and allocated between different classes of capital. A technical dilemma concerned preference shareholders who had prior rights of liquidation at nominal value, but whose shares stood at much higher market values because of low interest rates, thus creating a conflict of interest with ordinary shareholders. They in turn could find the valuation of their shares calculated in several different ways. The Coal Industry Bill published on 20 December 1945 laid down the principle that a compensation figure would be negotiated for each individual colliery, which in turn would itself allocate the compensation between its different classes of capital according to 'reasonable expectations of income'.

This touched on the fundamental question of whether or not all classes of shareholders and stockholders should receive compensation broadly to maintain income. The Coal Industry Bill recognised this point with its 'reasonable expectations' clause, but it was an unusual example of legislation that had appeared to set aside the contractual rights of classes of shareholder laid down in the articles of association of individual companies. It was a genuine attempt to ensure fairness in the sharing of compensation between classes of shareholders, but it did not deal with the principle of whether or not compensation should maintain income levels for all shareholders. It happened to be only a coincidence that compensation for the Bank of England shareholders had protected their income. Future nationalisations would involve the offer of government stock on the yield basis prevailing on vesting date when the change of ownership formally takes place. This was usually 3% to 3½%, irrespective of the existing yield on the stocks to be acquired, and often involving significant losses of income.

In its second year of office, the Government proposed in the King's Speech on the 12 November 1946 to nationalise inland transport and electricity supply. Inland transport mainly involved the four regional railways and London Transport, but it also included long-distance haulage, and the canals and docks.

It was for the nationalisation of the railway companies that the Government changed its policy on the calculation of compensation. On 18 November 1946, Mr A. J. Barnes, Minister of Transport, stated it would be based on market prices. The calculation for each security was to be based on the higher of, either the average of share prices in the first week of November 1946 or the average of monthly prices over the six months immediately prior to the last election in the first half of 1945. The market was taken completely by surprise by this decision. It was a simple and pragmatic alternative to the protracted negotiations already apparent in agreeing compensation for the individual coal mines. Vesting date for coal was only a few weeks away on 1 January 1947, but agreement on compensation had barely made any progress and would, in fact, still be incomplete when the Government left office in 1951. The use of market prices offered rough and ready justice rather than tortuous negotiation.

This decision provoked furious reactions in the *Financial Times* and the Stock Exchange. To illustrate just how emotive the subject of nationalisation had become, here were two bodies that might have been expected to believe that day-to-day share prices are reasonable indicators of value at a particular moment. In a scathing leader on 19 November, the *Financial Times* charged the Government that the income guarantees of the Bank of England acquisition had been overthrown, the net maintainable revenue concept and the interclass arrangements of coal had been overthrown, and, much more justifiably, stockholders would suffer considerable falls in income that could not be repurchased in the market. The leader concluded 'the terms bear out the cautionary view, repeatedly urged by the *Financial Times* that, under nationalisation, stockholders should expect only Greek gifts from the Treasury'.

The Stock Exchange took the unprecedented step on 12 December of making formal representations to the Government to point out that share prices were merely the result of 'hope, fear, guess work, intelligent or otherwise, good or bad investment policy and many other considerations', and were not a suitable basis for valuation. It concluded that share prices do not indicate the value of a company's assets and requested arbitration. A prime purpose of the Stock Exchange is to provide a forum for setting share prices and rarely can an institution have indicted its own product quite so comprehensively.

As a general guideline, share prices give a reasonable indication of value at a particular moment and the decision of the Government to resort to share prices as a basis for compensation was a practical, if rough and ready solution to the problem of valuation. However, there were two genuine grievances. First, daily share prices rarely include a premium for acquiring the control of a company and, second, in the case of known nationalisation candidates, the share price reflects public perception of the likely terms rather than an indication of value as a going concern.

Within a few weeks of deciding to use share prices for rail nationalisation, the Government announced on 10 January 1947 that a similar basis would be used for the nationalisation of the electricity supply companies. The formula for calculation was almost identical, using whichever was the higher of the prices in the first week of November 1946 or the monthly average between March and July 1945. This caused another outcry in the Stock Exchange, because, in this case, the proposed terms were believed to be confiscatory. For the railways, the Government paid an exorbitant price for a run-down industry slowly heading for bankruptcy, but electricity supply was a stable and growing utility industry with good prospects, and its assets were of much higher quality than the assets of the railway companies. The shareholders of the railway companies were lucky to be bought out at all, but the shareholders of the electricity supply companies could genuinely claim their investments had enough potential to justify the payment of a premium for control. In both cases, compensation in government stock would lead to a significant fall in income.

Despite outcries from the Stock Exchange, the market reaction to both announcements for rail and electricity on 18 November 1946 and 10 January 1947 was to push the FT Index to new highs. In both cases, private shareholders decided to sell holdings into the market and reinvest in other equities, although vesting date was a year or more away. The selling by private investors was just as quickly absorbed by institutional buyers using these stocks as substitutes for gilt-edged holdings, and they, too, were reinvesting in other equity shares.

For its third year in office, the government proposed in the King's Speech on 22 October 1947 the nationalisation of the gas supply industry. No reference was made to the iron and steel industry, but the intention to nationalise it within the life of this Parliament was reiterated in debate.

Nationalisation remained much in the headlines as it formally took place in 1948. Vesting dates saw the creation of the British Transport Commission for the railways on 1 January 1948 and the new British Electricity Authority on 1 April 1948. On these dates, shareholders of the original companies learned the details of the government stock to be allocated to them, British Transport 3%

1978–88 stock for the railways, and Electricity 3% 1968–73 for the electricity industry, both issued at par.

The acquisition of the railway companies was much the largest of all the nationalisation issues, with a total of £1,023m, of which £963m was to acquire the debenture and preference stocks of the four railway companies – LNER, LMS, GWR and SR – and London Transport. The capital structure of the railway companies was very highly geared, with only £60m of the total consideration – some 6%, issued in exchange for equity stock, and 94% for fixed interest debentures and preference shares. Such excessive gearing suggested an industry facing severe financial problems beyond recovery.

The acquisition of the railways at a cost of around £1,000m – or some £20,000m in current prices – must rank as one of the most expensive acquisitions ever made. The industry was visibly in decline with ageing assets and, in the context of the capitalist system, heading for bankruptcy. However, the fact that the gross income from the issue of the Transport stock of some £30m was much less than the dividend and interest payments of some £45m previously being paid by the railway companies had nothing to do with doubtful prospects, as will be seen from the acquisition of the electricity supply industry.

The Government acquired this industry cheaply for the issue of some £350m Electricity Stock 3% 1968–73, or £7,000m in current prices. Although it may not have been fully appreciated at the time, the railway stockholders were lucky to be bought out at all, but the terms of the acquisition of the electricity supply industry were confiscatory. Shareholders suffered an even greater reduction in income than those in the railways, with the compensation producing some £9m compared with the £14m being previously distributed. Investors in electricity supply were taken out of a secure quality investment, deprived of future growth and made to suffer a 40% reduction in income.

Details of the nationalisation of the gas industry were published in a Bill on 23 January 1948 in between the two vesting dates for rail and electricity. Compensation for the stockholders was to be on the basis of whichever was higher of Stock Exchange prices over six consecutive business days in mid October 1947 or over six monthly averages for the first half of 1945. Total compensation was estimated to be in the range of £180m to £200m, of which some £110m would be compensation for quoted securities. Vesting date for the creation of the new Gas Board was to be 1 May 1949.

The momentum of nationalisation now slowed down. In three years, the Government had seized coal, rail, electricity and gas – four large, basic industries, the products and services of which were believed to be so important to the daily lives of the people that only a State monopoly could guarantee availability and delivery at common prices to everybody. The people would no longer be exploited for profit, and more than two and a half million workers would now be working for themselves and the people rather than shareholders. Pricing policies would favour the people, who happened to have the vote, rather than face-less industries. This was the emotional appeal of nationalisation.

However, the importance of these basic services and products to the industrial base of the economy was overlooked. Industrial consumers relied on the provision of efficient basic services to keep down their own costs, but with pricing policies geared against them, nationalisation became a long-term burden. Its adverse effects on industry were, for a long time, underestimated or ignored for political convenience. It is also to be noted that, although strongly opposed in Parliament, at every step, no pledges of denationalisation were ever made by the Conservative Opposition over coal, rail, electricity or gas.

By this time, some members of the Labour cabinet were beginning to have second thoughts about the wisdom of taking nationalisation any further, preferring to give these new State industries time to evolve and develop, but no such doubts existed within the left wing of the party or in the trade unions. They both insisted that the commitment to nationalise the iron and steel industry should proceed, and this proposal was included in the King's Speech on 26 October 1948. A few days later, the Iron and Steel Nationalisation Bill was published on 30 October 1948 and, following recent practice, compensation was again to be based on stock market prices and by the issue of government stock.

Total compensation was estimated at around £300m, involving the acquisition of 107 firms 'extensively' engaged in iron and steel. For the 25 quoted companies, compensation would be based on the average of Stock Exchange prices between 21 and 25 October 1948, or the average of monthly prices over the six months prior to the 1945 election, whichever was higher. In the case of iron and steel, a difference was that all nationalised firms would retain their identity and businesses without being absorbed into a single State organisation. The issue was central ownership by the State rather than management control, thus recognising the commercial role this manufacturing industry had in a competitive marketplace.

The nationalisation of iron and steel was extremely controversial and driven by dogma from the left wing of the Labour Government. For the next 40 years, the steel industry was to become piggy in the middle of political argument, squabbled over by Labour and Conservatives, nationalised twice and denationalised twice. In 1948, it was a successful industry, achieving regular production records, and nationalisation was an irrelevance. For this industry, the Opposition gave a firm pledge that a Conservative government would return it to private ownership.

Iron and steel was the last industry on the list for this Parliament. The practical advantage of the decision to use stock market prices as the basis for calculating compensation was well illustrated in February 1949, when it was reported that the total cost of compensation for the coal industry was to be £165m, divided between 21 coal-producing districts. In a process that first began in December 1945, it had taken more than three years of negotiation to reach only this preliminary stage. Consideration had yet to be given to the question of how the individual sums for each district should be allocated between collieries, which in turn would then decide how to allocate the individual compensation between the different classes of shareholders. Many of these decisions still remained to be taken when the Government was defeated in October 1951.

In a similar vein, in February 1949, an arbitration tribunal determined that compensation for the nationalisation of Cable & Wireless, originally announced in November 1945, was to be £35.25m. In contrast, vesting date for the gas industry was 1 May 1949, when dealings started in a new government stock – Gas 3% 1990–95 issued at par – and the longest dated of the compensation stocks.

The debate on the nationalisation of iron and steel continued its bitter path through the House of Commons and eventually reached the House of Lords in November 1949. The Government was now well into its fifth year and, under threat from the House of Lords to hold up the legislation for one year, agreed that vesting date should be postponed from 1 May 1950 to 1 January 1951. This would allow a general election to take place first and, subject to this clause, royal assent was given to the Iron and Steel Act on 24 November 1949.

The Government was returned at the election with a bare majority of six. No reference was made to the nationalisation of iron and steel in the King's Speech on 7 March 1950, but, in answer to a question in debate, the Prime Minister said that the Government intended to proceed with the Iron and Steel Act. A final debate was survived and vesting date was announced for 15 February 1951. One famous British name Guest Keen & Nettlefolds – escaped from the original list because its steel subsidiary was able to be nationalised separately, and on vesting date, United Steel was removed from the FT Index and replaced by Tube Investments. A total of £200m of a new Steel stock 3½% 1979–81 was issued at par and, with further values agreed, later the eventual amount of compensation issued for the steel companies was £230m.

Although the election manifesto had promised the nationalisation of cement, sugar and industrial life assurance, nothing more was heard about these commitments during this second period in office.

Iron and steel completed the programme of taking five major industries into State control. It was undeniably an act of great political will and is often described today as one of the achievements of this famous reforming Government. It was undertaken much more aggressively than the comparable privatisations of the 1980s and 1990s.

Table 5.1 sets out the nationalisation programme in order of vesting dates. Thomas Tilling is included as the nationalised owner of extensive bus operations, taken over separately under inland transport.

Table 5.1
The nationalisation programme

Candidate	Terms announced	Vesting date	Stock issued	Amount (£m)
Bank of England	10 October 1945	1 March 1946	Treasury 3% 1966	58
Coal	20 December 1945	1 January 1947	Treasury 3½% 1977/80	229
Cable & Wireless	24 April 1946	1 January 1947	Savings 3% 1965/75	35
Rail	18 November 1946	1 January 1948	Transport 3% 1978/88	1,023
Thomas Tilling	18 November 1946	8 January 1948	Treasury 3½% 1968/73	25
Electricity	10 January 1947	1 April 1948	Electricity 3% 1968/73	350
Gas	23 January 1948	1 May 1949	Gas 3% 1990/95	200
Steel	29 October 1948	15 February 1951	Steel 3½% 1979/81	230
				£2,150

Academic discussion of nationalisation tends to be concerned with the principles of public or private monopoly, the confusion of political interference and management responsibility, and the setting of financial criteria and pricing policies. Very rarely is the issue of cost discussed. When adjusted for inflation, the total cost of £2,150m is equivalent to more than £40,000m today. It was a huge financial venture and its scale may be judged against the annual level of Government expenditure at the time, typically in 1949/50 some £3,400m.

The acquisitions were financed by the issue of government stock with a 3% to 3½% coupon. The annual interest payments amounted to £67m, which, in theory, should have been covered by surpluses generated from managing the businesses. The stocks were long dated and the cost of their ultimate redemption would in the event, though unforeseen at the time, be much reduced in real terms by the ravages of inflation. Nevertheless, the issue of £2,150m of stock was a large addition to the national debt at a time when Government expenditure was financed from revenues rather than deficit borrowing, and although the rates of interest were initially modest, they would later require refinancing at higher levels.

The eventual resale of some of these industries in the privatisations of the 1980s is the subject of later analysis. It produced buoyant paper profits from gas and electricity, but devastating losses from coal and the railways. In particular, British Gas was privatised in 1986 to raise £5,430m, several years before the original nationalisation issue of £200m Gas 3% 1990/95 was finally redeemed.

The theory behind the creation of the nationalised industries was that each would bear the interest cost of the compensation stock, creating a financial structure with capital formed wholly of debt without any equity. This puts a severe financial strain on any organisation and financial discipline was quickly lost as the line between management responsibility and political control became blurred. Financial deficits in railways and coal emerged almost immediately, and the obligation to finance capital expenditure from fixed interest borrowing led the nationalised industries into an ever-deeper financial quagmire.

This gearing of the balance sheets without equity was one of three serious weaknesses of nationalisation. The second weakness was that the creation of large State monopolies led to the creation of equally large trade unions with immense power. They were able to negotiate national pay deals by skilfully playing off management against the Government of the day, and in rail and coal they were always ready to use the strike weapon. The debilitating effect of these large unions became ominously apparent when deficits emerged in the early years of the Transport Commission. Management felt able to deal with deficits only by passing them on to the consumer in the form of price increases, rather than tackling the overmanning and restrictive practices so endemic in these industries.

The third weakness was that political interference seriously weakened management authority. Ministers would set the prices, usually loading them against commercial and industrial users so as to be hidden from the domestic users. When push came to shove, the unions would take their demands to Downing Street. It was the country that paid the price of long-term cost pressures passed on to manufacturing industry, which for three decades suffered a chronic competitive disadvantage in the battle to secure exports and resist imports.

The nationalised industries were a living illustration of the structural problems facing much of the British economy during these 30 years or more after the war. In a triangular conspiracy of self-interest, successive Labour and Conservative governments passively conspired with complacent management and backward-looking trade unions to enjoy together the comforts of apparent prosperity with as little disruption or change as possible. This theme comes alive more in the 1950s, 1960s and 1970s, but it was epitomised by the nationalised industries. The fundamental question remains as to whether or not it was right to take these industries out of private enterprise, switching them from large sectors of the preference and equity stock market into a significant proportion of the gilt-edged market.

In the day-to-day business of the stock market, nationalisation was an undoubted benefit. The announcement of terms or the occasion of a vesting date were oases in a desert of high taxation, dividend controls and a hostile government, and the bursts of market activity they created kept brokers and jobbers alive. Nationalisation amounted to the only takeover activity of any significance in the six years of this Government. The terms ranged from unfair and confiscatory for gas and electricity to tough for coal and steel, and generous for the railways. The industries themselves, the financial press and the Conservative opposition fought desperately against nationalisation.

The coal, electricity and gas industries had already recognised that they were far too fragmented. There were 900 collieries, many quoted but the majority privately owned; 575 companies and municipalities distributing electricity with two-thirds of the total in the hands of municipalities; and 1,120 gas undertakings, a third owned by local authorities. Even at the time of the 1945 election, the need for greater concentration had been recognised in each industry. The Reid Report into the coal industry was published in March 1945 and advocated the concentration of the industry rather than nationalisation.

The British Gas Federation in a report in 1943 opposed nationalisation and recommended a programme of voluntary geographical and functional integration. William Shearer, head of several electricity supply companies, sought on behalf of the electricity industry its consolidation under private ownership in January 1946. Although not nearly as fragmented, the iron and steel industry submitted plans for rationalisation through its federation in April 1946. The railways had already rationalised into the four regional railway companies.

None of these industry proposals would deflect the Labour Government from nationalisation. These were basic industries supplying a universal need, where the creation of profit was regarded as little more than the exploitation of captive consumers. The idea that profit might be a measure of efficiency was an idea whose time had not yet come in the community at large, let alone in the Labour Government. In *The Economist*, the trenchant editorials of Geoffrey Crowther displayed a contempt for industrialists that was as withering as his contempt for trade unionists. The price fixing and non-competitive cartels of the former were as iniquitous to him as the restrictive practices and resistance to change of the latter.

Nobody can ever know whether or not these industries would have been successfully rationalised if the Conservatives had won power in 1945, but undoubtedly damaging through the six years of the Labour Government was the deadening hand of nationalisation. Year by year, it slowly worked its way from industry to industry, curbing initiative, delaying investment and distracting management. This was especially so for the steel industry and for those other industries threatened in the 1950 election manifesto. The legacy of nationalisation was a confusion of responsibilities, the absence of the sanction and discipline of making profits, and a lack of management incentive. Management and unions sheltered under these giant State umbrellas, leaving their customers standing out in the rain enduring frequent shortages and disruption, and paying ever-higher prices.

Although the Conservatives vigorously opposed nationalisation, the fact is that on their return to office they made no attempt to reverse it except in the case of the recently nationalised iron and steel industry. The more liberal elements in the Conservative party were reconciled to it, and the appointment in 1951 of R. A. Butler as Chancellor of the Exchequer pushed the only possible opponent,

Oliver Lyttelton, to the sidelines. Lyttelton's financial and industrial experience favoured his appointment as Chancellor and he might have taken a Conservative government down a more radical path.

The majority view on nationalisation was well described by Harold Macmillan in his memoirs (*Tides of Fortune*, Macmillan, 1969) published many years later, when he wrote that:

> many of us on the Conservative side have long recognised that for a variety of reasons certain undertakings – the coal mines on historic and sentimental grounds; the railways on financial; and the public utilities and other monopolies like gas and electricity on technical – stood in a wholly different category from the great mass of productive industry and commerce.

The fairest judgement is that the dependence of the economy on coal and the parlous financial state of the railways required State intervention of some kind and, indeed, they remained the two most difficult problems in the privatisation programme. While they needed to be greatly concentrated, there is no convincing evidence that gas and electricity required to be nationalised. The nationalisation of iron and steel was an act of political expediency.

Over the next four decades, the steel industry was unlucky to find itself becoming the victim of border disputes between the parties, bouncing in and out of the stock market as the companies were denationalised by the Conservatives from 1953, re-nationalised by Labour in 1967, and eventually returned to the market as a single company by the Conservatives in 1988. This was a strand linking the Attlee era of nationalisation to the Thatcher era of privatisation.

Chapter 6

REVIEW
1945–51

The performance of a stock market in real terms over a particular period is calculated by taking the percentage change in a relevant index, and adjusting this percentage for the rate of inflation over the same period. The adjusted figure is known as the real return. It is a different calculation from the more theoretical total return, which assumes the reinvestment of dividends.

Table 6.1 shows the movement of the FT Index over the life of the Attlee Labour Government, and performance in real terms after adjusting for changes in the Retail Price Index.

Table 6.1
The FT Index and inflation, 1945–51

Date	FT Index		
25 July 1945	118.4		
23 February 1950	108.0		
25 October 1951	138.3		
	FT Index (% change)	*Inflation (% change)*	*Real return (%)*
25 July 1945–23 February 1950	(8.8)	11.0	(17.8)
23 February 1950–25 October 1951	28.1	13.9	12.5
25 July 1945–25 October 1951	16.8	26.3	(7.5)

Stock market performance and inflation figures are very different for the two periods of office. The Labour Government sought re-election in February 1950, when the FT Index was down 9% since it was elected in July 1945, and down by almost 18% after adjusting for inflation. During the 20 months of the second period in office, the FT Index recovered smartly with a 28% increase from 108.0 to 138.3, but accompanied also by higher inflation over those twenty months than for the whole of the previous 5 years. This recovery in share prices was influenced by the belief that a Labour government with a tiny majority would probably be driven to an early election and the return of a Conservative government.

Over the six years as a whole, the FT Index rose by 17% from 118.4 to 138.3, but with inflation of around 26%, the Index showed a loss in real terms of 7.5%. Investors in the gilt-edged market suffered much worse returns, illustrated by two benchmark stocks – the undated Consols 2½% and War Loan 3½% (see Table 6.2).

Table 6.2
Losses in the gilt-edged market during the Labour Government (1945–51)

Stocks	Price 25 July 1945	Price 25 Oct 1951	Change (%)	Inflation (%)	Real return (%)
Consols 2½%	83.25	66.5	(20.1)	26.3	(36.7)
War Loan 3½%	104.25	86.5	(17.0)	26.3	(34.3)

The performance of these and other gilt-edged stocks was of real significance to investors in the late 1940s, because the safe portfolio that would today be invested largely in equities was then invested largely in fixed interest investments. Indeed, the Trustee Act required trusts to invest wholly in fixed interest securities.

There are always investment lessons to be learned in stock markets and some of them date from this period of the Labour Government. The first is to sell equities on the announcement of dividend controls or dividend limitation. This is the opposite of the long-standing advice never to sell on a strike because they rarely last for long, whereas dividend controls tend to stretch out well into the future, sometimes without any end in sight. If they last for a number of years, equities assume the character of a fixed interest investment, but without any guarantees. The converse is also true – buy immediately dividend controls end or are confidently expected to end. Companies like to restore long-term dividend trends and are more likely to regard the effect of controls as a postponement of increases to a later date rather than a forfeit.

The second lesson is to buy after a devaluation. This particularly applies in Britain because a significant proportion of corporate profits are earned in foreign currencies, either from overseas subsidiaries or from exports. In both cases, the currency gain flows straight through to the bottom line of the profit and loss account, which also benefits from the competitive advantage created by devaluation.

The third lesson is that a positive reinvestment effect occurs when companies are taken over for cash or near cash and the proceeds are reinvested. This effect may apply to the market as a whole or to shares in a particular sector when one company has been taken over and cash is reinvested in other companies in the same sector. This is the simple equation of a reduced supply leading to higher prices in the face of new demand. This Labour Government nationalised nearly 20% of the ordinary share market in its first three years in office. A substantial reinvestment demand was created in a shrunken market and prices rose to all-time high levels in early 1947. However, takeovers are sometimes prompted by the euphoria of a bull market when the reinvestment attraction becomes a trap. In buoyant markets, it can be difficult to resist selling one expensive stock to a bidder and reinvesting the proceeds in another.

These three lessons are drawn from the examples in the late 1940s of dividend controls, devaluation and State acquisitions. These were new experiences for the investor of the 1920s and 1930s, now returning to the stock market after the war, but raised on a different diet of deflation and slow change. All three factors have reappeared on the investment scene on several occasions, but their provenance was from the late 1940s.

An example of simple stock market psychology at work was the reaction to the eight budgets produced under Labour, many of which discriminated against shareholders. Despite hostile measures, the FT Index rose on the day following seven of these eight budgets, because advance pessimism had already discounted even the worst news. As a general rule, if markets are aware of impending news, good or bad, they will usually have already more than discounted its effect, and thereby mystify the lay investor, irritate the company chairman and infuriate the politician, all baffled by the sight of shares apparently falling on good news and rising on bad news. When the news is good, it is better to travel hopefully than to arrive; when the news is bad, the medicine may leave a nasty taste, but at least it is time to think of travelling hopefully again.

Although the market rose by 17% during the six years of the Labour Government, equities failed to protect the investor against inflation and any benefits from the real growth of the economy were denied. However, increases in dividends were much more in line with economic indicators. The demobilisation of millions of people from the armed forces and their return to productive industry led to steady economic growth and export markets were reopened. The gross domestic product increased by 45% in money terms and adjusting for inflation showed real growth at an annual rate of around 2½%. Underlying dividend growth on the 30 shares in the FT Index matched the growth in the economy, but in an altogether different annual pattern (see Table 6.3).

The effect of three years of dividend limitation is clear to see. Over the six years, the underlying dividend index rose by 49%, a source of constant criticism from Labour because, over the same period, average weekly wage rates rose by around 35%, just ahead of inflation. Dividend increases in the two years after the end of the war were intended to compensate shareholders for having passed six years without any increases at all, whereas average weekly wage rates had

Table 6.3
Dividend growth of FT Index shares

Year	Dividend % increase
1946	11.0
1947	10.0
1948	0.5
1949	4.0
1950	2.5
1951	13.0

surged ahead during the war against an inflationary background. The share-holder could not win this argument and frustration with dividend increases drew hostile comment from Dalton at the beginning of the Labour Government, led to dividend control during the middle years from Cripps and provoked the threat of controls from Gaitskell in its last year.

It is fashionable to look back on the Attlee Government as one of the great reforming governments of the twentieth century, bringing basic industries under State control, removing the stigma of poverty and unemployment by the intro-duction of social security measures and creating the landmark reform of the National Health Service. This is a simplified analysis of a common perception, but through the eyes of the stock market it was a government staggering from one financial crisis to another, making bad and irrelevant decisions.

Quite apart from the chronic long-term inefficiencies created in large sectors of the economy by nationalisation, it is in the financial and economic fields that this Labour Government is open to criticism. First, an obsession with income and wealth led to the Government being one of high taxation, with standard rates of tax of 9/- rising to 9/6d and a rate of surtax at all times taking the maximum rate to 19/6d in the pound. The maximum rate of death duty was 75%. High taxation breeds an immoral psychology. It rewards connivance and spawns a tax avoidance industry that makes the honest citizen seem naive. Worst of all, its disincentive effect reduces the appetite to work harder and drives the very ambitious into tax exile. Its foundations were laid by this Labour Government and were to last for more than three decades until dismantled in the 1980s.

Second, there was an instinct for controls. In 1946, Hugh Dalton introduced the Investments (Control and Guarantee) Bill and the Exchange Control Bill as part of his financial weaponry to enable the Treasury to control all investment and currency decisions. He foreshadowed this Bill in debate on 22 November 1945 when he stated: 'It is important that there should be someone who should say, from the national point of view – never mind the purely profit making point of view – that project A comes before project B'. Dalton introduced a degree of central financial planning that was to hold back and deter industry from making those rapid and instinctive investment decisions that only its leaders are best placed to make.

No bureaucracy could effectively cope with deciding the priorities of hundreds of projects, nor could it sensibly control the supply of materials or efficiently carry out the policy of bulk buying of imports and the allocation of indigenous resources such as steel, coal and electricity. The Ministry of Supply had the sole power and responsibility for the purchase and import of materials such as copper, lead, zinc and tin among base metals; oil and rubber products for industry; cotton and wool for the textile industries; and the whole range of food imports for the food manufacturing and distribution industries.

Was it a driven belief in planning or was it more to do with an instinctive antipathy towards profit? Calls for the various commodity markets to be reopened were rebuffed for many years, thus denying opportunities for generating foreign commission and trading revenues. The bulk buying of food was needed for the administration of rationing and food subsidies, which typically in 1946 involved the Ministry of Food in the purchase of £1,440m of food, its sale at £1,127m and a cost in food subsidies of £313m.

Controls extended to the building industry, where priority was given almost entirely to housing, schools and factories. As a result, the building of shops and offices, and leisure and tourist facilities were highly restricted. Also, for many years after the war, there was little or no new building to replace lost offices in the bomb-damaged areas of the City of London.

The philosophy behind this panoply of controls was to ensure fair shares for all, and to give priority to exporting industries. Industries and businesses involved in activities outside the basic needs of the people or not in exports were confined to the sidelines. The consequence of this philosophy was gradually to build up a series of distortions in the economy with discrimination against the domestic purchase of motor cars, the imposition of high levels of purchase tax to deter expenditure on so-called luxury items such as radios and television, and the emergence of a developed environment with factories but too few offices, houses without shops, and leisure and tourism without restaurants, hotels and other facilities. The psychological consequence was a wearying acceptance of the philosophy of rationing and shortages. The reality was that sharing the problems became more important than solving them.

There was a contradiction in these restrictive policies in that while imposing austerity on the consumer the Government at the same time pursued a cheap money policy, with Bank rate remaining at 2% throughout. Cheap money was of little help if the private consumer had too few goods to spend it on, or if the complexities of the controls surrounding business decisions deterred industrialists from investing to expand. With its left hand the Government wished to stimulate the economy with low interest rates, but with its right hand it made spending decisions difficult and unwelcome. It purported to fear inflation, but fuelled an already pent-up demand with cheap money, which it then constrained by rationing and taxation. These contradictions discouraged growth, curbed initiative and removed incentive.

Planning and controls were believed by Labour to be the way to deal with the severity of the balance of payments problem left over from the war. Would a Conservative government have handled the post-war period with any more success than Labour did? It would have created freer and more open markets and might have adopted the philosophy of Oliver Lyttelton to encourage domestic demand in order to create more growth from which would emerge larger industries producing more competitive exports. It would have left more of the day-to-day domestic and industrial decisions to the marketplace. There would have been none of the distractions of nationalisation. It would have released more spending power, taxation would have been lower, government borrowing would have been higher and economic growth would have been faster. Such measures would have enabled the country to capitalise on its technical skills in newer industries such as radio and television rather than lose ground.

The price to pay would no doubt have been higher levels of government borrowing, higher interest rates, higher inflation and possibly an earlier devaluation than was seen under Labour. Achieving vital coal production might have been more difficult. There would have been greater social strain and much less of the feeling that the population was sharing its problems together. Although a Conservative government would have shared Labour's philosophy of a full employment policy, there would have been fewer civil servants, less bureaucracy and more people made available for the productive economy.

Comparisons with West Germany are striking. In a background article on West Germany in February 1949, the *Financial Times* reported that, under occupation, the German steel industry was now being decontrolled and broken up into separate competing units. Furthermore, industry was freely able to bid for available raw materials. It was once observed that, in the occupation of Germany, the Russians took the agriculture, the British the industry, the Americans the scenery and the French the wine. It is extraordinary that an efficient structure was created in the British zone for the steel industry and the supply of raw materials while the diametrically opposite was proposed at home.

Visitors to Germany from this country were amazed at the speed of progress. Free enterprise was given its head and, in a building boom, 350,000 houses were built in addition to the offices and shops that were everywhere to be seen. West Germany still had three million people unemployed and wage levels were much lower than in Britain, so the motivation to succeed was intense, and became a formidable combination with the traditional discipline of the German worker.

The encouragement given to the German people to generate economic growth, the freedom from controls, and the much lower rates of personal taxation make poor reading when compared with Britain under Labour.

The influence of the United States in the occupation of West Germany obviously encouraged these policies, whereas in Britain policy seemed more inclined towards the central planning that Russia was imposing on East Germany. Ironically, at the time when Britain was negotiating huge dollar loans from the United States for survival, and obtaining much the largest share of Marshall Aid, the defeated Germany was about to turn itself into a world economic power by its own efforts and the judicious use of much smaller helpings of Marshall Aid.

To lament the deadening hand of post-war economic policy in Britain is all very well, but the question has to be asked as to whether or not industry would have seized the opportunities of a more enlightened policy. Manufacturing industry was held in contempt by some commentators because of its instincts to operate price-fixing cartels, make agreements not to compete in another's territory and accept an easier life by tolerating overmanning and restrictive practices. Unfavourable productivity comparisons with other countries mattered little because Britain's domestic and imperial markets were well protected.

A powerful proponent of these views was Geoffrey Crowther, Editor of *The Economist*, who, in 1945 and during subsequent elections, was scathing in his criticism of management as a proxy for the Conservatives and unions as a proxy for Labour. He lamented the awfulness of the choice presented to the British voter and the vested interests standing behind that choice. The implication of this analysis is that the typical British industrialist was quite happy sheltering behind the bureaucracy created by the Labour Government, knowing that for several years after the war there would be a pent-up demand worldwide for goods of every kind, that for some years German and Japanese manufacturing competition would be limited and being a shade uncompetitive in a sellers' market would make no difference. Would industry have relished the opportunities of bidding for raw materials in the markets? Would it have revelled in open competition? Would it have made itself more efficient by tackling overmanning and restrictive practices?

The answers are by no means obvious. A feature of these post-war years is the complete absence of takeover bids or mergers. No attempts were made to improve efficiency by greater concentration and stronger market positions. In most sectors of British industry, there was a proliferation of companies, and far greater fragmentation than in the same industries in comparable countries. For example, in the motor industry, the post-war investor could choose from the shares of 11 manufacturers – Alvis, Austin, Ford, Humber, Jaguar, Jowett, Morris, Rolls-Royce, Rover, Standard & Singer. Industry statistics suggested that 80% of total car production was shared by six of these manufacturers, but in the United States with a massively larger car market, 90% of car production was supplied by just 3 manufacturers. The choice among aircraft manufacturers was almost as bizarre, with nine quoted companies – Blackburn, Bristol, de Havilland, English Electric, Fairey, Handley Page, Hawker Siddeley, Rolls-Royce and Vickers.

After the war, several industry associations sent missions to visit the United States to compare manufacturing techniques and, one by one, they returned to report extraordinary differences in productivity. It was common knowledge that it took far fewer people in the United States to manufacture a ton of steel or build a motor car than it did to do so in the UK. In a typical attack on trade associations and industry practices, *The Economist* on 13 January 1945 stated:

> It is undeniable that the extensive growth between the wars of restrictive and monopolistic practices has done incalculable harm to British industry by increasing its costs and lowering its output. Agreements to restrict output, to fix prices, or to limit entry into a trade, have been for the most part informal so that their full extent is unknown.

The crucial point in that paragraph is regarding the informal nature of agreements. Here was the code of the unwritten word, the 'word is my bond' of the Stock Exchange, spread far and wide to the quiet word on the golf course, while shooting, or over cocktails before luncheon or dinner. It was the extraordinary strength of these unwritten agreements, sealed only by social codes, that impressed Henry Grunfeld, who escaped from Hitler's Germany in 1935 and later joined Siegmund Warburg, as an early founder of S. G. Warburg & Co., the merchant bank. He observed that in this country people would never breach the unwritten word, unwitnessed and unsigned though it may be, whereas in his native Germany everybody would pretend to agree to a particular policy, before rushing off to break it as quickly as possible to gain an advantage for themselves at the expense of their competitors.

The consequence of this peculiarly British trait was a proliferation of companies in most commercial and industrial sectors, giving an illusory impression of widespread competition and plenty of choice for the customer. It also provided a choice of many companies in most sectors of the market for the investor. It is one of the reasons for there now being several thousand companies quoted on the Stock Exchange – a far greater number relative to the size of the British economy than is the case in other stock markets. It was a time when pricing policies agreed at the local golf club were designed to keep the least efficient local manufacturer alive, whereas a primary function of competition is to drive the weakest out of the market.

This proliferation of companies provided employment for large numbers of directors and workers alike, and it succeeded as long as the domestic and imperial markets remained isolated from foreign competition. As technology inescapably made the world an ever smaller place, so competitive inefficiencies came to be exposed and the country's manufacturing base undermined. The most tragic example of this was the motor industry where much greater manufacturing concentration in comparable countries such as Germany, France and Italy had driven Britain out of the European league tables well before Japanese competition emerged.

Most domestic industries were fragmented in the late 1940s and remained so well into the 1950s. Exceptions included the creation of ICI in 1927 from the merger of four chemical companies and the consolidation of the cement manufacturing industry under the leadership of Associated Portland Cement, today known as Blue Circle Industries.

The absence of mergers and takeovers has already been noted. In 1945, however, there were two mergers – both eccentric for the way in which terms were agreed. Two steel manufacturers – Baldwins and Richard Thomas – agreed to merge in January, but some shareholders of the latter were unhappy about the terms. Their concern was effortlessly dismissed by their Chairman in a letter to shareholders observing that 'the basis on which the two concerns were valued for fusion was far too complex for it to be possible to present it to shareholders.'

In April, British Insulated Cables merged with Callenders Cable & Construction Company to form the company known today as BICC. In this case, the basis of the merger was 'determined by four distinguished chartered accountants', drawn one each from the two auditing firms and two from independent firms.

During the six years of the Labour Government, the only merger of any significance took place in July 1948 when United Biscuits came to the market following the amalgamation of McVitie & Price and Macfarlane Lang & Co. – two well-known biscuit manufacturers.

In October 1948, there was a variation of the merger theme when the two largest motor manufacturers – Nuffields and Austin – announced a technical but not financial merger, involving the pooling of factory resources to make substantial reductions in production costs. At that time, there were 17,500 workers in Austin and 20,000 in Nuffields and the shares of both companies, Austin 'A' and Morris both rose usefully on the announcement. Sadly the opportunity faded away nine months later when it was quietly announced that Austin and Nuffield were to abandon the proposed pooling of ideas and resources.

The absence of mergers illustrated the philosophy of allowing the weakest to survive, as also did the rarity of insolvency. The only insolvency of any note was that of Richard Crittall, a firm of heating and ventilating engineers that issued a tranche of cumulative preference shares in December 1947. The issue had been oversubscribed 5 times, but the profits estimate for the calendar year 1947 of not less than £100,000 later emerged as a loss of £607,000. There followed a well-mannered game of pass the parcel between issuing house, broker, auditor and solicitor, but as the issue had not been technically an offer for sale, no further action was taken.

Stock Exchange practitioners may not have participated in the volumes of takeover activity to which they would later become accustomed, but there was ample consolation from the Labour Government's programme of nationalisation, and from the purchase by the governments of Argentina and Uruguay of their quoted stocks in the foreign rails sector. There was also a modest flow of new issue business with steady volumes of around £150m each year. The largest issues attracting the most attention were in the fixed interest market. An issue by Beecham in November 1947 of 1,500,000 4½% redeemable preference shares was oversubscribed 26 times with applications for over 40 million shares. In an active period in the autumn of 1950, ICI raised £20m from a private placing of 4% unsecured loan stock 1958–60, quickly followed by another private placing by Distillers to raise £10m.

These two private placings were controversial because they were unquoted and outside the normal stock market pricing mechanism, leading to comments that the rate of 4% was too generous to the insurance companies, which were the principal lenders. In October, Imperial Tobacco used the market to raise £20m by a rights issue to its preference and ordinary shareholders of 4% unsecured loan stock, and Unilever raised £10m by a public offer of 3¾% unsecured loan stock 1955–75 which was 8 times oversubscribed. Within the space of six weeks, four of the UK's largest companies raised a total of £60m of fixed interest capital, equivalent today to issues of £1,200m.

Although the emphasis was towards the fixed interest market, there was also a steady flow of new companies coming to the equity market via offers for sale or placings, and existing companies raised capital by means of rights issues. Another source of capital was provided by the Industrial and Commercial Finance Corporation, known later as ICFC and today as 3i. ICFC had been created in 1945 to fill the investment gap between bank finance and public issues. It was owned by a consortium of clearing banks with an initial capital of £15m to lend amounts of £5,000 to £200,000 of medium- and long-term loans to small- and medium-sized businesses. In its first six years of operation it lent £25m to a wide range of applicants.

To the broker or jobber, the merchant banker or the investment manager going about his daily business, the City seemed to return to normal very quickly after the war. The gossipy ways, the dress code of white shirt with stiff white collar, umbrella and bowler hat, or top hat for some, the labyrinthine network of favourite locals and the smoky, foggy winter evenings and dimly lit alleys were comfortably familiar to those returning after many years. The uncanny reliance on the spoken word and the scribbled note, partners' rooms with coal fires, elegant desks and solid, black telephone handsets, a leisurely day with the market opening at 10 o'clock and the bars and pubs at 11.30, lunch in the City clubs or booths in Dickensian restaurants for some and queuing in cafeterias for others, the market closing at 3.30 before a civilised journey home at the end of the day's business and a choice of three evening papers, were happy reminders that little had changed. These were still the days when, for many in the City, the week was but a pleasant interlude between more pressing events of the weekend, and talk of sport as likely referred to hunting, shooting and fishing as to cricket or football, tennis or golf.

They were also the days when private clients still owned the majority of the shares and provided much of the business. However, there are some strange contradictions with the situation today. Stocks and shares belonged to a privileged minority, and their ownership was a more distant prospect for the majority of the population than it is today, but the children of the time were widely exposed to the concept of receiving interest and dividends when playing Monopoly, the dominant board game in an era before families were diverted by television. Furthermore, if they sat the 'O' level arithmetic paper there would always be one question on stocks and shares requiring some such calculation as how much interest would be earned after selling one holding and buying another. No such practical questions appear today in the equivalent GCSE paper.

The Stock Exchange was a curate's egg of well-planned innovation and stubborn refusal to change. It reformed its own structure by creating the Stock Exchange Council, restored its pre-war dealing practices as quickly as possible and was well to the fore in promoting greater disclosure in company accounts. In 1946, it allowed partnerships to incorporate as unlimited liability companies – to enable them to build capital and reserves at a time of high taxation. This option was taken up by a surprising number of leading firms' including Cazenove and Rowe & Pitman. In August 1948, the Stock Exchange opened a new centralised delivery department and, in March 1950, created the Compensation Fund to protect the public from the financial failure of a member firm. In the same month, the Stock Exchange required new minimum standards of information from companies in their announcements of preliminary figures.

These were constructive measures, but, on the negative side, the Stock Exchange resolutely refused to publish any information about dealing volumes, whether for the market as a whole or individual sectors or stocks, deferring to the pleas of the jobbers that the confidentiality of their dealing positions would be compromised, although this problem could have been avoided by the retrospective publication of dealing volumes. In fact, in April 1951, the Stock Exchange announced a plan to improve the range and quality of its published statistics, but it was quietly announced one month later that time would be needed to think further about this because of the paperwork involved and the breach of confidentiality. This was an opportunity sadly missed.

Another anomaly presided over by the Stock Exchange for many years was the method of charging commission, with different rates according to the price of the security rather than the more logical percentage of the value of the transaction. At its extremes, a share quoted at £20 generated a commission of less than ¾%

of its value, whereas a share quoted at 1s 0d generated commission of more than 4% of its value. This was the subject of a regular campaign by Lex in the *Financial Times*, but it is easy today to forget that machines for automatically making precise percentage calculations of this kind did not exist in the 1940s and 1950s. The details of contract notes were calculated longhand and handwritten in flowing copperplate.

Lex gradually achieved its reputation for leadership in the newly merged *Financial Times* and became the most quoted and best-known financial column of all those in the newspapers. Just as the Stock Exchange was bringing forward reforms and innovations, so also was the *Financial Times* strengthening its position as the leading financial newspaper and introducing new services for its readers. In November 1947, it began to publish the dividend yields of all securities on its prices page twice a week. In April 1948, it published, for the first time, a weekly list of the dollar prices of 140 leading US stocks, although it did not include IBM. In March 1950, it introduced its monthly table of the 'trend of industrial profits', dividing the analysis into 22 different industrial sectors.

The *Financial Times* dominated public stock market information, not least with its famous FT Index of 30 industrial ordinary shares. This began life on 1 July 1935 as the 'Financial News Index', designed to reflect in a single number the 'changing moods' of the market. Companies with dominant overseas interests were deliberately excluded, hence the absence of Anglo-Iranian Oil (later BP), British-American Tobacco, Lever Brothers (later Unilever) and Shell, but the absence of bank and insurance shares is more difficult to understand. Many of the names of the constituents in 1945 are recognisable today only as subsidiaries of other companies. They are listed below in broad industrial groupings that illustrate the perceived strengths of the economy, with half of the Index in engineering, motor, electrical and chemical shares and a remarkable cluster of four textile companies:

Associated Portland Cement	Imperial Chemical Industries
London Brick	Murex
Pinchin Johnson	Turner & Newall
British Insulated Cables & Callenders Cable	Coats J & P
Electrical & Musical Industries	Courtaulds
General Electric	Lancashire Cotton
	Patons & Baldwins
Bolsover Colliery	
Dorman Long	Bass
Guest Keen & Nettlefolds	Distillers
United Steel	Imperial Tobacco

Vickers	International Tea
	Tate & Lyle
Austin Motor	Watney, Combe & Reid
Dunlop Rubber	
Hawker Siddeley	Harrods
Rolls-Royce	Woolworth FW

In July 1950, the *Financial Times* introduced new weekly indices for 16 industrial and distributive sectors of the market and 6 commodity sectors, making 22 in total. The 16 industrial and distributive sector indices mirrored the components of the FT 30 Index and were based on the underlying prices of 94 different companies across the sectors. They also highlight the manufacturing diversity of that era and make interesting reading when compared with the component sectors of the current All Share Index:

- Aircraft
- Breweries
- Building Materials
- Chemicals
- Electrical equipment
- Engineering
- Foods
- Motors
- Plastics
- Radio and television
- Rubber manufacturing
- Shipbuilding
- Shipping
- Stores
- Textiles
- Tobaccos.

The six commodities were oil, rubber, tea, copper, tin and lead zinc, but, quite illogically, there was no representation for the financial sector, where banks and insurance companies were large segments of the market.

This was a time when correspondents in serious newspapers remained anonymous, but the *Financial Times* was ahead of its field allowing its best-known journalist, Harold Wincott, to write a weekly column under his own name in a Tuesday series named 'Periscope', first published in July 1950. Harold Wincott was to become the best-known financial journalist of his time, widely respected for the simplicity of his writing, his wisdom and insight, and a modesty quite at odds with the personalisation of his name.

A typical sample of his writing is to be found in his Tuesday column on 6 February 1951 in which he laments the divisive attitude of Labour politicians towards the City. He gives vent to his feelings when he defines the indefinable – trading skills and invisible exports.

Within the square mile I know many men who can, with the aid of a telephone, a stub of pencil and the back of an old envelope, earn more foreign exchange for this country in one day than the horniest handed miner ever earned in a year. How they do it is nobody's business. They sell things they haven't got and buy others they can't pay for. They will arbitrage here and sell forward there. They will, without leaving their offices, process raw materials in two or three different countries, manufacture them in a fourth and fifth, and ship the finished product to the ends of the earth. . . . all this, we know, is anathema to the socialists [but] we have in this country native genius for such work.

Harold Wincott was a rare personal name at a time when the institution or the company was far stronger than the individual, and the interested layman would have found it difficult even to name a list of candidates for 'Businessman of the Year'. In the City, the only person whose name appeared regularly in print was the Governor of the Bank of England. From industry, few names were mentioned with any frequency, with leaders of the motor companies, Lord Nuffield and Miles Thomas perhaps being the best known.

It was from this industry that two names became known for the less celebrated reason of financial greed, which afflicts the capitalist system somewhere in every decade. With personal taxation rising to 97½%, it was impossible for companies to pay high effective remuneration. In an early sighting of the tax avoidance industry at work, the 'restrictive covenant' was devised. This involved making a severance payment just before the retirement of a senior director in exchange for his agreement not to set up in competition in the same industry.

In November 1949, Sir John Black, Managing Director of Standard Motors, received shares to the value of £100,000 on his severance from the company and his agreement not to engage in the motor industry in the future. Later in the same month, Mr L. P. Lord, Chairman and Managing Director of Austin, received £25,000 and shares to the value of £75,000 on the termination of his services, and his agreement not to manufacture motor cars elsewhere. In judging today whether or not this was simply a pragmatic way to reward the successful, or whether it was the unacceptable face of capitalism at work, it should be remembered that £100,000 in 1949, adjusted for inflation, would today be equal to £2m, and it was all tax free. The short answer is that it did cause outrage at the time and, in the April 1950 Budget, the Chancellor not only banned these restrictive covenants, but also taxed them retrospectively to 1948.

The fact that these leaders of the motor industry were well known reflects the dominance of the industry in the UK economy after the war. Two other industrialists who attracted publicity were Billy Butlin, whose boardroom row with colleagues in 1949 put his name on the front pages to generate plenty of free publicity for his fast-growing holiday camp business; and Halford Reddish, the diminutive Chairman and Managing Director of Rugby Portland Cement.

Reddish became Chairman in 1939, where he remained for 30 years. His annual statements to shareholders were masterpieces of political and social invective containing many of those home truths of the kind that would later make Warren Buffett a legend in the US for the wit and wisdom of his annual reports. A typical example was at the Annual General Meeting in March 1947 when he belaboured the Labour Government: 'Sheer incompetence on the part of the present government, composed as it is mainly of men who have little or no experience of the problems of industry, has much to answer for'. This was a characteristic political fusillade, but he could be just as trenchant in his support of the dignity of the working man or the authority of the law. The collected statements of Halford Reddish would make splendid reading, as would the writings of Harold Wincott.

It is now October 1951. One political era has ended, another is about to begin, and the stock market will take things exactly as it finds them, as it always does.

Chapter 7

KEY EVENTS
1945–51

GOVERNMENT

Prime Minister

Clement Attlee	27 July 1945–26 October 1951	Election defeat

Chancellors of the Exchequer

Hugh Dalton	27 July 1945–14 November 1947	Resigned
Sir Stafford Cripps	14 November 1947–19 October 1950	Retired
Hugh Gaitskell	19 October 1950–26 October 1951	Election defeat

BUDGETS AND FINANCIAL STATEMENTS

Hugh Dalton

23 October 1945	Excess profits tax reduced from 100% to 60%. Income tax – standard rate reduced from 10/- to 9/6d. Surtax – maximum rate increased from 9/6d to 10/6d.
9 April 1946	Excess profits tax abolished. Profits tax of 5% (national defence contribution). Wartime purchase tax rates made permanent. Estate duty – maximum rate increased from 65% to 75%.
15 April 1947	Profits tax – undistributed rate unchanged at 5%. Profits tax – distributed rate increased from 5% to 12½%. Stamp duty on share purchases increased from 1% to 2%. Tax on bonus share issues of 10%.
12 November 1947	Profits tax – undistributed rate increased from 5% to 10%. Profits tax – distributed rate increased from 12½% to 25%.

Stafford Cripps

6 April 1948	Voluntary dividend limitation.
	Levy of 10% to 50% on investment income.
6 April 1949	Voluntary dividend limitation to continue.
	Tax on bonus share issues abolished.
	First year depreciation allowance increased 20% to 40%.
18 September 1949	Devaluation of the pound from $4.03 to $2.80.
27 September 1949	Profits tax – distributed rate increased from 25% to 30%.
	Profits tax – undistributed rate unchanged at 10%.
18 April 1950	Income tax – lower rates reduced.
	Petrol tax increased from 9d to 1/6d per gallon.

Hugh Gaitskell

10 April 1951	Profits tax – distributed rate increased from 30% to 50%.
	Profits tax – undistributed rate unchanged at 10%.
	Income tax – standard rate increased from 9/- to 9/6d.
	Surtax – maximum rate reduced from 9/6d to 9/-.
26 July 1951	Dividend freeze for three years proposed.

BANK RATE

27 July 1945–26 October 1951   2%.

FT INDEX: JULY 1945–OCTOBER 1951

High: 140.6   17 January 1947
Low: 99.8   10 November 1949

Bull and bear markets

Movement	From	To	From	To	Duration
+32.8%	105.9	140.6	2 August 1945	17 January 1947	1 year 6 months
+40.7%	99.8	140.4	10 November 1949	13 June 1951	1 year 7 months
−29.0%	140.6	99.8	17 January 1947	10 November 1949	2 years 10 months

Movements of more than 2% in a single day

Date	% change	From	To	Reason
20 September 1951	+2.44	135.3	138.6	General election date
13 November 1947	+2.18	114.9	117.4	Budget relief
26 July 1945	–3.97	118.4	113.7	Election result
9 February 1948	–3.65	120.6	116.2	Fear of dividend controls
27 July 1951	–3.46	132.9	128.3	Dividend freeze
10 February 1947	–3.34	131.9	127.5	Emergency power cuts
29 July 1947	–2.59	127.6	124.3	Economic crisis
24 February 1950	–2.22	108.0	105.6	Election result
29 November 1950	–2.21	117.4	114.8	China enters Korean War
21 September 1949	–2.18	110.3	107.9	Devaluation

PART II

THIRTEEN
CONSERVATIVE YEARS
1951–64

Chapter 8

HIGHER BANK RATE
October 1951–June 1952

FT 30 Index	25 October 1951	138.3	
	24 June 1952	103.1	Down 25.5%

The Conservative election victory in October 1951 was received in the City with an enormous sense of relief, but, in the way so baffling to the outsider, the stock market promptly went into sharp reverse after the FT Index reached its highest point in the election campaign on polling day – 138.3 (see Figure 8.1). The stock market adage that it is better to travel hopefully than to arrive was vindicated yet again. Euphoria at the ending of six years of socialism quickly gave way to a harsh assessment of the problems facing the new Conservative government.

In particular, the market feared, with good reason, an increase in Bank rate. The previous Labour Government preferred to use fiscal, or taxation, measures to curb excess demand and inflationary pressures, while at the same time allowing the easy availability of credit by means of low interest rates. The contradiction inherent in this policy was highlighted in the *Financial Times* on 6 November 1951 when it referred to an earlier comment in the summer from Hugh Gaitskell, the previous Labour Chancellor, that 'it is no use our withdrawing purchasing power by draconic higher taxation if, by the back door, large additional quantities of credit are being pumped into the system'. This was the reality facing the new Chancellor, R. A. Butler, and within two weeks of taking office he raised Bank rate from 2% to 2½%, the first change for 12 years. This was no more than a token increase because, in his first budget in March 1952, he raised it again from 2½% to 4%.

The stock market had other reasons for concern after the return of the Conservative Government. In the debate on the King's Speech on 6 November 1951, the Prime Minister, Winston Churchill, solemnly warned that the current balance of payments deficit was running at an annual rate of £700m, an amount precisely equal to the existing sterling reserves. The following day, the Chancellor added that, if there were no resolution of this problem, the country will 'be bankrupt, idle and hungry', setting the scene for urgent action to reduce government expenditure and increase industrial production. The promise in the King's Speech to denationalise steel was small consolation for a market now becoming badly rattled.

Figure 8.1
FT INDEX 1951–57

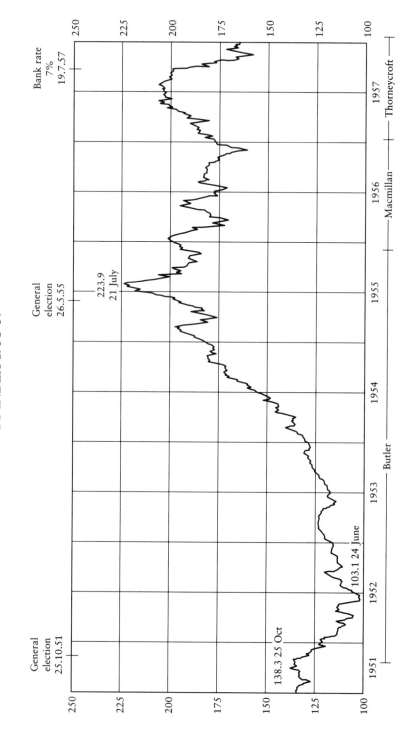

Source: Financial Times

Sentiment was not helped by the way the government announced measures in piece-meal steps. Bank rate had been increased in November, restrictions on bank lending were announced in December, and import cuts and hire purchase restrictions came in January. After these restrictive measures, the market now fearfully awaited details in the Budget of the excess profits tax promised in the election. It was not a happy background. In November, a £14m Unilever debenture issue had been almost entirely left with the underwriters, and a £20m rights issue from ICI in January put further pressure on markets.

From polling day to Budget day on 11 March 1952, the FT Index had fallen by nearly 20% in 4½ months from 138.3 to 112.7. There was worse to come. The increase in Bank rate from 2½% to 4% came as a surprise to a market wholly unaccustomed to increases on that scale, and there was bewilderment about the motives behind the newly proposed excess profits levy. The complexity of its detail would have done justice to those Labour Chancellors from whose clutches the market believed it had escaped. It was set at a rate of 30% of any profits exceeding a 'normal standard', defined as the average of the 3 years – 1947, 1948 and 1949.

Profits in 1950 and 1951 were judged to have been inflated to too high a level by the Korean War, and their exclusion produced an onerous base that took no account of genuine growth achieved in those two years. The levy was estimated to produce £200m, but compensating reductions in the two levels of profits tax – the undistributed rate from 5% to 2½% and the distributed rate from 25% to 17½% lowered the net burden of the excess profits levy to £100m, roughly the equivalent of some £2,000m today.

The effect was severe. Companies paid income tax on profits at the standard rate, just as though they were individuals, a fiction maintained until the introduction of a separate corporation tax in 1965. In addition, companies paid profits tax, a corporate equivalent of surtax on individuals, and with the new excess profits levy they faced a wide range of taxation. At its lowest, it would be from 50% on 'normal standard' undistributed profits, being 47½% income tax plus 2½% Profits Tax. At its highest, it would be 95% on distributed profits in excess of normal, being 47½% income tax, plus 17½% profits tax plus 30% excess profits levy.

The twin effect of the higher Bank rate on the gilt-edged market and the excess profits levy on equities overshadowed some helpful measures in the Budget to reduce personal taxation and attack food subsidies. On the day following the Budget – 12 March 1952 – the FT Index fell by just over 3% to 109.3 – the equivalent of a 180-point fall in the FTSE Index today. The Chancellor was widely criticised and the crudity of the excess profits levy led to questioning about his attitude to the private sector. 'Does he believe in capitalism?' asked Harold Wincott in the *Financial Times*. Unwittingly, he was laying the foundations of a financial policy that was later to be described as

'Butskellism' – Butler on the left of the Conservatives joining with Gaitskell on the right of the Labour party.

In fact, after debate some amendments were made to the excess profits levy. The base forming the 'normal standard' profits was raised by using the best two of the three years 1947, 1948 and 1949, but, in return, the proposed reduction in distributed profits tax from 25% to 17½% was amended to 22½%, thus creating a marginal tax rate on companies distributing higher profits in full to 100%. These amendments added further complication to an already unpopular tax.

In an investment letter to clients in April 1952, stockbrokers Read Hurst-Brown referred to 'an unexpectedly sharp rise in the Bank Rate and an Excess Profits Levy which was far more severe than had been anticipated', and whatever adjustments may be made 'the effect remains that the equity holder will this year have to provide £100m more than in 1951'. There are, the letter concluded, 'plenty of opportunities for meditation by even the most incorrigible optimists', and, indeed, the market was to continue to drift lower into the summer until it became completely becalmed in June.

The FT Index barely moved at all and eventually settled at what would prove to be its low of 103.1 on 24 June 1952. In the eight months since the election victory in October 1951, the FT Index had fallen by almost exactly 25%. Over the same period, the prices of gilt-edged stock fell by 10%, a lesser percentage fall than for equities, but in the context of gilts, probably more damaging to their investment status.

Chapter 9

DISCOVERING EQUITIES
June 1952–July 1955

FT 30 Index	24 June 1952	103.1	
	21 July 1955	223.9	Up 117.2%

It is only with hindsight that the precise date of 24 June 1952 marks the day when a bear market ended and a bull market began. Most bull markets take off slowly from a long runway – vertical takeoff is rare. This particular example, beginning in June 1952, started very slowly, but prices eventually more than doubled after a three-year journey.

Through the second half of 1952, the FT Index generally seemed to be going up, but it was only by a meagre decimal point or two at a time. By the end of the year, it had risen by 12% from its low of 103.1 to 115.8 against a background of low bargain volumes of barely 5000 per day. It was helped by a gradual perception that the Government's measures were beginning to work. Sterling strengthened as the balance of payments moved from deficit to surplus, and the next move in interest rates seemed likely to be downwards.

The stock market entered the new year in good heart and moved steadily ahead, but it remained a remarkably laborious process. For example, in early February 1953, the FT Index rose on 14 consecutive days. This is usually a sign of great market strength, but this sequence only took the index from 118.8 to 123.2 – a rise of 4.4 points at a daily average of 0.3. In these leisurely days of the 1950s investors seemed to be agreed about the direction of the market, but still found plenty of time to make decisions.

There was optimism about a helpful Budget and the Chancellor duly announced on 14 April 1953 a policy to 'lighten our burden and liberate our energies' by reducing taxation on all fronts. The standard rate of income tax for individuals and companies was reduced from 9/6d to 9/-, (47½% to 45%), and purchase taxes were reduced by a quarter. Initial allowances were restored at 20% for first year depreciation and, most welcome of all, the excess profits levy was to end on 1 January 1954.

For the first time in any budget since the war there were no new taxes and no increased taxes. It was, indeed, an incentive budget for individuals, industry and investors, and £170m was released into the economy. However, the good news had been discounted and the stock market wobbled in the face of poor company results announced during the traditionally busy spring reporting season. The FT aggregate profits table showed a 15% fall from companies reporting in the first quarter, and a fall in annual pre-tax profits from £53.9m to £38.9m from a company of the stature of Unilever was highly unsettling.

Confidence returned to the market in the second half of 1953. There was a surprise reduction in Bank rate, from 4% to 3½% in September. The economy was performing well, prospects for profits were improving and Wall Street had turned round following the return of a Republican government under President Eisenhower. As bargain levels approached 10,000 a day, there was talk of a bull market gathering pace, and the FT Index ended the year at 130.7.

Quite apart from improving cyclical trends, an entirely new and decisive factor for equity investment had appeared in 1953 – in the name of Charles Clore. In January, Clore made a successful takeover bid for the shoe chain J. Sears & Co. He bid 40/- for 2.25m shares and, in so doing, drew attention to the underlying value hiding behind the share prices of quoted companies. His bid for Sears was a catalyst for change in both the complacent attitude of company directors towards their shareholders, and in the passive and undemanding attitude of shareholders towards their investment.

Investors valued ordinary shares almost entirely by reference to dividend yield, and the relationship of that dividend yield to the yield on government stocks. This attitude stemmed from the influence of actuarial thinking within the dominant institutional investors of the day, the life assurance companies. For them, the purpose of investment was to provide assets to match as closely as possible liabilities stretching years into the future over the lifetime of individual policyholders. If an equity share allowed for its greater risk by yielding sufficiently more than its gilt-edged alternative, it mattered little in its valuation whether that dividend was covered three times or ten times. 'Whether we like it or not, it is quite certain that it is dividend yields which govern security values', wrote Harold Wincott on 24 March.

Because of restrictive policies, dividends had not been growing as fast as profits since the war, and they were now becoming increasingly well covered. In the 1950s, the extent to which a dividend was covered was expressed by a calculation known as the 'earnings yield', which is the yield on the shares if all the earnings were paid out as dividends. In simple terms, if a share yielded 5% and its dividend was covered 5 times, the earnings yield was 25%. If covered three times, it was 15%.

Dividends and earnings were both confusingly expressed as a percentage of the nominal capital, whereas today they would be stated in 'per share' terms. An earnings yield of 25% would today be described as a price to earnings ratio, or PE ratio, of 4, the one being the reciprocal of the other. An earnings yield of 10% would be a PE ratio of 10, and 5% would be inverted to a PE ratio of 20. When Charles Clore looked at J. Sears, the shares stood at around 20/- on an earnings yield of 33%, or a PE ratio of 3. In fact, he eventually bid twice that price and so purchased the company on the equivalent of a PE ratio of 6.

Although dividend restraint had made it genuinely difficult for companies to increase dividends in line with earnings, these restrictions suited the instinctive conservatism of many Boards of directors. Until National Provincial Bank took the lead in 1953, the dividends of the clearing banks had been unchanged for 21 years. The low valuation of equity shares in the 1950s was a consequence of the liking of directors for a cushion of earnings and assets, and the tendency of investors to value shares almost exclusively by reference to dividend yield. The extent of dividend cover was largely ignored, as was the fact that share prices frequently stood well below asset value in the balance sheet.

This undervaluation is well illustrated by examples drawn from investment letters to clients at the time. In October 1952, the ordinary shares of Joseph Lucas and Glaxo Laboratories were recommended by brokers Read Hurst-Brown. Lucas shares stood at 33/6d to yield 4.35%. The dividend was covered nine times by historic earnings, and good results for the current year were expected. The historic earnings yield was 38%, and, even with better results, this well-known manufacturing company in the motor sector was only valued in PE ratio terms at between 2 and 3. Furthermore, the 1951 balance sheet was stated to show 'a position of great strength and net liquid assets alone equivalent to approximately 48/- per share'.

Glaxo Laboratories was a growth stock by the standards of the 1950s and its shares yielded 3.85%. The dividend was covered nearly 12 times by earnings to give an earnings yield of 45%, or PE ratio of just over 2. Both companies had excellent reputations, but with yields already below average, their extremely high dividend cover counted for little, seeming almost to inhibit rather than encourage investor interest. Among higher-yielding stocks was Peninsula and Oriental Steam Navigation Company, or P&O as it is better known. In February 1953, the shares yielded 5¼% with the dividend covered 9½ times by earnings to give a PE ratio of precisely 2. The shares stood at 58/9d with an estimated asset value of £9.

For some time, the use of earnings yields was not encouraged by an absence of information. An aggregate dividend yield was calculated daily for the FT Index, but it was not until December 1954 that an earnings yield was first published. With the Index at 179, the first published earnings yield was 11.3%, roughly equal to a PE ratio of 8.8. When Clore had bid for J. Sears & Co. two years earlier, the FT Index stood at around 115 to yield just under 6%. Dividends were probably covered around three times on average, suggesting an earnings yield for the FT Index of around 18% and a PE ratio of 5.5.

Close analysis of the valuation of equities in the early 1950s is relevant because an important sea change was about to take place. The takeover bid, personified by Clore, drew the attention of investors to values waiting to be unlocked and jolted companies into becoming more liberal with their dividend policies. It prompted the first step in a long process that, over some 40 years, would, in broad terms, take the accepted valuation of equities from a 15 to 20% earnings yield in the 1950s, or PE ratios of 5 to 6, to around 15 regularly and, on occasions in the 1970s, 1980s and 1990s, over 20. Equity values would come to be multiplied some three or four times, simply because of a change in the basis of valuation. Profits have multiplied some 20 times or more over the last 50 years or so, but share prices have risen 75 times because of the change in valuation.

Charles Clore had thrown a large stone into calm waters and sent many a ripple through boardrooms across the country, although the fear of being taken over was out of all proportion to the number of bids that actually emerged. In addition to Clore, only Isaac Wolfson of Great Universal Stores made any regular forays into the market. Nevertheless, the psychological effect in 1953 and 1954 was to encourage companies to increase dividends, even if profits were lower. Despite the benefits his actions brought to shareholders, there was a general outcry about Clore himself. It would be idle to pretend that his was an attractive personality or charismatic presence, but he undoubtedly changed the thinking in many boardrooms.

His activities led to the extraordinary situation of prominent Labour leaders Hugh Gaitskell and Roy Jenkins coming to the aid of industry. Gaitskell asked a question in Parliament on 11 December 1953 as to whether 'takeover bids lead to encouragement to higher dividends, dissipation of reserves and abandonment of conservative financial polices'. Roy Jenkins proposed a motion on 12 February 1954 that 'this House deplores recent manifestations of the technique of takeover bids in so far as they have put large untaxed capital profits into the hands of certain individuals and seriously undermined the policy of dividend restraint'.

Clore was a reticent person, but, possibly goaded by the question from Gaitskell, he was drawn into discussing his philosophy in a speech on 20 December 1953, when he said:

> I have been accused in various places of having little regard to the well-being of businesses in which I am interested with the suggestion that my views and policies will lead them straight to ruin and destruction. Ruin and destruction will certainly come – but not to us. It will come where the rigid preservation of the status quo is the order of the day, where enterprise is regarded as speculation and the full uses of resources as dissipation . . . neither this country nor any business can afford to have its resources remaining stagnant. It is only directors who are either unwilling or unable to face up to reality who have cause for apprehension. I am surprised that their cries for help have been heeded in the light of their self-confessed failure.

The stock market gathered pace in 1954 in one of those rare years (since matched by the All Share Index in 1968 and 1983) when the FT Index moved from its low point on the first day of the year to its high point on the last day of the year – a rise of 40% from 131.1 to 184.0. This momentum continued well into the first half of 1955, to a peak of 223.9 on 21 July 1955, thus completing a three-year bull market in which share prices more than doubled, with a rise of 117%.

As well as takeover threats, there were other ingredients for the bull market. The economy was growing fast at between 5 and 6% in both 1953 and 1954 under the incentive of the Government's economic policies and companies reporting in 1954 reflected this with earnings up by 15% and dividends up by 25%. The Budget in April 1954 was possibly the most innocuous of all post-war budgets, without any tax changes or new taxes, but it was followed by a further reduction in Bank rate from 3½% to 3% in May 1954 and the removal of all hire purchase restrictions in July 1954. The economy was growing fast and the balance of payments improving as the trade gap was steadily reduced.

The freedom and incentives provided by government policy were reflected in a new phenomenon for the stock market – the emergence of company-wide profit-sharing schemes. This practice had spread very slowly in Britain, with schemes dating from before the war from only two companies of any significance – Rowntree and Associated Portland Cement. After the war, Joseph Lucas and Tate & Lyle introduced new schemes, but the plan introduced by ICI in May 1954 attracted particular attention as the first from a major national company. ICI's scheme involved the annual investment on behalf of employees of around £1m in ICI shares, with the shares handed over to each employee once an amount worth £25 had been accumulated. For many years, the annual sale of profit shares by ICI employees became a talking point in the stock market, partly because it was a large transaction, but more because of cynical comments about thousands of ICI employees selling their shares as soon as they could get hold of them.

An important election commitment in 1951 had been to denationalise the steel industry, but the Government moved very slowly. The passing of the Iron and Steel Act in May 1953 created the Iron and Steel Realisation Agency, a holding company for the ownership of all the nationalised steel companies. Denationalisation would be effected by a series of individual offers for sale expected to run to a total of £300–£350m. The first was one of the best-known companies in the sector – United Steel, when 14m shares were offered for sale at 25/- in October 1953, valuing the company at £17.5m.

This and all subsequent offers were to be handled by a rather splendid consortium of eight issuing houses and six stockbrokers. This decision was justified publicly by the need to ensure the absolute success of this and future issues, but it was probably more influenced by the agency heading off petty jealousies in the interests of a quiet life. The names of these issuing houses and stockbrokers give a good indication of the dominant firms in the new issue market in the early 1950s. The issuing houses were Barings, Robert Benson, Hambros, Helbert Wagg, Lazards, Morgan Grenfell, Rothschilds and Schroder. The stockbrokers were Cazenove, W. Greenwell, Hoare & Co., Panmure Gordon, Rowe & Pitman and Joseph Sebag.

The United Steel offer was reasonably successful and oversubscribed three times. No priority was given to former shareholders whose holdings had been nationalised except to the extent that payment for the offer could be made by the tender of government compensation stocks at specific prices. The offers for sale of Lancashire Steel in January 1954 and Stewarts & Lloyds in June 1954 were less successful, with the former undersubscribed and opening at a discount, and the latter only one and a half times subscribed. In October 1954, it was the turn of John Summers, followed by Dorman Long in November. As the stock market levels strengthened, the later issues were more successful. Indeed, in January 1955, the offer of 10m Colville shares at 26/- was oversubscribed 13 times.

After 6 disposals over a 15-month period, the consortium of 8 issuing houses and 6 stockbrokers was disbanded as there remained only the smaller steel companies and 2 large enterprises not yet believed to be in suitable shape for denationalisation – Richard Thomas & Baldwins and Steel Company of Wales. Consett and South Durham were returned to the private sector at the end of 1955, followed in March 1957 by the successful offer for sale of the Steel Company of Wales at a value of £40m.

The denationalisation of the steel industry was a belaboured exercise, taking the Conservatives six years to fulfil an election promise made in 1951. The proceeds of around £150m were modest compared with the £230m of steel stock issued in 1951, although the figures are not fully comparable because of changing capital structures. No advantage was taken of an opportunity to bring about any consolidation within the steel industry, and all the original fiefdoms were preserved. The only other commitment to denationalisation was for the fragmented road haulage industry. At no stage in the life of this Conservative Government was there any suggestion of further denationalisation.

As markets surged ahead, Lex commented in October 1954 that 'many members are having their busiest time ever' and it was, indeed, a highly profitable time for the Stock Exchange. The FT Index closed at new all time highs on more than 60 occasions in 1954, and bargain levels were regularly around 15,000 a day, compared with 6,000–7,000 in 1952. The equations of profitability in stockbroking are dramatic. If volumes more than double and prices are 50% higher, commissions received will treble as the feast or famine cycle takes effect.

When the FT Index closed at 184.0 at the end of 1954, it was a long way into new high ground. It had passed its previous 1947 peak of 140.6 in April after an interval of 7 years and 2 months – much the longest interval between all-time highs in the entire post-war era. Stock markets were also strong in the United States and, on 24 November 1954, the Dow Jones Index reached a new all-time peak of 381.60, after more than doubling since the end of the war. However, this was a cyclical peak of altogether different proportions, because the previous high of 381.17 had been recorded on 3 September 1929. It took 25 years to recover from the devastation of the Wall Street collapse that began in 1929. Less fortunate was the long-term shareholder in American Telephone and Telegraph, one of the largest companies in the United States, whose shares at $173 were still a long way below the 1929 high of $310.

There was widespread optimism in London at the end of 1954. Industrial production was 5% higher for the year and, after an increase of 6% in the previous year, the growth rate of the economy over the two years was at levels rarely seen before or since. The traditional manufacturing industries were bursting at the seams to provide for both home and export markets, but exciting new industries were contributing to economic growth and providing new opportunities for investors.

Plastics and man-made fibres, nuclear power, long-playing gramophone records, filter-tip cigarettes and commercial television were investment alternatives to the traditional sectors of aircraft and motors, oil and chemicals, television and radio, and housing, roadbuilding and construction. The 1950s was a manufacturing decade for the economy and the fashionable sectors for the investor in this bull market were in capital goods. It was also the time, on 20 December 1954, when the Anglo-Iranian Oil Company, formed at the beginning of the century to develop the oil resources of Persia, was renamed British Petroleum Company, and, with a market capitalisation of £480m, a stock market leader then and ever since.

Investors and newspaper readers today are swamped with pages of City comment and advice, but in the 1950s there was very little. *The Observer* newspaper allowed the stock market three columns in the bottom corner of an inside page, and it would be a long time before the professional economists were writing regularly in the City. A consequence was that the effect on the economy of growth rates of 5–6% for two successive years was not well understood by investors. The FT Index sailed on to all-time highs nearly every day in the new year until 27 January 1955, when, much to general surprise, Bank rate was increased from 3% to 3½%.

It took another three weeks for the message behind this modest increase in Bank rate to sink in. The economy was overheating, domestic demand had to be curbed and, on 18 February, the gilts market suddenly weakened in fear of further rises in interest rates. The FT Index fell by more than 2% on that day from 190.4 to 186.1. After time for reflection, over the weekend, it fell by a further 4%. On 24 February, Bank rate was duly increased a second time, from 3½% to 4½%, hire purchase restrictions were reimposed and the FT Index collapsed by nearly 4% on the day from 184.0 to 177.0, equal to more than 200 points in the FTSE Index today.

The stock market settled down at these lower levels, but investors were about to face an extraordinary combination of events. Without a word of warning to their readers of any impending problem, all national daily newspapers were closed down by a trade union dispute from 26 March to 20 April. During these four weeks, in the complete absence of press reporting, Winston Churchill retired as Prime Minister, Sir Antony Eden succeeded him, income tax was reduced from 9/- to 8/6d in an electioneering budget and a General Election was called for 26 May 1955.

With television reporting in its infancy and barely a mention of the stock market on radio, investors faced an information vacuum, but they took the market into higher ground in the belief that the Conservative Government would be re-elected. They were not to be deterred during the election campaign by ASLEF calling a rail strike to start on 28 May, two days after the General Election and by polling day the market had recovered all the losses following the Bank rate shock. Investors responded to the result of an increased overall Conservative majority of 58 seats with a 2% rise in the FT Index – to a new high of 199.4 – before pushing through the 200 barrier the following week.

Despite the announcement of a state of emergency within a week of the election because of the rail strike, and its settlement a week later on terms widely perceived as a surrender, the market continued to forge ahead, taking the FT Index to 223.9 on Thursday, 21 July 1955. It was on this day that the Chancellor, R. A. Butler, announced that he would be making an economic statement on the following Monday. It was an ominous sign that the party was over and a brilliant bull market had run its course.

Chapter 10

STOP–GO

July 1955–February 1958

FT 30 Index 21 July 1955   223.9
            25 February 1958   154.4   Down 31.0%

Practitioners today with experience of 20 years in the stock market may find it difficult to envisage drifting bear markets lasting for two or three years at a time. With the obvious exception of Tokyo where the stratospheric prices of the 1980s could take a decade or two to correct, a bear market today prefers to get itself over and done with as quickly as possible – in a matter of months – or even weeks. If a 20% or 30% correction is required, so be it, but do it now and avoid all that uncertainty and inactivity.

In London between 1945 and 1975, there were five bear markets, each lasting more than two years, and inactivity lasted not just for a few days, but for months on end. Bargain levels would fall to 5,000–6,000 a day, and individual share prices would remain unchanged day after day.

The bear market that began on 21 July 1955 was to last two and a half years and take the FT Index down by just over 30% by 25 February 1958. It was a bear market notable for its duration and drift rather than collapsing prices. The Index moved gently downwards amid low activity with a prevailing boredom that, for the fund manager of today, would seem like a life sentence (see Table 10.1).

Table 10.1
FT Index, 21 July 1955–25 February 1958

Dates	FT Index	% Fall
21 July 1955	223.9	
31 December 1955	200.4	10.5
31 December 1956	178.8	10.8
31 December 1957	165.3	7.5
25 February 1958	154.4	6.6
Overall		31.0

Circumstances were different in so many ways. During the 'stop–go' economic cycles of the 1950s, 1960s and 1970s the recessionary leg of each cycle would see investors preparing for a long siege while they waited for the economy to turn. Today there is a greater willingness to regard a recession as a hiccup in a long-term growth trend, and to look across the valley to the welcoming hills of recovery on the other side. Equities formed a minor proportion of most institutional portfolios in the 1950s, whereas today their portfolio dominance has created a massive vested interest in sustaining their value.

Fixed interest investments formed the dominant part of most portfolios as a genuine alternative to equities, whereas today a hedge against a fall in equities is as likely as not be sought in cash or currency or derivatives. In the 1950s and 1960s private investors owned a much greater proportion of issued equities than they do today, and they depended for information and advice on stock-brokers, who were themselves part of the spiral of inactivity and drifting prices. Investors were not exposed to the daily anxieties and enthusiasms of financial journalists or to pages of newspaper advice or to regular stock market reports on the radio, all of which encourage short-term activity.

Although not always visible at the time, there is usually a catalyst for a change of direction in markets and, on 21 July 1955, it was, the sudden announcement by the Chancellor, R. A. Butler, that, in four days' time, he would be making an economic statement. When the mood of a market changes, all those reasons used to justify rising markets are quickly abandoned, and those straws in the wind, timidly noted by some on the way up and contemptuously dismissed by the majority, suddenly become danger signals.

In particular, there had been two messy strikes caused by inter-union squabbles. A strike by 70,000 ASLEF train drivers had been called off after 17 days on 15 June 1955 following acceptance of a peace offer from the British Transport Commission. Some would say it was better described as an appeasement offer, and it was immediately followed by a beer and sandwiches meeting between the Prime Minister and TUC leaders at Downing Street of the kind that was to become symbolic of the 1950s and 1960s. On 5 July 1955, a strike of 20,000 dockers locked in an inter-union squabble was brought to an end after 6 weeks. Other straws in the wind had been an 18% increase in the price of coal in early July and a sharp rise in the monthly retail price index from 147 to 150, announced on 19 July 1955 just before the Chancellor's economic statement.

Rising prices and high wage claims had begun to plague this Conservative Government and were to continue to do so over the next two years. Although there was some evidence that the two increases in Bank rate and the hire purchase restrictions had begun to work, tougher action was required. In his economic statement on 25 July 1955, the Chancellor increased hire purchase deposits from 15 to 33%, and required the banks to make a 'positive and significant reduction in lending'. This announcement turned the market decisively downwards and produced one of those rare occasions when the FT Index fell by more than 3% in a day, from 221.3 to 214.6.

The implications of the seriousness of the current situation began to sink in over the following week, when the FT Index fell by a further 8%. Significantly, this latest fall was accompanied by the danger signal of high bargain volumes, and fears of the adverse effect of government measures on the economy proved stronger than fears of inflation for which equity investment continued to be the best defence.

There followed another crisis indicator – the autumn budget. At the annual party conference in October, the Chancellor warned that the 'restraint of wage payments and distribution of profits' was required, and it came as little surprise that in the Budget on 26 October 1955 he increased the distributed profits tax from 22½% to 27½%, increased each of the 3 rates of purchase tax by 20%, and imposed rent increases by reducing housing subsidies. He also made a specific attack on 'dividend stripping' a practice involving artificial Stock Exchange bargains in gilt-edged stocks, when it suited individual high taxpayers to sell their dividends for cash as untaxed capital, and it suited pension funds as nil taxpayers to buy dividends and reclaim the tax.

The Budget was criticised because it did nothing to curb the inflationary wage demands that in the next annual round would cancel out increased purchase taxes and higher rents. Meanwhile, inflation continued to rise with another two point jump in the Index in November. In a cabinet reshuffle on 20 December 1955, a reasonably successful but tired Chancellor, R. A. Butler, was replaced by his political rival, Harold Macmillan.

The FT Index closed the year 1955 at 200.4 and was very weak in the first 2 months of 1956. The Government seemed powerless to deal with a flood of wage increases demanded by the major unions. The engineers were asking for a 15% increase and the railway unions, despite the settlement of their strikes in the previous summer, were now asking for a further 7½%–10%. It was estimated in the *Financial Times* that 8 million workers were asking for increases totalling £400m. The government resorted to exhortation. In a major policy speech in Bradford on 18 January 1956, the Prime Minister proclaimed that 'the battle against inflation is on' and emphasised that 'increased profits should be passed on in the form of lower prices rather than increased dividends'.

On 16 February 1956, Bank rate was increased from 4½% to 5½% and the next day the new Chancellor announced yet another package of measures, the third of its kind outside the normal timetable since the Budget. He suspended investment allowances, demanded a 'vigorously critical' attitude to new issues – and imposed swingeing increases in hire purchase deposits, both for the consumer and for the commercial purchaser of capital goods. In debate, he made a strong plea for wage and dividend restraint, but investors in the stock market were cynical. Just before his statement, a 7% wage increase had been agreed for the railway unions and this was quickly followed by 8% for the engineering unions – settlements that flew in the face of exhortation and restrictive economic measures.

There was nothing more to do in the normal April Budget of 1956 and it is largely remembered for the introduction by Macmillan of the celebrated Premium Bonds. The introduction of taxation relief for the payment of premiums into self-employed pension schemes corrected an anomaly and was welcome to many professional partnerships. However, there were also further niggling increases in profits tax, from 2½% to 3% for the undistributed rate and 27½% to 30% for the distributed rate, raising the latter to the level imposed by the previous Labour Government.

After its initial fall in the first 2 months from over 200 to around 170, the FT Index barely changed for the remaining 10 months of the year, and, against a background of low volumes, it ended 1956 at 178.8.

Moments of weakness in the market during the year were usually prompted by strikes or wage claims. It is surprising how little impact was made on the stock market by one of the most traumatic events in Britain's political history – namely the nationalisation of the Suez Canal by Colonel Nasser in July 1956 and the ill-fated invasion of Egypt in November 1956. On the day of the seizure of the Canal on 27 July 1956, the FT Index fell from 185.6 to 183.2, but it changed hardly at all through the following months of political turmoil, invasion and ignominious retreat. However, it was different for the shareholders of British Petroleum and other oil companies. The Suez Canal was crucial to the transport of oil from the Middle East to Europe, and its blockade and indefinite closure caused heavy falls in oil shares. On the day of the seizure in July, BP shares stood at 174/-, but by the end of November they had fallen by 37% to 109/9d.

The stock market was philosophical about the resignation of Sir Anthony Eden as Prime Minister on 9 January 1957. The *Financial Times* reported the general expectation that R. A. Butler would succeed him, but the emergence of Harold Macmillan as Prime Minister, and his appointment of Peter Thorneycroft as Chancellor had no discernible effect on the stock market. Indeed, there was a positive reaction to an early speech by the new Chancellor referring to the need for incentives and rewards, and expressing the belief that 'competition is the mainspring of Britain's industrial growth'.

In this context, Thorneycroft praised the recent passing of the Restrictive Trade Practices Act, which made price cartels illegal and encouraged the concept of a European Free Trade Area. A week later on 7 February 1957, he reduced Bank rate from 5½% to 5% and the FT Index had by now recovered to 185.5. In the Budget on 9 April 1957, his first, he announced tax concessions of £98m, mainly from adjustments in earned income allowances and some reductions in purchase and fuel taxes. Stock markets responded positively and, over the summer months, the FT Index stayed just above 200.

The problems of high wage settlements and rising prices remained unsolved.

Strikes were fewer but 5–6% settlements with major unions were widespread. 'Buying Peace' was one of the headlines from the leader columns of the *Financial Times*. On inflation, the Government was beset by a continuing spiral of price increases from the major nationalised industries – a problem it had been wholly unable to deal with since its return in 1951. The worst culprits were the National Coal Board and the railways. A consequence of the effect of wage settlements was that both were continually running into deficits, and the instinct of the nationalised industries was to deal with deficits by simply passing them on to customers in the form of price increases.

A typical example was the announcement on 25 June 1957 by the National Coal Board of average price increases of 8%, which were required to meet a prospective deficit, of which £13m resulted from a recent wage settlement. The Coal Board's 3 biggest customers – electricity, gas and rail – saw their costs rise by £11m, £10m and £5m respectively from this price increase alone. They in turn were pushed into deficit by these increases, which they simply passed on to their customers, although usually at the expense of the industrial user rather than the private consumer. In this particular case, within a week of the increase in the price of coal, British Rail announced a 10% increase in freight charges.

This was a disastrous spiral that coloured much of the economic history of the 1950s. As well as having a direct effect on the Retail Price Index, it invariably fed through to the prices charged by manufacturers of all kinds, whether their products were for the man in the street or for highly competitive export markets. The strength of the unions in the nationalised industries was much greater than the resolve of management or the Government. Restrictive practices prevailed everywhere. Under the threat of national strikes, wage demands were regularly pushed through without productivity agreements. A culture of over-employment was institutionalised by the unions, tolerated by management and condoned by the Government. Hidden from public view, it was paid for by the consumer in higher prices, who then demanded higher wages, and by the manufacturer in higher costs who in turn sought higher prices.

Investors in equities in 1957 walked dangerously along the tightrope of inflation, sometimes comfortable with the protection given by equities, other times fearful that prices were too high if inflation spun out of control. The FT Index settled nicely at just over 200 through the summer months before optimism began to fade. The inflationary spiral in the nationalised industries was out of control as the railways, post office and steel industry announced successive price increases, all feeding into the retail price index and setting up the next round of wage claims. In speeches before and during the annual TUC conference in September, there was bitterness and aggression in a campaign for the outright rejection of any form of wage restraint, led by Frank Cousins of the Transport and General Workers Union.

Aware of the urgency of the situation, the Government reacted dramatically and unexpectedly by increasing Bank rate from 5% to a crisis level of 7% on 19 September 1957. Money supply was to be severely restricted, cutbacks were announced on capital expenditure by the Government, nationalised industries and local authorities, and a ceiling put on loans by the banks to the private sector – all in a bid to halt inflation and maintain the value of sterling.

At this point, investors in equities fell off the tightrope. The market was caught completely unawares, by both the timing and severity of the announcement. The FT Index fell by 4½% on the day from 192.2 to 183.5, and War Loan fell from 65¾ to 61½, and although a Bank rate at 7% sounds modest enough today, it was of crisis proportions to a generation that had lived with a 2% Bank rate for most of its life. 'The increase in Bank Rate to 7% – the highest rate since the early 1920s – is a consciously dramatic decision designed to create a shock', stated the leader in the *Financial Times* on 20 September. Less charitably, it may be described as a measure driven by panic and helplessness. The burden of these measures would fall on borrowers, whether they were the Government, corporate or private, and on capital investment rather than consumption. They would not deal with the inflationary pressures of prices and pay. The *Financial Times* leader continued that, the latest restrictions were 'being sent to the wrong address'.

After falling by 4½% on the day the measures were announced, the FT Index fell by a further 3½% on the following day – the equivalent in two days of a 400 point fall in the FTSE Index today. These were messy times. Within a week, Harold Wilson had requested an investigation into an alleged Bank rate leak that was to hang over the City for the next three months. ASLEF demanded a 10% increase for its 75,000 footplate staff. Harold Wincott speculated on 24 September that it was as much a moral crisis as it was a financial crisis in which 'a City of London which washes more bond interest than the government pays out' is just as culpable as any trade union that condones the actions of its workers. In a mood of increasing gloom, the market continued to fall during the remaining months of the year, influenced not only by immediate domestic problems, but also by weakness in the United States where the Dow Jones Index had also been falling sharply because of recessionary fears. The FT Index fell to 159.0 on 5 November 1957, nearly 25% below its earlier July high.

In fact, the Government began to take a harder line on wages and salaries. The Chancellor warned at the end of October that pay claims on the scale currently demanded would be disastrous and that as an employer, particularly in the nationalised industries, the Government would not be a party to unjustifiable claims and 'will not falter if claims lead to strikes'. Within a few days, it picked a soft target for decisive action by vetoing a 3% pay rise that had already been negotiated with 32,000 administrative and clerical workers in the National Health Service.

Of all the post-war years, 1957 was one of the unhappiest. It ended with Bank rate at 7%, the FT Index barely above its low for the year, a bear market still running after 2½ years and aggregate corporate earnings down by 2% after previously rising by 35% over the previous 2 years.

No sooner had the new year begun than events went from bad to worse. In a day of unexpected drama on 7 January 1958, the Chancellor, Peter Thorneycroft, and his Treasury team, Enoch Powell, Financial Secretary and Nigel Birch, Economic Secretary, all resigned. The Chancellor had been taking an openly strong line on wage increases and his resolve to defeat inflation drove him to resignation. Estimates of government expenditure for the next financial year were running at £150m higher than the current year and the Chancellor, believing the Government should impose on itself the same tough measures it was imposing on the economy, demanded the elimination of this overrun by cutbacks. After discussion in Cabinet, the figure was reduced to £50m and the balance could only be achieved by cutting back expenditure on social services or increasing national insurance. The Cabinet was unable to accept any further cutbacks and the Chancellor resigned, not just on a matter of £50m, but on principle.

In a simple resignation statement on 14 January that perhaps never achieved the influence it deserved, the Chancellor said, 'I am not prepared to approve estimates of the Government's current expenditure next year at a total higher than the sum that will be spent this year'. In his view, the Government had imposed financial disciplines on everybody during the year of crisis and it must share that same discipline. In this belief, he lacked the support of both the Prime Minister and other colleagues, and he was left with no alternative but resignation.

He was supported out of belief and loyalty by his two Treasury colleagues. The Prime Minister, Harold Macmillan, used his great political skills to disparage their resignation by alluding to 'these little local difficulties', as he flew out of Heathrow on a tour of the Commonwealth, and announcing that Derick Heathcoat Amory would be the new Chancellor. Today this would be described as a defining moment in the country's economic history when a Conservative Prime Minister gave government expenditure a higher priority than financial responsibility.

A philosophy that was to run as a common thread through Conservative and Labour thinking for the next two decades was set in place at this fateful moment. At the very highest level of the Government, the political will to confront inflation had weakened, and expediency was put ahead of principle. The reaction of the stock market was philosophical and the FT Index drifted by less than a point on the day. The market was already discounting enough.

Meanwhile, the Bank rate Tribunal had been speeding ahead under its Chairman, Lord Justice Parker, who published a 39-page report on 21 January 1958. The terms of reference of the Tribunal had been to discover whether or not there had been 'any improper disclosure' of information about the increase in Bank rate from 5% to 7% and whether or not 'use was made of such disclosure for the purpose of financial gain'. Political suspicion had originally fallen on Oliver Poole, who had been briefed to a limited extent by the Chancellor because he was Deputy Chairman of the Conservative party, but he was also a Director of Lazards, a leading merchant bank.

The Tribunal's hearings were held in public and they provided interesting insights into the relationships between City editors, financial journalists and their Stock Exchange sources. One of the best-known witnesses was Frederick Ellis, City Editor of the *Daily Express*, who boasted unconvincingly of seeing many stockbrokers in a typical day without remembering any of their names. One of the strongest rumours concerned heavy selling of gilt-edged securities by the Royal Exchange Assurance Company, and it originated from a conversation between Frederick Ellis and a partner in Joseph Sebag, a leading firm of stockbrokers. For the first time ever, the Stock Exchange revealed turnover figures in gilts on the relevant days. The aggregate of sales and purchases of government stock were £21.5m and £18m respectively on the day before and during the morning of the change in Bank rate.

The sales that particularly attracted attention were those of Royal Exchange Assurance, which sold an unprecedented amount of £1.4m, the British Match Company, which sold £310,000 of liquid assets held in gilts, and Lazards, which sold £750,000. These three apparently random sales were connected by the coincidence that Lord Kindersley, a Director of the Bank of England who had been informed two days earlier of the Bank rate decision, happened to be the Governor of Royal Exchange Assurance, Chairman of Lazards and the Chairman of British Match. He claimed in evidence that he only knew of these sales after they had been made, but admitted to having unsuccessfully tried to persuade Morgan Grenfell to abandon a forthcoming £30m debenture issue for Vickers.

In its report, the Tribunal stated there had been no leak and found that:

> there is no justification for any allegation that Lord Kindersley disclosed either intentionally or unintentionally, any information about the impending increase in the Bank Rate or about the proposed restrictive measures or that he used that information for the purpose of private gain.

In those deferential post-war days, this judgement was accepted without demur. The heavy selling of gilt-edged securities on the day before the Bank rate increase emanating from an insurance company, a merchant bank and an industrial corporation, that all just happened to be headed by Lord Kindersley, was purely coincidental.

Quite clearly these transactions did not involve immediate personal financial gain and, by the standards of the day, a nod and a wink in the right direction was believed by many to be the purpose of having cross-directorships. In answer to its terms of reference, the Tribunal was correctly able to say that information about the change of Bank rate was not improperly disclosed nor was it used for private gain. The possible expression of bearish murmurings about the gilt-edged market for the financial benefit of institutions or companies without revealing why, fell outside the terms of reference of the Tribunal. The admission by Lord Kindersley that he tried to have a corporate issue abandoned, presumably to save underwriting losses, elicited no comment. The Bank Rate Tribunal reflected poorly on the City and confirmed the worst suspicions of many outside. As is often the case, it is the forum where the activity takes place, the Stock Exchange, that suffers the image of being a den of thieves, rather than the clients who use the stock market for their own ends.

With a new Chancellor and the publicity of the Tribunal, the stock market continued to drift until the FT Index reached its low point of 154.4 on 25 February 1958, down 31% from the peak of July 1955. The dividend yield on the Index was now 7.1% and the earnings yield within a whisker of 18% or a PE ratio of 5.6. With exemplary timing Manchester Corporation announced its intention to invest in equities for the first time in its pension fund to the extent of £500,000, and was thus able to lay retrospective claim to have marked the moment when the market changed direction from bear market to bull market. Over the next two years' share prices would again more than double, just as they did between 1953 and 1955.

Chapter 11

....

CULT OF THE EQUITY
February 1958–January 1960

FT 30 Index	25 February 1958	154.4	
	4 January 1960	342.9	Up 122.1%

The timely decision of Manchester Corporation to enter the equity market was rewarded within three weeks when Bank rate was unexpectedly reduced on 20 March 1958 from 7% to 6%, a pleasing announcement that prompted a rise of over 2½% in the FT Index from 160.2 to 164.5. The sequence of bull and bear markets in the 1950s shows a reasonably strong correlation with changes in the direction of Bank rate.

This most simple of yardsticks has been underestimated as a guide to the direction of equity markets. It was to prove to be the perfect indicator in 1958 when there were 4 further reductions in Bank rate, in ½-point steps, to 4% on 20 November 1958, and the FT Index established a new all-time high of 225.5 on literally the last day of the year, passing its previous peak of 223.9 set 3½ years earlier in July 1955.

The reason for a correlation between changes in direction of Bank rate and the occurrence of bull or bear markets is simple. Bank rate sets the interest rate for money on deposit and the yield earned on government securities. If it falls from, say, 4% to 3%, yields will settle at lower levels, prices of government securities will rise, and money on deposit will earn less. Conversely, if Bank rate is increased from 5% to 7%, as happened late in 1957, yields rise, the prices of government securities fall sharply and money on deposit earns more.

Two consequences follow for equities. There is always some broad correlation between the yields on equities and government securities, and equity yields will move upwards or downwards in the same direction as government securities. Second, if money on deposit earns more, it will make equities seem less attractive and cash more attractive, or if it earns less it will make equities look more attractive and cash less attractive. Subsequent changes in Bank rate will also tend to move in the same direction, upwards or downwards, and will further enhance the strength or weakness of equities. When this sequence is approaching its extreme of very low or very high interest rates, the clamour will be that interest rates are now so low that equities are a better bet than cash or else so high that equities are not worth the bother, in both cases sending a strong signal of a change in direction.

The relationship between equity markets and interest rates is a continuing feature in stock markets, but an indicator peculiar to the 1950s and early 1960s was the correlation between the direction of share prices and trends in the figures for unemployment and job vacancies. In his blunt and simple way, Ernest Bevin once described full employment as the moment when the number of job vacancies was higher than the number of registered unemployed. Almost unbelievably by the standards of today, there were times in the 1950s when the line on the chart of vacancies crossed over and above the number of unemployed. When this happened, the economy was probably overheating, with competition for labour, aggressive pay demands and fears of inflation. Credit and hire purchase restrictions would follow close behind to bring the bull market smartly to a halt. The resultant bear market would last for a year or so as restrictive economic policies worked their way through the system.

Both the Labour and Conservative governments shared an unshaken electoral commitment to full employment – it was an article of faith for the former, more of a guilty postscript from the 1930s for the latter. Neither party ever paused to consider the economic consequences of this strongly held conviction. From time to time, published surveys would make international comparisons of indicators such as unemployment and inflation. One such analysis compared unemployment percentages and inflation rates in different countries for the period 1950 to 1955. Was it just a coincidence that unemployment of only 1% in Britain and 1.4% in Sweden was matched by inflation of 30% over those 5 years, whereas in the United States, Germany and Belgium unemployment ranging between 3.6% and 6.7%, was matched by inflation of only 10%?

This analysis suggested that full employment leads to higher inflation, and this was particularly illustrated in Britain by surges in inflation after 1950–51 and 1954–55 when unemployment percentages fell below 1%. In July 1955, the bull market peaked at the moment when unemployment fell to 185,000, its lowest post-war level. Full employment may have been a desirable policy for political and social reasons, but it was also a source of many of the problems that came to plague the British economy. It had too many negative consequences.

First, it influenced employers, whether in industry or government, only rarely to consider measures involving redundancy. Nationalised industries never tackled their recurring financial deficits by seeking a more efficient use of labour, and in the private sector productivity agreements were little known. Second, the very low level of unemployed, at around 1% encouraged employers to hoard labour, through fear of being unable to recruit. The result was a structural overmanning, tolerance of restrictive practices and lack of job mobility. It led to relatively static workforces and a false illusion that because everybody was at work, all was well with the status quo. Third, full employment inevitably has inflationary consequences as the marginal shortages of labour will drive up the price. This was exploited by trade unions, and particularly by those able to demand national agreements universal to all their members.

Shortly after the reduction in Bank rate from 7% to 6% in March, the new Chancellor, Heathcoat Amory, presented his first Budget. He took the welcome opportunity to get rid of the distortions of the two rates of distributed and undistributed profits tax by replacing them with a single rate of 10%, at a modest cost to the Treasury of £16m in a full year. He increased initial allowances from 20% to 25% for plant and machinery and, for the consumer, he consolidated 7 rates of purchase tax into 4 at a cost of £41m. The market continued its recovery despite problems in industrial relations, when unofficial strikes erupted among dockers and bus drivers in London, and difficult negotiations continued with the railway unions.

In July, the Chancellor announced further relaxations in the economy. The ceiling on total bank advances was dropped and replaced by a new and less onerous special deposits scheme, but banks were still not allowed to give consent to borrowing for the purpose of financing the speculative purchase of shares, commodities and real property. In September, hire purchase controls were relaxed and the stock market continued to make steady progress through the year, symbolically breaching its all-time high on a busy New Year's Eve when 17,800 bargains were recorded and the FT Index closed at 225.5.

Two quite different factors contributed to this buoyancy. The broad influence was a worldwide bull market in equities, led by New York where the Dow Jones Index also reached its all-time high on New Year's Eve at 583.65. US equities were only yielding 3½% compared with over 5% in Britain, where the yield gap between equities at 5.15% and Consols 2½% at 4.85% was closing. In Australia the yield gap had closed towards the end of the year and City opinion suggested that it was only a matter of time before British equities would yield less than government stocks.

Indeed, this forecast was made by George Ross Goobey, Investment Manager of the Imperial Tobacco pension fund. Ross Goobey was a colourful personality who had for some years been openly investing new money in his £30m pension fund almost entirely in equities, but had also sold off all his holdings of gilt-edged stocks. His fund was invested approximately 80% in equities, an asset distribution wholly different from any conventional funds of the day. He was a pioneer in his field, but constrained himself by looking for high-yielding equities offering a minimum of 6%, resulting in the exclusion of many growth stocks and market leaders. Ross Goobey operated from Bristol and was less susceptible to City conventions. He enjoyed being successfully different and, as a keen golfer of no mean ability, he was once introduced at an investment conference by Harold Wincott as 'the only pension fund manager with a golf handicap lower than the yield on his fund'.

The second factor influencing activity in the stock market was the 'Aluminium war' – an event that was to shake City conventions. It began on 27 November 1958 with an innocent statement from British Aluminium – a company of modest size – that 'discussions are taking place with other parties in the industry, the outcome of which is as yet uncertain', and was to last for an eventful six weeks when new precedents were set for the future conduct of takeover bids.

The cricketing world was about to decide that it could no longer sustain its traditional annual match between the Gentlemen and the Players because those who were previously amateurs or professionals had all become cricketers. However, in the City, the gentlemen still set the rules within the ranks of the major merchant banks. Suddenly they found their conventions rudely challenged by an upstart player – Siegmund Warburg – who cared little about the idea that everybody should know their place and abide by the rules.

The day after it announced that discussions were taking place with 'other parties in the industry', British Aluminium further announced that it was considering two alternatives. The first was that the Aluminum Company of America (Alcoa) should subscribe for shares in British Aluminium on a basis that would give them a one-third stake in the equity. The second was a bid worth 78/- a share from Tube Investments, in association with Reynolds, another US aluminium company. Without providing any convincing reason, British Aluminium perplexed the market by favouring the former alternative. The Lex column on 29 November noted that the Tube offer would 'fully justify the present share price of 71/6d, while the Alcoa plan would not', and criticised the Board for taking steps without seeking the approval of shareholders. Lex further asked whether or not Tube's bid would be communicated to the shareholders, observed that whereas this bid would retain UK control, the company's proposed course of action would not, and concluded that 'the battle, in short, has already been joined'.

It quickly became apparent that the shareholders of British Aluminium had been wholly excluded from consideration of the alternatives. It was revealed that Tube Investments had informed British Aluminium of its intention to bid as long ago as 5 November, and British Aluminium had signed its agreement with Alcoa to subscribe for shares on 10 November, dismissing the letter from Tube Investments of its intention to bid as 'too vague'. On 5 December, British Aluminium advised its shareholders that Alcoa would subscribe for 4,500,000 shares at 60/- compared with a share price fluctuating around 70/-, rather grandly adding that the Board 'has never done a better piece of business'.

Tube Investments had by now announced it would be sending out its bid direct to British Aluminium shareholders on 12 December 1958, which it duly did in the names of Helbert Wagg and J. Henry Schroder for Tube Investments, and S. G. Warburg & Co. representing Reynolds Metal Company. British Aluminium responded by raising its dividend from 12% to 17½%, except for the shares to be issued to Alcoa, but this was only of marginal advantage because the offer of one Tube Investment share plus 78/- for two British Aluminium shares could be made to produce a higher income by a modest increase in the four-times-covered dividend of Tube Investments.

In some desperation at seeing their plans frustrated, and bewildered at the challenge to their judgement, the British Aluminium camp led by Lazards and Hambros organised a consortium of 14 banks to announce on 31 December an offer of 82/- in cash for up to half of each British Aluminium shareholding, but to an aggregate limit of £7m, or enough to purchase just under a fifth of the existing shares. During the first two days of the New Year, massive dealings in the shares of British Aluminium were reported, 500,000 shares changing hands on the first day and 800,000 on the next, as S. G. Warburg bought aggressively to pursue outright control and keep the price above the consortium offer. On 5 January 1959, Tube Investments raised its offer by adding 10/- to the cash element of the bid, announcing at the same time that it now owned three million shares out of an issued total of nine million. Four days later, control had extended to over 80% of the capital and the bid had been successful.

British Aluminium was a landmark in post-war financial history. Conventions had been challenged and new practices highlighted in four different ways. First, this was a hostile takeover bid. British Aluminium was implacably opposed to a bid from Tube Investments that proved to be successful, despite a recommendation to shareholders not to accept. Second, it openly revealed a takeover battle taking place between the teams of advising merchant banks as much as between the companies, pitting, in this case, S. G. Warburg, J. H. Schroder and Helbert Wagg against Hambros, Lazards, Morgan Grenfell and Flemings.

Hostile takeover bids fought by opposing merchant banks were to become common ground in future battles. Bidding companies would ruthlessly pursue their target, whether or not their bid was recommended by the directors of the company, seeking only to gain acceptance from a majority of the shareholders, and there would be a parallel battle between the advising merchant banks as they faced each other with that same adversarial aggression of the barristers for the prosecution and the defence. Like barristers they, too, would be enemies one week, before happily working together in a future battle, but during the British Aluminium affair tempers between the merchant banks ran very high.

The third aspect of the bid was the practice initiated by Siegmund Warburg of aggressively buying shares of the target company in the market on behalf of the bidder. Until control was announced, there was no requirement to reveal how many shares had been purchased or what prices had been paid, practices that would later become closely regulated. Fourth, was the attempted defence of the bid by British Aluminium's plan to issue 4.5m shares to its preferred suitor, Alcoa, at a price of 60/-, the equivalent of a third of the issued capital of the company at a price some 10/- below the market price at the time. This transaction was agreed by the directors without reference to their shareholders, who had no power to prevent the scale of dilution of capital involved, another practice that would later require permission.

British Aluminium was not a large company and the value of the bid was around £38m, or the equivalent to a modest £500m today, but as an event it was a landmark in the financial history of the City. It signalled a more confrontational future for the merchant banks and thrust S. G. Warburg along its path to eventual leadership of the merchant banking sector. Above all, it was a victory for shareholders and displayed for the first time the power of the shareholders to act against their directors and advisers. It truly disrupted the control over events that close City relationships believed they had always exercised, and, after the event, its significance was unintentionally painted in a letter to *The Times* on 12 January from Olaf Hambro, Chairman of Hambros Bank.

In the letter, Hambro revealed that the consortium bid had the support of many more banks than its 14 signatories and continued:

> It is, therefore, quite clear that, except for the two houses who were connected with Tube Investments as financial advisers, and who would inevitably have to back their client, practically the whole of the representatives of the City were supporting the British Aluminium Company and its resistance to the American-dominated takeover. This being so it is very unclear why the majority of the City editors of the press seemed to be against City opinion and openly wrote in favour of the takeover bid.

The letter reflected the views of many whose entrenched belief was that the control of a company rests with the directors and their advisers, and who had not come to terms with the reality that it is the shareholders who actually own the company. It was an uncomprehending protest, sharply rebutted in the same columns by Esmond Durlacher, the most famous jobber of his generation, who wrote that City editors better reflected the views of the wider City – that shareholders would have been worse off following the advice of the consortium, and both bids involved strong American influence.

After the excitement of reaching an all-time high on the last day of 1958, the stock market was quiet in the first quarter of 1959 and share prices moved very little either way. The next election now lay within sight of the market's discounting mechanism and its outcome was by no means certain. However, there was nothing that a brazen election budget would not put right and on 7 April 1959 the Chancellor, Heathcoat Amory, perfected the art of the vote-catching budget. He reduced the standard rate of income tax from 8/6d to 7/9d, reduced the 3 purchase tax bands each by 20%, reduced the duty on beer by 2d a pint, and he restored investment allowances at rates of 20% for plant and machinery and 10% for buildings. In releasing £366m into the economy – the equivalent today of some £4bn to £5bn – he displayed exquisite timing to allow the benefits of these measures to seep through in time for an opportunist election later in the year.

The market reached new high ground towards the end of April and thereafter before the end of May the FT Index recorded new all-time highs on 18 out of 25 successive business days in climbing to 240.1. With growing confidence during the summer months, the market responded enthusiastically and, in the month of August, the FT Index recorded new highs on 15 out of 20 business days. It was during this latest surge that equities moved into the 'reverse yield gap' when, on 27 August 1959, the yield on the FT Index at 4.76% was, for the first time, lower than the yield on Consols 2½% at 4.77%. 'Through at Last' was the front-page headline of the *Financial Times* on the following morning, and no longer would the investor expect to obtain a higher yield on an equity than on a government stock. When allowance is made for economic growth, higher dividends and modest inflation, it seems remarkable that it should have taken 14 post-war years to set aside the convention that, because of greater inherent risk, an equity should yield more than a gilt. Its existence had for a long time provided fine opportunities for investment trusts to raise fixed interest capital and invest it in equities to gain a higher yield than the cost of borrowing.

In the midst of steadily rising share prices, it was announced on 8 September 1959 that a general election would be held on 8 October 1959. The FT Index responded to the news with a rise of 4 points from 251.2 to 255.2. By polling day, it had moved further ahead to 268.6. In its customary election day leader, the *Financial Times* summarised the policies of the two parties, preferred those of the Conservative Government, and stated confidently that 'we believe that a majority of the electorate will share this view and return the Conservative party to power today'.

The strength of the market and this ringing endorsement might suggest this was an easy election for the Conservative Government, with an outcome never doubted by investors. However, hindsight cannot convey just how nervous investors felt throughout the election campaign, ever fearful that the opinion polls would narrow at the last moment to produce the wrong result. Neither can it convey how much was at stake.

While the two political parties have always been far apart in their beliefs and policies, both had much greater power in the 1950s than would be the case today to impose extremist policies on the electorate and the economy. In 1959, the United Kingdom was one of several independent self-contained developed economies within well-defined boundaries, and, by the standards of today, almost isolated by the inadequacy of telecommunications. Today, all are cogs in an integrated global machine that is vastly bigger economically, but far smaller geographically. Investors in 1959 had every good reason to fear the measures awaiting them from a Labour government, and members of the Stock Exchange feared for its future under a hostile administration. The barometer of electoral uncertainty was the steel sector, newly denationalised by the Conservatives, but promised renationalisation on onerous terms by a Labour government.

In the event, the Conservative Government was returned with a much increased majority and the morning after the election, on 9 October 1959, witnessed some of the most frantic activity ever seen in the Stock Exchange. The FT Index rose by 6% from 268.6 to 284.7, the equivalent of a rise of more than 300 points in the FTSE Index today. At 10.19, the Extel tape reported 'Veteran members with up to forty years' experience on the floor are prepared to admit that the scenes witnessed this morning exceed anything they have ever seen before'.

'Conditions, particularly in the steel market, were the most hectic in living memory', reported the *Financial Times* on the next day and steel shares surged ahead by 20% or more with market leader United Steel moving from 44/6d to 55/-. The *Financial Times* published weekly sector indices every Wednesday and on the day before the election, the steel sector index stood at 147.0. One week later, it had risen by 32% to 194.6. On the first three days of the week following the election, the number of bargains marked exceeded 30,000, with a peak of 32,655 on 14 October 1959. The FT Index quickly broke through the 300 level on 30 October 1959 and the yield on the Index fell below 4% for the first time since 1947.

The mood of the nation was reflected in the euphoria of the market. 'You've never had it so good' was the message from Harold Macmillan. There was an insatiable demand for motor cars, the Mini had been recently launched, the first section of the M1 had been built, monthly indices of industrial production showed rises of 7%, 8% or 9% over the previous 12 months and retail sales were 5% higher. Frenetic activity on the Stock Exchange caused serious settlement pressures as a cumbersome paper-driven transfer system kept hard-pressed settlement clerks working late into the night.

Fears for the future of the Stock Exchange under a Labour government may have been exaggerated, but they were genuinely believed, and a measure of this was the price of membership. All intending members were required to purchase one nomination, or share, in the Stock Exchange. The transformation in prospects caused by the election result was illustrated by the rise in the price of a nomination from only £175 in March 1959 to £1,800 eight months later in November.

Towards the end of the year a further boost was given to equity shares when the Government announced its intention to reform the Trustee Act and allow trustees to invest up to 50% of trust funds in equities. The beneficiaries of trusts had suffered grievously from the legal requirement that their assets must be invested in fixed income investments. As the decade of the 1950s closed, reviews showed that, in broad terms, equities had trebled, gilt-edged stocks had fallen by a third and inflation had risen by 50%, illustrating all too well the fate of those trapped within the constraints of trustee investment.

Everything was now conspiring to drive the market higher. The value of invested funds in the unit trust movement had doubled in 1959 from £100m to £200m, and more than half a million unit-holders had average holdings of £386. The year had seen much takeover activity. It was dominated by mergers in the brewing and insurance industries, but there was a three-way battle for Harrods – won by House of Fraser ahead of Debenhams and United Drapery Stores – and an unusual takeover battle between Nestlé and Fisons for Crosse & Blackwell, a soup manufacturer with a strong brand image. It was won by Nestlé and was unusual because it was an early example of two later fashions. It was a bid for a 'brand' name – and, second, Fisons, as a fertiliser manufacturer, was indulging in diversification to a degree that baffled the market at the time.

When a bull market finally boils over, it is always easy to pick out those danger signals that become glaringly obvious with hindsight but are never quite so visible at the time. The problem is that those investors whose antennae successfully respond to danger signals will all too often have sold out before the bull market has hardly begun. Stock market timing is an art. It was once famously pointed out that investment discussions are almost always prefaced by some sort of statement along the lines that 'it's difficult just now', often accompanied by the throwaway line that 'three months ago it was all clear cut'.

However, the danger signals in this particular bull market would probably be better identified today than they were in 1959, when there was less understanding of the pressures caused by a very high growth rate in the economy of the kind created by the election boom in 1959. In the event, this bull market peaked on 4 January 1960, when the FT Index reached 342.9, a rise of 122% in just under 2 years (see Figure 11.1). This chapter began with an announcement from Manchester Corporation Pension Fund that it was to invest in equities for the first time with £500,000. It was a psychological signal that the bull market had run its course when the same fund announced it had successfully invested £2.9m in equities with a current market value of £4m, and was now raising its target for equities to 25% of the fund.

Similarities between the bull markets of 1954/55 and 1958/59 are uncanny. In both cases, share prices rather more than doubled. Stock markets mirrored an identical two years of quite exceptional rates of economic growth, both triggered by the creation of consumer booms timed opportunistically to straddle election dates. Both came shuddering to a halt within three months of the elections. When this bull market peaked on 4 January 1960, unease about the state of the economy was already beginning to grow. Unease turned into reality when, on 21 January 1960, Bank rate was increased from 4% to 5%.

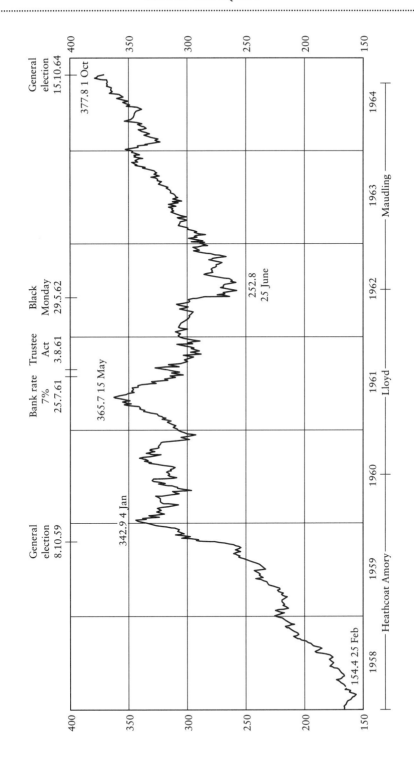

Figure 11.1
FT INDEX 1958–64

Source: Financial Times

Chapter 12

DRIFT

January 1960–October 1964

The last few chapters have followed the course of clearly defined bull and bear markets, but the closing quarter of this long period of Conservative rule was less well defined. It was a time of little overall progress and short-term fluctuations, but some important individual events. In some ways, it was the prelude to the unrewarding decades of the 1960s and 1970s, characterised by political weakness, economic failure and runaway inflation.

The 1959 election boom ended on 4 January 1960 when the FT Index reached 342.9 before drifting disappointingly through the rest of the year to below 300. The market was turned by an increase in Bank rate from 4% to 5%, and there followed a mildly deflationary Budget on 4 April 1960, when Heathcoat Amory raised profits tax from 10% to 12½% in what would be his final appearance as Chancellor. He promised an attack on tax avoidance schemes that artificially turned highly taxed income into untaxed capital gains, and he brought the so-called 'golden handshakes' into the tax net.

However, the unusual feature of the Budget was a warning that he would not hesitate to use monetary rather than budgetary weapons in the course of the year if further restraint were required. The Chancellor was giving himself discretion to use Bank rate, hire purchase controls and special deposits at will, and he wasted little time before doing so. On 28 April 1960, he imposed 20% deposits on hire purchase transactions, limited repayment to two years, and he raised 1% special deposits from the banks. Within another two months he had taken action on all three fronts by raising Bank rate from 5% to 6%, and doubling the special deposits required by the London clearing banks from 1% to 2%.

Heathcoat Amory had already indicated his wish to leave office and, on 27 July 1960, he was succeeded as Chancellor by Selwyn Lloyd. By now, the mood of the economy was swinging too far in the wrong direction, with four-day weeks in the motor industry and serious overcapacity in television manufacturing. There followed token reductions in Bank rate from 6% to 5½% in October 1960 and to 5% in December. Whether this was elegant fine-tuning by the Government or swaying with the breeze, the market responded by recovering very sharply in the first quarter of 1961.

The FT Index broke into new high ground in April 1961, 15 months after its previous high, and continued to rise until 15 May 1961, when it peaked at

365.7. It is a moot point as to whether this 15-month period should be counted as the final leg of the 1958/60 bull market, or the first leg of an indecisive four years of drift. In this narrative, the latter interpretation has been adopted because the previous economic and stock market cycle had already conclusively ended.

The market had taken little note of a mildly deflationary first Budget from Selwyn Lloyd on 18 April 1961, in which he further raised profits tax from 12½% to 15%, partly to offset the cost of an increase in the starting point of surtax from £2,000 to £4,000. In fact, a summer crisis was looming and the market suddenly lost its nerve in the face of a series of unwelcome strikes and a substantial pay claim from the railway workers, followed by the announcement of a 5-year low of 258,000 in unemployment and a rise in vacancies to 395,000 in July – a definition of full employment if ever there was one. The market cracked and, from its all-time high of 365.7 on 15 May 1961, the FT Index fell away sharply to 301.4 on 17 July as concern mounted and sterling came under pressure.

The crisis came to a head on 25 July 1961 in an emergency Budget. The Chancellor raised Bank rate from 5% to 7%, imposed 10% surcharges on all rates of purchase tax and excise duties, and raised special deposits from the banks from 2% to 3%.

He added two further significant announcements for the stock market. In the context of requesting a pause in pay demands, he exhorted companies not to increase dividends unless fully justified and, second, proposed the introduction of a capital gains tax in the next, April Budget. This was the first tentative step in the direction of those fateful income and dividend controls that in one form or another, were to become the signature of the 1960s and 1970s, discredited by their identification with some of the highest rates of inflation ever seen in the history of the British economy and unceremoniously bundled out in 1979.

The promise of a capital gains tax from a Conservative Chancellor was seen by a perplexed market as something of a betrayal. The stock market reaction to these July measures was unusual. From time to time, an extra day is required to absorb sudden and unexpected news, be it bullish or bearish, and, on the day following the Budget, the FT Index was steady. It was only on the next day that investors understood the seriousness of the situation and, in one of its sharpest falls, the FT Index fell by nearly 3% on the day, from 316.0 to 307.3.

Within a week of the Chancellor's statement, the stock market took fleeting comfort from the coming into operation of the new Trustee Act on 3 August 1961. On that day alone War Loan fell by more than 1 point to 51½, and, over 3 days, the FT Index rose by nearly 6%.

The Government continued in schizophrenic mood, reducing Bank rate in October and again in November, but at the same time ruling out any relaxation in the search for a pay policy. In this pursuit, the Chancellor met with the TUC, when he confirmed his plan to introduce a short-term capital gains tax in a move widely interpreted as a sop to encourage the unions to cooperate with a guideline for pay increases of 2½%. Bank rate reductions continued in 1962 and, within days of the Budget on 10 April 1962, it was down to 4½%.

In an otherwise broadly neutral and uneventful Budget, the Chancellor introduced his long-promised short-term speculative gains tax. Capital gains taken within six months on stocks and shares, and within three years on land, were to count as income liable to tax and surtax for individuals and profits tax for companies. A marginal tax rate of 17/9d, or 88¾% was close to confiscation for some taxpayers. Meanwhile, the Government continued to run into serious industrial relations problems, with strike threats from the engineering and ship-building unions, the dock workers, and also from the railway workers who were beginning to understand some of the consequences of the much-publicised appointment as Chairman of the British Transport Commission a year earlier of Dr Beeching, a former director of ICI. Pay settlements were widely breaching the guidelines of 2½% and a general air of crisis prevailed.

After a long dull period – with the FT Index marooned at around 300 – the market was caught by the backwash from a sudden collapse on Wall Street on 28 May 1962. This day came to be known as 'Black Monday'. There was a panic among US investors about the inevitability of a severe recession in 1963 and the Dow Jones Index fell by 5.7%, from 611.88 to 576.93 – its largest single-day fall since October 1929. On the following day, a tidal wave flooded the London market and it too incurred its largest single-day fall since the introduction of the FT Index in 1935. The Index fell by 18 points, from 279.3 to 261.3, or by 6.4%, thus exceeding the previous biggest percentage fall on a single day of 5.4% on 26 September 1938, when Hitler issued his ultimatum to Czechoslovakia.

Tidal waves vanish as quickly as they arrive and, on the following day, the FT Index recovered most of its lost ground, with a rise of 5.9% to 276.6, justifying the overnight words of Lord Ritchie, Chairman of the Stock Exchange, that 'My advice to the small investors is to put their heads down and let the wind blow over them'. However, these two days revealed the highly nervous state of the London market in the face of many economic problems. They also provided a good example of the sometimes hypnotic effect exercised over the London stock market by overnight trends on Wall Street, which regularly influenced the direction of opening prices in London.

The low point was reached on 25 June 1962 when the FT Index touched 252.8 – down 30% from its May 1961 peak – and it was barely changed 2 weeks later on 13 July 1962 – the dramatic 'night of the long knives'. Harold Macmillan sacked seven of his ministers, including Chancellor Selwyn Lloyd, who made it perfectly clear in his resignation letter that he had been forced to leave office against his wishes – uncanny in its resemblance many years later to the dismissal of Norman Lamont. 'You have told me that you would like me to resign and this I willingly do', wrote Selwyn Lloyd in his resignation letter to the Prime Minister, and 'I realise that the policies with which I have been associated are unpopular'.

He had been unlucky to inherit the remnants of his predecessor's electoral boom in 1958 and 1959, and had no option other than to introduce restrictive policies, but he was not helped by a poor manner on television and a visibly uneasy body language. Perhaps less noticed was the second failure of the Prime Minister, Harold Macmillan, to support his Chancellor in difficult times, just as he failed to support Peter Thorneycroft in 1957. In a highly perceptive article in the *Financial Times* on 17 July, Harold Wincott wrote that 'the truth is that Mr. Macmillan is and always has been an inflationist. He still lives and thinks in the atmosphere of Stockon-on-Tees in the early thirties and his book *The Middle Way* might have served as an election manifesto for the socialists'. This judgement of Macmillan is more commonly heard today than it ever was when he was Prime Minister.

The market had now reached such low levels that the yield gap returned on 19 July 1962 when equities yielded 6.01% and Consols 2½% yielded 5.95%. It remained for two months, returned briefly in October, and has since only ever returned for a few days in July 1996.

However, attention in a gloomy year was attracted by exciting corporate developments involving some of the largest British companies. It was always known that Imperial Tobacco owned 28½% of the capital of British-American Tobacco, arising from a division of the spoils at the turn of the century whereby Imperial Tobacco agreed to sell its brands only in the United Kingdom, allowing British-American Tobacco to sell the same brands only in the rest of the world. However, in July 1961, it was revealed in a Monopolies Commission Report that Imperial Tobacco also owned 42½% of the equity of Gallaher, its leading competitor in the United Kingdom, where together they controlled more than 90% of the cigarette market.

This was one of the best ever kept corporate secrets, and received with incredulity by the market. It transpired that in 1932, Imperial Tobacco bought a controlling stake in Gallaher, which then had a tiny 1% share of the cigarette market. In 1937, Gallaher acquired the highly successful Senior Service brand and, in 1946, the 51% shareholding fell below controlling level when Imperial Tobacco did not subscribe for a rights issue. The holding had remained secret for 30 years. Imperial Tobacco was roundly criticised for concealing from its shareholders an important element in calculating the real underlying value of the shares. The Monopolies Commission later decided that Imperial Tobacco should be allowed to keep its Gallaher shares subject to a binding commitment not to interfere, or be involved, in the management of the company's affairs.

The second and more startling corporate event was the bid by ICI for Courtaulds announced on 18 December 1961. It was then, by a large margin, the biggest ever UK takeover bid and the offer in ICI shares valued Courtaulds at £180m, equivalent to some £2,200m today. In a stock market more accustomed to agreed mergers than takeover bids, and less well informed by rumour, the announcement of this bid aroused strong emotions across the marketplace. It was perceived as breathtaking in size and outrageous in concept because ICI was the fourth-largest company after Shell, Unilever and BP, and Courtaulds was not far behind in thirteenth place. It was barely within most people's perception that bids could happen for companies the size of Courtaulds.

In fact, negotiations for an agreed merger had been continuing for several months but were now in danger of leaking. ICI broke ranks and aroused the hostility of the directors of Courtaulds by going public with an offer. One month later, on 17 January 1962, ICI raised its bid to £200m, or 46/3d per share compared with 30/- before the first bid. This 'final, final' offer from ICI was promptly rejected by Courtaulds, which in a statement to shareholders said that it 'would seriously under-value the earnings' capacity of Courtaulds relative to that of ICI'.

A week later, Courtaulds forecast that profits would rise over the next three years from £17.5m to £28.5m, producing steadily rising dividends, and estimated an asset value of 50/- per share. Courtaulds claimed that an earlier decision last year to cut its interim dividend had been 'political' and was now regretted. ICI responded with an option within the bid using a convertible unsecured loan stock to produce a higher income, but, in an atmosphere of growing bitterness, Courtaulds produced its plan to defeat the bid. Out of the hat came promises of dividend increases of at least 10% over the next 2 years, a cash distribution out of capital profits over the next 3 years, a £40m capitalisation issue in 7% unsecured loan stock and the creation of a £40m investment trust. These proposals raised shareholders' income well above the offer from ICI and the shares jumped to a new high of 51/-.

The confrontation between the two companies was now deeply hostile, with pride at stake on both sides. Although the prospect of victory was fast receding, ICI pressed on and made its bid unconditional before acceptances had even been counted, on the mistaken advice that this would lead to a flood of acceptances. On 12 March 1962, ICI announced that its bid had failed, with acceptances for 37.4% of the capital of Courtaulds. As the directors and senior employees of Courtaulds took themselves to church for a service of thanksgiving, ICI, as the owner of 29.6m Courtaulds shares, stubbornly announced it had no intention of either adding to or selling its holding.

This was another landmark in the history of corporate activity in the London market. It showed that size offered no immunity to a hostile bid. It demonstrated sophisticated defence tactics by using dividend forecasts well into the future, creating new pockets of income and actively using a friendly third party to buy its shares – namely the Courtaulds pension fund. Another feature of this battle between two large, well-established public companies was the emergence of personalities from behind the conventional corporate facade. The investing public became aware of the name of Frank Kearton who was now to emerge as a major figure in the textile industry.

Paul Chambers, the highly respected Chairman of ICI, probably suffered some loss of reputation during this takeover battle. His tactics made him appear arrogant and overbearing, and allowed Courtaulds to play for public sympathy as the underdog. This was an unfair judgement of a man who gave much thought to the problems and challenges of industry. Chambers was far-sighted and, in the course of the bid, he explained in an address to the American Chamber of Commerce his thinking behind a merger that would control 90% of the UK man-made fibre market. 'Much of modern industry was bound to be concentrated into big units as the requirements of capital, research and development increased the optimum size of the economic unit', was an observation some years ahead of its time in 1962 in Britain where an instinct remained within industry to share the spoils among competing companies and, within government, obsessively to fear monopoly. He lamented that 'legislation against large concentrations of economic power, necessary fifty years ago, was now out of date'.

The outcome was a popular, but undeserving, victory for Courtaulds. But how it was possible to paint so brightly a future that only a few months earlier had been dismal enough to require the dividend to be cut was a question neither put nor answered. The outcome was a setback for industrial concentration in the short term, but it also propelled Frank Kearton to a position of autocratic power in Courtaulds that he ruthlessly unleashed over the next decade in an endless series of acquisitions to rationalise a declining UK textile industry.

After Selwyn Lloyd's forced resignation on 13 July 1962, he was succeeded as Chancellor by Reginald Maudling. A candidate for the future leadership of the party, Maudling was a younger man of cheerful countenance and more likely to win votes than his gloomy predecessor. He began as he meant to continue by reducing the special deposits from 2% to 1% in September, followed a few days later by announcing further relaxations in the annual Mansion House speech. Post-war credits were to be released, £175m of public investment was announced for next year and restraints on bank lending were to be removed with immediate effect.

The Chancellor continued to hand out good news like confetti. On 5 November 1962, he released £50m to stimulate the economy by cutting purchase tax on motor cars from 45% to 25% and raising investment allowances for plant and machinery from 20% to 30%. British Motor Corporation shares rose by more than 10% on the day from 14/3d to 15/10½d. Three weeks later, he released the remaining 1%, or £80m, of special bank deposits. The Chancellor's urge to boost the economy was now becoming addictive. On 1 January 1963, at a cost of £30m, he abolished the top rate of purchase tax and lowered the tax on television sets, radios, perfumes and cosmetics to 25%. Two days, later Bank rate was reduced from 4½% to 4%.

There was still plenty left for his first Budget on 3 April 1963, when he injected a further £270m into the economy making a total of £420m from the measures already announced. He increased personal allowances, made concessions at the lower levels of income tax, improved depreciation allowances, and, much to the pleasure of the Stock Exchange, halved stamp duty on share transactions from 2% to 1% to take effect on 1 August 1963. 'The theme of this Budget is expansion; expansion without inflation, expansion that can be sustained', claimed Reginald Maudling. Harold Macmillan, a few decades ahead of his time, called it 'a people's Budget'.

However, hidden between the lines was an emerging borrowing deficit for the year of £597m. The stock market was sceptical and only marginally gave the new Chancellor the benefit of the doubt through this cycle of measures. The FT Index was 266.3 when he took office, 283.1 at the year end, and 303.3 on the day after this Budget. The market was preoccupied by other concerns. At a parochial level, the introduction of capital gains tax undoubtedly had an adverse effect on business volumes in the Stock Exchange, with daily bargain levels in the second half of 1962 typically in the 9,000–12,000 range, compared with 14,000–17,000 over the previous 12 months.

On an economic level, there were concerns about inflation and the painfully slow but stubborn intent of the Conservative Government to set guidelines for pay increases. This had first surfaced at the time of the emergency Budget of July 1961, when, at an acrimonious meeting with the TUC to discuss a pay pause, the TUC demanded a 'pause in profits' to match any pause in pay increases. In a one-sided dialogue, the Government talked about pay guidelines of 2½% and, in July 1962, the Prime Minister announced the setting up of an impartial advisory National Incomes Commission to make a permanent incomes policy acceptable nationally, despite failure to win TUC support.

At the party conference in October 1962, the Chancellor claimed the 'need for a permanent Incomes Policy' and in the April 1963 Budget he outlined a target range of 3–3½% for the growth of incomes. These hesitant steps served more to illustrate the strength of the unions and the sight of the Government being constantly rebuffed as it tried to make friends with the TUC was not a happy one. Investors were well aware that pay restraint would lead to dividend restraint and a return to the days of the last Labour Government.

On a political level, the market had other concerns. With the next election coming into view, the opinion polls were consistently showing large Labour leads. Under Edward Heath in October 1961, the Government had begun the process of applying to join the European Community. It gradually became apparent that the problem of reconciling the agricultural policies of the European Community with traditional Commonwealth trading links was insoluble. After 15 months, negotiations were deadlocked and on 14 January 1963, President de Gaulle made his famous intervention to say that the United Kingdom was not yet ready to join. Talks continued until 29 January 1963, when entry was formally blocked by a French veto.

The failure of these talks may have contributed to the general gloom of another dull year in the stock market, but investors probably shared the wait and see attitude of the general public. Stock markets were still largely domestic and international events such as the confrontation between President Kennedy and Mr Khruschev over Russian missile bases in Cuba had surprisingly little general effect in London. International incidents are usually felt in only the narrowest of senses, as, for example, when oil shares were hit by the closure of the Suez Canal in 1956, and tea shares collapsed by 24% in a single day when China threatened to invade India in November 1962.

The market remained in the doldrums after the new Chancellor's first Budget in April 1963, and was not helped by the resignation of War Minister John Profumo in June 1963. Even in the *Financial Times*, the Profumo scandal held the front-page lead every day for a whole week and further extensive weekend coverage led to a 7 points fall in the FT Index on 10 June 1963, a delayed reaction to possible disarray of the Government. In fact, this marked a low point in the market's fortunes and sentiment was helped by the announcement of another huge takeover bid.

BP and Shell announced a joint £290m bid for Burmah Oil on 27 June 1963. This was not an orthodox takeover bid because Burmah's principal assets were a 24½% stake in BP and a smaller stake in Shell, both of which, under the terms of the bid, would be distributed to Burmah shareholders, thereby unlocking assets of £200m. Motivation for the bid was fear on the part of BP that a foreign company could acquire a significant stake in it by making a bid for Burmah. In the event, the bid was quickly withdrawn on 4 July 1963 after failure to obtain agreement from the directors of Burmah.

The stock market continued its recovery from the Profumo episode and, in quick succession, brushed aside the resignation on medical grounds of Harold Macmillan on 10 October 1963, the unexpected emergence of Sir Alec Douglas-Home as his successor as Prime Minister, and the assassination of President Kennedy on 22 November 1963. The market ended 1963 in good spirit, at its highest point for the year, and the FT Index at 348.3 reached its highest point for 2½ years.

The election was now in sight and stock markets in 1964 were dominated by opinion polls. As the Conservatives slowly pulled back the Labour lead, so confidence returned. Economic events were largely neutral, although weak trade figures showed an ominous doubling of the trade gap to £121m for January, and Bank rate was increased from 4% to 5% on 27 February 1964 to help sterling and curb too rapid an expansion in the economy. Maudling's second Budget on

14 April 1964 was mildly deflationary, with the only feature a 10% increase in beer and tobacco duties in a Budget so simple that it might well have been prepared with a spring election in mind.

By-elections in May showed a further fall in the swing to Labour and the stock market continued to edge upwards in line with increasingly favourable opinion polls. The FT Index reached a new all-time high of 365.9 on 13 August 1964 when a National Opinion Poll showed a Labour lead over the Conservatives that had been reduced to 0.6% compared with 13.1% in April. Not even the announcement on 15 September 1964 of the actual date of the forthcoming General Election deterred investors and the FT Index eventually reached its high of the year, and for some 3 years to come, of 377.8 in the midst of the election campaign on 1 October 1964.

The stock market was more volatile in the course of this election campaign than in any other since the war. Fear and greed exchanged places from day to day, as investors nervously or expectantly awaited the verdict of every opinion poll. Early in the campaign, the Labour lead in the opinion polls was narrowing and the market surged to new all-time highs. 'The market smells a Tory victory' ran the *Financial Times* leader on 3 October 1964.

Two days later, a Gallup opinion poll showed Labour to be 4½% ahead. The FT Index fell by 7.1 points and steel shares – the most highly geared counter in a highly political market – fell by 8%. A few days later, an opinion poll in a critical constituency showed an 8% swing to Labour and down again went the FT Index by another 7 points and steel shares by 6%. Two days before the election, the market surged ahead by 8.8 points on the back of a wave of public buying as hope returned to investors at the very last minute.

The emotional gyrations triggered by this election were based on genuine fear by private investors that their assets would be attacked by a Labour government by the use of controls and taxation that in one form or another would amount to expropriation. These fears were all too easily fed by memories of the postwar Labour Government, still fresh in the minds of many people even after an interval of 13 years. It is conventional thinking today that no government could impose controls on the movement of capital as long as London remains at the heart of one of the three financial trading centres that make up the 24-global market. The sophistication of technology and communications would not allow it. In 1964, world markets simply did not exist in this way and there were genuine reasons to fear that a Labour government could easily erect barriers to contain and control financial assets within a highly effective ringed fence.

Everybody knew that the election was going to be a close call, and for private investors – hopeful one moment, fearful the next – much was riding on the outcome of as little as half a dozen seats either way. In the event, these frequent changes of mood were correctly forecasting the closeness of the election, which produced the smallest ever majority of 3 seats for Labour. It brought to an end the 13 years of the Conservative government, under which investors had prospered. A much less happy era was now about to begin, in which successive Labour, Conservative and Labour Governments would, over 15 years, preside over some of the worst inflation the country has ever experienced, and equities would fail by a long margin to be the hedge they are often assumed to be.

Chapter 13

....

REVIEW
1951–64

The 13 years of Conservative rule were highly rewarding for investors in equities, but disastrous for investors in gilt-edged and other fixed interest securities. The Conservatives took office on 26 October 1951 when the FT Index stood at 138.3, and left office on 15 October 1964 with the FT Index at 364.9 – an increase of 163%. Inflation over the same period was 51%, giving real capital appreciation of around 75%, or around 4% per annum, together with an average dividend yield of around 5%. The contrast with the lot of the fixed interest investor could hardly be more stark. The benchmark stock – Consols 2½%, fell by a third from 60 at the beginning of the period to 40 at the end, and had more than halved in real terms after allowing for inflation.

There was little change in the yield on the FT Index from 5¼% at the beginning to 4¼% at the end, but the yield on Consols rose from 4% to 6% as the reverse yield gap came into play. Table 13.1 sets out the details using the FT Index and the retail price index.

Table 13.1
The FT Index and inflation, 1951–64

Date	FT Index	Change (%)	Inflation	Real return (%)
25 October 1951	138.3			
15 October 1964	364.9	163.8	50.9	74.8

The FT Actuaries All Share Index was introduced in 1962 and quickly became the benchmark for performance calculations, but the FT Index is the only index available throughout the period being received here. Folding in the new index over the last two and a half years to October 1964 lowers the long-term calculation, but unfairly so because of weakness in financial shares during that brief period, when their previous strength had not been captured by the FT Index.

It was undeniably a successful era for the equity investor, but the journey was very uneven. Closer analysis shows that the capital appreciation was almost entirely achieved during the course of two remarkable bull markets, 1953–55 and 1958–60, when, in both cases, share prices more than doubled. Although the second of these spilled over into the first few days of 1960, both bull markets were creatures of the 1950s. Little further progress was made in the first half of the 1960s.

Stock market returns of the scale enjoyed by investors during these 13 years might suggest they were the rewards for glowing management performance across a wide range of industries against a background of rapid growth. Nothing could be further from the truth. They were largely the rewards of liberal dividend policies and a willingness on the part of investors to value shares on a constant dividend yield. The alternative explanation is that investors were prepared to put a higher valuation on earnings, but this is hard to justify on the basis of only modest earnings growth.

The economy grew by 46% in real terms between 1951 and 1964 – an annual growth rate of around 3%, after allowing for inflation of 51%. The *Financial Times* first published an earnings yield on the FT Index in 1954, enabling an underlying earnings index to be calculated. From 1954 to 1964, earnings grew by 31%, and an estimate for the 3 previous years based on dividend cover suggests that overall growth in earnings on the FT Index from 1951 to 1964 was 47%. This is close to inflation for the period, but signifies no real growth in earnings. The FT Index was an industrial share index dominated by manufacturing companies, a relatively successful segment of the economy in the 1950s, and did not include companies from the financial and oil sectors. However, a calculation based on a more widely based Moodies Services Index of 60 companies shows an almost identical figure for earnings growth.

In simple terms, the increase of 163% in share prices during the 13 years may be attributed to dividend growth of 170%, as measured by the underlying dividend indicator on the FT 30 Index. Alternatively, it may be attributed one-third to growth in earnings broadly in line with inflation in the economy, and two-thirds to a change by the market in its valuation of earnings from, in modern terms, a PE ratio of around 6 in 1951 to around 13 in 1964. The erosion of dividend cover from three to one and a half was partly hidden from view by the continuing influence of dividend yield on the valuation of shares, by the use of the obscure measure of the earnings yield and by a lack of market information. Investors were undoubtedly attracted by persistent increases in dividends at a rate well above inflation.

The change in valuation was partly a response to the chronically low valuation of equities towards the end of the post-war Labour Government, after years of dividend controls. The return of the Conservative Government in 1951 provided an immediate impetus for higher dividends and further weight was added by the predatory activities of Charles Clore in the 1950s. The cult of the equity led to persistent portfolio switching from gilts to equities on the part of pension funds and insurance companies.

The private sector was undoubtedly operating under a more liberal political regime, which allowed it to hand out much higher dividends, but little was done to confront the structural problems of a business culture where competition was sheltered by price agreements and insolvency was almost unknown. The easy growth of post-war recovery and hungry export markets allowed industrialists to prosper without seeking economies of scale and extra market share by acquisition, and concealed from view a lack of will to deal with the restrictive practices and demarcation lines of powerful trade unions. The private sector all too readily followed the example of the Government in its constant appeasement of the trade unions in the nationalised industries, as is well described by Andrew Roberts in *Eminent Churchillians* (Weidenfeld & Nicholson, 1994). The spirit of industry in the 1950s was epitomised by the classic film *I'm All Right Jack*.

The driving force behind the rise in equities was a constant flow of institutional funds that exercised the simple laws of supply and demand over share prices. Insurance companies and pension funds shed their actuarial inhibitions and discovered equities, typically building their percentages in them from around 10% of assets to some 30–40%, and generating the weight of money that lies behind all bull markets. Board of Trade figures for the life assurance companies show an aggregate investment at book value in 1951 of £411m in equities, amounting to 11% of total assets of £3,590m. By 1964, equities had risen to £2,253m, or 22% of total assets of £10,102m, and probably closer to 30% at market value. There is less long-term information available about pension funds, but Board of Trade figures show invested funds at market value in 1964 of £4,847m, of which £1,964m, or 40%, was in equities, presumably almost entirely in the UK.

In contrast, investment trusts and unit trusts had always been committed to equities. The same Board of Trade figures show the investment trusts in 1964 with assets of £2,887m and unit trusts with £406m, with just over 90% of assets in both cases invested in equities. However, there was a difference that whereas equities owned by investment trusts were more or less equally divided between the UK and overseas, those owned by the unit trusts were largely in the UK.

There is no precise information available about the total ownership of UK equities, and much credence is placed on different sampling surveys. A broad brush estimate based on the Board of Trade figures, above, and on the assumption that the published year-end valuation of the All Share Index at £18,741m represented 90% of the value of all equities, draws the picture shown in Table 13.2.

The cult of the equity was the principal feature of the 1950s, although it was not until the late 1950s that the market value of UK equities quoted on the Stock Exchange exceeded the value of government securities. The cult of the equity was the discovery of undervalued assets providing both rising dividends and protection against inflation. Closely identified with this discovery were George Ross

Table 13.2
Estimate of the institutional ownership of UK equities, 1964

	Total assets (£m)		UK equities Est. (£m)	%
All Share Index			20,800	100.0
Life Assurance Companies	10,102	(book)	3,000	14.4
Pension Funds	4,847		1,800	8.6
Investment Trusts	2,887		1,300	6.3
Unit Trusts	406		350	1.7
Total			6,450	31.0

Goobey, Investment Manager of the Imperial Tobacco pension fund, whose activities have already been described, and Lewis Whyte, Investment Director of the Equity & Law until 1953, when he joined London and Manchester Assurance, where he eventually became Chairman. He combined the academic with the practical in the shrewdest possible way.

A formative influence in Whyte's early working days as a stockbroker with Buckmaster and Moore was Maynard Keynes – the famous economist and inveterate stock market enthusiast. In 1951, Whyte published a textbook in two volumes entitled *The Principles of Finance and Investment* (Cambridge University Press, 1951) – at the time, the only available book of its kind – and throughout his career he was a wise investor and enthusiastic writer. For the immediate post-war generation, he was remembered as the man who bought investment trusts at very large discounts. In the 1950s, he argued strongly that equities should yield less than gilts because they participated in rising profits and dividends, and he anticipated the emergence of the reverse yield gap.

He placed great emphasis on the value of dividends, stemming from a simple belief that if you 'look after the income the capital will look after itself'. In a discussion paper in 1973, he defined the ordinary share in simple terms – 'The true worth of an equity share is the discounted value of the dividends over the period held together with any other casual distributions, plus or minus the profit or loss on realisation'. This reminds the shareholder that equities may involve the ownership of physical assets, but the return is only through the medium of paper money, in the form of dividend payments and the proceeds of sales.

Information and advice for the investor were sparse. Stockbrokers and jobbers regularly published statistical lists of stocks, prices and yields, and stockbrokers embellished these statistics with a few descriptive paragraphs in investment letters to clients. These letters offered general comment about the market, but were essentially written in the language of the private client. Press coverage was thin, with advice rarely extending beyond the language of the tip, and the specialist magazines – the *Investors Chronicle* and the *Stock Exchange Gazette* – tried to address all shareholders as one.

Stockbrokers were the prime source of market information. They had a professional advantage over many of the investment managers of pension funds and insurance companies who were often appointed to that role from elsewhere within the organisation without investment experience. Two statistical card services were available on subscription for stockbrokers and investment managers – Extel, with its large and small cards, and Moodies, with its folding cards. They were useful but unsophisticated and, for example, for many years did not adjust a sequence of earnings or dividends for the effect of scrip and rights issues. A true picture of a company's five-year record had to be worked out manually.

The more perceptive stockbrokers saw that the future lay with the institutions where the orders were large and repeating. They understood the more demanding needs of the investment manager and grasped the opportunities to develop new and distinctive skills to generate business. Some began to concentrate on particular aspects or sectors of the market and, although not necessarily realising it, they were creating the new skill of investment analysis. Ideas were developed in more depth and published as circulars to institutional clients, but headed 'Strictly Private and Confidential' because Stock Exchange rules were very strict about advertising or solicitation. In the good tradition of *The Times* newspaper, circulars were written anonymously.

For the first time, stockbrokers were able to attract business on the basis of *what* they knew rather than *who* they knew. In a business hitherto dominated by the old school tie and personal contacts, new career opportunities were available for university graduates with good degrees and for qualified actuaries and accountants who came from family backgrounds without any previous connection with the Stock Exchange. At first it was only a trickle, and surveys of graduate destinations at the time showed such a predominance for industry, teaching and public services that the numbers entering finance and accounting were insufficient to be reported as an identifiable group.

In many firms of stockbrokers, the 'statistical department' of little more than clerical status was turned into an upgraded and expanded 'research department'. Many firms thrived on this new challenge, but others found these new skills intrusive. Just as Siegmund Warburg was regarded by other merchant bankers as a player intruding into a gentleman's game, so investment analysts were regarded suspiciously by many stockbrokers as players straying on to a field occupied by gentlemen. It was a development not entirely welcomed by firms or individuals whose businesses were built on relationships. The absence of published factual information about companies actually suited the traditional new issue firms and those stockbrokers whose institutional links were founded on personal contacts. The rather secretive world of the gentleman stockbroker was based on discreet personal friendships. The analyst pushed against these barriers and, in a clash of culture, 'analyst' was sometimes a pejorative word.

Absence of information is usually a vacuum waiting to be filled and investment analysis offered an exciting future. It was formally created as a profession on 2 May 1955, when a small, enthusiastic group of seven stockbrokers and investment managers formed the Society of Investment Analysts, under the leadership of Francis Andrews – the distinguished Investment Manager of the Unilever Pension Fund, whose idea of holiday reading was the *Stock Exchange Official Year Book*. The Society's objectives were:

> to improve the general quality of investment analysis and analytical techniques, to foster the interchange of ideas and information among investment analysts, to promote fuller understanding of the function of investment analysis and financial research and the operation of security and commodity markets.

The inclusion of commodity markets now reads oddly and has since been dropped.

The Society of Investment Analysts is known today as the Institute of Investment Management and Research and, in 1997, it had some 3,800 members. The Society attracted many of the younger graduates and professionals then being recruited by stockbrokers and by investing institutions. They formed a natural peer group in a forum where eager brokers could meet their opposite numbers in the institutions.

The prime purpose of the Society in its early years was to seek information, encourage disclosure, improve the quality of company accounts and improve the standards of analysis. The chairmen, managing directors and finance directors of quoted companies were invited to make presentations to well-attended and interested audiences in a programme of regular meetings. It was on such occasions that the Board of Courtaulds used a previously arranged date to present their defence to the City in the middle of the ICI bid in February 1962, and John Bloom of Rolls Razor had the audience eating out of his hands with a comedy performance in October 1963, just nine months before his washing machine company went bankrupt.

For many analysts and investment managers it would be their first opportunity actually to see, hear and meet famous names in the corporate world. Equally important was the opportunity to discover basic information about a company whose report and accounts was typically a thin and poor-looking document. Contact between a company and the stockbroking community or its shareholders barely existed outside the formal relationship with its official stockbroker. It was technically a breach of Stock Exchange rules for a member firm to make contact with a company without first seeking formal approval from the company's official brokers.

These were exciting, pioneering days for investment analysts. With no apparent limit to their horizons, they enjoyed the satisfaction of pure research and discovery in a competitive search for basic information. It was very different from the prospect today for the trainee analyst entering a mature business with a high level of shared information. Surfing the Internet for prized snippets of information would be its nearest equivalent today.

In the 1960s an analyst could obtain a strong lead by piecing information together. Working out from press information something like the number of cars sold in a year by Jaguar, a figure cloaked in corporate secrecy, and estimating the profit per vehicle, presented an exciting challenge. Another example, from the insurance world, was the little-known fact that companies operating in the State of California were required by the Insurance Commissioner to deposit quarterly operating figures for their entire United States business. These figures were available for public inspection well before half-year or annual results were published by the three major British insurance companies with up to half their business in the United States, and this source of price-sensitive information was, for several years, kept a well-guarded secret by those who knew about it.

The analyst's pursuit of information, or 'disclosure', ran into the barriers of corporate privacy for many years. In an article on investment analysts on 16 January 1962 in the *Financial Times*, Harold Wincott wrote:

> It is not just that analysts everywhere – in common with financial journalists – are regarded by some industrialists as direct descendants of Oliver Twist and Mrs. Nosey-Parker; in countries where investment is traditionally done through the Old Boy Network there is understandable resentment at this dangerous importation from the New World, which, if it really gets going may do the Old Boys out of their privileges.

Clear leaders of this new age were Phillips & Drew, the stockbrokers whose employment of actuaries provided intimidating competition. Under the determined leadership of Dennis Weaver, the company raised investment analysis to new high standards in the 1950s. They provided market coverage of all the larger companies in the stock market, and introduced a new level of expertise in the forecasting of company profits and the provision of comparative analysis between shares and sectors across the market. Closest rivals in overall market coverage were Hoare & Co. They alone of the major brokers successfully combined leadership in both corporate finance and research and, in the 1960s, pioneered the use of computers for marketwide research.

Several small- and medium-sized firms pursued niche opportunities by being among the first to specialise in a particular sector of the market. Savory, with a long-term specialisation in insurance shares; Read Hurst-Brown in property and insurance shares, two homogeneous sectors where comparative statistical information between companies formed an important component of the research;

Kemp-Gee in retail and building materials; Stirling in chemicals and Milln Robinson in building materials and engineering are prime examples.

It was nevertheless difficult for a firm of stockbrokers to market their new research products. Under Stock Exchange rules, advertising was strictly forbidden, although two firms managed to circumvent this rule by publishing annuals for general sale. Thomas Skinner, publisher of the weekly *Stock Exchange Gazette*, published *Savory's Insurance Share Annual* at a price of 7/6d. This was followed by *Skinner's Property Share Annual*, produced by Read Hurst-Brown, and published for sale to surveyors and estate agents. Stockbrokers were not allowed to approach an institution without an introduction, and the idea of a mail shot to all institutions simply did not arise. One of the most important skills of a stockbroker in the 1960s was to contrive to obtain an innocent introduction to an investment manager.

The City was innately conservative. It was governed by the public school ethos that customs and rules are there to be learned and obeyed, not challenged. Deference was to be shown to those above and expected from those below. People were set in their ways. Some investment managers seeking access to research from a new broker would be inhibited by the conventional thinking of their superiors – the trustees and directors. Many were content to give all their business to a small number of traditional houses without the complication of more telephone calls. Some enjoyed flattery from important brokers and hospitality at exclusive events. Others enjoyed their power of patronage.

Although Phillips & Drew led the field in producing new and innovative research, Dennis Weaver remembers the difficulty of obtaining introductions to many of the large institutions where there was no existing relationship. Indeed, the firm was forced to search for clients new to the stock market, and an important part of their success stemmed from persuading a succession of local authority pension funds to invest in equities under their guidance. These were the antecedents of Phillips & Drew Fund Managers – a major fund management group today.

As investment analysis gathered pace, a dissenting voice attracted attention. In a publication in January 1963, 'Higgledy Piggledy Growth', I. D. M. Little, a Fellow of Nuffield College, disparaged the efforts of the analysts by claiming there was no correlation to be found between the past record of a company and its future prospects. It was a similar argument to the theory of the 'Random Walk', which, in essence, claims that past price movements are irrelevant to future prices.

Although in its infancy in the late 1950s and early 1960s, investment analysis grew steadily in importance, putting constant pressure on companies and legislators for more and more disclosure of information. This pressure was a vital early stage in the shift of financial power to the shareholder – a characteristic shared by the more open Anglo-Saxon financial systems of the United States,

Britain and the English-speaking countries of Australia, Canada and Hong Kong. In contrast, shareholders were second-class citizens in the countries of continental Europe, particularly in France and Germany, and in Japan. In Europe and Japan, the 'stakeholder' corporate model bound banks and companies so closely together in a multitude of cross-shareholdings that any need for public disclosure of information was simply disregarded.

It was during the 13 years of Conservative rule that the institutions moved decisively along the path towards dominance of the market as the cult of the equity took hold. The insurance companies remained much the largest institutional investors, and the investment trust movement retained its attractions for both the private investor, by spreading the risk, and the institutional investor, by offering assets at a discount. Both grew in line with the market, although their share of the total changed very little.

However, their pre-eminence in the 1950s meant that the best-known investment managers hailed from within their ranks. Lewis Whyte of London & Manchester and Leslie Brown of the Prudential have already been mentioned, but Louis Ginsberg of Legal & General was well known for his intellectual rigour, and Cecil Hampton of Royal Insurance was a spirited presence, despite his having suffered terrible wartime burn injuries. In the investment trust movement, a mystique for investment skills was created in the early post-war years in Scotland, where the names of Alan Brown and David McCurrach of Alliance Trust and Carlyle Gifford of Baillie Gifford were highly respected in the investment community.

 The fastest growth occurred in the field of pension funds. Contributions paid into pension funds rose faster than the economy, as benefits were improved and widened, and many new independent pension schemes were created as companies withdrew funds from insurance company schemes. Unit trusts remained the poor relation of the institutions, although by 1964 total funds under management had grown to £400m.

After the cult of the equity, the second major feature of this era was the emergence of agreed mergers and hostile takeover bids. Three tactical landmarks have already been described in some detail. These were the acquisition of J. Sears by Charles Clore in 1954, the British Aluminium battle in 1958, and the bid for Courtaulds by ICI in 1961. All caused anxiety at the time, upset conventional thinking and set precedents for new practices, but each was different in character. Clore was an individual acting on his own behalf, and his is the first name on the list of post-war personalities whose takeover activities have led to indignant questions in Parliament. British Aluminium is remembered for its bitter tactical battle between opposing merchant banks, and ICI/Courtaulds was the first direct confrontation between two well-known industrial giants.

Although different in character, these mergers and bids shared important common ground – raising the profile of the shareholder. Clore caused many a nervous shiver in the boardroom and reminded directors that their companies were owned by their shareholders. British Aluminium witnessed the shareholders exercising their powers of ownership to resolve a contested bid against the wishes of the directors. Courtaulds demonstrated the dangers of taking shareholders for granted, but then set a precedent for future defence strategies by showing what can be done for the shareholders when a company really tries.

Curiously, in view of his legendary reputation, Clore made two failed bids where he quickly walked away after being rebuffed. In May 1959, he was attracted by the development potential of Watney Mann, then the country's second-largest brewer, and bid £27m for the company. In February 1961, his newly merged property empire bid £64m for City of London Real Property. Both bids were withdrawn after strong opposition from the target companies.

A consequence of these tactical battles was recognition in the City that ground rules were needed to govern the behaviour of companies and their advisers during the course of takeover bids. An initiative was taken by the Issuing Houses Association when it published *Notes on Amalgamations of British Businesses* in October 1959, but it failed to deal with the tricky question of bidders buying shares in target companies in the market. After discussion, the Board of Trade issued a draft code of Take-over Bid Practice in May 1960, which came into force in August. This was to be the forerunner of the Take-Over Panel and the Take-Over Code in 1968, later to prove to be a remarkable example of effective self-regulation.

The bids that attracted the headlines were mostly those that crossed the boundaries between different industries. There was a general feeling that bids within an industry were acceptable, and the standard fare of the late 1950s and early 1960s was the more gentlemanly agreed merger. An early stray example had occurred in November 1951 when the merger of Austin and Morris was announced. The two companies were of equal size and the shareholders of both were given 20 million shares in a new holding company valued in the market at £35m. They had a combined market share of 50% of the British motor market and became the fourth largest motor manufacturer in the world after the big three Americans.

With 42,000 employees producing 24 different models, there should have been scope for rationalisation, but, in the event, it proved to be an example of the worst kind of merger when companies of equal size join together. Almost invariably this is a recipe for fudging decisions about people and products, and for arguing about the past rather than looking to the future. If a merger is to be successful, there can be no room for ambiguity about leadership responsibilities.

The first merger boom occurred as the 1950s were drawing to a close. It was particularly concentrated in the insurance and brewery sectors where companies in two homogeneous and fragmented industries sought to establish market leadership. In the insurance industry, the four largest of several mergers that took place in 1959 and 1960 were Commercial Union with North British, Sun Insurance with Alliance Assurance, Northern Assurance with Employers Liability, and Royal Insurance with London and Lancashire.

A spate of mergers followed in the brewery industry in 1961 and 1962, including Bass Ratcliffe with Mitchell & Butlers, Charrington with United Breweries, and a three-way merger of Ind Coope, Tetley Walker and Ansells. The combined market capitalisation of each of these mergers in the two industries ranged from £40m to £90m, figures that in current terms need to be multiplied 11 times to account for inflation alone, and perhaps something more to reflect real growth in the economy.

There were other significant mergers in this particular cycle. The largest was when the two leaders in cotton and wool, J. & P. Coats and Paton & Baldwins, merged with a combined market capitalisation of £120m in 1960. In the same year, two business tycoons – Charles Clore, wearing his property hat, and Jack Cotton – merged their quoted property vehicles, City and Central Investments and City Centre Properties. Merchant bankers Kleinworts merged with Robert Benson, and, in 1962, Rio Tinto and Consolidated Zinc joined together to create the RTZ of today.

The aggregate value of mergers and acquisitions of £680m in 1960 and £844m in 1961 were the two highest figures then recorded, although misleading when the market value of both companies in the many agreed mergers is included. The scale of this activity can be compared with the peak years of later bid cycles by expressing the value of acquisitions as a percentage of the aggregate market capitalisation of all equities. The respective percentages for 1960 and 1961 were approximately 3½%, and well below percentages in later peak years of 8% in 1972 and 7½% in 1989.

The emphasis may have been placed on the agreed merger, but, in fact, this was often a polite phrase for a takeover to obtain control of a higher market share in fragmented industries. Negotiations were conducted in gentlemanly fashion with sensitivities that are wholly absent today. The outcome of the merger was usually expressed in a simple aggregation of the accounts of the two companies, and any mention of benefits for the shareholders would be couched in the medium or long term. There would be little reference to cost savings or redundancies, and nothing about 'synergy' and other management jargon. It was discreet without the aggression and humiliation that is sometimes heaped on the target company today.

If the ICI bid for Courtaulds had been successful in 1961, it would have headed the league tables as the biggest ever acquisition in the London market, with a closing value of £200m. In turn, it would have been superseded by the £290m joint bid for Burmah Oil from British Petroleum and Shell in 1963, but that bid was withdrawn. In fact, the biggest acquisition was in November 1960, when Ford Motors bid £129m for the 46% of the capital that it did not already own of its quoted subsidiary, Ford UK, and it was such a large bid that photographs of the cheque appeared on the front pages. In terms of transactional value, it was exceeded in April 1964 when ICI cancelled its ill-fated 37% stake in Courtaulds in exchange for Courtaulds' half share in the jointly owned British Nylon Spinners. The value put on this transaction was £140m.

Takeover cycles are usually prompted by bull markets. Rising share prices boost corporate morale and drive or flatter corporate egos. Some will rush to acquire a target before the price rises too high, some will hurry to offer their own highly priced shares in exchange for cheaper assets, and others delude themselves into believing that a high share price is a sign of corporate invincibility. One of the oldest stock market adages is that it is difficult to tell the difference between 'brains and a bull market'. The ICI bid for Courtaulds was a rare example, at the time, of an opportunist bid for a company the fortunes of which happened to be at a low point. This tactic was a decade or two ahead of its time and companies today are well aware of their vulnerability to an unwelcome bid at moments when their shares are depressed or at the wrong point in a cycle.

Buoyant markets and takeover activity were a good combination for the Stock Exchange, although the pattern of feast and famine for stockbrokers and jobbers continued unchecked. However, it is significant that, at the comparable stage of each successive cycle, the number of bargains each time grew. The 1955 bull market produced 19,397 bargains at its highest point, just below the previous record of 19,438 set in 1947 in the midst of nationalisation. The 1959 election bull market saw a new peak of 20,000 bargains exceeded many times, and, on 14 October 1959, just after election victory, a new record of 32,655 bargains was established. Conversely, in a dull market in the immediate post-war years, bargains averaged 5,000 a day, whereas the dull years of 1956–58 produced averages of 7,000–8,000 bargains a day, and the same dull years of the early 1960s were producing some 12,000 bargains.

While many stockbrokers successfully turned to research as a new source of business in the widely competitive 'secondary' market, a small number of major brokers enjoyed a highly valuable franchise in the 'primary' market. Every time a new company was brought to the market or an existing company raised capital from a rights or debenture issue or a company sought to build a stake in another company or became involved in a takeover battle, the corporate finance stockbrokers would swing into action, working closely with the companies for which they acted as official broker and the advising merchant banks. A quotation would be arranged, subunderwriting would be distributed or stakes would be purchased. It was very lucrative business, and tightly controlled by those brokers with strong links with the leading merchant banks. Because every corporate finance transaction is individual and so important at the time to all concerned, there is no room for failure, and only those merchant banks and stockbrokers that knew and trusted each other would get involved. The art of the broker was to price the issue and get it underwritten.

The job was usually done well and companies rarely changed their advisers. Throughout the entire post-war period, Cazenove has consistently featured at the top of the list of number of companies for which it acted as official broker, and in the 1960s, under the leadership of Sir Antony Hornby, it retained its pre-eminent position. Relationships between a small number of stockbrokers and the merchant banks were much coveted and closely guarded in an 'old boy' network of senior partners making daily visits to their opposite numbers in the merchant banks. Other leaders at this time included Rowe & Pitman, also consistently at the top throughout, Joseph Sebag and Hoare & Co, the latter under the leadership of the legendary Kit Hoare – an abrasive character who fitted less easily into the ritual dances of the system.

Another group of specialists operated in the gilt-edged market, where high commissions were earned from the switching activities of the pension funds and life assurance companies. Mullens & Co, as the long-established government broker, and Pember & Boyle were two smaller specialist firms in competition with the gilt-edged teams of some of the major brokers, in particular W. Greenwell, Grieveson Grant and Phillips & Drew.

While the Stock Exchange provided the forum in which the cult of the equity prospered, it was not a great agent of change itself as an institution. The Stock Exchange Council was an instinctively conservative elected body made up of some senior and respected partners of firms of brokers or jobbers and a generous helping of partners whose time was easily spared by their firms.

The size of the Council and the need for any controversial measures to be approved by a vote of the whole membership made it an unpromising candidate for reform. Under the chairmanship of Sir John Braithwaite – who retired in June 1959 at the age of 74 after 10 years as Chairman – some successful new measures had been introduced. The creation of the Compensation Fund, the introduction of charges for quotations, the mechanisation of settlement, the opening of a visitors' gallery in November 1953 and the restarting of option dealing in October 1958 after an interval of 18 years were all positive steps.

Under the chairmanship of his successor, Lord Ritchie of Dundee, the Stock Exchange eventually tackled the problem of its anachronistic scale of commissions based on a series of bands of a fixed amount per share according to the price of the share. It weighed too heavily on low-priced shares and too lightly on high-priced shares, and was replaced in December 1960 by a logical flat percentage rate of 1¼% of the consideration for both sales and purchases, with a scale of reducing percentages for larger orders.

An important decision was made in March 1961 to rebuild the Stock Exchange. The existing building would be demolished and replaced on the same site with a new building and, despite the prospect of considerable disturbance, the decision was generally welcomed. The existing building dated back to 1801, had been reconstructed in 1855 and extended in 1885 with the addition of a new building. On the day of the announcement, it was aptly described in the 'Men and Matters' column of the *Financial Times* – 'Apart from its awkward shape and inadequate floor space, business is handicapped by the old-fashioned speaking tube communication, manually operated lifts and wretched ventilation'. Although it purported to inspire much affection, it was an overcrowded rabbit warren of a building, with jobbers packed so closely together it was difficult to see where one firm began and another ended.

Less impressive was the Stock Exchange's prevarication on the publication of information about stock market turnover, and the issue of non-voting shares. The failure or unwillingness of the Stock Exchange to publish any meaningful information about business volumes in the stock market was a contentious issue. An attempt in 1951 had petered out under pressure from the jobbers who argued that their system of making markets and willingness to deal would be hopelessly compromised if the value of purchases and sales in individual shares were to be published. The normal practice for a broker with a very large sale or purchase would be to confide in one jobber, who would start the order in decent size, in return for being left with the balance to unwind over a period of days or even weeks. 'My word is my bond' worked very effectively, and both broker and jobber would protect the confidentiality of the order.

The Stock Exchange put the matter to one side and continued only to publish in the Daily Official List the prices at which bargains had been executed on the previous day, and the number of bargains marked by stock and sector. The weakness was that the system was only voluntary, and permission could easily be gained for bargains at special prices not to be marked. The information was of little real value. On 19 August 1959, the Radcliffe Report was published, and widely praised as a masterpiece of analysis of the country's monetary and financial systems. It commented that 'Such information as is available about the volume of business done on the Stock Exchange is inadequate' – a rebuke perhaps too gently put and stubbornly ignored.

Nothing at all happened for another five years until, in September 1964, the Stock Exchange began the publication of monthly totals of aggregate turnover by value and number of bargains in each of five separate sectors. Only two were of much significance – namely equities and gilts with a life of over five years. For the first time, accurate figures were available to enable member firms to calculate their market share of equities and gilts. The Stock Exchange never explained why retrospective figures could not be published for turnover and numbers of bargains, analysed either by sectors or by leading individual stocks of the kind published daily today for the FTSE Index.

An instinct for secrecy still prevailed in the higher reaches of the City and

across the boardrooms of British industry, and this attitude was aptly characterised at the time at a conference on gold. A senior participant in the daily ritual
of fixing the gold price, when asked why the value of transactions was not published, replied after some thought that the publication of turnover in gold would
be 'misleading'. This view was to prevail for many years until daily turnover
began to be published in 1997.

Non-voting shares were a controversial matter in a wider forum than the
Stock Exchange alone. They were a simple and blatant means of allowing a
minority of shareholders with special voting rights to exercise control over a
company. The existence of non-voting shares would either date back to the
company's formation or arise from later scrip issues in non-voting shares to the
shareholders of a quoted company or the issue of non-voting shares to facilitate
an acquisition. In particular, it would enable the founders or founding families
to retain control of an expanding company while owning only a small proportion of its capital. It was a favourite of the retail sector and of companies
founded by autocratic entrepreneurs reluctant to cede control.

Doubts about their validity first began to surface in the 1950s, when some
companies seeking growth by acquisition issued non-voting 'A' shares to avoid
loss of control, and shareholders in companies receiving bids found that the
prices offered to ordinary and 'A' shares would widely differ. Although companies could not be forced to enfranchise existing non-voting shareholders, the
Stock Exchange could have prevented any further enlargement of this practice by
refusing to give a quotation to new issues in non-voting shares.

Non-voting shares were usually designated 'A' ordinary shares and were first
issued in 1918 by J. Lyons. By 1957 it was estimated that 7% of the market
value of the commercial and industrial sector of the equity market was held in
'A' non-voting shares. The two largest, by a long margin, were Marks &
Spencers, with voting shares valued at only £8m and non-voting at £200m, and
Great Universal Stores, with voting shares valued at £16m and non-voting shares
at £88m. Other examples were Allied Bakeries, House of Fraser and Sears
Holdings. In a carefully considered but complacent decision, the Stock Exchange
determined that it was too late to deal with the problem, arguing that shareholders do not use votes even if they have them, and the price differential in the
two classes of shares was usually no more than one shilling in the pound.

It was left to the Birmingham Stock Exchange to set an example that London
was unwilling to follow when, in June 1959, it announced that it would not
grant a quotation in non-voting shares for companies whose principal share
market was in Birmingham. The power of a controlling minority of shareholders to dictate decisions about the company's future, irrespective of the wishes of
the majority of the shareholders, and the ability of voting shareholders to extract
a high premium for their shares in the event of a takeover bid were genuine crit-
icisms of companies wanting the benefits of a stock market quotation without

ceding control. The New York Stock Exchange had banned dealings in non-voting shares for many years, but in London the eventual disappearance of all but a few 'A' shares owed more to the pressure exerted by institutional share-holders than to any efforts by the Stock Exchange.

The *Financial Times* continued to thrive as another great City institution, expanding its coverage and introducing from time to time new features to give its readers more information. An important landmark was the launch on 26 November 1962 of the new FT-Actuaries Indices, led by an All Share Index comprising the market capitalisation of the largest 594 companies. Within this total was an Industrial Index of 500 shares, separated from a financial group of 94 shares, and the Industrial Index was divided into subgroups of Capital Goods, Consumer Goods (Durable), Consumer Goods (Non-Durable) and Others, which became known as 'Cosmo' because it included chemicals, oils, shipping and miscellaneous.

These subgroups were further divided into 32 individually defined sectors. All groups and sectors began with a common base of 100, as at 10 April 1962, and each was published daily with its own index, yield and earnings yield. The reason for the separation of the Industrial 500 Index was the problem that most of the financial sectors did not then publish earnings per share, and an aggregate earnings figure for the market could only be calculated by excluding the financial sector. A complication in calculating an aggregate earnings and PE ratio for the market as a whole arose from the oil sector, which was dominated by BP and Shell and was so large that its volatile figures distorted the total. It was later separated from the Industrial Index.

This new initiative was widely welcomed, and the All Share Index quickly became the most relevant index for the calculation and comparison of investment performance. The simplicity of its arithmetic calculation of aggregate market capitalisation was an attraction, compared with the more obscure geometric calculation of the FT. However, more importantly, it embraced 90% of the value of all quoted equity shares, and truly reflected the real performance of the market. It also highlighted the scale of the long-standing omission from the FT Index of financials and oils, which together made up 31% of the market capitalisation of the new All Share Index, which, at 10 April 1962, amounted to £18,170m.

Although it was not published until November 1962, the new FT-Actuaries Indices had been calculated back to base figures of 100 for all sectors as at 10 April, when the FT Index stood at 306.6. In fact, during the bullish phase between April 1962 and October 1964 there was a wide disparity in the performance of two indices. The FT Index rose by 19% to 364.9 but the FT-Actuaries All Share Index only rose by 7% to 106.85. The explanation for this discrepancy is that the base date of the FT-Actuaries Index coincided with the peak of a bull market in the financial sector, particularly in insurance shares, which, for the purposes of trustees freed by the Trustee Act, had been labelled as 'gilt-edged' substitutes.

The industrial and consumer sectors then recovered to the advantage of the FT Index and at the expense of the new All Share Index. However, for daily usage the FT Index continued to command the headlines for many more years because it was calculated at intervals during the day, and, being focused on leading shares, was more volatile than its far larger rival. The All Share Index contained too many shares to calculate during the day, and even on volatile days many shares would be left unchanged. The role of playing the headlines for newspapers and television news remained with the FT Index until it was overtaken by the FTSE 100 Index in 1984.

The 13 years of Conservative rule became part of electoral folklore. They are fondly remembered as years of derationing, lower taxes, fewer controls, building lots of houses and the phrase 'you have never had it so good'. Shareholders enjoyed two remarkable bull markets and dividends rising at a cracking pace through most of those 13 years. These headlines compared so favourably with the post-war Labour Government that when Harold Wilson in his 1964 election speeches referred time and again to 'thirteen wasted years of Tory Rule', it seemed a churlish line thrown in for political purposes.

It may well be that his description of 13 wasted years was closer to the truth than realised at the time. Despite strong electoral majorities, successive Conservative administrations singularly failed to rise to the challenge of making Britain competitive and creating new industries for the future. The complacency of management and the greed of trade unions was never challenged or exposed. The chronic problems of over-manning and inefficiency that plagued almost every corner of the public sector and far too many corners in the private sector were swept under the carpet. The legacy of 13 years of Conservative government was to hand over an economy unprepared in the long term to cope with foreign competition.

Time and time again, it was a government that, within its own nationalised industries, made the public pay for excessive demands conceded to the unions with inflationary price increases. Restrictive practices and demarcation rituals took precedence over productivity agreements, and many private-sector industries were equally reluctant to face up to the same problems. The 1950s was an apparently successful manufacturing decade, but so many structural inefficiencies were cemented in place that the legacy for the 1960s and 1970s would be the self-destruction of the motor, shipbuilding and other heavy industries, quite unable to cope with competitive markets, where all that mattered to the customers was price, delivery and quality.

The post-war commitment of both parties to policies of full employment prevented a more rigorous allocation of labour resources that would have forced efficiencies on manufacturing industry, and released labour to encourage the growth of new industries. It might even have filled some of the job opportunities that attracted such a wave of immigration in the 1950s and 1960s. Instead, there was an unspoken conspiracy between government, management and unions to protect jobs in the name of full employment, each for their own reasons riding complacently on the back of post-war recovery. The seeds of the unemployment of the 1980s and 1990s were sown in these two decades after the war.

The last few years of a tiring government produced meagre returns for the investor, particularly as a better understanding emerged of the weakness of economic policies identified as 'stop–go'. The consumer boom which successfully preceded both elections in 1955 and 1959, was seen to have more to do with cynical political expediency when attempted again in 1964 and less to do with serious long-term economic policy. The first two had ended in tears, with balance of payments crises and 7% Bank rates. The third would follow suit, and it is explained in the next chapter.

Towards the end of the Conservative Government, there was increasing talk of the need for incomes policies and ceilings of 2½% or 3% for pay demands. These early seeds would germinate in time for the next phase in the political and stock market cycle – 1964 to 1979 – when the successive Labour, Conservative and Labour Governments would stumble from crisis to crisis, and endure the pain of a stock market crash comparable to that on Wall Street in 1929.

Chapter 14

KEY EVENTS

1951–64

GOVERNMENT

Prime Ministers

Winston Churchill	26 October 1951–5 April 1955	Retired
Sir Anthony Eden	5 April 1955–10 January 1957	Resigned
Harold Macmillan	10 January 1957–18 October 1963	Resigned
Sir Alec Douglas-Home	18 October 1963–15 October 1964	Election defeat

Chancellors of the Exchequer

R. A. Butler	26 October 1951–20 December 1955	Reshuffle
Harold Macmillan	20 December 1955–10 January 1957	Promoted
Peter Thorneycroft	14 January 1957–7 January 1958	Resigned
Derick Heathcoat Amory	7 January 1958–27 July 1960	Retired
Selwyn Lloyd	27 July 1960–13 July 1962	Dismissed
Reginald Maudling	13 July 1962–15 October 1964	Election defeat

BUDGETS AND FINANCIAL STATEMENTS

R. A. Butler

11 March 1952	Bank rate raised from 2½% to 4%.
	Excess profits levy set at 30%.
	Profits tax – undistributed rate reduced from 5% to 2½%.
	Profits tax – distributed rate reduced from 25% to 22½%.
14 April 1953	Excess profits levy to cease in January 1954.
	Income tax – standard rate reduced from 9/6d to 9/-.
Purchase tax bands reduced – 100/66/33% to 75/50/25%.	
6 April 1954	–
18 April 1955	Income tax – standard rate reduced from 9/- to 8/6d.
26 October 1955	Profits tax – undistributed rate unchanged at 2½%.

Profits tax – distributed rate increased from 22½% to 27½%.
Purchase tax bands raised from 75/50/25% to 90/60/30%.

Harold Macmillan

17 April 1956   Profits Tax – Undistributed rate increased from 2½% to 3%.
Profits tax – Distributed rate increased from 27½% to 30%.
Premium Bonds introduced.

Peter Thorneycroft

9 April 1957   Income tax allowances increased.
Purchase tax – 30% band reduced to 15%.

19 September 1957   Bank rate raised from 5% to 7%.

Derick Heathcoat Amory

15 April 1958   Profits tax – undistributed and distributed rates abolished.
Profits tax – single rate of 10%.

7 April 1959   Income tax – standard rate reduced from 8/6d to 7/9d.
Purchase taxes reduced from 60/30/15% to 50/25/12½%.

4 April 1960   Profits tax – rate increased from 10% to 12½%.
Discretion to allow future use of monetary measures.

Selwyn Lloyd

18 April 1961   Profits tax – rate increased from 12½ to 15%.
Surtax starting band raised from £2,000 to £4,000.

25 July 1961   Bank rate raised from 5% to 7%.
10% surcharge imposed on indirect taxes.
Special deposits from banks raised from 2% to 3%.

10 April 1962   Six months' short-term capital gains tax introduced.
10% Surcharge on indirect taxes consolidated.

Reginald Maudling

27 September 1962   Special deposits reduced from 2% to 1%.

5 November 1962   Investment allowances – plant and machinery 20% to 30%.
Investment allowances – buildings 10% to 15%.

29 November 1962   Special deposits released.

3 April 1963   Stamp duty on share purchases reduced from 2% to 1%.

BANK RATE

From	%	From	%	From	%
26 October 1951	2	19 September 1957	7	8 December 1960	5
7 November 1951	2½	20 March 1958	6	25 July 1961	7
11 March 1952	4	22 May 1958	5½	5 October 1961	6½
17 September 1953	3½	20 June 1958	5	2 November 1961	6
13 May 1954	3	14 August 1958	4½	8 March 1962	5½
27 January 1955	3½	20 November 1958	4	22 March 1962	5
24 February 1955	4½	21 January 1960	5	26 April 1962	4½
16 February 1956	5½	23 June 1960	6	3 January 1963	4
7 February 1957	5	27 October 1960	5½	27 February 1964	5

FT INDEX: OCTOBER 1951–OCTOBER 1964

High: 377.8   1 October 1964
Low: 103.1   24 June 1952

Bull and bear markets

Movement	From	To	From	To	Duration
+117.2%	103.1	223.9	24 June 1952	21 July 1955	3 years 1 month
+122.1%	154.4	342.9	25 February 1958	4 January 1960	1 year 10 months
+49.4%	252.8	377.8	25 June 1962	1 October 1964	2 years 3 months
−25.5%	138.3	103.1	25 October 1951	24 June 1952	0 year 8 months
−31.0%	223.9	154.4	21 July 1955	25 February 1958	2 years 7 months
−30.9%	365.7	252.8	15 May 1961	25 June 1962	1 year 1 month

Movements of more than 3% in a single day

Date	% change	From	To	Reason
9 October 1959	+5.99	268.6	284.7	Election result
30 May 1962	+5.86	261.3	276.6	'Black Monday' rebound
29 May 1962	−6.44	279.3	261.3	US 'Black Monday'
19 September 1957	−4.53	192.2	183.5	Bank rate 5% to 7%
24 February 1955	−3.80	184.0	177.0	Bank rate 3½% to 4½%
20 September 1957	−3.43	183.5	177.2	Bank rate 5% to 7%
25 July 1955	−3.03	221.3	214.6	Credit restrictions
12 March 1952	−3.02	112.7	109.3	Bank rate 2½% to 4%

PART III

INFLATIONARY YEARS
1964–79

Chapter 15

LABOUR RETURNS
October 1964–November 1966

All Share Index	1 October 1964	109.87	
	8 November 1966	87.74	Down 20.1%

The general election of 15 October 1964 was the closest of all post-war elections, with an overall majority of three seats for Harold Wilson and the Labour party. The London stock market was buoyant during the first half of the election campaign, and the FT Index registered all-time highs on 7 out of 8 successive days to 1 October, when it reached a record 377.8. It was helped by the Dow Jones Index reaching all-time highs on Wall Street, and by lingering hopes of a Conservative victory, but in the last two weeks of the campaign the opinion polls pointed to Labour, and on election day the FT Index had slipped to 364.9.

On the Friday morning of the result being known, the market opened nearly 4% lower, with steel shares down 10% or more, but this was quickly reversed and the FT Index ended the day only modestly lower at 359.5. In muted mood, it held its ground in the 350–360 range for the next 3 weeks. Among a community that feared for its future at the hands of vindictive elements in a Labour party deeply hostile to the City, there were some who had been persuaded by Harold Wilson's 'white heat of technology' speech, and by his insistence that under his Government there would be 'no room for restrictive practices'. However, the greater relief was that a majority of three would prevent any extremist policies and make steel renationalisation unlikely.

Sentiment slowly changed. Harold Wilson decided to govern boldly, as if he had a large working majority, and on 3 November the renationalisation of iron and steel was duly promised in the Queen's Speech. It slowly dawned on City opinion that he had only to govern with a straight bat for a year or so before calling a snap election for a proper majority and a full term of socialism.

The economic situation was gloomy. The Conservative's pre-election dash for growth had very nearly worked for the third successive time, but at the price of a balance of payments crisis of disturbing proportions, as the boom in consumer spending sucked in imports on an unprecedented scale. On the morning after the election, one of the worst ever monthly trade gaps of £111m was announced for September. In a flurry of activity, the Labour Government flaunted its inheritance of a balance of a payments deficit forecast at £800m for the year, and in an economic statement on 26 October imposed an immediate import surcharge of 15% on all manufactured and semi-manufactured goods.

In an atmosphere of crisis management, a ban on new office building in Greater London was announced, mainly as a reprisal for unlet offices, and on 11 November there was an autumn Budget. The new Chancellor of the Exchequer was James Callaghan, who at a City lunch before the election when asked by his host how he would raise money, disarmingly replied 'from people like you'. He raised the standard rate of income tax from 7/9d to 8/3d, and put 6d on a gallon of petrol in a deflationary Budget, but, disconcertingly for the stock market, he indicated that he would extend capital gains tax to all disposals, and introduce a new corporation tax to replace income tax and profits tax in his spring Budget. A bemused market responded over the next two days by returning the FT Index almost to its pre-election levels.

Lots of positive action may have calmed the stock market, but it was not enough to satisfy the impassive faces of the owners of sterling. They were coldly unimpressed by the return of a socialist government trumpeting an £800m deficit and imposing an import surcharge without warning or consultation. Private individuals were not allowed to sell sterling, but foreign banks with short-term deposits and British companies with import bills to pay or export proceeds to receive in foreign currency, were entirely free to act. It only required an almost subconscious decision by a proportion of these trading companies to buy their foreign currency ahead of their needs or sit a little longer on their foreign currency proceeds for sterling to come under pressure, not from unpatriotic speculation, but from the exercising of native business caution. In this kind of market, a modest amount of selling will go a long way, and all the signs were that sterling was under severe pressure.

The stock market suddenly took fright and share prices fell away sharply. Bank rate was raised from 5% to 7% on 23 November, 'to strengthen the international position of sterling'. Modest though it may sound today, 7% was a symbol of crisis in the 1950s and 1960s. In fact, this very act prompted another surge of selling of sterling and, two days later, a $3,000m credit was put in place from central banks worldwide. History later revealed that the Government lived to regret a decision at the time to rule out devaluation, thereby merely postponing the inevitable.

Investors ended the year in indecisive mood, the FT Index standing at 335.0. Profits were growing from the pre-election boom, dividends were rising, yields of 5–6% were generous and equities offered a hedge against possible inflation under the Labour Government. In contrast, gilts were performing badly and the economy was overstretched. The Retail Price Index was up nearly 5% for the year to December 1964, and unemployment was at its lowest January level for many years, at 376,000 – barely ahead of vacancies of 311,000. The only cure was a prolonged bout of deflation, and investors were then, in fact, only three months into a bear market that was to last for two full years.

There was little change in the months leading up to the Budget of 6 April 1965. Most budgets are to do with tightening or relaxing taxes and duties, but, from time to time, they introduce fundamental changes affecting investors. Callaghan's Budget of 1965 was one such example, because it reformed corporation tax and extended capital gains tax.

The reform of corporation tax was fundamental. Companies had previously been taxed under the fiction that they were individuals, paying income tax on profits at the standard rate of 8/3d, or 41¼%, and profits tax at 15%, making a total of 56¼%. Dividends were passed on to shareholders net of tax, although there might be further liabilities to surtax for private individuals and profits tax for corporate shareholders. Reform of the fiction that, for tax purposes, a company was an individual was overdue, but the Government was more interested in ending the relief from income tax enjoyed by the personal shareholder.

The Chancellor planned for the new corporation tax to take effect from April 1966, when he would announce the rate. It was expected to be in the range of 35–40%, and these two rates were used later in the year to illustrate the theoretical effect of corporation tax on earnings in the FT Actuaries Indices. Dividends paid out of these profits would be gross, and liable to income tax and surtax in the hands of the shareholder. The effects are best illustrated by an example of a company with profits of £100 (see Table 15.1).

Table 15.1
Illustration of the effects of the 1966 changes in corporation tax

Previous (£)		Proposed (£)		Effect
Profit	100	Profit	100	
Income tax	41.25	Corporation tax	40	
Profits tax	15			
Total tax	56.25	Total tax	40	
Net profit	43.75	Net profit	60	
Gross dividend (*fully distributed*)	74.45	Gross dividend (*fully distributed*)	60	Reduction of 19%
Retained profits (*nil distribution*)	43.75	Retained profits (*nil distribution*)	60	Increase of 37%

Behind the new corporation tax was a strong political purpose of discouraging the payment of dividends and encouraging the retention of profits. The example given in Table 15.1 shows how successfully this was achieved. Under the old system, the distribution in full of the profits of £43.75 would create a gross dividend for the shareholder of £74.45, but under corporation tax, the full distribution arising from the same pre-tax profit would only generate a gross dividend of £60, a reduction of 19%. Conversely, a company choosing to pay no dividend would retain £60 under the new system, compared with £43.75 under the old system, an increase of 37%.

An important consequence for the stock market was that corporation tax brought about a fundamental change in the method of valuing shares. In the United States, the PE ratio had, for many years been the prime determinant in the valuation of shares. The PE ratio is the division of the share price by the earnings per share, and, in simple terms, a high PE ratio of 20–25 suggests a growth stock and a low PE ratio of 7–10 indicates poor quality of earnings or little expected growth. The PE ratio makes it easier to compare the value of shares within the same sector or across different sectors. Furthermore, under corporation tax the earnings per share is simple to calculate, this being the profit after tax divided by the number of shares in issue.

Earnings in the London market had previously been calculated theoretically, on the basis of the maximum dividend payable if all profits were distributed, which is the notional £74.45 in Table 15.1 above. This figure would be used to calculate an 'earnings yield', whereby a share with a twice-covered dividend yielding 6% would have an earnings yield of 12%. As this was an artificial figure arising only in the unlikely event of all profits being exactly distributed in full, it was unsuitable as a basis for a PE ratio. The attraction of the new system was that the earnings after tax of £60 is a constant figure, whatever dividend is paid, whereas under the old system, fully retained profit was an actual £43.75, and fully distributed profit was £74.45. The Chancellor's new corporation tax expedited the use of PE ratios, brought Britain into line with other stock markets, and as will be seen in a later chapter, had some dramatic effects on the valuation of equities.

The short-term capital gains tax was introduced by Selwyn Lloyd in April 1962, and meant that gains taken within six months were treated as income and charged for income tax at the marginal rate. Callaghan extended this period to 12 months. With income tax at 8/3d and surtax rising to 10/-, the maximum rate incurred on capital gains taken within twelve months was a confiscatory 91¼%. For gains taken *after* 12 months, he introduced a new long-term flat rate of 30%. To avoid retrospective legislation, gains tax calculations were to be based on the higher of the original cost or the share price on 5 April 1965.

In fact, the Chancellor's reforming tax budget caused resentment in the stock market because it targeted both dividends and capital gains. It also achieved notoriety because its authors were commonly believed to be two Hungarian economists, Nicholas Kaldor and Thomas Balogh, personal confidants of the Prime Minister, the former with a reputation for imposing disastrous taxation policies on the economies of emerging nations, and the latter believed to hold extreme left wing views.

Events moved on with the publication on 30 April of the proposals for the renationalisation of the steel industry. A total cost of £660m would be met by the issue of government stock for all or part of the assets of 14 companies. Of this total, £555m would be issued in exchange for the quoted securities of 9 companies, divided £137m for fixed interest and £418m for equities. The balance was mainly to purchase the steel subsidiaries of Guest, Keen & Nettlefolds, Tube Investments and Vickers.

These terms were much more generous than the market had anticipated, although equal only to two-thirds of asset values, and the steel sector of the FT-Actuaries Index shot up by 21.3% on the day. Among the leaders, Colvilles rose from 28/- to 41/9d, United Steel 27/6d to 35/3d, and Steel Company of Wales 19/9d to 28/-. The announcement had a remarkable effect on the market as the reinvestment implications came into play. The FT Index had one of its sharpest daily rises – up by 3½% to 352.2. The equity compensation of £418m. was roughly equal to the total annual net acquisition of equities by all UK investing institutions, and the Lex column on 1 May commented that 'the inflation of equity prices looks inevitable'.

The imposition of new capital gains taxes had an instant effect on Stock Exchange transactions, particularly the extension of short-term gains to 12 months. For the last two years, the number of bargains marked had typically been in a daily range of 11,000–14,000, but immediately after the Budget, and through the summer, numbers fell by a third to a range of 7,000–10,000. These desultory volumes also reflected listless markets. The brief spurt for steel renationalisation took the FT Index to its high for the year of 359.1, but for most of the year it meandered along in a narrow trading range of 315 to 355, ending the year more or less where it began at 339.7.

After much activity in its first few months, the Government now began to play for time. The import surcharge was cut from 15% to 10%, and Bank rate was lowered in June from its crisis level of 7% to 6%. Aubrey Jones had become Chairman of the newly created National Board for Prices and Incomes in March, and the TUC gave its blessing to a 3–3½% norm for pay increases. Dividends were outside any such norms, and enjoying higher profits but fearing future controls, companies were able to afford generous dividend payments that did not endear them to their new political masters. George Brown, Minister for Economic Affairs, managed to get the message right but the detail wrong, when he warned that the 28% increase in dividends in the first quarter of 1965, was 'excessive'. The actual figure – he later apologised for the mistake – was 19%.

The Ministry for Economic Affairs was newly created by the Prime Minister for a number of reasons. He wished to underline the importance of the economy, he sought to create a Ministry strong enough to stand up to the Treasury and needed to satisfy the conflicting ambitions of his two most powerful colleagues – George Brown and James Callaghan. Brown brought energy and enthusiasm to his new department and, on 16 September 1965 ceremoniously launched his National Plan, the likes of which had never been seen before, or since.

It predicated a 25% increase in national output from 1964 to 1970, equal to an annual growth rate of just under 4%, based on export growth of 5½%, and productivity gains of 3.4%. Highly detailed targets were set for a wide range of industries, but its master's enthusiasm was a long way ahead of the Plan's credibility, particularly on productivity.

There was more reality about the next initiative – the formation of the Industrial Reorganisation Corporation (IRC) on 25 January 1966, with Sir Frank Kearton as its first Chairman. Its brief was 'to provide rationalisation schemes which could yield substantial benefits to the national economy' and it was endowed with a capital of £150m for providing loans or taking equity stakes.

Its purpose was regarded with suspicion in the City and in many parts of industry – thought of as an invasion by an agent of the public sector into the provinces of the private sector. However, it was not as if the City or industry or the trade unions or successive Conservative governments had shown any serious interest in the rationalisation of industry. It was to be another two years before the name of Arnold Weinstock would appear on the scene, as its pioneer in the private sector.

As natural custodians of the free market, Conservative governments might from time to time have been expected to attend to reforms of Company Law. In fact the last major Companies Act was brought in by the Attlee Government in 1948, and it remained for another Labour Government to introduce further reforms. The President of the Board of Trade, Douglas Jay, published a Companies Bill on 3 February 1966, with proposals of particular interest to a gathering crusade on the part of investment analysts for more disclosure of information.

New requirements for company accounts included the publication of turnover or sales, divided by business class and exports; a five year record; details of trade investments in other companies of 10% or more; and the Chairman's remuneration and that of other directors grouped in salary bands. 'Letting in some Light' was the heading of the Lex column the following morning, which observed that 'shareholders are at last on the way to being treated as the proprietors of their company'. The analyst of today may find it unbelievable that companies successfully resisted publishing such a basic item as turnover for so many years, although a small number of more progressive companies had been volunteering sales information for many years.

It was as long ago as 11 May 1954 that Harold Wincott wrote in the *Financial Times* that if turnover figures were disclosed: 'I suspect British capitalism would be a good deal more virile and competitive than in fact it is.'

The stock market was now treading water while it waited for a general election in the first quarter of 1966. Since October 1964, the Government had retained the political initiative and comfortably dealt with any problems arising from its tiny overall majority, even when this was reduced to one in September 1965 with the death of the Speaker. The opinion polls firmly pointed to Labour, while Edward Heath, the newly elected leader of the Conservative party, was no match for Harold Wilson and he dared not provoke an election he looked certain to lose.

The trade unions had given little trouble, even though the pay norm was lagging behind inflation, but pressures began to emerge in the first quarter of 1966 from the railways and the coal mines – the two most prized of the Attlee nationalisations, and yet the source of constant industrial strife throughout the post-war years. The National Union of Railwaymen threatened strike action in February because the Prices and Incomes Board refused their further demands. The strike was averted after the personal intervention of the Prime Minister over beer and sandwiches in Downing Street on 11 February – the first of many such meetings that were to become a hallmark of the 1970s. The National Union of Mineworkers had decided in the previous December to ignore TUC policy on pay restraint and threatened a ban on overtime and weekend working in February after the National Coal Board rejected a 6% pay claim.

The Prime Minister announced on 28 February that the general election was to be on 31 March. Share prices were already grounded in the first quarter of 1966 and the four-week campaign proved to be the quietest election market on record. With scarcely a ripple from the opinion polls, the FT Index barely moved at all in range of less than 2% between 344.9 and 351.7. In its leader on 30 March, the *Financial Times* did 'not regard the return of a Labour government with a reasonable majority with any misgiving'. It was all over before it began and Labour was returned with an overall majority of 97. The certain knowledge of a full working Labour term in office had been discounted, and over the following month the market was no more active than it had been before and during the election.

The Budget was delayed because of the election to the unusually late date of 3 May 1966. The Chancellor confirmed the rate of corporation tax at 40%, and the import surcharge was to be abolished in November, but in a deflationary Budget he took £386m out of the economy. This was largely raised from the introduction of a new and controversial selective employment tax (SET). All weekly national insurance contributions paid by employers were increased by

25/- for men and 12/6d for women. In a bureaucratic merry-go-round, employers in manufacturing industries would have their additional contribution repaid 6 months later together with a 30% premium – that is, 25/- plus 7/6d for men. Employers in government, local authorities and nationalised industries would preserve their neutrality and immunity from competitive pressures, by having their additional contribution repaid in full after six months, and the burden of the tax would fall on employers in service industries who paid the tax in full without any recovery.

The purpose of SET was both practical and political. There was no equivalent of purchase tax or excise duty on the output of service industries, and widening the net to include these was a legitimate and practical objective that would eventually be better served by value added tax (VAT). Politically, it nicely satisfied the prejudices of the Labour party in favour of making things at the expense of providing services. This discrimination was widely criticised, but the most scorn was reserved for creating a cumbersome bureaucracy to transfer backwards and forwards the contributions of millions of workers.

It was estimated that 8.25m workers would attract the additional contribution and its refund with a premium, 6.0m were in the neutral public sector, and 7.5m workers in the service sector would bear the burden of the new tax. In the Budget debate, on 5 May, a rising opposition star ridiculed the SET proposal:

> What the Chancellor is proposing to do in a time of labour shortage is to take away from a large number of people 25/- a week in order to repay the same amount six months later. This is sheer lunacy. Why does the Chancellor have a system whereby he takes away 25/- to repay 32/6d six months later? This is absolute nonsense. The Chancellor needs a woman at the Treasury.

Many years later this particular Chancellor moved on to Downing Street where, in due course, he was replaced by this particular woman.

Although the Budget was deflationary, it was barely felt in people's pockets because there were no increases in direct taxes or excise duties, except for those caught by a new betting tax. The stock market had feared a higher rate of corporation tax, and the FT Index responded with an increase of 4.3 to 354.4, and gradually edged upwards over the next two months to within sight of its all-time high of 377.8. This it narrowly failed to surmount despite remaining above 370 for 14 consecutive days, but the more broadly based All Share Index just managed to struggle into new high ground, before being washed away by the seamen's strike.

Rarely has an already difficult economic situation been more exacerbated by events than on the occasion of the seamen's strike in the summer of 1966. It began on 16 May over a demand for a reduction in the working week from 56 to 40 hours. Employers calculated that the overtime cost would be equal to a 17% increase in earnings and so proposed phasing in the reduction over two years. Beer and sandwiches in Downing Street with the Prime Minister failed to stop this strike. The Government refused to breach its incomes policy, declared a state of emergency and appointed a court of inquiry under Lord Pearson. The employers had offered to reduce the 56 hour week immediately to 48 hours, with a phased reduction to 40 hours over 2 years, and, on 7 June, Lord Pearson quickly returned with the inevitable compromise to phase it in over 1 year.

The atmosphere now turned nasty. The seamen rejected the compromise and the strike continued into its fourth week. The executive of the union was called into Downing Street for a second time on 16 June, but adamantly refused to budge, declaring it was 'now a fight with Government, not with the shipowners'. The stock market, trusting the adage of never selling on a strike, continued to test new highs – the FT Index came close to its all-time high on 16 June – seemingly oblivious to the damage caused to trade and unconcerned by the overtly political nature of the strike. The Prime Minister was now trapped in a personal confrontation and, in a famous statement in Parliament on 20 June, blamed the strike on a 'tightly knit group of politically motivated extremists' acting outside the executive of the union. The strike ended suddenly on 2 July after the Executive overruled its militants to accept the compromise of the Pearson Inquiry.

On the last day of the strike, the Government published its Steel Nationalisation Bill. The original Bill in April 1965 had come as a pleasant surprise, but this came as a shock because the total compensation of £580m now proposed was some £80m lower than before, and out of line with assurances given by the Prime Minister during the election campaign. The shortfall fell mainly on the equity capital of the 9 quoted companies, where compensation was £352m compared with an original £418m. The formula was based on whichever was the higher of the average of Stock Exchange prices over periods of 61 months or 6 months to April 1966. Steel share prices stood higher than this formula, and the sector fell by 7.3% on the day.

Nationalisation had been one of the props sustaining the market during the seamen's strike. After disappointment with the terms, the market began to fall apart within a matter of days. Attention switched to the scale of the damage caused by the seamen's strike, sterling began to weaken and the seriousness of the pay situation was ominously highlighted by the resignation from the cabinet of Frank Cousins, Minister of Technology, in protest against the newly published Prices and Incomes Bill, and his return to the Transport and General Workers Union. The stock market fell for 13 successive days, taking the FT Index down by more than 10% to 332.3, and culminating with sharp falls over the last two of these days after Bank rate was increased from 6% to 7% on 14 July.

On 20 July, amid the glow of England's progress in the World Cup, a dramatic package of economic measures was personally announced by the Prime Minister. Most startling of the measures was a six-month freeze on pay, followed

Figure 15.1
FT INDEX 1964–70

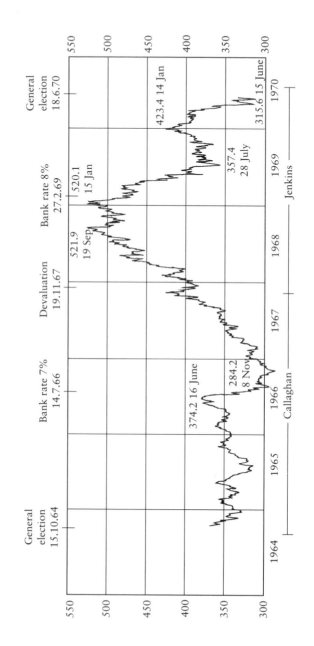

Source: Financial Times

by severe restraint for a further six months. Perhaps better remembered was the £50 limit on travel allowances outside the sterling area, enabling travel agents suddenly to discover the holiday attractions of Gibraltar. Altogether, more than £500m was taken out of the economy, almost as much as the last two deflationary budgets put together. Hire purchase controls were tightened, the regulator was used to raise purchase taxes and excise duties by 10%, and government expenditure was cut back. A surcharge of 10% was imposed on surtax for one year.

A Prices and Incomes Bill requiring the notification of increases had already been published earlier in the month, and it included dividends. It was now strengthened to include the pay freeze, and a voluntary freeze was separately demanded for both prices and dividends for one year. The market tumbled away and, by the end of July, the FT Index at 318.1 had fallen by nearly 15% in the month. For a second time, the Labour Government considered and rejected devaluation.

Investors were numbed, and remained so for the rest of the year – as bargain levels fell to a paltry 6,000 to 8,000 a day. In a period of inactivity difficult to comprehend today, the total value of all purchases and sales of equities for the entire month of September 1966 fell to £180m, equivalent in real terms today to the turnover of a single busy day. The FT Index drifted to its low for the year of 284.2 on 8 November when the yield on equities rose to 6¾% and the reverse yield gap disappeared briefly for a few days. This same day also marked the low point for the All Share Index at 87.74, and the two indices had fallen 24% and 21% respectively from their recent high points in June.

Chapter 16

DISCOVERING PE RATIOS
November 1966–January 1969

All Share Index   8 November 1966   87.74

                       31 January 1969   180.97   Up 106.3%

The low point of the bear market, as seen in the last chapter, was on 8 November 1966. Easy to identify in hindsight, but was less so at the time, because, as has been observed many times, bells do not ring to announce the turn, and most investors think they are still in a bear market. These turning points are difficult to identify, but there are usually some clues that might be useful on future occasions.

The brief disappearance of the reverse yield gap for a few days in early November, when the yield on Consols 2½% fell below the yield on the FT Index, might have offered a clue. The new conventional wisdom was that equities should yield less than gilts because they participate in growth, pay rising dividends and offer protection against inflation. Dividend freezes and deflationary measures put a dampener on any market and short-term pessimism sometimes obscures value, but when the plots on the simple graph of the yields of equities and gilts briefly crossed over, investors sensed long-term value beyond a prevailing gloom.

The publication of the Companies Bill on 4 November was another clue. It was little different from the outline given in February, but, by requiring the full disclosure of assets held by many companies in the form of trade and other investments of more than 10% in other companies, it was about to reveal values previously hidden. The requirement to publish sales figures would also provide good material for inventive analysts.

A third clue was the sudden return of takeover activity in the last two months of the year. In a series of bids in the £20–£30m range Philips and Thorn Electric fought over Pye, British-American Tobacco bid for Yardley, General Electric for Telephone Rentals, Hawker Siddeley for Crompton Parkinson, and Leyland for Rover. A spate of bids in depressed markets is a good signal that industrialists believe stock market valuations have fallen to a level where it is cheaper to buy a company than to build it, and this view was reinforced by four of the bids having to be raised to be successful and one failing. Conversely, when markets have been rising upwards to ever higher levels, frenetic takeover activity can be a warning signal, but the difference will be that bids at the bottom will tend to be in cash, but those at the top will be financed by paper, whether it be a share exchange or via a rights issue.

The market slowly picked up from its November low and dealing volumes improved in the new year. The Bank rate was reduced from 7% to 6% in ½-point steps in January and March 1967. In March, it was announced that the one-year dividend freeze would end on its July anniversary. In practice, exceptions had been allowed for dividend increases in defence against takeover bids or the restoration of a dividend after a profits recovery. However, companies would still be expected 'to exercise moderation' on a voluntary basis after July.

The Chancellor signalled a return to normal with a neutral Budget without any tax changes on 11 April, followed by another ½-point cut in Bank rate to 5½% in May. The market recovered its confidence in gradual matching steps and the FT Index reached 350 in June, boosted by the reinvestment of steel nation-alisation proceeds in advance of vesting date of 28 July 1967, when the government stock to be issued was a short-dated Treasury 6½% 1971. It was ironic that this stock was due to be redeemed 10 years earlier than the Treasury 3½% 1979–81 stock issued in 1951 for the *first* steel nationalisation.

There were other positive factors. In particular, the decision to apply for membership of the Common Market was well received on 2 May, and through-out the year increasingly buoyant sales figures were claimed for Concord (not yet with an 'e'), much encouraged by government and industry. The high point was a projection of sales of 400 for the supersonic airliner by 1980. Both the Common Market and Concord would flatter to deceive. By summer, the econ-omy was responding to the deflation of the last two years, and the August unemployment figure of 555,000, or 2.4%, was the highest post-war figure for the month. Indeed, the Chancellor relaxed hire purchase controls in a moment of mild reflation in August and, on 5 September, the All Share Index reached a new all-time high of 111.47, followed 2 weeks later by the FT Index at 380.9. The two indices had risen by 27% and 34% respectively from their November lows less than a year earlier.

The first phase of a bull market often happens against the better judgment of majority opinion, which struggles to distinguish between a technical rebound from a low point and the beginning of a change in direction. A bull market is like a river. The early trickle of investors at its source expands very slowly. The stream gradually becomes a river, and the river swells into a torrent of flood-water in the full spate of a bull market. The most skilful investors will enjoy a journey along the full length of the river, but the majority will have shorter jour-neys. Because individual psychology rarely changes, the same people will find their journey is of more or less the same length in every bull market, as captive to their instincts as migrating herds on the plains of Africa.

Investors need to know where their investment psychology leads them because those regularly finding themselves taking only a short, stressful journey in the floodwaters would do better to employ the services of professionals who are operating upstream. The same applies to knowing instinctively when to seek dry land. Many investors are quite good at the top or the bottom, but very few get it right at both ends.

Supply and demand were both now working strongly in favour of the market. Institutional demand for equities continued to grow unabated while the supply of equities was reduced for other reasons. Capital gains tax discouraged profit-taking, and, under corporation tax the higher real cost of dividends discouraged rights issues. The flurry of takeovers at the end of the previous year had turned into a steady flow, quite apart from steel nationalisation. Up and up went the market, taking the FT Index through the 400 barrier and on to an all-time high of 420.7 on 16 November 1967, followed by the All Share at 127.90 on 22 November both now nearly 50% higher than a year ago.

Two landmarks in the post-war history of the stock market were about to happen, the first helping to drive the market upwards, the second taking markets completely by surprise. First was the takeover bid on 28 September by Arnold Weinstock of General Electric for a rival company twice its size, Associated Electrical Industries (AEI). Second was the devaluation of the pound on 18 November, just 2 days after the FT Index reached its all-time high.

The General Electric bid for AEI in 1967 ranks in importance with Tube Investments/British Aluminium in 1958 and ICI/Courtaulds in 1961. When completed a year later with the acquisition of English Electric, it was the first example of the rationalisation of a basic industry by means of aggressive use of the stock market. It was the first major post-war bid where the name of the per-sonality – Arnold Weinstock – became bigger than the already well-known name of his company. Last, the creation of an electrical giant by the merging of the three largest companies put the cause of rationalisation ahead of conven-tional and obsessive concerns about monopoly, and put profitable productivity ahead of the mantra of full employment.

AEI shares stood at 43/6d when the first bid of 52/- in a mix of cash and shares was made on 28 September 1967, valuing the company at £120m. After strenuous opposition from AEI, the bid was increased in two stages to 72/6d or £160m, and General Electric narrowly obtained control on 9 November. In an atmosphere of much bitterness, the smaller company from the lighter end of the electrical industry, led by a man who today might be thought of as something of a control freak, had toppled a giant from the heavier end. An interloper who believed in profit had invaded a boardroom more concerned with corporate pride and traditional values. Weinstock immediately rubbed salt into the wound by closing down AEI's head office of 650 staff in Central London within 3 weeks of winning control, and in the following year he pointedly disclosed that the profits forecast of £10m made by the directors of AEI was an overstatement of the real position by £14.5m. During the course of the bid, it became apparent that Weinstock's initiative carried the support of the IRC – never a crucial factor, but helpful in weakening the defence.

The General Electric/AEI battle lasted for six weeks; devaluation happened more quickly. Bank rate was increased from 5½% to 6% on 19 October after currency rumours had begun to surface, and a few days later the Chancellor was surprised to be asked in the House of Commons to give an assurance that it was not his intention to devalue sterling in the next few months. 'Yes, sir', he replied, but perhaps unwittingly defined the question as unwelcome by the pointed use of the word 'sir'. Sterling continued to weaken and Bank rate was raised for a second time to 6½% on 9 November, just ahead of the announcement of one of the worst ever trade deficits for October. Britain was now negotiating a $1,000m loan from the Bank of International Settlements to strengthen reserves, and rumours gathered pace that devaluation would be a condition of the loan. On the afternoon of Saturday 18 November 1967, a devaluation of the pound by 14.3% from $2.80 to $2.40, was duly announced.

Devaluation was accompanied by another package of emergency measures. Bank rate was raised to a new post-war crisis level of 8% and hire purchase controls were tightened. Corporation tax was raised from 40% to 42½%. Immediate talks were proposed with the CBI and the TUC on controlling prices and incomes, and a 'strict watch' would be kept on dividends.

It all happened with bewildering speed. Two days earlier, the FT Index had been cruising happily into new high ground. Devaluation demanded the closing of the Stock Exchange on Monday 20 November, and, after a reflective Tuesday, the market surged ahead by more than 2% on Wednesday, attracted by the benefits for company profits following devaluation. The following day, the market gave way to serious second thoughts after the Chancellor referred to possible further economic measures and, on one of its worst ever days, the FT Index fell by more than 4% from 420.6 to 403.1. A few days later, on 29 November, in a simple exchange of jobs, James Callaghan resigned as Chancellor to be succeeded by the then Home Secretary, Roy Jenkins.

The new Chancellor recognised the need to ensure that the advantages given to the economy and to exports by devaluation were not eaten away by excessive domestic demand and inflation. The threat of further measures continued to hang heavily over the market and, within two weeks of the devaluation, the FT Index had tumbled by 8½% to 385.0. Sentiment was not helped by the 'non' from General de Gaulle on 27 November to Britain's application to join the Common Market and a work-to-rule by ASLEF, the train drivers union, in a messy dispute over the need for guards. This was finally resolved over beer and sandwiches with the Prime Minister in Downing Street – a meeting that went on into the night. This was the third such gathering hosted by Harold Wilson.

The snap reaction of the market mentioned above proved to be the full extent of devaluation blues and more positive thoughts returned. First, devaluation would lead to higher company profits, because of the extensive overseas interests of many companies either as newly encouraged exporters or as owners of foreign subsidiaries. Second, in the face of rising inflation, a flight from currency was taking place worldwide and its effect washed beneficially over equities. In particular, a flight from the dollar into gold was happening on an alarming scale, and demand in the UK for investment dollars overseas to diversify pushed the dollar premium up to 30%, even after devaluation.

Demand for equities gathered pace in the new year. There was speculation about another package of measures due to be announced by the Government. This came on 16 January 1968, when the Prime Minister announced a series of expenditure cuts, including the cancellation of an order for 50 F-111 US fighter-bombers, withdrawal of the Navy east of Suez, the postponement of raising the school-leaving age, and higher prescription charges – amounting to a total of £700m over 2 years. The policy of a 3½% guideline for the voluntary restraint on prices and incomes was reiterated. However, as the package contained nothing to curb consumer expenditure and, as the *Financial Times* leader put it, 'the mountain has given birth to a mouse', the stock market took off vertically. Marks & Spencer shares rose by more than 10%, and, on an extraordinary day, the FT Index rose by precisely 5% from 386.0 to 405.3 – one of its biggest ever percentage rises for a single day.

Buyers returned, quickly followed by another round of takeover bids and mergers. Schweppes bid for Typhoo Tea, a company claiming to be the largest one product manufacturer in the UK. Thorn Electrical bid for Radio Rentals, and was lucky to succeed with a combined market share of a third of both the television rental and manufacturing markets. There were more mergers in insurance, and two huge mergers planned among the clearing banks, where Westminster Bank successfully merged with National Provincial, but the proposal to merge Barclays, Lloyds and Martins Bank failed to survive a reference to the Monopolies Commission.

In a different vein, there was a strong sense of *déjà vu* about the merger announced on 17 January between British Motor Corporation and Leyland. Austin and Morris had merged on equal terms in 1951 to form BMC, then the fourth largest motor manufacturer in the world. After slipping well down the global league tables, BMC now merged on equal terms with Leyland to move up to equal fifth position, but it would prove too late to save an overmanned industry riddled with labour disputes and ineffective management.

The strength of the market was underlined by the combination of rising share prices and rising volume – a powerful signal in a bull market – and equities benefited from a worldwide stampede out of paper currency into gold. The United States allowed dollars to be freely convertible into gold at $35 an ounce, but demand became so great that, in March 1968, the US Government was forced to act. Gold markets and stock exchanges around the world were closed on Friday 15 March, pending a statement from Washington. On Monday, it was announced that there would be a two-tier gold price, remaining at $35 for transactions between central banks, but otherwise left to supply and demand in a free market. On the first day of dealings, the price opened at $45 and closed at $39.

Events in the gold market just preceded the new Chancellor's first Budget on 19 March. The market was not to be put off by a tough Budget, which raised most of the indirect taxes, put selective employment tax up by 50%, and altogether took £550m out of the economy. Furthermore, the Chancellor imposed an investment income levy for one year based on surtax, ranging from 2/- to 9/- on surtax over £8,000. This was a variation on the 10% surcharge on surtax introduced by Callaghan in July, 1966, but it raised £100m or four times as much tax. 'I recognise and intend that in the higher ranges it will be a small charge on capital', said Roy Jenkins in those civilised tones in his Budget speech, but it was a pity to see an intellectual Chancellor pulling out one of the chestnuts of the last Labour Government by banning scrip issues because they are a 'source of misunderstanding to many people, and their issue during the next crucial phase of incomes policy could become an impediment to full cooperation in the policy'.

The stock market had more confidence in the new Chancellor than in his predecessor and responded positively to his policy of securing the benefits of devaluation by squeezing personal consumption. There were other strong tides flowing in the market's favour.

The introduction of corporation tax had tightened the definition of earnings and focused attention on the comparative value of different sectors and of companies within sectors. Dividends and yields, the traditional drivers of the stock market for many years, now gave way to earnings and PE ratios. These allowed greater discrimination in valuation and, as major growth stocks such as Beecham, Glaxo, Marks & Spencer and Thorn Electrical were identified, so their values were driven up to PE ratios in the high twenties.

A new enthusiasm gripped the market. Institutional investors were as intent as ever on increasing the equity content of their portfolios, the cash inflows into pension funds and life assurance companies were reaching new records each year and the unit trust industry surged through the £1,000m barrier in total funds under management. A new phenomenon emerged – the cult of 'performance'. It was first displayed in the league tables of competing unit trusts, but soon spread to the far larger pension funds and insurance companies.

The merchant banks were beginning to compete openly to attract new funds and the traditional portfolio of a defensive spread of blue chips gave way to more actively managed portfolios. It was in 1969 that S. G. Warburg secured one of the largest pension fund mandates for the British Rail Pension Fund. Its successful management of this fund together with the BBC Pension Fund was to lay the ground for its leadership of the pension fund market – originally as S. G. Warburg Investment Management and later as Mercury Asset Management.

Investment views shortened dramatically and shares were re-rated very quickly under the pressure of aggressive institutional buying or selling. The distinction between capital and income, much influenced by actuarial thinking, became blurred by the concept of the total return. With their favourable tax position, the institutions became the new speculators in the marketplace, replacing the private client, now paralysed by the short-term capital gains tax. Much of this was influenced by trends in Wall Street, where aggressive young fund managers were known as 'gunslingers' and core holdings in portfolios were focused on a smaller number of leaders so that large gaps opened out in the rating and performance of the faster-growing 'nifty fifty' stocks at the expense of worthy, but slower-growing, names. One name particularly associated with this trend in the UK was a young Dutchman working in Edinburgh – Peter de Vink, an aggressive fund manager in Ivory & Sime.

These trends led to exciting opportunities for stockbrokers as rising prices and active dealing led to a surge in equity turnover. Official Stock Exchange figures show the sharply rising aggregate annual turnover in equities – from £3,566m in 1966 to £5,804m in 1967 and £9,118m in 1968. While partly reflecting higher share prices these figures also signalled the beginning of a new trend for a higher proportion of a company's capital to change hands in a year. If assumed to be half of turnover, sales in 1966 were equivalent to 8% of the value of all equities. By 1968, they had risen to 13%, and this percentage has been gradually rising ever since.

Greater institutional demand for equities was complemented by a quantum leap in the quality of investment advice and services offered by inventive stockbrokers to enthusiastic investors. Investment analysis had, in any case, been making steady progress from its beginnings in the late 1950s. A youthful Christopher Hogg, searching for basic information about different industries for the IRC in 1966, identified the best available source to be the research provided by specialist stockbrokers. Today he would endorse that decision and speak with praise for the standards of research set by the top analysts. However, he would also share the opinion of many fund managers consistently held for 30 years that while the best research is excellent, far too much of it is repetitive and second-rate.

Some of it was too enthusiastic. The modest one-paragraph summaries of the early 1960s had, by the end of the decade, turned into bibles of unnecessary and numbing detail about the technicalities of chicken farming or making bricks. Research of this kind needed the support of the companies being analysed, and a particular catalyst was the 1967 Companies Act.

This Act required companies to publish more information about sales and profits, both by division and geographical area. It encouraged analysts to probe more deeply and so served to open up lines of communication between companies and the stock market. The better-managed companies became aware of the importance of improving the quality of their accounts to attract more investment interest from institutional shareholders and, for the first time, welcomed an open dialogue with both investment analysts and shareholders.

Companies became aware of the advantages of a higher share price, whether for raising capital, issuing shares for acquisition, building a corporate reputation or deterring a bid. It was a sea change that suited shareholders, analysts and directors alike. It also marked another important step forward in the gradual shift of power from the company to its shareholders.

Two firms of stockbrokers – Hoare & Co. and Wood Mackenzie – were at the leading edge of new research products covering the whole equity market, while Phillips & Drew maintained the excellence and spread of their research coverage first established in the late 1950s.

Hoare & Co. was built to a position of strength as a leading firm of London stockbrokers under the leadership in the post-war years of Kit Hoare – a legendary corporate broker, who was shameless in his aggressive pursuit of companies and their merchant banks. Hoare & Co. announced in July 1968 the launch of their 'dataSTREAM' computerised information service on terminals available in clients' offices. The service stored a 5-year record of more than 100 items drawn from the accounts of 1,000 companies quoted on the London Stock Exchange. The information could be manipulated in clients' offices by analysts and fund managers to provide favourite ratios, and search programmes could list shares meeting any chosen criteria. Hoare & Co. seized an early lead in the computerisation of investment analysis. This initiative was led by Graham Blease, who had joined from the Airways Pension Fund, but it was more in the nature of a sophisticated information service than a creative source of ideas.

The frontiers of investment analysis were extended not in London, but by Wood Mackenzie – a small and fast-growing Edinburgh firm of stockbrokers, which launched three entirely new research services for institutional investors in the late 1960s– relative value analysis, business analysis and financial analysis. The firm was built by John Chiene, who joined a small one-partner firm in 1962 and by the mid 1970s had transformed it into the Stock Exchange's leading research house. Chiene had strong family roots in the Edinburgh investment community and possessed vision, drive and energy in equal measure. He was influenced by professional research skills witnessed at first hand in the United States, which, in his judgement, made the London stock market look like a backwater and so wide open to opportunities for new research ideas and products.

Wood Mackenzie was breaking new ground with its first new product, 'Focus' – relative value analysis system in chart form on a single sheet covering the leading companies. It set out for each company, initially over five years, the share price and its relative performance against the All Share Index; longer-term charts of the yield and yield relative; and the key items of PE ratio and earnings per share relatives, with two-year projections for individual shares and for the market. This gave Wood Mackenzie and their clients unique raw material to exploit opportunities in a stock market where the sorting and sifting of PE ratios was a dominant theme of the closing years of the 1960s.

This initiative was quickly followed in 1969 by a series of single, in-depth business analyses of selected companies, written in cooperation with the companies to ensure factual accuracy and with consultant help for longer-term business forecasting. Companies to be placed early under this microscope included Beecham, United Biscuits and Grand Metropolitan Hotels. The depth of the analysis, the extent of the probing into the business activities and the boldness of the forecasting was on a pioneering scale in the London market, and it set new standards for company research.

The third leg was launched later in the same year with the financial analysis service. This extracted and standardised financial items from the profit and loss accounts and balance sheets of leading companies to calculate a wide range of ratios and comparisons.

Although Wood Mackenzie would later be in the forefront of computerised research, the data for the relative value analysis was compiled manually using electro-mechanical calculating machines, the best available machines at the time before the electronic calculator. At least they were ahead of the calculating contraptions of the early 1960s, when a sort of mechanical abacus required intense coordination of hand and eye, as handles whirled and the top of the machine was bodily lifted sideways. Even slide rules were still widely used in the early 1960s for quick, visually observed calculations that would be as unacceptable today as using a stopwatch to time a 100-metre race.

In marketing these new products, Chiene challenged the traditional relationships between stockbrokers and their clients. Stockbrokers normally sent all their research to all clients, gratefully receiving far too much business from some clients and passively accepting too little or none at all from others. Conversely, too many institutions handed out business to brokers based purely on old relationships, where the regular provision of long lunches with fine wines in panelled rooms or exclusive invitations to cherished events, before the days of hospitality units, counted more highly than any other factor.

Chiene adopted the simple no-nonsense approach of the businessman. The research services offered by Wood Mackenzie were clearly defined, and priced in terms of an amount of commission expected in return from the client. The same concept was more loosely used by Hoare & Co. for its DataSTREAM service, although it was more in the nature of an information service that would normally be paid for by subscription, except that it happened to be provided by a stockbroker to clients. Wood Mackenzie and Hoare & Co. pioneered the practice of institutions giving specific commission allocations to brokers in return for research or other services. In due course, it would have consequences for the Stock Exchange. It drew attention to the high level of commissions on gilt-edged securities by comparison with equities, added pressure to the campaign before Big Bang for the abandonment of fixed commissions, and eventually it would lead to the practice of 'soft' commissions.

A strong influence on the market in the late 1960s was the charismatic presence of Jim Slater. A trained accountant, he abandoned a successful management career in Leyland to form an investment vehicle to indulge his personal fascination for the stock market. This became Slater Walker and, for a few years in the late 1960s and early 1970s Jim Slater aroused the same range of feelings from awe and admiration to fear and trepidation – once reserved for Charles Clore in the 1950s. They shared many characteristics. They were both attracted like moths to a bright light by assets at a discount. They both lent their personal names to phases in the market when their activities led many an uneasy boardroom to fear it might be taken over. They both resented the label of asset-stripper, believing that the shareholders of many companies deserved better of their complacent directors, and that the capitalist system was better served by their influence.

In other ways they were quite different. Clore was short, secretive, uncommunicative and unpopular. Slater was tall, open, a man who freely expressed his views and had an engaging personality. Clore's interest in assets was driven by an instinct for the value of property; Slater's interest was the financial manipulation of assets of all kinds. Clore built a strong business empire that easily survived him; Slater's empire collapsed when his financial assets evaporated into thin air. The passing of time has enhanced Clore's business reputation, but done nothing to improve his personal reputation, whereas Slater's business reputation was destroyed by manipulative financial accounting, but his personal reputation has strengthened through his success as a writer and investment guru. Clore ran his empire with a small group of loyal colleagues, whereas Slater bred acolytes and spawned them off into the marketplace to create a band of imitators in his own image.

In the late 1960s the name of Jim Slater was that of a widely acclaimed entrepreneur seeking out badly managed companies and undervalued assets, and his predatory influence contributed to the prevailing bullishness. He was featured in an interview in the *Financial Times* on 8 May 1968 – a rare accolade in those days – when he talked of quadrupling the market capitalisation of Slater Walker from £50m over 5 years. In another article on 7 September, Slater Walker was identified as the leading example of the new 'conglomerate', a concept imported from the United States and displacing the industrial holding company. Also identified in the same article as another example of the new conglomerate was Wiles Group, which later changed its name to Hanson

Trust. Slater Walker collapsed in the bear market in the 1970s, but Hanson survived to become an industrial giant in the 1980s.

A final factor contributing to bullish markets in 1968 was the scale of takeover activity when the value of mergers and acquisitions reached £2,312m, nearly treble the figure for the previous year. The highlight was the second instalment of the creation of GEC as an electrical giant by Arnold Weinstock.

Amid gathering rumours, Plessey, with a market capitalisation of £246m, made a pre-emptive bid of £263m for English Electric on 21 August 1968, offering 67/- a share against a market price of 53/-. English Electric rejected the bid, and within two weeks it was announced that General Electric and English Electric had agreed to merge. Talks between the two companies had been taking place over the last year and, in an unusual intervention during the course of a bid battle while terms were still being worked out, the IRC publicly gave its backing to the merger. Although in no way critical to the achievement of Weinstock's ambitions to create an industrial giant, the support of the IRC eased the way forward politically.

On 19 September, General Electric offered a package to English Electric shareholders worth 79/6d, compared with the Plessey bid now worth 74/-. Plessey withdrew and General Electric acquired English Electric for £312m – a bargain price agreed in hurried negotiations. The market value of the combined group was around £950m and, initially at least, the company was to be named General Electric, English Electric, with Lord Nelson from the latter as Chairman and Arnold Weinstock as Managing Director.

As the year drew to a close, the *Financial Times* on 7 December headed an article 'Gigantomania'. It was on the spate of mergers in 1968, prompted not only by GEC/EE but also by a merger announced on 29 November between Unilever and Allied Breweries. This would have created another giant company valued at just under £1,000m, but, in the event, it merely joined the list of famous mergers proposed but never consummated, failing like many others to survive the hurdle of being referred to the Monopolies Commission. Adjusting for inflation, these mergers would today be in the area of £8,000–£9,000m, and considerably more if growth is taken into account.

With new research ideas feeding a ready institutional appetite for equities, and a flow of mergers and takeovers spiced with the excitement of Slater Walker, it is not surprising that the market was continually breaking into new high ground through the summer of 1968. International markets were also enjoying booming times. In the early part of the year, London had enjoyed and participated in an Australian mining boom that witnessed the birth of Western Mining – one of today's major mining companies. Based on a huge nickel discovery, the shares shot up from 51/6d to £21 in the month of January 1968. In the United States the Dow Jones Index finished the year strongly, and shrewd investors were beginning to notice some remarkable growth rates being achieved in Japan.

The FT Index broke through the 500 barrier in August, peaked on 19 September at 521.9, and closed the year at 506.4, up 30% over the year. The more broadly based All Share Index illustrated the all-round strength of the market, and strongly outperformed the FT Index because of its exposure to a very buoyant oil sector. It ended the year at its all-time high of 173.72, up 43% on the year, and went on to peak at 180.97 on 31 January, 1969, up 106% from its low of 87.74 on 8 November 1966.

This was a memorable bull market that ranks in scale and timing with the two great bull markets of 1953–55 and 1958–60, when indices also more than doubled in little more than two years. All three were driven by the weight of institutional money pressing on to the market. The bull markets of the 1950s were prompted by the discovery of dividends. In the 1960s it was the discovery of earnings. At its peak on 31 January 1969, the FT All Share Index valued the earnings of 500 companies on an aggregate historic PE ratio of over 23, compared with 13 near the beginning of this bull market. This high figure has never since been reached, but later historic PE ratios are not properly comparable because of changing corporate tax systems and changing rates of corporation tax.

A decade of memorable events was drawing to a close – the Trustee Act, the FT-Actuaries Indices, the Takeover Panel, a new Companies Act, the emergence of the PE ratio, the first sighting of institutional supremacy, the performance cult and the ICI/Courtaulds and GEC/AEI/English Electric takeover battles. Together these events raised the profile of the securities industry, putting in place strong foundations on which it would thrive and prosper.

Chapter 17

THE DAM BURSTS
January 1969–June 1970

All Share Index	31 January 1969	180.97	
	12 June 1970	114.73	Down 36.6%

Memories of a powerful bull market in 1967–68 help sustain the myth that stock markets have performed well under Labour Governments. The simple fact is that, over the life of the three post-war Labour Governments' stock market indices consistently failed to keep up with inflation, and memory tends to overlook the bad times that either preceded or followed the bull markets.

In the case of the 1964–69 Labour Government, the bull market that enjoyed a doubling of share prices was preceded by a 20% fall during its first 2 years in office, and, as will be described in this chapter, was followed by a fall of around 35% in its last 18 months. Harold Wilson entered Number 10 in October 1964 with the FT Index at 364.9 and left in June 1970 when it was 334.6, although the more representative All Share Index more fairly shows him in at 106.85 and out at 120.63, an actual rise of 13% but still lagging well behind inflation of just under 30%. Far worse was the fate of the luckless investor in the gilt-edged market. The price of the benchmark Consols 2½% fell by 37% from 41 to 26 over the same period, as its yield rose from around 6% to over 9½%.

Stock markets began the new year of 1969 in fine fettle. The indices were riding high, many takeover bids were on the table, unit trusts reported an increase in funds under management of 73% for the year to a record £1,480m, Slater Walker shares had almost trebled in a year, company profits were rising at over 20% in the last quarter as devaluation benefits came through and Stock Exchange figures showed monthly turnover in equities topping £1,000m for the first time in January. Just the moment to trap those luckless investors whose psychology makes them wait until the news is absolutely favourable before casting their carefully guarded savings into the market.

A few clouds had been gathering towards the end of 1968. A full year after the devaluation, the Chancellor had still not acted sufficiently to cut domestic demand and make room for more exports. After tightening hire purchase controls earlier in the month, he cut demand by £200m in a minor package on 22 November by sharply raising petrol and cigarette duties and by using the regulator for a 10% increase in the rates of purchase tax. More significantly, he showed his concern for the adverse effect on the balance of payments of high levels of personal spending by introducing an import deposit of 50% covering around a third of imports other than food, fuel and raw materials. The deposits would be refundable after 180 days and the scheme was to last for a year. The FT Index fell on the day by 2.6% to 483.9, but quickly recovered.

In earnest, Roy Jenkins now began the crusade for financial rectitude that some critics would later claim lost the 1970 general election. In the then traditional New Year's Day message to readers of the *Financial Times*, the Chancellor wrote 'I have one clear and overriding objective for 1969. Last year was the fifth year in succession that we have run a deficit in our balance of payments. I am determined it shall be the last'. In February, he said that government borrowing would be 'nil' this year and, speaking to the Committee of London Clearing Banks, he said, 'I expect to be a net repayer of debt on a substantial scale'. He would prove to be as good as his word and become the first post-war Chancellor to run a surplus on both the balance of payments and the public-sector accounts.

Pressures were emerging to threaten his good intentions. The Bank of England had sent a directive in December to the clearing banks to reduce lending by 2% over the next quarter, but the buoyancy of the economy frustrated this and, on 27 February, Bank rate was raised from 7% to 8%.

At the same time, labour relations took a turn for the worse after a relatively peaceful year. Ford Motor has always been the bellwether for pay settlements in the private sector and, in February the company agreed a 7½%–10% pay offer, but because it breached the 3½% norm and lacked the necessary productivity proposals, Government approval was required. Within days, the unions were demanding a higher offer with no strings attached and unofficial strikes broke out. A total of 46,000 workers were called out on an official strike that lasted for 3 weeks until a compromise was cobbled together. The strike was damaging to the balance of payments and put pressure on a stock market that was beginning to lose its nerve.

The more serious political consequence was that the Prime Minister became determined to force through the trade union and labour relations reforms set out in the White Paper, 'In Place of Strife'. This intent was sufficiently strong for the Chancellor to announce in his Budget on 15 April that, in view of impending legislation, the statutory powers in place to control prices, incomes and dividends would not be renewed when they expired at the end of the year.

The Budget offered no relief, raising £272m mainly from the corporate sector with a 25% increase in selective employment tax from 37/6d a week to 48/- – now almost double the rate when it was first introduced in 1966 – and from another increase in corporation tax from 42½% to 45%. Commenting in his Budget speech on the latter, the Chancellor said, 'if this means a somewhat less buoyant Stock Exchange, I would not regret that either. There is undoubtedly a relationship between a Stock Exchange boom and the level of consumption'. The boom was now fading fast. The FT Index fell by nearly 5% in the 3 days after the Budget, more or less equal to the reduction in earnings per share that followed from the higher level of corporation tax. However, there was some consolation from the exemption of gilt-edged securities from long-term capital gains tax, and gilts enjoyed an upwards blip of 2 points or so in their long downwards trend.

The stock market adage of 'sell in May and go away' served well in 1969, with the FT Index falling roughly from 450 to 360 by the end of July. Serious Cabinet divisions over trade union reform were unsettling and recessionary problems in the United States had worrying implications for the British economy. In fact, the biggest one-day fall of the year in London was directly influenced by Wall Street, when the FT Index fell on 10 June by more than 3% from 411.3 to 398.6. The US prime lending rate, the equivalent of Bank rate, was increased from 7½% to 8½% and the market was unable to believe that interest rates could remain for long at a lower level in the UK than in the US. The gilt-edged market had been weak in London for some weeks. In May, a small debenture issue slipped through with, for the first time, a coupon in double figures at 10%, and a £10m unsecured loan stock for market leader Metal Box attracted comment because of its record coupon of 10½%. The same pressures led to a £400m government issue on 17 July requiring a record high coupon of 9%.

The stock market was now in schizophrenic mood. The Industrial Relations Bill was dropped on 18 June after the Prime Minister had been undermined by a campaign from within his Cabinet openly led by Home Secretary James Callaghan, and there was widespread disbelief when it was replaced by the famous and much parodied 'solemn and binding' undertaking from the TUC to tackle the problem of unofficial strikes. The market fell sharply. A week later, the terms of a $1,000m standby credit from the International Monetary Fund (IMF) imposed severe limits on the expansion of domestic credit and set a target for achieving a balance of payments surplus. The stock market saw the IMF as a better taskmaster than the TUC and the market bounced back.

However, the trend was firmly downwards and, by the end of July, the FT Index fell to 362.4, down 30% since the beginning of the year, and the All Share Index was down 25%. Against such a gloomy background, it is interesting to note that, in early July, the prospectus of Dalton Barton Securities – a small banking services group, where profits had doubled in successive years and were forecast to do so again – attracted so much attention that it was oversubscribed 54 times. The *Financial Times* referred to the 'astoundingly good reception' given earlier in May to a similar banking services business, London and County Securities. These were the stock market vehicles of Gerald Caplan and Jack Dellal, both producing profits that everybody believed but nobody understood, and basking in the warm, protective glow given to this sector of the market by Slater Walker.

In 1969, two famous names of the 1980s and 1990s, Robert Maxwell and Rupert Murdoch – the one little known and the other unknown – first came to the notice of the stock market. Sharing the same initials and aggressive ambition, they were thrown against each other in a battle for control of the News of the World. The shares of this famous newspaper group were languishing at 29/3d when Maxwell made an opportunist bid of 41/6d through his company, Pergamon, on 16 October 1968, quickly raising it to 50/- just 5 days later to a total value of £34m. News of the World was one of those quoted companies in the 1950s and 1960s that were run more or less as personal fiefdoms by the principal family shareholders, in this case Sir William Carr. He was aghast at the thought of the bumptious Maxwell stealing his empire, but realistic enough to see the problem of heading off a bid set at such a premium over the market price.

Within a few days, it was announced that News Ltd., a barely known Australian newspaper group, was seeking a 40% stake in News of the World, and a certain Rupert Murdoch was to be joint Managing Director. This stake, combined with the family shareholdings, would be sufficient to control the company, but Pergamon responded by raising its bid to 52/6d. In the event, News Ltd. transferred assets into News of the World in exchange for a 26% stake in the enlarged company and this, together with shares purchased by News Ltd. in the market, enabled News of the World to claim on 1 January 1969 that the proposal to purchase assets from News Ltd. had been carried. Few have jumped more elegantly out of the frying pan into the fire than Sir William Carr in his haste to be saved from Robert Maxwell by Rupert Murdoch. Six months later, he was ousted as Chairman.

There was some sympathy for the frustration of Maxwell's plans by this backdoor ploy, but, less than a year later, his own reputation was compromised by events that would eventually leave it in tatters after a damning DTI report. Leasco, the US conglomerate vehicle of Saul Steinberg, bid £25m in June 1969 for Maxwell's company, Pergamon. Two months later, the bid was withdrawn amid a welter of accusations by Leasco about weaknesses in Pergamon's accounts and profits forecasts, and the Board of Trade set up an inquiry into the affairs of Pergamon. Independent reports by Price Waterhouse would later show that Pergamon's last reported profits of £2,104,000 were a figment of Maxwell's creative imagination and, in reality, they were only £495,000. The DTI Report, published in July 1971, stated that Maxwell 'is not in our opinion a person who can be relied upon to exercise proper stewardship of a publicly quoted company'. It was a judgement vigorously denied by Maxwell and, over the next 20 years, any repetition of it was aggressively fought with streams of writs, but, in the end, it was to prove all too chillingly accurate.

Having fallen by 30% in seven months, the stock market stagnated for the rest of 1969, and bargain levels subsided to 8,000 to 10,000 a day. Dull days were enlivened by the second leg of three in an Australian mining boom that would eventually be remembered for fortunes made or lost in Western Mining (1968), Poseidon (1969) and Pancontinental (1976) – the first two in nickel, the last in uranium. It was now the turn of Poseidon. On 29 September, the shares all but trebled in a day from 20/9d to 59/6d on news of a nickel find. By the end of the week, they had touched £11. Four months later, in February 1970, they peaked at £124, where Poseidon was capitalised at over £300m. Many UK investors were now hopelessly locked into the shares by the penal 91¼% rate of capital gains tax.

Poseidon prompted many a speculative Australian mining dream in a market driven by rumour and trickery, where hope became confused with hype, hearsay became confused with evidence and the most frequently asked question was 'How do you spell that?' One such name was Tasminex whose shares on 27 January shot up from 45/- to £40, before closing at £21, after the Chairman was quoted as saying of his nickel find, 'I reckon it could be better than Poseidon'. Rarely has so much been achieved so quickly by a throwaway line. The market value of Tasminex closed at £44m, not even deterred by the further information that they had stumbled on the find while drilling a borehole for water and 'we have not got on to the geologists yet'. They eventually did get on to the geologists, whose report, received a few weeks later, sent the shares down to 40/-, lower than on the day the rumours started.

The incomes policy was falling into disarray as 1969 drew to a close. After the collapse of the industrial relations legislation, the government talked about replacing the Prices and Incomes Act. The Queen's Speech in November referred to the need to retain Part II, which allowed price and pay settlements to be delayed by up to four months, until new legislation would be introduced in 1970. By now, the unions had moved in to occupy the ground left vacant by the abandonment of 'In Place Of Strife' and public-sector workers were obtaining increases of 10% or more. Nevertheless, there was some surprise when, on 6 November, the Treasury announced that the powers to restrain dividends and the present ceiling of 3½%, would be abolished on 31 December, although companies were expected to 'observe moderation'.

It was as if the Government was suddenly exhausted by controls. Companies seized the moment to push through much needed price rises and the lights were green for unions seeking pay increases. Dividend control had been effective and severe. From July 1966 to December 1969, the underlying dividend index of the 594 companies in the All Share Index rose by only 3.1%, well behind both earnings growth of 15.3% and inflation of 15.2% during the same period. It was a gloomy end to a decade that may be remembered as the swinging sixties for many aspects of British life, but not for stock market investors. The FT Index began the decade at 339.0 on 1 January 1960 and ended at 407.4 on 31 December 1969 – a rise of 20%, or just under 2% annually, but inflation rose by 43%, or just under 4% annually, and equities failed to meet one of their prime objectives.

However, there were some bright spots. Oil shares had enjoyed a major bull market for several years and property shares illustrated how political decisions sometimes achieve the opposite of what is intended. An early decision of the incoming Labour Government in 1964 had been to ban all new office buildings in Greater London. When the surplus of vacant properties was eventually absorbed, and without new supply, the market became a seller's paradise. A rent spiral without equal caused serious problems for anguished tenants and created many a fortune for even the least imaginative of property developers. Many a glass was raised in a toast to George Brown.

The reality of this was vividly illustrated by takeover battles attracting three different bidders, first, for City of London Real Property Co. and, later, for London County Freehold. City of London Real Property was the jewel in the crown of the property market, with a fine portfolio of offices mainly in central London. The shares had already moved up to 105/- in November 1968 when Trafalgar House made a sighting bid of 103/- in a package worth £94m. Metropolitan Estates entered the bidding with an offer of £148m, but the prize went to Land Securities with a bid of 177/3d, or £161m, in January – 72% higher than the opening bid. This was as fruitful an outcome as any for the shareholders of a major company in receipt of competing bids.

Less exciting, but by way of consolation, Metropolitan Estates made an opening bid of £42m for London County Freehold in November 1969 that had to be raised twice to £47.5m before heading off competing bids from two other companies. By this time, the psychological barrier of £10 per square foot for City rentals had been breached in Bucklersbury House, creating a new benchmark for unfortunate tenants caught in the trap of a rent review or lease renewal, and there were rumours of rents of £15 being asked in Winchester House.

The 1970s began with a ludicrous corporate hoax. On 15 January, the shares of E. J. Austin were suspended to allow the announcement of plans to acquire El Sobrante Mining Corporation of California, a company claiming to have invented a new process that dramatically improved the yield from refining gold. The Chairman of E. J. Austin, Kenneth Howarth, claimed that this 'crock of gold' would be producing profits for E. J. Austin of £10m by the end of 1970, compared with a current £500,000. The shares were suspended at 18/9d, but one large institutional shareholder, Surinvest, sold part of an overlarge holding at 45/- in unofficial dealings.

E. J. Austin was to acquire El Sobrante for £6.8m in shares, but the deal began to wobble when it emerged that the Chairman of E. J. Austin, Kenneth Howarth, just happened to be the majority shareholder of El Sobrante, along with Wayne Chambers, an Australian mining expert who had invented the 'process' that produced yields of $5,000 a ton compared with a normal $35. A party of investors was flown out to see the mine, but saw no more than barbed wire around a mine entrance. It all fell apart and, on 16 March, a receiver was appointed, followed by a Board of Trade Inquiry.

Quite apart from this diversion, the shackles of controls in the economy were now being broken in spectacular fashion. Price increases were coming through in basic materials such as cement, coal, paper and steel. The *Financial Times* highlighted an 'avalanche' of pay claims in the 10–20% range; Ford workers denounced an offer of 18–20% as 'not remotely acceptable'; ICI offered 19–22%, and, in the public sector, the nurses were awarded a 20% increase. Company dividends announced in March rose in aggregate by 10% in the busy reporting season.

The stock market was active, but little changed in the new year – confused by fears of inflation from price and pay rises on the one hand, and the expectation of a further stimulus to the economy in the April Budget on the other hand as the Government entered its last year in office. This latter view was encouraged by a call from the National Institute for Economic and Social Research for a £650m stimulus to the economy, and by a reduction in Bank rate in early March from 8% to 7½%. The Chancellor's professed caution and the needs of an electoral timetable made for nice debate. The political commentator David Watt penned an imaginary letter to the Chancellor in the *Financial Times* on 13 March about his dilemma between following the experts with a neutral Budget and losing the election by a 100 seats, or following demands of the left wing of the party for expanding into more inflation and winning by a comfortable majority. Watt perceptively concluded, 'it is suspected that you are more concerned with your reputation as Chancellor than for the good of the party'.

And so it proved. The Chancellor secured his financing double of a surplus on the balance of payments and the public-sector accounts, but he was as concerned as any about the emerging pay spiral, and, in his Budget on 14 April, he allowed only a modest stimulus of £220m. He lowered Bank rate by a ½-point to 7% and removed the ceilings on bank lending, but raised special deposits from 2% to 2½%, and gave tax incentives only by increasing personal allowances. It would seem that an election announcement was not on his agenda when he told the Parliamentary Labour party that he could always adjust for any overcaution later in the year

The market would probably not have enjoyed either of the policy options facing the Chancellor, and, from this moment, it went into free fall of some 20% in 5 weeks. The FT Index fell from 397.6 on Budget day to 316.0 on 26 May, although bargain levels were unusually low for a fall of this severity.

Sentiment was not helped by a combination of unexpected or unwanted events elsewhere. In the United States, the Dow Jones Index fell in the same proportions against a background of economic uncertainty and the escalation of the Vietnam war. These events triggered a fall of 9% on a single day in Tokyo on 29 April, when the local Dow Jones Index fell from 2,315 to 2,114. Another bearish influence was the collapse of international fund management group, Investors Overseas Services (IOS), whose Chairman and founder, the 'Do you seriously want to be rich?' Bernie Cornfeld, resigned to make way for new ownership. Urgent action was needed to stem a flood of redemptions from weak policy-holders sucked into IOS funds by high-pressure selling. Nothing drives share prices down quite so rapidly as the scent of the forced seller, and redemptions in his funds across the world put pressure on all markets.

Meanwhile, investors at home were discouraged by a never-ending succession of pay claims, and dismayed by encouraging political news for Labour from good municipal election results on 7 May and a Gallup opinion poll lead of 7½% on 13 May. Five days later, Harold Wilson seized the moment he would later regret and announced that a general election would be held on 18 June.

The market was despondent for most of the campaign, recovering only in the final week, when the FT Index went up each day, and, on polling day itself, small buying was noticed from all parts of the country. Although the final opinion polls on the day of the election gave leads for Labour of 7% in Gallup and 4.1% in NOP, the man in the street knew better and, in a shock result, the Conservatives won with an overall majority of 30.

Chapter 18

GOING FOR GROWTH

June 1970–May 1972

All Share Index	12 June 1970	114.73	
	1 May 1972	228.18	Up 98.9%

The newspaper headlines proclaimed opinion poll leads for Labour of 7% from Gallup and 4.1% from NOP on polling day in the 1970 general election, but the stock market was telling a very different story. Two days before the election, the FT Index enjoyed one of those rare sharp rises of more than 3% in a day from 315.6 to 325.7, followed by a further 1% rise on the day before the election (see Figure 18.1). Most unusually for an election day, the market moved strongly ahead, taking the FT Index up by 1.6% to 334.6.

A particular clue was buying from across the country of small parcels of property shares by private investors. This is a textbook example of the stock market's predictive abilities at work. All it needed was a handful of alert private investors in a dozen or more marginal constituencies to translate into a flutter in property shares their realisation that support for the Conservatives was far stronger than indicated by the pollsters. Positive activity in the most politically sensitive sector of the market amounted to a real-time sampling process of what was actually happening out there. This occurs all the time in the stock market, where unconnected people of like mind come to an identical conclusion, and follow their noses by buying or selling. It has something in common with a television advertising campaign, where a successful advert requires only a modest but identical response.

The buyers were proved right. 'Tories head for shock win' ran the headline of the *Financial Times* on the morning of Friday 19 June, and for Edward Heath, 'no politician since Harry Truman has had a bigger and more satisfying last laugh', as he was returned with an overall majority of 30. The reaction of the stock market was electric. In early dealings, the FT Index was up by 7% at 358.4. Bargain numbers through the day doubled to more than 15,000, and the FT Index closed 5.1% higher, from 334.6 to 351.5. Even more remarkable was the 5.4% rise on the day, from 120.63 to 127.10, in the wider-ranging All Share Index. This was the measure of the relief felt by investors at the defeat of the Labour Government, which was caught out in a moment of complacency and equally shocked by the result, and the return of a Conservative Government

Figure 18.1
FT INDEX 1970–75

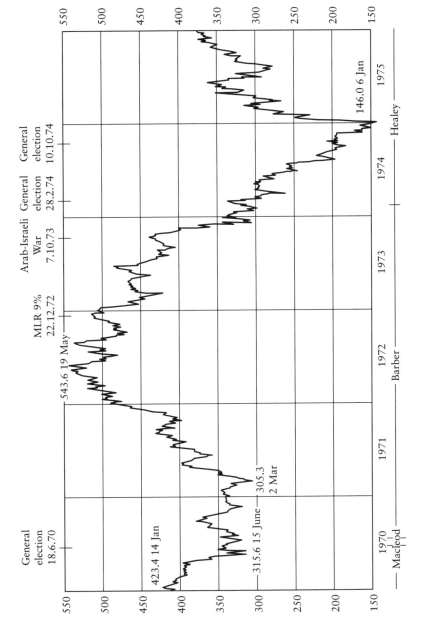

Source: Financial Times

promising 'substantial' reductions in the burden of high personal taxation, and freedom for the economy to grow and prosper.

An early tragedy befell the new Conservative Government on 20 July 1970, when the Chancellor of the Exchequer, the highly respected Iain Macleod, collapsed and died, exactly one calendar month after his appointment. He had time only to define inflation as the most serious problem faced by the Government, and to announce that there would be no autumn budget, with a reminder that the 'regulator' was always available to increase purchase taxes. It was in the nature of a posthumous decision that, within days of his death, it was announced that Labour's import deposits would be reduced from 30% to 20% from 1 September, and abolished from December. He was succeeded by Anthony Barber, who remained Chancellor through the Heath administration.

After the euphoria of the election victory, the stock market drifted down and business quickly reverted to its desultory levels of 6,000–7,000 bargains a day. The inheritance of a flood of inflationary pay claims after 3 years of Labour controls was to haunt the Conservative government, and, by the summer, claims ranged against them included 33% for the miners and 40% for teachers. The judgement of hindsight may well be that the situation facing Edward Heath was almost unplayable. The stock market suffered a one-day fall of over 3% on 15 July, when a national dock strike over a pay dispute was called. On the following day there was a declaration of a state of emergency and an inquiry was set up under Lord Pearson. Robert Carr, Secretary of State for Employment, stated that the country was 'heading for another economic disaster' unless cost inflation was brought down, and the Prime Minister announced he would be holding talks with the TUC and CBI about the problem of escalating pay and prices, so continuing the Wilson tradition of welcoming trade union leaders to Downing Street.

Inflationary pressures built up in the autumn with the miners, bus workers and local authority workers all rejecting 10–25% offers, and price increases coming through for letter post and steel. On 27 October 1970, the new Chancellor announced an economic package signalling the Government's policy of seeking to curb inflationary pay claims by offering tax cuts and encouraging growth. In a mini-Budget that released £330m, he reduced the standard rate of income tax from 8/3d to 7/9d, and corporation tax from 45% to 42½%, the first reductions in either tax for 11 years. He replaced investment grants with initial allowances of 60%, and allowed free depreciation in development areas. He also announced the winding up of the Industrial Reorganisation Corporation. The stock market responded enthusiastically with a 2½% rise and at 372.6 the FT Index now stood above its post-election level. The package was intended to discourage pay claims and encourage investment rather than reflate consumer demand, and the Chancellor raised the special deposits from the banks from 2½% to 3½%.

The rally proved to be short-lived as investors became alarmed by the scale of union pay demands and their readiness to strike. Typical indices at the time for the year to November 1970 showed the Retail Price Index up by 7½% and the index of basic wages up 13½%, with a queue of substantial claims still to be settled. Nobody was willing to relinquish the precedent of somebody else's settlement and, all too often, strikes were brought to an end by setting up an inquiry. Pearson, Scamp and Wilberforce – the names of those heading inquiries into striking dockers, council workers and power workers – sounded more like a firm of local solicitors, but the inevitable compromise of their reports produced settlements that did nothing to lower expectations elsewhere.

Harold Macmillan once said that 'events' were the greatest problem facing governments, and one such unexpected and unwanted event for the Heath Government was the sudden financial crisis besetting Rolls-Royce – one of Britain's finest technology companies competing worldwide in the manufacture of aero-engines. Without any previous hint of a problem, it was announced on 11 November 1970, that Rolls-Royce would receive £60m in a public rescue package to cover a £48m loss on the cost of developing a new RB-211 aero-engine for the Lockheed Tri-Star, a project originally estimated to cost £65m, but now heading for £135m. Rolls-Royce shares fell from 11/6d to 7/9d. The situation continued to deteriorate and, on 4 February 1971, a receiver was appointed, the Lockheed contract was to be terminated, the Government was to take over the essential assets of the company, and there would be substantial redundancies. The shares were suspended at 7/6d – little different from the time of the first announcement in November.

This was an anguished moment for a government that had set its face against bailing out lame ducks, and had closed down the IRC, a vehicle for corporate rescues. The Prime Minister emphasised that Rolls-Royce, with its unique reputation, was an exception because of its defence implications, and its emergency nationalisation did not change the policy of refusing to intervene. A Bill was rushed through Parliament in less than three weeks to take over the company and create Rolls-Royce (1971) Ltd.

Meanwhile, dealings quickly resumed on 10 February and, in high turnover, the shares closed at 1/6d. Ironically, on the next two days, the Stock Exchange was closed to implement decimalisation and in unofficial dealings outside the market the shares rose to 3/- (15p). When Rolls-Royce (1971) Ltd. was formed on 23 February, dealings were suspended for the last time at 18.5p, compared with an all-time high of 275p. In its last few days, there was a huge turnover in Rolls-Royce shares, and much of the buying was rumoured to be from the United States.

This buying would later be justified by the realisation of assets obtained by the receiver, and it was a good example of a home truth about the London stock market. From time to time, the price of a particular share will be driven much higher than London valuations are willing to support by aggressive buying from the United States. 'Beware Americans buying shares' would be a suitable motto for the London stock market, because they have an uncanny habit of picking up bargains at the expense of sceptical British sellers, particularly in one-off situations or when the shares of a company are in a sector of the market new to investors.

At the time when Rolls-Royce was nationalised, the market appeared to have fallen well below its post-election levels, with the better publicised FT Index as low as 305.3 in early March (see Figure 18.1) compared with 351.5. However, the All Share Index stood at 129.47, a shade higher than its post-election level of 127.10. This is a good example of the weakness of the FT Index. It contained only 30 shares, drawn mostly from traditional industrial sectors, with each given equal weight, whereas the All Share Index was the aggregate market capitalisation of the largest 594 companies, drawn from all sectors of the market. Since the election, two of the best-performing sectors in the market had been financials and oils, both more than 20% higher. Neither was represented in the FT Index, but they formed 21% and 13% respectively of the value of the All Share Index, or a third of the entire equity market.

The FT Index attracted the headline interest in the stock market because it was calculated several times during the day, and it alone could express the changing mood of the market through the day in one familiar figure. The All Share Index was calculated only once a day, after the close of the market, and was less expressive of short-term price movements than the FT Index because it contained so many shares where price changes lagged behind changes in the leaders. Its lack of immediacy was less suitable for newspaper and television headlines and market gossip, but it was better suited as the benchmark for performance measurement.

The FT 30 was superseded in 1984 by the FTSE 100, a simple aggregation of the value of the 100 largest equities, updated in real time at 1-minute intervals, but the All Share Index continues to provide much the best long-term data for price performance, earnings and dividend growth, as well as PE ratios and yields of both the market and its individual sectors. The FT 30 Index is now hardly ever mentioned, but is still calculated daily for the continuity of its historical record.

The stock market was unsettled by strikes in 1970, when the 11.1m days lost was the worst year since 1926, but that paled in comparison with the 9.5m days lost in the first quarter alone of 1971. There was a fruitless six-week strike by postal workers and a more serious strike by Ford workers, who rejected an 8–10% offer on the last Friday in January and went on strike on the following Monday. Five weeks later, they rejected a 14% offer before eventually returning to work on 3 April for an agreed 33% over two years. This crippling but victorious 9-week strike cost Ford £91m in lost production, but far greater was the

Government's dismay at the scale of the final settlement, a dismay shared also by many companies in the private sector for which Ford acted as benchmark.

With the Ford strike and rumblings from steel and rail unions, the stock market might well have spiralled on downwards, but it was shaken out of its gloom by a remarkable Budget on 30 March 1971. Anthony Barber's reputation has not survived well, but he presented the most tax-reforming Budget of any in the entire post-war period, and the market responded with one of the biggest ever single-day rises in the FT Index of 6.2% from 331.7 to 352.2.

It is a rare Chancellor who abolishes four taxes in one Budget, but that is what Barber did with purchase tax, selective employment tax, surtax and short-term capital gains tax. He made three major reforms in taxation that have survived to this day. Value added tax, (VAT) was introduced to replace purchase tax and selective employment tax from April 1973. A single graduated income tax with a probable basic rate of 30% and an implied maximum of 75% was to replace the existing income tax and surtax from April 1973. Corporation tax was to be reformed to remove its bias against distributed profits. Last of all he extended the flat rate of 30% capital gains tax to all gains by abolishing the separate short-term tax.

There were other details to savour. Having already reduced corporation tax the previous November, he further reduced it from 42½% to 40%, and he halved the rates of selective employment tax in advance of its abolition. By changing income tax reliefs the Chancellor reduced the maximum rate of tax on earned income from 88¾% to 75%, but, less happily, he left in place the 15% surcharge on investment income. The Budget released £546m into the economy, making an accumulated total of £951m including the November measures. Less convincingly, he built into his forecasts a financial deficit of £378m compared with a surplus of £313m achieved for the year just ending, but he forecast increased growth in the economy from 2% to 3%. Two days later, Bank rate was reduced from 7% to 6% on the traditional weekly Thursday.

In its leader on the following day, the *Financial Times* praised the Chancellor for changes that 'constitute the most comprehensive and far-reaching reform of the tax system this century'. The effect in the City was remarkable. Here was a Budget full of positive statements – higher growth was expected, penal rates of surtax were to be lowered, corporation tax was to be friendlier to dividends, and the twin weaknesses of purchase tax as a tax on goods and not services and selective employment tax as a tax on exports, were both to be resolved by VAT. It was a constructive and imaginative Budget that put to one side those cares about pay inflation and striking unions and, from this moment, everybody became a buyer. The market set forth on a major bull run that would lift the indices by 40–45% by the end of the year.

In fact, after the two expansionary budgets in November and March, the Chancellor returned for a third time on 19 July when he released a further

£400m in a mini-Budget by removing hire purchase controls, cutting purchase taxes by 20% and raising first-year allowances from 60% to 80%. He raised his forecast of growth in the economy to 4–4½%, but, more significantly, he announced an agreement with the CBI for a voluntary restraint on price increases to a limit of 5% over the next 12 months, to which the nationalised industries would also be a party. The Chancellor had earlier hinted that he would support a genuine voluntary incomes policy and, by winning support on prices, he hoped the unions would play their part with regard to pay. He was to prove sadly out of touch with reality if he had hoped to shame the National Union of Mineworkers into withdrawing their 35–47% claim, put in on behalf of 290,000 members only 2 weeks earlier.

However, his hopes were shared by a stock market now seized by bull market enthusiasm and lots of silver linings to threatening clouds. Inflation had tipped into double figures in June, but there was good news to be found. Industrial activity was buoyant, with attendant prospects for profits and dividends. Negotiations for entry into the European Economic Community had been proceeding apace for many months, and the announcement of agreed terms on 23 June was hailed as a triumph for future prosperity. The balance of payments was improving, North Sea oil was imminent, and sterling was strong. In contrast, the US economy was running into such problems that President Nixon suspended the convertibility of dollars into gold on 15 August 1971, and imposed an import surcharge of 10%. The pound was allowed to float and moved upwards against the dollar. In September, Bank rate was cut from 6% to 5% and, on 1 October, the Bank of England's proposals to introduce greater competition in the money markets came into force, by removing credit ceilings on banks and finance houses, and ending the clearing banks' cartel on interest rates.

In the Stock Exchange, the abolition of the short-term capital gains tax immediately led to higher activity, and daily bargains jumped from 7,000–8,000 to 11,000–14,000, and, although takeover activity was generally modest, the market witnessed two highly competitive bids. Grand Metropolitan Hotels and Watney together made a total of six bids for brewers Truman Hanbury Buxton. In the narrowest of final counts, Grand Metropolitan claimed 47% and Watney 46%, before the Imperial Tobacco Pension Fund switched sides to give Grand Metropolitan an edge that led to victory. Truman shares stood at 254p before the first bid of 311p, or £34m, on 1 July, and were finally bought out at 453p, or £51m, on 25 August.

At more or less the same time, two retailing giants – United Drapery Stores and Great Universal Stores – fought a battle over the tiniest of mail order companies, A. & S. Henry, which just happened to own a prime site in central Manchester. The shares stood at 56p when the bidding began on 18 August from UDS at 59p, or £6.5m. Two months later, after a total of four bids from UDS and three from GUS, the latter won the day, at 110p or £11m. It is hardly surprising that surveys have shown that shareholders in target companies do quite well out of agreed bids, better still from hostile bids, but best of all from competing bids. In these two examples, the shares were finally bought out at prices respectively 78% and 96% higher than pre-bid prices.

Discoveries of hidden value on this scale always excite stock markets, and these were the prelude to a period of bid fever that began inauspiciously in the autumn of 1971 with the failure of three major bids. Bids that fail quickly slip from memory, but looking back at what might have been, in November 1971, Ready Mixed Concrete bid £74m for Redland, and Allied Breweries bid £132m for Trust House Forte. Both failed – the latter defended in style by Sir Charles Forte, who personally spent £5m of his own money – the equivalent of £50m today – to add to the family's 23% holding in a battle fought against both the bidder and most of his fellow directors on a divided Board. He emerged triumphantly with a tactic that his son Rocco was unable to repeat 25 years later when Forte succumbed to Granada.

The third failed bid would have changed the face of the stock market of the 1980s and 1990s if it had succeeded. On 2 December 1971, Beecham, then one of the market's finest growth stocks, bid £290m for its pharmaceutical rival, Glaxo, in what would have been the biggest merger since GEC and English Electric, with a combined market capitalisation of £735m. The bid of 421p against a market price of 366p was immediately rejected. On 12 January 1972, Boots made a surprise intervention with an agreed bid of 503p, or £346m. This was quickly followed with a substantially increased offer from Beecham of 560p, or £385m, and a matching second and agreed bid from Boots, taking Glaxo shares more than 50% higher than the pre-bid price. One week later, on 3 February, the shares tumbled from 530p to 470p when both bids were referred to the Monopolies Commission with a brief to report within 5 months. Very few bids survive these references and Glaxo lived to become a major growth stock – at times, the largest quoted company on the London stock market.

With all this excitement and a booming economy, the market ended 1971 with a flourish at its high for the year, up by around 40%, with PE ratios for the market of just under 19 and the yield on the All Share Index at 3¼%. The yield gap between equities and gilts was now 5.20%, despite gilt-edged stocks standing at their best levels for 4 years. The mood of the moment was reflected in the Prime Minister's speech at the Conservative party conference, when he claimed that Britain was 'on the threshold of a period of growth and prosperity unparalleled since the war'.

In a flurry of news in the week before Christmas, the market shrugged off the decision by the National Union of Mineworkers to call a national strike from 9 January following the breakdown of talks on a 30% pay claim, and it calmly accepted an effective 8½% revaluation of sterling to a rate of $2.60 at the Smithsonian conference on 19 December, which realigned all major currencies against the dollar. The market cared more for the news from BP that the £150m development of the huge Forties Field would bring North Sea oil ashore in 1974, and looked forward to the imminent signing of the Brussels Treaty.

In his traditional New Year's Day message in the *Financial Times* for 1972, the Chancellor flaunted the drive for growth, claiming that 'No government has ever before taken so much action in the space of one year to expand demand. The economy is expanding at twice the rate of the average of the last six years'. The stock market was at its all-time high, and siren voices were few and far between. Economic policy was still driven by the influence of one of the great founding economic thinkers, Maynard Keynes, that, in times of recession, government spending should be the vehicle for raising demand. However, a new school of thought was emerging. Monetary theory, or monetarism, had first been brought to wider public attention in London by the name most often associated with it – Milton Friedman, a Chicago economist – when he was invited to give the first Harold Wincott Memorial Lecture on 16 September 1970.

The central theme of his theory was that 'There is a consistent, though not precise, relation between the rate of growth of the quantity of money and the rate of growth of national income'. He identified the correlation that an increase in money supply will, after a period of around 18 months, flow through to higher demand, push up the price of goods and services, and cause inflation. This relationship was not widely understood, because a government using fiscal measures to increase demand at the appropriate time was assumed to be pursuing sensible Keynesian policies, but, in simple terms, Friedman's theory was that the greater the increase in money supply, the greater the risk or, indeed, the inevitability of inflation.

Friedman's monetarist theory was attracting support. In January 1971, the economist Alan Walters lamented that the UK economy faced both mild recession and inflation of prices and pay, a combination that is as 'unusual as it is unwelcome'. He warned how the slow and difficult battle of dealing with inflation was not helped by pay rises injecting more spending power into the economy, with more to come from the cut in the standard rate of income tax. After the April Budget, Sam Brittan wrote a visionary article on 8 April 1971 in the *Financial Times*, entitled 'When the Cheering has to Stop', in which he described the debate in the House of Commons as a 'fine example of the national capacity for self-delusion and wishful thinking'. The Chancellor was parading a big increase in central borrowing, only to be capped by his shadow, Roy Jenkins, who demanded even more reflation. Brittan explained that money supply would rise and simply underwrite inflation, for which the Government had no policy except exhortation. Another voice endlessly challenging the Government's failure to control the money supply was that of Gordon Pepper, a partner in W. Greenwell, a leading firm of stockbrokers.

The practice of stockbrokers using economists to provide commentaries for their institutional clients blossomed in the 1980s to such an extent that Nigel Lawson would irritably refer to them as 'teenage scribblers'. However, Gordon Pepper was the doyen of economists in the gilt-edged market, and his regular economic bulletins were influential in both stock market and Treasury circles. He understood the consequences of money supply well ahead of his time.

So, there were a few voices crying in the wilderness as the Government's measures fuelled money into the economy, pay rises outstripped inflation and high levels of borrowing were deliberately planned. It was at this time that the phrase well known today, the public-sector borrowing requirement, (PSBR) first came more widely to public notice. For most of the post-war years, governments planned for budgetary surpluses, but in his March 1971 Budget, the Chancellor had planned for a financial deficit of £378m. Together with capital expenditure, this pushed the estimated PSBR from an unintended £617m, in 1970/71 to a deliberate £1,209m for 1971/72. Borrowing on this scale would, in due course, distort the demand for money, fuel inflation and exacerbate monetary pressures.

Nevertheless, this powerful bull market surged ahead in the early part of 1972, and the All Share Index hit new highs as often as not in the days of January and February. Such strength was surprising against the background of a miners' strike with political overtones and the widely televised violence of picketing. This began on 9 January and led, a month later, to the declaration of a state of emergency and power cut rotas on 9 February. Never selling on a strike has been mentioned as a stock market motto, but aggressive buying is another matter. The National Coal Board had offered a 7.9% increase in response to a 30% claim and, in rejecting this offer out of hand, the President of the NUM, Joe Gormley, borrowed the language of the seamen's union in 1966 that the strike was a challenge on behalf of the trade union movement against the Government's pay policy in the public sector. Further talks collapsed, and as the power cuts were biting and industry was facing a three-day week, the Government unilaterally announced the setting up of an inquiry under Lord Wilberforce, with a brief to report within a week.

The Government had lost control of events. Recently published unemployment figures for December had taken the number through the one million barrier for the first time since the 1930s, and now a further one million workers were laid off because of the strike. It was time again for sandwiches in Downing Street, and peace was reached with the miners at 1 am on 19 February after a five-hour session. Wilberforce concluded that the miners were justified in seeking above-average increases, and recommended proposals with an overall cost of 20%, including some rises in basic wages ranging up to 30%.

The Government was widely criticised for its handling of a strike that imposed widespread misery and served only to reveal the chilling ability of a major trade union to exert power. The rail unions representing 200,000 workers wasted no time in looking for a post-Wilberforce settlement as they rejected a 10% increase within days of the ending of the coal strike. While the public found the implications of the strike disturbing, investors responded to its inflationary consequences by buying more equities, taking the FT Index over 500 and the All Share Index into new high ground.

Although the economy was growing at 4% or more, talk persisted of the need for another reflationary budget. Contradictory messages came on one and the same day in March from the respected National Institute for Economic and Social Research, which called for tax cuts of £2,500m in the forthcoming Budget, and the Bank of England, which reported an increase in money supply of 23% over the last 3 months. Milton Friedman's monetary theories suggested that money supply rising unchecked at this rate would guarantee an inflationary spiral, yet influential demands were being made for further substantial injections into the economy.

This background helps to explain the strength of the bull market in equities in 1971 and into 1972. Investors enjoyed a two-way option. The economy would enjoy growth or it would suffer inflation, and the best way of participating in either was to buy equities. As the bull market progressed, the emphasis shifted to the latter and, for the first time in their lives, many investors in the UK were buying equities solely as a hedge against inflation. The scale of this buying is illustrated by successive record monthly peaks in turnover of equities in the early months of 1972, reaching £2,000m in May, and record monthly cash inflows into unit trusts.

However there was also another factor. With the easy availability of money, the opportunity for capital gains from rising share prices and rising property prices simply proved irresistible. Individuals from all backgrounds, in their own name or through private companies, fell prey to the temptation to borrow capital to invest in these unmissable opportunities. When borrowing is easy and prices rise ever higher, the temptation becomes impossible to resist. The more the story is publicised the greater the pressure put on those not already on board. It was this bull market more than any in the post-war era that was built on the sands of borrowed money, and when it crashed the pain was intense. When values plummet, it is the borrowers who are forced to sell, and each tranche of selling uncovers more borrowers in a vicious downward spiral, made worse by the uncanny ability of the marketplace to sniff out the forced seller and drive the hardest of bargains. At least shares were saleable, but many investors found property assets unsaleable at any price and so were forced into bankruptcy. Those banks once so eager to lend found their loan books devastated by write-offs.

However, this is dealing with the problems before they happened. Assets holding their real value may offer protection against inflation, but they are very vulnerable to the collapse of an artificial price spiral caused by excessive demand for them. The search for assets spread well beyond equities. House prices suddenly jumped by 20% in 1971, and for new houses in the South-East by 45%. Commercial property enjoyed strong demand, particularly from pension funds and life assurance companies. Works of art and antiques rose sharply in price as collectors found themselves competing with investors. After the convertibility of dollars into gold was suspended in 1971, the official price of gold was raised from $35 to $38 an ounce, but in the free market, the attraction of gold as a hedge against inflation quickly took the price to $45. Ordinary shares enjoyed the advantage of liquidity – that is, a market where large volumes could be bought and sold at will. This was their attraction to institutional investors, and, as strong as any among the sectors, were property shares which offered a double play of being an equity in a company owning property.

The call for further reflation was met in the Budget on 21 March, when the Chancellor released another £1,211m into the economy by raising income tax allowances, reducing purchase tax and making large concessions on depreciation to encourage investment. This was his fourth successive stimulus to the economy, and it enabled him to set a new growth target of 5%. Combined with higher growth was the deliberate decision to allow the PSBR to rise to £3,300m, regardless of the risk of an inflationary spiral. He also spelled out more details about the major tax reforms proposed in his Budget the year before that were due to come into effect from April 1973. VAT would provisionally be 10% subject to discretion of 2½%; the standard rate of income tax would be 30% rising to a maximum of 75%; and the new corporation tax would be the imputation tax system. This meant that where dividends are declared out of profits taxed under corporation tax rate, the shareholder is 'imputed' to have already paid the standard rate of income tax of 30%.

The Budget offered encouraging prospects for the stock market from the positive reforms of corporation tax and income tax, and from a higher growth rate for the economy. Interest was also enlivened by one of the most famous of all post-war takeover battles. Watney Mann had responded to its recent defeat by Grand Metropolitan Hotels in the battle for Truman Hanbury Buxton by taking over International Distillers and Vintners (IDV) for £153m in February 1972. However, no sooner was this acquisition completed than Grand Metropolitan proceeded to bid for Watney Mann itself, the third largest brewery company with 6,100 pubs. It was to be a bitter, hostile and expensive battle. Amid a flurry of rumours, Watney Mann shares had raced up from 160p to 212p in the few days before the first bid of 227p, or £353m, was made on 10 March 1972. The bid was raised to £401m, or 258p, on 12 May, making it the largest post-war takeover bid, only to be followed by a surprise intervention from Rank Organisation on 25 May, offering a package worth £430m.

Rank Organisation was a famous name in the post-war years, as the maker of

British films with the large gong introducing the credits, and as an owner of cinemas. In the City, and for a large number of transatlantic investors, it was better known for a remarkable, if fortuitous, decision in 1956 to purchase for £600,000 a 50% stake in Rank Xerox, a subsidiary set up by a small US company, Haloid, to market overseas its newly invented copier that a Rank Organisation executive happened to read about in a scientific magazine.

Xerox, like Hoover and Biro, became one of those market leaders in a fast-growing industry, its name becoming the generic word for the product in the marketplace. Serendipity rarely plays any part in the unsentimental world of the stock market, except perhaps in the mining sector, but it created in Rank Organisation one of the famous post-war growth stocks in the London market, attracting huge US investment interest in a technology stock that happened to own a few cinemas. Rank's intervention in this battle for Watney drew much criticism from shareholders on both sides of the Atlantic for pursuing an unnecessary and expensive diversification, and, in the face of a falling share price, the bid was dropped less than two weeks after it was made.

The Board of Watney Mann remained resolutely hostile to Grand Metropolitan Hotels, viewing Maxwell Joseph as an interloper into the cosy, paternal ranks of a traditional industry, and rejected a third and final bid notionally valued in the bid document at £435m, or 293p, made on 16 June. Grand Metropolitan, meanwhile, was steadily buying shares in the market up to the maximum of 15% allowed under the Takeover Code, and these shares proved decisive at the final count on 2 July, as acceptances amounted only to an unenthusiastic 38.5%. Together they were just enough to give narrow overall control. There were critical last-minute acceptances by Prudential for their 3½% stake, and by 2 former IDV directors for one million shares, the latter exacting revenge for the recent unwelcome bid from Watney Mann by advising others to accept an 'extremely fair offer'.

The market continued to fall and the closing value of the bid of £405m exceeded, both in actual and real terms, the previous highest bid of £310m by GEC for English Electric in 1968. Equivalent to £3,000m today, this was an expensive bid valuing Watney Mann on a prospective PE ratio of 26. It was made doubly expensive by Grand Metropolitan having to pay one premium to buy Watney Mann, and indirectly picking up the premium that Watney Mann had only recently paid to buy IDV. This is one of the landmark takeover bids of the post-war era. It was the largest successful hostile bid in its day, and remained the largest in real terms until Guinness first bid for Distillers in 1986. It highlighted Maxwell Joseph as being one of a select group of people running major corporations whose name was bigger than that of his company.

It happened at the peak of a bull market, when PE ratios were stretched to a market average of around 20, and was one of those events of grandiose proportions that sometimes signals the top of a bull market. The average yield on all equities in the All Share Index had fallen below 3% when it peaked at 228.18 on 1 May, and the FT Index peaked at 543.6 on 19 May. These peaks would not be scaled again for five or six years, and about to begin was a traumatic bear market that lasted for more than two and a half years – one that would see these two indices lose more than 70% of their value.

Chapter 19

TRAUMATIC BEAR MARKET
May 1972–January 1975

All Share Index	1 May 1972	228.18	
	13 December 1974	61.92	Down 72.9%
FT 30 Index	19 May 1972	543.6	
	6 January 1975	146.0	Down 73.1%

Although history shows the indices peaking in May 1972, most investors at the time hoped or believed for the rest of the year that they were still in a bull market. There is a natural instinct to linger longer in the good times, and this bull market had been as good a party as any could remember. Equity portfolios had just about doubled in two years. Many shares had performed much better than that, and a confiscatory short-term gains tax of up to 91¼% had been replaced by a more agreeable 30%. At moments like this, a bull market almost enters into a conspiracy with itself, fuelled by excitement and greed. Even at the end of the year, the FT Index was still standing at over 500, and the All Share Index at 218.18 was only a precise 10 points below its all-time high in May.

There were some ominous signs. Monthly Stock Exchange turnover in equities reached £2,000m for the first time in May 1972, but by the year end was averaging a much lower £1,400m. Daily bargains averaging 12,000–14,000 for the first 5 months of 1972 subsided to 8,000–10,000 through the second half of the year. Was this a pause for breath or the calm before the storm?

The uppermost concern was the control of inflation. After some alarms in 1971, when inflation reached double figures for 3 months in a row and averaged 9.4% for the year, the Government had pulled it back to 6% by the middle of 1972, but only by persuading industry to impose a voluntary 5% freeze on prices and exhorting unions to curb pay claims to 7–8%. The price freeze was now about to run out and pay guidelines had been badly breached by the miners obtaining 20% and the railwaymen 13%, both after weeks of disruptive industrial action. The situation was very nearly unplayable.

Public concern about inflation was focused more on headlines about prices and pay than on the less widely understood contribution to it from rising government expenditure and a sharply expanding money supply. In a feature article in the *Financial Times* on 20 June 1972, its former editor and distinguished economist, Lord Robbins, observed that current rates of inflation had been pre-viously experienced only in times of war, and lamented that 'preservation of the purchasing power of money has yet to acquire a major political appeal'. However, he reserved his harshest criticism for the trade unions, continuing:

> it is not to be thought of that in a civilised and non-totalitarian society the value of money is to be left for ever to the whims and fancies of monopolistic associations, asking for any increased rate of income which comes into their heads and then, in a milieu of elastic credit, forcing the dire consequences of inflation on all who are not in their fortunate position.

In the summer of 1972, the country was hit by a sterling crisis. Sterling had been weakening from $2.65 in March, and a massive flight in the few days before Bank rate was raised from 5% to 6% on 22 June suddenly took it down to $2.56. The next day, the Chancellor announced that sterling would float as a 'temporary measure'. Within days of this announcement, sterling had fallen to $2.46, amounting overall to a devaluation of 7%. The Bretton Woods and Smithsonian post-war systems of fixed currencies were collapsing and the pound would continue to float for nearly two decades until it entered the European Exchange Rate Mechanism (ERM) in 1990.

The Wilson Government had learned the hard way that foreign exchange markets coldly judge the situation as they find it – namely, that inflationary pres-sures depreciate the value of the currency. Edward Heath now joined that long list of indignant politicians who blame the speculators for their currency prob-lems. If the guardians of the currency neglect to protect it, the owners will take action to avoid losses. Speculators only make it happen more quickly.

The stock market was erratic during these difficult summer months, and shares were being out-performed by the 17% rise in the price of new houses during the first half of the year. Industrial relations were failing in the docks, where Lord Aldington and Jack Jones – drawn together from the two extremes of the social spectrum – were wrestling with the problem of overmanning caused by the spread of containerisation. Meanwhile, the miners sought to drive yet another coach and horses through any pay guidelines with a range of claims from 14–30% only a few months after the Wilberforce settlement.

The first signs of the U-turn that would prove to be so damaging to the long-term reputation of the Government appeared when the Prime Minister chaired a tripartite meeting with representatives of the CBI and TUC in Downing Street on 18 July 1972 with a view to finding a voluntary solution to the problem of inflation. This was to be the first of many meetings which although they took place in August against the background of a ten-week strike at Jaguar and a five-week dock strike that led to the declaration of another state of emergency on 3 August – the stock market responded by taking the indices to within a whisker of their May peaks. Investors wanted to believe these meetings would succeed and were partly swayed by the rustic charm of the TUC General Secretary, Vic Feather, into believing that trade union power would be exercised responsibly.

To allow a breathing space for these talks, the CBI had agreed to extend its voluntary 5% price restraint for another 3 months, up to 1 November, subject to the nationalised industries being given the necessary financial support to allow them to be included. Earlier pay awards to the miners and the railwaymen were causing financial havoc for the nationalised industries, where the normal practice of handing costs straight on to the customer was prevented by means of price restraint. A further burden on government borrowing was inevitable.

With a timetable set by the CBI's gesture, the tripartite talks began in earnest and covered many hours at 11 separate meetings in Downing Street or Chequers. As differences emerged, thinking shifted away from a voluntary to a statutory solution, and talks hardened around the conflicting wishes of the Government for some form of matching pay and price restraint, and the TUC for statutory controls on retail prices, but not on pay. The TUC also pressed for a solution on pay aimed at helping the lower paid.

Towards the end of the talks on 26 September, the Government tabled proposals for voluntary limits of £2 on weekly basic pay and £2.60 on earnings, 4–5% on prices, and a commitment to a 5% growth rate in the economy for each of the next 2 years. The TUC responded on 16 October with £3.40 on weekly pay, and statutory controls on certain prices. As the deadline approached, meetings took place nearly every day, and an exasperated Chancellor was eventually driven to complain that the 'TUC want statutory controls in every area except the one that concerns them', and he referred to their 'manifest humbug'. The talks collapsed on 2 November.

In a background article in the *Financial Times* on 4 November it was explained that 'the Prime Minister and the TUC had two completely different views of what they were doing in Downing Street. The TUC thought they were negotiating, the Prime Minister only that they were discussing an economic package'. The TUC may have convinced themselves of this because of the strength of their team, which included three of the most powerful trade union leaders – Hugh Scanlon, Jack Jones and Sidney Greene. Furthermore, the TUC attitude was coloured by bitterness about the Industrial Relations Act, which had led to the imprisonment of five dockers in July.

A few days after the collapse of the talks, the Government introduced its Counter-inflation (Temporary Provisions) Bill on 6 November. This imposed a 90-day freeze on pay, prices, rents and dividends, with a possible extension of a further 60 days. A statutory 'Phase two' Bill would follow later. This was a defining moment in the fortunes of the Heath Government, and, on that same day, in the House of Commons, no one was more scathing than Enoch Powell:

Do you not know that it is fatal for any government to seek to govern in direct opposition to the principles on which they were entrusted with the right to govern? Have you taken leave of your senses?

This was the fourth post-war freeze, following those of 1948–50, 1961–62 and 1966–67, and the seriousness of the position was underlined later in the month when official figures showed weekly wages rates to be up by 17.3% in the year to October, compared with inflation of 7.9%. The stock market remained remarkably calm, moving up on the day of its announcement and gradually picking up through to the year end.

There were some encouraging pointers for the market. Takeover activity may have been limited, notable only for Imperial Tobacco's diversification into brewing by the acquisition of Courage for £286m, and the bid by P & O for Bovis, which Inchcape failed to frustrate by bidding for P & O, but profits were running strongly, up by 17% for the year, a growth rate last seen in 1964 and 1969, with the prospect of another buoyant year ahead. Attempts were being made to deal with an explosion of money supply of such magnitude that, in August, the Bank of England had asked banks to curb lending for property and Stock Exchange speculation, areas where much of the growth in lending had taken place. In November, the Bank of England called for special deposits of 1%, followed by another 2% in December, thereby mopping up some £670m.

It was also time for change for one of the most famous ceremonies in the Stock Exchange. For the last 270 years, the government broker, who was usually the senior partner of gilt-edged stockbrokers Mullens & Co., had walked the short distance from the Bank of England to the Stock Exchange every Thursday at 11.45 am to announce Bank rate to the assembled market. There was an element of old-fashioned drama in this ceremony, although, of course, Bank rate was usually unchanged – especially when it remained at 2% for 12 years from 1939 to 1951.

However, on 9 October 1972, the Bank of England announced that Bank rate as it then stood was to end and be replaced by a Minimum Lending Rate. MLR, as it quickly became known, would be announced every Friday, and be the minimum rate at which the Bank of England was lending to the discount market. This new rate would be more sensitive to trends in the money markets, would lead rather than follow and, although trends would be influenced by the Bank of England, MLR would be automatically set by formula. It would change more frequently than did Bank rate, but with less political drama. Bank rate had become something of an anachronism, tending to lag behind the market, and its political overtones had, for example, made a much-needed increase difficult to achieve while the tripartite talks on inflation had been in progress, whereas an automatic adjustment based on a formula would have been acceptable.

Its effect was immediate. MLR started life on Friday 13 October at 7¼%, compared with the closing Bank rate of 6%. It quickly rose in two stages to 8%, partly to help the pound, which had drifted to $2.34, before being raised to 9% on 22 December – the highest official rate of interest since the outbreak of the Great War in August 1914 when Bank rate was briefly raised to 10%.

Gilt-edged yields were pushed higher and, at the year end, Consols 2½% yielded 9.85%, compared with a dividend yield of 3.15% on the All Share Index, creating a reverse yield gap of 6.70%. It has since become common practice to monitor the ratio of gilt yields divided by equity yields, and the ratio of 3:1 in the above example would today be regarded as expensive for equities. Elsewhere, equities were riding high. In New York, the Dow Jones Index closed for the first time above the 1,000 barrier at 1,003.16 on 14 November.

New Year's Day 1973 was an historic date. Britain, Denmark and Ireland joined the European Economic Community, taking the number of member states to nine. It would be idle to pretend that the Common Market had any great influence on the stock market, however. There was a belief that it would increase trading opportunities for British companies and force them to become more efficient. Investment analysts struggled to find beneficiaries, but much of the debate concerned the breaking of ties with the Commonwealth, the consequences for agriculture and fisheries, and the cost of entry. Negotiations for terms of entry had been concluded as long ago as 23 June 1971, and the Treaty of Brussels was signed on 22 January 1972.

Edward Heath's persuasive conviction about Europe disguised what may all along have been an obsession, and his extraordinary reported declaration in France in June 1971 just before negotiations were completed, 'Do we have the wisdom to achieve by construction and cooperation what Napoleon and Hitler failed to achieve by destruction and conquest?' does raise some questions about his interpretation of history. His anxiety to join the EEC may also have led to some weakness in the negotiation of terms of entry, judging by later concessions obtained by Harold Wilson and Margaret Thatcher.

Most people took the 'Common Market' to mean exactly that and thought little about the long-term implications, although the intention to achieve economic and monetary union was always clearly stated. It was reinforced in a communique from the EEC summit in October 1972, just before Britain's entry: 'The Heads of State or Government reaffirm the determination of the member-states of the enlarged European Community irreversibly to achieve economic and monetary union . . . with a view to completion not later than 31 December 1980'. What was missing from the debate at the time was the view held more widely today that *monetary* union cannot be achieved without *political* union. Any doubts were put to one side by the Prime Minister's assurance in a Parliamentary statement in May 1971 that there was 'clear evidence that joining the Community does not entail a loss of national identity or an erosion of essential national sovereignty', an assurance that today seems to have been less than frank.

Practitioners in the London Stock Exchange and the investment community felt very little in common with Europe. Their natural links were with the English-speaking Anglo-Saxon stock markets of the United States, Canada, Australia and Hong Kong. By contrast, European stock markets seemed backward, and accounting practices so impenetrable that nobody trusted European companies to disclose any worthwhile information on which to base investment decisions. As a result, British institutions were only modest investors in Europe, and European institutions took little interest in investing in Britain because of the chronic weakness of sterling. There remains to this day a considerable distance between the shareholder-dominated markets of the Anglo-Saxon financial systems and the protected and less open European systems. This is a subject for analysis in Chapter 33.

In any case, the stock market had other matters to worry about early in 1973. On 17 January, the government announced that the 90-day freeze would be extended for a further 60 days, and tabled its plans for Phase Two to follow the end of the freeze. Pay increases would be restricted to £1 a week plus 4%, with a maximum of £250 a year from 'shop floor to boardroom', and controlled by a Pay Board. Prices would be rigorously controlled by a Price Commission and dividend increases would be restricted to 5%. Phase Three was planned for the Autumn, but more unexpected was a Counter-inflation Bill to give the Government power to regulate prices, pay, dividends and rent for three years.

Enoch Powell scornfully predicted on the following day that the Government's policy was 'destined to end in ridicule and failure'. The stock market took fright at such a stranglehold on the economy so far into the future and share prices fell away sharply. After adverse weekend press comment, the FT Index fell by 3.7% on 22 January, from 488.1 to 470.1, a reaction shared by a 3.3% fall in the widely based All Share Index. This was the beginning of two years of collapsing share prices on a scale for which the investing public was totally unprepared.

The trauma may be illustrated by sharing the experience of a hypothetical private client investor with a portfolio of leading shares. He might have been a reasonably affluent individual with a mortgage that was looking smaller by the day as house prices surged ahead by 40% in 1972. He would probably have been a long-term investor with no more than a passing interest in the day-to-day events of the stock market, and a portfolio worth some £20,000 or the equivalent of £200,000, today. In the 1970s, he would probably have followed the advice of a stockbroker and owned a portfolio of equities, whereas today he would be more likely to invest in unit trusts or hand over his investments to a discretionary fund manager.

His capital could typically have been invested in equal amounts in a selection of ten leading equities. The portfolio would provide a mix of capital growth and income drawn from the major sectors of the market – capital goods, consumers, oils and financials – with Slater Walker added to give a little spice in a bull market. It would, essentially, be a 'blue chip' portfolio, yielding a shade more than the market at 3½%, and intended to avoid sleepless nights (see Table 19.1).

Table 19.1
Hypothetical portfolio of a private investor, 31 December 1972

Holdings		Price (p) at 31 December 1972	Yield (%)
880	A. P. Cement	228	4.1
1,210	Courtaulds	165	4.2
1,350	General Electric	148	2.5
550	Guest, Keen	363	3.5
1,945	Imperial Tobacco	103	5.7
695	Marks & Spencer	288	2.7
430	National Westminster	465	1.9
1,005	Prudential	199	2.9
570	Shell	350	4.2
770	Slater Walker	260	3.1

In the first week of January 1973, he receives a year-end valuation from his stockbroker, probably with comments to the effect that the market was holding up well at a difficult time, and he was invested in a good spread of long-term equities. However, 1973 was starting badly. The market was disturbed by the severity of Phase Two, especially from a Conservative government, and in the space of two weeks from mid January, the FT Index fell by 10%, from 505.5 to 455.5. It was helped on the way down by the outright rejection by the National Union of Mineworkers (NUM) of a pay offer from the National Coal Board based on the new Phase Two formula.

Tensions increased when gas workers took industrial action in February, angry to have been caught at the head of the pay queue when the barriers came down. On 14 February, the Prime Minister appealed to the nation 'your government is engaged in a fierce fight against inflation, and this is something in which we all have a part to play', but 52,000 Ford workers were not listening when they called for an unofficial strike from 1 March unless they received a better offer. In the midst of gathering anarchy, the FT Index fell on 12 consecutive days in February.

The market now paused to puzzle over a White Paper on Phase Two and a Green Paper on Phase Three of controls on incomes and prices. Ministers seemed almost to celebrate the cleverness of highly detailed and bureaucratic procedures for establishing which cost increases were allowed to be passed on in price increases. Sir Geoffrey Howe, Minister for Trade and Consumer Affairs, appeared to take pride in debate that the Government's price controls under Phase Three would be the 'most stringent ever introduced in this country'. Meanwhile, Phase Two came into effect on 1 April, with dividends limited to 5% increases, and the new Price and Pay Boards were established.

The Government claimed that there had been 'intensive consultations', but, in fact, the TUC had declined to be consulted, being more concerned with organising a national one-day protest strike on May Day, and the CBI had made little impression in putting the case for those many companies that had faithfully followed voluntary price restraint for 15 months prior to the November freeze. Not even a Labour government trying hard could have thrown itself into controls with more relish and purpose, and rarely has such virtue been made of necessity than by the Heath Government when it embraced controls.

Anthony Barber presented his third Budget on 6 March 1973. It was broadly neutral, and the three newly reformed taxes were introduced at their indicated levels of 10% for VAT, 30% for the basic rate of income tax and 40% for corporation tax. A growth target of 5% was set for the economy, but, more ominously, the PSBR was forecast at £4,423m for 1973/74 against outcomes of £2,855m for 1972/73 and £495m for 1971/72. City opinion instinctively felt there was something wrong about borrowing on this scale, and these concerns were best articulated by Gordon Pepper of stockbrokers W. Greenwell, who waged a one-man campaign against the Government's monetary policy in his regular economic bulletins.

These arguments were essentially for the professionals, but everybody was worried by the Conservative Government's sudden conversion to controls. Rather than just straying into natural Labour territory, the Government had rushed in headlong – intent on proving it could handle controls with more panache than Labour. The prospect for the investor was a commitment to controls lasting at least for three years and a political philosophy now embraced by both parties. What future was there for equity investment under never-ending controls?

Lord Robbins took up this theme in an article in the *Financial Times* on 24 April 1973, headed 'Crisis for the Free Economy?':

> There are sophisticated reasons why, as an emergency measure, some control of prices and incomes is sometimes to be recommended. But the belief that price and income controls by themselves can be effective in solving the fundamental problem, or that they are likely to endure without either erosion or the imposition of even more far-reaching controls, is founded on delusion, and very dangerous delusion at that.

These words of a distinguished economist exactly paralleled the earlier words of Enoch Powell.

Wise words are often spoken before the audience is ready to hear them, and the market preferred to take comfort from continuing rapid growth in the economy, rising company profits of 20% or so and lower interest rates as MLR drifted down from 9% to 7½%. Perhaps owing more to inertia than belief, share prices recovered in time for the opening by the Stock Exchange on 11 June 1973 of its new spacious and airy trading floor with its smart hexagonal jobbers' pitches showing off an uneasy combination of new technology and old-fashioned boards annotated with red and blue coloured pencils.

Any celebration of the first day of trading was rather spoiled by a 2% fall in the FT Index and, two days later, the worst ever recorded trade deficit for any month of £290m for May was published. Over the next six weeks, the FT Index fell by 11% to under 430, partly undermined by the decision of the NUM at its annual conference to ignore the pay formula of £2.29 a week and put in a claim for between £8.20 and £12.70. Investors were now alarmed by the display of power by the miners, and their ill-concealed intent to defy the legislation of the land.

Another concern was a question mark hanging over Slater Walker – the name that epitomised the bull markets of both 1968/69 and 1970/72. Its success as a growth stock prompted the Stock Exchange listing of many imitators in the late 1960s and early 1970s, all given warm welcomes by commentators and investors alike. However, doubts were emerging about the quality of the earnings being reported by these providers of specialist banking services.

There was a wider aspect to this question. Earnings and PE ratios had come to exercise a dominant influence over the valuation of shares, and comparisons would be drawn between a PE ratio of 15.1 or 15.6 with a precision that was absurd when compared with the imprecision of published earnings – or the 'E' that forms the basis of the PE ratio. The calculation of earnings was subject to a range of accounting practices available to less scrupulous companies.

Quality of earnings is a subjective concept. In setting PE ratios for individual companies, the market is fairly adept in deliberately or subconsciously allowing for uncertainties about the consistency, credibility or comparability of published earnings. There are always some companies that use accounting practices to 'massage' earnings to make them look better than they really are, and, once identified, earnings from these companies will be given a lower PE ratio to reflect their poor quality. The two most common methods of massaging earnings are to hide away in the balance sheet negative items that properly belong in the profit and loss account or transfer into the profit and loss account positive items that properly belong in the balance sheet.

Shifting costs into the balance sheet is known as 'capitalising', and examples include research and development costs, interest charges and exchange losses on transactions. The balance sheet item most commonly shifted to the profit and loss account is a capital profit made on the sale of assets or businesses. Many of the financial failures of the last 25 years can be traced back to an accumulation of accounting abuse in one or both of these areas. With earnings per share still a relatively new concept in the early 1970s, companies were more easily able to hide behind a single profit figure without any explanation, whereas today the demands of disclosure require notes to the accounts to explain and quantify unusual items, and 'creative accounting' is a widely analysed subject.

In the case of Slater Walker and the new banking services companies, later to be known dismissively as 'secondary banks', so little information was disclosed that nobody knew how profits were generated. The biggest weakness was the unknown extent to which profits were derived from capital gains on stock market or property transactions.

Short-term capital gains on investments are elusive, unpredictable and have no consistency. They fall into a grey area between capital and income, belonging in the balance sheet but more valuable in the profit and loss account. If a company can demonstrate a long-term record of the regular disposal of assets for capital gain – as perhaps in the case of a mature property company, retailer or life assurance company with long-term invested funds – there is a possible argument for their inclusion in the calculation of earnings per share. But simply to apply a PE ratio of 20, or whatever, to capital gains on investments in the stock market is grossly misleading. In reality, they merit a PE ratio of little more than 1, because that is the amount they add to the asset value.

When a bull market is running fast, people are less inclined to listen to quibbles about accounting niceties, and so it was that the likes of London and County Securities, Dalton Barton and Keyser Ullmann were able to prosper in their early years. Another member of this band of financial cavaliers, Triumph Investment Trust, took creative accounting one step further by including 'unrealised' capital gains in its profits and earnings per share. The accounts of Slater Walker were just as difficult to fathom, but fewer questions were asked because Jim Slater's personal reputation, although beginning to wobble, still stood ahead of those of his imitators.

It was therefore a matter of general surprise and some mystery when an agreed merger was announced on 26 April 1973 between Slater Walker and the merchant bank Hill Samuel. The merger was to be implemented by the issue of shares in Slater Walker, having twice the market capitalisation of Hill Samuel, but the name of the merged group would be Hill Samuel, and Sir Kenneth Keith would be Chairman.

Two months later in a joint statement on 19 June, the merger was abruptly called off after discussions had 'revealed fundamental differences of work-style and personalities'. During those two months, so many questions had been asked about the rationale of the merger that Slater Walker shares had fallen from 240p to 184p, and Hill Samuel's from 170p to 144p. Hill Samuel was a merchant bank with clients and a continuing business for the future, but Slater Walker was a predator with a reputation for asset-stripping and financial manipulation, and its future in a bear market was much less certain. It had no clients in a conventional sense, although it owned stakes in many of its target companies.

Slater had created one of those umbrella structures that are so confusing to investors because of his penchant for spawning off quoted subsidiaries. One such subsidiary was the Slater Walker Dual Trust, a repository for parcelling together a collection of holdings in satellite investments, launched early in 1972. Its disparaging nickname in the market of the 'Dustbin Trust' was damaging to his slipping reputation, and the failure to merge with Hill Samuel brought these concerns to the surface, leaving Slater Walker badly wounded.

Bull markets are sometimes remembered by the fame or notoriety of personalities who caught the headlines at the time. Jim Slater was a one-time hero now heading for bankruptcy. There were other prominent names in 1973. Lonrho – a conglomerate with mining interests in many parts of Africa – was a company personified by its charismatic Chairman, Tiny Rowland, a wartime immigrant of German descent. He owned a large stake, in the company, ran it with an iron fist and, unusually for a company of its size, was supported by small private shareholders rather than institutions. Rowland ran it as a personal fiefdom with scant regard for what anybody thought, least of all his fellow directors. Matters came to a head in May 1973 when eight directors took action in the High Court to have Rowland removed as Chief Executive, but the judge ruled that this was a matter for the Board to resolve with its shareholders.

In the course of this action, it emerged that Rowland had been living for many years in a £350,000 mansion in Bourne End, bought and owned by Lonrho, which he had personally undertaken to purchase, but apparently had not. Furthermore, some salaries were being paid to directors into tax havens such as the Cayman Islands, including, in particular, to Duncan Sandys, a recent Conservative cabinet minister, who had joined Lonrho as prospective Non-executive Chairman. These events led to a question in the House of Commons and on 15 May, Edward Heath made one of his best-remembered remarks, that the Lonrho row had disclosed an 'unpleasant and unacceptable face of capitalism'.

The fine company house and bank accounts in the Cayman Islands were regarded, according to taste, as examples of either corporate benefits or corporate greed. However, public companies are not usually in the business of buying mansions for the use of the chairman and chief executive, and directors of public companies are not expected to have their salaries paid into offshore tax havens. Rowland was quite unabashed as he romped home at the shareholders' meeting with a massive majority in his favour for continuing as the Chief Executive, and the eight dissenting directors were unceremoniously voted out of office.

Another controversy concerned a former Lord Mayor of the City of London – Sir Denys Lowson, a long-standing figure in the field of investment trusts and unit trusts. His reputation already preceded him in some quarters of the City when it was learned in July 1973 that he had made a personal profit of £5m from the purchase and sale of 80% of the shares in the National Group of Unit Trusts. He personally purchased them from 11 different investment trusts and companies within his own empire at a price of 62.5p in July 1972, and sold them four months later to Triumph Investment Trust at a price nearly 14 times higher, at £8.67 per share.

Following the publication of a scoop about the details of this transaction in the *Investors Chronicle*, Sir Denys Lowson issued a statement on 11 July 1973 that 'Although I considered the terms of the acquisition to be fair and reasonable, I have now come to the conclusion that it would be wrong for me to retain the benefits of the sale and that it would be in accordance with the best tradition of the City of London, which I have served for some 45 years, for me to restore the position'. He would therefore give up £5m of profit on the transaction. Any connection between Lowson and 'best City traditions' elicited many a wry smile in the City, and a Department of Trade investigation was promptly announced.

His statement did not stand up well in the light of the report published a year later in July 1974, when the Inspectors accused Lowson of 'grave mismanagement' of the companies involved. He had ignored legal advice questioning the purchase, he did not obtain a proper valuation of the shares and to push the acquisition through 11 different companies required a calculated determination 'to obtain a very substantial gain for himself and his family'. Unit trust groups were typically valued at around 4% of funds under management in 1972, or around £5m for the £130m of funds under management in the National Group. His purchase of 80% of the shares for £427,000 was grotesque.

By way of a postscript to the Lowson revelation, Rowntree announced on the following day that it had incurred losses on cocoa trading of £20m, and although there was no suggestion of fraud or personal gain, two senior cocoa buyers had been suspended. Rowntree shares fell by 15% from 220p to 186p. Between January and July, the price of cocoa had soared from £300 to £600 a ton, and it later transpired that, having sold short, the two buyers had attempted to trade out of trouble by doubling up. Arguing with commodity prices in a bull market is positively dangerous.

It was in July 1973 that a famous name came to the stock market, when shares in J. Sainsbury were offered for sale at a price that valued the company at £117m, making it the biggest ever new issue. At this price, the family holdings were worth £85m – the prelude to the legendary fortunes these would later become when Sainsbury joined Glaxo and Hanson Trust as one of the great growth stocks of the 1980s.

The previous biggest new issue had been that of another famous family firm, Pilkington Brothers, in November 1970, in an offer for sale that valued the company at £96m. Pilkingtons has retained a remarkable world dominance in glassmaking and has been one of Britain's most famous manufacturing companies, but operating in a more competitive marketplace than J. Sainsbury, which has focused entirely on food retailing in the UK, the shares have not fared nearly as well. Pilkington was brought to the market by Schroder Wagg with London stockbrokers Cazenove and Rowe & Pitman. The later issue of Sainsbury was handled by S. G. Warburg and Rowe & Pitman.

Comparing these two issues is an example of the deception of inflation. Sainsbury was pronounced to be the biggest ever new issue at the time, valued at £117m, compared with Pilkington three years earlier at £96m. However, in real terms, the Pilkington issue was the larger of the two, after allowing for inflation of 26% between the launching of the two issues.

After nervous weeks in the market in June and July 1973, MLR was increased in successive weeks from 7½% to 9%, and from 9% to a record 11½% on 27 July. Sterling was suffering from another loss of nerve, and paralysis spread over the Stock Exchange where average daily bargains were now running at 7,000, roughly half the levels of the beginning of the year. The Government was struggling to gain agreement for Phase Three of its incomes policy and wasted a fruitless day of negotiations in August at Chequers with the members of the TUC whose interest lay in a return to free collective pay bargaining, but with strict restraint on prices and a sustained commitment to economic growth. Sterling wobbled again, despite high interest rates, and the stock market lost its nerve for the third time in the year. Between June and September, sterling suffered a devaluation of 7%.

The Government eventually produced its Phase Three proposals on 8 October 1973. Controls on pay were to be more flexible, with weekly increases of £2.25, or 7%, to a maximum of £400 a year, but controls on prices and profit margins remained strict. A threshold agreement would allow an extra 40p a week for every 1% increase in inflation over 7%, a step that would later cause havoc. The limit of 5% on dividend increases remained and business rents continued to be frozen. The stock market had picked up a little from its September low and acquiesced at these levels.

Since its election three years earlier, the Government had continuously battled against powerful trade unions and the persistent pressures of inflation. It was now about to be attacked on a third front. On 6 October, two days before the publication of the Phase Three proposals, Egypt invaded Israel and a brief war was fought to a standstill on 16 October. At this point, the Arab states joined forces to declare economic war on the developed world by doubling the price of oil from an average of $2 a barrel to $4. Oil amounted to 10% of Britain's imports and the immediate effect would be to add some £500m to the import bill. The Arab states agreed among themselves to cut back production by a minimum of 5%, and, while few doubted their ability to impose these higher prices because they controlled 60% of the world's oil exports, there remained an element of disbelief that it would actually happen. The stock market remained phlegmatic, with shares even moving *up* over the following three weeks, as though expecting something to turn up.

This relaxed veneer cracked only after weekend reflection on the rejection by the NUM of the Coal Board's pay offer on Thursday 8 November, and notice was given of an immediate overtime ban. This would put more pressure on electricity supplies, which were already adversely affected by a ban on standby duties by power engineers over the previous two weeks. On Friday 9 November, Wall Street suffered one of its biggest ever one-day falls as a belated reaction to the oil shock. Many investors in London must have fallen into the trap when their instincts told them that all was not well, but they had the weekend to think it over. By the time they thought it over and read the weekend press along with everybody else, they were wishing they had sold at those attractive closing prices that would have vanished out of sight on the Monday morning.

And so it proved to be. The FT Index fell by nearly 2% on Monday, from 430.3 to 422.9, followed by a 4% fall on Tuesday 13 November to 405.5. The latter fall was exacerbated by all sorts of bad news on the same day. The declaration of a national state of emergency following a warning that industrial action by the NUM would threaten coal supplies within seven to ten days; an immediate prohibition on floodlighting and display advertising; restrictions on space heating in public offices; a huge trade deficit of £298m for October; and a crisis increase in MLR from 11¼% to 13%. This was a demoralising combination for share prices – a dispute that threatened to overwhelm the government; a serious trade deficit even before a doubling of the oil price; and interest rates suddenly raised to their highest ever level. Gilt-edged stocks suffered falls of between 2 and 4 points, and War Loan fell to its lowest ever price of 29¼.

This was the beginning of one of the fastest and steepest falls ever experienced in the stock market. The FT Index fell by 29% from 430.3 on 9 November to 305.9 exactly 5 weeks later on 14 December, and the All Share Index fell by 28% over the same period, from 185.89 to 134.36. Both indices fell on 21 out of 25 business days and by the equivalent of some 1,800 points in the FTSE 100 today.

The combination of events on 13 November may have triggered the fall, but the news then worsened by the day. The Arab oil producers stood firm, with planned production cuts of as much as 25% and spot prices at oil auctions soared way above the doubled price of $4 a barrel. Oil deliveries at home were cut by 10%, petrol coupons were issued and a speed limit of 50 mph. was introduced. Heating and lighting restrictions were extended to commercial offices.

Meanwhile, industrial action by the coalminers gradually assumed the political overtones of a challenge to the Government by holding the nation to ransom. The Prime Minister urged them to settle under Phase Three, warned that they were confronting the elected representatives of the people and, to no avail, asked their leaders to hold a pit ballot after a meeting in Number 10. The power engineers were still banning standby duties and, as if these problems were not enough, pay talks broke down with ASLEF, the train drivers' union, which announced an overtime ban and no Sunday working from 11 December.

In the second week of December, an already demoralised market faced the prospect of cuts in the supply of coal, petrol and electricity, and of disruption on the railways. This impasse prompted a fall of 12% in the fifth and final week of this bear market within a bear market. Far more serious was the gradual strangulation of business activity, a matter of greater concern to industry than to a public still not made fully aware of the seriousness of the situation by a government veering between panic measures and complacent exhortation. By now, there was a fatal air of desperation and paralysis hanging over the government, and investors concluded that, in times like these, cash is best.

The culmination of these five weeks was a broadcast to the nation by the Prime Minister on the evening of 13 December, and the announcement of the three-day week starting in the new year with a target of reducing electricity demand by 20%. Furthermore, there was to be a mini-Budget on 17 December. The three-day week came as a shock to the public, but it offered no solution for ending a battle between the Government and the miners that neither side was prepared to lose. On the day following the broadcast, the FT Index fell 3% and the All Share Index fell 5.4%.

The Chancellor prefaced the mini-Budget on 17 December 1973 with the sombre warning that the country faces 'our gravest situation since the end of the war', but his measures hardly seemed to match the gravity of the situation. He took £1,200m out of the economy in the form of public expenditure cuts, which mostly affected the nationalised industries and roads. Hire purchase controls were reimposed to require 33% deposits and maximum repayment over 2 years. He imposed a 10% surcharge on surtax incurred in the year to April 1973, the last year before its abolition.

Last, the Chancellor took action against property developers who were disliked by this government because of their exploitation of sharply rising property values. Newly built offices were deliberately being kept empty to curb supply and exacerbate a shortage that was forcing rents ever higher. The Government had already imposed a freeze on business rents, and, in this Budget, now proposed to tax development gains under corporation tax for companies and under income tax for individuals. Within three days, the property sector of the All Share Index had fallen by 10%, in contrast to the market as a whole, which recovered by nearly 5% from its recent low.

In fact, the market recovered some lost ground in the last few days of the year. The three-day week came as unexpectedly to the TUC as it did to everybody else, and its response was to propose that the miners be considered as a special case outside Phase Three. This led to a belief that a solution was possible and the market ended the year strongly with the FT Index at 344.0.

The battle with the miners had taken precedence over all other events for the last two months and had pushed into the background the seriousness of the doubling of the price of oil for the economies of all developed countries. On Christmas eve, the Arab countries announced that oil prices were to be doubled for a second time from January 1 1974. This would add another £700m to UK imports and an estimated $25,000m to the world's fuel bills. The stock market barely blinked and between Christmas and New Year went up by 7–8%.

Amid these events, little notice was taken of the collapse of two of the banking services groups or 'secondary banks'. Their depositors were rescued by a 'lifeboat' operation set up by the Bank of England in cooperation with the clearing banks. On 29 November 1973, the shares of London and County Securities – once at an all-time high of 305p – halved in price to 60p, and were suspended the following day at 40p, when it was announced that emergency rescue talks were under way. On 20 December, Cedar Holdings followed suit, the shares suspended at 12p against a peak of 90p.

Although the market ended the year on a slightly more optimistic note, shares had lost roughly a third of their value over 12 months. The hypothetical long-term private investor with his £20,000 portfolio of leaders will have noted the advice of his stockbroker along the lines that it had been an 'annus horribilis' for shares, but at these levels he could hope for some gradual recovery, and it was probably too late to sell Slater Walker. His portfolio was now valued at £13,400.

The portfolio would be unlikely to have included any gold shares. Their strength had been a rare redeeming feature of 1973 when the FT Gold Mines Index had more than doubled, and they were to feature strongly again in the first few weeks of 1974. In the United States, the right to convert dollars into gold at $35 an ounce had been abandoned for individuals in 1968 and for central banks in 1971, so creating a free market in gold. The price initially responded by rising to $45, but, after successive 10% devaluations of the dollar in December 1971 and February 1973, it had more than doubled to around $70, before peaking at $126 in July 1973.

The strength of the price of gold was partly a correction for the devaluation of the dollar, but it was becoming an attractive refuge from disturbing signs of inflation all around the world. The doubling of the price of oil – or 'black gold' as it became known – after the Arab-Israeli war in October 1973, gave a new impetus to the price of gold and to gold shares. They had already enjoyed a bull market through 1973, but the second rise in the oil price just before Christmas led them to move dramatically ahead in the New Year.

The FT Gold Mines Index stood at 207.1 on 2 January 1974. In the space of 5 weeks it rose by 60% to 330.4, while the price of gold rose from $112 to $144 over the same period. This Index was, in effect, an index of the shares of South African gold mines, and its rise was driven by a worldwide investment demand. The oil crisis affected all developed economies alike, and fears were gathering of a new economic phenomenon of 'stagflation' – an ugly word describing the unwelcome combination of stagnation and inflation. There was a spontaneous reaction to the oil crisis across world markets – a common enough feature today, when every fund manager and dealer in every country has the same Reuter's terminal, but a rarer event in the 1970s, when information was absorbed at different speeds in different places.

The stock market in London held steady in early January, although the miners' strike was becoming ever more entrenched. Under the leadership of its new General Secretary, Len Murray, the TUC offered a lifeline to the Government by proposing that the miners should be regarded as an 'exceptional case', which the TUC itself would recognise on behalf of its members. The Chancellor dismissed the proposal out of hand, but, on the following day, the Prime Minister agreed to convene talks on this proposal. These were held on 14 January, but they ended in deadlock and collapsed after a second meeting on 21 January. Genuine dismay was etched on those lugubrious features of Len Murray, later to become so familiar to the country, when he said 'I am very sorry to report that the government has turned down our proposal'.

The stock market was very sorry as well, and the failure of the talks prompted yet another of those drastic sell-offs that were becoming a feature of this bear market. In 5 days, the FT Index fell 10% from 333.2 to 301.7 on 28 January – a scale better appreciated today by calling it 600 points on the FTSE Index. The miners reacted to the failure of the talks by calling for a strike ballot after 11 weeks of industrial action.

Idle speculation over Christmas about a general election now turned into a flurry of rumours. Further talks with the TUC made no progress and, on 5 February, the NUM called a full strike to start five days later. This decision prompted a fall in the FT Index to below 300, a level first reached more than 14 years earlier in October 1959 in the 'never had it so good' days of Harold Macmillan. On 7 February, the Prime Minister called a general election for 28 February, the earliest date possible after a minimum of a three-week campaign.

Opinion polls were encouraging for the Conservatives over Labour throughout the campaign, but assessment of the result was complicated by high Liberal support. Anticipating a Conservative victory, the stock market recovered by some 6–7% during the campaign, but the electorate was confused by the ambiguity of the question posed by Edward Heath, 'Who rules Britain?' The dusty answer he received from the saloon bars was 'Not you', while the middle classes took the easy way out and voted Liberal.

The result was a 'hung' Parliament, with 301 Labour seats, 296 Conservatives, 14 Liberals and 23 others. The stock market opened in disarray on the Friday morning and, at 9.30 am, the FT Index had tumbled 10%, from 337.8 to 305.0, before closing at 313.8. This was a fall of 7.1% on the day, fully matched by a fall of 7.3% in the All Share Index, and the politically sensitive property sector was down by 16%. Despondent investors had nowhere to turn.

In fact, the Conservatives polled more votes than Labour, and this may have encouraged Edward Heath to seek, in vain, a coalition with the Liberals. He delayed his resignation before bowing to the inevitable, and Harold Wilson returned to Downing Street on the Monday evening to lead his minority Government with an indication of Liberal support.

His choice of ministers was not welcomed in the City. The Chancellor was Denis Healey, who had recently repeated Tony Crosland's famous comment about squeezing the wealthy until 'the pips squeak' and had predicted his tax policies would provoke 'howls of anguish' from the better off. The appointment of two left wingers – Michael Foot and Anthony Wedgwood Benn (later known as Tony Benn) – as Ministers of Employment and Industry respectively, was received with foreboding, as these areas straddled the boundaries between the public and private sectors.

Fears about the neutrality of the patrolling of these boundaries were confirmed within 48 hours of taking office when the National Coal Board put £100m on the table against the £43m previously offered under Phase Three, in order to settle the miners' dispute. The FT Index promptly fell by 20 points in 2 days as the inflationary consequences of this settlement were digested, and it fell below 300 again after the highest ever post-war rate of annual inflation was reported for the year to February at 13.2%, thus triggering threshold payments to millions of workers.

Denis Healey produced his first Budget on 26 March 1974, and he was as good as his word on personal taxes. The standard rate was raised from 30% to 33%, and the top rate from 75% to 83%. The threshold for the 15% surcharge on investment income was reduced from £2,000 to £1,000, and the marginal top rate of tax was taken to the notorious level of 98% on investment income. He promised a Green Paper on a wealth tax, and abolished tax relief on interest payments, except on mortgages up to £25,000. He increased corporation tax from 50% to 52% and doubled stamp duty on share purchases from 1% to 2%.

These tax measures raised £1,400m, and he raised a further £1,200m by permitting price increases in the nationalised industries of 48% for coal, 30% for electricity, and 25% for steel. His target was to reduce the PSBR from a projected £3,400m to £2,700m.

The tax changes were unwelcome but not unexpected. For many in the Labour party, they were the first step on the road to that long-standing pledge of an 'irreversible transfer of wealth and power to working people and their families'. The bigger issue waiting for the Budget was how the Labour Government would deal with its inherited controls over pay, prices and dividends. Phase Three was to run its course, but reforms were planned to bring prices firmly under the control of a new Secretary of State for Prices and Consumer Protection, Shirley Williams, who could limit the frequency of price rises by manufacturers and empower the Price Commission to order reductions in profit margins. In return for regular consultation, strict controls over prices and a promise to repeal the Industrial Relations Act, the TUC agreed to initiate measures on pay to stem inflation and honour the unwritten side of a 'social contract' with the Government, thus marking the return of the fictional 'Solomon Binding'.

The immediate response of the stock market was another despairing 20-point fall in two days to a new low of 272.5, where average yields now stood at around 7% and PE ratios of 8, a far cry from the 3% and 20 enjoyed at the peak of the market in 1972. There was deep cynicism about the ability of the TUC to deliver meaningful controls over pay, but two other factors were emerging as acute causes for concern.

These were the state of corporate liquidity and the effect of inflation on profits. The first stemmed from the different treatment of prices and costs – the two vital components of profits. Restraint on prices of one kind or another had been in force for nearly three years, since July 1971, when the CBI initiated a voluntary 5% limit on price increases. This lasted for 15 months and was followed by a freeze for 5 months to April 1973. Thereafter, Phases Two and Three weighed heavily on prices and, as a result, price increases lagged well behind inflation of 31% recorded since July 1971. Now there was the prospect of never-ending price controls under a Labour Government. These controls were already putting pressure on corporate profits, which, by any measure, were touching a post-war low. Datastream figures show that aggregate profits as a percentage of GDP fell to some 8–9% in 1974, well below existing long-term trends of some 13–14%, and very different from the 18–20% levels later to be witnessed at times in the 1980s and 1990s.

While prices were held back, costs had been spiralling out of control at a faster rate than inflation – commodity and raw material prices had recently shot up after the oil price rise; the weakness of sterling over the period had exacerbated the cost of imported materials; financing costs had roughly doubled as interest rates moved up from 6% to 12%; and controls had failed to hold pay rates below inflation. The last was the most insidious factor of all because large segments of the population were well enough protected from inflation to be indifferent to its malign effects elsewhere.

Shareholders were also shielded from its worst effects by the significant profits earned by foreign subsidiaries and by exports, both of which benefited from the weakness of sterling when converted into sterling in company accounts. Overseas profits could often be a third to half of the total, but are of little help to liquidity in the UK if they largely remain in the country of origin for further investment or because of practical difficulties of remitting them home. In simple terms, many apparently profitable companies were fast running out of cash in the UK, and some were facing bankruptcy. The latest budget had added more pressure by raising corporation tax, and by requiring the earlier payment of advanced corporation tax on dividends. Denis Healey acknowledged in his auto-biography that this was a practical problem he unwittingly made worse.

The second factor was the effect of double-digit inflation on the validity of profits. Companies use conventional historic cost accounts to calculate profit and are required so to do by the Inland Revenue as the basis for charging cor-poration tax.

Inflation was causing particular problems for depreciation and stocks. Using a simple example, a company may invest £100,000 in a machine and write off this asset over its life of 5 years by charging depreciation of £20,000 against profits before tax each year. This generates a cash sum for the purchase of a new machine, but if inflation has pushed up the cost of the new machine from £100,000 to £150,000, then depreciation of the historic cost will have been inadequate to fund the new machine. A small number of capital-intensive com-panies, including Pilkington and Guest, Keen, dealt with this problem by charging extra depreciation in the profit and loss account to fund the replace-ment cost of their assets, but without receiving tax relief and at the expense of earnings per share. However, investment analysis was sophisticated enough to allow for this.

Stocks are the products made by a company for known or possible future sales, and profit is earned from the difference between, for illustration, the cost of a stock item of £100 and its sale price of £130. If these are constant, then the proceeds of the sale will cover the cost of replacing the stock at £100 and leave a clear profit of £30. However, if inflation has pushed up the cost of replacing the same item of stock to £110, then the real profit is only £20. Under historic cost accounting, the profit is £30, whatever the cost of replacing stock. A par-ticularly extreme and misleading example was the declaration of spectacular profits from British Petroleum in June. Oil prices had doubled and doubled again, so stock costing £100 might sell for £200 at a profit of £100, but replac-ing the same stock now cost £400.

At the time of the Budget in March 1974, inflation in the UK was firmly into double figures, at 14%, and rising. Companies were paying tax on illusory prof-its, much of which were required to finance replacement stocks and to fund the shortfall of depreciation when replacing assets. This was becoming a matter for serious debate in the accounting profession, the academic world and within the forum of the Society of Investment Analysts on behalf of two of the most impor-tant users of accounts – investment analysts and fund managers. A war of words was about to take place between two schools of thought – those favouring replace-ment cost accounts, which specifically allows for the depreciation and stock problems described above, and those favouring current purchasing power accounts, which adjust relevant items by reference to the RPI. The battle was never convincingly won by either side, and historic cost accounts survive to this day.

After the March Budget, the stock market quietened down in a mood of forlorn acceptance of seemingly insoluble problems. There were occasional fretful rallies, but turnover dwindled away and revenues fell below the levels required to cover the costs of the typical firm of stockbrokers, all of whom were shedding staff. There never seemed to be any good news, only negative moments, such as a record monthly £480m trade deficit or Jim Slater announcing 'cash is best' or Alan Clements of ICI warning of hyper-inflation or slump if inflation reaches 15%, or Tony Benn savouring opportunities for the Government to step in to save capitalism from itself or the sudden collapse of Herstatt Bank in Cologne, each of which, in turn, prompted uneasy selling and another ten points off the Index.

A depressing landmark was reached on 19 June 1974, when the 53% fall from their peaks of both the FT Index and the All Share Index exceeded the fall experienced in London during the crash and slump of 1929–32. Yet pessimism still prevailed so widely that nobody dared call a buying opportunity. The outlook remained deeply gloomy. The world economy was heading for recession and still remained fearful of accelerating inflation. In Britain, there was a minority Government hostile to the private sector, unaware or uncaring of the crises faced by many companies, and quite indifferent to the massive loss of institutional and personal wealth suffered in the stock market crash.

Matters came to a head again in July. Inflation for the year to June rose to another post-war high of 16½%, but pay rates were also up by a matching 16.2%, underwritten by the threshold provisions of Phase Three, which triggered a 3% increase for the month of June alone. Phase Three was due to expire at the end of July, to be succeeded by the voluntary pay policy of the Social Contract devised by the TUC.

In advance of this, the Chancellor announced on 22 July a small package of measures designed to reduce the RPI by 1½%, including a cut in VAT from 10% to 8%. He also raised the limit on dividend increases from 5% to 12½%, but a pessimistic market was more concerned about the addition of another £750m to the PSBR. The Chancellor was subscribing to the policy advised by the International Monetary Fund that developed countries should absorb the impact of higher oil prices by borrowing rather than inducing deflation, but this was a politically convenient, if unconvincing, method of dealing with an irreversible change in the price of oil.

The responsibility for controlling pay and setting guidelines was now handed to the TUC, but, in reality, it lacked the power and failed to assume responsibility. The miners, railwaymen and nurses had all received 'special case' awards under Phase Three and, after controls lasting for nearly two years, a pay explosion was looming in both the private and the public sectors. The TUC indicated that 16–20% increases would be needed in the next pay round if only to ensure that 'real incomes are maintained', brushing aside any responsibility for inflation in a year's time. Denis Healey has since bluntly written that 'the unions defaulted on their part of the contract'. (*The Time of My Life*, Michael Joseph, 1989). The stock market had believed little else from the start, and yet another sell-off followed the Chancellor's July package, taking the FT Index down by 25% in 4 weeks from 264.4 on 23 July to 199.8 on 19 August, breaking down another psychological support barrier of 200, and matched by a 23% fall in the All Share Index from 109.37 to 84.47.

This latest fall was accentuated by another daunting monthly deficit in the balance of payments, and two unwelcome policy statements from the Government. Despite being in a minority the Government was not to be deterred from its commitment to nationalisation, and detailed plans to nationalise 26 shipbuilding and ship-repairing companies were published on 31 July. Two weeks later, Tony Benn published a White Paper entitled 'The regeneration of British Industry', in which he proposed the creation of a National Enterprise Board and the securing of planning agreements with major companies in key sectors. The latter brought back unwelcome memories of his campaign in the Labour party in 1973 to take controlling interests in 25 leading manufacturing companies.

The FT Index had now fallen below 200, a level first reached 19 years before in June 1955. Two months earlier, the extent of the bear market had exceeded that of 1929–32, and when the FT Index fell to 199.8 it marked the worst ever bear market recorded in London, exceeding the 61% fall between 1936 and 1940, the low point for Britain in World War II.

The fall below 200 had a devastating psychological effect, and a paralysing pessimism took hold of a significant number of stock market practitioners, fund managers and company directors. Some genuinely believed that the capitalist system faced collapse. Stockbrokers had been cutting costs to the bone and reducing staff for months on end, but with revenues still well below expenses, many partners began to contemplate the horror of unlimited liability and its stripping of their houses and furniture. Fund managers accustomed to big and growing surpluses in the market value of their investments now looked in shock as the capital profits accumulated on investments over a generation were wiped out. Alarming shortfalls were appearing in assets held against liabilities to guarantee life policies and pensions. Institutions dared not invest ever-larger cash balances for fear of further losses. Companies were running out of cash and forced to borrow at record rates of interest. Many feared bankruptcy.

This state of demoralised inertia was so widespread that shares standing well under asset value failed to attract takeover bids. The absence of bids was a feature of this bear market. Only two years earlier, in 1972, takeover activity had reached record levels, approaching £2,500m, but, towards the end of that year, Sir Geoffrey Howe announced, in marginally disapproving terms, that the Government planned to tighten up its policing of mergers by making greater use of the Monopolies Commission and giving special scrutiny to mergers of a conglomerate or asset-stripping nature.

This put a dampener on takeover activity in 1973, when several large bids either failed or were referred to the Monopolies Commission, and in 1974 only one company of any note was subject to a bid. Commercial Union offered £76m for St Martin's Property on 12 August, at 115p per share compared with a market price of 80p. However, Kuwait Investment Office won the day on 6 September with a bid of £91m, or 140p, and it later became apparent that the Commercial Union bid had been a disguised form of rights issue because of an urgent need to strengthen its balance sheet after depletion from falling stock prices.

This intervention from Kuwait was an early reminder of the massive transfer of resources taking place from the oil-consuming countries to the oil producers, and it brought to wider notice the existence of the Kuwait Investment Office as a portfolio investor. Under the management of Bruce Dawson, this highly secretive investor was well known only to those few stockbrokers fortunate to deal for them as aggressive buyers of equities throughout this bear market. It was later believed to be second in size in the UK only to the Prudential as an investing institution as it pursued its government's policy of investing oil revenues in assets to provide for the day the oil would run out. In the event, its assets were depleted to finance the expulsion of Iraq after its invasion of Kuwait in 1990.

In the midst of these August days of unrelieved gloom, an alternative view was put by the famous, now veteran, investor, Lewis Whyte, described in an earlier chapter as one of the investment gurus who founded the cult of the equity in the 1950s. He wrote a visionary article in *The Daily Telegraph* on 23 August entitled 'The coming recovery in Ordinary shares'.

He argued in this article that the 'fundamental arguments for investing in equities' remain, and that there were 'logical and practical reasons' for suggesting that 'the majority of equity share prices will be very much higher than they are today', because, 'sooner or later intrinsic values will emerge as the predominant consideration'. He was particularly influenced by liquidity of more than £1,000m that the institutions were believed to have accumulated to wait for the eventual turn in the market, of which 'it is certain that only a small fraction will ever get into the market at anywhere near its lowest levels' when the 'current extreme pessimism burns itself out'.

He vividly foretold exactly what happened, later in January 1975:

> Once an upturn is established and when incipient optimism returns a buying spree of near panic proportions could take place. Nearly all investors in equities know the distress of holding shares which go down day after day, but the investment manager who by his own choice stays out of a market which rises strongly and unexpectedly can suffer an even greater agony.

A fine illustration of the psychology of markets and the crucial importance of timing.

Whyte's article prompted a 4% rise in the FT Index, from 212.6 to 221.1, on the day of its publication. It was written primarily from the point of view of institutional investors – then unanimously shunning equities and building cash mountains. This was an early example of the more widespread trend today for major institutional investors to cluster their asset allocations around similar percentages – a defensive mechanism that deflects criticism for failing to read market trends when everybody fails together, as in 1974 when there was safety in numbers for investment managers as their portfolios all collapsed at the same time.

Many institutions have steady cash inflows that smooth the path of their investment decisions, but the individual investor with a fixed amount of capital is more dependent on timing, and more vulnerable to the psychological pressures of volatile markets. When Lewis Whyte was telling him to buy, the hypothetical private client with his portfolio of leaders is sitting on the beach on holiday, sorely distracted by a quick calculation that his £20,000 equities portfolio has now shrunk to only £8,700, and agonising whether he should sell up and protect what little capital now remains or, instead, should he cobble together another £5,000 to put into the market after reading Whyte's rather convincing article? In fact, either decision would inflict more agony – and agony is not too strong a word for the psychological strain caused by rapidly vanishing assets in 1974 .

If he responds to Whyte and invests more capital, he will, over the next four months see its value, and that of the original portfolio, fall by another third. If he loses his nerve and seeks respite from the pain by selling, he will enjoy a short remission, but suffer later the even greater agony so vividly predicted.

The experience of 1974 is visited on investors perhaps only once in a lifetime, but, when it happens, it leaves behind deep scars that last for many years. Many private investors abandoned the stock market for good. The institutional investor had the easier option, building a cash mountain, safe in the knowledge that all his competitors were doing the same.

Timing is no less difficult for the shrewdest of investors, who may have brilliantly judged the time to sell out somewhere near the peak in 1972, and then reinvested after the market has halved, only to find it halve again. Contrarian investors face serious timing difficulties. Individual shares stay in or out of favour for longer than might be expected and it is easy to be reckless in buying too soon. A fashionable growth stock will collapse to a quarter of its price if the forecast doubled earnings of 10p per share, valued on a prospective PE ratio of 40, turns out to be an unchanged 5p, then valued on a PE ratio of 20. But it might halve again if the disappointment continues and many a once fashionable share will fall to around 10% of its high. It is said that fortunes were lost in the Wall Street crash in 1929 by those who sold out at the top but reinvested too soon.

In the event, Whyte's article offered no more than a brief respite before rumours of an impending second general election began to circulate. The Conservatives were well behind in the opinion polls and when Harold Wilson announced on 18 September that polling day would be on 10 October, the FT Index promptly fell through 200 for a second time. Within a week, it had suffered another 10% sell-off, to 181.6, with the All Share Index following suit, moving from 84.25 to 75.35.

The Commercial Union rights issue on 24 September was one of the milestones of this bear market and a contributing factor to this latest fall. The bid for St Martin's Property had been lost to Kuwait, but the need to increase its capital base and meet the legal requirement of the solvency margin led to the announcement by Commercial Union of a one for two rights issue at 60p to raise £62.5m. The shares fell from 84p to 72p on the news, where the market capitalisation of the company was £150m. This was, by any standard, a heavy rights issue relative to the existing capital, and a severe burden to impose on shareholders, particularly private individuals who might have neither the capital nor the will to put up such amounts. Furthermore, the new shares were being offered on a yield basis of 17% – an extraordinarily expensive way of raising capital that sent out a message of corporate crisis.

There followed a lacklustre election that nobody enjoyed. The Chancellor acknowledged in the campaign on 23 September that there was a 'very real problem in the liquidity position of companies' and promised a reflationary Budget. All three parties appeared to subscribe to some variation of the 'Social Contract', and, given the consistent Labour lead of 5 to 8 points in the opinion polls, Edward Heath probably entertained hopes of a national coalition as being his best chance of retaining influence. Fredy Fisher wrote in the *Financial Times* on 7 October about the election's 'total irrelevance to the economic problems faced by this country'. Lord Robens, a former Labour minister, made an extraordinary attack on the Government, in an article in the *Financial Times* on 3 October warning that a majority Labour Government would take the electorate 'hell-bent down economic paths which this country will regret very much', led by the 'academic revolutionary' Anthony Wedgwood Benn.

In the event, the voters again fooled the pollsters. The headlines of News at Ten on ITV famously predicted a Labour majority of around 60 on the evidence of exit polls, but, in fact, the Labour vote was 3 to 4 percentage points below what was forecasted and, in a repeat of his 1964 victory, Harold Wilson finished with an overall majority of only 3. Although his name will always be in the history books for winning four elections out of five, the actual results, in terms of overall majorities, make a less impressive sequence of plus 3, plus 97, minus 28, minus 14 and plus 3, and it can be argued that two of his victories were no more than replays.

The Queen's Speech on 29 October 1974 promised the nationalisation of the shipbuilding, ship-repairing and aircraft industries – the latter affecting General Electric, Vickers and Hawker, as the shareholders of British Aircraft Corporation. Tony Benn's voluntary planning agreements were included, along with the new National Enterprise Board. On the same day, State aid was announced for the country's largest machine tool manufacturer, Alfred Herbert, to keep it alive after losses for three successive years.

It is in the nature of markets that the cavalry will eventually come riding to the rescue and it was the unlikely figure of Denis Healey who took the first step that was to lead to the rescue of the stock market. It was a vital turning point when he announced on 12 November relief of £1,600m for industry, spread equally between relaxations in the price code and tax relief from stock appreciation. He also planned a phasing out of the combined deficits of £1,000m of the nationalised industries, while reporting a much higher than expected PSBR for the year of £6,330m, and, above all, warned how much depended on the social contract.

Turning points are easily identified with the benefit of hindsight, but are not always recognised at the time by the stock market, and this was the case with the Chancellor's concessions to industry. Indeed, on this occasion, it was doubly worse because the reaction of the stock market to the economic package was yet another sell-off. Above all, it was the daunting task of funding a PSBR of more than £6,000m – more than twice the level forecast in his March Budget – that undermined any remaining confidence in the gilts market.

Government borrowing is financed in the form of small personal savings from National Savings and longer-term savings from the sale of government securities, mainly to life assurance companies and pension funds. The market had depleted the size of the funds of the life assurance companies to an estimated £20,000m and pension funds to £10,000m, and their cash mountain was believed to be £1,000m or more. By comparison, a PSBR of £6,000m seemed to be many bridges too far and, over the 2 weeks, following the package, equities suffered falls of 14% in the FT Index, from 191.4 to 164.6, and 16% in the All Share Index, from 77.74 to 65.26.

Concerns in the stock market were now heavily focused on the financial sectors. The lifeboat launched by the Bank of England at the beginning of the year to recycle deposits to replace those withdrawn in panic by depositors from secondary banks had been picking up many more passengers than was generally appreciated. Originally it was believed that £500m would be sufficient, but the latest estimate now suggested that £1,300m had already been committed to some 30 secondary banks out of a likely total heading for £2,000m.

The clearing banks in the syndicate were now concerned that their commitment to the lifeboat was beginning to threaten their own stability, being equal to around half of their reserves. The most insidious of many spreading rumours centred on National Westminster Bank, shares in which had fallen below their par value of £1 to a price of 90p. The significance of this was that a rights issue of the kind launched by Commercial Union had become impossible, because shares cannot be issued at below par value. In the feverish conditions of the time, National Westminster was forced, on 1 December, to send a circular to all its branches denying rumours of problems. A withdrawal of depositors from a bank of this size would have been catastrophic.

In early December, a combination of alarm over National Westminster, a National Institute of Economic and Social Research (NIESR) forecast of 25% inflation in 1975, the need of British Leyland for State aid of £50m to avert financial crisis, and a claim from the coalminers for a 60–90% rise in basic pay rates, sent the market for the fifth and final time in 1974 into a short-term sell-off of more than 10%. The FT Index fell from 166.6 on 2 December to 150.0 on 12 December, breaching a level first reached more than 20 years earlier in May 1954, and the All Share Index fell to what was to prove to be its all-time low of 61.92 on 13 December.

Most insurance companies and many pension funds have an accounting year that runs to 31 December, and the current prices of equities and gilts was about to devastate balance sheet and year end valuations. Shortfalls in the actuarial valuations of assets of life assurance funds and pension funds could twist the downward spiral of the market even further, and large one-off contributions to pension funds might be needed from companies already woefully short of cash. One of a series of regular but informal meetings of the investment managers of a small group of leading insurance companies is believed to have been held at that time, and it prompted a buying campaign in the month of December. The All Share Index did indeed rise by some 8% from its low point, but, in the event, by the time the accounts and the actuarial valuations were completed in the new year, the market had already solved the problem, as will be seen in the next chapter.

However, at the time, no such comfort was available and for investors alike, Christmas 1974 was the most worrying they would ever experience. Institutional fund managers were dreading the details of their year end valuations, and private shareholders were traumatised. In 1974, the two indices fell by around 55% – the worst post-war performance over a calendar year. Towards the end of the year, in one of his expressive market reports for stockbrokers Rowe & Pitman, James D'Albiac opined, 'This bear market is the financial equivalent of the Great War. Lamps going out, end of an era, casualties numbered in millions, will it ever end?'

The hypothetical private investor is now looking at the remnants of his portfolio of blue chips in a year end valuation. In 2 years, £20,000 has shrunk in line with the market to £6,000, as shown in Table 19.2.

Many private investors are dependent on the income produced from a portfolio of investments, but for many others an equity portfolio acts as a financial reserve or cushion to finance or underwrite personal expenditure. The devastation

Table 19.2

Holdings		Price (p) at 31 December 1972	Price (p) 31 December 1974	% fall	Value (£)	Yield (%)
880	A. P. Cement	228	71	68.9	625	14.7
1,210	Courtaulds	165	56	66.1	678	13.7
1,350	General Electric	148	56	62.2	756	7.5
550	Guest Keen	363	105	71.1	577	14.0
1,945	Imperial Tobacco	103	36	65.0	700	17.9
695	Marks & Spencer	288	100	65.3	695	8.7
430	National Westminster	465	100	78.5	430	11.1
1,005	Prudential	199	57	71.4	572	12.0
570	Shell	350	126	64.0	718	12.8
770	Slater Walker	260	35	86.5	270	12.9
Total				69.0	6,021	12.5

of that reserve, as in the hypothetical portfolio shown in Table 19.2, acts as a strong psychological deterrent to personal expenditure, sufficient in the aggregate to have an adverse effect on the economy. This was a factor in the 1974 recession.

It was a year in which the market suffered short-term collapses of 10% or more on 5 occasions, and only in the month of February did any technical recovery last for more than the briefest moment. The short-term sell-offs were all triggered by specific events, either a general election or its announcement or Budget or mini-Budget and, in all cases the market had recovered little or no ground from its previous low point. The events were as given in Table 19.3.

In conditions of unparalleled volatility, the FT Index recorded a daily fall of 2% or more on fifty occasions. It was not as if this volatility was accompanied

Table 19.3
Events triggering collapses in the market in 1974

Event	Date	Number of days	FT Index from	FT Index to	% fall
Election	28 February–8 March	6	337.8	295.0	12.7
Budget	26 March–1 April	4	293.2	263.6	10.1
Mini Budget	23 July–19 August	19	264.4	199.8	24.4
Election	18 September–26 September	6	204.9	181.6	11.4
Mini Budget	12 November–25 November	9	191.4	164.6	14.0

by high trading volumes. In the last 8 months of 1974, monthly turnover averaged less than £850m, compared with a peak in May 1972 of £2,088m, although it remained high relative to the shrinking capitalisation of the market as a whole. There was a similar trend in the number of bargains, peaking at 732,000 in May 1972, but averaging only 260,000 from May to December 1974.

A partial explanation of the volatility and the scale of short-term sell-offs lies with the unique jobbing system in the London stock market. Jobbers – known today as market makers – operated a quote-driven system as opposed to the order-driven systems used in other stock markets. It is more expensive because the spread between bid and offer prices is the source of the jobbers' profit, but it is more liquid because jobbers are required to quote bid and offer prices in a minimum number of shares, whatever the state of the market, and for day-to-day business in marketable stocks they are usually willing to start an order in large quantity. The result is greater certainty, immediacy and a degree of confidentiality for the buyer or seller. By comparison, in an order-driven system, buyers and sellers need the existence of each other in matching amounts when they then deal at a common price.

Another important difference is that the details of matched orders are published immediately, as on the famous ticker-tape in Wall Street, whereas a jobber needs time to work through a large order in confidence. This factor is defined as transparency, which is obviously greater in the order-driven system.

The existence and survival of the jobbing system and its lack of imitation elsewhere is a tribute to the native skills that have put the City of London at the forefront of financial markets, and for large or aggressive fund managers it is a neat choice between better liquidity or cheaper cost. However, the jobber is also an investor, even if this is over a very short timescale, and being forced to deal can be painful if everybody to a man is a buyer or a seller. For jobbers to have survived in the bear market of 1973 and 1974, they could never afford to be bulls of stock. To run their books short of the market they had to sell more shares to reluctant buyers than they were willing to buy from eager sellers. In a bear market, the jobber expresses his reluctance to buy by marking prices sharply lower to discourage sellers and, at the same, making his short position more profitable. It was this constant downward pressure that contributed to the volatility of prices on so many days in the closing months of 1974.

One of the largest firms of jobbers, Akroyd & Smithers, became a publicly quoted company in June 1975. Earlier in the year, it revealed profits for the half-year to 30 September 1974 of £3.55m, up by more than 50%. These figures were achieved in the midst of the most volatile year ever known to the stock market and they shone brightly amid the disasters suffered by other financial institutions. They could only have been achieved in a bear market by resolutely running short positions. The jobbing system brings with it a subjective first call

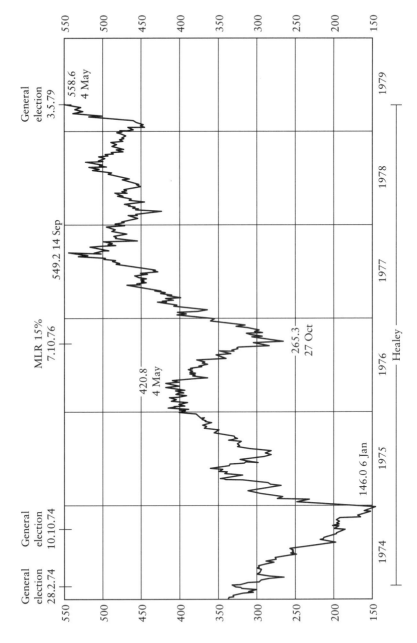

Figure 19.1
FT INDEX 1974–79

Source: Financial Times

to the jobbers in setting prices, whereas there is an element of neutrality in an order-driven system. In broadly stable markets, the liquidity of the jobbing system is its attraction, but in volatile markets it will accentuate the swings in prices. The attempt by a group of insurance companies to call the market higher in December was partly frustrated by the willingness of the jobbers to keep their short positions in place by feeding stocks to them.

It was on a Friday the thirteenth that the All Share Index fell to its all-time low of 61.92 in December 1974. The dividend yield on the aggregate of 594 shares was 12.71% and the aggregate PE ratio on the 500 shares in the industrial index was 3.6 – figures that now seem incomprehensible. In a bear market lasting more than two and a half years, the Index fell 72.9% from its peak of 228.18 on 1 May 1972. On the narrower front of the FT Index, the low was marked on Monday 6 January 1975, in the aftermath of the financial collapse of Burmah Oil and its rescue by the Government (see Figure 19.1). The FT Index fell by 73.1% from its peak of 543.6 on 19 May 1972 to 146.0.

The low point of the FT Index is the better remembered of the two.

Chapter 20

VERTICAL TAKE-OFF

January 1975–May 1976

All Share Index	13 December 1974	61.92	
	3 May 1976	171.66	Up 177.2%
FT 30 Index	6 January 1975	146.0	
	4 May 1976	420.8	Up 188.2%

Burmah Oil faced disaster on New Year's Day 1975. The company was unable to repay loans of $650m, and to avoid bankruptcy the Government agreed to guarantee these loans against a collateral placed with the Bank of England of Burmah Oil's stakes of 21.6% in British Petroleum and 2% in Shell. Dealings were suspended in the shares of Burmah Oil at 100p.

For many years, Burmah Oil had been treated as little more than an investment trust offering an alternative route into BP, and stockbrokers created steady business by switching between the two. BP was always uneasy that an unwelcome outsider could too easily become a large shareholder by acquiring Burmah, and BP, together with Shell, in 1963 mounted what would then have been the biggest ever takeover bid for Burmah in order to unravel these holdings, but this came to naught.

Burmah responded by pursuing a policy of diversification, including thwarted attempts to buy chemical company Laporte in 1970 and merge with US oil company Conoco in 1971. The problem was that any attempted diversification paled in size by comparison with a 21.6% holding in BP. Those investors who habitually switch between any two stocks on a mechanical basis also learned a painful lesson that if the link between the two is ever broken, the switching investor is bound to be out of the one that breaks upwards or in the one that collapses downwards.

The news of Burmah Oil's collapse came as yet another shock to an already stunned market. On Thursday, 2 January – the first day of dealing in the new year – the FT Index fell by 6.7% from 161.4 to 150.6, and the All Share Index fell by 6.4% from 66.89 to 62.60 – two of the largest one-day percentage falls on record. The oil sector alone fell by 10.3% and in the gilt market the yield on War Loan rose to 17.6%. Friday was quiet, but, after reflection over the weekend, the FT Index fell further on Monday 6 January to its low point of 146.0 and the All Share to 62.16, within a whisker of its December low.

This was the turning point – recognised only slowly over the remaining days of the week, but then gathering speed with a rate of acceleration never seen before or since, inducing a buying spree of panic proportions, exactly as Lewis Whyte had predicted. Almost everybody who had wanted to sell had already done so. The institutions had built up their liquidity to unprecedented proportions, with unit trusts averaging 31% in cash and short-term assets, and pension funds and investment trusts 18% each. Institutional liquidity added up to a much larger total than was generally appreciated at the time, evidenced by later published returns showing institutional cash of £1,850m and deposits and other short-term assets of a further £1,900m.

The market value of the assets of three of the principal investing institutions, and assets at book values for the life companies, as at 31 December 1974 were later published by the Central Statistical Office (see Table 20.1).

Table 20.1
Cash and short-term assets of principal investing institutions, 31 December, 1974

	Total assets (£m)	Equities	Cash	Deposits and short-term assets	Total liquidity (%)
Pension funds	10,200	3,688	787	1,021	1,808 (17.7)
Life companies	20,718	4,258	484	365	849 (4.1)
Investment trusts	3,743	2,708	294	376	670 (17.9)
Unit trusts	1,407	941	285	151	436 (31.0)
Total	36,068	11,595	1,850	1,913	3,763

The unit trust movement had been so mesmerised by the bear market that its liquidity had reached extraordinary levels for funds marketed as being invested wholly in equities. The pension funds had seen their customary percentages in equities reduced to only 36%, and like the investment trusts, took refuge in cash. The life companies were less committed to equities, had invested cash in December and could look for future cash flow from their long-term business with some certainty.

The entire UK equity market was valued at a mere £17,000m – a commonplace value for a single market leader today. Average equity dividend yields of 12% and PE ratios of 4 suddenly seemed absurdly cheap. Lastly, as potent a factor as any, the jobbers and many professional bears entered the new year resolutely short of stock.

There was a veritable explosion of buying, best illustrated by the weekly

turnover in equities by value and volume reported by the Stock Exchange that
through the second half of 1974, had averaged £185m and 55,000 bargains.
Table 20.2 shows the weekly figures for January 1975.

Table 20.2
Weekly turnover in equities, January 1975

Date	Weekly value (£m)	Weekly bargains	FT Index % change
January 6–10	217.3	63,800	+9.4
January 13–17	263.2	79,700	+9.7
January 20–24	386.6	110,600	+23.9
January 27–31	661.2	180,000	+9.2

This intensity of buying culminated in a sequence over eight business days
towards the end of January that lifted the FT Index by 49% and the All Share
Index by 44% – performance familiar for the occasional growth stock, but
rarely, if ever, seen for the whole of a major stock market. Included were two of
the most hectic days ever known to the market on Friday 24 and Monday 27
January. A rise of 10.1% on the Friday is the biggest one-day percentage rise
ever recorded in the FT Index, as is the 9.4% rise for the All Share Index on the
same day. This was the last day of the fortnightly Stock Exchange account,
when speculators who had disbelievingly sold the market short were forced to
close, in competition with jobbers and professionals who were desperately short
of stock, while equally desperate institutions were panicking into the market
before it was too late and running headlong into unit trusts, bearing liquidity
problems compounded by money pouring in from the public. This remarkable
sequence is set out in Table 20.3.

Turnover on the Friday was £138m, with 33,438 bargains, but even these figures paled beside those recorded on the first day of a new account on the
Monday, when turnover soared to £162m from 45,048 bargains. Following its
record rise of 10.1% on Friday 24 January, the stock market opened with
another rise of 10.2%, taking the Index to 239.1 at its 10.00 am calculation,
whereupon it subsided through the day to 223.9.

With scarcely a pause for breath and with daily turnover regularly over
£100m, the market continued relentlessly upwards through February, until, on
the very last trading day of the month, the FT Index broke through to 301.8, and
the All Share Index to 126.44, both on the same day having doubled in 8 weeks.
The weekly sequence of the two indices and the percentage changes were as
shown in Table 20.4.

Table 20.3
Daily measurements in the FT Index,
21–30 January 1975

Date	Closing FT Index	Daily change %	Cumulative change %
Monday 20 January	169.4		
Tuesday 21 January	178.4	+ 5.3	+5.3
Wednesday 22 January	185.6	+4.0	+9.5
Thursday 23 January	197.1	+6.2	+16.4
Friday 24 January	217.0	**+10.1**	+28.1
Monday 27 January	223.9	+3.2	+32.2
Tuesday 28 January	224.3	+0.2	+32.4
Wednesday 29 January	235.0	+ 4.8	+38.7
Thursday 30 January	252.3	+7.4	**+48.9**

Table 20.4
Weekly movement of the market, 6 January–28 February 1975

Date	FT Index	% change	All Share Index	% change
6 January	146.0		62.16	
10 January	159.7	+9.4	65.96	+6.1
17 January	175.2	+9.7	74.55	+13.0
24 January	217.0	+23.9	91.29	+22.5
31 January	236.9	+9.2	102.13	+11.9
7 February	256.8	+8.4	108.22	+6.0
14 February	275.1	+7.1	117.81	+8.9
21 February	260.4	−5.3	111.99	−4.9
28 February	301.8	+15.9	126.44	+12.9
		———		———
Total		+106.7		+103.4

The value put on the quoted private sector of the British economy shifted in eight weeks from £17,000m to £35,000m. Shares that had yielded 12% now only offered 6%, and PE ratios of 4 were now 8. The best performance came from the most depressed sectors, with merchant banks up 175%, or near to trebling, followed by contracting and construction up 163% and hire purchase up 155%. Gold shares lagged well behind, with a rise of 16%, followed by the highly defensive sectors of tobacco, up by a mere 67%, and wines and spirits, up 75%.

These eight weeks amount to the most astonishing single period in the postwar history of the stock market, although few investors would admit to having enjoyed this frenzied feast while it was happening. Many simply looked on, paralysed like rabbits caught in the headlights. Many suffered intense frustration. Far too many institutions had husbanded their cash resources for sunnier days, complacently believing that the time would come when wonderful buying opportunities would be there for the taking at their leisure. In the event, these wonderful opportunities vanished like melting snow in a sudden thaw and, to quote Rowe & Pitman's Market Report, 'most investors were wrong-footed by the sudden change and remained imprisoned by the seemingly irrefutable logic of their gloom'.

After spending months at a time fighting off the sellers, the jobbers now found themselves fighting an even bigger battle with the buyers. A small number of funds, particularly in the Rothschilds stable, had beaten their competitors into the ground through the bear market by buying gold shares – the shining light of equity markets in 1973 and 1974 – but now found themselves stranded at the foot of the performance tables. Perhaps the greatest psychological damage was inflicted on private investors. Many had sold out on the way down; others who sat through the recovery were now disillusioned beyond repair and never wished to own a share again. To many an outsider, the gyrations of the market were beyond comprehension.

There is only one simple explanation for the bewildered outsider – all stock market peaks and troughs are driven to extremes by those two imperatives of greed and fear. The dramatic scale of the recovery in January and February was the corollary of the extraordinary and unprecedented extent to which investors were gripped by fear in 1974.

At the end of it all, feeling in the City was one of overwhelming relief. The patient had returned to good health after months in delirium. Portfolios had survived. The Stock Exchange did have a future after all. Commissions and fees were rolling in again. Normal service had been resumed. The hypothetical investor from the last chapter was profoundly relieved to discover that his portfolio had all but doubled, from £6,000 to £11,700, but was now irritated that he had failed to seize such a blindingly obvious opportunity to invest in the first week of January.

The usual influences of company profits and economic statistics played no part in these dramatic events. It was a purely local affair, fought on the floor of the Stock Exchange, where the bulls overwhelmed the bears to restore a semblance of value to their shares. The FT Index was at 300. It was time for a pause.

Away from the stock market, trends in the real economy in the early months of 1975 were, if anything, looking rather worse. They were also looking bad for

Edward Heath, who was replaced as leader of the Conservatives by Margaret Thatcher in February. The 'Social Contract' was collapsing in the face of widespread expectations of 30% increases for the public-sector unions. Roy Jenkins described inflation as 'the biggest menace since Hitler', but who cared when the year end wage rate index was up by 28% against a mere 19% for inflation. Concerns were also growing about an exploding PSBR for 1974/75. The Chancellor's first estimate of £2,700m in March 1974 had been revised to £6,300m in November, and market estimates now suggested it was heading for £8,000m–£9,000m, or 10% of GDP, for 1975/76.

On 15 April, in his fourth Budget within a year, Denis Healey had to face reality. He openly punished the failure of the Social Contract by raising the tax burden by £1,250m. He lifted the standard rate of income tax from 33p to 35p, applied a new VAT rate of 25% to a wide range of consumer products and lifted all the usual excise duties. He acknowledged its effect on the Retail Price Index of nearly 3% and forecast a rise of a quarter in unemployment to the headline level of one million, but even after the severity of these measures, he was unable to forecast a PSBR any lower than £9,000m for 1975/76. There was some comfort for companies and their shareholders when he announced the continuation of his stock relief measures, and this, together with an acknowledgement of the grim reality of the Budget, led to a sharp rise of more than 11% in the FT Index over the 2 days following the Budget, from 305.4 to 339.9.

This may seem to have been a perverse reaction, but a more sinister reason was coming into play. Sterling was weakening fast as inflation went over 20%, and while the Chancellor had punished pay increases averaging 30%, he had done nothing to curb them. Figures for the year to March showing wage rates up 32½% and inflation up 21.2% were published within a couple of days of the Budget. The market was now living in fear of inflation, and the equity ownership of assets provided a far safer home than either cash or fixed interest assets, particularly as interest rates were perversely falling while inflation was rising.

'Hyperinflation' was appearing as a new word in the vocabulary of many people, and photographs of Germans pushing wheelbarrows full of paper currency were plucked from newspaper files from the 1920s. Hedges against inflation took various forms. The most obvious was to invest overseas, and the dollar premium soared through 100% within a few days of the Budget. An attractive alternative was in UK stocks with a strong overseas flavour. Property shares rebounded strongly and direct property remained a core holding for the pension funds and life companies. The British Rail Pension Fund was actively pursuing its new policy announced in February of investing up to 3% of its fund in works of art – an innovative if eccentric step for an actuarially calculated portfolio.

The institutional appetite for equities was fed by a succession of rights issues, as many companies took advantage of the stock market recovery to replenish their balance sheets. The first of any size had been Midland Bank, raising £52m in March, followed in the spring by issues in the £30m–£50m range from Guest Keen, Prudential and Glaxo. Unlike today, when a rights issue often signals positive expansion, in the 1970s they were regarded more as a sign of weakness, forced by a need to rebuild balance sheets ravaged by inflation rather than as a source of new funds to finance future growth.

A smaller well-intentioned, but ultimately disastrous rights issue was the £14m raised by EMI to finance the development of a scanner – a new invention at the leading edge of medical technology. Sadly, it was dogged by too many problems for it to succeed, and its fate was later ironically if cruelly reduced to a Lex headline, 'A Scanner in the Works at EMI'. By the end of the year, some £1,200m had been raised by rights issues from a long list of companies. Imperial Tobacco also took advantage of the market in April to raise £77m by reducing its large holding in British-American Tobacco from 26% to 16%, in one of the biggest ever placings of its kind in the London market.

The frenzied activity of the first quarter of 1975 had benefited all stockbrokers, but as the year progressed and turnover settled down at quieter levels, the advantage swung strongly in favour of the corporate finance brokers. The two with the largest client lists were Cazenove and Rowe & Pitman (known briefly at that time as Rowe & Pitman, Hurst-Brown, following a successful merger with a smaller, research-based firm), followed by Hoare & Co., Govett and W. Greenwell. Rights issues were particularly lucrative for the brokers. They generated a fee of ¼ per cent for carrying out the subunderwriting of the issue with a wide range of institutions, and commissions followed from placing with institutions the usual rump of 5–10% of the issue not taken up by shareholders.

Pay demands of 30% continued unabated through the early summer in both public and private sectors, although the attention of the country at large was diverted by the referendum on the renegotiated EEC terms held on 5 June and its decisive 67% yes vote. This was also a time when segments of the private sector fell deliberately or haplessly into the Government hands. Earlier in March, terms had been announced for the nationalisation of the shipbuilding industry, with compensation prices based on average prices between September 1973 and February 1974, when the market was generally higher but shipbuilding shares stood at large discounts to asset values, as for example Swan Hunter at 90p with assets of 250p.

In quick succession in April and May, both British Leyland and Ferranti fell under State control. At British Leyland, the long reign of Sir Donald Stokes ended with a massive financial crisis and his resignation. He was succeeded by Sir Don Ryder, journalist turned industrialist. State aid of £700m was promised over 3 years and, with the shares suspended at 6p, shareholders were offered 10p a share by the Government. Sir Donald Stokes had long lamented that the City put a higher value on an office block than on the whole of British Leyland and at last he may have understood why. Ferranti was a simpler transaction – State aid of £15m was given in return for 50% of voting control. Alfred Herbert – once Britain's leading machine tool manufacturer – was taken into the Government's portfolio of 'lame ducks' in October, via a bid of 6p a share from the National Enterprise Board and the injection of £25m.

The spiral of 30% pay claims came to a head in June when the National Union of Railwaymen rejected an arbitration award of 27.7% and announced a strike. However, after another beer and sandwiches gathering in Downing Street, the strike was averted with a 30% offer. At this point, the Government, now down to an overall majority of one, began to talk of a pay target of 10%, or £6 a week. The market took fright at the prospect of a freeze bearing hard on prices and dividends, and the FT Index fell away during June from 365.3 to 291.8 on the last day of the month.

Action quickly followed. On 1 July, the Chancellor gave the unions one week to agree a 10% voluntary limit, failing which there would be statutory legislation, and he tightened the limit on dividend increases from 12½% to 10% with immediate effect. The market responded with its then biggest ever rise in points in a single day in the FT Index of 23.7 to 315.5, or 8.1%, having feared worse and been impressed by decisive action. The measures duly appeared in an anti-inflation White Paper on 11 July, on the basis of a universal limit of £6 a week on annual pay of £8,500, above which no increases were allowed, and they were to run for a year from 1 August.

The rest of the year was one of those periods when the stock market rises as the headlines worsen. During the first week of the new incomes policy in August, the FT Index drifted down to 277.7, but, by the end of the year, it was 35% higher at 375.7. Unemployment surged through the million forecast by the Chancellor to 1.25m in August, or 5.4%, a post-war high. MLR was raised in 2 steps, from 10% to 12%, sharply raising the cost of funding the PSBR. Government expenditure for the first half of 1975/76 was officially reported to be up by an alarming 47% compared with revenues up by 31%, two percentages that illustrate as well as any the chilling nature of rampant inflation in Britain at the time. The PSBR target of £9,000m was abandoned and there was talk of a figure heading for £12,000m, or more than 10% of GDP.

Other background negatives served as positives. Sterling had been weakening through the year in what amounted to a devaluation of around 10%, but a high overseas and exporting content ensured benefits for company profits. Crises in British Steel with its well-publicised problems of overmanning, and in Chrysler, where a State rescue package of £160m was agreed, encouraged a belief that the Government at last understood the importance and need for profits. Nothing better concentrated the mind than the imminent collapse of the motor industry, and the arrival in June of the pragmatic Eric Varley as Minister of Industry in place of the anti-capitalist Tony Benn had been widely welcomed. And so, rather against the odds, London enjoyed steadily improving markets through to the end of 1975.

In the New Year, the market quickly mounted an assault on the 400 level for the FT Index. Institutional buying was strongly underpinning the market with cash flows into pension funds and life assurance swollen by inflation, and unit trust funds under management overtook their 1972 peak to reach £2,700m. After its autumn increase to 12%, MLR was now retracing its steps in almost weekly falls to 9% by the first week of March. The incomes policy was holding, not least with the miners and the railwaymen, and the Government's hands were neatly bound by a majority of just one. Company profits were buoyant. An external factor was the strength of markets worldwide, and in Australia euphoria surrounded the uranium prospects of Pancontinental, which in two years had risen from 35p to £19, thus completing the third and final leg of the remarkable Australian mining treble of Western Mining (1968), Poseidon (1969) and Pancontinental (1976) – a saga worthy of its own telling, but in each case driven mainly by buying in the London Stock Exchange.

Talk of a reflationary Budget helped the market along in early 1976, and investors were deceived by a benign attitude on the part of the Bank of England to an incipient currency problem. On 5 March, the pound was allowed to slip below $2 for the first time – apparently encouraged by a reduction in MLR on the same day – and within a week it had fallen to $1.91, where the depreciation of the pound against a trade-weighted basket of all currencies was 34% below the Smithsonian levels set in December 1971. Over the shorter timeframe of a year, the pound had been devalued by 15%, seemingly beneficial for the market, but in reality about to become a time-bomb waiting to explode in the Chancellor's face.

On 16 March, there was a fall of 2½% in the equity market for the rarest of reasons – the sudden resignation of the Prime Minister, Harold Wilson. He was succeeded by James Callaghan on 5 April, the day before the Budget. The Chancellor set a precedent by proposing tax cuts of £1,300m, mainly by raising income tax allowances and thresholds, but making the bulk of these – £1,000m – 'conditional' on achieving a pay norm of 3% in Phase Two of the incomes policy, due for renewal in August. He forecast a growth rate of 4% in the economy and a PSBR of £11,900m, close to market estimates. There was some encouragement for the Stock Exchange with the abolition of the 2% stamp duty on fixed interest stocks to bring them into line with government securities, and for industry by making stock appreciation tax relief permanent.

The pound continued to wobble, touching a new low of $1.80 on 22 April and forcing a sharp increase in MLR from 9% to 10½% on the next day. The Government continued active talks with the TUC, now in effect responsible for the standard rate of income tax, and, on 5 May 1975, announced a package for the next stage of incomes policy to take effect from 1 August. Weekly increases would be allowed to a maximum of £4, and a minimum of £2.50, with an over-riding 5% limit. The Price Code would be modified to encourage investment, but no mention was made of dividends – then subject to a 10% limit. Although the Budget condition of a 3% norm was not achieved, the conditional tax concessions were allowed to stand.

It was at this moment that the stock market peaked – the All Share Index at 171.66 on 3 May, up 177% from its 1974 low and the FT Index one day later at 420.8, up 188%.

Chapter 21

BEAR TRAP
May 1976–October 1976

All Share Index	3 May 1976	171.66	
	27 October 1976	116.29	Down 32.3%

This chapter covers the shortest time-span of any of the defined bull and bear markets, but it deals with a mean bear market that drove the two indices down by 32% and 37% in less than 6 months. A bear trap, means a sudden, severe downturn in a market or a stock that 'traps' the bears by recovering as sharply and as quickly as it falls. The chapter could equally have been headed 'Goodbye TUC, hello IMF'.

Early in this period, in mid-May, ICI took advantage of rising markets to launch the biggest ever equity rights issue in the London market to raise £204m – well ahead of the only issue of any size during the year, from Lloyds Bank in February which raised £76m. Timing a rights issue when the market is high sparks a mix of grudging respect and suppressed irritation. The company may have skilfully timed its call for money, but shareholders may be unenthusiastic about adding to a holding at a high level.

However, this was a mere domestic detail compared with the currency crisis that began on 21 May. The incomes policy announced earlier in the month had been weaker than indicated in the Budget and despite an increase in MLR from 10½% to 11½%, the pound began to fall sharply. The stock market took fright and by 2 June the FT Index had fallen by 11% from 410.3 to 364.7, as the pound fell from over $1.80 to $1.72, and the trade-weighted devaluation from December 1971 widened from 37% to 41%.

The seeds of the currency crisis lay in the prospective size of the PSBR at around 10% of GDP – a level leading to an attack on the Chancellor for living in a fool's paradise from Gordon Pepper of W. Greenwell, much the most influential of all the stockbroking economists at the time. As sterling continued to slip away, the Chancellor gained a breathing space on 7 June by announcing a $5,300m standby credit from the central banks of the Group of Ten countries. No conditions were attached, except that the Government must go to the International Monetary Fund (IMF) if the need for the standby remained after six months.

It became increasingly obvious that, without any spending cuts, the standby credit was a toothless gesture – and, after earlier Government resistance, the Chancellor announced on 22 July an economic package to bring down the PSBR in stages to a target of £9,000m in 1977/78. He imposed cuts of more than £1,000m in Government spending across a broad front, much of it in capital projects, and raised a further £1,000m by increasing national insurance contributions from employers by 2 percentage points. It was an act of desperation to have to announce deflationary measures just as unemployment was reaching a post-war high of 1,450,000, or 5½%, and there was deep political unrest in the Government and the TUC.

Since its fall in early June, when the standby credit was agreed, the stock market had been trapped in one of those periods of bewildered inactivity, and the FT Index stayed in the 370–90 range for many weeks until nerves began to fray in mid-August. In some years, a winter freeze will drag the market down, but it is a rare year when a summer drought has the same effect. In 1976, the country was experiencing its hottest, driest summer in living memory and towards the end of August, talk of a three-day week in industries dependent on water helped to unsettle the market.

The market was entering a phase that happens from time to time when, for no definable reason, an uneasy mood prevails. In the psychology of markets, the successful investor will recognise that mood the moment it occurs. Lex paid a rare tribute to the stock market in the *Financial Times* on 31 August, when, reviewing the continuing decline from the peak in May, he wrote that 'the equity market is one of the best leading indicators of economic activity that we have, and when it turns down to any significant degree, for any considerable length of time, it deserves to be taken seriously'.

In September, the cracks began to spread. Sterling weakened further as a seamen's strike was called. MLR was increased from 11½% to 13%. The Bank of England's intervention failed to stem a declining pound. Special deposits were raised from 3% to 4%, calling in £350m. Government stock was issued at a record high coupon of 14½%. The seamen's strike was averted with a settlement that breached the spirit of the incomes policy. And still the market remained passively uneasy.

On 28 September 1976, there occurred another of those defining moments of post-war financial history. The pound was falling fast as the Chancellor drove to Heathrow to catch a flight to the Commonwealth Finance Ministers' Conference in Hong Kong. The situation became more serious by the minute, so, when he arrived at Heathrow, he cancelled his flight and turned round to return to London. The pound had slipped two cents to $1.68 the day before, and by the end of the day of his return from Heathrow it had fallen another 5 cents to $1.63.

The Government had lost control and exercised the only remaining option by seeking a $3,900 loan from the IMF on the following morning. The Chancellor rushed to address the Labour party conference on the following day and argue the case for the loan, only to be met with noisy disapproval from many sections of the audience. Handing over the economy to the IMF was a humiliation. It was deeply resented by many in the party who would solve the problem with a siege economy, import controls and nationalisation of the banks and insurance companies, but it was rhetoric of this kind that prompted holders of sterling to sell through the summer.

In the midst of a financial crisis, the stock market is driven by rumour, exaggeration and speculative headlines, because nobody outside a small magic circle is privy to the detail of exactly what is happening, and events move so quickly there is never time to explain. With exaggerated visions of the Chancellor stopping the plane on the runway as it was taking off, and the pound dropping by the hour, the market was now tumbling day after day. It received another shock, driven by crisis, on 7 October when MLR was raised from 13% to 15% to bring the money supply under control, and special deposits were raised from 4% to 6% to take another £700m out of circulation.

The deflationary package in August was now being reinforced by a major credit squeeze at exactly the wrong point in the economic cycle. The market was completely unnerved. Gilt-edged stocks fell on the day by 3–4 points and the FT Index by nearly 5% to 296.0, making a fall of more than 15% in 9 days since the Heathrow saga. The mortgage rate was set at a record 12¼%, but the root cause of the problem was the sheer scale of Government borrowing, which could only be financed at higher and higher rates of interest and by crowding out other borrowers.

Negotiating the terms and conditions attached to an IMF loan is a slow and serious process, because it is a loan of last resort. There is plenty of time for rumour to play havoc in a demoralised market, and one last sell-off occurred after a weekend newspaper article on 24 October claimed that the IMF wanted sterling to be set at $1.50, a devaluation of a further 10%. The two indices fell sharply over the first 3 days of that week, and both together reached the low point of this very unsettling bear market on 27 October, at 265.3 for the FT Index and 116.29 for the All Share.

However, there was a critical difference with this bear market. Volume remained at a low level throughout, suggesting that prices were driven down as much by sentiment as by genuine selling pressure. It was time for the rebound.

Chapter 22

LABOUR BULL MARKET

October 1976–May 1979

All Share Index   27 October 1976   116.29

4 May 1979   283.82   Up 144.1%

A new chapter as the market turns. Would it be so easy. Hindsight is history's great advantage, but the turning point of a bear market is obscured by dark clouds. Fear – the prevailing emotion of the bear market – is quick to snuff out flickers of hope.

A particular uncertainty in 1976 was how to interpret the fragmenting of the roughly consistent and overlapping 4-year economic, electoral and stock market cycles that had guided investors over a generation for some 20 years. The four-year cycle was cynically put in place by successive Conservative Governments inducing consumer booms in time for general elections in 1955, 1959 and 1964, but the electoral link was broken by the six-year period of Labour governments from 1964 to 1970. However the stop–go economic cycle continued unchecked to produce business and stock market peaks in 1968 and 1972, with the usual symptoms of overheating in the economy, cured by a dose of high interest rates.

In 1976, the picture was confused. The bear market described in the last chapter started from a stock market peak in May, exactly in line with the four-year cycle, except that it had not recovered to the levels of the previous peak in 1972. Furthermore, the economy was in a disastrous state and wholly out of kilter with its four-year cycle. In previous crises, Bank rates of 7% in 1957, 1961 and 1966, 8% in 1969, and MLR at 13% in 1973 had brought each economic cycle to a juddering halt. In 1976, MLR was at a comparable crisis level of 15%, but at a time when the economy was already struggling and hardly needed stopping any further.

The stock market was gently rising as it awaited the outcome of talks with the IMF, but its mood was fragile. The wheels of negotiation turned slowly, as the Chancellor fought and won a hard battle to limit further cuts in Government expenditure to no more than £1,000m, which he announced on 15 December 1976. Forecasts of the PSBR for the current and following years were lowered to under £9,000m, including the benefit of estimated proceeds of £500m from the sale of a 17½% stake in BP. The controversial purchase of a 21% stake from Burmah Oil by the Bank of England for £180m in February 1975 had trebled in value to show a large profit. The knee-jerk reaction of the market to the IMF package was disappointment at another list of half-hearted measures, and a 3.2% fall in the FT Index to 313.8. However, over the next 2 days there were second thoughts and a rebound to 339.5.

In essence, the stables had been cleansed. The pound had been stabilised, interest rates should start to fall, and the economy for the next year or two would be in the hands of the IMF, with whom, in the words of the Chancellor, an agreement is 'like the seal of *Good Housekeeping*'. These were handcuffs that appealed to the stock market, further comforted by the Government's bare over-all majority acting as a sanction against extremism.

Another strength was an increasing awareness of the potential significance of North Sea oil to the economy. Export revenues from oil were just beginning to flow in 1976, but new forecasts for the next ten years showed its dramatic effect on the balance of payments – a negotiating point used to good effect by the Chancellor with the IMF. The year ended in good spirit and the FT Index at 354.7 was already some 33% above its October low. The bear trap was snapping shut.

In January, the Bank of England released the 2% special deposits imposed during the autumn crisis and completed its financing of the PSBR for 1974/75 with a record £1,250m issue of 13¼% stock in January. By this time, MLR had already ticked lower in ¼-point steps to 14%, but these two measures marked the end of the credit squeeze and left the way open for further falls in interest rates – always a positive sign for stocks and shares.

With sterling apparently secured at around $1.70, there now followed some of the steepest sustained falls in interest rates ever witnessed. MLR was reduced 21 times from its peak of 15% on 19 November 1976 to 5% on 14 October 1977 – a fall of extraordinary dimensions in 11 months. The gilt-edged market enjoyed one of its strongest ever bull phases, with the FT Gilts Index rising from a low of 58.06 on 27 October 1976 to a peak of 79.85 on 30 September 1977 – a rise of 37½%. Among individual stocks, War Loan rose over the same period by 71% from 22½ to 38½.

Given the structural security of an investment in government stocks, except against inflation, the returns of around 40% or more in a year were extraordinary, but they illustrated another general rule that in inflationary times if the climate is good for gilts, it will probably be even better for equities. Over the same 11 months, the FT Index rose from 307.2 to 500.0, and the All Share from 132.46 to 217.70, rises of 63% and 64% respectively, with the FT Index briefly for one day on 14 September 1977 hitting a new all-time high of 549.2. It was a good example of the yield gap at play. In broad terms, the yield on gilts fell from 15% to 10%, while the yield on equities fell from 8% to 5%.

There is a case study to be made of the price the institutions exacted in the autumn of 1976 to fund an excessive PSBR of the Government's own making, and the dramatic return the institutions made on their investment over the following year. In the eyes of some members of the Government, the institutions indulged in a reprehensible strike against the national interest. In the eyes of the City, the deeper a financial hole is dug, the higher the cost of rescue, and a PSBR of around 10% of GDP was a hole in the ground of Kimberley proportions.

There was nothing new about protesting politicians. History shows that soon after the Stock Exchange came into existence in 1716, Sir Robert Walpole's Government attempted to raise £600,000 at 4%, but the issue failed with only £45,000 subscribed. In great anger, Sir Robert reported to the House of Commons, 'I know that the members of the Stock Exchange have combined not to advance money on the loan. Everyone is aware how the administration of this country has been distressed by stockjobbers'. Such was the distrust of stock markets in those days that, in 1734 an Act of Parliament was introduced to 'Prevent the Infamous Practice of Stock Jobbing'. This sounds worse than intended because it referred to the settlement of 'time' bargains, whereby the balance between the cost of purchase and proceeds of sales was delayed many months into the future. Bargains extended over long time periods led to gambling on a ruinous scale and this Act merely made these bargains unenforceable.

The ground lost in the five-month bear market to October 1976 of around 33% was made good in the next 5 months, and the recovery formed a 'V' shape on the charts, remarkable for its steepness and symmetry. This recovery carried on upwards into one of those powerful bull markets in which share prices more or less doubled.

The reasons for this bull market may initially have been more apparent to foreigners looking in than to investors at home wrestling with an IMF crisis. In simple terms, yields of 15% were obtainable on a currency the value of which was more or less underwritten by the IMF at around $1.70 and covered by the security of North Sea oil. This combination held an irresistible attraction to currency investors and speculators, and persistent foreign currency inflows were instrumental in driving interest rates down and down.

In the equity market, the mood quickly changed from despair to relief, and from relief to hope. Investors were enjoying the grip of the IMF and the protection of the Government's majority of one. They could see the benefit to company profits and future competitiveness of what amounted to a devaluation of the pound from $2.40 to $1.70 over the previous 18 months. They were not to be deterred by fractious argument between the Government talking of the inevitability of a third phase of pay restraint and unions seeking a return to free collective bargaining, nor the musings of Roy Hattersley, Secretary of State for Prices and Consumer Protection, that the Price Code was not just to keep prices down, but also to regulate the profits of different sectors of the economy, nor the call from Jack Jones, leader of the Transport and General Workers' Union, for a price freeze in return for pay restraint.

The market took in its stride the formation of the Lib–Lab Pact on 23 March 1977, which added 13 Liberal votes to give the Government a working majority for the remaining two years of this Parliament, and postponed any hopes of a return of the Conservatives. In the Budget a few days later on 29 March, the Chancellor attempted a contingent tax cut for the second successive time. He increased the allowances and extended the bands for income tax to release £1,300m, and set aside a further £960m to reduce the standard rate from 35% to 33% – the latter contingent on the agreement of a successful pay policy. He forecast a PSBR of £8,500m.

The lower rate of income tax, at 33% was important for dividends because the 10% limit applied to the gross level, allowing an increase of 13.3% at the net level. However, the administration of dividend limitation had become relatively benign. Since it was first imposed in 1972, companies had been allowed to increase dividends in three ways – to restore them to former levels, in defence against takeover bids and on the occasion of a rights issue. Bid activity had been at a low level for some time, but rights issues were a more frequent route round the controls. A recent example had been Guest, Keen raising £67m in April 1977 – the third largest rights issue outside the financial sector after ICI with £204m in 1976 and British Petroleum with £120m in 1971.

The stock market was being driven upwards by institutional demand for equities. Cash inflows to pension funds and insurance companies were growing relentlessly and now approaching a combined annual rate of £7,000m. Although the Government was struggling to find a successor to Phase Two when it expired on 31 July, the feeling was that some sanity had returned to the economy. Inflation was falling, there was a reluctant awareness of the need for profits and less fear of permanent dividend controls. Share prices still lagged a long way behind in real terms when adjusted for inflation – and, above all, the prospect of North Sea oil offered a heaven-sent release from chronic balance of payments problems.

A new expression 'stock shortage' took hold in the marketplace, as though to imply that while the market was rising, it was not actually cheap. It was, in fact, a euphemism for the simple driver of all bull markets – more buyers than sellers. The scale of institutional activity was illustrated by monthly Stock Exchange figures for the month of May showing an all-time record for turnover in equities of £2,130m. An expression commonly used today about bull markets is 'wall of money'. The two bull markets of the late 1940s were driven by reinvestment from nationalisation, shared alike by the institutions and the private client. From the 1950s through to the 1970s, the 'wall of money' was primarily the cash flows of the institutions. In the 1980s and 1990s institutional liquidity was joined by corporate liquidity, but that is a subject for Chapters 28 and 31.

Interest in equities was heightened through the summer of 1977 by new disclosure rules coming into force in April under a new Companies Act. The existing requirement that any shareholding in a company of 10% or more must be publicly disclosed was amended to 5% or more, and there followed a steady stream of announcements that tickled the curiosity of the professionals and surprised the general public. The Prudential, as the largest investing institution, was required to report dozens of holdings, and the size of its holdings in two of the leading growth stocks of the 1960s and 1970s – namely, 6.2% of General Electric, worth £59.8m, and 6.3% of Marks & Spencer, worth £48.7m – attracted attention. These were significantly ahead of the next largest holding of 6.3% of the property sector leader, Land Securities, worth £16.8m, followed in turn by holdings in Coats Patons, United Biscuits and Cavenham.

The disclosure of holdings by Kuwait Investment Office was awaited with greater interest. Kuwait came into public awareness in 1974 when it bid for St Martin's Property, and it was believed to have been an aggressive but secretive investor in equities during the throes of the 1974 bear market. This was duly confirmed, but with a very different emphasis from the Prudential – towards the financial sector. Large holdings were disclosed in the insurance sector, where Kuwait owned 7.2% of General Accident, 5.9% of Guardian Royal Exchange and 6.2% of Legal & General, worth £23.3m, £13.8m and £10.1m respectively. Other large holdings included Reckitt & Colman and Trafalgar House. Capital inflows into Kuwait jumped dramatically after the price of oil quadrupled in 1973, and the speed of accumulation of equities thereafter was remarkable.

Although Kuwait's openly declared policy of investing its oil revenues in financial assets around the world as a safeguard against the day the oil runs out was widely praised for its prudence and originality, it was not widely advocated as a precedent or example for Britain as an emerging oil producer. Sam Brittan strongly argued the case in an article in the *Financial Times* on 15 September, suggesting the abandonment of exchange controls, the encouragement of outward investment and debt repayment. The Netherlands was already known for its 'Dutch disease', having allowed massive new revenues from natural gas to be used for consumption and benefits, and Brittan scorned those who would waste oil revenues by forcing capital into inefficient and uncompetitive domestic investment. The debate over the proper use of North Sea oil revenues would continue unresolved through the 1980s and 1990s.

Stock shortage in the market was partly met by the sale on 14 June 1977 of a 17% stake in British Petroleum by the Government when 66.7m shares were successfully underwritten at a price of 845p to raise £560m. This was the largest Stock Exchange equity issue of any kind and it was handled by an array of leading City names. It was masterminded by S. G. Warburg with ten other merchant banks and five stockbrokers – Mullens, Cazenove, Hoare Govett, Rowe & Pitman and J. & A. Scrimgeour. Mullens was involved as the Government broker, but otherwise the pecking order of leading corporate stockbrokers was much the same as in any post-war decade. In contrast, the choice of S. G.

Warburg as lead merchant bank illustrated its redoubtable progress to the top since its formation in 1946.

In size and complexity, the BP issue was a forerunner of those sales of government holdings and later tranches of privatisation issues in the 1980s and 1990s. The underwriting was spread across 782 institutions at a price of 845p – a 3% discount below the overnight closing price of 870p, which had already fallen sharply over the previous 3 days from 912p.

With the help of US investment bankers Morgan Stanley, the issue was extended to include the United States, where underwriting practices are very different. The advantages of the British practice of underwriting over the US system are that the issuer or seller is guaranteed to receive the proceeds; the rights of existing shareholders to participate are protected; and a much wider public participation can be achieved. The disadvantages are a higher underwriting cost; a longer timetable for external events to invalidate the agreed price; and a tendency to price an issue conservatively to ensure success. In the United States, a process of book-building is used, whereby institutional interest is solicited and expressed until a price for an issue can be established from a form of polling process. It will cost less, have a tighter timetable and will probably be at a price closer to the market, but it will provide little opportunity for the smaller shareholder to participate and gives no priority to existing shareholders.

In the event, there was widespread interest in the BP issue, and the 25% proportion of the issue allocated to the US was cut back to 20% – a controversial decision, not least because the book-building process had established a price of 890p a share compared with the 845p arising from the traditional UK underwriting method. This segment of the issue raised £119m, of which £6m was due to the higher price.

In the late 1970s, the seasons were never allowed to pass without an economic package from Denis Healey, who, in his 6 years as Chancellor, broke all records with a total of 15 Budgets and mini budgets. Since the Budget in March 1976, the Government had been trying to agree Phase Three of the incomes policy, and there had been strong hints of a reflationary package. This duly arrived on 15 July, when the Chancellor announced the first step in his contingent policy of reducing income tax by lowering the standard rate from 35% to 34%, but he also made further increases in income tax allowances. In a rare example of Liberal influence from the Lib-Lab Pact, he abandoned the previously announced increase in petrol duty of 5½p in the face of strong opposition from the Liberal party and its rural constituents.

The reflationary part of the package was needed because the economy was growing at only 1–1½%. For the incomes policy, the Chancellor sought moderation 'enough to secure that the national earnings' increase is no more than 10%', and he relied on the strict enforcement of 12-month intervals between settlements. Inflation was slowing down at only 4.3% over the 6 months to July.

Dividend increases were to be limited for another year at 10%, after which controls would lapse without further legislation.

The market drifted lower after the July package amid anxieties about the autumn pay round, and seemed set for an inactive summer. It is often assumed that the traditional holiday weeks of summer and Christmas are quiet because far too many fund managers are away. In fact, there are many examples of sharply rising markets in August and December, as though the mice rush out to play while the cats are away, leaving some fund managers stranded on holiday, mildly irritated that so much could be happening in their absence. This happened in August 1977 after a surprise decision by the Bank of England on 27 July to adopt a more flexible exchange rate policy by allowing sterling to float.

The pound immediately strengthened against the dollar and other currencies. Although it was only to a marginal and cosmetic extent, it had a dramatic effect on morale. There was a surge in demand for gilt-edged securities, enabling the successful issue of two large government stocks, and triggering a sequence of ½-point cuts in MLR that would lower it from 8% in early August to 5% by mid-October. The equity market fully shared in this sudden reversal of mood. From a low of 430.1 on 26 July, the FT Index rose for 10 consecutive days and reached 500 on the last day of August before surging to a new, all-time peak of 549.2 on 14 September 1977. The All Share Index fell just short of its all-time high, but enjoyed a 23% rise over the same 7 weeks.

The City was in celebratory mood. The FT Index had passed 500 – a level last seen on the way down in January 1973 – and reached its all-time high, if only for a fleeting moment. Suddenly, the traumas of 1974 had been exorcised and it was good to be alive in a roaring bull market. Without trying to spoil the party, some of the more sober spirits, such as Lex in the *Financial Times*, pointed out that inflation had been 100% since the last time the FT Index had been 500 in January 1973 and, of its 30 shares, only Vickers (up 104%), Beecham (102%) and GEC (101%) had matched inflation. Later calculations suggested that, in the All Share Index, only 1 share in 10 out of the 600 had matched inflation in a list headed by Ladbroke, Dixons Photographic and Associated Dairies – the latter two known today as Dixons and Asda.

In the last part of the year, equities marked time and were strongly outperformed by gilts. As MLR continued its downwards path towards 5%, the gilt-edged market enjoyed some remarkable days – particularly in the last week of September when some long-dated stocks rose by up to 8 points, to complete the surging bull market in gilts described earlier in this chapter. At its outset, the newly issued Treasury 15½%, a record high coupon, had stood at 95½, but less than a year later it had risen to 136½, a rise of 43%. It also introduced a new phenomenon to post-war investors – gilt-edged securities standing at prices well above their redemption price of 100, and guaranteeing an eventual capital loss to a new purchaser, offset by a high-running yield.

The pressure to invest remained intense. Official figures show that, at the end of 1977, life assurance company assets were around £35,000m, pension fund assets were in excess of £20,000m, each with buoyant cash inflows of £3,000m, and unit trusts were at a new peak of £3,400m. However, the total market capitalisation of all equities was only £60,000m. Unlike today, these assets were more or less ring-fenced within the UK by exchange controls. The dollar premium had drifted down to 25–30%, but the 25% surrender of the premium on any sales was a heavy portfolio tax. Demands were heard for the abandonment of controls in the face of a strong pound, but the Government resisted calls from the Bank of England, partly under the negative influence of the TUC.

There were other ways of feeding an insatiable institutional appetite. Commercial Union and Midland Bank were quite unabashed in returning for second helpings of large rights issues, seeking £74m and £96m respectively. ICI sold its 63% holding in Imperial Metal Industries for £68m. However, another initiative was more controversial and it created bitterness and hostility in the Edinburgh financial community.

On 18 October 1977, the National Coal Board Pension Fund announced its intention to make a takeover bid for British Investment Trust – one of the largest independent quoted investment trusts, based in Edinburgh, with an equity market capitalisation of £88m and gross assets of £125m. On 27 October, a bid of £106m was formally confirmed and, on the same day, the British Rail Pension Fund bid £75m for Edinburgh and Dundee Investment Trust – one of several investment trusts managed by distinguished Edinburgh investment managers Baillie Gifford.

One of the original purposes of investment trusts was to provide a quoted vehicle for the private investor seeking a balanced portfolio, although in that role today they have been upstaged by the unit trust movement in what is now called the retail market. In round terms, investment trusts were twice the size of unit trusts in the late 1970s, managing assets of £6,000m–£7,000m compared with some £3,500m for unit trusts – quite the reverse of the position today when assets of the unit trust movement in 1997 were in excess of £150,000m compared with £60,000m for investment trusts.

Another attraction was that investment trusts traditionally diversified their portfolios by investing overseas, particularly in the United States. The problem for investment trusts has been that the quoted prices of their shares have almost invariably stood at a discount to the underlying value of the assets. It was this factor, together with their spread of investments, that made them attractive to insurance companies, and Lewis Whyte was described in an earlier chapter as an active buyer of investment trusts at large discounts in the immediate post-war years.

In the late 1970s, discounts stood typically at 25% or more, on the theoretical basis of realising the investments at market value, paying off the prior charges at par and distributing the balance to the ordinary shareholders, as though in a liquidation. However, the existence of a discount can be justified by reference to income rather than capital. A proportion of the assets of an investment trust, broadly similar to average discounts over the years, is working to provide income to pay for the expenses of management, taxation and interest rather than providing earnings and dividends for the shareholder. Nevertheless, stockbrokers quickly discovered that calculating these discounts on a daily basis for their clients was a useful application for the computer resources now becoming available to their research departments. More attention was focused on the amount of the discount than on the investment record, and it was calculated solely on the capital value of the investments.

These two unwelcome bids tossed large rocks into a sheltered pool. There were many conflicts. Aggressive, upstart pension funds were raiding long-established investment trusts. London was attacking Edinburgh. Undeserving nationalised industries were trespassing in the private sector. Faceless institutions were evicting private investors from their natural home. Privileged tax-free institutions were creating unwanted capital gains tax problems for private investors.

Above all, there was resentment that carefully constructed long-term portfolios were being opportunistically sacrificed to resolve the investment problems of two major pension funds. The managers of both trusts toured widely to fight hard to retain the loyalty of their shareholders, and many a stockbroker sat uncomfortably in the crossfire between opposing clients. As with most takeover bids, money talks more loudly than loyalty, and in December both trusts fell with acceptances of around 75%, but the failure of the National Coal Board ever to reach the mandatory 90% led to structural complications in having to retain the identity of the British Investment Trust.

There can be no complaint that exposure to a bid is a price to be paid for being part of the stock market system, but normally the price is only exacted after management failure has created an opportunity for others who believe they can manage the business better or a successful company facing a bid can extract a substantial premium for its shareholders. In the case of these two investment trusts, the system was turned on its head. Nothing was to be gained by a good record because the basis of acquisition was the market value of the underlying portfolio, whether the trust was the best managed or the worst. British Investment Trust and Edinburgh and Dundee had good records, and it was galling for their managers that the higher the quality of their portfolios, the more likely their elimination from the scene.

Yet, British Rail and National Coal Board Pension Funds cannot be blamed for buying the better portfolios if they were available at the same price. The cash inflows into the pension funds of the huge nationalised industries were impossible to invest in any normal sense – a problem illustrated at the time when the Post Office Pension Fund, then including British Telecom of today, reported a cash inflow for the year of £367m.

By now, it was the autumn session and time for another package from Denis Healey. On 26 October 1977, he released a mildly reflationary £1,000m, almost entirely by means of a 12% increase in income tax allowances, and – at the same time, forecast a reduction of £1,000m in the PSBR for the year to £7,500m. The market succumbed to extended bouts of profit-taking after the package, partly losing its nerve after a ballot of miners rejected a high-paying bonus scheme, and a call for a firemen's strike over a 30% pay claim. However, a quiet December saw the two indices ending the year with impressive gains of around 40%, and the pound riding high against the dollar at $1.95.

The year 1977 had been a splendid one for fund managers, stockbrokers and jobbers alike. All were pleased with a Christmas gesture from the Treasury, when on 21 December the surrender rule of 25% of the proceeds of the sale of the dollar premium was abolished, 12 years after its introduction.

Little information was available to the public about the profitability of Stock Exchange firms, but eyebrows were raised when leading jobbers Akroyd and Smithers announced profits for the year to 30 September 1977 of £15.5m, after paying 358 employees an average of £9,940 and 41 directors and employees over £20,000 – modest by today's standards when adjusted for inflation, but well ahead of corporate culture for the time.

Barely noticed amid the general euphoria in the Stock Exchange was a small dark cloud just becoming visible on the horizon. In 1976, the legislation on restrictive practices had been extended to include services, and the Stock Exchange had submitted its rule book to the Office of Fair Trading. On 31 October 1977, the Office reported that it was placing the Stock Exchange's rule book on the register of restrictive practices, for a hearing not expected before 1979. The Stock Exchange was not singled out for special treatment – the Office of Fair Trading placed around 200 agreements and rule books on the register for hearings before the Restrictive Practices Court out of some 600 originally submitted from across the range of all services. The Stock Exchange was locked into a journey that would end nine years later with Big Bang.

Although this bull market was to last for another 18 months, share prices had more or less doubled in less than a year and both indices touched their low and high points of this phase on the same days:

	27 October 1976	14 September 1977	% change
FT Index	265.3	549.2	+107.0
All Share Index	116.29	225.72	+94.1

This remarkable consistency was to change in 1978 when they diverged quite significantly. Both drifted away in the first quarter, but while the All Share

Index surged into new high ground in August and September, the FT Index fell back well below its all-time high of 549.2.

Denis Healey produced his thirteenth Budget on 11 April 1978, shortly after completing his fourth year in office. It was reflationary on a grand scale, releasing £2,000m by raising income tax allowances and introducing a new lower rate of 25% on the first £750. The threshold for the maximum rate of 83% was raised to £23,000. Growth in the economy was forecast at 3% and the PSBR at £8,500m, or just over 5% of GDP. A target of 8–12% was set for growth in the money supply and MLR was raised from 6½% to 7½%.

At this stage of the electoral cycle, the Budget bore the hallmarks of recent cynical election exercises carried out by successive Conservative Chancellors, but it was not particularly described in those terms. The country was desperately tired of endless years of financial crisis, and the latest measures were seen as just another throw by this struggling coalition Government. The stock market was particularly concerned about the funding pressures caused by the continuing scale of Government borrowing and rises in the money supply already well above the new target of 8–12%.

Yet again, Government borrowing was threatening to crowd out the normal demands of the private sector. The PSBR is largely funded by the issue of gilts to the life assurance companies and pension funds, and these institutions in 1978 had combined cash flows of new money of around £8,000m, most of which would be swept up by the Government. They were, in any case, more intent on investing their new money in equities for a variety of good reasons. With inflation unconvincingly back into single figures, they preferred a yield of 5–6% on equities to 12% on gilts, particularly as the ending of controls in July offered the prospect of fat dividend increases. Furthermore, there were many pension funds still passing through the phase of raising the equity percentage of their portfolios towards long-term targets approaching 50%.

In late spring of 1978, the Government faced a potential funding crisis that would require higher interest rates to tempt the institutions or, as many on the left of the party would put it, the price to be paid to buy off striking investors. At this moment, the Government ran into a problem with its Liberal colleagues, who called for further cuts in income tax to stimulate the economy. The Conservative opposition seized an opportunity to impress its tax-cutting credentials on the electorate by proposing an amendment to the Finance Bill to reduce the standard rate of tax from 34% to 33%, and, with Liberal support, this was passed by 312 votes to 304. It was quickly followed by another successful amendment to raise the starting point for higher rate tax from £7,000 to £8,000 – these amendments together depriving the Chancellor of revenues of some £500m.

Back came Denis Healey with his fourteenth Budget on 8 June. To compensate for the lost revenues, he imposed a 2½% surcharge on employers' national insurance contributions. He dealt with excessive growth in the money supply by applying a penal 'corset' on the banks to restrict lending, and he eased the funding problem by raising MLR from 9% to 10%, having already twice raised it from 7½% since his April Budget.

The latest increase in MLR was more significant than usual because it was the first change made since the Bank of England announced in May that it was abandoning the automatic calculation of MLR by reference to Treasury Bill rates – the practice followed for the last five and a half years. It was a deliberate decision with both financial and political overtones. The squeeze enabled the Government to issue £1,000m of stock on the following day, but the equity market remained subdued.

Through the year, the Government had said very little about a further stage of its incomes policy after the expiry of Phase Three, and it was not until 21 July that a White Paper laid down a ceiling of 5% on pay and a limit on dividends of 10%, to take effect on 1 August. The total pay bill was permitted to rise to a total of 7% to allow for drift and anomalies, and, where profit increases exceeded 10%, dividends were allowed to be raised by the same percentage.

With a funding crisis averted and the link between dividends and earnings restored for the first time in six years, there now followed a second successive busy and buoyant August that took the All Share Index into new high ground and returned the FT Index to 500 and above. London was sharing in a world-wide pattern of booming equity markets, mostly at their highs for the year, including Japan, where the Nikkei Index reached a new all-time high of 5,650. Unusually, the price of gold was also reaching new highs, at over $200 an ounce – largely reflecting weakness of the dollar and inflationary pressures during Carter's presidency.

The bullish move into new high ground petered out in September. The TUC voiced opposition to the 5% pay ceiling, confirmed later by a formal vote at its conference, and talk of pay claims of 20–30% was in the air. On 7 September, the Prime Minister surprisingly announced that there would be no autumn election, appearing to miss a window of opportunity before his pay policy crumbled. The market had, all along, drawn some comfort from the probability of the return of a Conservative Government committed to a free economy, but the postponement of the election for six months or more now exposed it to deteriorating economic prospects in the face of industrial unrest.

This unrest quickly surfaced. Ford made an offer of 5% in line with official policy, only to prompt an immediate strike and shut down on 25 September, while the NUM rattled nerves with talk of a 40% claim. The Ford strike lasted for a bitter 9 weeks before eventually being settled on 22 November with a second 'final' offer of 17% that visibly destroyed the Government's incomes policy.

Meanwhile, well-founded fears of a resurgence of inflation had already led to a sudden increase in MLR from 10% to 12½% on 9 November, and the economic prospects were bleak. In earlier years, against this background, shares might have fallen much further than the modest 12% falls they suffered from their September highs. Partly, this was because the United States was afflicted with similar problems. Indeed, in October, President Carter introduced the American people to a rare territory for them, an incomes policy, based on limiting pay increases to 7% and price increases to ½% below the average of the last 2 years.

However, a more important reason stemmed from structural changes in shareholdings that limited downside pressure on share prices. The influence of rising cash flows had almost turned the institutions into permanent buyers, and negative influences in the market that might previously have prompted active selling now merely led institutions to cease buying. At the same time, private investors were of decreasing importance, a long-term trend that accelerated after the traumatic experience of the 1974 bear market led to many shareholders switching into cash deposits or unit trusts. As long as insurance companies and pension funds remain the principal channel for private savings, their presence brings an element of stability to markets.

Around the turn of the year, institutional appetites were fed by two large rights issues – £83m from Beechams and £62m from Rank Organisation – and two corporate disposals. Plessey sold its 24% stake in ICL for £34m in January and, in March, Imperial Group sold its remaining 15% stake in BAT Industries for £154m – the largest ever Stock Exchange placing of 49.5m shares at 310p. This was carried out by Morgan Grenfell and Barings, with stockbrokers Cazenove, Rowe & Pitman, and De Zoete & Bevan, but at a substantial discount of 11% to the overnight market price of 350p.

Although the market wobbled in February against a background of increasing industrial and trade union chaos – particularly from lorry drivers and local authority workers – and another jump in MLR from 12½% to 14% to ease funding pressure, share prices were sustained by an increasing awareness that this was a dying Government waiting to be put down. A powerful leader in the *Financial Times* on 13 January 1979 described a state of chaos in which the Government could not influence the TUC, the TUC could not influence union leaders and union leaders could not influence militant members. When the Prime Minister announced yet another pact with the TUC in February, it was dismissed as a 'boneless wonder' by Margaret Thatcher. This was the period that would later be known as 'the winter of discontent'.

Shortly after MLR was raised to 14% to break a deadlock in Government funding, there occurred an incident that became known as the 'Battle of Watling Street'. Public offerings of government stocks require application forms and cheques to be received by the closing time and date, usually 10.00 am, at a City office of the Bank of England in Watling Street. It was common practice for institutions to leave to the last minute an assessment of the likely success of an issue and, to facilitate this, stockbrokers would undertake to deposit forms for their clients by messenger delivery, having agreed at the last minute the amount to be applied for just before the issue closed at 10.00 am.

On 22 February, two issues were offered to raise £1,300m and, with one voice, the institutions decided that MLR at 14% was a temporary expedient and the new issues would be highly successful. Because a part payment of only £15 was required on application, a very attractive return was possible, and this proved to be all too true when, on the first day of dealing, the two issues closed at premiums of £3¾ and £2¾. Unfortunately, the issues were so wildly attractive that just about all the messengers in the City found themselves jostling and scuffling with each other and with numerous private individuals, too, in a huge queue in Watling Street. The reception counters were unable to cope and when the shutters were closed on the dot at 10.00 am, dozens of messengers were stranded outside with their applications from City institutions.

It was an expensive episode for the stockbroking community, whose motto 'my word is my bond' prompted without question the immediate payment to clients of compensation of at least £1m. The newly created Council for the Securities Industry (CSI) later ruled in a statement that the Bank of England was at fault in 'failing to provide such facilities for the receipt of applications as the investing public was entitled to expect', particularly in the context of partly paid issues which are designed to attract applications. However, the CSI stopped short of recommending the payment of compensation by the Bank of England, and the character of the City at the time was encapsulated in a comment by Lex on 16 March that 'in a more litigious country the Bank would no doubt already be facing challenges in the courts'.

The public sensed the death throes of the Callaghan Government on 2 March 1979 when plans for devolution for Scotland and Wales – a centrepiece of policy – were undermined by the results of referendums showing only a bare but wholly inadequate majority in favour in Scotland and decisive rejection in Wales. 'Around lunchtime yesterday the stock market woke up to politics' wrote a perceptive Lex on the following morning, and the market gathered pace in anticipation of an imminent election and the return of a Conservative government.

The end came on 28 March, when the Government lost a vote of confidence by a single vote – 311 to 310. The next day, James Callaghan recommended to the Queen the dissolution of Parliament and announced a general election for 3 May. Denis Healey's long reign as Chancellor ended with the anticlimax of a 'caretaker' Budget on 3 April.

The atmosphere in the Stock Exchange was electric in the two months between the devolution defeat on 2 March and the general election on 3 May, and daily dealings in equities frequently exceeded 30,000 bargains. The dollar premium plunged in anticipation of an end to currency controls. Wholly confident of a Conservative victory between these two dates the FT Index rose by 17% from 476.1 to 558.6, and the All Share Index by 20% from 236.35 to 283.82 – both indices standing at all-time highs on election day. It was reminiscent of the return of the Conservatives in October 1951 when the FT Index rose to within a whisker of its all-time high on election day.

The Conservatives duly swept home in the election, with an overall majority of 45. The market celebrated on the Friday, pushing both indices to new highs, whereupon the euphoria faded away. Once more it had been better to travel hopefully than to arrive.

Chapter 23

REVIEW
1964–79

The 15 years from 1964 to 1979 form the most consistently negative post-war period for the stock market investor, and many would say the same 15 years form the most dismal of any for the state of the economy and the failure of political leadership.

The investor found no favours from either political colour – the Conservative Government sandwiched between the two Labour Governments. The public was exposed to the ravages of steadily worsening surges of inflation that peaked in 1975 at 27% – a level never before experienced in peacetime in Britain.

The purpose of holding equities is to participate in the growth of the economy and to protect against inflation. The outcome for each of the 3 periods in office of the two parties, and for the total over the 15 years, shows the failure of equities to match inflation, let alone participate in growth (see Table 23.1).

Table 23.1
The All Share Index and inflation, 1964–79

Government	Dates	All Share Index	Change	Inflation	Real return (%)
Labour	15 October 1964	106.85	100.0	100.0	
	18 June 1970	120.63	112.9	129.7	(13.0)
Conservative	18 June 1970	120.63	100.0	100.0	
	28 February 1974	149.27	123.7	139.4	(11.3)
Labour	28 February 1974	149.27	100.0	100.0	
	3 May 1979	280.28	187.8	212.3	(11.5)
Overall	15 October 1964	106.85	100.0	100.0	
	3 May 1979	280.28	262.3	383.8	(31.7)

Equity shares lost almost a third of their real value with a depressing consistency over the 15 years. In simple terms, annual inflation averaged 9–10% while shares averaged annual gains of over 6–7%. The real growth in the economy overall was a shade over 2% annually, but lagging well behind an OECD average of around 3%. The yield basis of the All Share Index was little changed between October 1964 at 4.60% and May 1979 at 4.75%, with annual dividend increases averaging around 6%.

Losses in real terms were far worse in gilt-edged and fixed interest investments than in equities, thus continuing the same sorry message for the third time in these sectional reviews. The unfortunate investor in War Loan was consistently failed by one government after another (see Table 23.2).

Table 23.2
Losses in War Loan, 25 July 1945–3 May 1979

Date	Price	Change (%)	Inflation (%)	Real return (%)
25 July 1945	104¼			
25 October 1951	86½	(17.0)	26.3	(34.3)
15 October 1964	57½	(33.5)	50.9	(55.9)
3 May 1979	33½	(41.7)	283.9	(84.8)
25 July 1945–3 May 1979		(67.9)	631.7	(95.6)

In simple terms, inflation over these three political eras rose cumulatively more than 7 times, while the price of War Loan stock fell by two-thirds, amounting to a capital loss in real terms of 95%. The fifteen years now under review merely continued the pattern. 'Describe the economy today if governments since 1945 had only been allowed to issue index-linked securities', would be a testing question for the brightest of economics graduates.

The consistency of the losses in real terms in equities under each of the three governments over these fifteen years might suggest a story of steady decline throughout, with shares standing roughly on the same yield basis at the beginning as at the end. Nothing could more deceptively disguise the quite exceptional volatility of share prices, because, hidden within these fifteen years, there was a most vicious and sustained bear market of the kind that afflicts investors and practitioners only once in a lifetime, and bull markets in 1967/68, 1971/72, 1975 and 1976/77, each of which led to share prices roughly doubling.

Rising share prices alleviated the damage wrought by inflation, as did rising house prices, and the problem of inflation was not all that obvious to the man on the Clapham omnibus. One pound in 1964 may have been worth barely more than 25p in 1979, but average earnings rose from £1,000 to £5,000. It is against this yardstick that the rise in the value of equities from an equivalent £1,000 to £2,620 should be judged and found wanting.

A potent image of these years is of trade union power so rampant that their leaders attained unprecedented political influence in the heart of government. Collective bargaining and a readily used strike weapon compelled employers in private and public industries both to concede high pay increases and, at the same time, maintain overmanned workforces, with disastrous consequences for the competitive efficiency of the economy.

For twelve of these fifteen years, governments of both colours struggled with some form of incomes policy in a succession of fruitless endeavours to dam the river for a year or two, before it collapsed in the face of ever-larger flood tides of inflation. Incomes policies were abandoned after 1979.

Emergency measures to control incomes and reduce inflation were imposed three times in July 1966, November 1972 and August 1976, each followed by annual stages lingering for two, three and even four years. Initially the controls would bring down or contain inflation, only for it to surge forward again to higher levels. The rising peaks and troughs of each inflationary cycle are shown in Table 23.3 based on year to the month figures for the Retail Price Index.

Table 23.3
The peaks and troughs of the inflationary cycles, 1966–1980

Year to	Peak (%)	Year to	Trough (%)
February 1966	4.5	August 1967	1.4
June 1971	10.3	July 1972	5.8
August 1975	26.9	June 1978	7.4
May 1980	21.9		

Dividend controls are invariably a negative factor for equity shares, and they were in place in one form or another for three and a half years from July 1966 and six and a half years from November 1972. Table 23.4 sets out the dividend limits year by year, the actual annual increase achieved in the underlying dividend index on the All Share Index and annual inflation.

Dividend increases lagged behind inflation for 10 out of the 11 years from 1966 to 1976. The effect was particularly severe between 1972 and 1975, when dividends overall rose by 26%, compared with inflation of 65%, but in the late 1970s some ground was recovered when total dividend payments exceeded the control percentages. Exceptions were allowed, in the form of rights issues, defence against takeover bids and the restoration of previously cut or passed dividends.

Dividend controls are a crude weapon. Values become distorted. Successful,

Table 23.4
Dividend controls, 1965–79

Year	From	Limits	Dividend increase (%)	Inflation (%)
1965		None	7.8	4.5
1966	July	Freeze	0.4	3.6
1967	July	Voluntary	(2.4)	2.5
1968	March	3½%	4.2	5.9
1969		3½%	2.7	4.7
1970		None	5.5	7.9
1971		None	5.2	9.0
1972	November	Freeze	9.2	7.7
1973	April	5%	3.9	10.6
1974	August	12½%	9.7	19.1
1975	July	10%	10.5	24.9
1976		10%	12.3	15.1
1977		10%	16.7	12.1
1978		10%	12.5	8.4
1979 to May	10%			

growing companies are prevented from rewarding their shareholders, whereas other companies that could ill afford to pay higher dividends pretend they have no choice. However, it would be misleading to blame dividend controls alone for slow dividend growth. Profits were being squeezed hard by controls that were more effective in holding down prices than labour costs, and at the same time were subject to tax charges on a figure that was unadjusted for the adverse effect of inflation. Many companies endured a liquidity squeeze that made even the maintenance of dividends difficult.

By any measure, profits in real terms as a percentage of the GDP reached all-time low levels in the 1970s, but, because of changes to the methods of calculating corporation tax in 1965 and 1973, and the introduction of stock relief in 1975, it is difficult to illustrate this by reference to the sequence of earnings aggregated within the FT Actuaries Indices. Datastream figures show profits falling to 8–9% of GDP compared with a post-war trend of 14–15%.

The accounting problems caused by inflation have been described in an earlier chapter. The debate was at its fiercest in 1974 when there was deep conceptual disagreement in academic and professional circles about the most appropriate accounting method for dealing with the effects of inflation. British governments prefer pragmatic solutions rather than conceptual debate and Francis Sandilands, Chairman of Commercial Union Assurance, was asked in January 1974 to lead a team to investigate and report on inflation accounting.

A fundamental question was whether a new system should replace historic cost accounts or merely embellish them. Another question was whether a solution should only concern the practical problem of replacing stocks and assets when historical prices have been outpaced by inflation or should extend to the theoretical revaluation of monetary assets and liabilities. The latter involved crediting gains for the benefit of having loans that will cost less to repay in real terms and debiting losses for the depreciation in the value of cash held in the balance sheet. With debt well in excess of cash in most balance sheets the inclusion of monetary items would partly offset the swingeing forecast reductions of 50% or more in the UK profits of many companies arising from the adjustment for stocks and depreciation.

The problem was that replacing stocks and assets cost real money, whereas crediting gains for borrowings only created paper profits. There was a credibility problem about a solution that penalised a cash-rich company such as GEC that was clearly able to survive the strain and made over-borrowed companies suddenly look more profitable when they were actually desperately short of cash and struggling to stay afloat.

Although the Sandilands Report was published in September 1975 at the moment when the rate of inflation stood at its highest point, liquidity problems had been defused by the Chancellor's allowance of stock relief in the November 1974 Budget. This pragmatic measure took precedence over the theoretical niceties proposed in the Report and, in any case, many investors believed that the market had always been discounting the problem by the selective use of PE ratios, both for individual companies and for the market as a whole. Although the market had more than doubled from its low point when the Report was published, average PE ratios still only stood at a historically low level of around 8, which was another way of saying that the market recognised that true profits were between a third and half lower than reported.

The Sandilands Report proposed a new system of 'current cost accounting', with industry-specific adjustments to assets, the exclusion of monetary assets and liabilities, and the definition of stock profits as non-distributable holding gains. In December, the Accounting Standards Committee of the Institute of Chartered Accountants published an Exposure Draft, ED 18, proposing a system of current cost accounting broadly along the lines of the Sandilands Report. The adjustment for monetary assets and liabilities was sidelined as a weak voluntary option.

There was a long consultation period during the first half of 1977. Opinion was widely divided. Companies were torn between the attraction of lower profits leading to lower taxation and making it easier to resist pay claims, and a concern that dividends would become more difficult to justify to the disadvantage of share prices. The accounting profession was divided between the larger and smaller firms, with the latter opposed to the complexity and workload of the proposed system. In the event, the Institute lost the argument in the face of a grass roots revolt led by two young Sussex accountants and ED 18 was withdrawn. However, a positive consequence of the debate on inflation accounting was the emergence in company accounts of a statement of the source and application of funds – better known today as cash flow statements. This valuable extra page provided a link between the profit and loss account and the balance sheet.

Interest in inflation accounting was now waning fast. In October 1977, a compromise was reached in the introduction of the Hyde Guidelines, named after William Hyde, Chief Accountant of Oxford University, who was chairing a working party on the subject. These guidelines simply required that the relevant adjustments for depreciation, stocks and gearing be shown in the form of a note to the accounts, while leaving the historic cost accounts unchanged – a harmless outcome to what had become a tiresome issue. It was a neat compromise that a solution should be found by an accountant from the heart of academia.

The linking themes that join together these 15 years of stock market history are the continuity of controls over incomes and dividends, accelerating inflation and poor stock market experience. However, from an alternative perspective, the period could be divided into two halves, before and after 1970.

For some 25 years since the end of the war, countries had become accustomed to systems of fixed prices, for currencies, gold and oil. Currencies were fixed at Bretton Woods in 1946 and, although occasional devaluations were permitted as a last resort, every country strived to maintain the value of its currency. The price of gold had been fixed at $35 an ounce in the 1930s, and the price of oil was fixed at around $2 a barrel.

With an uncanny congruence of timing in the early 1970s, these fixed prices collapsed within a short space of time. The convertibility of dollars into gold at the fixed price was abandoned for private individuals in 1968 and for governments in 1971. Fixed rates for currencies fell apart in 1971, to be replaced by new, flexible 'Smithsonian' rates that have become little more than benchmarks for measuring the extent to which currencies have since floated. The price of oil was twice doubled in 1973.

Apart from local attempts to fix currencies – in particular, in Europe – the major currencies – dollar, yen, mark, pound and Swiss franc – have since mostly floated one with another, and gold and oil have become market commodities. From a fixed price of $35 an ounce, gold has been as high as $835, and from $2 a barrel, oil has since reached a high of $40. The liberalisation of currencies, oil and gold is a feature that divides the Wilson/Heath/Wilson/Callaghan years right down the middle. Edmund Dell, in a history of the post-war Chancellors (*The Chancellors*, HarperCollins, 1996), marks 1970 as a defining year for closing one chapter and opening another because of the shift from fixed to floating currencies.

However, it could be argued that the fixed prices of currencies, gold and oil simply fell victim to the pressures of an inflationary era that more or less began in 1964 and peaked in 1979. They could no longer be sustained. Fixed currencies collapsed in the face of different rates of inflation within individual countries, the fixed price of gold was undermined by widespread inflation and oil fell to a combination of inflation and producer power.

Inflation in double figures provided a new challenge to the public, the governments and City practitioners. Apart from a small number of people who had escaped from Germany in the 1930s, people in the City had no experience of living with inflation and had only a textbook understanding of its horrors. In Britain, the man in the street with a house and a decent job or the typical member of a trade union actually felt they were doing rather well as inflation took hold. The weaker voice of the pensioner living on a fixed annuity or fixed pension was barely heard.

New challenges were presented to the investor. The ending of fixed prices of currencies, oil and gold brought with it the volatility of the free market, where prices are no longer centrally imposed, but set by buyers and sellers, investors and speculators. This turbulent period was characterised by a flight from cash into assets. Commodities were one such hedge, but they produced no income. Gold was an obvious choice among the precious metals, with silver and platinum having some attractions, too, and there was support for copper among the base metals. Works of art were acquired by the British Rail Pension Fund, but, like commodities, they produced no income.

Fund managers focused on property and equities. A certain mystique attached itself to commercial property, and the institutions built up core holdings of commercial property that peaked in 1979 at 24% of total assets of the life assurance companies and 18% of the pension funds. It had many attractions. Severe planning and political constraints on the building of offices acted to limit the supply of city centre offices to such an extent that rents and, hence, capital values not only matched inflation but rose sharply in real terms. There was a large, unsatisfied demand from fast-growing service businesses and professions. Office blocks in the City of London were the cream of commercial properties, followed by offices in the rest of London and the main provincial cities. The pecking order continued to include small office developments, shops, trading estates and warehouses, each in turn offering a higher yield.

The tentacles of property reached many corners of the economy. The property sector of the equity market was a star performer, and the development of new properties was led by the principal quoted property companies. Many worked in conjunction with an insurance company or pension fund, which supplied the finance in a joint venture. Rising values created a property spiral and many outsiders were sucked into second-rate developments, financed by the banks on the basis of extravagant projections of rental income. Many of the bankruptcies after the 1974 crash were caused by the value of properties plummeting below the loans advanced to build or buy them, and it was at this time that the prime weakness of property investment was seen at its starkest – namely that it is illiquid.

There is no day-to-day market in office blocks. Individual transactions are infrequent, but, when they occur, they exercise a disproportionate influence on the valuation of the whole of the property market. On the upward leg of the cycle, the price may be exaggerated by competing institutions being required to tender sealed bids. On the way down, a forced seller may be squeezed hard by a sole buyer. In either direction, the yield basis on which the latest transaction is completed becomes the benchmark for the valuation of all comparable properties.

The scramble to buy and develop commercial property by the institutions was mirrored by a scramble for residential property by private individuals and developers, and the level of bank lending for property development became a matter for concern in the 1970s. Illiquidity led to property becoming unsaleable and the long-term financing of property developments from short-term deposits played the leading role in the crash of the secondary banks in the mid-1970s.

It is ironic that an overcommitment to unsaleable property led directly to the fall of Slater Walker in 1976 as few people seemed as alert to the perils of inflation as Jim Slater. He expressed home truths during those inflationary years – for example, warning at his AGM in 1974 about the illiquidity of assets perceived as hedges against inflation: 'many people in recent months have found you cannot always turn property into cash, large lines of shares into cash, pictures into cash. Cash you can always turn into other things'. By then it was already too late.

However, the most liquid hedge against inflation remained equity shares. Department of Trade figures show that, in aggregate, the pension funds had built up their investment in equities from 40% of assets at market value in the mid 1960s to a peak of 60% in 1972. The percentage then fell with the market and stood at 47% in 1979. Until 1975, the life assurance companies confined published information only to investments at book value, which consistently through the 1960s and 1970s showed equities at 20% of total assets, but later market value figures from 1976 showed percentages at around 30%.

The industry figures for 1979 show a remarkable concurrence in the value of assets owned by these two drivers of the stock market, with totals of £42,700m for the life companies and £42,300m for the pension funds.

Since 1979, the equity percentages of both have continued to rise in the UK, particularly in overseas equities following the dismantling of exchange controls in 1979. Industry figures for 1996 show that the UK percentage has risen modestly to around 55%, but the overseas equities have added a further 15%. The life companies now have 60% of assets in equities. Conversely the percentages in property has dwindled to a mere 5% for pension funds and 7% for life companies. As inflation has gradually been defeated, so property has fallen out of favour – a victim of slow rental growth and illiquidity. Whereas equity holdings in the late 1970s were barely twice the size of property holdings, today they are ten times higher.

There was a double play in the impact of pension funds on the equity market because they were increasing their equity percentages at the same time as the funds they had available for investment were growing rapidly. This was for a combination of reasons. Many new pension funds were being created and all employers came under pressure to improve pension benefits for their employees. Inflation was lifting the pay bill in nominal terms for all employers and contributions paid into pension funds simply followed suit. Finally, most pension funds were relatively immature in the sense that they had very few pensioners in receipt of payments compared with the numbers contributing for future payments. For many years, therefore, cash inflows greatly exceeded outflows – a position that only began to be reversed in the 1990s.

The growth of the long-term funds is illustrated in Table 23.5 by the net cash inflows to the pension funds and life assurance companies over the same period.

Table 23.5
The growth of cash flows of pension funds and life assurance companies, 1966–79

Year	Life Assurance	Pension Funds	Total (£m)
1966	610	437	1,047
1970	837	673	1,660
1975	1,733	2,209	3,942
1976	2,084	2,972	5,056
1977	2,863	3,180	6,043
1978	4,028	3,720	7,748
1979	4,451	5,590	10,041

This was a formidable pool of new money flowing into the investment market, much of it seeking equity investments, and it explains why pension funds and insurance companies came to own an ever-increasing percentage of the shares of the average company. The weight of money driving the bull markets of this period came, as in the 1950s, from the institutional investors, but clearly was now led by the pension funds, which pursued equities more aggressively than did the insurance companies. At the same time, a third institutional vehicle was accelerating rapidly in the outside lane.

This was the unit trust movement, which barely participated in the early years of the cult of the equity in the 1950s. It was seen as the poor cousin of the long-established investment trusts – not especially popular with the stockbroking community and hampered by discouraging regulations. It was only in 1965 that total unit trust funds reached £500m from just over 100 individual trusts and, at that time, the movement was still overshadowed by the investment trust movement with assets of £3,100m. Growth thereafter was dramatic, as shown in Table 23.6.

Table 23.6
The growth of the value of unit trust funds, 1965–80

Year	Value of funds (£m)	Number of trusts
1965	500	121
1970	1,320	240
1975	2,550	353
1980	4,250	493

Table 25.6 represents only a segment of the long-term growth of a movement that today manages funds of over £150,000m, but it was an important component in the changing picture of the register of shareholders of the typical company between 1964 and 1979. The unit trust industry might have felt it had arrived in 1969 when the *Financial Times*, for the first time, devoted a separate page to the prices of some 230 trusts.

The growth of pension funds, insurance companies and unit trusts changed the structure of share ownership. Information about shareholders has never been precise, but various surveys and estimates broadly tell a consistent enough story for a reasonable estimate to be made of the percentage of quoted shares owned by the principal categories of shareholder, shown in Table 23.7.

The four conventional investing institutions together owned less than a fifth of equities in 1957. This rose to a quarter in 1963, and to more than half in 1979. Their growth is mirrored in reverse in the decline of private individual ownership, particularly after the experience of the 1974 bear market, although unit trusts became an alternative vehicle for private investors.

The 'miscellaneous' heading is made up of groups of investors that would largely be regarded as institutional. In roughly equal proportions they include overseas investors; industrial, commercial and financial companies; charities; and the public sector. Since 1979, shareholdings of the four conventional investing institutions have risen close to an estimated 60% of the total, private individuals have drifted to around 20%, and overseas investors have emerged as a powerful separate grouping at around 15%.

Overseas investors reflect the emergence of cross-border investment as a

Table 23.7
Estimated percentage ownership of UK equities, 1957–79

Year	1957 (%)	1963 (%)	1969 (%)	1973 (%)	1979 (%)
Pension funds	3.4	7.0	9.0	12.2	23.0
Insurance companies	8.9	10.6	12.2	16.2	21.0
Unit trusts	0.7	1.3	2.9	3.4	3.5
Investment trusts	5.0	6.7	6.6	6.5	4.8
Total	18.0	25.6	30.7	38.3	52.3
Private individuals	66.0	54.0	47.4	42.0	28.7
Miscellaneous	16.0	20.4	21.9	19.7	19.0

legitimate avenue for reducing portfolio risk by diversifying away from being too dependent on domestic markets. It was always talked about in theory, but has only been made possible in practice by the relaxation of financial controls and the use of technology. Overseas investors have become significant shareholders in the London market because the new fashion of cross-border investment has coincided with the greater appeal of the British market in the 1980s and 1990s.

Just as 1971 marked the liberalisation from a fixed past to a flexible future in currencies, so also the middle years that cover this section of the history of the post-war stock market witnessed the beginnings of major changes in the stock market, whether it was in the institutions, the practitioners in the Stock Exchange or in the shift in power to the shareholder. Although these changes came to be later expressed in Big Bang and the freedom of the 1980s and 1990s, the seeds of change were sown in these more turbulent years of the 1970s.

Fund management had been a fragmented business of different methods and structures, but it was now beginning to consolidate into more focused fund management groups. These would eventually form a successful segment of the quoted equity market and establish for Britain a reputation as a world leader in fund management. The City again displayed its ability to capture a large market share in a new financial service, and the merchant banks showed their traditional adaptability by taking the lead in defining a new and profitable business.

The contrast between common practice in 1964 and 1979 is striking. In the 1960s many companies paid pension contributions into insured schemes operated by life assurance companies, until they became large enough or aware enough to form an in-house pension fund. The majority of large companies already managed their own pension funds from an in-house team, usually reporting to the chief executive or the finance director.

The post of investment manager would probably have been filled by a random choice from within the company, and some of these managers would become prized clients for stockbrokers and influential names in the City, such as Geoff Morley of Shell, John Mulligan of Courtaulds and William Broadfield of Unilever. Jack Butterworth of British Petroleum was another, but he usually chose to meet the jobbers face to face in a brokers' box in the Stock Exchange and hand out his business direct to them before parcelling it out to the brokers later in the day. Others kept a lower profile, such as the National Coal Board Pension Fund, which operated on pound averaging principles with regular orders to invest an exact £5,000 or £10,000 in chosen equities. It later came under the control of Hugh Jenkins, a leading City name in fund management in the 1970s.

External fund managers were rare. Particular exceptions were the local authority pension funds, which were mostly managed by stockbrokers Phillips & Drew, and the pension funds of corporate clients managed or advised by various stockbrokers. No fees were charged, but commissions were generated from handling all the transactions.

Cost factors slowly began to work against these in-house departments. The administration and settlement of large portfolios became ever more complicated, and fitting City salary scales for investment managers into an industrial salary structure created unwanted friction. At the same time, incipient asset management divisions were growing within the leading merchant banks, charging a fee on the funds managed, and as in-house management teams began to be closed down, there was competition for the management of their funds.

The leading contestants for this business emerged from the investment management division of the merchant banks – led from first to last by S. G. Warburg, later under its independent name of Mercury Asset Management. It was in the 1970s that this switch to external fund managers gained ground. They were able to offer objective advice, performance analysis and freedom from unnecessary churning in exchange for a fee that compared favourably with the cost of running an in-house department. Thereafter, it became a performance battle consistently won in the 1970s and 1980s by S. G. Warburg, where, despite an in-house cultural horror of personal publicity, the mantle of the best-known pension fund manager passed to Leonard Licht.

Licht was an especially astute judge of value and people. He developed an encyclopaedic knowledge of companies, but, above all, displayed a boldness in backing his judgement. While the majority of fund managers and their directors or trustees were essentially risk-averse and did not stray too far away from the balanced portfolio, Licht would willingly build 10–20% stakes in companies he favoured, and hold nothing in sectors or leading companies he disliked. Given good judgement, this was a recipe for success, but it is easier said than done.

Rothschilds were strong competitors to S. G. Warburg in the early 1970s and carried the headlines in the 1974 bear market for their commitment to gold shares and cash, but they were left stranded in 1975, and never recovered their reputation.

The investment departments of the life assurance companies were almost invariably headed by an actuary. Details of the holdings of the investment funds and their performance were closely guarded secrets, and actuarial influence tended to lead to conservative investment policies. Gilt-edged holdings formed a larger part of the portfolio than for pension funds. Large property holdings were common to both, except that a proportion of the portfolio of the life company would comprise its own head office and branch office buildings. There was a reluctance to reveal the market values of investments, and the analysis of holdings in the annual accounts at book or cost value under different categories of investment was largely meaningless.

The life fund was an aggregation of investments designed to provide the necessary returns to support the many different types of life policies in issue and, in most cases, bonuses would be declared once every three years after an actuarial valuation of the fund. Life assurance companies were havens of conservatism surrounded by actuarial mystique. Bonuses were declared on the basis of investment income, capital appreciation on equity investments seemed to be ignored and few things were more confusing to the outsider than a policyholder's bonus statement.

Large hidden surpluses were steadily accumulating in the life funds and this was recognised in 1969 when the concept of the terminal bonus was introduced, allowing part of the capital appreciation earned over the life of a policy to be paid to the policyholder. These same surpluses had also come to the notice of predators, and some of the smaller quoted life companies were acquired at high prices. They had also come to the notice of Jim Slater, who accumulated holdings in the sector before coming to the conclusion that an attack on a major life company would not be welcomed.

The life companies were no longer able to surround themselves with actuarial mystique. Prudential Assurance broke the ice by marketing new policies based on its own newly launched unit trust in 1968, although this was trifling in the context of its life fund. The life assurance industry next found itself facing new competition in the form of linked life policies, where the ultimate return to the policyholders was transparent in that their premiums were invested in a specific fund with an openly quoted market price.

The pioneer of this new form of life assurance in the UK was Mark Weinberg – a young, engaging and very astute South African lawyer who created the business of Abbey Life, jointly owned by two US companies. The company was subject to an arcane capital structure, whereby if one party chose at any time to make a bid for the shareholding of the other party, the latter had either to accept that bid or buy the bidder's stake at the same price. It was poker writ large, but when the option was exercised in 1970, Weinberg and four of his most senior colleagues left Abbey Life and, with the aid of Hambros Bank, founded the highly successful Hambro Life, which became a quoted company in 1976.

Linked life assurance with its dedicated funds leads naturally to unit trusts, the third leg of the institutional investment market. They grew rapidly in the 1970s, although at nothing like the rate of growth to be seen in the next two decades after tight regulatory restrictions on charging were removed in 1979. The two market leaders were long established. Municipal and General Securities, popularly known as M&G, was founded in 1931, and Save & Prosper, owned by merchant bank Robert Fleming, in 1934. They were primarily aimed at small, private investors, for whom investment trusts had been the more traditional alternative, but they had the advantage of a daily valuation and exact price in the financial pages, whereas the investment trusts had a fluctuating market price that usually stood at a significant discount to the underlying asset value.

Unit trusts traditionally offered private individuals a diversified fund of UK investments with an emphasis either on capital growth or income or a combination of the two. Specialised funds were also provided, some of the earliest examples being in the financial sector, followed by funds investing in overseas markets, with particular emphasis on the United States.

By the end of the 1970s there were more than 400 unit trusts managed by nearly 100 management groups, many formed in the late 1960s. Much the largest was Save & Prosper with over 400,000 unitholders spread across some 20 different funds with an aggregate value approaching 25% of the industry total. It also managed by far and away the largest unit trust, Investment Trust Units, invested solely in quoted investment trusts, offering the ultimate example of diversification to reduce risk.

An attraction for the buyers of unit trusts was the ease with which past performance was measured, published and compared in league table form. This is taken for granted today, but it was a welcome new feature when first introduced. M&G was the second largest unit trust group, approaching 15% of the total market and it also had the second largest unit trust, M&G Dividend Fund, another veteran fund like Save & Prosper's Investment Trust Units. A sample league table published in March 1978 – reproduced in Table 23.8 – showed the top five performers across all unit trusts over one, two, four and six years.

There are intriguing differences between these tables and comparable tables published today. A top five table drawn from all unit trusts today would be dominated by a proliferation of trusts that happened to specialise in the narrow market area that was the best-performing market or country at the time. There might be 100 or more trusts in a single specialist sector today compared with

Table 23.8
Unit trust performance table, March 1978

One year	%	Two years	%
M&G Recovery	+67.3	M&G Recovery	+90.1
Piccadilly Small Companies	+60.3	Framlington Capital	+80.1
Allied Hambro Smaller Cos	+59.7	Framlington Income	+71.8
Framlington Income	+58.2	Allied Hambro Smaller Companies	+66.8
Framlington Capital	+56.2	London Wall Extra Income	+66.6
FT All Share Index	+17.6	*FT All Share Index*	+25.2

Four years	%	Six years	%
Framlington Income	+193.0	M&G Recovery	+142.0
Gartmore High Income	+169.0	Framlington Income	+134.8
GT Japan & General	+167.6	Arbuthnot Commodity	+104.4
M&G Recovery	+165.7	Framlington Capital	+104.0
Framlington Capital	+161.7	Henderson High Income	+103.0
FT All Share Index	+54.0	*FT All Share Index*	+12.7

only 400 trusts across *all* markets in 1978. Only one overseas trusts appears in Table 23.8 – GT Japan – and one fund investing in commodity shares appears in the listing for six years.

The most striking difference between then and today is the scale and extent of the outperformance of the All Share Index achieved over all periods, not only by the top five, but also by a succession of trusts following just behind. The apparent ease and scale of outperformance reported in 1978 suggests that the stock market was far less efficient than it is today. Development in research, the greater accessibility of companies, and the speed and ease of communication have raised common knowledge to such a high level that opportunities for beating the market have been much reduced. Almost all the trusts ranked in the top five in 1978 were investing in the UK for capital growth or income, or in smaller companies, and they were able to take advantage of opportunities that no longer exist. Another difference observed by Leonard Licht in the context of pension funds is that in the 1970s it was easier to shine because the overall standard of fund management was far lower than it is today. It had not yet become a glamorous part of the City and so was not attracting the best graduates.

The star performer – with three first places and one fourth place in Table 23.8 – was M&G Recovery, managed by David Tucker, and investing in companies out of fashion or passing through hard times. Under the leadership of the evangelical David Hopkinson, M&G was much the most successful group, with three other funds appearing in the top ten. Hopkinson drew together a team of highly individual fund managers who were given a free rein to perform. The M&G Recovery Fund was the most successful of all, and David Tucker used his earlier experience as the buyer of struggling textile companies for Joe Hyman's Viyella empire to good effect, applying an entrepreneurial approach to the risks and rewards of companies falling on hard times. Tucker rose to fame in fund management, suddenly retiring in the late 1980s.

Also ranking in all four parts of Table 23.8 were two other outstanding performers – Framlington Income and Framlington Capital. They were examples of another trend emerging in the late 1960s for stockbrokers to form and manage in-house unit trusts for their smaller, private clients. Small bargains had become uneconomic and, rather than turn clients away, some 20 firms of stockbrokers formed unit trusts between 1968 and 1973, despite not being allowed to advertise under Stock Exchange rules.

Their performance in most cases was middling to poor, but notable exceptions were the two Framlington trusts, formed under the aegis of Laurence Prust, but with a controlling outside interest that enabled the ban on advertising by the Stock Exchange to be avoided. The two Framlington trusts specialised in small companies and were managed by Bill Stuttaford and Anthony Milford. Stuttaford's enthusiasm and panache blended perfectly with Milford's cerebral skills as an international bridge player. Bridge is as good a grounding as any for fund management. It requires the ability to make a rapid and accurate assessment of the cards, the discipline to pass for much of the time and the confidence to make successful game and slam bids – all perfect ingredients for the successful fund manager.

While unit trusts thrived, the investment trusts struggled, becoming the weakest of the four legs of the institutional market. The widely discussed discounts to asset value were a marketing director's nightmare – difficult to explain and seemingly unpredictable, varying according to the whims of the market. Furthermore, the discounts widened over the period from around 10–15% in the late 1960s to either side of 30% in the mid to late 1970s, culminating in controversial bids for two leading Scottish investment trusts in 1977 from two nationalised industry pension funds.

The morale of the manager of an investment trust was little helped by an acute awareness that a takeover bid to liquidate the trust was probably the best solution for the shareholder. The inevitable discount has also operated against the issue of new investment trusts, where skilful promotion is required to induce subscribers to put up money for shares at par value when those shares will almost inevitably drift to a discount – rather like buying a new car.

Many investment trust managers were highly skilled, while others were passengers, enjoying a quiet life. It would be no exaggeration to say that the reputation of Scotland as a centre of investment excellence was based on investment trust management skills in Edinburgh, Dundee, Aberdeen and Glasgow. The Alliance Trust in Dundee could lay claim to the finest single name of all investment trusts. Groups of investment trusts were managed in Edinburgh under the names of leading firms of accountants and solicitors of the likes of Baillie Gifford, Ivory & Sime, and Martin Currie, and in Glasgow by McClelland Moores. Other individual trusts carried names resonant of an earlier era, such as Investors Mortgage and Scottish-American Investment Trust.

Edinburgh played on its reputation and made a virtue of the greater time for reflection allowed by its distance from London. It emphasised the long-term view in contrast to the assumed shorter-term pressures of London, rather like the equally proud investment community of Boston looks down on New York. Edinburgh had a distinct edge over London in terms of its expertise and contacts in the stock markets of the United States, and with high proportions of their portfolios in dollar stocks the typical investment trust in Scotland offered the best option for investors seeking an exposure across the Atlantic.

Edinburgh is also host to two of the largest life assurance companies – Standard Life, modestly second in size only to the Prudential, and the rather more flamboyant Scottish Widows. However, the influence of the investment community north of the border was probably at its peak in the 1960s and 1970s. Investment trusts have survived but not flourished, their diversified, general character working against them in times of specialisation, and Scotland has signally failed to make much impact in the thriving world of unit trusts.

Those were the days when distance lent enchantment, but it carries less weight in the electronic age. Stockbrokers in London would spend the better part of a week in Scotland, visiting some 20 or more institutions, in an annual pilgrimage that was daunting in the face of penetrating questions or the sudden aside, 'I have a note here that tells me last year you said . . .'. The constant repetition of the story was tiring, but pleasurable for the courtesy and hospitality that once earned was gladly given. Those days have been overtaken by the screen, the fax and the conference call – all quite indifferent to the physical location of the desk.

Fund management was emerging as a growth business, and some individual fund managers were tempted to break away to form their own business – a common enough practice in the United States, but relatively rare in the City. It was risky because an innate conservatism inhibited the trustees and directors of investing institutions from pursuing the unconventional route of backing an individual. The earliest notable example was the formation in 1969 of GT Management by Tom Griffin and Richard Thornton – two fund managers from Foreign and Colonial. At an older age, Geoffrey Morley formed a successful pension fund management group under his own name in 1973, after retiring as the fund manager of the Shell Pension Fund.

These examples involved names already well known in the investment field, but outstandingly successful was the formation of Perpetual Fund Managers in 1973 by Martyn Arbib in the then seemingly eccentric location of Henley. The concept of locating away from London was far-sighted, as has been the decision to specialise in unit trusts, and by 1997 Perpetual had built itself into the fourth largest unit trust manager and a company with a market capitalisation of £800m. Another example was set by Stewart Newton, who left Ivory & Sime in 1977 to form a successful fund management business, now well known in his own name, managing funds of some £12bn. However, examples of fund managers going it alone are few and far between, and far less common than in the US.

These were also years of change in stockbroking and jobbing. The decline in ownership of shares by private clients has been illustrated in an earlier table. For most firms of stockbrokers in the mid-1960s, an active private clients' department was still an important part of the business. Many partners had long lists of well-satisfied private clients, others hung on to a loyal few. Some partners were scornful of faceless institutions, some were frightened, others were uneasily aware that private clients were slipping down the agenda in a business increasingly driven by institutions. In the good years, any business was welcome, but in a downturn closer analysis would reveal that the staffing of many firms was built around the need to support the much higher volume of bargains levels produced by private clients and by the large branch bank business for customers of the clearing banks.

Stockbroking is a highly geared activity and questions are only really asked when business activity falls away and profits fall twice as quickly. One such downturn was in 1965/66, when the effects of falling markets were exacerbated by the introduction of a short-term capital gains tax aimed specifically at the private individual. For the first time, the stark contrast between the profitability of institutional and private client business became apparent to many firms.

Smaller private clients were the first to come under pressure. Many stockbrokers refused to handle unprofitable branch bank business. Some formed unit trusts as a vehicle for small clients and some of the established unit trusts encouraged stockbrokers to buy units for their private clients by offering reciprocal business of a multiple of the amount invested. M&G was justified by good performance in being especially active in this direction, but for less well-managed funds, it was little more than bribery.

Private client departments became more commercial. Some started to charge clients for an annual valuation and, in the mid-1970s, others for the first time charged their clients a fee based on the size of the portfolio, although this was often rebated against subsequent commissions. Another development was the formation within the partnership of a fund management company. An early example in 1976 was Rowan Investment Managers, a wholly owned subsidiary of Rowe & Pitman, which took over the management of private clients on an advisory or discretionary fee-paying basis and the management of in-house unit trusts and pension funds on a basis comparable to that of external fund managers. It also asserted its freedom to deal with brokers other than the parent firm.

A particular significance of this step was the principle of charging a fee. Stockbrokers had collected many smaller pension funds from client companies, charging no fee but taking commissions from handling all transactions. This practice provoked complaints of unfair competition and conflict of interest from professional fund managers. Most vociferous of all were the merchant banks whose investment departments charged fees for managing pension funds and paid commissions to the same stockbrokers for executing business.

The merchant banks were emerging as powerful investors in their own right and, with their widespread investing needs, they had become the most prized of all clients for the leading stockbrokers. Their corporate finance departments might be buying stakes for corporate clients in target companies or buying shares in a defence. Some managed investment trusts, others managed unit trusts – as, for example, Robert Fleming and the unit trusts of the Save & Prosper stable.

Much the fastest-growing area of pension funds has already been described and the merchant banks also managed personal portfolios, but only those with high minimum values of £250,000 or an amount exuding that air of wealth and exclusivity suitable for the image of both client and merchant bank. Lastly, the merchant banks invested their own capital.

It was from these fragmented forms of fund management – in-house pension funds, life assurance companies, unit trusts, investment trusts, merchant banks and stockbrokers – that there emerged the fund management companies that stand today as both large and small specialist businesses, either wholly independent or as largely independent divisions of their merchant bank parents. Their evolution is a subject for the 1980s.

As the merchant banks became a major force in the stock market, they grew restless at the millions of pounds of commission they were handing out to stockbrokers each year, on fixed commission scales that were insensitive to rising volumes of business. In August 1972, the Issuing Houses Association confirmed circulating rumours that the merchant banks were to develop a new computerised dealing system to compete directly with the Stock Exchange. It was called the Automated Real-time Investments Exchange Limited, to be known as Ariel.

The shareholders of Ariel subscribed capital in roughly equal proportions to the amounts of Stock Exchange commission paid, and this gave an insight into the ranking of the investment activities of the merchant banks at the time:

- 10% Hambros, Hill Samuel, Lazards, Rothschilds, Schroder Wagg, S. G. Warburg;
- 8% Kleinwort Benson, Samuel Montagu, Morgan Grenfell;
- 5% Barings, Guinness Mahon;
- 1% Antony Gibbs, Arbuthnot Latham, Wm. Brandt's, Brown Shipley, Charterhouse Japhet, Rea Bros.

Ariel was to provide an automated order-matching system modelled on the

Instinet system used in the United States. It would guarantee anonymity and be open to all institutions. It planned to charge an annual subscription of £3,000 and a commission rate of 0.3% up to a maximum of £2,000. Its objective was to secure 10% of institutional business, or an estimated 4% of the total equity market.

The plan for Ariel rattled the Stock Exchange and was a factor in prompting some sizeable and overdue reductions in commission rates for both equities and gilts in August 1972, in a year that was easily a record for equity turnover. Even these recently reduced commission rates would be halved by Ariel on a sample equity transaction of £100,000 and there would be no jobber's turn. Individual reactions ranged from philosophical calm to panic among the institutional firms of stockbrokers most closely threatened. However, when Ariel actually opened for business in February 1974 with some 40 subscribers, share prices had already fallen and activity was in rapid decline. In its first 8 months it obtained 1% of stock market turnover.

Ariel was always a better idea in theory than in practice. Its proponents under-estimated the psychological reluctance of fund managers to declare their hand openly and their preference for having an intermediary to take into their confidence when executing a large transaction.

The Stock Exchange itself was not immune to change during this period, although its critics might say otherwise. It faithfully remained the curate's egg – good in parts, a mixture of sensible reform spiced with refusal to change. The process of consolidation in the numbers of firms in London continued apace through the period 1964 to 1979 (see Table 23.9).

Table 23.9
Consolidation in number of Stock Exchange firms, 1964–79

Year	Number of firms of stockbrokers	Number of firms of jobbers
1950	364	191
1960	305	100
1964	271	66
1970	192	31
1975	124	16
1979	110	14

Events that culminated in the crash of 1974 led to many firms closing down, merging or being 'hammered'. The latter is the Stock Exchange ritual announced on the floor of the House that 'Messrs. . . . are unable to comply with their bargains'. When a firm is made bankrupt, the public is protected from losses by the compensation fund, but this was depleted by a succession of 'hammerings' and had to be topped up in 1974 by an unpopular levy of £300 per member. Many stockbrokers endured the nightmare of unlimited liability and many jobbers were driven out of business by lack of trade and shortage of capital. The total numbers employed by the firms in all Stock Exchanges in the UK, including members, reached a peak of 35,000 in May 1972 and fell to its lowest point of 16,200 in February 1977.

Every firm of stockbrokers was forced to consider its future in 1974 as business contracted to levels insufficient to cover expenses. Turnover in equities dwindled from a monthly average of £1,700m in 1972 to £800m in the latter half of 1974. Corporate activity in new issues, rights issues and takeover bids almost disappeared. Most firms allowed staff numbers to contract by natural wastage, a freeze on recruitment and discreet redundancies, particularly in settlement departments now handling bargain numbers less than half of the peak.

In many firms, these measures were still insufficient to generate worthwhile profits, and it is at this point that the stark difference between a partnership and a company becomes apparent. Partners are the equivalent of the directors and top executives of a company, but when costs are cut by a company to bring them into line with revenues, they still include realistic salaries for the directors and executives. When a partnership cuts its costs into line with revenues, it is before any profits are earned for the partners. If notional salaries for partners had been included in costs in 1974, most firms would have been heavily in loss.

The personal pressure on partners was intense. With barely any profits being earned, the personal capital resources of each partner were required to cover their own day-to-day living expenses and meet any losses in the business under the laws of unlimited liability. For many younger partners, their capital resources were already subscribed to the partnership. Other partners with capital had suffered the same depletion of their investment portfolios as any other investor, and their asset of last resort, their house, had become unsaleable at any worthwhile price. With the increasing risk of clients announcing bankruptcy without notice, unlimited liability for losses became, for some partners, a nightmare.

The pressure was greatest on the medium-sized generalist firm. Private clients tend to stop dealing in bear markets and institutions became choosy about which brokers to use when they had less business to give. Many mergers took place between the smaller names and others simply disappeared, but the major firms survived largely intact. Many mergers were contemplated, but ran into obstacles on closer examination. Cost savings could be achieved, but partnership pride was often a stumbling block, and there was no market for surplus office space and complicated leases. Maintenance of revenue from the institutions was the greatest uncertainty in any merger, with the danger that one plus one, far from equalling two, would all too often equal a tiny margin over one.

In fact, very few large mergers have ever taken place. De Zoete and Bevan was the product of a successful merger in 1970, and leading corporate broker Rowe & Pitman successfully merged with the smaller research specialist Read Hurst-Brown in 1975. The major casualty was Joseph Sebag, merging to form Carr, Sebag in 1979, which, in turn, ceased trading three years later. Sebag had been one of the largest firms in the 1960s, but it came to depend too much on business from Slater Walker, believed at one time to produce 25% of its revenue, and became prone to destructive personality clashes within the partnership.

The major broad-based firms to survive from the crash of 1974 were James Capel, De Zoete and Bevan, W. Greenwell, Grieveson Grant, Hoare Govett, and Phillips & Drew. They were helped in all cases by a substantial presence in the gilt-edged market, where business volumes remained more constant than in the equity market, although only at modest levels. Cazenove retained its prime franchise in corporate finance, strengthened by recruiting Michael Richardson from Panmure Gordon, but the paucity of business in that area in 1973–74 led to some firms shedding resources. When corporate activity returned with a vengeance in 1975, it was dominated to a greater extent than before by Cazenove, Rowe & Pitman and Hoare Govett.

A franchise of similar strength had now been built by Wood Mackenzie in research. It was in 1974 that Continental Illinois launched the first survey of investment managers ranking the research output of stockbrokers, and this showed Hoare Govett well ahead of the field – a remarkable achievement for a firm also strongly placed in corporate finance. Wood Mackenzie moved into first place overall in 1975 and, during the 1970s traded the first four places with another research specialist, Kemp-Gee, and two of the broader-based firms, Hoare Govett and James Capel.

The number of jobbers continued to contract, but, during the crash of 1974, there was only one significant casualty. Akroyd & Smithers and Wedd, Durlacher remained the two dominant firms, covering both gilt-edged and equities. Bisgood Bishop, Pinchin Denny and Smith Bros survived as equity specialists, but Berger & Gosschalk slipped from the ranks when it ceased trading in December 1974.

In September 1965, the plan to rebuild the Stock Exchange was agreed at a cost of £11.5m – the equivalent of some £125m today. A tower block of 26 floors would rise above a new dealing floor, and it would take 7 years to complete the project before its formal opening by Queen Elizabeth in November 1972. The old building was much loved by the traditionalists, with its rambling shape, different ceilings, wooden floors, panelled walls and marble pillars. It was a study in asymmetric informality, with the air of a chaotically disorganised assembly hall, presided over by waiters on high wooden stands summoning the attention of members by calling their numbers in a constant monotone. By the end of the day, discarded notes and slips littered the floor, and, in the last 15 minutes of the day, the atmosphere thickened when smoking was permitted.

Because of the image it projected and the needs of modern technology, cabling and screens, it was hopeless and quite rightly had to go.

It was a noisy, extroverted, crowded, male environment, suitably spartan, yet, for many of its occupants, reassuringly reminiscent of public school or regimental days long gone. An abundance of sharp humour mingled with practical jokes. On the last day in February 1970, there was a carnival atmosphere – newspapers were set alight, toilet rolls were thrown and 'Auld Lang Syne' was sung many times. After its demolition, all members received a cigarette box sculpted from the marble pillars, and all hoped that their box of white marble would be decently flecked with those bluish Gorgonzola streaks.

For the next three years, the market existed on an even more crowded temporary floor before moving to its fine new floor on 11 June 1973. It was spacious, airy, well-lit and designed round a series of large, hexagonal dealing positions with price boards on the outer walls, and room for technology within the hexagonal. It was suitable for its time, if clinical and more formal than before.

A contentious issue at this time, precisely because of the male-dominated character of the market, was the question of allowing women members into this male preserve. In the rather arcane ways of the Stock Exchange, changes in the rules could only be authorised by a poll of the members.

In February 1967, the principle of allowing women to obtain membership without access to the trading floor was approved by a 55% to 45% vote, but this fell well short of the 75% required. Rather surprisingly, attitudes hardened and in May 1968 a second attempt was strongly rejected by 1,366 votes to 663 – only 32% in favour. In May, 1971 a third attempt was rejected by 57% to 43%. Backwoodsmen to the fore, the members of the Stock Exchange were making it look ridiculous. Stockbroking was assuming a professional character with important advisory and research roles, a picture reinforced by the introduction of examinations in 1971. Many women were achieving successful careers, some deserving of partnership and, in any case, they were not demanding access to the floor of the market, where opposition was strongest.

The matter was resolved by the completion of another reform being pursued at the same time, which was the proposal to amalgamate all the provincial Stock Exchanges with London to form The Stock Exchange as a single entity. It was the completion of this amalgamation that enabled women to be recognised in a new constitution in March 1973.

The amalgamation was one of several constructive reforms introduced by the Stock Exchange. The Market Price Display System (MPDS) was launched in 1968, making screen-based prices for the 692 stocks in the All Share Index available in members' offices, almost in real time, with changes marked for rising and falling prices.

Until this innovation, stockbrokers worked from their offices with limited price information. If you were very senior, you might have a second handset for access to the 'Box', as the tiny dealing rooms off the market floor were called, where, on the walls, would be white price boards, kept up to date in coloured crayon by young trainee clerks known as 'blue buttons'. White price boards might be located somewhere in the office, but probably not amid the traditional furnishings of large, Edwardian partners' desks and coloured prints of scenes of old London on the walls. There would be occasional clip boards placed discreetly in suitable places around the office, with a roneoed list of leading stocks, updated every hour by a clerical assistant.

As MPDS was about to be launched, stockbrokers W. Greenwell stole a march on the competition by installing screens in the offices of selected clients and transmitting live, fixed coverage of a price board, regularly updated by the sudden appearance of a hand in large close-up. The electronic age had indeed arrived in the stock market, but only by the merest whisker was it ahead of the landing on the moon.

The proposal to amalgamate all Stock Exchanges in the UK was first published in August 1969, but was not achieved until March 1973. Its importance lay in its harmonisation of the rules and bringing to an end the ban on members of one Stock Exchange opening a branch office within the area of another. A consequence ahead of this reform was the abolition in March 1970 of the need for a new member in London to purchase a nomination in the marketplace, and its replacement by a fixed entrance fee of £1,000.

An important step was taken in June 1971 with the introduction of Stock Exchange examinations as a future requirement for membership. This was a controversial issue that divided members. Stockbroking was attracting graduates and qualified professionals in increasing numbers and was regarded by many as a profession in its own right. However, such recognition was impossible without professional examinations, and the Stock Exchange was anxious to enhance its reputation.

Recruitment into the Stock Exchange now extended more widely than the traditional ranks of the public school, the services and the streetwise school-leaver – all attracted to stock market careers because of the absence of exams. At senior levels fund managers were crossing over to the stock market, attracted by much higher financial rewards. Newly qualified actuaries and accountants were being recruited, but the biggest difference from a decade or so earlier was that stockbroking had become a glamorous area for graduates. The work offered variety and interest, promotion was fast, earnings were high, and, above all, the City offered the attraction for graduates of working among a large peer group. From the late 1960s onwards, allowing for a hiatus during the 1974 crash, Oxbridge came to the Stock Exchange.

While examinations presented few problems for young graduates, many older members believed that stockbroking skills fell outside the scope of any conceivable examination, and the jobbers feared that many of those possessing the instinctive trading skills of the born dealer would not have the academic ability to pass examinations at a professional level. With some concessions to meet the latter concern, four compulsory papers were introduced – Stock Exchange practice, technique of investment, interpretation of company accounts and taxation.

It was in the late 1960s and early 1970s that financial journalism spread its wings and the broadsheet newspapers expanded their coverage of the stock market. This was a reflection of a widening interest in the stock market and a better understanding of its role in the economy in harnessing the savings of the pension funds and life companies.

Under the leadership of well known City Editors, such as Kenneth Fleet in the *Daily Telegraph*, Patrick Hutber in the *Sunday Telegraph* and Ivan Fallon in the *Sunday Times*, ever larger and sometimes separate sections of the newspapers were devoted to finance and the stock market. However, the doyen of them all was Patrick Sergeant, City Editor of the *Daily Mail* from 1960 to 1982. He was the last of the flamboyant City Editors and his annual choice of 'share of the year' in the late 1960s was eagerly awaited by his many readers.

It was at the same time in the late 1960s, early 1970s that the rigid City dress codes began to weaken. The black, rolled umbrella remained as a practical accessory, but the bowler hat was no longer regarded as essential to a successful career and quickly fell out of fashion. However, the top hat continued to be used by an exclusive minority that included the partners of Mullens, the government broker and members of the discount houses. The separate, stiff white collar fell out of use at the same time, to be replaced by softer materials and shirts in pastel colours. One of the rituals of the City was squeezed out of existence – the sight of people of all backgrounds carrying rigid brown cardboard boxes to and from the office, containing the stiff, white collars hired out and laundered by Collars Ltd.

In June 1965, Sir Martin Wilkinson had succeeded Lord Ritchie of Dundee as Chairman of the Stock Exchange. When he retired in June 1973, he was, somewhat surprisingly, succeeded by George Loveday, a partner in the medium-sized stockbrokers, Read Hurst-Brown. Loveday, aged 64, was a compromise candidate and in his short reign, he handled the difficult years of the market crash with aplomb and was obliged to preside over a dramatic contraction as numerous firms merged, closed down or collapsed. Loveday was succeeded in June 1975 by Michael Marriot, a senior partner of Williams de Broe, and, at the age of 49, the youngest ever Chairman. Sadly he died in December 1975, within months of taking office, and so in January 1976, Nicholas Goodison, at the even younger age of 41, was elected to a reign that would last almost 13 years, until November 1988.

In the 1970s, the Stock Exchange became involved in attempts to confront the difficult subject of insider dealing. Nobody actually knows the scale of insider dealing or the extent to which it has flourished at any particular moment. It is impossibly difficult to know where to draw the line in its definition, let alone prove it.

At its most blatant, it is visible in the sudden, sharp rise in a share price in the days before a takeover bid is announced. There are obviously occasions when knowledge of a takeover is leaked or abused for personal gain. The finger then points either to directors or their families within the bidding or bid for companies or to the many advisers involved, be they merchant bankers, corporate financiers, stockbrokers, analysts, fund managers, accountants, solicitors, advertising and PR agents or even printers. There are other times when news leaks out for wholly innocent reasons or as a result of nothing more than careless indiscretion. Other 'leaks' follow from clever deduction or careful observation, but without actual knowledge.

The market has acute hearing for the quietest of whispers and nothing moves faster than a share price beset by a flurry of buying by sharp-witted observers of the scene, none of whom possesses an iota of inside information. The snowball effect drives prices sharply higher, and to the outsider it appears that everybody knows. Without *any* knowledge, some investors will systematically buy shares betraying sudden price movements. When the bid is announced, the public talks of illegal profits and outraged sellers protest, but they never comment on the many more occasions when such rumours come to naught.

There have been quite specific examples of insider dealing. Relatives of a company director carelessly buy the shares just before the bid or the City executive telephones his bank in some distant tax haven. Systematic abuse is rare because no individual or professional firm involved in bid situations can afford to risk their reputation by being the common thread in a series of investigations into suspected leaks, and, as a general rule, the leading City firms have high ethical standards. Nevertheless, rogue examples will always slip through and the biggest obstacle to their discovery is the inability of investigators to identify the names or nationality of clients buying via foreign banks, which shelter behind a wall of silence on the grounds of confidentiality.

Knowledge of a takeover bid is the single most clearcut example of inside information. Close behind is knowledge of company results that are well above or below market expectations. In 1977, the Stock Exchange discussed with the CBI the question of a code of conduct to ban company directors from dealing in their company's shares in the two months prior to the announcement of half-year and full-year results, and most companies now have strict controls in place along these lines. Outside the company, it is difficult to draw a line between actual knowledge and intelligent guesswork. So many investment decisions relate to how well or badly a company is performing that 'inside information' to some is legitimate research to the majority.

Just as restrictions began to be imposed on company directors in the 1970s, so also at the same time securities and fund management firms began to formulate rules for the personal dealings of their executives. Attitudes to personal dealing had previously been very loose, and there were individual examples in the 1950s and 1960s of behaviour that would be wholly unacceptable today. Some fund managers or their dealers with a large buying order would first purchase a holding for their personal account. Others would personally accept the gift of shares at the placing price in an oversubscribed new issue. Some analysts holding choice information, or salesmen with a large order, would get their personal orders in first. Some journalists would buy shares they were about to recommend. None of these practices was widespread, but they happened enough to tarnish the system, and the names of some of the regulars were touted around the marketplace.

Whatever its scale, insider dealing was producing harmful publicity for the Stock Exchange and so, in February 1973, the Takeover Panel and the Stock Exchange recommended in a joint statement that insider dealing should be defined as a crime. Little happened because self-regulation was seen to be the essential culture of the City. In April 1977, the Stock Exchange set up an Investigations Department to monitor and investigate unusual price movements. In November 1977, the Government issued a White Paper, with City backing, proposing that, in certain circumstances, insider dealing should be a criminal offence, subject to imprisonment for up to two years.

It was a subject that nobody wished to pick up. The White Paper lay on the table and, meanwhile, another voluntary self-regulatory body, the Council for the Securities Industry, came into being in May 1978. Once the Takeover Panel had exerted its authority to continue to act independently, the purpose of the new Council became less apparent. At its first meeting, it decided that a prime function was to maintain ethical standards. Insider dealing duly became a criminal offence in June 1980, as outlined in the White Paper, but it has proved impossible to secure any significant prosecutions.

At the close of the 1970s, two new Stock Exchange ventures came into operation. In April 1978, a market in traded options was opened – much along the lines of the highly successful Chicago Board Options Exchange. It was launched in the face of a wall of indifference on the part of the large majority of leading institutions, but it was well supported by a small band of devotees.

The typical fund manager viewed traded options with suspicion and reluctance, and was unimpressed by theoretical examples showing how to improve the yield on an equity holding by replacing it with a much lower-priced traded option and a parcel of short-dated gilts. Their native instinct told them that traded options would be difficult to explain to their trustees or directors and, on balance, were probably more profitable for the provider than the user. They were initially available on a modest scale for the shares of ten leading companies and those selected offer an interesting cross-section of perceived market leaders in the late 1970s:

- British Petroleum
- Commercial Union
- Consolidated Gold Fields
- Courtaulds
- GEC
- Grand Metropolitan
- ICI
- Land Securities
- Marks & Spencer
- Shell.

The second innovation was the introduction in March 1979 of Talisman, a newly designed and much simplified central Stock Exchange settlement system that was to prove highly successful. Originally proposed in response to settlement chaos in the bull market in 1972, it was many years in gestation and, as its launch approached, bargain levels were typically less than half the peak totals of 1972. Its costs were split 70:30 between brokers and jobbers, and although there was initial concern about the cost of charges, it did produce significant savings in clerical labour and its introduction was timely in advance of the buoyant markets of the 1980s.

The 1964–79 period showed dramatic growth in total Stock Exchange business, illustrated by official turnover figures (see Table 23.10). These began to be published by the Stock Exchange on a regular monthly basis for the major categories of securities in October 1964, when equity turnover for the whole of the month of £380m would today be regarded as a slow start to the day.

Turnover was published only after a long rearguard action from the backwoodsmen, then familiar in most City institutions, and resolute in their belief that information is private and its release is dangerous. Interest focused on the value of aggregate sales and purchase in the two largest categories of equities and gilts with a life of over five years, partly to examine trends, but more particularly because firms could at long last measure their market share. Publication was later extended in 1977 to cover the principal subsectors of the All Share Index. This enabled stockbrokers to judge the effectiveness of specialist research teams working in individual sectors, and for jobbers to monitor business generated by the different books.

Table 23.10 shows the link between high volumes and bull markets, seen in the surges in turnover and bargains in 1968, 1972, 1977 and 1979, just as the troughs in 1974 and 1976 are equally marked. A feature is that the number of bargains is only modestly higher overall, but the average value of each bargain has risen nearly six times to reflect the dominance of the institutions as the performance cult took hold in the equity market. Turnover increased nearly 7 times compared with under 4 times for inflation, and the stock market emerged as a

Table 23.10
The annual turnover in equities, and number of bargains, 1965–79

Year	Equity turnover (£m)	Equity bargains (000)	Average bargain value (£)
1965	3,479	3,417	1,017
1966	3,566	3,119	1,143
1967	5,804	3,891	1,491
1968	9,118	5,313	1,716
1969	8.713	4,539	1,919
1970	8,813	4,097	2,150
1971	13,375	5,258	2,543
1972	20,066	6,725	2,983
1973	17,079	4,955	3,446
1974	12,616	3,935	3,205
1975	17,547	4,769	3,679
1976	14,163	3,567	3,970
1977	20,168	4,435	4,548
1978	19,215	4,130	4,652
1979	24,106	4,112	5,863

'growth stock' in its own right, with equity turnover sustaining a 15% annual growth rate over 14 years, combined with productivity savings from the number of bargains to be processed growing at little more than 1%.

For government securities, the meaningful turnover figure was for stocks with a life above five years, as commissions on short-dated stocks up to five years were negligible. This category also showed strong overall growth, but in a more erratic pattern. From 1964 to 1974, the nominal value of government securities rose gradually from £20,000m to £27,700m, but over the next 5 years to 1979, the nominal value more than doubled to £59,000m to finance excessive government borrowing. Turnover in the gilt-edged market followed the same pattern, growing from around £6,000m in the late 1960s to £15,000m to £20,000m in the early 1970s, to a record £63,000m in 1979.

The ever-increasing level of activity in the stock market brought with it, in the late 1970s, new methods and theories about the principles of fund management, mostly originating from the United States where academic research into the stock market has a long history. Two developments gained a limited following in London – chartism and a series of mathematical principles loosely described as modern portfolio theory (MPT).

Chartists believe the patterns of behaviour of a share price when drawn in a series of vertical lines on a 'point and figure' chart indicate its future behaviour.

Trend lines between successive highs or lows are broken or different shapes are formed such as a 'head and shoulders', each shape carrying a message for future prices. MPT is more mathematical and involves the measurement of risk by ascribing to an individual share a 'beta' factor to measure its volatility against movements in the index. Portfolio diversification and efficient markets are examples of other elements of MPT.

Neither chartism nor MPT has gained the following in Britain achieved in the United States, and active proponents are few in number. Both methods attempt to introduce an element of science into stock market investment, but it is more widely regarded as an art than a science. An efficient market assumes that shares are correctly priced on the basis that all known information has been taken into account. The art and the skill of the successful investor is in correctly forecasting the information that will come to be known and taken into account at future dates. As many theories about beating the stock market have been produced as systems to beat the roulette wheel. They tend to have one factor in common – they work until the moment they are published.

A central theme of the post-war history of the stock market is the changing status of the shareholder, from an uninformed poor relation to a controlling power. Although obtaining only modest financial returns from the market between 1964 and 1979, the equity shareholder made great strides forward in strength and status.

This revealed itself in different ways. First, new company legislation and the rise in investment analysis broke down resistance to the disclosure of information. This exposed companies to regular dialogue with analysts and fund managers, and to a rigorous analysis of their financial and business performance, which, in turn, prompted a virtuous circle of better management, better results and a higher share price. The advantages of a higher share price showed up in cheaper financing, cheaper cost of acquisitions, less likelihood of takeover and higher morale. In what would prove to be for the later benefit of the economy as a whole, the uncompetitive producer mentality of the immediate post-war years began slowly to shift towards a more competitive consumer and shareholder mentality.

Second, the power of the shareholder was boosted because the growth of the investing institutions consolidated the register of shareholders into fewer hands. These shareholdings became so large that the traditional response to management failure – selling the shares – was no longer possible. This led to further dialogue, and there were many examples where management change at the top was brought about behind the scenes by institutional shareholder pressure, often led by the Prudential or other major institutions. Examples in the 1970s included John Brown and Plessey. If pension funds had existed in France and Germany, the Anglo-Saxon financial culture might have made earlier inroads into the bank- and director-dominated financial systems of the Continent.

Third, the creation of the Takeover Panel served to protect the rights of shareholders from abuse, while in no way inhibiting the culture of takeover bids as a remedy for failure and a vehicle for change. Whereas self-regulation was slow to respond to insider dealing, it has been outstandingly successful in the evolution of the Takeover Panel – a uniquely flourishing creation that no other country has had the confidence or the culture to imitate.

The Takeover Panel was created in March 1968. Its antecedents lay in an initiative by the Issuing Houses Association in October 1959, which led to a code of Takeover Bid Practice issued by the Board of Trade. In July 1967, the Stock Exchange, concerned about the inadequacies of control of bid practices, requested that the Issuing Houses Association should again convene a working party on the matter. This initiative was given greater authority two months later when it was picked up by the Bank of England, which proposed setting up a panel to supervise a new bid code, and from this followed the publication of the City Takeover Code and the creation of a Panel on Takeovers and Mergers. As it was succinctly put on 27 March 1968 by Lex, 'This is the City's last attempt to put its house in order. If it fails a statutory code must be a certainty', but the infant Panel ran headlong into an early conflict of exactly the kind it was intended to curb. It was an episode that brought no credit to the participants or the system.

The sequence of events began when Imperial Tobacco's 36% holding in Gallaher, a fast-growing UK cigarette manufacturer based on the success of the Senior Service brand, was placed by Cazenove with institutions in May 1968 at 20/- a share. The existence of this holding had astonished the market when it was first revealed in 1961, but its placing now exposed Gallaher to the threat of takeover, and the US tobacco company Philip Morris made a partial takeover bid of 25/- a share for 50% of the shares of Gallaher on 26 June. On 16 July, American Tobacco, which had owned 13% of Gallaher since 1962, made a sharply higher counter-bid of 35/- for 50% of the company. It was an agreed bid, but immediately after its announcement, Cazenove went into the market and bought some 20 million shares at 35/- to take American Tobacco's holding to 28%, enough to block a counter-bid. On the following day, Morgan Grenfell, acting for American Tobacco, bought, through Cazenove, a further 12.2 million shares at an average price of a fraction below 35/-.

In the flurry of selling in the market, many shareholders sold their entire holdings to Cazenove, who knew exactly where to find stock, as they had placed the Imperial Tobacco stake only two months earlier. Cazenove's action was roundly condemned in the financial press as a challenge to the Takeover Panel and a breach of Paragraph 7 of the general principles of the Takeover Code, which ensures equal treatment of shareholders, and Clause 26, which prescribes that partial bids are to be made pro rata to existing shareholders. The Takeover Panel, having no disciplinary powers of its own, but with the support of the

Bank of England, advised the Issuing House Association and the Stock Exchange of its findings that the Takeover Code had been broken. This prompted an immediate rebuttal from Lord Harcourt, Chairman of Morgan Grenfell, and Sir Antony Hornby, Senior Partner of Cazenove.

In a decision described by Lex as 'pitiful but predictable', the Stock Exchange accepted the breach but proposed no action. This decision merely confirmed the worst suspicions held by many that the Stock Exchange was nothing more than a gentleman's club protecting its best-known member, whereas many a lesser firm would have had the book thrown at it for similar behaviour.

At the time, these two eminent firms epitomised the image of the City stockbroker and merchant bank. This was still a time when the stock market and its leading practitioners were governed by a public school ethos, which, at the highest levels, was dominated by a powerful Etonian influence stretching across the boardrooms and partners' rooms of the leading houses. This ethos was probably at its strongest in the late 1960s and early 1970s. Its contribution was to bring to the City a resolute self-confidence that, within its network, any problem could be solved, and it promoted the highest standards of courtesy, commitment, loyalty and service to the client. On the other hand, it tended to produce autocratic leadership and an instinctive resistance to change. The Etonian influence was formidable in its day and at its most effective when the tentacles of the network were widely spread. It is a network that has today been weakened in a more confrontational and individualistic City culture.

The 'Gallaher affair' is described in detail in David Kynaston's history of Cazenove (*Cazenove & Co.: A History*, B. T. Batsford, 1991), a firm that has thrived under a degree of autocratic leadership and simple, traditional rules of behaviour. Kynaston describes how, in the post-war years, at Cazenove the philosophy was that 'shoes have laces and cars are black'. Gallaher was an aberration for Cazenove. Autocracy joined with inflexibility, and when Sir Antony Hornby protested like an American lawyer that 'We did not breach the Code as it is. We may have breached the Code as they wish they had written it', he was propounding something that Cazenove was not.

It was a controversial episode that threatened the existence of the new Takeover Panel and, in the views of many commentators, brought nearer the statutory equivalent of New York's Securities and Exchange Commission (SEC). The consequence was a strengthening of the Panel, with the announcement in February 1969 that Lord Shawcross was to be its Chairman and Ian Fraser of S. G. Warburg its Chief Executive, and it was to be located in the Stock Exchange building. This placed it at the heart of the action and gave it a proper structure. It opened for business with the launch of a new Takeover Code on 28 April 1969.

Its first new measure was to strengthen the procedures for the forecasting of profits in bid situations. Under the strong leadership of Ian Fraser and the intimidating legal mind of Lord Shawcross, the Takeover Panel quickly achieved an authority that commanded the respect of all practitioners. It built its own case law out of practical decisions made in good time and rules were allowed to evolve or emerge with a flexibility not possible in a statutory system.

Many future headlines would follow from one such new rule introduced in June 1974, which required that a 30% stake in a quoted company trigger a bid for the remainder of the capital. Out of this rule would emerge many a dawn raid to acquire a 29.9% stake in a target company, but that is a theme for the 1980s and the Thatcher years.

Chapter 24

KEY EVENTS
1964–79

GOVERNMENT

Prime ministers

Harold Wilson	16 October 1964–18 June 1970	Election defeat
Edward Heath	18 June 1970–28 February 1974	Election defeat
Harold Wilson	28 February 1974–5 April 1976	Retired
James Callaghan	5 April 1976–3 May 1979	Election defeat

Chancellors of the Exchequer

James Callaghan	16 October 1964–29 November 1967	Reshuffle
Roy Jenkins	29 November 1967–18 June 1970	Election defeat
Iain Macleod	18 June 1970–20 July 1970	Died
Anthony Barber	20 July 1970–28 February 1974	Election defeat
Denis Healey	28 February 1974–3 May 1979	Election defeat

BUDGETS AND FINANCIAL STATEMENTS

James Callaghan

11 November 1964	Income tax – standard rate increased from 7/9d to 8/3d. Corporation tax to replace income tax and profits tax. Capital gains tax to be proposed on all disposals.
6 April 1965	Capital gains tax – 30% after a year. Capital gains tax – income tax/surtax under a year.
3 May 1966	Corporation tax 40%, dividends gross. Selective employment tax 25/- per week.
28 July 1966	Price and pay freeze. Dividends – 12 months voluntary freeze.
11 April 1967	–
19 November 1967	Devaluation of the pound from $2.80 to $2.40.

Bank rate 6½% to 8%.
Corporation tax increased from 40% to 42½%.

Roy Jenkins

19 March 1968   SET increased from 25/- to 37/6d a week.
Investment income levy.

15 April 1969   Corporation tax increased from 42½% to 45%.
SET increased from 37/6d to 48/- a week.
Gilt-edged securities exempt from capital gains tax.

14 April 1970   Caretaker budget.

Anthony Barber

27 October 1970   Income tax – standard rate reduced from 8/3d to 7/9d.
Corporation tax reduced from 45% to 42½%.

30 March 1971   Corporation tax reduced from 42½% to 40%.
SET reduced from 48/- to 24/- a week.
Short-term capital gains tax abolished.
VAT to replace purchase tax and SET in April 1973.
Surtax to be abolished from April 1973.

19 December 1971   Smithsonian Agreement – pound revalued to $2.60.

21 March 1972   VAT to be 10% from April 1973.
Corporation tax – Imputation system from April 1973.
Income tax – standard rate to be 30% from April 1973.
Income tax – maximum rate to be 75%.
Investment income surcharge to be 15%.

6 November 1972   Pay and prices freeze for 90 days, plus 60 days extension.

6 March 1973   Corporation tax rate set at 50%.
Income tax – standard rate set at 30%.

Denis Healey

26 March 1974   Income tax – standard rate increased from 30% to 33%.
Income tax – maximum rate increased from 75% to 83%.
Investment income surcharge 15%.
Corporation tax increased from 50% to 52%.
Stamp duty on share purchases increased from 1% to 2%.

22 July 1974   VAT reduced from 10% to 8%.
Dividend limit increased from 5% to 12½%.

12 November 1974   Stock appreciation relief introduced.
Capital transfer tax to replace estate duty.

15 April 1975	Income tax – standard rate increased from 33% to 35%. Higher rate of VAT of 25% on electrical products.
6 April 1976	Higher rate of VAT reduced from 25% to 12½%.
7 October 1976	MLR raised from 13% to 15%. Special deposits from banks increased from 4% to 6%.
15 July 1977	Income tax – standard rate reduced from 35% to 34%.
8 May 1978	Income tax - standard rate reduced from 34% to 33%.
8 June 1978	National insurance surcharge 2½% imposed on employers.

INDICES: OCTOBER 1964–MAY 1979

Financial Times Index

High: 553.5   3 May 1979
Low: 146.0   6 January 1975

FT Actuaries All Share Index

High: 280.28   3 May 1979
Low: 61.92   13 December 1974

Bull and bear markets

All Share Index

Movement	From	To	From	To	Duration
+106.3%	87.74	180.97	8 November 1966	31 January 1969	2 years 3 months
+98.9%	114.73	228.18	12 June 1970	1 May 1972	1 year 11 months
+177.2%	61.92	171.66	13 December 1974	3 May 1976	1 year 5 months
+144.1%	116.29	283.82	27 October 1976	4 May 1979	2 years 6 months
−36.6%	180.97	114.73	31 January 1969	12 June 1970	1 year 4 months
−72.9%	228.18	61.92	1 May 1972	13 December 1974	2 years 6 months
−32.3%	171.66	116.29	3 May 1976	27 October 1976	0 years 6 months

FT Index

Movement	From	To	From	To	Duration
+188.2%	146.0	420.8	6 January 1975	4 May 1976	1 years 4 months
−73.1%	543.6	146.0	19 May 1972	6 January 1975	2 years 8 months

Movements of more than 5% in the All Share Index in a single day

Date	% change	From	To	Reason
24 January 1975	+9.36	83.48	91.29	Bull market surge
10 February 1975	+8.60	108.22	117.53	Bull market surge
30 January 1975	+7.20	99.09	106.22	Bull market surge
7 February 1975	+6.24	101.86	108.22	Bull market surge
27 January 1975	+6.10	91.29	96.86	Bull market surge
29 January 1975	+5.53	93.90	99.09	Bull market surge
22 April 1975	+5.48	139.31	146.94	Bull market surge
16 April 1975	+5.38	123.56	130.21	Budget relief
19 June 1970	+5.36	120.63	127.10	Election victory
13 January 1975	+5.28	65.96	69.44	Bull market surge
23 January 1975	+5.07	79.45	83.48	Bull market surge
26 February 1975	+5.01	112.94	118.60	Bull market surge
1 March 1974	−7.28	149.27	138.40	Election defeat
2 January 1975	−6.41	66.89	62.60	Burmah Oil crisis
11 March 1975	−6.07	134.73	126.55	Market correction
6 December 1973	−5.49	151.16	142.86	Oil crisis
14 December 1973	−5.39	142.02	134.36	Three-day week
17 February 1975	−5.03	117.81	111.88	Inflation fears

Movements of more than 7% in the FT Index in a single day

Date	% change	From	To	Reason
24 January 1975	+10.10	197.1	217.0	Bull market surge
1 July 1975	+8.12	291.8	315.5	Budget relief
10 February 1975	+7.44	256.8	275.9	Bull market surge
30 January 1975	+7.36	235.0	252.3	Bull market surge
1 March 1974	−7.10	337.8	313.8	Election defeat

Note: In 1975, daily changes in the FT Index of more than 5% were recorded on 15 occasions, and in the period under review, from 1964 to 1979, daily changes of more than 3% were recorded on 130 occasions.

INTEREST RATES

Benchmark	Peaks (%)	Date	Troughs (%)	Date
Bank rate	7	23 November 1964	5½	4 May 1967
	8	19 November 1967	5	2 September 1971 (Bank rate ceased 9 October 1972)
MLR	13	13 November 1973	9¾	18 April 1975
	12	3 October 1975	9	5 March 1976
	15	7 October 1976	5	14 October 1977
	17	15 November 1979		

PART IV

THE THATCHER YEARS
1979–90

Chapter 25

SETBACK

May 1979–November 1979

All Share Index	4 May 1979	283.82	
	15 November 1979	219.85	Down 22.5%

Margaret Thatcher's victory produced a stock market reaction very similar to that of Winston Churchill in 1951, when, in both cases, a sea change in political opinion swept the Conservatives back into power. In 1951, it was under the slogan of 'Set the people free', and in 1979 under 'Labour isn't working', whereupon, on both occasions, the stock market promptly fell sharply.

General elections have frequently been accompanied by buoyant stock markets. In 1955 and 1959, confident expectations of Conservative victories were well satisfied, but, in 1964, similar hopes were frustrated. The sea changes of 1951 and 1979 were both well discounted by the stock market, with the All Share Index, in the latter case, surging to a new all-time high (see Figure 25.1) on polling day. Only once out of these five elections, in 1959, did the market avoid serious reverses in the year or so following. In 1979, the triumphal return of the Conservatives was welcomed on the day after the election with another new high of 283.82 before a fall of nearly 30% in the remaining months of the year.

As has been seen before, it was indeed better to travel hopefully than to arrive. On 3 May 1979, the morning of the election, the *Financial Times* advised its readers that 'The time to arrest the trends of decades of post-war history is now. No one can be certain that the Tories will succeed. But they must be given the chance to try'. With an overall majority of 43 and a full term ahead, the moment had arrived.

Trade union reform, lower taxation, a reduction in Government borrowing and the denationalisation of aerospace and shipbuilding had been specifically promised in the manifesto. The Queen's Speech on 15 May further explained the Government's philosophy for the economy. There was to be a switch to a free market, the abolition of the Price Commission, the elimination of State intervention, and a review of the National Enterprise Board to dispose of its profitable assets.

On 12 June, the new Chancellor of the Exchequer, Sir Geoffrey Howe, took the programme another step forward when he presented his first Budget. He

· 287 ·

Figure 25.1
All Share Index, 1979–84

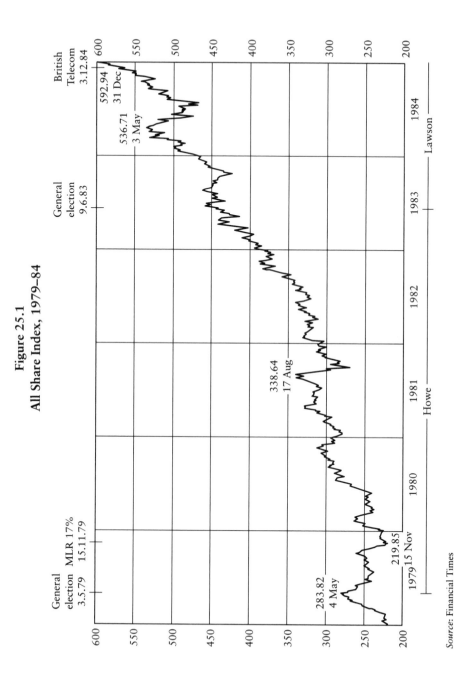

Source: Financial Times

reduced personal taxation and shifted the balance from direct to indirect taxes. He raised personal allowances, lowered the standard rate of income tax from 33% to 30% and the top rate from 83% to 60%. He left the investment income surcharge in place, but raised the starting threshold to £5,000.

These measures reduced direct personal taxation by £3,500m, but £2,500m of this was clawed back by consolidating the 8% and 12% rates of VAT to 15%, and by raising excise duties. He forecast a reduced PSBR of £8,250m or 4½% of GDP, after allowing for lower public expenditure and revenues of £1,000m from the sale of shareholdings in British Petroleum and businesses in the British National Oil Corporation.

Dividend controls would end on 31 July, and relaxations in exchange controls were planned. The Chancellor described it as an 'opportunity Budget', but his strongest commitment was to attack inflation by a monetarist squeeze. Government spending would be pinned down, a target of 7–11% was set for the growth of money supply, and bank lending was further curbed by raising MLR from 12% to 14%. It was setting the economy free, but in a monetarist strait-jacket with no lifeboats. The *Financial Times* of 13 June 1979 referred to its election advice: 'Six weeks ago the country voted for a radical change in direction and yesterday it got it'.

During those six weeks since the election, the market had been slipping away from an all-time high of 558.6 for the FT Index on 4 May. The election victory had been fully discounted, planned asset sales would need to be absorbed and the strength of sterling was hurting profits. In the short term, the Budget added to selling pressure. Radical monetarist policies sounded more like an old-fash-ioned credit squeeze, and, at first glance, adding 4 points to the RPI by raising VAT did not seem to be helping the battle against inflation. The market's reac-tion to the Budget was to push the Index decisively below 500, with a fall of 12.5 points to 488.9, and it continued drifting down through the summer months.

Powerful factors were pulling in both directions. On the positive side, the long-term determination of the Government was clear. Government borrowing was going to be reduced, releasing pension funds and insurance companies from their annual obligation since 1975 to invest some £3,000m in gilts. The removal of controls on prices and dividends left companies free to seek profits and reward shareholders. North Sea oil production was growing fast and, in June 1979, was equal to 85% of UK consumption, close to self-sufficiency at a time when the world price of oil was rising. A stronger currency was to prove espe-cially important in allowing the Government to stand firm against strikes in the public sector without being undermined by a sterling crisis.

On the other hand, the economy was facing a ferocious monetarist squeeze to drive out inflation that would undoubtedly trigger a serious recession. The out-look for profits was bleak. With no prospect of Government help, many companies would barely survive and the recession would add further pressure on profits already being eaten away by a rising pound. In the short term, inflation was rising towards 20% and, in June, the miners were talking of rises of 30% and more. For the current year, a large PSBR still needed funding and asset sales were promised.

The dilemma for the investor was neatly described in Rowe & Pitman's Market Report for July 1979: 'In explorer's language the valley threatens to be rather deeper than expected but the light across it is that much brighter'.

The ending of dividend restraint led to the declaration of some large increases for payment in August. British Petroleum more than doubled its dividend from just under 25p to 55p and threw in a special dividend of over 8p. GEC increased its dividend by 55% and set its cover at 5 times, only to find it was grumpily received by shareholders who had fancied something more generous. In the third quarter of 1979, the underlying dividend index of the All Share Index rose by 15%.

October 1979 was a critical and eventful month for the stock market as a portent of things to come. At the annual Mansion House Dinner, the Chancellor reiterated that monetary policy was at the heart of a battle against inflation that will be 'long and difficult' because 'inflation has become embedded in expectations'. Only a week earlier had come news of the first large casualty in a traditional manufacturing industry, when Singer announced its factory in Clydebank was to close with the loss of 3,000 jobs. In the 1950s, this manufacturer of sewing machines had been Scotland's largest employer, with 14,000 people. Singer was the first of many large manufacturing casualties in the early years of the Thatcher Government, when cold water was at long last prescribed as the much-needed medicine for an ailing industrial base that had become hopelessly uncompetitive.

Two announcements were made on the same day, 23 October, that would have profound consequences for the stock market. The first was the removal with immediate effect of all remaining exchange controls. The second was a decision that the Stock Exchange rule book would not be removed from the scope of the Restrictive Practices Act, where it had earlier been placed by the previous Government. The decision to abolish exchange controls was the catalyst for change. It redefined portfolio investment in the UK and set in train the changes to the structure of the Stock Exchange that led to Big Bang. Although not understood as such at the time, both decisions would later be seen to epitomise some of the political values of the Thatcher years – namely, the willingness to challenge institutions and to be rid of controls. The abolition of exchange controls has long been regarded as one of the best and boldest moves made by the Thatcher Government.

These two decisions, with closely connected consequences, were made in quite separate departments under different governments. Ending exchange controls was a spontaneous decision that would only have been taken by a Conservative government, whereas the reference of the Stock Exchange to the Restrictive Practices Court was a simple endorsement of a decision previously taken by the Labour Government.

The surprise for the stock market was the speed with which exchange controls were dismantled. In a first step in July 1979, all direct foreign investment by companies in existing businesses or in acquisitions had been freed from restriction. Portfolio investment in Europe was freed, leaving in place the dollar premium for the far larger volume of investments held in North America and the Far East. Three months later, all further restrictions on portfolio investment were removed. The dollar premium, quoted at 23–26% overnight, became worthless on the morning of 24 October 1979. The biggest losers were the investment trusts, which, over the course of a year, saw the dollar premium fall from an average 8% of their total assets to nil.

The reality of this decision was brought home to the City not just by the disappearance of the dollar premium, but more starkly by the immediate dismantling by the Bank of England of its exchange control department, which employed more than 500 people. A large bureaucracy was simply taken out. The decision was warmly welcomed in the House of Commons by Enoch Powell and damned as irresponsible by Denis Healey, but the broader issues were admirably summarised by the leader in the *Financial Times* on 24 October:

> The abolition, at a stroke, of the remaining Exchange Controls is most welcome. It removes a market distortion which has tended for a long period to keep sterling overvalued. It removes an important restriction on the freedom of British savers and should encourage thrift. It also, and perhaps more important in the long run, makes it possible for Britain to resume her traditional role as a capital exporter, as is vital if the windfall of North Sea oil is to provide any lasting benefit to the economy.

The practical, short-term purpose of the decision was to relieve upward pressure on the pound by allowing portfolio investment into other currencies. The strength of sterling stemmed, in part, from the windfall discovery of North Sea oil, and it was logical that Britain would be forced by a rising currency to concede manufactured exports and encourage imports as the benefit of North Sea oil transformed the balance of payments. That is the penalty of becoming a petrocurrency.

The last sentence in the *Financial Times'* leader quoted above is the most significant of all, because it flags, well in advance of its time, the need for oil revenues to be turned into assets overseas to provide future flows of income for when the oil runs out. Exactly the same principle had been guiding the Kuwait Investment Office and the Abu Dhabi Government for many years. It is a difficult principle to grasp, because an immediate instinct is to use the oil revenues to reinvest and re-equip industry in Britain, although this would probably have driven the pound to even higher levels and made any such investment even more uncompetitive. By means of a combination of direct investment and acquisition overseas, and foreign portfolio investment, Britain has, in effect, recycled North Sea oil revenues into overseas assets.

The knee-jerk reaction of the stock market on the day of the news was a fall of nearly 3% in the FT Index from 462.0 to 449.5, with concern focusing on the extent to which pension funds and life companies would divert their cash flows to build up their equity holdings overseas, which were widely believed to be no more than 3–4% of their assets. For no particular reason, it was immediately, and correctly, assumed that targets of up to 10% of assets would be set, and Phillips & Drew produced an estimate on the same day that such a target would require investment in foreign equities of £6,000m by the pension funds and life companies, thus diverting large cash flows away from the UK market.

After a stunned initial response, the City quickly awoke to the opportunities presented by the removal of controls. They had been in place for 30 years and a whole generation of stock market practitioners had been inoculated against involvement in foreign securities. With only a few exceptions stockbrokers and jobbers had come to focus their entire activities on UK markets.

In the 1930s, many brokers and jobbers participated in a thriving market in London in US, Canadian, Australian and South African shares. In the immediate post-war years a desperate shortage of foreign currency and newly imposed controls reduced these markets to a shadow of their former selves and, in 1979, nobody pretended they could be fully restored. The time was passing when London stockbrokers could advise institutions on foreign equities from an operation conducted wholly in London. Those who did, like Cazenove, Kitcat & Aitken and Rowe & Pitman, found themselves competing with US brokers based in offices they had opened in London, and, with the advent of direct call transatlantic dialling in the late 1960s, US brokers calling from New York.

To carry credibility, research in foreign markets now had to emanate from the country concerned. The response from London was for a small number of firms to open offices overseas. In 1967, Cazenove bought a seat on the Pacific Coast Stock Exchange in the United States, and two years later opened an office in Australia. Among others, Rowe & Pitman followed suit in San Francisco, and later opened offices in Johannesburg and Hong Kong. These new ventures were still hampered by exchange controls and restrictive rules about foreign ownership and dealings across Stock Exchanges, although the London Stock Exchange had allowed its members to operate overseas under local rules since 1970. However, the prospect for jobbers to win back lost business was more promising, because trading is a skill that crosses boundaries more easily.

Ironically, it was at this point that the decision of the Treasury and Bank of England to abandon exchange controls coincided with the separate decision of John Nott, Secretary for Trade, to reject a request from the Council of the Stock Exchange that its rule book be removed from the scope of the Restrictive

Practices Court. However, he amended procedures to give bodies similar to the Stock Exchange nine months to revise their practices in the light of any judgments made by the Court, which were normally made with immediate effect.

At the time, the Stock Exchange thought that the original decision to put its rule book before the Court was a political gesture by a Labour minister. Nicholas Goodison protested that John Nott's decision was 'purely political' and some dismay spread through the ranks of a membership confident that a Conservative Government would rescue them from the net.

Two particular rules were under threat. The first was that commissions charged by stockbrokers were fixed. The second concerned the demarcation drawn between the activities allowed to be carried out by stockbrokers and jobbers.

It was easier to understand the challenge to fixed commissions because the alternative of negotiated commissions between broker and client had been introduced in Wall Street in 1975. Many institutions believed that fixed commission scales were an anachronism in modern times and were particularly incensed about the commissions charged on gilt-edged bargains. With the rapid expansion of Government borrowing in the late 1970s, the size of individual transactions in gilts had become much larger, and a relatively painless purchase or sale running into many millions in a liquid market attracted far too high a commission.

The separation of 'capacity' between broker and jobber is a feature unique to the London Stock Exchange. It was a separation between principal and agent. The broker was only allowed to act as an agent for his client, seeking the best available price in the market, for which he charged a commission. The jobber was a principal making a profit from the difference between bid and offer prices quoted to the broker. He was required to quote prices in a minimum number of shares at all times and was not allowed to talk to or approach any client or member of the public. He could only pass bids and offers to interested parties via a broker.

The system was known as 'single capacity', whereby all members of the Stock Exchange were either principals or agents, jobbers or brokers, as opposed to 'dual capacity' where the same firm both advises clients and runs books in shares for its own account. The purpose of this rule was to ensure that, by using an agent, clients were not exposed to any conflict of interest and so would obtain the best price available from jobbers competing for business.

Because the jobbers were required to make prices in all shares on their books, the system is known as 'quote-driven' as opposed to 'order-driven', where purchases and sales are matched at a single price – the system that operates in some form in all other stock markets. Order-driven systems lend themselves to computerisation and are cheaper to operate, but the quote-driven system offers better liquidity.

In London, the separation between jobber and broker was, in practice, breaking down under the weight of business. Stockbrokers were receiving ever larger orders in individual equities. As a result of increasing specialisation and client relationships, they were well aware of potential buyers or sellers who could take or provide stock to satisfy these orders, and they were well aware of the extra commissions they could generate by handling both sides of the transaction. This particularly applied to selling orders, where the practice of 'placing' the stock with clients became the norm. Stock Exchange rules required that the order must first be taken to a jobber, who would agree the prices at which the stock would be 'put through' his book, with a fraction of a penny's difference between the two prices to allow the jobber a turn on the transaction. The larger brokers had in place well-organised sales teams who, within minutes, were able to place the shares with a wide range of institutions. The price to the buyers would be at a small discount to the middle price and attractive to the institutions with cash inflows to invest, and the seller would be content to obtain a decent price for a large holding.

It may have been against the spirit of the rules, but it worked. It enabled institutions to deal in much larger size without destabilising the price, but it shifted the balance of power to the broker at the expense of the jobber, who already had problems enough. The institutions tended to move together in the same direction on active days in the market, creating a one-way pressure that made jobbing difficult, and the shrinking of private client business had led to fewer bargains. While a large number of stockbrokers were growing in size, the jobbers were contracting and, by the end of 1979, the jobbing community had shrunk to only 17 firms, of which 12 were only small, specialist traders.

Only five firms of any size remained. The two largest were Wedd Durlacher and Akroyd & Smithers – both cushioned by their joint dominance of the gilt-edged market. Wedd Durlacher was the result of a merger between powerful names in the gilt-edged and equity markets, not least that of Durlacher, probably the best-known name of any jobber in the equity market. Akroyd & Smithers was traditionally stronger in the gilt-edged market, but had now built up a strong presence in the equity market. Smith Brothers were in third place as equity specialists with well-developed overseas interests, and more broadly based than Pinchin Denny and Bisgood Bishop, which were both dependent on the UK equity market.

However, the abolition of exchange controls created new opportunities to recover lost ground in foreign markets. Stockbrokers would find it difficult to compete with local brokers in providing research on shares in foreign markets without having a presence in the particular country, although some institutions still welcomed a friendly face to stand between them and the overseas brokers. The greater potential lay in trading opportunities for the jobbers.

But the Stock Exchange was caught in a trap. In preparation for the Restrictive Practices Court it was defending the rule on single capacity that made it impossible for jobbers to offer a trading facility in foreign securities to clients they were not allowed to approach, an absurd restriction in the eyes of foreign investors. The brokers would make little headway without a dealing capacity, and the jobbers could do nothing if they were denied access to clients. A clear example was the market in South African gold shares, an international market once dominated by London, but eroded away because the dual cost of a broker's commission and a jobber's turn could not compete with net prices offered by foreign dealers. Fears were being expressed that dealings in market leaders, such as BP and ICI, might also migrate to cheaper foreign markets.

This erosion could not be prevented, or lost markets recovered, unless dual capacity were allowed. The dilemma was obvious to the Stock Exchange and an idea first floated in 1974 of allowing an 'international dealer' to operate under dual capacity in foreign stocks was given new life, but progress towards this was tortuous. Many members feared it would be the thin end of a wedge that would break single capacity apart in the UK market, and others could see no logic in the Stock Exchange mounting a defence of single capacity in the Restrictive Practices Court while conceding dual capacity in foreign markets. The events of 23 October 1979 have been described in some detail. It was, and will remain, a key date in the history of the stock market.

Quite separately from these issues, the stock market was now losing its nerve. Wall Street was in crisis as a monetary squeeze was driving interest rates to record levels, the dollar was falling and the price of gold rising ominously. The FT Index stood at 486.8 on 8 October, but a 3% sell-off in the Dow Jones Index triggered a collapse in London that, at one point, saw shares fall on 16 out of 17 successive days from 472.5 on 16 October to 412.2 on 8 November.

In the midst of these falling markets, the Government made its first step in selling off assets by announcing on 31 October an offer for sale of 80m shares in British Petroleum at 363p to raise £290m. It was sponsored by an array of 6 leading merchant banks and 5 stockbrokers, and the underwriting was spread across 800 institutions at a modest discount of 4% below the overnight price. This was a sale of just over 5% of BP, a mere portion of the government holding of 51%, including the frozen holding of 20% acquired from Burmah Oil in 1975, but it was enough to relinquish overall control.

The market was passing through a deeply pessimistic phase. Business surveys were especially gloomy, official forecasts were confirming an approaching recession, money supply was still growing too fast and the miners ominously rejected a 'final' 20% pay offer. As markets slid away, the Prime Minister reiterated at the Lord Mayor's Banquet her uncompromising intent to defeat inflation. Two days later, on 15 November, the City was shocked by an increase in MLR from 14% to a record 17%. The All Share Index had fallen far enough already and lost only a few more points on the day to 219.85, where it stood 23% below its all-time high of 283.82 reached at the election, a little more than 6 months earlier.

A sudden increase in Bank rate or MLR had, in the past, signalled an economic crisis. In the 1950s and early 1960s, the crisis rate on three occasions was 7%, rising to 8% in 1969 and 13% in 1973, and, on each of those five occasions the equity market suffered heavy falls in the months following. The crisis rate was now an unprecedented 17%, but the nature of the problem was altogether different.

On the previous occasions, action was prompted by an overheated economy leading to a run on sterling and balance of payments problems. In November 1979, the economy was heading fast into recession and sterling was riding high. Hence, the stock market reacted quite differently. It looked for the positive message that 17% did not, on this occasion, signal weakness, but the strength of conviction of the Thatcher government to defeat inflation and transform the economy. So it was that the All Share Index touched its low point of this bear market at 219.85 on the day that MLR was raised to 17%. In the words of the earlier Rowe & Pitman analogy, the valley had indeed been deeper than expected, but the light across would prove to have been shining more brightly than in any other post-war phase of the market.

Chapter 26

A LONG BULL MARKET – PART ONE

November 1979–June 1983

All Share Index	15 November 1979	219.85	
	9 June 1983	442.80	Up 101.4%

The first half of 1980 witnessed some of the most dramatic and contradictory events of any post-war period. A new stock market expression, the 'dawn raid', was born. The classic indicators of inflation were rampant. Gold and silver reached prices that have not been remotely seen again in two decades and may stand for generations. Interest rates in Britain and the United States reached record post-war levels with MLR at 17% in London and prime rates at 20% in New York. In Britain, inflation depressingly went over 20% again in April, where it remained for 3 months, peaking at 21.9% in May.

Yet, there was an underlying belief that the ingredients for a bull market were in place. Margaret Thatcher and Sir Geoffrey Howe communicated a resolution lacking in previous governments that, whatever the price, inflation was there to be defeated not accommodated. The price would prove to be a monetary squeeze of unprecedented proportions that would shock many leaders of industry too long accustomed to those comfortable surroundings that had made so many of them so perilously uncompetitive. A bull market that would last for seven years was just beginning.

Both major indices touched bottom on 15 November 1979 – the FT Index at 406.3 and the All Share Index at 219.85. The FT Index fell again to 406.9 on 3 January 1980, by which time the All Share had marginally risen to 225.06.

Between these two dates, the world was coming to terms with a surprise Russian invasion of Afghanistan on Christmas Eve. Wars and invasions are quite unpredictable in their effect on stock markets. The Korean War in 1950 sparked an inflation in commodity prices that fed through to economies world-wide, and the Arab-Israeli war of 1973 had dramatic consequences for the price of oil, but the invasions of Hungary, the Suez Canal, Czechoslovakia and the Vietnam conflict had little or no overall effect on the stock market. The uncertainty created by the invasion of Afghanistan fuelled the prices of gold, silver and platinum, and the shares of the mining companies.

Gold had performed strongly through 1979 as the classic hedge against inflation, rising from $226 an ounce at the beginning of the year to $530 at the year end, and the FT Gold Mines Index almost doubled over the same period, from 141 to 268. For many people in the stock market, this was the year of the Krugerrand – a fine glistening coin made of one ounce of pure gold, and selling for a bare margin over its underlying value. Demand was so great that the South African Government ran out of supplies in November.

Many Stock Exchange members had been tinkering with holdings of Krugerrands for some years, but they presented a trickier settlement problem than stocks and shares because they arrived in a plastic tube of 25 coins. Some were delivered to safe deposits, others were taken home to the family safe. One member, hastening to catch a train on the platform of the Monument station, transferred his tube of coins from pocket to hand for greater convenience. He raced for the train with his thumb pressed hard over the wrong end of the tube, the top burst open and coins cascaded over the platform and on to the line. He remained ever grateful to the helpful staff who eventually recovered all his coins.

The tension caused by the invasion of Afghanistan spilled over into the gold market to produce a price spiral worthy of a case book study of the behaviour of markets. Gold is a huge market, traded at times in hundreds of millions of dollars, and, during 1979, a series of large auctions of official holdings of gold by the US Government had been regularly attracting bids well in excess of the amount being sold. By the end of December 1979, the price had already doubled to $530 an ounce and it reached $600 on 10 January. Over the next two weeks, the story continued as shown in Table 26.1.

Table 26.1
The price of gold, January 1980

Date	Price $ per oz.
10 January	600
11 January	623
14 January	656
15 January	687
16 January	755
17 January	760
18 January	835
21 January	825
22 January	690
23 January	700
24 January	705
25 January	670
28 January	635

The high of $835 an ounce has since become etched on the memories of gold enthusiasts and is for ever quoted in words written on the subject. What is extraordinary is the brevity of this moment and the steepness of the final peak for a commodity so widely held purely for investment. The price stood above $800 for only two days, rising by 20% in three days to the peak before falling away by 17% in a day. It quickly fell away to as low as $475 by the end of March, and was thereafter highly volatile for the remainder of the year, briefly recovering to $715 on the outbreak of the Iran-Iraq war in September, before closing the year at $590. These levels have never even remotely been approached since, and in the 1990s the price has become marooned at $300 and below.

Gold was not alone in surging upwards in January. In precious metals, platinum and silver were also recording new highs – the latter driven by the reckless attempt of American oil billionaire, Nelson Bunker Hunt, to corner the silver market. When this failed in a mountain of debt in April, the price of silver collapsed from a peak of £22 an ounce to £6.

Equities started the new year in fine fettle in both London and New York. It was an easy option – if the battle against inflation were to be won, interest rates would tumble; if lost, equities would fare as well as any.

Another indicator of value in depressed markets – the takeover bid – was making itself felt again after six dullish years for the corporate finance departments of the merchant banks. In January, the City enjoyed one of the fastest fought bid battles involving some of the finest names in the stock market. Decca, a famous post-war name in television and electronics, had drifted into sad decline, and institutional pressure, led by the Prudential, had failed to bring about change. There followed a rapid-fire shoot-out for the assets of Decca between Racal, a new and highly successful growth company in electronics and defence radio, under the leadership of Ernest Harrison, and the redoubtable GEC, long established as one of Britain's finest companies under the leadership of Arnold Weinstock, but now just beginning to mature out of favour. The sequence of bids for the mix of voting and non-voting shares of Decca was:

- 25 January   Racal   £66.0m
- 4 February   GEC   £82.5m
- 7 February   Racal   £93.1m
- 8 February   GEC   £97.9m
- 14 February   Racal   £104.0m

It was all over in under three weeks. It is doubtful if the diaries of the proliferating numbers of professional advisers involved in a bid battle could accommodate such a timetable today.

However, the closing stages of the Decca battle, and the surprise incursion of Hong Kong shipping magnate C. Y. Tung in bidding £96m for another long-standing British name, Furness Withy, were overshadowed on 12 February when stockbrokers Rowe & Pitman launched a 'dawn raid' on Consolidated Goldfields.

Although it attracted little attention at the time, Rowe & Pitman had, in effect, rehearsed the operation several months earlier on 20 August 1979, when it bought 20% of the capital of Stenhouse Holdings in the market on behalf of Continental Corporation, the US insurance company, for £8.2m. Stenhouse was a small company with relatively few shareholders and the purchase was only just achieved and barely noticed.

Consolidated Goldfields was altogether different. It was a visible market leader in its sector, with an extensive list of institutional shareholders and was already aware of a possible problem. On the day before the raid, it had asked the Department of Trade to help track down a mystery buyer of its shares. A consequence of the dismantling of exchange controls had been the loss of basic information about inward and outward investment, which previously required permission or approval.

The speed, audacity and scale of the operation produced a shock wave in the stock market, and prompted cartoons likening it to the recent SAS swoop on the Iranian Embassy. Consolidated Goldfields had closed on the previous evening at 525p. Early the next morning, acting on behalf of De Beers within the Anglo-American Group in South Africa, Rowe & Pitman bought 16.5m shares at 616p at a cost of £101.5m, taking the Anglo-American holding from an existing 14% to 25%. The raid was all over by 10 o'clock, but it became controversial because the shares finished the day so far below the bid price at 510p.

Admiration for the nerve of the dawn raid was tempered with criticism. Rowe & Pitman's clients were in a prime position to sell their entire holdings and buy them back at a handsome profit. Akroyd & Smithers, the jobbers buying stock in the market, had been able to take a significant short position at the bid price. It all happened so quickly that private shareholders had no chance to participate, and a later investigation showed that 13.5m of the shares came from Rowe & Pitman clients, 1.2m from Akroyd & Smithers and only 1.8m from clients of other stockbrokers. The raid had been legitimately carried out under existing rules, allowing the acquisition of up to 29.9% of the capital of another company without any obligation to bid for the remainder, and, although it only involved a modest 11% of the shares, it gave the impression of something far bigger. It was perceived to have offended the principle that, in partial bids, all shareholders should be treated equally and, two days after the raid, the Stock Exchange announced it would mount an investigation.

The outcome led to criticism of De Beers, more for technical breaches of the rules while secretly accumulating its 14% holding prior to the raid than for the raid itself, which exploited, in a perfectly proper way, an opportunity available to those willing to seize it. Nobody better personified that nerve and boldness than Peter Wilmot-Sitwell, the Senior Partner of Rowe & Pitman. Wilmot-Sitwell, an outstanding corporate finance stockbroker of his generation, brought to his leadership instinctive qualities of self-belief, discipline and a strong sense of the practical.

There are no patents on new ideas in financial markets and although others copied the dawn raid, its provenance remained firmly with Rowe & Pitman, who varied the pattern with a 'siesta raid' after lunch on 27 May to buy 28.4% of Anderson Strathclyde for Charter Consolidated. The shares were 74p, the raid lasted for half an hour at 92p, and the shares closed at 79p. This was the sixth market raid, the third by Rowe & Pitman, and it occurred on the same day that the Council for the Securities Industry released a report on the subject that would shortly lead to new guidelines.

There were two genuine concerns about dawn raids. The first was a tactical question of the equal treatment of shareholders as they involved a significant stake of up to 30% being purchased very quickly, without notice, at a premium of 20–25% over the market price. The second was the more strategic principle of whether or not a stake large enough to give effective control of a company should be allowed to be acquired without giving the company any chance of commenting or advising its shareholders.

These concerns exercised both the Stock Exchange and the Council for the Securities Industry. In July, the Stock Exchange recommended that dawn raids should not happen before 9.30 am, should be announced formally to the Stock Exchange to allow the suspension of dealings for 30 minutes and jobbers should beware selling short. This was an attempt to secure more equal treatment for all shareholders. The CSI was more rigorous and, on 7 August, imposed a temporary ban while new rules were formulated.

The important new rule that emerged was the reduction in the level at which a bid for all the capital is triggered from 30% to 15%, and, on 21 October, Ward White bought 14.85% of K Shoes under the new rules. A particular difference occurred in this raid. The shares stood at 48p and the raid was at a 25% premium, at 60p, but the shares closed at the bid price of 60p. For the first time, it came to be realised that a dawn raid was likely to be the prelude to a full bid at a higher price and henceforth, it would become more difficult for brokers to persuade institutions to sell shares to a market raider.

Dawn raids were a talking point of constant interest to the stock market in 1980 and so this description has taken chronology ahead of other events.

To return to them, Geoffrey Howe introduced his second Budget on 26 March 1980. Tax changes were marginal, with income tax allowances raised by 18% in line with inflation and the usual excise duties were increased. He made unit trusts and investment trusts exempt from corporation tax on capital gains. However, City interest was drawn to his new 'medium-term financial strategy' projected ahead over four years with an absolute priority to slow down inflation by reducing monetary growth and cutting government spending and borrowing. He set a monetary target of 7–11%, reducing to 4–8% by 1983/84, and a PSBR falling from 4¾% of GDP to 1½% in 1983/84. The snap reaction of the market was to lower the FT Index by 12.0 to 423.1, but it quickly recovered.

The economy was now presenting all sorts of contradictions to the investor. The monetary squeeze and the strength of sterling put appalling pressure on manufacturing industry. MLR remained at 17%. Factories were closing as recession deepened. A steel strike lasted for 13 weeks until it was settled to no particular advantage in the first week of April. Yet inflation remained an implacable problem as it climbed over 20% in April. Monetarism was slow to work. Part of the inflation problem was self-inflicted, with higher VAT adding 4 percentage points, and the high price of oil being a mixed blessing as it pushed up prices, but strengthened the value of the now substantial North Sea oil flows.

Another problem was the inheritance of the Clegg Comparability Commission, set up under Professor Hugh Clegg by the Callaghan Government to ensure fairness between workers in the public and private sectors. Its credibility was damaged beyond repair in May 1980 when inflation was at its peak and it admitted that an earlier recommendation for teachers had been overstated in error by 4%. It was abolished in August 1980 and it was later estimated to have added 2% to the national earnings index by making recommendations over and above normally negotiated settlements in the public sector.

The problems of manufacturing were all too visible in the daily news headlines on television and in the press, and the mood of the market was still gauged largely by the manufacturing-dominated FT Index. Yields of 18% on market leaders like Courtaulds and Turner & Newall or 15% on Tube Investments suggested serious problems ahead. In the 13 months since the election victory, there had been glaring disparities between the performance of the manufacturing sectors, such as textiles down 35% and mechanical engineering down 25%, and the oil sector up 15% and a marginally higher financial sector.

It was almost precisely on this anniversary that the market moved decisively ahead. The FT Index had drifted back to 412.7 on 2 June, much the same as its low points in the previous November and in January, although the All Share Index at around 245 was some 10% off its low. Six weeks later, on 16 July, the FT Index had risen by 22% to 503.1, and, on the same day, the All Share Index reached a new all-time high of 286.58.

Sudden moves on this scale are usually accompanied by some items of good news. In early June, Lord Carrington successfully negotiated a £700m reduction in Britain's EEC contribution, to be used to reduce the PSBR, and, on 3 July, the onerous 8-month regime of MLR at 17% was relaxed for the first time with a reduction to 16%. On 7 July, British Petroleum announced an agreed record takeover bid of £410m for Selection Trust – a mining finance house with strong South African interests. Although their mining activities were overseas, the mining finance houses were companies stemming from the days of Empire, registered in London, widely held by the institutions and regarded as UK stocks for portfolio analysis.

After convincingly reaching new high ground, the market continued to move ahead in the autumn and the All Share Index recorded many new highs. The enticing prospect of lower interest rates was propelling world markets higher, but for Britain there was an additional intangible factor. It was identified in Rowe & Pitman's Market Report in July, when discussing whether the market surge was a watershed or a false dawn: 'We believe a turning point for the market has been reached and that the implacable resolve of the Government, still the greatest bull point of all, should ensure there is no turning back'. Three months later, in a speech at the Conservative party conference, Margaret Thatcher made her famous comment, 'You turn if you want to – the lady's not for turning'. Implacable political resolve was something entirely new for the stock market.

Indeed, this resolve remained unshaken in the face of ritual demands from the TUC for reflation, hang-dog pessimism from Harold Macmillan, rumblings from Edward Heath and angry threats of a 'bare-knuckle fight' from CBI Director-general Sir Terence Beckett. The only concession came in the form of an economic package on 24 November, when the Chancellor reduced MLR from 16% to 14%, but, as the PSBR was running higher than forecast, he raised national insurance contributions from employees by 1%.

The stock market remained buoyant. The Iran-Iraq war had given a fresh impetus to the price of oil, which touched $37 a barrel and was unilaterally raised to $41 by Libya on the last day of the year. Oil shares were booming and, within the sectors of the All Share Index, all set initially at 100 in April 1962, oil was the first to reach 1,000 on 30 October. A rise of 10 times over 18 years is equal to 14% per annum, approximately double the rate of inflation over the same period, and just ahead of the electricals sector, which had been winning the race but now stood at around 950.

Britain's previous vulnerability to the oil shocks of 1973 now gave way to an immunity in 1980, and there was a further hidden benefit. North Sea oil strengthened the pound and enabled the Government to stand up to those confrontational strikes that in the past would have caused a run on the pound and ended in ignominious defeat. The long, fruitless steel strike in the first quarter had demonstrated this point. However, there was a price to be paid for the discovery of oil – the rest of the world forced Britain to accept a reduction in revenues from manufactured goods in exchange for revenues from oil by the simple mechanism of driving up the price of sterling.

In other aspects, 1980 was a good year for the stock market. Stock Exchange figures would later reveal record turnover for the year of £30,800m in equities, nearly 30% higher than the previous record a year earlier. The All Share Index was up 27% over the year. While the Stock Exchange flourished, Ariel, the computerised dealing system set up in opposition by the merchant banks in 1974, was floundering in losses, and almost half the shareholders wanted out. In November, the Stock Exchange opened the new unlisted securities market, or USM as it quickly became known, with a mix of 11 companies drawn largely from oil exploration and technology.

Even the Wilson Inquiry, set up by James Callaghan in 1977, reported in June in more favourable terms than its rather forbidding terms of reference might have suggested. Its 18 members were drawn from the ranks of academia, banking, industry and the trade unions and, under the chairmanship of Harold Wilson, they were invited:

> To inquire into the role and functioning, at home and abroad, of financial institutions in the UK and their value to the economy; to review in particular the provision of funds for industry and trade; to consider what changes are required in the existing arrangements for the supervision of these institutions including the possible extension of the public sector; and to make recommendations.

Between the setting of the agenda and the result of the Inquiry, the same sea change that brought Margaret Thatcher to power seemed to influence its findings. The Wilson Inquiry found no case for nationalising any City institutions and approved the self-regulatory disciplines of the Stock Exchange. It recommended more disclosure and accountability for pension funds, and the introduction of lay members on the Council of the Stock Exchange.

Despite buoyant markets, these were still times of doubt. The headlines were ghastly. Government borrowing was obstinately high. Unemployment rose to 2,030,000 in October as factories closed by the day. GDP was heading for a fall of 2% for the year, with a further fall forecast for 1981. However, the annual leaders and laggards tables for 1980 made interesting reading. Under a certain Asil Nadir, the shares in a company called Polly Peck had risen by 2700%, from 7p in February to a recent peak of 190p.

The pressure on profits and dividends remained intense and, in the first quarter of 1981, the reporting season of results for the previous year was dismal. ICI cut its final dividend after profits were more than halved, and Tube Investments and Turner & Newall raised the total to 7 companies out of 30 in the FT Index with cut dividends. 'We are freezing to death' the Chairman of ICI had warned in October.

The pressures on companies of high interest rates and strong sterling, each reinforcing the other, and the burden of oil prices at around $40 a barrel, were all about to be relieved. In an early Budget, on 10 March 1981, the Chancellor lowered MLR from 14% to 12%. This, together with the emergence of an oil glut and lower oil prices, pushed sterling downwards from its cyclical peak in February, when it stood at $2.42. Relief on all three fronts, and the prospect of a profits recovery from the worst of the levels currently being reported, gave renewed encouragement to the market, and, in April and May, both indices reached new all-time highs of 597.3 for the FT Index, up 26% on the year, and 332.77 for the All Share, up 16%.

The discrepancy between the two indices reflected greater strength in industrials on the one hand and a collapse in oil shares on the other hand. The FT Actuaries oil sector – proud to be the first sector to reach 1,000 only the previous October, peaking at 1,065 was, 6 months later, down to 830 by the end of April, and the electrical sector was riding high at over 1,100. There is no protection for the largest of companies if the market does not like the fundamentals.

The March 1981 Budget released pressure from industry only to transfer it to the personal sector. No increases were made in income tax allowances, to save £2,500m, and heavy increases on tobacco, drinks and petrol raised another £2,400m. In his determination to bring the PSBR down by £3,000m to £10,500m and to defeat inflation, the Chancellor shifted the burden firmly on to the shoulders of the personal sector. He also indicated control over public-sector pay by imposing the same cash limits that had, in reality, been operating in many parts of the private sector through intense pressure on profits, and he uncompromisingly forecast that unemployment would rise to 2.5m in 1981/82 and 2.7m in 1982/83.

He made two strikes on the corporate sector. He raised £1,000m from higher taxes on North Sea oil, and imposed a 'windfall tax' on the clearing banks to raise around £400m. This was to recognise that the government's regime of very high interest rates, particularly MLR at 17% during the first half of 1980, had endowed the banks with a windfall profit they were scarcely able to avoid and had not earned through their own efforts. The basis of the tax was 2½% on average current account balances in the fourth quarter of 1980. It raised an amount equivalent to £1,000m in 1997, when a £4,000m windfall tax on the privatised utilities was proposed by Labour.

Although it lifted pressure from industry, the stringency of the Budget threatened further deflation in the economy. It led to the famous letter to *The Times* on 30 March 1981 from 364 university economists stating that, in their view, 'there was no basis in economic theory for the belief that deflating demand will bring inflation under control; that present policies will deepen recession, erode the industrial base, threaten social and political stability, and they reject monetarist policies'. Of the signatories, 54 were drawn from a Keynesian tendency in Cambridge, but none from Liverpool University, where the free market theories of Patrick Minford held sway, or from the London Business School. In the *Financial Times*, Samuel Brittan mischievously suggested it was the best possible sign that the Government's policies might be right. History shows that the economy was about to produce some of its finest years, and this letter was a classic example of a mass of people selling the economy at the bottom of the market.

The City was having nothing to do with it and the market went forward to new highs.

An innovation announced in the Budget was the issue of a £1,000m Index-linked government stock, where both the interest payments and the final redemption price would constantly be adjusted in line with inflation. The first issue of Treasury 2% 1996 was tentatively restricted to pension funds and over-subscribed on 27 March 1981. The second issue, by tender, in July of £1,000m Treasury 2% 2006 was less successful and not fully subscribed, and it would not be until the Budget of 1982 that Index-linked stocks were made available to private individuals.

In the equity market, there was plenty to occupy the institutions in these early months of 1981 with privatisation, takeover bids, dawn raids and rights issues. Privatisation is the subject of Chapter 29, but it was in February 1981 that the Government sold 50% of its stake in British Aerospace to raise £150m, and announced its intention to sell 49% of Cable & Wireless, which, later in October, raised £224m.

In March, Standard Chartered Bank announced a merger putting a value of £312m on Royal Bank of Scotland, only to be trumped by a £500m bid from Hongkong and Shanghai Banking Corporation. This was matched by an agreed bid from Standard Chartered, and if both bids had not been referred to and later blocked by the Monopolies Commission, they would have been the highest bids recorded in the London market

Another event emanating from overseas occurred on 1 June when Rowe & Pitman mounted a dawn raid to buy 14.9% of the shares of Eagle Star at 290p at a cost of £59.2m on behalf of Allianz, the leading German insurance company. The shares were 230p overnight and later in the same day, Morgan Grenfell announced a tender offer for a further 15% of the shares at the same price.

It was later in the same month, on 18 June, that British Petroleum announced a mammoth rights issue of 1 for 7 at 275p from its 287,000 shareholders to raise £624m – more than 3 times larger than the previous record of £204m for ICI in 1976. The rights issue was complicated by a decision of the Government not to take up the rights from their holding, but to sell them at a small premium at 290p. This was so close to the market price that less than half were placed, but the issue was more than 90% subscribed by the remaining shareholders.

These separate events amounted to calls for cash from shareholders of almost £1,000m. Cash inflows to the pension funds and life companies were approaching £14,000m, but a PSBR of around £11,000m needed to be financed, and the institutions were widely diversifying into overseas equities following the abolition of exchange controls. In the last quarter of 1980 and the first quarter of 1981, more than £2,000m was invested in foreign securities, by which time pension funds had roughly doubled their overseas percentage of total assets from 5–10%. The Prudential had reached 10% and was heading for 15%, and the larger unit trust groups found the bulk of their new sales originated from many newly launched specialist overseas funds.

The subject of foreign investment by institutions raises many questions. The first is whether the motive is primarily to diversify into foreign currency or foreign companies. For many years, portfolio strategy had probably been influenced more by the former, but in the detail there were many industries – such as electronics, information technology and utilities – where opportunities to invest in Britain were limited or non-existent. In the academic field, new theories of portfolio diversification lent weight to the argument to invest in foreign economies. However, an instinctive political response from the left was to condemn the investment of domestic savings in foreign companies when factories in Britain were being closed by the day, and call for the direction of these savings into new industrial capacity. The opposite argument was that taking advantage of a strong pound to invest in cheap foreign assets was making the best possible use of funds in the national interest.

In practical terms, the surge of foreign investment did help to curb the strength of sterling that was so crippling to industry. If these funds had been directed into domestic investment, sterling would have traded even higher and made both existing and new capacity even more uneconomic.

The institutions, now free to invest overseas, were still motivated to diversify away from sterling where long post-war experience had been so dismal, but more so to diversify their portfolios into the highly successful economies of the United States, Japan and Europe. The outcome has been unexpected and ironical. As a general rule, ever since 1981, the London equity market has performed outstandingly well and better than its larger and obvious rivals.

On the other hand, the business of fund management in London has benefited from the willingness of institutions to pursue portfolio diversification in the early 1980s. Diversification was much discussed in theory, but slow to become a generally accepted practice in other countries. Its greatest effect has followed from the obligation of pension funds in the United States to diversify part of their portfolios overseas. A modest percentage of their assets applied overseas was equal to a large cash flow into local stock markets. The experience and knowledge of fund management in foreign markets is one of the City's competitive strengths. It has also developed in a characteristically British way, displaying little interest in the academic theories of diversification, but as later with privatisation, quickly understanding its practical advantages.

Having the necessary skills to invest overseas provided fund management businesses with a major advantage over the in-house management of the pension funds of the larger companies. The economics of maintaining in-house teams was coming under increasing pressure. One estimate suggested that the cost of running and supporting a team of four might amount to £200,000, or 1% of a typical £20m pension fund, whereas a fee a fraction of that could be negotiated in the highly competitive fund management business. Influenced by overall cost, the disruption to salary scales demanded by investment managers and under pressure from consulting actuaries, companies increasingly closed down their investment departments and handed over their portfolios to external managers. To obtain that business, the fund management houses made presentations in 'beauty parades', where the strongest suit was proof of a good performance record. A league table of the leading pension fund managers as at March 1982 is given in Table 26.2.

Table 26.2
Leading pension fund managers, March 1982

Managers	Funds under management (£m)
Merchant banks	
S. G. Warburg	2,200
Robert Fleming	1,800
Schroder Wagg	1,800
Morgan Grenfell	1,785
Hill Samuel	1,667
Insurance companies	
Prudential	2,200
Legal & General	2,000

Pension fund management was now becoming a growing, profitable and competitive business. It was driven by performance, which led fund managers to shorter-term views and higher turnover, as pension funds enjoyed the benefit of tax-free opportunities for capital gains. The simplest measure of higher turnover is to take half the annual Stock Exchange equity turnover as sales and express that figure as a percentage of the average market capitalisation of quoted companies, for which the quarterly valuations of the All Share Index are assumed to represent 90% of the total.

The long-term trends of this rough calculation show the effect of the performance cult that started in the late 1960s, as described in Chapter 16. In 1965 and 1966, only 7% of the equity of the average company was sold in a full year. By 1970, the figure had increased to 13½%, before settling in the late 1970s and early 1980s at 15–17%. A second phase of increased competitive performance was now about to begin, and the percentage of the equity of the typical company traded in a year rose from 16% in 1982 to 44% in 1987. This is an imprecise but consistent calculation, although it does not mean that 44% of all shareholdings were sold in 1987. Much of the total is made up of parcels of shares changing hands with much greater frequency.

This trend later became identified as 'short-termism', a subject considered in Chapter 33. At this stage, it is worth noting that many a chairman, chief executive or finance director complaining of the effects of short-termism on the shares of their own company was often the same person demanding aggressive performance from the managers of their company pension fund.

To return to the events of 1981, the stock market continued gently upwards through the summer months and the All Share Index hit new all-time highs in August, giving credence to the view that better times lay ahead. This peaceful calm was shattered without warning and for no obvious reason when the market suddenly collapsed in the calendar month of September, displaying that fragility so offputting to many investors and bewildering to company directors, who cannot believe the value of their enterprise can possibly vary so much from day to day.

The last three days of August 1981 were a Bank Holiday weekend and investors left for home content with the FT Index at 573.8 and the All Share at 334.63. Sterling had been rather weak in the last two months and, in late August, the Bank of England abandoned MLR as a published symbol of interest rates without putting anything very visible in its place.

Gradual selling in the first half of September turned into a flood. In the two-week Stock Exchange account ending on 25 September, the FT Index fell by 14.3%, when a loss of confidence in stock markets worldwide turned into something far worse in London. On the following Monday, 28 September, an avalanche of selling by destabilised private investors pushed the FT Index down 29.4 points by midday to 445.3, before it closed at 457.5. In exactly 4 weeks, the Index was down 20.3%, a fall mirrored to within a decimal point by the All Share Index.

Within the narrative of bull and bear markets that divide the chapters of this book, a fall of more than 20% might constitute enough for the briefest of chapters for September 1981, but it was too short-lived. On Tuesday 29 September, the FT Index bounced back with a 5.2% rise, matched by 4.8% from the All Share Index.

It was a peculiar month. MLR had been abandoned at 12% in late August. Amid uncertainty about interest rates, the gilt-edged market also collapsed during September, pushing yields to over 16%, levels only ever seen before in the depths of the bear market in January 1975 and again during the sterling crisis of 1976. Without any published indicator, the best guide for interest rates became clearing bank base rates, lifted from 12% to 14% on 16 September and from 14% to 16% on 1 October, by which time what appeared to have been a flight into cash was all over. Strangely, when market turnover and bargain figures were later published, September proved to have been a very busy month for equities, but the quietest month of the year for gilts and fixed interest.

Over the remainder of the year, markets recovered some ground but remained fragile. The luck of timing for new issues was amply demonstrated by the contrast of an £87m rights issue announced by Trust House Forte on 2 September, just as the market was breaking down and 75% left with the underwriters, and the £20m offer for sale in calmer days in November of money brokers Exco, which was oversubscribed 62.5 times.

In popular memory, 1982 was the year of the Falklands. For the stock market, it was a year when equity values were firmly underpinned by falling interest rates. From a peak of 16% in October 1981, base rates had already been cut to 14% by the year end, and their steady downtrend during 1982 led to sharply higher gilt-edged prices, matched by higher equities. The effect can be seen from Table 26.3.

Table 26.3
Falling interest rates and markets, October 1981 to November 1982

Date	Base rate %	Consols 2½%	FT Gilts Index	All Share Index
2 October 1981	16	17½	60.60	282.78
9 November 1981	15	18½	62.89	306.11
13 July 1982	12	20½	70.88	324.49
6 October 1982	10	23½	79.60	361.64
4 November 1982	9	26¾	85.27	388.16
% change		52.9	40.7	37.3

The sequence of falling interest rates came to an end in November, but its effect was to produce an exceptional bull market in gilt-edged securities, comparable to that in 1976/77. The undated Consols 2½% and other long-dated stocks rose by some 50%, and the FT Gilts Index by 40%. It closely followed the pattern from October 1976, when MLR fell from its sterling crisis peak of 15% to 5% in 11 months, then also leading the way for a massive bull market for equities. However, whereas these crisis rates of 15% in 1976 and 16% in October 1981 sparked, almost to the day, powerful equity markets, the matching crisis rates of 7% in 1957, 1961 and 1966 and 8% in 1969 marked the onset of nasty bear markets.

The reason for the difference was that when high interest rates were imposed by the Government in the 1950s and 1960s, their purpose was to reduce overheating in the economy, whereas in the latter years they were imposed on the Government as the price at which excessive public-sector borrowing could be financed. The institutions held the upper hand and were able to dictate the terms. In 1976 and 1981, they marched the Government to the top of the hill to rates of 15% and 16%, and marched it down a steeply falling slope of lower interest rates and capital profits. In both cases, institutions with responsibilities for policyholders and pensioners refused to bail out extravagant Government borrowing, except at the right price, whereupon they were accused of making political gestures in a 'buyers' strike'.

The recovery was under way by the time of Geoffrey Howe's fourth Budget on 9 March 1982. He reduced taxes by £2,500m, shared between individuals, by raising income tax allowances by 2% more than inflation, and industry, by reducing the national insurance surcharge for employers from 3½% to 2½%. He forecast a PSBR of £9,500m, or 3½% of GDP, and inflation in single figures at 9%, followed by 7%. He described it as a pragmatic Budget, and it included two measures for investors. Henceforth, purchase prices of securities would be indexed for inflation for capital gains tax purposes, and, second, Index-linked gilts would no longer be restricted to pension funds and would be available to private individuals.

The Government had now been in power for almost three years, but in the economy 'green shoots' were slow to appear. The headlines were enough to make any fund manager feel insecure. Vivid pictures of rioting in the streets of London and Liverpool in the summer of 1981 stayed long in the memory and, in January, unemployment finally reached a total of 3 million, or 12.7%. The newly elected Chairman of ICI, John Harvey-Jones, when asked abroad in April why the recession was so hard, replied 'Well, we've got Thatcher', but there were some compensations. In January, the miners voted against industrial action to accept 9.3%, and later a national rail strike collapsed. In April, inflation returned to single figures for the first time in three years.

The reflationary Budget was well timed and confidence grew during the summer, helped now by falling interest rates worldwide. This was especially marked on 18 August when world markets surged, including a record rise in the Dow Jones of 38.81 points, or 4.8%, and a 3.8% rise in the FT Index. The All Share Index hit many new highs to reach 389.24 on 15 November, and the FT Index reached 600 for the first time in October before touching 637.4 on 12 November. The stoical belief of investors is marked by the extraordinary fact that, despite the depth and severity of the recession, 1982 was the fifth consecutive year in which the All Share Index reached a new high, although many would say it did not feel quite like that at the time. In that week of surging markets in August, unemployment reached 3,290,000.

Two major themes of the Thatcher years – Big Bang and privatisation – are the subject of Chapters 27 and 29 but they were both making first impressions in 1982. The first signs of foreign ownership of stockbrokers surfaced in June when Security Pacific purchased 29.9% of Hoare Govett and the intention to privatise British Telecommunications was revealed in July, with some awesome estimates of its possible market capitalisation.

Activity in takeovers and new issues was at a lower level in 1982, possibly affected by the Falklands war, but there were some unusual examples for the case book. There was an example of the biter bit in the long-running battle of commodity dealers S. & W. Berisford to buy the British Sugar Corporation, dominant refiners of sugar beet and 24% owned by the Government. It began in May 1980 when a bid of £120.6m from Berisford was referred to the Monopolies Commission which eventually gave its consent to the bid in March 1981. On 28 May, Berisford raised its bid to £142m, but, making little progress, carried out a dawn raid on 12 June to buy 23½% of the shares for £47m. The bid lapsed, leaving Berisford with a 38% holding and the Government still owning 24%. Takeover Code rules did not allow another bid for 12 months.

In July 1981, the Government sold its 24% stake in an institutional placing for £44m, making British Sugar more vulnerable to an eventual bid. Perhaps in an attempt to defend itself by diversification, British Sugar mounted a market raid in November on Rank Hovis McDougall, leading flour millers and bakers, to buy a 14.7% stake for £28m. The response of Rank Hovis McDougall was immediate. Six days later, it mounted a reverse market raid on British Sugar to buy 10½% of the shares for £24.3m, and thus be able to join with Berisford in assuming effective control. In July 1982, Berisford bought the holding from Rank Hovis for £29.6m to gain control, and its final bid valued British Sugar at £282m compared with the first bid in May 1980 of £121m.

Another example was the bid mounted for F. W. Woolworth, the quoted UK subsidiary of the famous US parent. Woolworth owned nearly 1,000 general merchandising stores in the high streets of towns and cities across Britain, but their best years were long behind them. The stores were too small, popular taste was moving away from cheapness for its own sake and specialist retailers were making inroads into their wide product range. The shares were languishing at 58p – well below an estimated asset value of 145p – when they were suspended in September 1982 because a bid was being prepared by Charterhouse Japhet. The market capitalisation was £220m.

The unusual feature of this bid was revealed one week later on 30 September, when an offer of 82p per share, or £310m, was made by Paternoster Stores, following its purchase of the 52.6% controlling shareholding from the US parent. Hitherto, almost all takeover bids involved the offer of cash or shares from an existing company, usually already quoted on the Stock Exchange, but in this case Paternoster was created specifically for the purpose of bidding for Woolworth. Its capital was provided by some 30 institutions in a consortium put together by Charterhouse and Rowe & Pitman. The concept proved to be highly successful under its renamed title of Kingfisher. There was a link between the ill-fated British Sugar Corporation and the new Paternoster. John Beckett and Geoff Mulcahy, previously Chairman and Finance Director of British Sugar, transferred their talents to the new company, an opportunity they would have missed if they had successfully fought off Berisford.

In the field of new issues, September 1982 marked the arrival on the London

Stock Exchange of International Signal & Control, an extraordinary American company in the defence field based in Pennsylvania under James Guerin. Strangely, it was not quoted in the United States, but was now seeking a full listing in London by way of an offer for sale to raise £33m, giving the company a market value of £86m. It was promoted by Robert Fleming and stockbrokers L. Messel, and, having an excellent five-year growth record with a forecast of surging profits in alluring 'special purpose defence systems', the issue was over-subscribed 34 times.

Apart from revealing basic sales and profits figures and dividing them 80% overseas and 20% in the United States, International Signal & Control and its advisers found it difficult to explain what it actually did and where. The company was coming to London because SEC rules in New York would have required the disclosure of information that would have 'broken the terms of its contracts' and 'jeopardised confidential aspects of its business'. It was a perfect example of Catch 22 in reverse – if we tell you what we do, we lose the business – and it would continue to fool everybody for seven years. It was taken over in 1987 by Ferranti, which, 18 months later, discovered to its horror that behind the barriers of secrecy, the business was largely a figment of James Guerin's fertile imagination. There is a lesson to be learned, which is beware companies quoted away from their natural home.

Stock markets entered 1983 in buoyant form. It was likely to be an election year with the probability of the return of the Conservatives for a second term. The long battle against inflation had been largely won, with the year end rate being 5.4% for 1982, at its lowest since 1969. Further relaxation could be expected in the Budget, following a cut in the employers' National Insurance surcharge from 2½% to 1½% in an economic statement in November. The prospect for company profits was improving, with forecasts of 20% increases suggested for 1983, as both interest rates and sterling had been easing for several months, although the consensus of forecasts of GDP growth for the year was only 1.7%.

The economy had taken a battering during the recession. Percentage growth rates of GDP published by OECD show the following sequence:

- 1979   1.4
- 1980   −2.2
- 1981   −1.3
- 1982   1.7

In the event, the consensus forecast of 1.7% for 1983 proved to be well below the outcome for the year of 3.7%, but the stock market was abreast of what was really happening in the economy and, during the first 6 months of the year, both indices frequently recorded new all-time highs. Stock Exchange figures for 1982 had shown record turnover in equities at a monthly average of £3,100m. In the first quarter of 1983, the monthly average moved sharply higher, to £5,000m, as a powerful bull market took hold in all corners of the market.

Showing their colours among the leaders were two of the great growth stocks of the 1980s, Glaxo and J. Sainsbury. Glaxo had trebled in 1982 to a market capitalisation of £2,750m, and Sainsbury had produced remarkable trading figures during the recession in comparison with its competitors. At the other extreme was the new Unlisted Securities Market (USM), where speculative fever spread across its 150 quoted companies, of which nearly half were in the technology or oil exploration sectors.

The same excitement spread to new issues. The Government's sale of 50% of Associated British Ports was oversubscribed 34 times, with a low price probably influenced by a disastrous earlier sale by tender of Britoil. However, a record multiple oversubscription of 95 times was set by Superdrug Stores in February, exceeding the previous record of 85 times for Eurotherm International in 1978. Superdrug attracted applications of £1,470m for a £15m offer for sale and the shares offered at 175p opened at 295p on the first day of dealing. It was the same story on the USM, and, typical of many companies where few people asked what it actually did, was Microgen, placed at 190p and trading up to 370p on its first day of dealing.

Elsewhere, Polly Peck, which caught the headlines in 1980 when it shot up 27 times to 190p, reached £35 in February 1983, with investors still no wiser about its unbelievable profit margins, before it spiralled downwards to £17. Asil Nadir had planned to merge Polly Peck with two smaller quoted companies under his control and the shares were suspended in some disarray. More unbelievable figures with even better profit margins were announced for the half year to March showing pre-tax profits up 164% to £8.1m on turnover up 134% to £18.2m. No explanation was offered and the market in the shares remained tightly under the control of stockbrokers L. Messel, fast becoming experts in impenetrable companies, with International Signal & Control also in its portfolio.

The mood of the market was helped by the reflationary Budget from Geoffrey Howe on 15 March. For a second successive year, he made substantial personal tax concessions by concentrating wholly on allowances that he raised by 14% compared with inflation of 5%, to release £2,500m in a full year. He continued to cut the national insurance surcharge from 1½% to 1% and was rightly able to claim that 'the trend of rising inflation that appeared irresistible has been decisively broken'. Both indices hit new highs on Budget day and continued upwards unchecked in April and May as rumours of a general election began to spread.

In the closing weeks before the election, there were three bid situations of note. First, Cable & Wireless purchased a 34.8% stake in Hong Kong Telephone Company for £143m from Hong Kong Land in March 1983. This holding would become of immense value and be the driving force behind the company's future growth.

Second, there was a battle for the control of United Drapery Stores (UDS) – owner of several chains of clothing stores – between a consortium company, Bassishaw, led by Gerald Ronson, and Hanson Trust, the industrial conglomerate led by James Hanson. The terms were closely matched after 3 bids from Ronson to 130p per share and 2 from Hanson to 133.5p, but the Board of UDS was divided between executives in favour of Ronson and non-executives preferring Hanson. The executives followed the unusual tactic of taking a full-page advertisement in the *Financial Times* on 20 April 1983 that began with the sentence 'If your sole interest is getting the maximum price for your holding, doubtless you will accept the Hanson Trust offer. But if you consider it more responsible to preserve a major independent . . .'. It was a suicide note – 3 days later, Hanson claimed 62% acceptances.

The third bid went to the day before the election and was to be a bitter battle between BTR, the flagship of the conglomerates of the 1980s and Thomas Tilling the flagship of the industrial holding companies of the 1960s. Their philosophies were very different. BTR managed businesses, whereas Tilling managed investments in businesses. It began with an attempted market raid by BTR to secure 14.9% of Tilling at 175p on 5 April at a large premium over the existing price of 126p. The raid failed dismally, with BTR obtaining a mere 6% of the shares at a cost of £30m. Just 6 days later, BTR made a full bid of 185p in cash, equal to £576m. On 17 May, the bid was increased to 225p, or £655m, and, despite strong rejection from Thomas Tilling, the bid was successful on 8 June.

These pre-election months may have brought glad tidings for excited fund managers, but these were painful times for many segments of manufacturing industry. In the early months of the Thatcher Government, Scotland lost one of its largest employers when Singer closed its sewing machine factory. More than three years later, in the closing months, it lost another long-standing employer when Timex closed its Dundee watchmaking factory. Unemployment had been 1,250,000; it was now over 3,000,000. GDP was lower in 1982 than in 1979. 'The bewilderment of the proverbial Birmingham manufacturer at the behaviour of the London stock market is a well-documented social phenomenon', was how Lex described the situation in his column, on 2 April 1983.

However, there was one big difference in the stock market. When Margaret Thatcher came to power in 1979, earnings were valued on a PE ratio of around 8, but although earnings only marginally increased over the period by 12%, when she sought re-election, the average PE ratio was 12.

On 9 May 1983, Margaret Thatcher called a general election for 9 June. The FT Index promptly surged over 700 for the first time and, exactly as in May 1979, both indices hit new all-time highs on polling day. The record over her first Parliament had been:

	3 May 1979	9 June 1983	% change
FT Index	553.5	716.4	+ 29.4
All Share Index	280.28	442.80	+ 58.0

The discrepancy in performance figures between the two indices was so great that the value of the FT Index was being increasingly questioned. Within a year, it would be replaced by the FTSE 100 as the real-time index of market sentiment. Its preponderance of industrial shares weakened it beyond repair during the 1980–81 recession, and its geometric calculation caused it to lag further behind. The true measure of portfolio performance was the 58% rise shown in the All Share Index, but even this no more than matched inflation of 56% over the same period. Dividends also fell within the same bracket, with a 55% increase in the underlying dividend index on the All Share Index.

Markets suffered few doubts during the election campaign and Margaret Thatcher was returned with a much increased overall majority of 144 seats. Her victory heralded the second stage of a powerful and sustained bull market.

Chapter 27

BIG BANG

The date of Big Bang was Monday 27 October 1986. It was a veritable explosion for the stock market, consigning to history the traditional Stock Exchange roles of broker and jobber, single capacity, fixed commissions and the individual flavour of membership of the Stock Exchange. The jobber was no longer to be a familiar face on the floor of the market, but the remote voice of a corporate trader sitting at a desk amid screens, from now on to be known as a market maker. The stockbroker more or less disappeared to become a corporate executive serving the institutions in sales, research or corporate finance, or replaced by independent financial advisers serving the public.

The stockbroker – for so long a symbol of wealth and large houses in fiction and newspaper articles – will largely remain, a character of the nineteenth and twentieth centuries. Nobody now claims to be a 'Member of the Stock Exchange', although a small number of private client stockbrokers remain. A few are in London, including some offshoots of the clearing banks, and there are many smaller firms in the provinces, all serving the public, but for the far larger institutional markets, stockbrokers have disappeared into securities firms.

Big Bang is defined in different ways according to choice. At one extreme, it was the Stock Exchange – a nineteenth-century club – being dragged, screaming, into the twentieth century. At the other extreme, it was merely part of the Thatcher Government's carefully planned programme of deregulation. In fact, it was a good example of British pragmatism at work, with all concerned edging forward one step at a time towards a successful conclusion. The proof of the pudding is that, for the securities industry, the City has secured the prime place at the hub of the European wheel, itself in the prime middle spot of the 24-hour clock passing from Tokyo to London to New York.

It was a long, slow-burning fuse set in 1976 that finally triggered the explosion of Big Bang ten years later in 1986. Although the Government had no direct control over the Stock Exchange, key ministerial decisions were taken on the way along by Roy Hattersley in February 1979, John Nott in October 1979 and Cecil Parkinson in July 1983.

The Restrictive Trade Practices Act of 1956 was first confined to the manufacturers of goods and products, but was extended in 1976 to include service industries. The Stock Exchange registered its rule book and, in 1977, it was placed on the Register by the Office of Fair Trading for formal investigation, along with some 200 others for a case unlikely to be heard before 1979.

At this early stage, the Stock Exchange was confident that its restrictions could be defended as being in the public interest. It believed that the principle of single capacity, the existence of the Compensation Fund and the rigour of the listing requirements served to protect the public, and that this structure could only be sustained by fixed commissions.

While the Office of Fair Trading continued its investigations, the Chairman of the Stock Exchange, the recently elected Nicholas Goodison, wrote to Roy Hattersley, Secretary of State for Prices and Consumer Protection, to appeal for exemption. Hattersley refused to intervene and, in February 1979, the Stock Exchange was formally referred to the Restrictive Practices Court for a hearing likely to begin in late 1980.

With the return of a Conservative Government in May 1979, the Stock Exchange made a further attempt to have the case removed from the Restrictive Practices Court, but such hopes proved to be naive when the Secretary of State for Trade, John Nott, himself a former merchant banker with S. G. Warburg, rejected this request on 23 October, on the same day that foreign exchange controls were abandoned. However, a serious problem in taking the Stock Exchange to the Restrictive Practices Court was at last recognised – namely that an adverse decision requires the immediate abandonment of any restrictive practices. Without an alternative structure in place, the Stock Exchange would be thrown into chaos. John Nott amended the procedures to give the Stock Exchange a still inadequate nine months to revise its rules in the event of an adverse decision.

In fact, the Stock Exchange was being thrown into chaos by the surprise abandonment of exchange controls, which revealed at a stroke just how far out of step with the rest of the world the London system of brokers and jobbers had become. Single capacity and fixed commissions were uncompetitive when it came to dealing in international markets and handling cross-border transactions and, once the Stock Exchange began to discuss concessions to be given to the proposed international dealer, the case for their retention in London began to be undermined.

With hindsight, it can be seen that the eventual reforms were made inevitable by the abandonment of exchange controls, and John Nott's refusal to remove the Stock Exchange from the Restrictive Practices Court held up the process for three or four years. Instead, the Stock Exchange was caught in a trap of conflicting interests. It was preparing the case for defending its rules in domestic markets, while negotiating those same rules away in international markets. Being trapped as a defendant in the inflexibility of a legal process made even-handed debate within the Stock Exchange difficult, and this point was well recognised by the report of the Wilson Committee published in June 1980. This Committee had been set up by James Callaghan in 1977 to look into various aspects of the City and, after three and a half years, its conclusions were widely favourable.

The Report attempted to smooth the way forward by recommending that 'public debate about possible alternatives has been muted by the Stock Exchange's understandable unwillingness to do anything which might weaken its position before the Court. We believe that consideration of alternatives is now urgent and suggest the Council for Securities is the body to undertake this task'. This recommendation fell on deaf ears, and the impasse remained, although another recommendation – that lay members should serve on the Stock Exchange Council – was readily adopted.

While the Stock Exchange and the Office of Fair Trading were beginning the long process of case preparation, the attention of most stock market practitioners was diverted by rapidly rising activity, the abandonment of exchange controls, dawn raids and takeover bids. Hardly anybody believed that fixed commissions would survive close examination, but opinion about the so-called 'link' argument between fixed commissions and single capacity was more divided. The argument was that a break in the link would cause the collapse of single capacity because stockbrokers would be driven to adopt principal positions to compensate for lost revenues and jobbers would retaliate by demanding direct access to clients. In fact, many firms of brokers put the matter to the back of their minds because they were too busy, preferring not to think too closely about an uncertain and unpredictable future.

In reflective moments, behind this cheerful facade of busy markets, there was undoubtedly a deal of pessimism about a future under negotiated commissions. The London stock market had long ago retreated into its own domestic world, with the barriers of exchange controls making outward investment difficult and the chronic decline of sterling making inward investment unattractive. Criticism that the Stock Exchange lost international ground as a result of its own inadequacies are exaggerated because there was little ground to gain or defend, but it had settled into a comfortable complacency that made the prospect of change difficult to achieve.

Meanwhile, some of the customers were getting restless. For many institutions, fixed commissions were a matter of the Stock Exchange defending the indefensible. Much of this institutional frustration had been self-inflicted by the Stock Exchange and allowed to build up over many years because of earlier, ill-judged decisions on commissions. At issue was the balance between commissions on gilt-edged securities and equities. They were perceived to be far too high on gilts, given the sheer size of the gilt-edged market after massive Government funding in the 1960s and 1970s, the comparative ease of dealing in amounts of millions of pounds, the limited economic advice required and the technical nature of much of the business of switching between holdings for small margins. By comparison, equities were disparate, required much more extensive knowledge and research, and it was more difficult to deal in large size.

The problem stemmed from as far back as 1971, when substantial cuts were made in commission rates for large deals in response to the threat of competition in equities from Ariel. The lowest rate for equities was reduced from ½% to ⅛% for consideration over £1.75m, but as gilts were not seen to be under threat their lowest rate was only cut from 0.14% to 0.1% for consideration over £1m. The lowest rates for equities and gilts were too close together, giving an impression to the outsider that the Stock Exchange perceived little difference between the two, but it probably owed more to the presence of a powerful gilt-edged lobby on the Stock Exchange Council.

This anomaly was never corrected. The next rate review in 1976 only tinkered at the edges in raising commissions overall by 3.9%, and a proposal to increase rates in 1982 ran into powerful opposition from the institutions before eventually being settled at 4.2% overall and primarily aimed at smaller bargains. Representations by the institutions that this review should incorporate reductions in gilt-edged commissions were rebuffed. Perhaps the gilt-edged specialists were always too powerful a lobby on the Stock Exchange Council, but this long-standing insensitivity to the underlying differences between transactions in gilt-edged securities and equities was a critical cause of antagonism towards the Stock Exchange from the insurance companies and the pension funds – the two most active investors in the gilt-edged market.

The reality of the situation had long been apparent because of the widespread and ludicrous practice of institutions being forced to instruct gilt-edged brokers to send participation cheques – often to the value of several thousand pounds – to equity brokers to bring about a fair allocation of total commissions to reflect the value of services provided. The later judgement of Big Bang was conclusive – institutional commissions disappeared altogether from the gilt-edged market, but remained for equities.

Hostility to Stock Exchange commissions was most strongly expressed by the insurance companies and pension funds. There was talk of the 'unbundling' of commissions, whereby institutions would pay stockbrokers only for those services they required – a pointed reference to being forced to pay for unwanted and surplus research material from too many brokers. The attitude of the fund managers of investment trusts and unit trusts was more equivocal because it suited many of them to have costs paid by their clients through commissions on transactions, and, being largely equity investors, the rule that purchases or sales could be aggregated over a three-month period meant that, in effect, commissions actually charged were little different from negotiated rates in New York. Furthermore, the unit trusts encouraged stockbrokers to purchase units for their private clients by offering in return reciprocal equity business to generate commission income.

The attitude of the merchant banks was coloured by an internal practice in their fund management divisions. Purchases or sales of a particular equity executed through one broker over a period of three months were allowed to be aggregated to generate the lowest possible commission rate, but when the merchant bank allocated these bargains across their many portfolios, they were able to charge each client the relevant and higher stock market commission for the smaller amount allocated. The difference between commission charged out and commission paid was retained as an undisclosed profit.

Institutions drew other advantages from the existing system. Stock Exchange firms provided extensive research services that, if curtailed would involve institutions in the cost of hiring their own analysts. Stockbrokers were also allowed to pick up the cost of fees for certain approved external services – in particular, valuation or performance measurement services. In return, the institution would agree to provide 'extra' commission of possibly twice the amount of the fee, but this could be impossibly difficult to verify. Many institutions would 'invite' stockbrokers to allow such invoices to be sent direct to them for payment, in return, of course, for extra commission. Some merchant banks invited stockbrokers to deposit capital in return for a multiple of the notional rate of interest paid in commissions. Commissions generated in this way are described as 'soft' and they amounted to an erosion of the minimum commission system, but it enabled many institutions to reduce their costs, and raise their profits, by indirectly hiding them in client transactions.

While stock markets were going from strength to strength in 1981 and 1982 with rising prices and record turnover, a *sub judice* paralysis stifled debate in the Stock Exchange as preparation for the Court case edged slowly forwards. Bull markets breed short-term horizons and 1984 still seemed a long time away. The battle for fixed commissions was deemed to have been lost, but single capacity had plenty of support, including that of David Hopkinson, the individualist Chairman of the most successful unit trust group at the time – M&G. He passionately feared for the integrity of the market should the separation between principal and agent be abandoned.

Nicholas Goodison had for some time lobbied the Bank of England about the rigidity of the legal process now slowly enveloping the Stock Exchange. In 1982, the Bank responded – now clearly aware how the abandonment of exchange controls had exposed the City to new competition and thrown the Stock Exchange into confusion. Change was inevitable and contingency planning was taking place, but nothing could be openly discussed in the light of the forthcoming court case. Behind the scenes, David Walker – transferred from the Treasury to become a new director of the Bank of England with City responsibilities – quickly concluded that the best interests of the City, and not least the Bank of England with its government fundraising responsibilities, were ill-served by pursuing this case in the Restrictive Practices Court. Discussion with the Department of Trade led to wider support for taking the case out of the court if suitable concessions for reform could be secured from the Stock Exchange.

After the 1983 general election, Nicholas Goodison approached the new

Secretary of State for Trade and Industry, Cecil Parkinson, to ask for the case to be dropped in return for a commitment by the Stock Exchange to bring about major reforms. Much of the groundwork had already been covered by Lord Cockfield, the previous Secretary of State, and the Government was already well briefed about the misgivings of the Bank of England. Like minds quickly negotiated an agreement to remove the case from the Restrictive Practices Court, in return for the abandonment of fixed commissions within three years and other reforms, such as admitting lay members to the Stock Exchange Council and allowing non-members to become non-executive directors of member firms. The vexed question of the survival of single capacity was rather left in the air. The implementation of the agreement was to be monitored by the Bank of England.

The agreement announced by Cecil Parkinson on 27 July 1983 was strongly criticised in some quarters as an unjustified circumvention of the law. It had appeared unexpectedly on the scene and appeared to many outsiders to be a hasty stitch-up between the Conservative Government and its friends in the City to give the Stock Exchange another three privileged years before having to put its house in order. It was by now widely agreed that fixed commissions were not sustainable, but opinions still differed about single capacity. Majority opinion in the Stock Exchange doubted its survival, but many stockbrokers genuinely believed that the separation of principal and agent was fundamental to the integrity of the Stock Exchange, and the National Association of Pension Funds openly supported its continuance. Ironically, at the same time, gathering clouds over the Lloyds insurance market were drawing attention to the problems caused by the blurring of differences between principal and agent, and just as Lloyds was looking to solve its problems by a clearer separation of the two, the Stock Exchange was rushing to abandon it.

The Stock Exchange immediately began to plan for major changes in the way the market operated, knowing it faced the difficulty of gaining approval for many changes in its constitution from around 4,500 individual members with differing interests. It was fortunate to have at this time an outstanding leader in Nicholas Goodison, the Senior Partner of a small- to medium-sized firm of stockbrokers, Quilter Goodison. He had for some time been a prospective chairman of the Stock Exchange, but was elected in January 1976 at the unexpectedly early age of 41, following the death of Michael Marriott who died within months of taking office.

His tall, slender figure and slightly ascetic manner exuded an authority and maturity beyond his years. The Stock Exchange had uncharacteristically found itself at the right time with a chairman for whom the word intellectual would be no exaggeration. During his stockbroking career, Goodison had found time to publish a standard work on barometers, was an expert on furniture and metalworks and carried extensive responsibilities in the world of the arts. For those wondering how all this could be, much was revealed of an iron discipline by a later admission 'I don't watch television, I don't read the Sunday newspapers and I don't play golf'.

If ever a cool head were required to handle a complicated situation it was now. The Stock Exchange is a forcefully opinionated place and it owes much to the leadership and patience of Nicholas Goodison that new structures were successfully brought into play with the backing of the majority of the members, when all could have collapsed into chaos and acrimony. The July agreement with Cecil Parkinson set a deadline for change and produced reactions ranging from excitement about new challenges to fear for any future at all. The Stock Exchange faced three major policy decisions. Would single capacity survive and, if not, what would take its place? What should be the timetable for abandoning fixed commissions? What constitutional changes were required concerning ownership and membership?

By the end of the year, the debate had moved decisively against the retention of single capacity, and the problems were well summarised in a *Financial Times* leader of 12 September 1983: 'In the face of strong commercial pressures the Bank of England would find it very difficult to maintain single capacity simply by exerting its moral authority. Legislation would be at least as tricky.' Its ending was publicly foreshadowed by the Governor of the Bank of England at a seminar in March 1984 and formally confirmed when the Stock Exchange published its discussion paper in April.

The alternatives to fixed commissions were a series of gradual reductions over three years or an overnight change on a single date – popularly referred to as 'Big Bang'. In February 1984, the latter course was proposed for equities on a date not before the autumn of 1985, but immediate cuts of around 20% were proposed for larger gilt-edged transactions.

The agreement with Cecil Parkinson included the powerful sanction that if the Stock Exchange failed to obtain the support of the membership for the necessary constitutional changes, the case would return to the Restrictive Practices Court. In October 1983, a vote massively in favour of the principle of change was successfully recorded. Later votes on the detail would prove to be more controversial.

When later described in cold print, the steps along the path to deregulation always seem more straightforward than they actually were. Every next step is beset with doubt and uncertainty, and so it was in 1983 and 1984 when it was known that the market systems of the Stock Exchange were to be dismantled by deregulation, but their replacement was not even yet designed, let alone built. Deregulation in any industry causes uncertainties for all involved, but it also provides opportunities for the bold, whether they be new entrants coming into the particular business or fund managers spotting new opportunities. It was now the turn of many City practitioners who had profited from opportunities following deregulation in other industries to face hard competition from within their own ranks, together with much sniffing in the air from outsiders looking in.

The merchant banks and clearing banks in London, the universal banks from the continent of Europe, the commercial banks, investment banks and stock-brokers in the United States, and financial institutions from the rest of the world circled round, sensing new opportunities in a revitalised London securities market that occupied the key position in the middle of the global day. Surrounded within were large numbers of gloomy stockbrokers and jobbers, under attack from their institutional customers who talked of negotiating com-missions into the ground. Suddenly the cavalry came along to the rescue in the form of outsiders waving large cheques. Never before had so many willing sell-ers run headlong into so many willing buyers.

A lone marker had already been placed much earlier in June 1982, well before the threat of the court case had been removed. The Stock Exchange had long been sensitive to the problem faced by many stockbrokers and jobbers of raising capital, particularly in partnerships where profits have to be distributed in full and the capital of retiring partners needs to be replaced by younger partners with limited resources. For this reason, it had allowed outsiders to sub-scribe for up to 10% of the capital of a firm as an investment as long ago as 1968, but without any management role or Board representation. In June 1982, this rule was relaxed to raise the limit for outsiders to 29.9%. Within days, it was announced on 9 June that Security Pacific – a Californian bank, ninth largest in the United States – had taken a 29.9% stake in one of the leading firms of stockbrokers, Hoare Govett, for an undisclosed price but believed to be in the region of £8m.

It was a surprise because of its speed and because little was known about Security Pacific. However, an attraction for Hoare Govett was the absence of any conflict of interest between its new partners and its existing client base. This remained the only transaction of its kind to be announced for the next 16 months, which is surprising because, during that time, there was much circling round and many a discreet approach. What is also apparent is that valuations rose sharply in the interval because the next transaction was the purchase in November 1983 of 29.9% of stockbrokers Vickers da Costa at an overall valu-ation of £20m by Citicorp – one of the major New York commercial banks – followed quickly by the announcement that Mercury Securities, parent of the leading merchant bank, S. G. Warburg, had subscribed £41m for a 29.9% stake in Akroyd & Smithers – a quoted company and one of the two largest jobbers.

In December 1983, N. M. Rothschild subscribed £6.5m in shares and con-vertible loan stock for a stake equivalent to 29.9% in Smith Bros – one of three medium-sized jobbers ranking well behind the two leaders. In January 1984, the first round of acquisitions was completed with the surprise announcement that Charter Consolidated, an industrial holding company with strong South African antecedents, had purchased a 29.9% stake in stockbrokers Rowe & Pitman for £16.2m. At the same time, it was announced that Rowe & Pitman and Akroyd & Smithers were to form a jointly owned international dealer, the first link of its kind between broker and jobber, and, in effect, casting the die for the eventual link between Rowe & Pitman and S. G. Warburg.

These transactions illustrate the thinking of the time. The leading firms of stockbrokers were concerned to avoid links causing conflicts of interest with their major clients, particularly where joining forces with one merchant bank might prejudice relationships with the others. As a result, Hoare Govett and Rowe & Pitman settled for neutral partners. The leading firms of jobbers were attractive because their numbers were so limited – there were only five of any significant size. Two of these were taken in the first round, both by merchant banks alert to the limited market-making skills available, and the other three were all snapped up by April.

The merchant banks faced a real dilemma. The separation of skills in the City had suited them well while they pursued their essentially advisory activities in mergers and acquisitions, corporate issues and fund management. These activities were client-driven, risk-averse, fee-paying and required relatively modest capital. They were different in character from the activities of American and European banks where more of the business was transaction-driven, risky, demanded capital and generated more speculative revenues.

They faced a dangerous choice. Remaining independent was attractive, but carried the risk of being relegated to a niche role in the face of an onslaught of competition from integrated houses able to handle both the pricing and the distribution of corporate issues, and from foreign banks and brokers forming large alliances to create investment banks capable of competing on a world stage. They particularly feared the loss of their corporate issues if their traditional links with stockbrokers were cut off and they did not have their own distribution capability. A particular question under debate was whether or not companies would continue their practice of retaining a merchant bank adviser and a separate company stockbroker. Big Bang offered the option of having a single adviser, possibly at a cheaper overall cost, and if this became common practice the integrated houses would have a powerful competitive advantage.

This dilemma sorely tested the merchant banks, which no more wanted to change than did the average broker or jobber. Furthermore, there were severe cultural influences at work. The typical merchant banker believed both himself and his business to be a cut or two above the typical stockbroker or jobber, yet it was the merchant bank that was now expected to pay large amounts of capital to buy out the stockbrokers and the jobbers.

The three foremost merchant banks at this time were Morgan Grenfell – renowned for its aggression in mergers and acquisitions – S. G. Warburg, equally renowned for its skill in defence – and Kleinwort Benson – much the leading player in privatisations. The reputations of Morgan Grenfell and S. G. Warburg were respectively in attack and defence in takeover battles, but in their approach to Big Bang these roles were reversed. It was S. G. Warburg that moved aggressively to buy Akroyd & Smithers, Rowe & Pitman and Mullens to form an investment bank of all the leaders, whereas Morgan Grenfell prevaricated, talking to the likes of Wedd Durlacher and Rowe & Pitman, but was reluctant to pay high market prices for quality, and so later finished with two of the lesser firms, which, within a few years, were closed down. It is ironic that neither followed the advice they would have confidently handed out to their corporate clients. S. G. Warburg would have strongly advised any company against entering into a four-way merger, and Morgan Grenfell would have advised paying the market price to buy the best.

The issues were the same for all the leading domestic practitioners in the different sectors of the London financial markets. The barriers between them were about to fall away. Should they remain independent or should they join forces with others? How would it be possible to manage the conflicts of interest between corporate finance, research, distribution, market making and fund management when housed together under one roof? Was there any certainty that the limit of 29.9% would be raised to allow control or full ownership? Table 27.1 is a broad estimate of the leaders in each sector at the time.

Table 27.1
Leading City houses, 1984

Clearing banks	Merchant banks	Stockbrokers	Jobbers
Barclays	Barings	James Capel	Akroyd & Smithers
Lloyds	Fleming	Cazenove	Bisgood Bishop
Midland	Hambros	De Zoete & Bevan	Pinchin Denny
National Westminster	Hill Samuel	W. Greenwell	Smith Bros
	Kleinwort Benson	Grieveson Grant	Wedd Durlacher
	Lazards	Hoare Govett	
	Montagu Samuel	Phillips & Drew	
	Morgan Grenfell	Rowe & Pitman	
	N. M. Rothschild	Scrimgeour Kemp-Gee	
	Schroder Wagg	Wood Mackenzie	
	S.G. Warburg		

In the event, only 5 of these 30 firms felt able to resist the temptation to become involved. Among the prospective buyers, Lloyds Bank, Schroder Wagg, Fleming and Lazards stood back, either choosing independence or preferring to build a securities business from a green field rather than pay the high price of acquisition. Among the brokers and jobbers, only Cazenove chose resolutely to remain independent. The number of stockbrokers and jobbers eventually acquired extended a long way below the leaders named in the table. The decision of Cazenove to remain independent was crucial. It had the longest list of corporate clients of any stockbroker and openly paraded its specialisation in corporate broking. As a result, those merchant banks remaining independent had a high-class alternative available for the distribution of their issues without building their own team, and Cazenove's name was so powerful that its client companies were content to continue with separate merchant bank advisers.

The first five acquisitions up to January 1984 have already been described. The feature of the earlier transactions was that the five leading jobbers had all been spoken for by April 1984, before the Stock Exchange had published any proposals about the future structure of the market (see Table 27.2).

Table 27.2
Acquisitions of jobbers, 1983–84

Date	Acquirer	%	Acquired
November 1983	S. G. Warburg	29.9	Akroyd & Smithers
December 1983	N. M. Rothschild	29.9	Smith Bros
February 1984	National Westminster Bank	29.9	Bisgood Bishop
March 1984	Barclays Bank	29.9	Wedd Durlacher
April 1984	Morgan Grenfell	29.9	Pinchin Denny

The Stock Exchange released a discussion paper in April 1984 recommending the abolition of the 29.9% limit, thus signalling acceptance of the principle of full control of member firms by outside companies. Thereafter, the pace quickened and, in 1984, not a month passed without the announcement of a further alignment or purchase – 32 in all in the year – followed by a further 7 in the first half of 1985.

The paper outlined how the single capacity division between broker and jobber would be replaced in equities by a new 'broker-dealer' who could elect to act as agent or principal or both. By July 1984, firm proposals were in place for a new dealing system of 'competing market makers', based on the National Association of Securities Dealers Automated Quotation system (NASDAQ). This was a fast-growing screen-based system, operated outside the New York Stock Exchange where for each security the prices quoted by all market makers were displayed on one page.

The system was 'quote-driven' by the display of competing prices rather than 'order-driven', where bargains are electronically matched. This was an attraction for the Stock Exchange as it enabled the quote-driven character of the jobbing system to be retained, and it met the general wishes of members that face-to-face negotiation of bargains should continue between dealers on the floor of the market. Under the new rules, all firms were to be broker-dealers operating under dual capacity, but with no obligation to be a market maker. Those wishing to act as market makers in specific stocks would apply, and be required to maintain two-way prices in minimum numbers of shares. Some would be expected to cover wide swathes of the market, others might concentrate on a narrower list – possibly confined to corporate connections or sector research.

A new Stock Exchange Automated Quotations system (SEAQ), would be developed over the next two years to operate the new proposals, and it would prove to be a highly successful system, meeting most of its objectives. The quote-driven character of the market was retained, but the speed of modern communications and computerisation quickly ended the tradition of face-to-face negotiation on the market floor. Within a few weeks of Big Bang the market floor was abandoned and replaced by office-based trading floors and telephone dealing. The timeframe required to develop the new systems amply confirmed the sense of the decision to take the original referral of the Stock Exchange away from the Restrictive Practices Court.

At the same time, a new structure was proposed by the Bank of England for the gilt-edged market that was along the lines of the 'primary dealer' system operating for government bonds in New York. While equity and gilt-edged teams had in the past operated happily side by side in the same firms, charging fixed commissions and talking to the same clients, a parting of the ways was becoming increasingly apparent. In equities, the concept of negotiated commissions at least implied the continuing existence of some form of commission, and prospective broker-dealers had a choice between the role of agent or principal. In gilts, it soon became apparent that commissions would not survive in the new primary dealer and it was a matter of making markets direct to clients or not at all. Furthermore, the cosy system much enjoyed by the jobbers, whereby the government broker released tranches of new stock into the market, would also be coming to an end.

The reality of the new structure in the gilt-edged market entirely justified the long-standing complaints of the institutions that commissions had been too high. However, the existing gilt-edged businesses employed many people and they were extremely profitable, and all the specialist brokers and jobbers wished to continue. In addition, many investment and commercial banks with primary dealer experience in New York were also keen to participate. When the Bank of England invited applications for primary dealers, it was surprised to receive as many as 29 – far more than the number of specialist gilt brokers and jobbers practising in the Stock Exchange. More alarming for these applicants was that the responses to a specific question asking each about its forecast market share revealed ambitions adding up to a total of around 200%. A dramatic increase in turnover would be required to allow profits even remotely comparable to those still enjoyed in a market dominated by two jobbers and six to eight stockbrokers.

As the new world of broker-dealers and primary dealers took shape, those planning to participate began to identify their needs. With many more brokers than jobbers, there was a desperate shortage of market-making experience, although it was by no means certain that yesterday's jobber would necessarily make tomorrow's computer-literate market maker. Most of the new broker-dealers had no alternative other than to recruit, train and build new in-house teams from scratch. The existing teams of jobbers generally remained intact, apart from a well-publicised splinter of a team from Wedd Durlacher to Kleinwort Benson. It is no coincidence that three of the most formidable broker-dealers in the years following Big Bang were those with strong jobbing foundations in Warburg Securities (Akroyd & Smithers), BZW (Wedd Durlacher) and Smith Bros.

In equities, there was a choice of roles between active market making, as in the three examples above, or remaining an agency broker as decided by the dominant research house and market leader, James Capel, or as a commission broker, with limited market making within a narrow list, as chosen by Cazenove. In gilts, the revenues would arise solely from trading the book. There was a vital need for access to an institutional client base to provide trading opportunities and obtain information about the market, but no longer to generate commission revenue. This was a dispiriting role for the former stockbrokers in the gilt-edged market, who would have to learn that the client was, at best, a competing investor and, at worst, the 'enemy', as the Americans put it. Brilliantly timed advice to enable a client to catch the turn of the market used to mean large commissions and goodwill for the future, but now it represented lost profit for the book.

By July 1984, the prospective shape of the new market was in place and six of the ten major firms of stockbrokers listed in Table 27.1 had formed links. The scramble to acquire a foothold in the new market gathered pace and buying interest moved just as enthusiastically to the medium-sized and smaller firms. With the notable exception of Cazenove, the major firms in the earlier list fell as shown in Table 27.3.

Of these unions only Hongkong & Shanghai Bank/James Capel remains today in broadly its original form. The ownership of S. G. Warburg and Union Bank of Switzerland has fallen to the Swiss Bank and Kleinwort Benson to Dresdner Bank. Hoare Govett and Wood Mackenzie have since been sold on to other hands, and W. Greenwell reduced to becoming a primary dealer. Scrimgeour Kemp-Gee has been ignominiously closed down and BZW, formed from the purchase by Barclays of Wedd Durlacher and De Zoete & Bevan has been broken up.

Among the remaining stockbrokers, only five had formed an alliance when the Stock Exchange proposals were approved in July, but eventually every medium-

Table 27.3
Acquisitions of leading stockbrokers, 1982–84

Date	Acquirer	%	Acquired
June 1982	Security Pacific (US)	29.9	Hoare Govett
January 1984	Charter Consolidated	29.9	Rowe & Pitman
March 1984	Barclays Bank	5	De Zoete & Bevan
March 1984	Samuel Montagu (Midland Bank)	29.9	W. Greenwell
June 1984	Hill Samuel	29.9	Wood Mackenzie
June 1984	Kleinwort Benson	5	Grieveson Grant
August 1984	S. G. Warburg	100	Rowe & Pitman
August 1984	Hongkong & Shanghai Bank	29.9	James Capel
September 1984	Citicorp (US)	29.9	Scrimgeour Kemp-Gee
November 1984	Union Bank of Switzerland	29.9	Phillips & Drew

sized firm was courted and won. The list in Table 27.4 records a further 22 groupings, including some smaller firms and one provincial firm.

Very few of these mergers survive today in any visible or significant form, and several no longer exist after being sold on or closed down. The 21 buying institutions in this list include 9 from the United Kingdom, 6 from continental Europe, 4 from the United States and 1 each from Australia and Canada.

The last group of acquisitions shown in Table 27.5 was made up of a number of small jobbers specialising in the gilt-edged market that were bought for their dealing expertise in the newly formed primary dealers.

In the approach to Big Bang, a total of 32 different financial institutions purchased stakes of between 5% and 100% of the capital of 42 Stock Exchange firms, leading ultimately in almost all cases to 100% control. The majority took place in 1984 – a long time ahead of the actual date of Big Bang in October 1986. The whole process turned into a desperate scramble as the better names were spoken for. Some of the purchases were calmly calculated, some derived from instinctive opportunism, but many were little more than a panic move to avoid being left out. All too often, a rash temptation to buy a barely understood business was met by an equally rash temptation to sell out to a little-known buyer or an ill-defined future.

The total cost of acquisition was high because the first stage of the initial purchase was followed by a second stage of capital investment. Few details of the initial purchase prices have been revealed, but reasonable overall estimates are possible from publicly available information.

For the major firms of stockbrokers, it appears that Hoare Govett sold its first 29.9% tranche too cheaply, for around £8m, but the next tranche – taking Security Pacific's holding to 80–85% was on a basis suggesting overall proceeds of £63m. The published listing particulars of the acquisition of Rowe & Pitman

Table 27.4
Further acquisitions of stockbrokers, 1983–85

Date	Acquirer	%	Acquired
November 1983	Citicorp (US)	29.9	Vickers da Costa
March 1984	Hambros Bank	29.9	Strauss Turnbull
April 1984	Skandia Life (Swedish)	29.9	Quilter Goodison
May 1984	Mercantile House	29.9	Laing & Cruickshank
May 1984	Exco International	29.9	Galloway & Pearson
July 1984	National Westminster Bank	5	Fielding Newson-Smith
July 1984	Australia & New Zealand Bank (Australian)	29.9	Capel-Cure Myers
July 1984	Shearson Lehman (US)	5	L. Messel
August 1984	S. G. Warburg	100	Mullens
September 1984	Dow Scandia	29.9	Savory Milln
October 1984	Morgan Grenfell	5	Pember & Boyle
November 1984	Chase Manhattan (US)	100	Laurie Milbank
November 1984	Chase Manhattan (US)	100	Simon & Coates
November 1984	Britannia Arrow	29.9	Heseltine Moss
December 1984	N. M. Rothschild	5	Scott Goff Layton
December 1984	Banque Bruxelles Lambert (Belgian)	29.9	Williams de Broe
December 1984	North Carolina National Bank (US)	29.9	Panmure Gordon
January 1985	Crédit Suisse (Swiss)	29.9	Buckmaster & Moore
February 1985	Royal Bank of Canada	29.9	Kitcat & Aitken
February 1985	Banque Arabe (French)	29.9	Sheppards & Chase
May 1985	Save & Prosper	5	Montagu Loebl Stanley
June 1985	Crédit Commerciel de France (French)	100	Laurence Prust

Table 27.5
Further acquisitions of jobbers, 1984–85

Date	Acquirer	%	Acquired
April 1984	Guinness Peat	29.9	White & Cheeseman
April 1984	Security Pacific (US)	5	Charles Pulley
June 1984	Kleinwort Benson	29.9	Charlesworth
December 1984	Baring Bros	29.9	Wilson & Watford
April 1985	Union Bank of Switzerland	5	Moulsdale
June 1985	Merrill Lynch (US)	100	Giles & Cresswell

by Mercury Securities – the quoted parent of S. G. Warburg – and Grieveson Grant by Kleinwort Benson, put respective values, after adding back the withdrawal of capital, of £60m and £55m. Other estimates have suggested figures of around £50m for De Zoete & Bevan, Phillips & Drew and Scrimgeour Kemp-Gee, and hinted at the highest figures of all for James Capel. Wood Mackenzie was sold for £21m, but ownership was retained of the valuable performance measurement and valuation computer company that later became WM Company.

The ten major stockbrokers listed in the Table 27.1 probably commanded overall market shares of all commissions from equities, gilts and foreign securities, and fees from corporate transactions in the range of 4–6%, adding, in total, to 45–50%. A rough and ready estimate is that a 1% market share was valued at roughly £10m, and, allowing for the exception of Cazenove, the nine leaders were valued at around £450m.

Figures suggested for the best of the larger medium-sized brokers appear consistent with a formula of around £10m for a 1% market share of Stock Exchange revenues, but rather less for the smaller firms. Vickers da Costa was valued at £20m, Laing & Cruickshank at £25m, and the two specialist gilt-edged brokers, Mullens and Pember & Boyle at £12m and £10m respectively. Altogether 22 firms were purchased in this segment with a market share of 1–3%, and around 45% in total, for an estimated £400m.

There are matching gradations in the value of the five dominant firms of jobbers. Akroyd & Smithers was valued at £145m by S. G. Warburg when first approached, and Wedd Durlacher is believed to have been initially valued at £100m by Barclays when making the initial purchase. Smith Bros was valued at £22m when N. M. Rothschild took its stake, Pinchin Denny at £21m and Bisgood Bishop at rather less. The five jobbing firms might have accounted for some £300m. These estimates are loose, but indicative in the aggregate of a total cost of purchase of around £850m for the stockbrokers and £300m for the jobbers.

This first stage was only the purchase of ownership, and most of the consideration was paid out in the form of goodwill. The only assets were the partners or directors and staff, and the client lists of each firm – the former able to walk out of the door and the latter often fickle. Partners and directors were almost invariably tied in with 'golden handcuffs', committed to remaining for up to five years on pain of loss of their individual share of the purchase consideration.

It was a fortunate time to be a partner in any of these firms at that precise moment when shifting partnership percentages were fortuitously converted into fixed amounts of capital or shareholdings. Any inhibitions about capitalising the goodwill of a partnership built up over generations and held in trust for future generations were quietly put to one side in the face of an uncertain future and prospective buyers waving large cheques, but there was one notable exception.

Among the partners of Cazenove there was, and remains, a strong sense of the 'trusteeship' implicit in being a member of a famous and historic partnership, although another powerful factor is described by David Kynaston in his history of the firm. Joint Senior Partner, John Kemp-Welch, in addressing the entire firm at the time spoke of a passion to remain independent: 'we do not see Cazenove's becoming part of the securities division of some large bank only to lose our identity a few years hence'. Cazenove remains a name familiar to the young City graduates of today, but how many of the other famous names will they ever know or remember?

Big Bang was a less fortunate moment for both retired and prospective partners. Some firms made arrangements to share part of the consideration with recently retired partners, but for the younger, successful members of a firm, the door to a junior partnership was suddenly closed. They wistfully described themselves as the 'marzipan' layer, near the top of the cake, but just below the icing. Many firms shared some of the consideration with the marzipan layer – in recognition of their position and to retain their services in a market where the demand for talent was about to explode.

Having spent over £1,000m on buying the firms, ambitious new owners next found themselves facing the cost of new investment in premises and technology – and in particular, planning for the new dealing systems proposed for Big Bang. The old technology was little more than a dealer standing on the market floor with a coloured pen for the price board and a sharp pencil for the book, with a little understood computer to process the bargains. When the market closed at 3.30 pm, the entire jobbing community exited the Stock Exchange, walking in procession back to their offices, followed by a file of blue buttons struggling to carry cumbersome dealing books.

Just as a spaceship is out of contact on the far side of the moon, so the stock market would come to a complete halt for some 15 minutes while dealers returned to little more than rows of telephone cubicles for trading over the last hour or so of the day. At the same time, dealers and blue buttons for the firms of stockbrokers left their individual dealing 'box' located just off the Stock Exchange floor and returned to their offices, with book and pencil, to continue dealing and to check bargains.

Big Bang shifted the heart of the action away from the market floor to literally hundreds of sophisticated dealing desks in offices – one for every person employed in market making, sales and research. Each desk would be equipped with a new SEAQ screen, probably a screen for internal systems and possibly a Reuters screen, but, most importantly, a telecommunications system of much improved capacity and sophistication. For proper cohesion and effective control of the business, all needed to be located close together on huge dealing floors. There was a scramble for space and much of it was provided by the massive and far-sighted Broadgate development next to Liverpool Street Station. However, when new space is at a premium it is never cheap, and moving whole businesses into new premises and fitting out the new dealing floors with all the necessary cabling required an investment estimated by some to have matched the cost of acquiring the businesses in the first place.

A vital factor in the successful launch of Big Bang was the liberalisation and deregulation of the telecommunications industry in the early 1980s by the new Conservative Government. New competition was allowed in the form of Mercury, many smaller companies offered new products, prices were freed and in 1984 British Telecom was privatised. The effect was a dramatic improvement in the price and quality of service, and the importance of the role played by BT and the telecommunications industry, both during and since Big Bang, has never been fully recognised. Deregulation and privatisation gave the industry a ten-year lead over its Continental rivals in terms of price, service and flexibility, and allowed London to build the worldwide telecommunication networks needed by the securities industry on a scale that would have been impossible in Frankfurt or Paris. In the language of the management consultant, the telecommunications industry in Britain became a 'competitive weapon' in attracting businesses to the City and to the wider British economy.

It was during the planning of this second stage that cultural differences first began to emerge. The newly acquired brokers and jobbers needed to plan and agree with their new owners their technology needs, where to locate in existing or new premises and how to merge parts of their operations to create new business structures in time for Big Bang. Decision after decision was required from participants already sorely stretched by highly active markets.

Even the best-intentioned now found themselves unprepared for the surprise of cultural differences between banks and brokers, brokers and jobbers, companies and partnerships, or country and country. There was a world of difference between the discipline of a corporate structure and the looseness of a partnership; between rigid reporting lines and collegiate partnership consensus; between a corporate executive with defined responsibilities and a general partner; between highly individualised performance-related remuneration and firm-wide sharing; between attitudes ranging from planning ahead for three to five years and 'How much did we make last week?'; between the risk-averse and the risk-takers; and between the American, the British and the European.

Shocks occurred on both sides as plans to merge were put in place. Many of the acquiring companies were shocked by the paucity of management among many of the brokers and jobbers, who in turn were appalled by the degree of interference and seeming bureaucracy imposed on them. Some of the newly formed businesses never really survived closer acquaintance and acrimoniously fell apart. Very few of the forays into the Stock Exchange by 32 buying institutions could be regarded as outstanding successes, and such was the random outcome that no particular category of institution was more successful than any other.

Overall, the merchant banks came out of their various acquisitions poorly. Their challenge was to create an integrated securities business along the lines of Goldman Sachs and Morgan Stanley – investment banks in the United States. Only S. G. Warburg came anywhere near this objective, with its successful integration with Akroyd & Smithers, Rowe & Pitman and Mullens to form Mercury International Group. It reverted to its more appropriate name of S. G. Warburg Group in 1987 and was widely regarded as the most successful of all the Big Bang mergers of the different cultures. An important factor in its success – something absent from the other merchant bank mergers – was that the three Stock Exchange firms together formed a securities group of matching weight and influence to the merchant bank, and were accorded equal representation at the Group's main Board level.

The other merchant banks were unable or unwilling to offer comparable status to their newly acquired partners. Kleinwort Benson immediately ran into problems with Grieveson Grant and only built a successful securities business after many unhappy years. Hill Samuel had an equally unhappy time with Wood Mackenzie before eventually selling it on to County Bank. Samuel Montagu reduced W. Greenwell to a primary dealer in gilts within 15 months. Morgan Grenfell defied any corporate logic by buying a gilt-edged specialist broker and a medium-sized equity jobber, foisting on itself a memorable Big Bang disaster when the whole operation was unceremoniously closed down in December 1988. However, N. M. Rothschild made a successful investment in Smith Bros, avoiding any cultural clashes by never attempting to integrate, and many years later Smith Bros was taken over by Merrill Lynch.

Barings, Flemings and Schroders resisted making acquisitions in the London equity market and expanded into overseas securities. Barings expanded aggressively into Japan, Flemings into the Far East with Jardine Fleming, and Schroders acquired Wertheim, a niche Wall Street stockbroker. In London, Schroders began the slow process of building an embryo securities business and Flemings ventured into the stock market in 1984 when they independently acted as jobbers in electrical, and later, pharmaceutical shares, an experiment abandoned in 1990.

The US banks and brokers were no more successful. Citicorp managed to destroy and close down one of the leading equity brokers – Scrimgeour Kemp-Gee – in January 1990, within five years of its acquisition, and Security Pacific eventually sold Hoare Govett on to ABN Amro in 1992. Chase Manhattan closed down its equity business in January 1989 and nothing much remains of Shearson Lehman's acquisition of L. Messel. Far more successful have been the US investment banks that simply continued to build their existing London operations organically rather than by acquisition. Indeed, the likes of Goldman Sachs, Morgan Stanley and Salomon have become formidable competitors in London, with managements more comfortable with rigid reporting lines back to New York.

Refusal to be drawn into change was, on the whole, well rewarded. Schroders and Lazards continued to flourish as traditional merchant banks. Cazenove has retained its cachet as the leading corporate stockbroker, admirably led through these turbulent years by Anthony Forbes and John Kemp-Welch. With its distinctive refusal to engage in market making, James Capel retained its unrivalled position as the leading research stockbroker, just as Smith Bros retained its distinctive role primarily as a market maker.

The greatest irony of all is that only one European bank made a move of any significance during Big Bang when Union Bank of Switzerland bought Phillips & Drew, but within ten years of Big Bang, the European banks had become the dominant owners of recognisably British investment banks. This is discussed in Chapter 33.

The countdown to Big Bang remained fraught to the last minute for Nicholas Goodison and the Stock Exchange. A crucial vote among the members was held on 5 June 1985 to agree the extension of corporate ownership of firms from 29.9% to 100% from March 1986. A second motion – to implement outside corporate membership, by splitting each individual membership share into five and permitting the sale of four of them – narrowly failed to gain its necessary 75% support, but corporate membership was later achieved in November when widespread changes were made to the rules. The particular point at issue was that members of the smaller firms were aggrieved that their individual rights were being sold out over their heads by the fait accompli of larger firms entering into direct financial transactions with outsiders. Eventually it was agreed that all members would receive compensation of £10,000 on reaching the age of 60.

Having wearily gained support for change from the membership, the Stock Exchange faced a new looming problem towards the end of 1985. Many of the new foreign banks and brokers were active dealers in Eurobonds – a huge, unregulated, fixed interest telephone market involved in raising corporate loans from the pools of dollars located outside the United States. The Eurobond market had originally been invented by S. G. Warburg in the late 1950s, but it was essentially a market of no fixed abode and so did not fall easily into a regulated Stock Exchange.

The immediate problem towards the end of 1985 was a threat by the foreign houses and banks as members of the Association of International Bond Dealers (AIBD) to stay separate from the Stock Exchange by setting up an International Securities Regulatory Organisation (ISRO) to regulate their own affairs, so fragmenting the market in international equities. The solution gradually emerged of a merger between the two bodies, which was agreed within a few weeks of Big Bang in September 1986. ISRO demanded and obtained equal representation on the Council of 'The International Stock Exchange in the United Kingdom and Republic of Ireland', to be known as 'The Stock Exchange'. The intervention of powerful overseas banks in a collective group formed less than 2 years earlier had secured concessions from an institution with a history of more than 200 years, but the central regulated securities market, so fundamental to Stock Exchange thinking, was secure.

Big Bang changed lives. It abolished the title of 'Member of the Stock Exchange'. It ended unlimited liability. It propelled thousands of practitioners into far larger businesses as corporate executives – change on a scale that either excites and invigorates or bewilders and destroys. The pace of business quickened, the opportunities proliferated and the rewards multiplied, but the pressures intensified. Many found there was no train on the timetable early enough to get them to their desks in time for the early morning meeting. They either moved to a flat in London or discovered how quiet the roads were at 6 o'clock in the morning. Tied to telephones and screens, their breakfast and lunch became the sandwich snatched at the desk. The 60-hour week and plenty to think about at the weekend became the norm. A competitive edge was added to personal contact. The short list for retirement started at 50 and today looks at 45. It has all speeded up, but as a place to work the stock market was and is as exhilarating and addictive as ever. It just happens to have lost much of its former charm and easy trust.

The institution of the Stock Exchange has found change less opportune and struggled to define its role. The trading floor quickly became deserted after Big Bang and, for many years, looked like the abandoned set of a well-known film. Thousands of individual members were replaced by powerful, self-interested investment banks and foreign houses. Regulation has become a tortuous subject that is slowly falling into the tentacles of government and the legal profession. The provision of information and settlement systems requires a scale of investment in technology better suited in the long term to the skills and resources of major companies supplying those services to a wider customer base than the Stock Exchange. The retention of the unique market-making system is having to be compromised by experiments in order-driven systems.

Andrew Hugh Smith, Senior Partner of stockbrokers Capel-Cure Myers, succeeded Nicholas Goodison as Chairman of the Stock Exchange in 1988. He in turn was succeeded in 1994 by John Kemp-Welch, after a long reign as joint Senior Partner of Cazenove. The Chairman's task has never been easy and the intractability of many of the problems has been apparent in the eventual resignation of successive Chief Executives, Peter Rawlins and Michael Lawrence. Big Bang may have successfully reformed the stock market, but it has served the institution of the Stock Exchange less kindly.

Chapter 28

A LONG BULL MARKET – PART TWO

June 1983–July 1987

All Share Index	9 June 1983	442.80	
	16 July 1987	1,238.57	Up 179.7%

A feature of Margaret Thatcher's three election victories is that, on each occasion, the All Share Index stood at or a whisker below an all-time high on polling day. Behind the dry statistic of a market reaching a new peak lies a collective euphoria that belies the image of the shareholder as that of a cold creature belonging to a privileged minority.

When the market is at an all-time high, optimism and enthusiasm prevails on a wide front across the economy, and there is an unspoken sense of well-being. When an individual share moves to an all-time high, these feelings are enhanced, because, at that moment every single shareholder in that company is making a profit. This makes for a powerful technical position and the daily list of shares reaching new highs is required reading in the *Financial Times* for many fund managers. In fact, the enjoyment of new highs is shared today by millions of individual shareholders, whether investing directly or indirectly as unit trust holders. Millions more have insurance policies or contribute to pension funds. Company directors and executives have option schemes, and employees have profit-sharing schemes settled in shares.

Chapter 26 has described how the first leg of the long bull market of 1979 to 1987 was achieved despite a background of slow growth, economic upheaval and a struggle to defeat inflation. The second leg reaped the harvest of these efforts with sustained economic growth. It also marked the most confident of the three Thatcher administrations, with major privatisations, tax reforms and the defeat of the miners.

This long bull market was quite different in character from others then experienced since the war. Most of the major bull markets had witnessed shares roughly doubling in two years or so, (1952–55, 1958–60, 1966–69 and 1976–79). The two exceptions were in 1975, when equities sprinted ahead to double in eight weeks, and in this long bull market, when equities made consistent progress in each of eight consecutive years and multiplied by more than five and a half times.

The year end sequence shown in Table 28.1, of the All Share Index, from its low point on 15 November 1979 to its peak on 16 July 1987, shows the consistency of the annual percentage increases.

Table 28.1
The All Share Index during the course of the bull market, 1979–87

Year ends	All Share Index	% increase	Cumulative
1979 (15 November)	219.85		100
1980	292.22	32.9	133
1981	313.12	7.2	142
1982	382.22	22.1	174
1983	470.50	23.1	214
1984	592.94	26.0	270
1985	682.94	15.2	311
1986	835.48	22.3	380
1987 (16 July)	1,238.57	48.2	563

The consistency of the increases over these years, and the gathering pace to a crescendo in 1987, may also be illustrated by the number of days each year when the All Share Index recorded an all-time high, and the extraordinary fact that the market recorded new all-time highs so many times in each of nine successive years (see Table 28.2).

Table 28.2
The numbers of daily all-time highs in the All Share Index
recorded during the bull market, 1979–87

Years	All-time highs
1979	13
1980	19
1981	12
1982	23
1983	36
1984	42
1985	37
1986	27
1987	59

Prior to this sequence, all-time highs in the FT Index or All Share Index had never been recorded in the post-war period for more than three consecutive years.

The market discounted the 1983 election victory. The Falklands factor was a reminder of past strengths, the economy was exhibiting growth, inflation at 3.7% was at its lowest level for 15 years and the Labour party was at its least electable. After the victory, the market gradually moved into higher ground, peaking in August and drifting back in October, before closing the year at an all-time high on New Year's Eve with the All Share Index at 470.50. Companies made leaner and more efficient by the pressures of a monetary squeeze and the 1980–81 recession discovered that productivity gains were feeding higher revenues through to real profits, no longer distorted by inflation. In turn, buoyant institutional cash flows were feeding through to equities.

Chapters 27 and 29 describe how Big Bang preoccupied the stock market at this time, and how privatisation generated much activity from 1984 onwards, but other events also attracted the headlines – in particular, a takeover battle for the Eagle Star insurance company. Earlier, in June 1981, the largest German insurance company – Allianz Versicherung – had purchased an unwelcome 27.8% stake in Eagle Star after a dawn raid and partial offer at 290p. An uneasy truce ensued until 19 October 1983, when Allianz carried out a small dawn raid at 500p to take their stake to 29.9% and made a bid at this price for the remainder of the shares, valuing Eagle Star at £692m. As the overnight price had been 468p, Eagle Star not unreasonably dismissed the bid as 'derisory'.

To general surprise, BAT Industries joined in the battle, announcing an agreed bid of 575p, or £796m, on 2 November. This tobacco giant had already diversified into paper and retailing and now sought a fourth leg in financial services, imitating the conglomerate fashion of the 1980s, personified in the market by BTR and Hanson Trust. Each side was to bid a further three times, as set out in Table 28.3.

Table 28.3
Allianz Versicherung and BAT Industries' bids for Eagle Star, October–December 1983

Dates	Bidders	Bids	Valuations
19 October	Allianz	500p	£692m
2 November	BAT	575p	£796m
28 November	Allianz	650p	£900m
28 November	BAT	660p	£913m
14 December	Allianz	665p	£920m
14 December	BAT	675p	£934m
22 December	Allianz	675p	£934m
30 December	BAT	700p	£968m

BAT shadowed Allianz as if they were yachts in an ocean race. It had counter-bids at the ready, producing one on 28 November within 13 minutes of Allianz's – almost certainly a corporate finance record – and another after 90 minutes on 14 December. The final bid of 700p was made after compromise talks secured the agreement of Allianz to sell its holding. Eagle Star – an individualistic and domestically oriented British insurance company – was more than happy to escape the clutches of a massive German insurer, and move to a haven lacking insurance expertise and with no overlapping activities requiring rationalisation. One year later, in December 1984, it would be joined by another highly individualistic company – Hambro Life, founded by Mark Weinberg in 1971, and leader in the linked life assurance market now mounting an effective challenge against the traditional ways of the life companies. Hambro Life was purchased by BAT in an agreed bid of £664m.

Whereas BTR and Hanson Trust would have issued highly rated paper for their acquisitions, BAT was able to use the prolific cash resources generated by tobacco to make a cash bid for Eagle Star. The sudden release of almost £1,000m for reinvestment in the stock market assisted a rapid rise into new high ground in the first quarter of 1984, when the All Share Index moved from 470 to 530. However, the market was also being driven by excellent prospects for profits and dividends. Increasingly, these were being built into market forecasts, and would eventually produce for 1984 increases of 21% in the underlying dividend on the All Share Index and 36% in the underlying earnings on the FT Actuaries 500 Industrial Share Index.

Another significant influence on market sentiment was the first Budget of the new Chancellor, Nigel Lawson, who had succeeded Sir Geoffrey Howe immediately after the 1983 election. Having been a City editor of considerable repute on the *Sunday Telegraph* before entering Parliament, Lawson was unique among post-war Chancellors in having an unusually deep knowledge of financial markets, and his political ambitions were focused exclusively on Number 11 rather than Number 10. His knowledge later displayed itself in another way. Most prime ministers and chancellors hardly ever refer to the stock market in their memoirs, but Nigel Lawson and Margaret Thatcher make frequent reference to it.

In his New Year message to the *Financial Times* on 2 January 1984, Lawson used his journalistic talents to good effect, concisely summarising that:

> The experience of the past four and a half years has clearly vindicated the policies on which we embarked in 1979 and to which we have adhered ever since; the medium-term financial strategy with its emphasis on lower budget deficits and declining monetary growth, and within that framework a greater reliance on market forces – including, not least, the eschewing of incomes policy. The result has been a sharp and lasting reduction in inflation and now a soundly based economic recovery.

His first Budget, on 13 March 1984, was radical in its thinking, with many positive consequences for the stock market. Overall, its effect was to release £1,700m to personal and corporate taxpayers, while at the same time forecasting growth in the economy of 3%, and achieving a reduction of the PSBR to £7,250m, or 2¼% of GDP. In the detail, it was an exercise in simplification. The investment income surcharge was abolished, along with tax relief on life assurance premiums and the national insurance surcharge of 1%. Stamp duty on the purchase of stocks and shares was halved from 2% to 1%. A reform that was gradually to have a profound effect was to allow the proceeds of share option schemes to be charged to capital gains tax at 30% in place of income tax at a marginal rate of 60%.

However, much the most important reform concerned the simplification of corporation tax. The Chancellor proposed the phased abolition of investment allowances and the immediate abolition of stock relief in exchange for significant reductions in the rate of corporation tax. Over the 3 financial years to 1986/87, investment allowances would fall from 75% to 50% to nil, and the rate of corporation tax, then 52%, would fall from 45% to 40% to 35%. The Budget was a cleansing of allowances and distortions, and it was received enthusiastically by the stock market because of its positive implications for earnings and dividends. The reduction in corporation tax from 52% to 35% would alone over 3 years generate a 35% increase in earnings from unchanged pre-tax profits. The FT Index responded to the Budget with a rise of 2½% from 844.1 to 865.0, and quickly followed through to reach 900. The All Share Index moved from 503.64 on the day before the Budget to reach 528.89 by the end of the week, a rise of 5% in 4 days.

A landmark at around this time was the launching on 13 February 1984 of the Financial Times-Stock Exchange 100 Share Index, FTSE 100, or 'Footsie' as it is commonly called. A simple weighted index by equity market capitalisation of the largest 100 companies, the FTSE 100 is displayed in real time at one minute intervals. On its first day of dealing, it closed at 1,018.3, from a base calculation of 1,000 on 3 January 1984, and simulated calculations as far back as 1978 were provided for continuity. The constituents are reviewed quarterly and, in aggregate, amount to some 70–75% of the total capitalisation of all quoted equities. It was devised to provide a better headline index for trends in the market than the FT 30, but never intended to compete with the statistical and performance data of the All Share Index. Of key importance was its suitability for trading as a stock index, or proxy for the equity market as a whole, in the Traded Options market and in LIFFE, the new futures exchange.

Today the FTSE 100 is widely quoted in market reports, but in its early days sentimental attraction remained strong for the FT 30 and the *Financial Times* continued to use the FT 30 for headline purposes for several years. When the FTSE 100 was launched, the FT 30 stood at 803, and the magical figure of 1,000 was in sight. This was reached perhaps sooner than expected, on 18 January 1985. If the FTSE 100 has a weakness, it is that its quarterly reviews regularly promote two or three winners and discard two or three losers, thereby flattering its long-term performance.

After nudging into new high ground in early May, the market wobbled in the face of the twin threats of an escalation in the long-standing miners' dispute at home, and concerns from abroad that high interest rates in the United States due to a banking crisis would force up rates in Britain or put sterling under pressure. Towards the end of May, there were several days when the FT Index suffered 20-point falls, and, by the end of the month, the All Share Index was 11% below its high. The miners' strike had become so bitter that no room for compromise was left between the National Coal Board and the National Union of Mineworkers, and pressure on the pound culminated in base rates rising from 9¼% to 10% on 7 July, and from 10% to 12% on 12 July, whereupon the All Share Index fell away to 464.90.

As so often happens when the bad news arrives, investors begin again to travel hopefully and so, thereafter, for the rest of the year, the market recovered strongly to new high levels and, eventually, for the second successive year, the All Share Index closed on New Year's Eve at an all-time high of 592.94. Quite apart from extensive negotiations ahead of Big Bang and the spectacular success of the BT privatisation, there was much activity for the year as a whole in new issues, takeover bids and rights issues – each in its own way a signal of opportunities perceived in rising markets.

A feature of the stock market in the second half of the 1980s was a steady stream of new large companies emerging from the private sector, in addition to the many new names from the public sector created by privatisation. For many years, Pilkington and J. Sainsbury had been lone examples of big, established companies coming to the market. It was in May 1984 that Reuters – later to prove one of the most dynamic growth stocks in the FTSE 100 – headed a list of big, new companies coming to the market that would later include Abbey Life, Wellcome, TSB, Abbey National and Eurotunnel.

Reuters was founded in 1851 by Julius Reuter as a news service, transmitting share prices between London and Paris. To ensure its independence in news dissemination it later came under the collective ownership of the principal newspaper groups. By the 1980s, Reuters had developed into a major international electronic information supplier to the banking and securities industries, and had successfully retained a powerful marketing and financial grip on the menu of services it supplied to individual screens on thousands of desks across the world. The newspapers wished to unlock the considerable hidden value of their holdings, but, at the same time, preserve the historical integrity of the company. The capital was ring-fenced not only by a 'golden share' in Britoil style, but also by dividing the equity a quarter into 'A' shares, to be retained by the newspapers, and three-quarters into 'B' shares to be offered to the public for sale by tender, with the 'A ' shares having four times the voting rights of the 'B' shares.

Two classes of equities with different voting rights made the issue controversial and the Investment Protection Committees of both the British Insurance Association and National Association of Pension Funds recommended their members to boycott it. The offer for sale was by tender at a minimum price of 180p, putting a valuation of some £700m on the company. It was launched in London and New York in the midst of falling markets in late May. The striking price was 196p, but within a week of the start of dealings, the price stood at 230p – valuing the company at over £900m – a rise influenced by the purchase of almost a third of the issue by the Abu Dhabi Investment Authority in building a 12½% stake. The familiarity of the distinctive green screen of the Reuters terminal lent special interest to this issue of shares in a company that would become a world leader in the provision of financial information services.

In the same year that Reuters was the first of several new companies to come to the market, there also emerged the first signs of another takeover cycle, with a series of bids across a range of industries. The largest included the £664m bid by BAT Industries for Hambros Life, £411m by Standard Telephone for ICL – the last surviving British computer manufacturer – and £400m by Sun Alliance for Phoenix Assurance. The sharp increase in 1984 is apparent from DTI figures for the annual total values of acquisitions, which also show for the early 1980s how recessions tend to bring takeover activity to a halt along with everything else (see Table 28.4).

Table 28.4
Value of acquisitions of quoted UK companies, 1980–84

Year	Value (£m)
1980	1,475
1981	1,144
1982	2,206
1983	2,343
1984	5,474

Source: DTI

The total of £5,474m for 1984 was much the highest ever recorded in money terms, but, when earlier years are adjusted for inflation, it was only half of takeover volumes in the peak years of the last major cycles in 1968 and 1972.

The biggest bid of the year failed after Thorn EMI's initiative in May 1984 to acquire and merge with British Aerospace was eventually rejected by the latter because the indicated terms of £812m gave it insufficient value. Thorn EMI was the larger and more profitable company, with revenues of £2.9 billion compared with £2.3 billion, but its extensive interests in television, domestic appliances and music seemed remote from the aerospace industry, and Lex in the *Financial Times* on 16 May was unable to decide whether this approach by Thorn EMI was 'one of the most imaginative corporate initiatives for years' or 'one of the most illogical pieces of opportunism'. This approach prompted GEC into exploratory talks with British Aerospace, but these came to nought.

Allowing also for the privatisation of British Telecom, 1984 was another buoyant year for turnover in equities. Official Stock Exchange figures show the trends over five years (see Table 28.5).

Table 28.5
Stock Exchange equity turnover, 1980–84

Year	Turnover (£m)	Bargains (m)	Average bargain (£)	All Share Index
1980	30,801	4.231	7,280	292.22
1981	32,387	3.944	8,212	313.12
1982	37,414	3.883	9,635	382.22
1983	56,131	4.726	11,877	470.50
1984	73,119	4.849	15,079	592.90

The acceleration in turnover was now drawing well ahead of the upward movement in the index, with the total for 1984 almost double that of 1982. The slower growth in the number of bargains and the larger size of the average bargain illustrates how institutional investors were becoming more aggressive in their dealings. However, these figures were to pale beside those for the next three years and prove to be only the beginning of a new trend of much greater institutional activity.

Two practices new to the market occurred towards the end of 1984. The first was the announcement by GEC in December that it had spent £57m to buy in 1% of its shares for cancellation, after obtaining shareholder approval to buy in up to 9% of the equity. Using surplus cash to buy in shares has been common practice in the United States, but it was illegal in Britain until it was allowed by the 1981 Companies Act. GEC was the first major company to take advantage of the change – buying 25 million shares at 228p and leaving the shares 5p higher at 230p as a result.

The justification for buying in shares is that the return on cash from short-term interest rates is much lower than the return on capital invested in a business, and using that cash to reduce the number of shares in issue will automatically increase earnings per share. Nevertheless, the immediate reaction of the stock market to this new practice was one of puzzlement. It was difficult to put a positive interpretation on a procedure implemented only by persuading shareholders to sell.

In reality, this transaction involved handing over £57m almost entirely to opportunist institutions able to respond quickly to a broker paying a small premium, and they probably reinvested the proceeds in other equities. This interpretation puts a casual air on the use of £57m, but the intention of buying back shares is to use surplus cash in the best interest of the shareholders, and the more obvious alternative of paying special dividends is tarnished by the widely differing tax status of various categories of shareholders. This particular transaction also attracted attention because it was carried out by GEC, which, having been the pride of the stock market in the 1960s and early 1970s, was now out of favour and probably better known for the size of its cash mountain than for the range of its business.

Arnold Weinstock created GEC from successful acquisitions in the 1960s and, rightly or wrongly, the market perceived that the company's huge cash mountain would have been better used to make further acquisitions than sitting in the bank earning short-term interest. And it was huge – around £1,600m in 1984 – £57m being a mere scratch on the surface. The issue of the cash mountain had previously been tackled more aggressively by GEC in 1977 when cash holdings were around £400m and shareholders were given £178m of a variable interest note worth 32.5p a share. Masters of control are always at odds with the uncontrollable and Weinstock was rarely at ease with the stock market. In a later interview in the *Financial Times* on 30 December 1996 he said that he believed it 'over-emphasises the short term and undervalues the long term', although, in the same interview, he rather contradicted himself by cautioning the market for having put the shares on a long-sighted PE ratio of 30 in 1969 after the completion of the triple merger, a valuation wholly justified by later events.

The second example of changing practice was the altogether more controversial subject of vendor placings. These occur when a company is taken over by the issue of shares, but the sellers wish to be paid in cash and, to enable this to happen, it is agreed in advance that the newly issued shares will be placed with institutions at a discount to the market price. Vendor placings of modest amounts have always been allowed, but in 1984 the practice was extended to placings of sufficient size to undermine the principle of pre-emptive rights, whereby existing shareholders have the legal right to participate in any significant increase in the equity capital of their company.

Saatchi & Saatchi first discovered in 1984 that the vendor placing was a quick and ready alternative to a rights issue as a means of financing a takeover bid. In a bull market with an insatiable institutional appetite for equities, the merchant banks and their stockbrokers became ever more confident of their ability to effect large vendor placings with ease and speed, and enable takeover bids to be quickly sealed.

The controversy came to a head in November 1984 over the purchase by Dee Corporation, a food retailer, of International Stores, an unquoted food retailing subsidiary of BAT Industries. The price was £180m and BAT wanted cash, but Dee Corporation was only able to offer shares. The deal was agreed on the basis that Morgan Grenfell would purchase for cash the 113.25m shares in Dee Corporation issued to BAT, and place these shares with a range of institutions at 160p. This was at a discount to the market price, which stood at 174p. In recognition of the attraction of the bid it rose during the day to close at 186p.

This placing constituted 45% of the equity capital of the enlarged Dee Corporation and was, to all intents and purposes, a rights issue to raise £180m, but the benefit of a 14p discount to the market price was handed to institutional shareholders at the expense of existing shareholders, thus denying the principle of pre-emptive rights. The placing was masterminded by Morgan Grenfell and stockbrokers Rowe & Pitman. Most existing institutional shareholders had the opportunity to participate, but individual shareholders were left to read about it in the newspapers on the following day.

This placing brought a gathering controversy to a head, and Peter Wilmot-Sitwell, Senior Partner of Rowe & Pitman, brokers to the placing, disarmingly commented that 'this deal will make it red hot'. It provoked a letter on 24 November to the *Financial Times* from David Hopkinson – Chairman of unit trust group M&G and ever a watchdog over the interests of the small share-holder – in which he expressed 'strong reservations' about an 'undesirable practice which almost always operates to the disadvantage of small sharehold-ers', who are deprived of an element of capital appreciation and unable to share with the institutions in the expansion of their company.

The criticism of this placing eventually led to a degree of protection for the individual shareholder in future placings. In June 1986, the ever-acquisitive Dee Corporation was again involved in the controversy following its purchase of the Fine Fare food retailing subsidiary of Associated British Foods for £686m, financed by the issue of 282m shares. AB Foods retained just under half of the shares, but 147.5m became the subject of a record £350m vendor placing. However, on this occasion, after strong institutional pressure, existing share-holders were allowed to claw back from the placing up to 75% of their proportional entitlement as though it had been a rights issue.

In effect, this moved the vendor placing closer to a rights issue, with a right to subscribe but without the right to sell the entitlement. In August 1986, Boots car-ried out a record vendor placing of £377m at an 18% discount to the market price, the third such placing under the aegis of Rowe & Pitman. This placing allowed a 100% clawback for shareholders wishing to subscribe, taking it even closer to a rights issue, and this has now become the standard practice for vendor placings.

Meanwhile, the stock market moved confidently forward into 1985, although excuses for caution were easy to find. Higher interest rates were feared to protect sterling, then passing through one of its weakest phases in the face of a strong recovery in the dollar and a background of falling oil prices. Measured against the basket of trading currencies and the dollar, sterling reached all-time low levels. On 28 January 1985, base rates rose sharply from 12% to 14%, but even this did not prevent the pound from touching a low point of $1.04 in February.

Furthermore, background forecasts for the economy were making miserable reading. Two of the more pessimistic were published in November 1984 – admittedly when the miners' strike was still unresolved – by Oxford Economic Forecasting and the National Institute of Economic and Social Research (NIESR). Their forecasts of the annual percentage growth in GDP, along with the consensus forecasts, were well below the actual outcome (see Table 28.6).

Table 28.6
Forecast and actual growth in GDP, 1984–88

Forecasts	1984 %	1985 %	1986 %	1987 %	1988 %
Oxford Economic	1.8	2.3	1.3	1.4	2.4
NIESR	2.0	3.3	1.4	and average 1984–89: 1.75	
Actual outcome					
OECD	2.3	3.8	4.3	4.8	5.0

It was a feature of the middle years of the Thatcher Government that the growth rate of the economy was consistently underestimated by most professional fore-casting bodies, although the evidence of rising markets suggested that investors took little heed of their predictions. The *Financial Times*, from time to time, pub-lished the average of some 20 published forecasts of the growth of GDP for the current and following years. These are shown in Table 28.7, together with the outcome based on OECD figures.

Perhaps the caution of the economic forecasters contributed to steady year-to-year progress in the market. For the typical portfolio investor, 1985 seems to have been exactly such a year. The All Share Index climbed to 600 for the first time in January and steadily moved up to reach 700 in the last week of November. The Budget on 19 March 1985 was cautious and uneventful after the reforms of the previous year. Inflation was ticking a shade higher at around 6% – a consequence of high interest rates and an effective devaluation of the pound over the previous year of some 30% against the dollar and some 10% in the basket of currencies – but dividends were growing at twice the rate of inflation at some 12%. The bull market remained in place, but it was patchy and

Table 28.7
Forecast and actual growth in GDP, 1985–88

Date of forecasts	1985	1986	1987	1988
March 1985	3.0	2.1		
December 1985	3.6	2.3		
December 1986		2.2	2.7	
January 1987			3.0	
January 1988				2.7
Outcome				
OECD	3.8	4.3	4.8	5.0

electricals/electronics and oils – two of the largest and most glamorous sectors of the market – were struggling.

However, behind the scenes, a volume of corporate activity was building up on a scale never before witnessed in the City. It happened despite the distraction for most of the leading practitioners of planning for the upheaval of Big Bang. As it drew nearer, there was confidence and mounting excitement about the potential it would release for the London securities industry, and it was in 1985 that some of the finest names in the corporate and financial world, and some of the largest egos, were drawn into a spider's web of activity. For some the entanglement would prove fatal.

On 4 March, the Al-Fayed family emerged into the limelight. Having appeared to be a passive purchaser of Lonrho's 29.9% stake in House of Fraser 4 months earlier in November for £138m, the family caught Tiny Rowland on the wrong foot by mounting a £615m cash bid for House of Fraser – the owners of Harrods. Rowland had been trapped by a Monopolies and Mergers decision in 1981 preventing him from bidding for House of Fraser, but, with unfortunate timing, this decision was reversed only three days after the Al-Fayed bid. By now it was too late and, on 11 March, within a week of their bid, the Al-Fayed family won control following a dawn raid and aggressive buying in the market. This included a 6.3% stake held by Lonrho, sold on the calculation that the bid would be referred and disallowed. It was not, and the reverberations of this bid continue to this day.

Two names at the forefront of bid activity were the highly fashionable conglomerates – Hanson Trust and BTR, which had both consistently outperformed the market over many years. Hanson Trust yielded 2.1% and BTR yielded 2½% compared with 4.3% on the All Share Index, and their PE ratios in the low twenties stood at around twice the market average of 12. Typical of their activities was the acquisition of tired leaders in maturing industries, and Hanson Trust – which took its name from its legendary founder James Hanson – had recently acquired London Brick in 1984. BTR – once known as the British Tyre and Rubber Company, and now under the leadership of Owen Green – ironically won control for a paltry £101m of tyre manufacturer Dunlop, now but a fading name with a long manufacturing history, and ripe in the eyes of many for the management efficiencies BTR would bring to bear.

Nevertheless, to achieve consistent long-term growth, these were both trapped in a search for ever-larger acquisitions. In a highly perceptive comment, Lex on 22 January 1985 observed that the 'logical conclusion of this argument is that the likes of ICI must eventually be swallowed up if the momentum is to be sustained'. In June, Hanson Trust prepared the ground for its next onslaught with a £519m rights issue – then the second ever biggest London rights issue after BP's £624m in 1981, and just ahead of the £513m raised earlier in the year by Barclays Bank.

The observation by Lex showed ICI in its historical pride of place as one of Britain's four or five largest quoted stock market companies, along with BP, Shell and GEC and recently joined by British Telecom. ICI became the first company outside the oil industry to reach profits above the £1 billion mark when it announced pre-tax profits for 1984 of £1,034m in March. Three weeks later, it was overtaken by BAT Industries – which, courtesy of the benefits of devaluation and its recent insurance acquisition, announced pre-tax profits of £1,405m – and BT was hinting at profits of £1,480m. It is a different story today as ICI languishes well down the list, after demerging its pharmaceutical subsidiary Zeneca.

Far more significant for the history and practice of takeover bids were two medium-sized hostile bids running together in the summer of 1984. In the stores sector, Burton, in conjunction with Habitat, bid £492m for Debenhams on 22 May, and, in the drinks sector, Guinness bid £327m for Arthur Bell on 14 June. Both bids introduced a new tactical ruthlessness on the part of companies and their advisers that would later intensify and tarnish the reputation of the system. By definition, hostile bids are unwelcome – rejected from the outset by the target company and bitterly fought – and these two were especially acrimonious.

The two bids featured controversial practices. The use of negative and promotional newspaper advertising reached new levels, with full-page advertisements regularly appearing in the financial pages of the quality newspapers. One typical day produced an advert in the *Financial Times* on 31 July showing Burton proclaiming 'Remember the price before we came along' over a close-up of the stores sector before and after, and, on another page, Guinness matching this with 'Why Guinness is Good for You' over a 12-month chart of the Arthur Bell share price. Burton and Habitat also ran a series of egotistical adverts featuring large photographs of their respective leaders, Ralph Halpern and Terence Conran, under the theme 'With Halpern and Conran there will be life after Debenhams'. Guinness applied all its marketing skills to an unprecedented advertising campaign in support of its bid.

Both bids eventually succeeded after Burton increased theirs from £492m to £553m, and Guinness from £327m to £356m, but success was achieved only by the use of a controversial new tactic. Burton reached 50% to claim victory only by including shares it 'had agreed to acquire', and the *Financial Times* on 3 August observed that a 'critical factor in its victory was the pledging of stakes totalling about 7% believed to have been held by Sir Philip Harris and his Harris Queensway Group and Mr Gerald Ronson and his Heron International Group'. These stakes were later reported as 2% and 6% respectively. In the closing stages of the bid for Arthur Bell, Morgan Grenfell, advisers to Guinness, purchased a 5% stake in Arthur Bell and placed it with institutions supporting the bid, to avoid taking the stake owned by Guinness over the limit of 15%.

These two bids brought out into the open the subject of 'warehousing', 'concert parties' and other stratagems for obtaining friendly support to help the success of a bid. Any purchases of shares of the target company made in the course of the bid by the bidder or its advisers must be reported, and if any purchase is made at a price higher than the bid, that price is triggered for the bid as a whole. The problem with so-called friendly parties concerns any inducements or guarantees against loss made to obtain support. The bidding company is not allowed to offer guarantees, but its advisers are free to do so – a thinly drawn line where the cost to the adviser can be reflected in their fee.

There is a further distinction to be made between friendly stakes and holdings aggressively built up by individuals or fund managers convinced that a higher price will be extracted or a counter-bidder will emerge. This is a legitimate activity, formalised as arbitrage, and carries with it the risk of loss. These were the matters that went to the heart of the Guinness trial several years later, but it was in these two bids – Burton for Debenhams and Guinness for Arthur Bell – that they first emerged in the public domain.

Burton and Debenhams pitted S. G. Warburg against Rothschilds, and Guinness and Arthur Bell put Morgan Grenfell against S. G. Warburg. An offensive role for S. G. Warburg was unusual for a merchant bank with a greater reputation for defence, but the role of Morgan Grenfell was much in keeping with its emerging image. A pattern had already been noticed that many of the hostile bids of the last year had been mounted by Morgan Grenfell – STC for ICL, Unilever for Brooke Bond, Dixons for Currys, Dee Corporation for Booker McConnell and BTR for Dunlop.

Morgan Grenfell adopted a higher profile than its more discreet rivals, allowing the personalities of corporate financiers George Magan and Roger Seelig to be identified with its aggressive City presence and smiling benevolently when Chairman and Chief Executive Christopher Reeves was observed to have a name similar to the film star playing Superman in the recently released blockbuster series. The promotion of named, individual corporate financiers is commonplace in New York, but the arrogance it breeds is less well received in

London. Perhaps inadvertently the names of Magan and Seelig were becoming bigger than the name of Morgan Grenfell, and the name of Morgan Grenfell was becoming bigger than the name of the clients it was acting for. Undoubtedly the acquisitive ambitions of a number of chief executives was perfectly complemented by the gung-ho spirit of the Morgan Grenfell corporate financiers.

In the last quarter of 1985, the size and number of hostile bids moved to a sharply higher level with an extraordinary series of billion-pound bids. The first occurred on 21 October 1985, when Elders – an Australian brewing and agricultural company famous for Foster's lager – bid £1,800m for Allied Lyons. The feature of this bid was that Elders was barely a quarter of the size of its target, and it was introducing to London the leveraged takeover familiar in New York. In essence, the bidder raises the finance against the security of the assets of the company it intends to buy, and later repays it by the issue of a huge 'junk bond' that introduces a dangerous level of gearing into the capital of the company. In this case, a consortium – Elders IXL – had been put together, of which 58% was led by Citibank and 8 other international banks, and 42% by a group of which Elders controlled 49%. Common they may be in the United States, but leveraged bids and junk bonds have been slow to find any following in London.

Takeover fever was now driving the market and the bid for Allied Lyons prompted the All Share Index to move into a succession of new highs on 18 of the next 24 days, from 649.16 on 22 October to 702.06 on 25 November. Billion-pound bids followed thick and fast in the last quarter of 1985 (see Table 28.8).

Table 28.8
Billion-pound bids, 1985

Date	Bidder	Target	Amount
21 October	Elders IXL	Allied Lyons	£1,800m
25 November	Habitat/Mothercare	British Home Stores	£1,520m (merger)
2 December	Argyll	Distillers	£1,860m
2 December	Imperial Group	United Biscuits	£1,220m
6 December	Hanson Trust	Imperial Group	£1,900m
9 December	GEC	Plessey	£1,180m

These were mostly topical names. Among the bidders, Hanson Trust had topped up its war chest with its £519m rights issue earlier in the year, and GEC shed a reluctance to spend its cash mountain. Among the targets were Imperial Group and Distillers – two dinosaurs that for too long had been complacently enjoying market dominance in cigarettes and spirits. Imperial Group had for years tried ineffectively to diversify out of the tobacco market, and as recently as September had reminded shareholders of its inadequacies by selling the US motel chain Howard Johnson for $314m, 5 years after purchasing it for $630m. Quite undaunted, Imperial Group mounted its bid for United Biscuits some weeks later, although in its defence the spirit of that bid was partly to buy in the highly regarded management of United Biscuits in a reverse takeover. Distillers had diversified modestly into chemicals, but was perceived as a remote and complacent company cocooned in Edinburgh.

Few tears were shed by investors when these two companies fell victim to predators and both were the subject of bidding battles after the turn of the year (see Table 28.9).

Table 28.9
The bidding battles for Distillers and Imperial Group, 1986

Date	Bidder	Target	Amount
20 January	Guinness	Distillers	£2,190m
6 February	Argyll	Distillers	£2,300m
17 February	Hanson Trust	Imperial Group	£2,320m
17 February	United Biscuits	Imperial Group	£2,560m
20 February	Guinness	Distillers	£2,350m
21 March	Argyll	Distillers	£2,500m

The list in Table 28.9 states the values ascribed to each of the bids on the days they were made and these are misleading to the extent that, in both cases, the apparently lower bidder won the day, but when the consideration is largely made up of shares in the bidding company, the value of a bid will fluctuate from day to day. Hanson Trust won control of Imperial Group and Guinness won Distillers partly because of the high stock market reputations at the time of James Hanson and Ernest Saunders, but there were other reasons.

The attempt to bring Imperial Group and United Biscuits together lost its credibility when the bids were switched round for reasons that appeared to attach more importance to corporate convenience than shareholder value. In the event, the shareholders of Imperial Group decided that the time was up for their company, believing Hanson Trust would create better value for its shareholders by disposing of assets than would United Biscuits for its shareholders. It was a close call, with United Biscuits conceding defeat on 11 April when acceptances, including shares already owned from market purchases, reached 34% compared with 45% claimed by Hanson Trust.

Guinness claimed control of 50.7% of Distillers on 18 April after a battle that left much bitterness in the Argyll camp, where James Gulliver believed he had been a victim of establishment sensitivities in Edinburgh about his Glaswegian origins, and would only later discover he had also been victim of a massive support scheme to push up the price of Guinness shares that would later lead to the criminal prosecution of some of those involved. The DTI Report would later show that 78 million Guinness shares – or a quarter of the capital – were purchased during the course of the bid by a range of supporters encouraged to help by means of a mixture of incentives and guarantees.

The bid had other unusual aspects. The appearance of Guinness as a counter-bidder in January was presented as an agreed merger, but the condition that all underwriting costs incurred by Guinness to finance the bid would be paid for by Distillers was seen as a mark of desperation on the part of Distillers to escape the clutches of Argyll. Soothing promises from Guinness about moving the head office to Edinburgh and seeking a non-executive chairman were cynically forgotten within a few weeks.

When Argyll raised its bid on 21 March to £2,500m, or 687p per share, the Guinness bid of a month earlier had risen to the equivalent of 690p, because of the strong rise in the price of Guinness shares. Although most unusual because the shares of bidding companies normally struggle to hold their level – especially if a competing bidder is putting on pressure – no particular comment was passed at the time because the stock market was performing so strongly. After reaching 700 at the end of the previous November, the All Share Index had drifted down to around 680 at year end. It reached 700 again, and, from 7 February, another long succession of new daily highs on 23 out of the next 30 days drove it up by 17%, to 820, on 21 March.

Only later at the Guinness trial would the secrecy and extent of the support operation to chase up the price of Guinness shares and push the value of the Guinness bid ahead of Argyll's be fully revealed, although, within a few days of victory, Guinness announced it was buying in for cancellation 90 million shares in Distillers, or 14.9% of the capital, held by Morgan Grenfell and other friendly parties. Argyll had been cheated out of its prize, and had good reason to feel embittered. Distillers had jumped out of the frying pan into the fire, reminiscent of the News of the World escaping from Robert Maxwell into the arms of Rupert Murdoch in 1969.

Although the battle for Distillers attracted the most publicity, events were unfolding in the other bids. The Elders/Allied Lyons and GEC/Plessey bids both lapsed after being referred to the Monopolies and Mergers Commission. The Imperial Group/United Biscuits merger was also referred because of overlapping products, but cleared when its reversal to a bid by United Biscuits enabled promises of disposals of overlapping products to be made.

This remarkable period of takeover activity was completed with three other major bids made early in 1986 – Rank Organisation £753m for Granada, Dixons £1,750m for Woolworth and Lloyds Bank £1,170 for Standard Chartered.

Perhaps the appetite was now waning or institutions were tiring of change, but these three bids have in common that they all failed, despite the latter two being raised. There were other constraints. In February, in the midst of the bids for Imperial Group and Distillers, Morgan Grenfell was taken to task by both the Stock Exchange and the Bank of England about its conduct. The Stock Exchange asked for clarification about its relationship with United Biscuits and Guinness following purchases of £360m of shares in Imperial Group and £70m in Distillers.

One week later, the Bank of England expressed concern about the practice of merchant banks committing their capital to buy share stakes to assist a client with a bid or to buy a subsidiary business from a client to enable it to escape a reference to the Monopolies and Mergers Commission. In the example above, Morgan Grenfell had used £430m to buy shares, but its shareholders' funds amounted only to £174m. The Bank of England formalised its concern by issuing a circular to the effect that not more than 25% of the equity capital and reserves of a merchant bank should be committed to the support of any one corporate transaction. Finally, in March, the Takeover Panel deplored the practice of aggressive advertising in the support of bids.

The questions asked quite separately by these three institutions – the Stock Exchange, the Bank of England and the Takeover Panel – reflected a common concern about excesses of behaviour in the marketplace. Many more bids were to take place in 1986 and 1987, but the tempo certainly slowed down after the culmination of the Guinness bid for Distillers. The market had lived through a frenetic seven months as those many billion-pound bids worked their way through the system.

Earlier tables in this chapter showed how the value of takeover bids and the turnover in equities both moved sharply upwards in 1984. These trends accelerated in 1985 and 1986 (see Tables 28.10 and 28.11).

Table 28.10
Value of acquisitions of quoted
UK companies, 1983–86

Year	Acquisitions value (£m)
1983	2,343
1984	5,474
1985	6,398
1986	16,550

Table 28.11
Stock Exchange equity turnover, 1983–86

Year	Turnover (£m)	Bargains (m)	Average bargain (£)	All Share Index year end
1983	56,131	4.726	11,877	470.50
1984	73,119	4.849	15,079	592.90
1985	105,554	5.568	18,957	682.94
1986	181,211	7.638	23,725	835.48

In 1986, the activity was at its peak in the first four months – thereafter the tempo of rising stock market prices slowed down. The All Share Index reached a new high of 832.39 on 3 April, whereupon it paused and only returned in the last two days of December to set new highs. Nevertheless, 1986 was an eventful year, with a second reforming Budget from Nigel Lawson and a long list of interesting new issues.

In his Budget on 18 March 1986, the Chancellor continued the reforms of his first Budget two years earlier. Corporation tax duly reached its promised level of 35%. Income tax was reduced from 30% to 29% and an eventual target of 25% was planned. Profit-related pay was encouraged. Releasing a total of £1,000m in tax cuts, the Chancellor forecast growth in the economy of 3% and an unchanged money figure of £7,000m for the PSBR, equal to 1¾% of GDP.

Two specific measures encouraged the stock market. Stamp duty on share purchases was to be reduced from 1% to ½% from Big Bang, but of greater long-term significance was the introduction of a new personal equity plan (PEP), whereby £2,400 could be invested in a financial year in individual shares in a separate portfolio incurring no liability to tax on capital gains or dividends. While initially intended to apply to the purchase of individual stocks, PEPs were extended to include unit trusts and investment trusts in 1989, and the amount allowable for investment each year has been steadily increased to its current level of £9,000. A notional investment of the annual PEP allowance in the All Share Index would show a total invested of £81,600, with a market value of £138,000 at December 1997.

The purpose of the PEP was to encourage wider share ownership by private investors, already a theme of the Thatcher Government in privatisation and employee share schemes. A successful precedent had been set in France in 1978 with the Loi Monory, under which an amount of capital invested in equities was allowable as a deduction from taxable income. The immediacy of this relief was closer to a bribe than the prospective relief offered by the PEP, and, in the short term, it had a galvanising effect on the French stock market. In contrast, PEPs have had a more cumulative positive effect, and latest estimates are that some

£50,000m is sheltered in PEP schemes in a market that has been successfully promoted by the unit trust movement.

New issues were a feature of 1986, quite apart from privatisation. Two of the largest were Wellcome and the Trustee Savings Bank (TSB). On 14 February, Wellcome became the largest private company to be floated on the Stock Exchange. Named after the American pharmacist who founded it, who later became a British subject, Wellcome was a pharmaceutical company wholly owned by the Wellcome Trust, which was set up by the founder on his death in 1936. The Trust reduced its holding to 75% by means of an offer for sale that was 17 times oversubscribed and attracted £4,500m. The shares opened at 160p compared with an offer price of 120p, valuing the company at £1,350m.

The scale of oversubscription was close to that for Abbey Life – the linked life assurance company originally founded by Mark Weinberg – that had come to the market in the previous summer, in June 1985, when just under half of the shares were offered for sale at 180p. That offer was 18 times oversubscribed, attracting a record £4,680m, and the shares opened at 235p, valuing the company at £650m.

The second big private issue of 1986 was TSB – a savings bank with strong traditions in the industrial towns and cities of the North of England and the Midlands, and, in many ways, the equivalent in the banking world of the traditional industrial life assurance companies that collected small weekly premiums from the working classes. Its ownership was obscure and, after long legal argument, the House of Lords ruled in July 1986 that its surplus assets did not belong to its depositors, although it had some of the characteristics of a mutually owned business. A later ruling laid down that its assets before 1985 belonged to the State, thus technically making it a candidate for privatisation, but by then the issue was well under way.

The issue prompted a huge response from 5m applicants – tempted by a 6% yield at a price of 100p, but only 50p partly paid – and the issue was 8 times oversubscribed, attracting £5,600m. The shares, 50p paid, opened on 10 October at a 100% premium at 100p before closing at 85p, valuing the company at £2,020m. The issue created 3.15m shareholders, well in excess of the 2.4m created by BT. More significantly, it raised nearly £1,500m for the bank, and, as events described later will show, rarely has money been seen to burn such a hole in the pocket as the largesse heaped on TSB.

Wellcome Trust and TSB came to the market as major new, but long-established businesses, both moving straight into the FTSE 100 Index. Two other new issues of 1986 were of a wholly different size and character, bringing to the market the private empires of Andrew Lloyd-Webber and Richard Branson. The Really Useful Group brought the musical talents of Lloyd-Webber to the stock market in January 1986 through an offer for sale by tender that valued the company at £35m. Those with long memories recalled the Beatles coming to the market by means of Northern Songs in 1965. The Virgin Group brought to the market Richard Branson's mix of businesses operating under the Virgin label, except the incipient airline, which this issue was designed to finance, through an offer for sale by tender of 25% of the capital at a minimum price of 120p in November 1986. The offer was modestly oversubscribed 3 times and, at the tender price of 140p, the company was valued at £242m.

Both proved to be salutary experiences for all concerned. Within two years, Branson had taken Virgin back into private ownership and, after four years, Lloyd-Webber followed suit – both disenchanted with the constraints of having external shareholders to consider and rules to follow. Both businesses were dominated by highly successful, driven personalities accustomed to control and impatient with the niceties of having to report to and accommodate questioning shareholders.

The year 1986 closed in buoyant mood. With hindsight, Big Bang on 26 October now seemed more like a carefree transition than the revolution it really was – in itself a tribute to the careful planning by all concerned and the long timescale rightly negotiated by Nicholas Goodison. It had been a year of records in takeover bids, new issues and rights issues, and, at the close of the year, achieved a record firgure for a privatisation, too, with the £5,430m British Gas issue in December. The economy was growing, profits and dividends were rising – little wonder that the All Share Index broke through to new highs on the last two days of the year to close at 835.48, completing a seventh successive year of rising markets.

The optimism that comes with the start of a new year needs little enough excuse to talk stock markets higher, but at this time there were prospects too good to miss. The momentum of the last two days of 1986 gathered speed to carry the All Share Index to new highs on 10 of the first 11 days of January. It moved relentlessly forward, passing through the 1,000 barrier on 17 March, at 1,001.08, before pausing on 24 March at 1,026.58, up by 23% over a period of 60 days when new daily highs were recorded more often than not.

Bull market fever was now gripping all investors, driven by three factors, of which the first was liquidity. The institutions were enjoying the increased liquidity and cheaper dealing costs of Big Bang. The public was actively investing in unit trusts, which reported total funds under management up by 60% during 1986, from £20,000m to £32,000m. Corporate liquidity was strong, but opportunities for applying it to successful takeover bids were fewer, and the decision of BTR, after taking soundings from the institutions, to abandon its hostile £1,160m bid for Pilkington Brothers in January helped to underline value in the market.

Second, the political and financial background could hardly be faulted. Optimism was fuelled by the prospect of an impending general election, and the likely return of the Conservative Government to a third term in office. The hard labour of the first term had given way to rapid growth and modest inflation in the second term – a recipe enjoyed by all investors. Exceptional profits growth was stimulated by remarkable productivity gains and a gradual devaluation of sterling from its 1980–81 peaks. The 'feel good' factor was enhanced by Nigel Lawson's fourth Budget on 17 March 1987, when he lowered the standard rate of income tax from 29% to 27%. He released some £2,600m into the economy, forecast growth of 3% and a PSBR of only £4,000m, or 1% of GDP. Bank base rates fell steadily from 11% in March to 9% in May.

Third, the London market was sharing in a worldwide boom in securities markets. The All Share Index had been no more than matching the Dow Jones Index in New York, which rose by 23% from 1,546.67 to 1,895.95, in 1986, and surged through 2,000 in the first week of January. In Tokyo stratospheric average PE ratios of around 60 were beginning to mesmerise investors as the Nikkei Index moved ahead from 13,000 to 18,800 in 1986, and by another third in the first quarter of 1987. The Morgan Stanley World Index rose by 39.1% in 1986.

In London, the All Share Index fell briefly below 1,000 in April, but returned to pass through another series of new highs in May, June and July, buoyed up by the return on 11 June of the Conservative Government with a majority of 101. On 16 July, it reached 1,238.57 – at that point up by 48% since the beginning of the year. Markets worldwide were surging ahead in a scramble for equities, driven in all markets by some common themes.

Deregulation and the abandonment of controls had produced a 24-hour global market open to all-comers. London was a particular catalyst for change because it opened up liquid markets not only in British equities, but also in French and German stocks where previously illiquid Continental markets suddenly found their business had been taken over by lively market makers in London. Cross-border investment and diversification – for long second nature to British fund managers – became fashionable elsewhere, and a trifling percentage of US funds amounted to a flood tide when it arrived for investment in overseas markets.

The rationale for investing in equities was common ground. Inflation had been defeated in the major economies, interest rates were low or falling, the private sector was triumphant, the public sector was privatising itself away – all pointing to a worldwide consensus to invest in equities. Mutual funds and unit trusts swept up personal savings, and pension funds shifted further into equities. The weight of money that fuels all bull markets stemmed from both institutions and corporations. In the summer of 1987, everybody agreed valuations were far too high, but few dared step off the escalator. Investors have an uncontrollable instinct to stay on board at such times. It was all very well for the April edition of the *Bank Credit Analyst* – possibly the most respected of all forecasters – to say that the 'benchmarks of rationality are rapidly disappearing', but the All

Share Index still had another 25% to go and the Dow Jones another 20%. And after that, why not another 25%? Such is the difficulty of calling the top of a rampant bull market.

In early July, the dividend yield on the All Share Index fell below 3%, while gilts yielded a shade over 9% – a rare yield ratio of 3 times. On 16 July, the Index reached 1,238.57 and the yield fell to 2.85%. The historic PE ratio on the 500 Industrial Index stood at 21.03 or 20.03 excluding oil shares. This was to prove to be the peak of a sustained Thatcher bull market that was domestic for the most part, but distinctly international towards the end. France and Germany had already peaked, but Japan and the Anglo-Saxon markets of the United States, Canada, Australia and Hong Kong continued climbing for another month or two. In Britain, the All Share Index reached an all-time high that would stand for four years until July 1991.

It also marked the end of a longer bull market trend that had begun in those despairing days at the end of 1974, when the All Share Index touched its low point of 61.92 in December. It had now peaked at 1,238.57 – at a quick glance, up about 20 times. In fact, it was more precise than that – it was up by an uncannily *exact* 20.00 times, correct to two decimal places.

Chapter 29

PRIVATISATION

A post-war history of the stock market begins with the great programme of *nationalisation* by the Attlee Government and ends with its natural corollary of *privatisation* on an equally grand scale by the Thatcher Government. The long-term rhythm of this will be familiar to students of market cycles, but, with this example, any claim that the one was waiting naturally to follow the other would have seemed absurd to observers of the scene in the 1950s, 1960s and 1970s.

Attlee and Thatcher are regarded as the two great 'conviction' prime ministers of the post-war era, but they approached nationalisation and privatisation in quite different ways. For Attlee, nationalisation was written in stone, and all members of the Labour party carried in their pockets a membership card with the words of Clause 4 printed on the back. As a prime commitment of the 1945 election manifesto, legislation for the public ownership of coal, rail, electricity and gas was executed with ruthless speed and largely completed in the first two years in office.

For Thatcher, the unwinding of these and other State industries was an altogether longer and more difficult process. Privatisation was not an article of faith in the 1979 election manifesto, but emerged in a series of ever-increasing deliberate steps. It was not until 1984, after five years in office, that the first major privatisation was achieved when British Telecommunications became a publicly quoted company. Attlee's nationalisation was a 'grand plan' of the kind favoured by the French, where the principle is proclaimed and the details are worked out later. Thatcher's privatisation was pragmatically British, where successful applications of the detail eventually allow a tested principle to be defined.

Attlee set the post-war agenda for future Labour and Conservative governments. Apart from denationalising steel in the 1950s, successive Conservative governments acquiesced in the State ownership of the utilities and transport. Harold Macmillan went further and described in his memoirs how this extent of public ownership was wholly compatible with his political philosophy laid down in the 1930s publication *The Middle Way*, and later, in the 1980s, he famously damned privatisation as 'selling the family silver'.

Siren voices against this political consensus were few and far between, but one such voice was from the ablest of minds in the Conservative party, and a great upholder of Tory traditions – Enoch Powell. In September 1968, he called in Parliament for 'wholesale denationalisation' as the solution to the ills of the nationalised industries, but this fell on the deaf ears of his leader, Edward Heath. This was partly because Heath had only recently dismissed Powell from the shadow cabinet for his notorious immigration speech, but far more likely because Heath no more contemplated denationalisation than had Macmillan.

Another strong critic of the nationalised industries was John Redwood, who wrote extensively about their problems and failures and, in 1980, his book on the subject – *Public Enterprise in Crisis: The future of the nationalised industries* (Blackwell, 1980) – was published. This was the first year of the Thatcher Government, but he did not propose denationalisation as a solution and the word 'privatisation' does not appear in the book.

The Conservative party manifesto for the successful general election in May 1979 promised only the denationalisation of three businesses clearly belonging in a competitive private sector – aerospace and shipbuilding, which had only recently been nationalised, and freight. The Queen's Speech in May further referred to the sale of State-owned businesses in the National Enterprise Board, and State shareholdings in quoted companies.

The word 'privatisation' appeared in a feature article in the *Financial Times* on 28 July 1979. It referred to this new word 'circulating in the corridors of power in Whitehall' that 'goes to the heart of government policy for reforming the ownership and bureaucracy of State-owned industries'. According to this article, initial thoughts centred on British Airways, British Aerospace, British National Oil Corporation, Cable & Wireless and National Freight Corporation, but questions were being asked about how to deal with the public utilities. 'Privatisation' was preferred as a more positive word for the transfer of assets to the private sector than 'denationalisation'.

The process began with the sale of some existing self-contained companies or holdings in companies already quoted. The first was the sale in November 1979 of a modest 5% stake in British Petroleum, at 363p (equivalent to 121p today) to raise £290m, a mere shaving of the Government's 51% holding, of which 20% was still disputed by Burmah Oil after its forced sale to the Bank of England in 1975. It was followed in July 1980 with the £54m sale of a 50% holding in Ferranti – a successful rescue investment of £8.7m in equity made in 1975 by the National Enterprise Board.

British Aerospace involved the offer for sale at 150p in February 1981 of 51% of the shares of the Government's holding in a company created by nationalisation in 1976, and one of Britain's largest exporters. This issue was successful and raised £150m. After the modest sale of a 24% stake in British Sugar in July 1981, there followed in October the offer for sale at 168p per share of 49.9% of the State-owned Cable & Wireless to raise £224m for half of a company originally nationalised in 1947 for £35m. This company operated telecommunications systems in the former British Empire and was dominated by its activities in Hong Kong, where 60% of the profits were generated. The offer was oversubscribed more than five times. The offers for sale of both British Aerospace and Cable & Wireless were handled by merchant bankers Kleinwort Benson, which was to play a major role throughout the privatisation process under the leadership of Martin Jacomb.

National Freight Corporation was handled quite differently, partly because of the disparate nature of its business, but also in response to the determined efforts of its Chief Executive, Peter Thompson, to achieve a management buy-out. Critical to the acceptance of his proposal was the widespread ownership of shares by employees, and, when he raised £53.5m in October 1981, it was then the biggest known management buy-out. It proved to be a very successful investment, but the only one of its kind allowed in the privatisation process, until parts of the former British Rail were sold to management syndicates in the mid 1990s.

Progress so far had amounted only to the sale of State holdings in existing companies, and purists will claim that the first *true* privatisation was Amersham International in February 1982 – a company created as a subsidiary of the United Kingdom Atomic Energy Authority for the development, manufacture and sale of radioactive materials. As a new business area it was difficult to value in the stock market, but the shares were offered by Rothschilds on an apparently expensive PE ratio of 19 at 142p, to raise £71m. The company was also made bid proof by a £1 special rights preference share owned by the Secretary of State for Energy, which empowered the Minister to prevent any change to a rule limiting ownership to a maximum of 15% of the voting capital.

In fact, the market was tempted by the glamorous look of the business, and the issue was oversubscribed 24 times. On the first day of dealing, the shares closed at 188p, a 32% premium of 46p. The Government ran into fierce political criticism for its failure to sell the shares on behalf of the taxpayer at a proper price, and was from the outset to learn about the difficulties of pricing new issues.

The success of a new issue often depends on the instincts of the 'stags' – a pejorative word for that mass of unconnected individuals who, with remarkable unanimity, will dictate whether a new issue will be comfortably oversubscribed and open at a decent premium or be largely ignored and flop, with rarely a middle way. Alternative methods to the offer for sale have been tried, but they have found little favour. In particular, an offer for sale by tender at a minimum price sounds sensible in theory, but it tends to deaden the issue and be difficult for the private individual to grasp. Attempts were made to persuade Rothschilds to use the tender option in the case of Amersham International. Another alternative used in New York is the book-building process, whereby prospective institutional demand is gradually measured, but this method more or less rules out the private individual, whose participation was a fundamental objective of the whole privatisation process.

Pricing problems haunted the Government in the two remaining privatisations of the first Thatcher administration – Britoil and Associated British Ports. After the experience of the oversubscribed Amersham International issue, the tender method was adopted by S. G. Warburg for Britoil, which was offered for sale by tender at a minimum price of 215p on 11 November 1982, to raise a minimum of £549m for 51% of the shares of the company. This method was risky for such a large issue, but it was hopelessly compromised by the main risk of any new issue – namely, its exposure to market movements during the extended period of many days between the publication of the prospectus and the first day of dealing. For Britoil, the market stood at an all-time high on the day of the prospectus, but fell heavily just before the issue closed, so all bets were off. The issue was only 27% subscribed, leaving the bulk of the shares with the underwriters, and, on the first day of dealing, the partly paid 100p shares closed at 81p.

It is all too easy to get on the wrong foot in the stock market, and this was the problem for the Government with the next issue – Associated British Ports – in February 1983. Mindful of the Britoil disaster, Schroder Wagg and Kleinwort Benson reverted to a traditional offer for sale at a low price to ensure success. The company was formerly known as the British Transport Docks Board, and its image under State control was that of a dull company with limited prospects – indeed, so dull that 50% of the shares were offered at a third of asset value at a price of 112p, to yield 9%. Perversely, on this occasion, the market rose sharply during the offer period, and the issue was oversubscribed 34 times, attracting £740m for a £22m issue. The shares closed on the first day of dealing at 138p, a premium of 23%.

Associated British Ports proved to be a spectacularly successful investment. It was the first of several examples emerging from the privatisation programme of how both advisers and investors failed to recognise the profit potential waiting to be unlocked in businesses that had laboured under the dead hand of State management and to value highly enough those industries or businesses new to the stock market where there are no existing benchmarks to provide comparative valuations. This double undervaluation supplied wonderful opportunities for those fund managers alert to their potential, but also provided hindsight material for political opponents to condemn the Government for appearing to give public assets away at far too cheap a price. Those same opponents overlooked the negative effect on values caused by constant Labour threats to renationalise privatised industries and confiscate any capital gains.

The first Thatcher Government raised some £1,400m from the sale of shareholdings and privatisations. It was a modest beginning and, curiously, was far less than the £3,500m raised from the sale of council houses. The first phase was as shown in Table 29.1.

Table 29.1
The first phase of privatisation, 1979–83

Date	%	Company	Price (p)	Value (£m)
November 1979	5	British Petroleum	363	290
July 1980	50	Ferranti	–	54
February 1981	51	British Aerospace	150	150
July 1981	24	British Sugar	–	44
October 1981	49.9	Cable & Wireless	168	224
February 1982	100	Amersham International	142	71
November 1982	51	Britoil	215	549
February 1983	49	Associated British Ports	112	22
Total				1,404

In the event, these sales were little more than a choice of first courses while awaiting the preparation of the main course – British Telecommunications (BT), which had for so long been an example of State management at its worst. Until separated in 1980, it had been part of the Post Office and, despite being in the forefront of technological change it had always been administered by the civil service as part of a government department. It had never been managed as a business and had failed to disabuse the public of an image of broken down telephone boxes and long waiting times for installations.

BT was separated from the Post Office for several reasons. Technological change was fast advancing and mounting investment needs could no longer be financed by higher customer charges or from the pot of government expenditure. Second, BT needed the freedom to prepare for new competitive pressures that the Government was intent on imposing by liberalising the State monopoly. New competition was allowed in the provision of telephone services by licensing Mercury in 1982, and outside suppliers were encouraged to provide new products to improve services. Lastly, the Government wished to transfer BT into private ownership and, in March 1982, plans were announced to sell 50% of BT in the current Parliament.

More details were announced on 19 July 1982 by Patrick Jenkin, Secretary of State for Industry, but the complexity of creating BT as a public company and preparing for an issue meant that actual privatisation would not happen until after the next election. The link between competition, financing and privatisation was emphasised by Jenkin:

> Liberalisation of telecommunications has started and we intend to see it through. The government believes that the only way forward is to free BT from government control. That means transferring BT's business to a Companies Act company and selling a

majority of the shares in it to the public. The company will then be free both to borrow outside the PSBR and to act independently of government controls.

The decision to privatise BT was a critical turning point. Until that moment, the Government had privatised on a small scale and taken the easy decisions to sell stakes in companies, but the implications of a proposal to privatise a utility on this mammoth scale stopped the City in its tracks. It was a powerful signal of intent and privatisation was suddenly taken more seriously across a broad range of City institutions. Here was a proposal to launch a company with a market capitalisation of around £8,000m – half as big again as the market leader, GEC. The open sale of 51% would require the underwriting and the subscription of fresh equity capital of £4,000m, dwarfing any previous issue. Even the largest gilt-edged issues were only a quarter of this size. Indeed, this would be the biggest equity issue ever undertaken in *any* stock market.

Two other major State-owned companies – British Airways and British Steel – were also being prepared for privatisation, but on a longer timescale. Both competed openly in international markets and required radical restructuring before they would be in proper shape for privatisation as major public companies. Key management appointments were made for both.

The most remarkable decision was to appoint Ian MacGregor as the Chairman of British Steel in May 1980 for three years. He was aged 67 and Lazard Freres New York required the payment of £1.8m to secure his release. MacGregor was born in Scotland, but his business reputation was made in the United States as Chief Executive of AMAX – the metals and natural resources company. These unusual circumstances made it a controversial appointment, and it was made in the immediate aftermath of a destructive three month strike by 100,000 steelworkers in the first quarter of the year. It ensured that the restructuring of British Steel continued apace, with dramatic productivity improvements, and severe job losses in an overmanned State industry that would later become the most efficient steel manufacturer in Europe.

Equally significant was the appointment in 1981 of John King as Chairman of British Airways. Now Lord King of Wartnaby, he was the feisty Chairman of Babcock who suffered neither fools nor journalists, and he set about the restructuring of British Airways with the same vigour that MacGregor was applying to British Steel. He too obtained major productivity gains from another overmanned loss-making State industry, and turned British Airways into the most successful airline in the world.

For both companies, it was a long haul turning frequent losses into records suitably profitable for public quotation. From the date of the appointments of King and MacGregor, it took British Airways six years and British Steel eight years before they were ready to stand alone in the private sector.

The privatisation programme moved into a higher gear in the second Thatcher administration. In ruthlessly attacking inflation in its first years in office, the Government had focused on improving the supply side of the economy, with harsh but ultimately beneficial results on industry. It was now time to tackle supply-side deficiencies in the public sector, and the manifesto for the 1983 election committed the Government to an extensive programme to follow the privatisation of BT with that of British Airways, British Steel, Rolls-Royce, British Shipbuilders, British Leyland, British Airports and the oil interests of British Gas. The hesitant steps of the 1979 manifesto, had become an ambitious crusade, fired by Margaret Thatcher's utter conviction, expressed in her memoirs (*The Downing Street Years*, Harper Collins, 1993) thus: 'The state should not be in business' because 'state-owned businesses can never function as proper businesses'.

Margaret Thatcher led from the front on privatisation. For the Labour party and the trade unions, she was plunging a knife into the heart of deeply held beliefs. Many in her own party would have left well alone, and many in the City were unable to comprehend the scale of her ambition or recognise the confidence she was placing in the capitalist system, but her analysis was impeccable.

In State-owned businesses, the discipline of the threat of bankruptcy is absent. The threat of takeover is also removed, and there are none of the sanctions of reporting to shareholders or being judged on performance by fund managers and investment analysts. Capital requests for investment are judged more by the political whims of government expenditure targets than by an objective assessment of the merits of the project. In Britain, the nationalised industries had become sheltered havens for the producers and the unions at the expense of customers. It was not until some years after the completion of privatisation, that the extent of over-manning and over-charging became apparent as, at one and the same time, prices fell in real terms and profits rose.

The Conservatives were returned in June 1993, with a resounding majority, and their immediate privatisation measures were sales of further tranches of British Petroleum, Cable & Wireless and Associated British Ports.

The first was an offer for sale by tender in September 1983 of 130m shares in BP at a minimum price of 405p (equivalent to 135p today), to raise at least £526m. It would reduce the government's holding from 38.9% to 31.7%, and the price was set at a 5% discount to the closing price of 426p. This was a large issue to underwrite and it was led by S. G. Warburg with five other leading merchant banks together with five stockbrokers – Mullens, Scrimgeour Kemp-Gee, Hoare Govett, Cazenove, and Rowe & Pitman. The issue was oversubscribed nearly 3 times and the tender price was struck at 435p, to raise £542m.

This was followed in December with the offer for sale of 100m shares in Cable & Wireless at a minimum tender price of 275p, to raise £262m, reducing the Government's stake from 45% to 23%. Although the market was firm and close to its all-time high, the shares surprisingly fell in 2 days from 300p to 270p, leaving the issue stranded and only 70% subscribed.

In April 1984, the remaining 48½% of Associated British Ports was offered for sale by tender at a minimum price of 250p, to raise £48m. A little more than a year earlier, the first tranche had been offered at 112p, and, although the All Share Index was some 30% higher, the shares had more than doubled in the meantime. Whereas the original issue had been 34 times oversubscribed, the second tranche was only just subscribed, but this unfashionable owner of ports and docks would prove to be an unsung hero at the top of the performance tables of all the privatisations, with loyal original applicants multiplying the value of their holdings by more than 10 times.

While these smaller morsels were fed to the market at suitable intervals, the major effort was concentrated on preparing for the privatisation of BT. Norman Tebbit had succeeded Patrick Jenkin as Secretary of State for Trade and Industry to lead the issue with Kleinwort Benson, and Hoare Govett was appointed as lead stockbroker. Kleinwort Benson was, at this stage, much the most dominant merchant bank in the privatisation league tables, with British Aerospace, Cable & Wireless and Associated British Ports to its credit as well as BT. The privatisation of BT was a project of enormous proportions. History often conspires to make figures in the past look small, but, by the standards of 1984, a prospective issue of around £4,000m was literally mindboggling.

However, BT was still some months away and two smaller privatisations – Enterprise Oil and Jaguar – were slipped into the queue. Enterprise Oil was a new company cobbled together from the North Sea oil-producing interests of British Gas, and it became involved in an extraordinary corporate episode. It was offered for sale by tender in June 1984 at a minimum price of 185p, to raise £392m, again led by Kleinwort Benson, and including a 'golden share', operative until 1988. The issue was poorly timed against a background of weakening oil prices and, although the price was pitched some 25% below asset value to allow for this, it was only 66% subscribed. However, the surprise to come was the news that subscriptions were dominated by the international mining company RTZ, which had applied for 49% of Enterprise Oil at well above the minimum tender price of 210p. Given the undersubscription, RTZ was entitled to an allocation in full.

There was embarrassment all round. If fully allotted, the 49% stake would, in theory, under the Takeover Code, require RTZ to bid for the remainder, but the company's independence was protected by the golden share. The Government intervened to frustrate RTZ when Peter Walker, Secretary of State for Energy, arbitrarily restricted the application to a 10% stake, thus raising the amount left with the underwriters from 34% to 73% of the issue. An 'inspired stroke of commercial opportunism' on the part of RTZ, as it was described by Lex, had been thwarted amid City anger.

The Government next offered for sale in August 1984 178m shares in Jaguar at 165p to raise £297m. The issue was oversubscribed 8.3 times and the shares closed at a modest premium at 179p on the first day of dealing. Patient share-holders were rewarded 5 years later in November 1989 when Ford made an agreed £1,600m bid at 850p per share.

While waiting for the star event, the stock market had raised more than £1,500m from 5 issues, but it was now the turn of BT. The first step was the release of a 'pathfinder' prospectus on 26 October 1984. This practice is now commonly followed in the case of large issues, where no price is indicated, but enough background information is provided to enable institutions to indicate interest and for the issuing houses to take soundings. The prospectus included a description of the business, preliminary details of the size of the issue of 3,012m shares, or 50.2% of the capital, a commitment to sell no further shares before March 1988 and a pre-tax profits forecast of £1,350m for the year to March 1985. Martin Jacomb of Kleinwort Benson, who was masterminding the issue, suggested that the shares would be issued on a yield basis of around 7%.

Three weeks later, on 16 November 1984, these details were confirmed with a formal offer for sale of 3,012m shares at 130p, to yield 7.14%, on a PE ratio of 9.3, to raise £3,916m. The institutions were allocated 47% of the issue, the general public 39%, and overseas investors in the United States, Canada and Japan 14%.

It was decided at an early stage that extensive public participation in the issue was essential to its success because of its daunting size. There was the added political attraction of being seen to sell a publicly owned asset to the public, and a genuine desire to encourage a share-owning culture across a wider public domain. The result was an onslaught of television advertising and the offer of a loyalty bonus to customers who held the shares for 3 years of a 7% rebate on the telephone bill or 1 free share in 10. Trade union opposition was deflected by the offer of free shares to BT employees, and a decisive factor in attracting public interest was to issue the shares in partly paid form. The price of 130p was made up of 50p payable on application, 40p in June 1985 and 40p in April 1986, so producing a very high short-term return by way of dividend yield in the first year, and also making talk of any normal premium on the full issue price appear as a far larger percentage return in the partly paid form. Whereas a long-term institution would look at an opening partly paid price of, say, 70p as a 15% pre-mium over the full issue price of 130p, to the public, it would appear to be a 40% premium above the 50p subscription.

It was a great success. The warning by John Smith that a Labour government would renationalise at 130p was ignored and the issue in the UK was 5 times oversubscribed with a total for applications for 12,750m shares from some 2.3m prospective shareholders, none of whom would be allocated more than 800 shares, however large their application. However, the institutions were guaranteed 47% of the issue from the earlier commitment during the under-writing. Dealings began on 3 December amid scenes on the floor of the stock market reminiscent of the crowded terraces of a football ground. The shares opened in the 50p form at 95p, touched 97p and closed at 93p, offering the best part of a 100% premium – a beguiling return for hundreds of thousands of individuals buying shares for the first time in their lives. It was a 'double your money' event that ensured public enthusiasm for future privatisations.

It was estimated that a million shares changed hands on the first day as institutions strove to build up their holdings in this new market leader with a market capitalisation now of over £10,000m. The issue presented a serious problem for performance conscious institutions and for the compilers of market indices. Here was a huge new company included in full to comprise 5.6% of the All Share Index by the close of dealings on the first day, although half of the shares were owned by the Government and not available to institutions competing to match their holding to the size of the company. To rub salt into the performance wounds of the institutions, the whole capitalisation of BT was incorporated into the All Share Index at the offer price of 130p, and largely for this factor it rose by 2% on the day from 560.26 to 571.94.

For investors, BT was a celebration. For issuers and advisers, it was a source of fees beyond their wildest dreams of more than £100m. For the Government, it was a mixed blessing. The precedent of a major privatisation had been successfully created, but only £3,900m had been raised for a holding now valued at £5,200m, and political opponents seized every opportunity to attack the Government for giving assets away to its friends in the City. Vulnerability to short-term trends in the market has always made the pricing of new issues an inexact science, but this becomes doubly so if there are no comparable companies to act as benchmarks of value. When the pathfinder prospectus was published in October, the All Share Index stood at 534.21, but, within a few days, the market was climbing to new all-time highs to reach 560.26 on the day before dealings began, and surging on to new highs month after month into 1985. Furthermore, critics always forget that the issue would never have been fully subscribed at a price approaching the closing price on the first day of dealing.

The Government neatly phased the receipts from BT over three financial years and continued the programme of other sales in 1985. In May, the remaining 49% holding of British Aerospace was offered for sale at 375p to raise £363m. The shares had comfortably outperformed the market since the sale of the first tranche in February 1981 at 150p. The issue was oversubscribed 4½ times and the shares quickly rose to 435p.

In August 1985 came the offer for sale of the remaining 49% of Britoil at 185p to raise £434m. This was a rare example where the price of the second tranche was lower than the first, previously offered three years earlier at 215p, but largely left with the underwriters. This time it was more successful, being 4 times oversubscribed and opening at a 24p premium. This sequence of disposals continued, with the offer for sale of the remaining 22.7% holding in Cable & Wireless at 587p to raise £602m in December 1985. In common with the British Aerospace sale, Cable & Wireless combined the sale with the issue of further shares to raise capital, and the package was 2 times oversubscribed. The shares had performed well since the first tranche was sold in October 1981 at 168p.

The success of the BT privatisation lifted the Government's aspirations to altogether new heights, and the Prime Minister now found strong supporters in her Cabinet. British Gas became clearly marked as the next candidate and, in July 1985, John Moore, Financial Secretary, summarised how the current programme up to the next election would be followed by electricity, water and the railways. The Chancellor, Nigel Lawson, was as strong an advocate as any and, on 30 October, he stated that 'Telecom has paved the way for gas. Gas will pave the way for water and so on. Each time the frontiers are pushed back, further possibilities emerge.' No comment better describes the essentially pragmatic flavour of privatisation in the 1980s. This was no grand plan on Continental lines – simply the outcome of instinctively radical thinking.

Nor was the Prime Minister to be put off by a censorious speech on 8 November 1985 by one of her predecessors, Harold Macmillan, now the Earl of Stockton. This skeletal figure of great age showed that he had learned nothing from the long years of decline of the nationalised industries, and the concept of privatisation remained as remote as ever from his understanding. However, in his attack on it, he reminded listeners of his political genius. Speaking with that impeccable timing of his, he drew a comparison between the Government's actions and those of a country estate in financial difficulties: 'first the Georgian silver goes, then all that nice furniture that used to be in the saloon, then the Canaletto', and so the erroneous image of the Conservatives selling the family silver joined the political vocabulary.

The bill to privatise British Gas was published in November 1985, and a White Paper setting out plans to privatise the water industry was published in February 1986. In the event, it was decided to delay British Gas until after Big Bang in the Stock Exchange in October, and the water industry until after the next election. The campaign to privatise British Gas began in earnest in October 1986 with a letter to all 16m customers offering a £10 rebate or 1 free share for every 10 shares held for three years and the famous 'Tell Sid' television advertising campaign was mounted to attract the widest possible range of applicants. Two years earlier, the £3,900m BT issue had seemed a mountain to climb, but, after its success, £5,400m for British Gas seemed easily possible.

Following the release of the usual pathfinder prospectus, it was announced on 21 November that the offer for sale of 4,025m shares would be at a price of 135p, yielding an attractive 6.8%. It would raise £5,430m and had been successfully underwritten under the lead of N. M. Rothschild with brokers Cazenove, Hoare Govett, James Capel and Wood Mackenzie. The BT success allowed for a tougher line to be taken on fees, and underwriting was completed at ¾%, half the normal rate. The shares were to be only 50p paid on application, with 2 further calls in June 1987 and April 1988, adding attraction to the issue and spreading the proceeds to the Government over 3 financial years, as in the BT issue. The shares were to be spread 40% to the public, 40% to institutions and 20% overseas.

Despite every effort being made to promote the issue, the public response was muted and so it was only two times oversubscribed, compared with five times for BT. Perhaps gas meters were simply less glamorous than telephones, but there were other differences. The whole of the capital of British Gas was offered, compared with 50% of BT's, and the stock market background was less favourable. BT enjoyed a 7% rise in the All Share Index between the pathfinder prospectus and the first day of dealings, whereas the market moved barely at all over the same period for British Gas. Dealings began on 8 December, when the partly paid 50p shares opened at 67p and closed at 62½p. The issue may have been disappointing by comparison with BT, but the privatisation of the second of the four major utilities was successfully achieved at a fair price for both the Government and the public.

British Gas was quickly followed by the issue on 8 January 1987 of a pathfinder prospectus for the offer for sale of the whole of the capital of British Airways, but this issue was aimed primarily at the institutions rather than the public. Whereas there was some familiarity with British Gas as a monopoly supplier to a captive domestic market, British Airways was a capital-intensive company with an erratic profits record operating in a fiercely competitive market and thought to be an investment best judged by the institutions. The issue was led by Hill Samuel, with brokers Cazenove, Wood Mackenzie, Rowe & Pitman and Phillips & Drew.

The issue was an offer for sale of 720m shares at 125p, to raise £900m, being 65p payable on application and 60p in August. The yield of 6.8% and low PE ratio of 6.3 seemed attractive, and so it proved as the issue was oversubscribed 11 times, attracting £9,750m compared to the recent £8,400m for the far larger British Gas. The public had only been earmarked for 20% of the issue, and this portion was oversubscribed 34 times. Dealings began on 11 February and the shares closed at 109p, at a 68% premium over the issue price of 65p, valuing the company at £1,215m. British Airways enjoyed the support of a strong bull market, which hit endless new highs during the 5 weeks between the pathfinder prospectus and the first day of dealings, when the All Share Index rose by 8% to match the equally successful BT issue.

Aeroplanes were quickly followed by aeroengines when the now customary pathfinder prospectus for Rolls-Royce was published by Samuel Montagu on 8 April 1987. Three weeks later, the price for the offer for sale of 801m shares was set at 170p, to raise £1,362m. The shares would be 60% pre-placed to the institutions, leaving 40% for the public, and the particular sensitivities surrounding the company led to a 15% upper limit being placed on foreign ownership.

The yield of 4.1% and PE ratio of 10.2 did not appear particularly tempting, but, aided by recent memories of British Airways and background market strength, the public tranche of shares was oversubscribed 9.4 times, attracting £5,270m. When dealings began on 20 May, the 85p partly paid shares closed at 147p, a premium of 73%, helped by a rise of 11% in the All Share Index in the 6 weeks since the pathfinder prospectus. At the end of the first day of its return to the stock market, Rolls-Royce was valued at £1,850m and ready to step straight into the FTSE 100 Index, 16 years after its ignominious rescue by the Heath Government.

In the midst of the Rolls-Royce issue, the general election was called for 11 June 1987. The first Thatcher Government had launched sales and privatisations valued at some £1,400m. The second Thatcher government multiplied this tenfold to more than £14,500m (see Table 29.2).

Table 29.2
The second phase of privatisation, 1983–87

Date	%	Company	Price (p)	Value (£m)
September 1983	7	British Petroleum	435	542
December 1983	22	Cable & Wireless	275	262
April 1984	48.5	Associated British Ports	250	48
June 1984	100	Enterprise Oil	185	392
August 1984	100	Jaguar	165	297
December 1984	50.2	BT	130	3,916
May 1985	49	British Aerospace	375	363
August 1985	49	Britoil	185	434
December 1985	22.7	Cable & Wireless	587	602
December 1986	100	British Gas	135	5,434
February 1987	100	British Airways	125	900
May 1987	100	Rolls-Royce	170	1,362
Total				14,552

Privatisation figured strongly in the Conservative party manifesto for the 1987 election, which planned that in the next parliament the two remaining major utilities – water and electricity – would be privatised, together with the less well-known British Airports Authority. Immediately after the election victory, the third Thatcher Government moved quickly ahead with the latter – the owners of Heathrow, Gatwick, Stansted and four Scottish airports. Privatisation opportunities for the merchant banks were by now being spread more widely than the initial emphasis on Kleinwort Benson and N. M. Rothschild, and for this issue it was the turn of County NatWest. An unusual formula was announced on 5 July 1987 that proposed an offer for sale of 500m shares partly at a fixed price and partly by a tender without any striking price, to raise a minimum of £1,225m at the offer price of 245p. The shares would be allocated 48% by a pre-placing to institutions and 52% to the public, with a clawback of up to 25% for allocation by tender at a higher price.

British Airports Authority was difficult to value as this was another example of a company with no existing benchmark for comparison. The yield of 3.7% and PE ratio of 15.3 appeared demanding for an unknown quantity, but it was received with acclamation – with the fixed price portion oversubscribed 8 times, and the tender offer 6 times. The cut-off price of the tender was 282p, producing extra proceeds of £56m, and, on the first day of dealings on 28 July, the 100p paid shares closed at 146p – a premium of 46% over the fixed price, but very little higher than the tender price.

The influence of background trends in the stock market over the success of an issue was again evident in the case of British Airports Authority, when the All Share Index rose by 5% in the 3 weeks to the closing date, thus encouraging applications. This previously benign influence over so many privatisations was to become horribly malign in the next Government disposal of the remaining 31.7% stake in BP – a £7,250m issue, of which £1,500m would be extra capital raised by BP. The story of this ill-fated issue forms an integral part of the October 1987 crash and so is described in Chapter 30. Save to say here that the Government received its £5,750m, but the underwriting institutions were sitting on losses of £700m at the end of the first day of dealing.

Over the 12 months following the crash, the Government was preparing behind the scenes for the major privatisations of the water and electricity industries, both of which raised complicated questions about structure and competition. A White Paper in February 1988 outlined the plan to privatise the distribution companies into 12 regional companies, and divide the generating industry into 2 companies in England and Wales. At this stage, ownership of the transmission company – National Grid – would be shared among the distribution companies. In July 1988, it was announced by Nicholas Ridley, the Environment Secretary, that the water authorities would be privatised into 10 companies in late 1989 to raise £5–7bn.

Meanwhile, two modest privatisations took place. In October 1987, after the crash, it was announced that the National Bus Company had been broken up into 72 subsidiaries for individual sale, of which 50 had already been agreed. An overall total of £300m was expected to be raised.

The second was unplanned. In March 1988, it was revealed that British Aerospace had entered into talks about the purchase of the Government's 99.8% stake in the Rover Group. The outcome was controversial when, on 29 March, the sale was agreed at £150m, or 2.7p per share, but only after the injection of £800m of State aid. British Aerospace shares responded with a rise of 60p to 412p, and it was none too cynical a comment that the Government had paid £650m to have a chronic problem taken off its hands. Political pressure, both at home and in the European Union, eventually led to an agreed reduction in the cash injection to £547m on 14 July, whereupon the shares rose another 40p to 490p.

Next it was the turn of British Steel, and details of its privatisation were announced by Lord Young, Secretary of State for Trade and Industry, on 23 November 1988. The terms reflected the cyclical nature of the steel industry when 2bn shares were offered by Samuel Montagu at 125p to raise £2,500m on a yield basis of 8% and a prospective PE ratio of 4.8. Lord Young explained in a uniquely British way that this particular offer was 'going slightly upmarket' and was 'aimed at Sidney rather than Sid'. The offer was well subscribed, with the 23% reserved for the public oversubscribed 3.3 times and triggering a clawback to a public allocation of 42%. Unfortunately, the issue caught a dull phase in the market, with the All Share Index falling from 957.58 on the day of the prospectus to 914.84 on the first day of dealing on 5 December, when the 60p partly paid shares closed at 63p.

The main event of 1989 was the privatisation of the water industry. The pathfinder prospectus was released on 3 November and the final prospectus published on 22 November, offering for sale 100% of the capital of 10 water companies, all at the same price of 240p, payable in 3 instalments and initially 100p paid. The average dividend yield was a generous 8.55%, but earnings forecasts ranged widely between the companies from 41.1p to 71.5p. The sale would raise a total of £5,239m from 10 regional companies ranging in market value from £922m for Thames Water to £157m for Northumbrian Water. The privatisation was led by Schroder Wagg and Rowe & Pitman.

Political opposition had been a common feature of all privatisations, but, on this occasion, there was strong public opposition, with opinion polls suggesting 70% against. In the event, the 23½% of the issue reserved for public subscription was oversubscribed 5.7 times, triggering a clawback to increase the public percentage to 47%. On the first day of dealing on 11 December, the average closing price of the 100p partly paid shares was 145p, ranging from 157p for Northumbrian to 131p for Severn Trent. Market trends continued to play a critical role in the success of privatisation issues. The All Share Index rose from 1,101.79 on the publication of the prospectus to 1,172.04 on the first day of dealing – a rise of 6.4%.

A full year passed before the next major privatisation of the electricity industry, which would complete the privatisation of the four major utilities – telecommunications, gas, water and electricity. It was planned in three stages, beginning with the regional electricity distribution companies in December 1990, followed by the two power generation companies in February 1991 and the two Scottish generators in June 1991. The uncertainty caused by the invasion of Kuwait was shrugged to one side and details of the offer for sale of the 12 distribution companies, led by Kleinwort Benson, were released on 21 November – the eve of the resignation of Margaret Thatcher.

Following the pattern of the water companies, all 12 distribution companies were offered at the same price of 240p, payable in 3 instalments, with the first at 100p. The total sale would raise £5,182m, with market capitalisations ranging from the two largest – Eastern and Southern – at £648m, and the smallest – South Wales – at £244m. The average yield was 8.4%, ranging from 8.03% from Eastern and Southern to 9.03% from Northern, and prospective PE ratios ranged from 6.9 to 9.0. The privatisation continued the practice set for BT, British Gas and the water companies of offering incentives to encourage long-term individual investment in the form of a 1 for 10 bonus share issue for a maximum of 300 additional shares after 3 years or the alternative of a cash rebate to customers worth around 7% of the fully paid price.

In the advertising campaign, a crude attempt was made to emulate 'Sid' of gas fame with 'Frank' for electricity. None the less, the issue was highly successful in attracting an oversubscription of 10.7 times for the public portion of the offer. The usual clawbacks applied and the public percentage was raised to 55% of the issue. With the following wind of a rising stock market, the shares closed at an average premium of 51% on the first day of dealings on 11 December 1990, with prices ranging from 166p for Manweb to 142p for Seeboard. Dealings also took place in a 'package' of 100 shares in each company, which closed at £1,508. The apparent scale of the premium at 51% elicited the usual accusations of underpricing, although the opening premium, based on a fully paid price of 240p, was only 21%.

The regular occurence of large premiums was a constant source of criticism of privatisation because it appeared that State-owned assets were repeatedly being sold too cheaply to the disadvantage of the taxpayer. Pricing new issues has never been easy under the British system because the time lapse between pricing and first dealings, which averaged 16 days for privatisations, makes the issue vulnerable to market movements. In the case of the major privatisations, there was a remarkably strong correlation between success or failure and rising or falling markets. Table 29.3 shows the percentage change in the All Share Index between the release of the prospectus and first day of dealings, and the premium over the issue price at the close of the first day of dealings expressed as a percentage of both the partly paid and fully paid prices.

Most of the privatisations enjoyed buoyant markets, except Britoil, Enterprise Oil and British Steel. Table 29.3 also illustrates how the spectacular premiums that attracted the most publicity were, in all cases, much more sober when expressed as percentages of the full prices.

Table 29.3
The percentage changes in the All Share Index between publication of the prospectus and closing prices on the first day of dealings

Company	Issue price (partly paid) (p)		Closing price (p)	Change in All Share Index (%)	Premium partly paid (%)	Premium fully paid (%)
British Aerospace	150	–	171	1.1	–	14.0
Britoil	215	(100)	81	(1.7)	(19.0)	(8.8)
Associated British Ports	112	–	138	3.1	–	23.2
Cable & Wireless	168	–	197	5.9	–	17.3
Jaguar	165	–	179	9.9	–	8.5
BT	130	(50)	93	3.1	86.0	33.1
British Gas	135	(50)	62.5	0.5	25.0	9.3
British Airways	125	(65)	109	4.1	67.8	35.2
Enterprise Oil	185	(100)	100	(1.4)	0.0	0.0
Rolls-Royce	170	(85)	147	7.4	72.9	36.5
BAA	245	(100)	146	2.1	46.0	18.8
British Steel	125	(60)	63	(4.2)	5.0	2.4
Water	240	(100)	145	6.8	45.0	18.8
Electricity	240	(100)	151	2.0	51.0	21.3

Table 29.4
The third phase of privatisation, 1987–91

Date	%	Company	Price (p)	Value (£m)
July 1987	100	British Airports Authority	245	1,280
October 1987	31.7	British Petroleum		5,750
October 1987	100	National Bus Company		300
March 1988	99.8	Rover Group		150
December 1988	100	British Steel	125	2,500
December 1989	100	Water Companies	240	5,240
December 1990	100	Electricity Distribution Companies	240	5,180
March 1991	60	National Power and PowerGen		2,160
June 1991	100	Scottish Power and Scottish Hydro		2,880
December 1991	25	BT	350	5,400
Total				30,840

The cycle of privatisation in the third Conservative administration was completed with the sale of 60% of the capital of National Power and PowerGen in March 1991 for £2,160m; 100% of Scottish Power and Scottish Hydro in June 1991 for £2,880m; and a second tranche of BT shares to raise £5,400m. This pattern of almost exponential growth in the value raised by privatisation over the 3 successive administrations continued – rising from £1,400m in the first, to £14,500m in the second and nearly £31,000m in the third. The final sequence was as shown in Table 29.4.

Chapter 30

CRASH
July 1987–November 1987

All Share Index	16 July 1987	1238.57	
	10 November 1987	784.81	Down 36.6%

Of the ten bear markets forming the subject of individual chapters in this history of the stock market, two have imprinted themselves indelibly on the memory of those practitioners and shareholders who were there. The first was the traumatic two-and-a-half year bear market that, by December 1974, reduced the London equity market to a quarter of its peak value. The second was the crash in October 1987, which, in a single day, lowered the Dow Jones Index in New York by 22%, and, in two days, removed 20% of the value of the All Share Index in London.

These two bear markets were quite different in character. In the first, a slow Chinese torture left behind a mass of whimpering shareholders. In the second, a guillotine simply lopped off a sizeable chunk of the body. The first was essentially a domestic affair, the second was a shared experience with the rest of the world. The first was a consequence of chronic economic and political problems, the second was the bursting of a valuation bubble.

Many an image is used to portray these two bear markets. A fashionable word today is 'meltdown'. A constant image is the erupting volcano. The first bear market was a slow-moving wall of lava that gradually enveloped three-quarters of the land before halting in full view of what little remained. The second was a torrent of red-hot lava that stopped as abruptly as it started. Such images may seem extravagant, but, within the daily lives of those involved at the time, they help to convey the shock of a dramatic bear market.

The October crash is vividly remembered in City circles, and, in most years, its anniversary is the subject of articles in the financial press. It is probably the most widely remembered single post-war stock market event because it dominated the television, radio and newspaper headlines for several days. Just for once, there was a genuine air of menace behind the normally vacuous headline about billions of pounds being written off stock market values when, on each of two successive days, the figure was 50 billion pounds.

The October crash occurred in New York on Monday 19 October and in London on Monday and Tuesday, 19 and 20 October. Popular memory might assume that it was a crash from an all-time high. In fact stock markets had already peaked in July in London and in August in New York. In London a sharp increase in the June trade deficit had an unsettling effect when announced on 22 July, and an unexpected increase in base rates on 6 August from 9% to 10% shook confidence by raising fears of recession. Further unease was caused by two large rights issues from WPP and Blue Arrow to finance ambitious transatlantic bids, and barely a month after reaching its peak of 1,238.57 on 16 July, the All Share Index had fallen by 10% to 1,114.81 on 20 August (see Figure 30.1).

However over the next two months, equities recovered to within sight of their peak in the first week of October. The All Share Index was 4% below its high on Friday 16 October, at which point the crash in London came to most people out of a clear blue sky – with the train hitting the buffers travelling flat out and fully loaded, as it was put at the time by Sir David Scholey, Chairman of S. G. Warburg Group.

The reason for this was that the crash had its origins in New York in the space of a few days in October, and the chronology of events in New York is important to an understanding of events in London. While London was falling away in July and August under the local pressures of higher interest rates and a worsening trade deficit, Wall Street continued to race ahead to a peak in the Dow Jones Index of 2,722.42 on 25 August before it paused to draw breath. Historic PE ratios were over 20, dividend yields were around 2½%, and, in an indicator used more widely in New York than in London, share prices stood at a record 2½ times book value.

The market cracked on Tuesday 6 October when the Dow Jones Index suffered a 3½% fall of 91.55 points to 2,548.63 after the prime rate in New York was raised from 8¾% to 9¼%. In the following week, the index fell away rapidly over 3 successive days after disappointing trade figures on Wednesday 14 October and another ½-point increase in the prime rate to 9¾% on Thursday 15 October, as shown in Table 30.1.

Table 30.1
Movements in the Dow Jones Index leading up to the market crash, October 1987

Date in October 1987	Dow Jones Index		Fall (points)	Fall (%)
	From	To		
Tuesday 6	2,640.18	2,548.63	91.55	3.5
Wednesday 14	2,508.16	2,412.70	95.46	3.8
Thursday 15	2,412.70	2,355.09	57.61	2.4
Friday 16	2,355.09	2,246.73	108.36	4.6

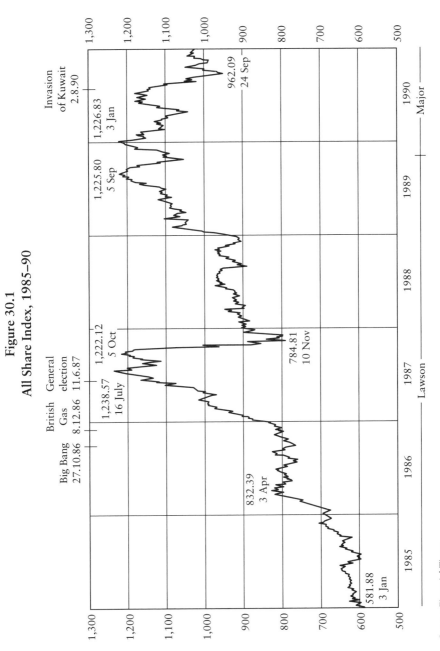

Figure 30.1
All Share Index, 1985–90

Source: Financial Times

On the eve of the crash, the Dow Jones Index had already fallen by 15% in 10 days in the face of the looming threat of recession and, in terms of points, had suffered its 3 largest ever one day falls. Worse still, this downwards spiral was exacerbated by uneasy rumours in the heart of the marketplace about problems in Salomon Brothers – an aggressive investment bank widely regarded to be the leading bond trader on Wall Street. It was from among its ranks that Sherman McCoy might well have been drawn – the fictitious bond trader and so-called master of the universe, whose downfall is rivetingly portrayed in Tom Wolfe's novel *Bonfire of the Vanities* (Farrar Straus Giroux, 1987). With uncanny foresight, this novel was written before the crash, as was the screenplay of the film *Wall Street* in which Michael Douglas eulogises on greed in his portrayal of the fictitious investment banker Gordon Gekko. Both vividly described the excesses of the 1980s and were surely warnings of events to come.

Salomon Brothers had epitomised the long Wall Street bull market of the 1980s, and, in an uncontrolled expansion, its staff numbers had risen by 40% in the previous 12 months alone to a worldwide total of 6,500. When Salomon Brothers announced on Monday 12 October that, because business in the third quarter had been only 'marginally profitable' it was closing down segments of its trading operations and cutting staff numbers by 12%, this came as a shock to the Wall Street community. It sent out a signal clearly understood by the professionals in the investment banks and fund management world that the party was over. When the professionals lose their collective nerve, the results for the public can be catastrophic.

Although in those final few days before the crash the London market was beginning to weaken, there was none of the sense of imminent danger pervading New York. The All Share Index fell on 5 consecutive days from Friday 9 October to Thursday 15 October, but only by some 2.4% overall. At this point, fate played a strange hand. On the night of Thursday 15 October, London and the South East of England suffered a devastating hurricane. London became inaccessible because so many trees had fallen on to roads and railway lines, and was rendered largely inoperable because of widespread power cuts and failed telephone exchanges. A few market makers made their way through trees and fallen masonry, only to input indicative prices to absent clients, and no indices were calculated. London was cut off from events from the moment prices were tumbling in New York after hours on the Thursday evening until the following Monday. Investors were thrown back to the conditions of an earlier century when news of momentous events in other capitals took a day or two to arrive and frustrated sellers were trapped.

Despite its New York origins, the crash actually began in London on Monday 19 October. Apart from Hong Kong, the Asian and Australian markets had closed at lower levels, but not especially so, and in Tokyo a 5% fall in Saturday trading had been partially recovered. In London, the FTSE 100 lost 250 points, and the All Share Index fell by just under 10%. Dramatic this may have been, but as the global market moved westward to New York, it paled beside the unprecedented 22% fall of 508 points in the Dow Jones Index on a record turnover of 603m shares, exacerbated by waves of automatic selling from computerised portfolio systems. It was from this single day in New York that the October crash achieved its fame and notoriety.

It caused the floodgates to open in the Far East the next morning – Tuesday 20 October – when the Nikkei Index in Tokyo fell by 12% and the Ordinary Index in Australia by 25%. The Hong Kong market was so overwhelmed with sellers that trading was suspended for the rest of the week, and when it reopened on 26 October the local Hang Seng Index recorded a net fall of 41%. The collapse continued as the clock moved round again to London where the indices recorded a fall of 11%, matching over two days the fall achieved in one day in New York. There it ended as New York recovered some of the lost ground with a 6% rise on the Tuesday.

Table 30.2 shows the indices of the major world stock markets, with the percentage falls that occured given in brackets.

Table 30.2
Actual and percentage falls in the major stock market indices during the course of the crash, October 1987

Country-index	16 October 1987	19 October 1987	20 October 1987
UK–All Share Index	1,189.92	1,074.47 (9.7%)	951.95 (11.4%)
UK–FTSE 100	2,301.9	2,052.3 (10.8%)	1,801.6 (12.2%)
USA–Dow Jones	2,246.74	1,738.42 (22.6%)	1,841.01 (+5.9%)
Japan–Nikkei	26,366.74	24,866.06 (5.7%)	21,910.08 (11.9%)
Hong Kong–Hang Seng	3,783.20	3,362.39 (11.1%)	2,241.69 (33.3%)
Australia–All Ordinary	2,145.1	2,064.9 (3.8%)	1,549.5 (25.0%)
Canada–Composite	3,598.6	3,272.1 (9.1%)	2,952.0 (9.8%)
France–CAC	369.6	352.4 (4.7%)	331.9 (5.8%)
Germany–FAZ	613.67	569.85 (7.1%)	540.90 (5.1%)
FT World Index	117.20	104.95 (10.5%)	97.41 (7.2%)

The cumulative percentage falls over the two days were as follows:

- Hong Kong   40.7
- Australia   27.8
- UK–FTSE 100   21.7

- UK–All Share Index   20.0
- United States   18.1
- Canada   18.0
- FT World Index   16.9
- Japan   16.9
- Germany   11.9
- France   10.2.

Table 30.2 and the above list show how the smaller and more speculative Australian and Hong Kong markets suffered worst of all, and how the 'Anglo-Saxon' markets suffered much more severely than the 'stakeholder' markets of Europe and Japan. At this particular time in the late 1980s, there was lively debate about the comparative benefits of these two different forms of capitalism, with much support for the consensual stakeholder systems that had apparently served the economies of West Germany and Japan so well, and rather better than the confrontational Anglo-Saxon systems elsewhere. Since then, as will be discussed in Chapter 33, the argument has swung decisively the other way, but at the time of the October crash the stability of the stakeholder economies provided better protection for equity shareholders.

The list above also shows how the Japanese managed to preserve their instinct to conform by exactly matching the fall in the FT World Index, before surging ahead over the next two years. The fall in London over the two days produced another uncannily precise calculation for the All Share Index, comparable to the 20.00 times increase from trough to peak between 1974 and 1987 referred to on page 358. The percentage fall in the All Share Index over the two days was a precise 20.00%, correct to 2 decimal places.

Behind the pain of paper losses from depleted portfolios lay a separate problem causing financial distress for many investment banks and investing institutions around the world. The crash occurred in the midst of the world's largest ever equity offering – £7,250m of British Petroleum shares, being the sale of the Government's remaining 31½% stake combined with an issue by the company to raise £1,500m. Masterminded by N. M. Rothschild, this was larger than the £5,430m British Gas issue, although simpler to handle because the shares were to be issued into an existing market.

Outline details of the offer for sale were released on Thursday 15 October just before the crash. The price was set at 330p, a 5% discount to the opening price of 347p, but the true discount was higher because only 120p was to be paid on application, with the balance spread over two further dates. The offer of 2.2m shares was divided equally between applications from the public at the fixed price and from institutional investors worldwide at a minimum tender price of 330p, closing on 28 October. The prospectus was published on Monday 19 October.

It was also announced that the issue had been successfully subunderwritten by some 400 institutions in London and various syndicates in the United States, Canada and Europe. The successful completion of the underwriting and the decision to use a tender for the institutional half of the issue illustrates just how wholly unexpected was the market crash only 3 working days later, although anxieties about the general weakness of markets led to the issue price being some 20p lower than expected only a few days earlier. However, perhaps taking note of weakening markets, Lex had observed in the *Financial Times* of 16 October that 'Much can happen, of course, between now and first dealings on 30 October, but it would take a fall of over 10% in the fully paid – from 350p to 310p – to wipe out the premium entirely'.

This is almost exactly what happened on the following Monday, when, on the same day, the newspapers carried the prospectus and the market fell apart. BP fell from 350p to 316p, followed by a further fall on the second day of the crash to 286p. This huge issue was now well and truly under water. The Chancellor, Nigel Lawson, vividly describes in his memoirs, *The View From Number Eleven* (Bantam Press, 1992) the intense pressure put on him to use a *force majeure* clause in the underwriting documents to call off the issue and release the underwriters from potential losses of some £1,000m.

In London, the traditional underwriting system had at least spread the losses widely among the institutions, but in New York the small number of investment banks to the issue, led by Goldman Sachs, suffered harshly from the different system in the US of retaining their underwriting liability until the shares are actually distributed after a gradual process of book-building. The US portion of the issue was 480m shares, each bearing a prospective loss of around 50p. The greatest suffering was in Canada, where stockbrokers Wood Gundy led a consortium for 105m shares and barely had the resources to cope with their losses.

As a result, Lawson was put under intense pressure from all quarters to pull the issue. He received calls from high-level transatlantic political sources, from the Bank of England fearful of the rippling effect of losses, from BP itself and from Michael Richardson, who, in 1981, had seamlessly moved from Cazenove to N. M. Rothschild, where he was leading the issue. The question at issue was whether or not a stock market crash counted as *force majeure*. The Chancellor rightly and courageously considered that the crash did not share those characteristics of a natural disaster – be it an act of God, a revolution or an outbreak of war – that would normally justify the abandonment of a contract. In his view, underwriting was clearly embedded in the system as an insurance policy against falling stock market prices, and in the House of Commons he feigned to express surprise that underwriters had even asked the question. However, he finally compromised to the extent of undertaking to repurchase shares issued in the partly paid form of 120p should they fall to 70p. In the event, the shares opened at 90p on the first day of dealing on 30 October before closing at 85p, and underwriters collectively faced paper losses of £700m.

Quite apart from BP, it was a devastating experience for two such major and mature Stock Exchanges as London and New York to have 20% or more of the value of quoted equities wiped out in a matter of hours. Hindsight shows that 19/20 October proved to be a stinging slap on the wrist to punish investors for what, in a different context, was described more recently by Alan Greenspan as 'irrational exuberance'. But that was not how it appeared at the time to those many participants in securities markets whose confidence was shattered. Commentators were comparing events with the Wall Street crash in 1929, when the initial fall spiralled on downwards for a further three years, and during that third week in October nobody knew what to expect next. Panic was afoot and nerves were stretched for many weeks.

Morale was low after successive falls of more than 10% in the indices on the Monday and Tuesday, but a steadier overnight Wall Street prompted a rebound on Wednesday 21 October. The All Share Index bounced back over 1,000 with a 5.8% rise, from 951.95 to 1,007.47, and the FTSE 100 rose by nearly 8% amid frantic activity that produced more than 100,000 bargains. However, it was only a technical rally and, on Thursday, these gains were wiped out as bargain numbers peaked at almost 115,000. On Friday, the All Share Index drifted lower, to 930.33 – a fall of 21.8% on the week.

It had been a week of records, with business volumes easily surpassing the levels experienced through the long summer bull market. The daily totals were as shown in Table 30.3.

Table 30.3
The week of the crash, 19–23 October 1987

Date	FT All Share Index	FTSE 100	Equity Bargains	Equity value (£m)
16 October	1,189.92	2,301.9		
19 October	1,074.58	2,052.3	55,708	2,525
20 October	951.95	1,801.6	80,974	2,814
21 October	1,007.47	1,943.8	109,235	2,838
22 October	953.46	1,833.2	114,974	2,689
23 October	930.33	1,795.2	99,151	3,022
Totals			460,042	13,888

The changes to dealing systems following Big Bang in October 1986 and the expansion in the numbers of market makers led to a significant increase in the number of equity bargains and their total value, and much higher volumes were sustained during the bull market in the spring and summer of 1987. Nevertheless, until the week of the crash, daily bargains rarely exceeded 70,000, daily turnover rarely exceeded £2,000m and previous weekly totals had never approached the totals for the week of the crash.

Another feature of the week was a surge in traded options contracts to a daily record of 120,840, as investors sought to cover positions and take advantage of volatile prices. There was some evidence over the week of a flight to quality. Glaxo and Marks & Spencer fell by some 15% but BTR, Hanson Trust and ICI fell by around 25%. Speculative shares fared badly.

At the end of a gruelling week, investors were numbed by uncertainty as the speed of the crash evoked memories of 1929, and for the next two weeks nerves would be tested to the limit by volatile markets continuing to fall. On Monday 26 October, the All Share Index fell by 7.2% and the FTSE 100 by 111.1 points to 1,684.1, although both steadied through the rest of a week when the Chancellor put in place the floor under the new partly paid shares in the BP underwriting,

The next week was almost as alarming as the crash itself, as London went into its own daily free fall, and, over 7 business days, the All Share Index fell another 11½%, taking the cumulative loss in just over 3 weeks to 34% (see Table 30.4).

Table 30.4
The second week after the crash, 2–10 November 1987

Date	All Share Index	% change	FTSE 100	% change
30 October	887.33		1,749.8	
2 November	876.00	– 1.28	1,723.7	– 1.49
3 November	844.14	– 3.64	1,653.9	– 4.05
4 November	813.85	– 3.59	1,608.1	– 2.77
5 November	824.90	+ 1.36	1,638.8	+ 1.91
6 November	815.68	– 1.12	1,620.8	– 1.10
9 November	787.64	– 3.44	1,565.2	– 3.43
10 November	784.81	– 0.36	1,573.5	+ 0.53

These were painful days. Portfolio values had suffered grievously. Quite apart from losses of some £700m from BP, there were justifiable concerns that some £500m of other rights issues were about to be left with the underwriters, including £254m from Ladbrokes. There was also a widespread belief that economic growth worldwide would be hit by the after-effects of the crash, reflected in an immediate shaving of forecasts of growth rates for 1988. The Government attempted to allay such fears by raising its spending targets in the autumn statement in the first week of November, and reducing base rates from 9½% to 9% inadvertently adding inflationary pressure.

A nice dilemma presented by the crash was the fate of earlier takeover bids mounted at prices that were now made to look excessively generous. A. B. Foods allowed its £767m bid for S. & W. Berisford to lapse, despite receiving 59% acceptances, but TSB, amid angry scenes at an EGM, agreed to proceed with its £777m cash bid for investment bank Hill Samuel. This was especially controversial because even the shares of the market leader, S. G. Warburg, had fallen by 40% since the crash. Having received a windfall of £1½bn on its flotation, TSB had now followed its £220m bid for Target – an unquoted linked life company – earlier in June with a fulsome bid for a lesser investment bank, seemingly intent on proving the old saying that money burns a hole in the pocket.

The indices are set out in detail for the first few days of November because, although hardly anybody believed it then, the FTSE 100 on 9 November and the All Share Index a day later marked the low points in this short and vicious bear market. At the time, investors, advisers and practitioners were genuinely frightened of an uncontrollable free fall comparable to that in 1929. Apart from brief setbacks in 1976 and 1979, investors had lived through a stunning bull market that had witnessed shares multiplying 20 times from 1975 to 1987. The sheer growth of the securities and fund management businesses over this period meant that only a minority of participants – in their mid-thirties and above – had experienced a proper bear market. The bewildered majority saw a third of their assets wiped out in three weeks.

The outsider finds it difficult to believe the value of all companies can fall by a third in three weeks, and the 'efficient market' theorists have to run for cover. As these extremes will happen again, investors look for clues to identify the problem next time and, in two aspects, the market was sending out warning signals. The first was the simple question of valuation. At its peak in July, the yield on the All Share Index had fallen below 3% and the historic PE ratio on the industrial sector had risen to over 20 – levels last seen in 1972. Similar extremes were evident in New York. There are, of course, always good reasons to be found to justify the high valuations of a bull market, and a factor in 1987 may have been the mesmerising effect on all investors of the Japanese market.

The economy of Japan had, for many years, been displaying astonishing rates of growth based on manufacturing skills of the highest quality, huge trade surpluses, negligible inflation, minuscule interest rates, a powerful currency and an extraordinary propensity of its people to save. These strengths had combined to produce in the 1980s an equity bull market of phenomenal proportions, driven by both domestic and foreign demand.

The culmination of that market in 1989 is a subject for the next chapter, but its average PE ratios of 50 to 60 were already legendary in 1987, making 20 or so in Britain and the United States seem commonplace. Nippon Telegraph & Telephone, the domestic equivalent of BT, was privatised in February 1987. In subsequent dealings its market valuation exceeded £200bn. A second tranche of shares was later offered on a yield basis of 0.2% and a historic PE ratio of 270 and its market capitalisation was believed to exceed that of the whole West German stock market. It was in 1987 that the capitalisation of the Tokyo equity market exceeded that of New York for the first time, and for the next two years Japan acquired a mesmeric mystique in financial circles.

The second warning signal of the extremes of a bull market in 1987 is more subjective, and it concerns identifying moments of excess. There were some examples of this in London in the summer of 1987.

There was the massive oversubscription of two tiny new issues in the retail sector, Sock Shop and Tie Rack, soul mates on many a railway station concourse. Sock Shop had a retail network of 43 shops and a £4.9m offer for sale of shares at 125p, on a prospective PE ratio of 24.2, was oversubscribed 53 times, attracting £260m. When dealings began on 14 May 1987, the shares opened at 205p and rose to 290p before closing at a 106% premium at 257p. At this price, the market capitalisation was £56m and the prospective PE ratio was 50.

Much encouraged by the welcome given to Sock Shop, Samuel Montagu raised the stakes when bringing Tie Rack to the market some two weeks later in early June. Tie Rack was larger with 115 shops, and £12.5m of shares were offered for sale at 145p, on a historic PE ratio of 31.5. The response was even greater and the offer was oversubscribed 85 times, attracting £1,060m. When dealings began on 16 June, the shares opened at 195p, reached 202p before closing at only a modest 16% premium at 168p, and a similar market capitalisation to Sock Shop of £58m.

The publicity surrounding new issues like Sock Shop and Tie Rack attracts the private investor, particularly in the person of the stag, ever willing to fill in dozens of application forms to improve the odds in the ballots for shares when new issues are heavily oversubscribed. 'Stagging' was a profitable pursuit over many post-war decades – a hobby for many and a professional occupation for some. As an activity, it bordered on the parasitic, for its purpose was to obtain as many shares as possible and follow the golden rule of selling on the first day of dealing, without any intention of investing as a shareholder.

Stagging was a poor advertisement for the system and eventually procedures were changed in many new issues to reject multiple applications. This presented a challenge to the persistent stag who spread confusion by making applications in the names of different members of the family, sometimes even the family cat, and posting them from different places. Finally, the Government took the extreme measure for the large privatisation issues of making multiple applications a criminal offence. With the support of modern technology for sorting and identifying multiple or suspicious applications, and a willingness to prosecute, an effective deterrent was put in place.

Sock Shop and Tie Rack were extreme examples, but still of modest size.

Summer madness on a far larger scale occurred when two medium-sized companies – WPP and Blue Arrow – followed broadly similar paths by making acquisitions in the United States of companies far larger than themselves. Both were financed by burdensome rights issues that heavily diluted the equity capital and were poorly subscribed.

On 10 June 1987, WPP – a fast-growing marketing services group with a market capitalisation of £130m – bid $460m, or £277m, in cash for JWT Group – a US company owning J. Walter Thompson – the world's fourth largest advertising agency. It was an audacious bid for a much larger company on foreign soil and, advised by Samuel Montagu, the bid would be financed by a rights issue to raise £177m and a $260m bank loan. WPP had been built up from the shell of the small quoted company Wire and Plastic Products by the former finance director of Saatchi & Saatchi, Martin Sorrell. In May 1985, the shares stood at 38p, but only two years later, on the day of the bid, they rose marginally above £11.

The opening bid for JWT Group of $45 a share was raised to $50.50, and raised again to $55.50 to secure agreement on 26 June. The total cost was now $566m, and a very heavy rights issue on the basis of 2 for 1 at 875p to raise £213m was announced on 26 June. The issue was only 34.7% subscribed, leaving a large overhang of shares with the underwriting institutions, and by early August the shares had fallen below the issue price to 865p. On the second day of the crash, the shares fell to 690p, and in the early 1990s the company was nearly brought down by the recession and by excessive gearing in the balance sheet.

There were remarkable parallels with the equally audacious bid announced on 4 August 1987 by Blue Arrow – an employment and recruitment agency that joined the Unlisted Securities Market in 1984 as a tiny £3m company. Under the aggressive leadership of Tony Berry it had grown and expanded to its current market capitalisation of £420m. Here was another fast-growing company in a services industry making a bold, if reckless, foray into the United States to buy a company twice its size.

Blue Arrow bid $1,200m, or £760m, for the US company Manpower – the largest employment agency in the world. This bid was also to be financed by a rights issue to raise £837m, and advisers County NatWest were not to be deterred from launching the largest rights issue then known in the London market – ahead of the likes of National Westminster, Midland Bank and British Petroleum – for the purpose of trebling the size of a smallish company. The shares responded badly, with a 15% fall from 1075p to 918p on the announcement of another very heavy rights issue on the basis of 5 for 2 shares at 830p. On 22 August, Blue Arrow increased its bid from $75 per share to $82.50 to secure agreement, and the total cost of the acquisition was $1,300m, or £800m.

Before this ill-fated rights issue went ahead, the shares were split five times, reducing the price of the rights issue to 166p, but not affecting the amount raised. Its success was threatened by Blue Arrow shares falling close to the issue price by the time of the closing date, and there was surprise in the market when it was announced on 29 September that the issue had been 48.9% subscribed – rather better than the 34.7% achieved by WPP – and furthermore, that the remainder of the shares not taken up had been placed with institutions by stock-brokers Phillips and Drew at 166.25p. The issue was claimed as an achievement because no shares had been left with the underwriters, and Phillips & Drew had successfully completed one of the largest ever placings of shares of £435m.

The reality, however, was rather different. The issue had been only 38% subscribed, which, if known, would have made the placing impossible. The advisers, County NatWest and Phillips & Drew, did not reveal that they had subscribed for shares after the closing of the offer, thus taking the published figure to an apparently respectable 48.9%. They then participated in the placing to secure its completion. An illusion of strong institutional support had been created by a smokescreen which, once blown away by heavy losses on these secret holdings in the October crash, would ruin the careers of many of those involved. The Blue Arrow affair of concealment and false words would later join the Guinness affair as twin testaments to some of the worst aspects of the City in the 1980s. They illustrated the lengths to which people would take an obsessive concern to avoid being seen to fail to complete a transaction, be they chief executives pursuing their ambitions or advisers intoxicated by the fumes of huge fees. The Blue Arrow concealment was all the more reckless because it happened shortly after details of the Guinness support operation had become public and Ernest Saunders had been charged with criminal offences.

WPP and Blue Arrow both invited their shareholders more or less to treble their holdings by subscribing for new shares when stock markets were at high levels by any standards of valuation. Many private shareholders patently could not afford to subscribe, many institutions preferred not to subscribe, and many underwriters of WPP and in-house supporters of Blue Arrow became reluctant shareholders. In both cases shareholders were used rather than served. and a lasting instability was created. Both suffered badly from the October crash, when, over 2 days, WPP fell from 880p to 690p, and Blue Arrow from 169p to 118p.

As summer moved into autumn, there were other isolated moments of bull market fervour. Its rewards were highlighted by the emergence of the Managing Director of a securities subsidiary of a merchant bank as the highest-paid executive in corporate Britain. He was Christopher Heath, the Managing Director of Baring's Japanese securities subsidiary, with remuneration of £2.5m, reflecting his role in building up a highly profitable and rapidly growing subsidiary in Tokyo, which had grown from a mere 15 employees in 1983 to 370 in 1987. Through no fault of his own, Heath will be remembered as the name at the top of the first annual league table of seriously high corporate remuneration.

Ironically, after his later retirement this same subsidiary would acquire notoriety of a different kind from the name of one of its employees – Nick Leeson.

Events out of all proportion continued on 27 September, when Benlox Holdings – a little-known quoted company with a market capitalisation of £45m – bid £2,040m for Storehouse, on the basis of 11 shares in Benlox at 91p for 2 shares in Storehouse, supposedly worth 501p a share. Storehouse – the newly named parent for the merger in November 1985 of the former British Home Stores with Habitat and Mothercare – had been struggling to make progress under Sir Terence Conran, and had no sooner resisted a speculative £1,800m bid approach to break up the company from property developer Mountleigh than it received this bid of grotesque proportions from Benlox Holdings. It drew an immediate angry response from the beleaguered Conran: 'This bid is opportunistic financial engineering at its worst. This kind of ridiculous behaviour has got to be stopped'.

New heights were also scaled in early October by MFI, the self-assembly furniture specialists purchased by Asda for £615m in March 1985 in a merger of two fast-growing retail empires. Too many talents sometimes spoil the broth, and there was insufficient room for Derek Hunt, who had built MFI from its early beginnings as Midland Furniture Industries. It was another unhappy retailing merger and, in October 1987, Hunt led a management buyout at a record cost of £705m, buying back the original MFI for £505m and the kitchen furniture subsidiary Hygena for £200m.

The management buy-out (MBO) came into the limelight in the late 1980s as a variation of the American practice of taking over public companies by means of the leveraged buy-out (LBO), where an outside syndicate makes a takeover bid financed almost entirely by debt for an existing quoted company. The difference in the MBO is that the syndicate is put in place by the existing management either to buy a quoted company from its shareholders or, more commonly, a subsidiary or division from its parent company. From slow beginnings in 1980, the value of MBOs in the UK rose to around £800m in 1986, but suddenly accelerated to some £3,000m – £5,000 in each of the years 1987 to 1989.

They became a symbol of the enterprise economy created by the Thatcher revolution. Many a subsidiary has escaped from the inhibiting clutches of a remote parent to become a thriving business, but others might say that, in many cases, they have allowed opportunistic groups of directors to become extremely rich for modest risk. The capital structure of a typical buy-out is usually highly geared. In the case of MFI, the equity capital of £190m was supported by borrowings of £485m, but in many of the smaller examples at least 90% of the consideration would be in the form of debt. The selling parent is concerned only to receive the cash consideration, not how it is financed, and a highly geared capital structure is made possible because the purchase is of an existing business. The rewards flowing to a narrow equity base from future success can be huge. It is an area full of conflicts and contradictions that is considered in more detail in the next chapter.

This series of events – Sock Shop and Tie Rack, WPP and Blue Arrow, Christopher Heath, Benlox and MFI – were not the cause of the crash, but symptoms of conditions that can only thrive when markets stand at excessively high levels. The crash was the culmination of a universal drive into equities to unsustainable valuations. The difference between this and any previous crash was the common thread of global investment, able to cross boundaries due to political deregulation, and easily implemented due to technology. The result was a global rush into equities without any safety valves to let down the inevitable head of steam. Indeed, technology itself accentuated the problem in Wall Street, when, on the day of the crash, an uncontrolled selling spiral was triggered by computer-programmed portfolios. Computers chased each other downwards as each signal of falling prices automatically triggered yet further sales.

It is alarming enough for the typical private investor to watch helplessly as capital suddenly disappears and the comfort of that personal financial cushion is removed, but the institutional investor is no less dismayed. By 1987, pension funds had raised their domestic and foreign equity holdings to approaching 80% of total assets and the sudden removal of a third of this value raises doubts about the wisdom of investing so extensively in equities, and concern about the solvency of the fund. Policyholders in a life assurance company see the value of their terminal bonuses falling. A maturing personal pension policy suddenly buys a pension a third lower than a month earlier. Unit trusts face demands for redemption and sometimes become forced sellers in a falling market at the worst possible time.

The practitioners are as much dismayed as any by a market crash, be they stockbrokers, market makers, fund managers or corporate financiers, the more so when it is entirely new to their experience, as in 1974 and 1987. Bear markets of that depth or severity produce a lethal combination of negatives for the profit and loss account.

The uncertainty and loss of confidence caused by a market collapse induces inertia. Investors deal less or not at all. Companies abandon or postpone takeover bids and issues to raise capital. New companies postpone or cancel their plans to go public. Activity in the securities and new issues businesses falls away. Not only are volumes reduced, but what little business remains is executed at lower prices. Fees and commissions charged by securities houses, fund managers and corporate financiers tend to be based on a flat rate of the sum involved and revenues are a function of the level of share prices. Trading revenues are hit by both lower turnover and lower prices, and by the simple fact that it is easier to make trading profits in rising markets.

As a result revenue forecasts deteriorate alarmingly, but the cost base of the business remains stubbornly unchanged because some 70% of costs will be staff related and much of the balance will be in office space and computer systems. Even worse, the cost base will have been driven sharply higher during the bull market that preceded the crash, when the euphoria of rising volumes at rising prices pushes up the demand for staff and makes remuneration levels the subject of newspaper headlines.

Psychologically, the October crash could hardly have happened at a worse time of the year because most firms have a December or March year end, and business planning for the following financial year would have been well in hand. Suddenly, all those revenue forecasts used to justify an ever-higher cost base disappeared out of sight. At its simplest, a fund management business based on revenues of a percentage of £1,000m of funds under management is looking at the same percentage of £700m, and profits are decimated. A corporate finance business fears takeover bids and issues will dry up, and a securities business sees turnover dwindling away. It is no coincidence that by the end of November the shares of leading fund managers M&G and Mercury Asset Management were among the worst performers in the market, closely followed by investment banks Kleinwort Benson and S. G. Warburg, all of whose shares had more than halved in six weeks.

A cost base previously flourishing on rising bull market revenues suddenly appears dangerously unsuitable for lower revenues, but action to reduce costs is difficult to achieve and slow to have any effect. It is an unavoidable equation that leads to extreme volatility in the profits of the securities and investment banking business at the peaks and troughs of bull and bear markets, often made worse by delusions of grandeur during long bull markets of the kind witnessed in the 1980s and 1990s. The problem is that it is nice in theory for an investment bank to decline to recruit extra people in sales and research to service an expanding securities business, or extra corporate financiers to deal with widening client needs, just because the whole thing might collapse next year. But it rarely happens in practice – just as investors rarely sell booming equities into cash.

It is no coincidence that the long bear market of 1974 led to a mass of mergers and closings down in the Stock Exchange. The crash of October 1987 may have bottomed out in November, but it left behind a long tail of pessimism and much-reduced activity. Total equity turnover in the Stock Exchange would fall by a third from £283bn in 1987 to £192bn in 1988 and many of the business combinations put together for Big Bang would fall apart.

Chapter 31

BID FEVER

November 1987–January 1990

All Share Index	10 November 1987	784.81	
	3 January 1990	1,226.83	Up 56.3%

British Petroleum occupied most of the headlines in the last two months of 1987. Intriguing rumours circulated that the Kuwait Investment Office was taking advantage of unwanted shares to build up a stake in BP. Anguished investment banks on both sides of the Atlantic reported or alluded to the tens of millions of pounds or dollars they had lost in the BP underwriting. Phillips & Drew cleverly put together a huge 'bread and breakfast' deal at a fraction above the 70p support price to enable a group of insurance companies to set up a tax loss of £53m on a total of 105m BP shares they had underwritten. Lastly BP mounted a dawn raid to buy 15% of Britoil, and a tender offer to take the holding to 29.9%, at 300p compared with a market price of 185p.

The rumours of a Kuwaiti stake were quickly confirmed – initially at 4.9% on 5 November, but rising in a series of disconcerting announcements to the level of 17.4% on 30 December. Millions of these shares were bought just above the Treasury support price of 70p, probably saving the Government from having to spend no more than £27m to buy 1.8% of the new shares, but creating serious strategic concerns about their intentions towards BP. The pace of buying slowed down, but when the holding reached 21.7% in May 1988, Lord Young, Trade and Industry Secretary, asked the Monopolies Commission to 'consider the implications' of the Kuwaiti holding.

Meanwhile, BP mounted its dawn raid on Britoil at 300p on 8 December, whereupon Atlantic Richfield entered the fray by buying shares and tendering for a 29.9% stake at 350p. This immediately prompted a £2,270m bid for Britoil from BP at 450p a share on 18 December, by which time Atlantic Richfield claimed control of 14.7%, later rising to 23.7%. For the first time, the 'golden share' – retained by the Government in the majority of privatisations to prevent control passing to unwelcome hands – became subject to a bid, but the Takeover Panel cleverly avoided any controversy by allowing the bid to go forward on the basis that ownership and control were separate matters. On 22 January 1988, Britoil agreed to buy the Atlantic Richfield stake at 500p and raised its bid to that price. In due course, the Government announced it would not be exercising its golden share.

After the Index lows in early November, investors remained nervous and prices returned close to those levels in early December, influenced particularly by dollar weakness. Thereafter, prices remained volatile, but earlier fears of a global economic crisis began to recede because governments were responding to the crash by lowering interest rates and introducing other measures to stimulate activity. As the year closed, the All Share Index at 870.22 was 11% above its low, but the mood within the investment banking and securities houses about business prospects in 1988 remained deeply pessimistic.

The widespread belief was that companies would cancel or indefinitely postpone all those bids and issues that generated fees and commissions. There was hard evidence that new issues had been withdrawn, including a £1,000m company formed from the separation of Courage public houses from the brewing business and a £300m Sotheby's issue. However, the closing months of 1987 had not been entirely devoid of interest in this area and in takeover bids. There was, for example, the successful financing and launch of Eurotunnel.

A complicated and highly geared capital structure was needed to enable Eurotunnel to finance and complete a project costing an estimated £4,800m, all of which would be spent before any revenue could be earned. Work on this was taking place well before the October crash and the timing of the launch was unfortunate, but the prospectus for the offer for sale of equity units was published on 18 November 1987, seeking the subscription of £770m, divided equally between London and Paris at a price of 350p. In the event it was only 80% subscribed and, on 10 December, the shares opened at 284p and closed at 250p – a heavy discount on the issue price of 350p. In the early years, the shares performed well on optimistic revenue forecasts, but, as the costs spiralled, the original equity was nearly wiped out. Costs on huge projects often do spiral, but the dilemma is that many construction projects would never be authorised or financed in the first place without lip-service being paid to the original estimate.

In takeover activity, there were other bids apart from Britoil. In a decisive move, Hongkong & Shanghai Bank moved closer to the Midland Bank, still troubled by its disastrous 1980 Crocker National Bank venture in California. Unable, because of banking constraints, to give the few minutes' notice of a hostile dawn raid, Hongkong & Shanghai Bank secured its link in more friendly fashion by negotiating to subscribe £400m for a 14.9% stake in new shares at 475p – a 33% premium over the market price of 358p. No further stake would be acquired for 3 years without mutual consent, and, when the deal was announced on 13 November, the shares of Midland Bank rose from 358p to 388p five years later. Hongkong & Shanghai Bank would complete the acquisition of Midland Bank and, in the mid-1990s, become one of the largest quoted companies on the London stock market, alongside BP, Shell, Glaxo and BT, in the £50bn range. However, for Midland Bank, the episode was an object lesson in how a disastrous acquisition can destroy the independence of a successful business.

An intriguing David and Goliath battle emerged on 17 December when tiny Barker & Dobson – with a market capitalisation of £130m and once well known for toffees – made a £2,000m bid for Dee Corporation. Barker & Dobson was run by John Fletcher – formerly Managing Director of Asda – and it had a 1% share of the food retailing market as a result of its acquisition of Budgens. Dee Corporation, under Alec Monk, had built up a 13% share via a disparate range of names now being rationalised under the Gateway name. These included the former International Stores and Fine Fare, mentioned in Chapter 28 because of their controversial financing by vendor placings. Barker & Dobson had put in place £1.6bn of loan finance in a textbook example of the leveraged buyout, but was no more able to summon enthusiasm or support for this kind of approach than the similar Benlox bid for Storehouse, although it fared better, with acceptances of 23.9% than the derisory 1.8% obtained by Benlox. The London market remained suspicious of what it perceived as opportunist financial engineering from little-known quarters.

The market recovered its equilibrium in the new year, comfortable that the worst was over, and encouraged to expect tax cuts in the Budget, but 1988 proved to be no more than a year of consolidation. The All Share Index rose by a modest 6% over the year, to 926.59, with its a high and low only 11% apart – one of the narrowest ranges on record.

The Budget duly arrived on 15 March 1988, and the Chancellor released a net £4,000m in a series of cuts in income tax. The standard rate was reduced from 27% to 25% and a long-term target of 20% was established, but more remarkable was his decision to sweep away 5 bands of higher rate tax up to a maximum 60% and replace them with a single maximum rate of 40%. Capital gains tax was changed from a flat 30% to an individual's marginal rate of 25% or 40%, later creating a serious disincentive to sell for long-term investors. At the same time, he swept away 4 bands of inheritance tax, replacing them with a single rate of 40%. The PEP allowance was raised from £2,400 to £3,000.

The reduction in the top rate of income tax caused such outrage among the opposition in the House of Commons that proceedings had to be suspended in mid-speech. Its purpose was to establish a level playing field that drew no distinction between the taxation of remuneration, dividends and capital gains, and, for the purpose of creating incentive and rewarding enterprise, to set maximum rates that compared favourably with other leading economies. It was probably this single measure of reducing the top rate of income tax so abruptly from 60% to 40% that would later fuel critical propaganda about the transfer of wealth from the poor to the rich under many years of Conservative rule. The missing element in that debate has been whether or not the starting point of a maximum rate of 83% inherited by the Conservatives in 1979 had pushed the balance so far the other way that a correction was inevitable.

The remainder of 1988 presented a mixture of problems and opportunities. The tax cuts in the Budget were at first accompanied by further cuts in base rates from 9% to 7½%, partly in an attempt by the Chancellor to hold down the pound, but, from June onwards, this policy was rapidly reversed. A gathering consumer boom was reflected in a record trade deficit of £1,200m for May, followed by a dramatically worse deficit of £2,150m for July. Sterling came under pressure and worrying signs of inflation emerged. On 2 June, there began a succession of ½-point increases in base rates from 7½% to 11% – 7 times in 10 weeks – culminating in a full point increase to 12% on 25 August. Inflation was nudging higher every month, exacerbated by the inclusion of higher interest rates in its calculation. This problem is avoided in many countries by the exclusion of interest rates from any calculation of inflation because the effect of an increase in rates is not an added price increase, but simply a transfer of income from the borrower to the lender.

The market overall reached its high point of this dull year in August, but, quite separately, many major companies were setting new precedents on a grand scale in the areas of financing and acquisitions. In a mix of triumph and disaster, those involved included Barclays Bank, Rowntree, Harris Queensway, British & Commonwealth, BAT Industries, Grand Metropolitan and Racal.

Barclays Bank shared a widespread banking problem of having to write off loans to Third World countries, and, in April, launched a rights issue to raise £924m. It was unusual in being a deeply discounted rights issue on the basis of one new share at 250p for every two held, compared with an overnight price of 481p, which immediately fell to 429p. The purpose of the deep discount is to avoid underwriting costs, but it is an unpopular route for private shareholders, who are often faced with an unwelcome sale of new shares, and it has a negative element if the existing dividend rate cannot be maintained.

Takeover bids also fell outside their traditional pattern. The first was a battle between two foreign companies for the ownership of a major household British name. The Swiss confectionery groups Jacobs-Suchard and Nestlé fought as if in the auction room to acquire Rowntree in the following sequence of hostile bids given in Table 31.1.

Table 31.1
The sequence of bids for Rowntree, April–June 1988

Date	Bidder	%	Price (p)	Value (£m)
Overnight			477	1,130
13 April	Suchard	14.9	630	
26 April	Nestlé	100	890	2,100
4 May	Suchard	29.9	925	
26 May	Suchard	100	950	2,320
23 June	Nestlé	100	1,075	2,550

Many aspects of this bid were disquieting to the public. Rowntree was founded in York in the nineteenth century by a Quaker family with strong paternalistic instincts for the welfare of its workers. It was an unorthodox company within a capitalist society, and there was local distaste, that two foreign companies should be allowed to battle over its fate. In the City, there was hostility to the principle that Swiss companies were allowed a freedom to acquire a major British company that would be denied under Swiss law to a British company seeking a similar acquisition in Switzerland. In particular, it was perplexing that a well-known, successful company, valued in April at little more than £1,000m, should, just 2 months later be worth more than £2,500m.

The last point is easily answered. First, two determined competing buyers will always pay a higher price than one, and, second, they were fighting over a textbook example of the latest management fashion. This was the pursuit of brands, and Rowntree was a prime example in the confectionery market, with KitKat, Polo mints, Smarties and Yorkie chocolate bars. The value of established brands in consumer markets became an accounting issue at this time, with some companies seeking to capitalise their value as an additional invisible asset in the balance sheet. Later in the year, Ranks Hovis McDougall – a company under threat of takeover – valued its brands in the balance sheet at £678m. However, there were immediate difficulties over depreciation and this practice was strongly resisted by the accounting profession because of the problems of finding a consistent basis for the valuation of brands.

Nestlé might have paid a full price for Rowntree, but at least it acquired long-term value. Other bids at this time proved to be ill-timed disasters. Harris Queensway was a highly successful carpet retailer, founded and run by a classic entrepreneur, Phil Harris, who announced a bid approach on 5 May that lifted the shares from 125p to 171p. On 6 July, James Gulliver – recently retired from Argyll after being frustrated in his attempt to buy Distillers – formed Lowndes, which was a corporate vehicle to make an agreed bid of 190p, or £447m, for Harris Queensway. In the immediate aftermath of four successive rate increases and in the midst of a consumer boom, it was a brilliantly timed sale by Harris, who later watched the acquisition fall apart before starting all over again in the 1990s with Carpetright. It was a sad finale to Gulliver's business career, after building Argyll and rightly identifying Distillers as a prime target.

Another disastrous acquisition was the £407m bid by British & Commonwealth made in July for the computer leasing company Atlantic Computers. The shares had already fallen from a peak of 800p to 364p when the bid of 509p was agreed, and critical questions had been asked about the validity of its accounting practices. These doubts proved to be all too well founded, and the consequences for British & Commonwealth would later be fatal.

A disaster in the making was happening in Ferranti following its merger in November 1997 with International Signal & Control. In the summer of 1988, the merger was reported to be going 'exceedingly well' but the business of the impenetrable International Signal was, in fact, largely non-existent.

Whereas the acquisition of Harris Queensway was an error of judgement, acquisitions of deeply flawed companies such as Atlantic Computers and International Signal, and the later rapid demise of Polly Peck, are often attributed after the event to the failure of auditors to detect and reveal accounting problems. The reality is that the independence of the auditor is occasionally challenged and trampled over. It is easy to underestimate the power of the personality of the dominant entrepreneur, who, in companies that fail, is often driving the company single-handedly. Such were the personalities of John Foulston of Atlantic Computers, James Guerin of International Signal, Asil Nadir of Polly Peck and, later, Robert Maxwell. 'Buyer beware', applies just as strongly in corporate acquisitions as in any other market, and it is the judgement and instinct of the bidder and his advisers that is often put to the test and fails.

There were other variations on this bid cycle. Two major acquisitions were made in the United States by British companies in 1988. After a long struggle, BAT Industries extended its insurance interests by means of the $5,200m (£3,070m) purchase of US insurer Farmers Group in August, although it was gradually pushed higher from its original bid of $60 a share to $75. In December, the US food group Pillsbury – owners of fast food chain Burgerking – was purchased by Grand Metropolitan for $5,750m (£3,160m), at a price of $66 a share after an initial bid of $60.

Another variation was the launching of a subsidiary that was to become far larger than its parent. Under the leadership of Ernest Harrison, Racal became one of the most successful growth stocks in the stock market in the 1960s and 1970s, with its defence electronic and communications systems thriving from high levels of defence expenditure in the Cold War years. It was the supreme technology stock in the days before 'technology' had been identified as a sector of the market in the way it is today. Nevertheless, its shares were languishing, along with those of other defence stocks, in the late 1980s, although locked within it was a leader in a prospective growth market of the 1990s – mobile telephones.

The potential for Racal Telecom – or Vodafone as it came to be known – was not recognised by the stock market, and Racal resolved the undervaluation by initiating its separate flotation by an offer for sale in October 1988 as a £1,700m company, dwarfing what little remained as Racal. The flotation required that 20% of the shares were made available, of which 75% were offered to Racal shareholders on a pro rata basis at 170p, and 25% reserved for overseas investors. At this price, the shares stood on a prospective PE ratio of 30.5 – a high valuation, justified only by reference to comparable US companies, and, initially, a deterrent to British investors.

Racal and Vodafone was much the largest example of a quoted company floating a subsidiary. An earlier example had been the offer for sale of 25% of Mercury Asset Management by S. G. Warburg Group in 1987, and it had happened before with the occasional flotation in overseas markets of the local subsidiary of a British company. An immediate question to ask is why shareholders should have to pay a price for something they already own, and the more likely course today would be a demerger. However, a parent company may still wish to retain control of its subsidiary for good business reasons of long-term value or it might use this route as a means of raising capital.

These are only the leading examples of a high level of corporate activity. As 1988 drew to a close, British Steel was privatised, Lloyds Bank cleverly obtained control of Abbey Life without paying a premium by creating a merger with its own life assurance subsidiary, and GEC – having been frustrated two years earlier by a reference to the Monopolies Commission – now joined forces with Siemens to bid £1,700m for Plessey. However the economic background remained gloomy. There was talk of 10% pay deals and, on 25 November, base rates were raised from 12% to 13% following a record monthly trade deficit of £2,400m in October. Routine stock market business remained at depressed levels and share prices were drifting lower.

The year end is the time for critical decisions in the securities business. Deregulation always brings with it a quantum leap in competition and capacity, and Big Bang was no different for the Stock Exchange. For the first year, the effects of over-capacity and reduced commission rates were hidden by the stock market boom that culminated in the crash of October 1987, but by the end of 1988 many of the Big Bang combinations were unravelling in the face of declining revenues and emerging losses.

Commission rates had settled at around 0.2% for institutional business in equities compared with 0.3–0.4%, and had disappeared altogether in gilts. The spreading practice of 'soft commission', whereby a broker would agree to pick up an institution's bill for terminals or performance measurement services of, say, £1,000 in return for guaranteed commission of £2,000, in the ratio of 2:1, was price-cutting under another name. Competition in market making was ruthless as those previous jobbing experience took advantage of the inexperience of their fledgling rivals in the new firms.

The institutions took advantage of all market makers by the new, but misnamed, practice of 'programme trades'. An institution would let a number of firms know that it wished to sell a portfolio of stocks, unnamed but categorised by size of company, and reinvest in a matching, but unnamed, portfolio. The firm bidding to do the transaction closest to quoted middle market prices won the bid, only then to discover the names of unmarketable stocks hidden away in the list. James Capel was an early leader in these trades and, within a few weeks of Big Bang, it had carried out a £300m programme trade for the Post Office

Pension Fund, followed in August 1987 by another £300m trade for the Shipbuilding Industries Pension Scheme. The latter transaction was arranged to bring the portfolio closely in line with the market index – a practice gathering pace under the leadership of BZW, where its fund management division was a market leader in the provision of Index Funds for institutional clients.

While revenues were being squeezed, at the same time cost pressures remained intense, with remuneration levels for the better staff as high as ever. To ensure their retention, many were locked in with generous guaranteed bonuses that had to be paid from non-existent profits. The 'golden handcuffs' that retained the services of partners from the original purchases were now joined by expensive 'golden hellos' offered to entice star analysts, market makers and salespeople to jump ship. The expansionary pressures of the boom had led to trainees with flimsy experience moving elsewhere for large salaries. Staff costs and numbers had run out of control, but, by the end of 1988, business revenues had fallen by a third and there was no particular reason to suggest that there would be any improvement in 1989.

One notable casualty had already happened at an early stage. W. Greenwell announced in March 1987 that it was ceasing to make markets in equities after incurring losses of £6m in the 6 months after Big Bang, and, in January 1988, closed down its equities business with the loss of 200 jobs. Wood Mackenzie, another notable firm, began to lose its way in 1987. The necessary chemistry was lacking in its merger with Hill Samuel, but it might have recovered if an expected bid from Union Bank of Switzerland to facilitate a merger with Phillips & Drew had not been withdrawn at the last moment in August 1987. In its place, there followed in October the bid for Hill Samuel from TSB, and contingent sale of Wood Mackenzie to County NatWest in December for a figure believed to be £30m. The merger of the firms led to redundancies of 165.

The market was well aware of redundancy programmes taking place discreetly throughout the year, and the number of gilt-edged market makers had been steadily reducing, but few were prepared for the announcement on 6 December 1988 that Morgan Grenfell was closing down its securities business with immediate effect and the loss of 450 jobs. It had been an ill-fated business with mismatched acquisitions of an equity jobber with a gilt-edged broker, and its reputation suffered badly from the resignation in November 1986 of Geoffrey Collier, newly appointed joint Director of the Securities Division, and his subsequent conviction for a blatant example of insider dealing. The brutality of the Morgan Grenfell decision came as a shock to the system, but it also acted as a catalyst for others elsewhere to take action.

In January 1989, Chase Manhattan – formerly Laurie, Milbank and Simon & Coates – closed down its equities business with 135 redundancies, and Hoare Govett became the seventh gilt-edged market maker to close down, leaving 22 out of the original 29. Hoare Govett had been a leading gilt-edged broker before

Big Bang, but it failed to develop market making skills and found it had joined a crowded marketplace that, in total, had lost £190m in two and a quarter years since Big Bang. Losses were also widespread in equities and some depressing estimates suggested the securities industry as a whole lost £500m in 1988. Figures began to appear for individual firms. Phillips & Drew admitted to losses of £115m since April 1987, and Citicorp Scrimgeour Vickers and James Capel lost £42m and £32m respectively in their latest financial years. Smith New Court, the quoted independent firm of market makers, announced a loss of £12.6m and passed its dividend.

Losses on this scale reflected poorly on the reputation and judgement of many of the participants in Big Bang. Morgan Grenfell had squandered millions of pounds in a fruitless foray into the stock market, but the culmination of this first round of closures and retrenchment came in January 1990 when Citicorp closed down the core equity business of Citicorp Scrimgeour Vickers with the loss of 215 jobs. The prime stockbroking firm of Scrimgeour Kemp-Gee – a market leader up to Big Bang – had been destroyed in three years. The US experience had been dismal, with Shearson Lehman publicly lamenting the failure of its acquisition of L. Messel, and Chase Manhattan having closed down its newly acquired equity business. The publicity given to these widespread industry losses served the reputation of the City badly in the light of so much earlier attention given to salaries and bonuses, believed by outsiders to have reached absurd and indefensible levels – whether it was million-pound packages for stars or salaries for 25-year-olds with minimal experience matching director-level salaries elsewhere.

The aftermath of Big Bang was a chastening experience. The strongest combinations remained those with a strong market-making base, able to sustain thin margins on a much higher turnover and capitalise on the success of SEAQ International – a dealing system in foreign stocks that mirrored the SEAQ system in domestic stocks launched at Big Bang. SEAQ International provided a far greater liquidity in leading European stocks than was available in any of the domestic Continental stock markets, and it quickly captured a significant share of the market in Continental stocks for both international and British institutions. The new primary dealers in government securities struggled to make profits, no longer benefiting from privileged access to new issues, earning no commissions and solely dependent on positioning of the dealing books.

The reforms of Big Bang were planned to bring the securities industry into line with common practice elsewhere. It was clearly achieved in ending single capacity, but the next stage of combining the issuing activities of the merchant bank with the distribution of the stockbroker to form an investment bank offering 'one-stop' shopping for corporate clients was only partially successful. British companies widely continued to prefer advice from two places rather than one, even if at extra cost, and this preference was facilitated by the decision of the likes of Lazards and Schroders from among the merchant banks and, vitally, Cazenove, from among the stockbrokers, to remain independent.

Although the prospects for 1989 may have been muted, it proved in the event to be a good year for investors and a busy year for corporate financiers. The All Share Index rose by 30% from 926.59 to 1,204.70, close to its all-time high, flying in the face of increases in base rates from 13% to 15%, but enjoying a takeover boom and participating in a worldwide recovery in equities.

The year began with a flourish in the first week of January when BP spent £2,400m to buy back for cancellation an 11.7% stake from the Kuwait Investment Office. This reduced the Kuwait holding to 10% and fulfilled the rather arbitrary findings of the Monopolies Commission. The shares were bought at 247p, which, with a tax rebate, allowed Kuwait a modest profit. BP financed the transaction by the coincidental sale of its minerals holdings to RTZ for an identical £2,400m.

This was merely the prelude to a flood of corporate transactions of unprecedented size and ingenuity, for which the freedom of opportunity released by deregulation acted as a powerful catalyst. With the exception of Hoylake's bid for BAT Industries, which lapsed but indirectly served its purpose, the takeover bids set out in Table 31.2 were successfully won.

Table 31.2
Major takeover bids of UK companies, 1989

Month	Bidder	Target	Value (£bn)
May	Smith Kline/Beecham	Agreed merger	4.700
July	Hanson Trust	Consolidated Gold Fields	3.500
July	Isosceles (consortium)	Gateway	2.220
August	Hoylake (consortium)	BAT Industries	13.500
September	GEC/Siemens	Plessey	2.000
November	Ford	Jaguar	1.600

In the same year, the new issues given in Table 31.3 were successfully launched.

Table 31.3
Major new issues, 1989

Month	Company	Value (£bn)
February	National Freight Corporation	0.890
July	Abbey National Building Society	1.700
October	EuroDisney	1.200
November	Water privatisation	5.240

It is the variety of transactions that makes these two lists so intriguing. The new issues included a major privatisation of ten separate water companies, the successful flotation of a privatised management buy-out, the first building society to incorporate and seek a public quotation, and an example of a US company using corporate expertise in London to finance a new subsidiary building a project in Paris.

There was similar variety in the takeover bids. The merger between Smith Kline Beckman – a leading US pharmaceutical company – and Beecham Group – a prime British name in pharmaceutical and associated consumer products – was the first transatlantic merger of its kind. It was a forerunner of similar cross-border mergers later formed between British and Continental companies, and a reminder of the Royal Dutch-Shell and Unilever mergers much earlier in the century.

Hanson Trust's acquisition of Consolidated Gold Fields was an uncharacteristic intervention in the rather incestuous world of South African mining. Consolidated Gold Fields was a holding company with a portfolio of gold-mining interests that had been the subject of a bid in September 1988 from Minorco, an offshore company in Luxembourg with South African mining interests. Consolidated Gold Fields was one of a small number of long-established mining finance companies with a registered share capital in London, but with mining interests around the world and mostly in countries coloured red in turn of the century atlases. RTZ was another prime example of the tentacles of early City influence in many parts of the world. As the Minorco bid involved a UK-registered company, it was referred to the Monopolies Commission, where it was duly cleared, but ran into the ground in the courts in the United States, whereupon Hanson Trust won the day.

Another bid was also working its way through the Monopolies Commission. Three years earlier, in December 1985, GEC bid £1,180m, at 163p, for Plessey, only for it to be ruled against by the Monopolies Commission. In November 1988, GEC joined forces with the German company Siemens to make a joint £1,700m bid at 225p. This bid was also referred, but was later cleared by the Monopolies Commission and an increased bid of 270p, or £2,000m, was successful in September 1989. However, there was a twist to this affair. Ever a feisty company under the influence of the Clark family, Plessey responded to the first bid from GEC and Siemens by working with Lazards to put together a consortium to make a reverse £7,000m bid for GEC. In the event, these much-publicised plans came to nought and Plessey was duly dismembered.

Two major consortium bids were put together in 1989. One for the supermarket chain Gateway was successfully won, but ultimately proved disastrous for its new shareholders, while the other bid for BAT Industries was unsuccessful but stung the company into action.

On 18 April 1989, a newly formed company, Isosceles, made a £1,730m bid for Gateway, at 195p against an overnight price of 184p. It was a leveraged bid involving layers of borrowings and an intention to recover some of the cost by breaking up and selling off parts of the business – including 62 superstores to Asda for an agreed £705m – but retaining the core of 730 supermarkets collected together by Alec Monk under its former name of Dee Corporation. Barker & Dobson had attempted a similar manoeuvre in December 1987, but, on this occasion, a stronger consortium was led by S. G. Warburg. On 30 May, Isosceles raised its bid to 210p, or £1,870m, only to be trumped by an agreed bid of 225p, or £2,000m, from Wall Street – the home of leveraged bids. Wasserstein Perella – a boutique investment bank newly formed by two leading Wall Street corporate financiers – joined forces with the Great Atlantic & Pacific Tea Company to make the bid.

Gateway was now doomed – a victim of two investment banks fighting for fees and reputation in equal measure. On 22 June, Isosceles raised its bid to 230p, followed on the same day by a bid of 237p from Wasserstein Perella. Both bids were in cash, but Isosceles now played a winning card by having as an alternative to its cash bid of 230p an offer of 215p in cash plus a small equity stake in the consortium, (or 'equity stub' as it became known), valued at arms' length by Salomon Brothers at 30–35p. Wasserstein Perella responded with a third bid at 242p, or £2,150m, on 30 June, but Salomon helpfully made a 'grey' market in the equity stub at 26–31p and, on 13 July, Isosceles claimed victory with 50.9% acceptances, compared with 34% held by Wasserstein Perella. It was to prove to be a Pyrrhic victory when the consortium company later foundered in the recession and became a costly venture for investors and lenders alike.

As this rather esoteric City battle for Gateway was concluding, a far more dramatic bid unfolded. Gateway was largely fought over in the City pages, but the £13,000m bid for BAT Industries on 11 July 1989 was headline news on the front pages. A newly formed consortium – Hoylake – announced its intention to make a bid of 850p per share, compared with a market price of 694p, prompting a rise in the shares of 206p to 900p. It was headline news for two reasons. First, it was, by a long measure, the largest bid ever made in the London stock market, and the second largest worldwide after the $24,700m bid for RJR Nabisco. Second, the consortium was led by Sir James Goldsmith, Kerry Packer and Jacob Rothschild – a trio respected in the City for their financial acumen but equally well known as international celebrities. The name Hoylake cultivated the image of fashionable golf clubs as it followed an intervention only a few weeks earlier when the same three set up another consortium – Sunningdale Holdings – to purchase a 29.9% stake in Rank Hovis McDougall.

Patrick Sheehy, Chairman of BAT Industries, immediately joined battle and, on the same day, contemptuously dismissed the bid as 'an ill-conceived attempt at destructive financial engineering designed to remove value from BAT shareholders to the benefit of an *ad hoc*, troupe of financiers', but he quickly realised that, behind the celebrity froth, there was the deadly earnest of a consortium controlled by Sir James Goldsmith. Few people have ever expressed cold financial logic in such chilling tones as Goldsmith, and his image of merely acting as a catalyst to help subsidiary businesses free themselves from the stranglehold of a cumbersome conglomerate parent was very powerful.

The bid was formally made on 8 August at 874p, or £13,500m, in secured and subordinated notes and an equity stake in Anglo – the Goldsmith vehicle created for the bid. The intention was to break up an ill-assorted conglomerate, and the first step was to announce an agreement to sell the US insurance subsidiary Farmers to the French insurer Axa Midi for $4,500m or £3,000m. Hoylake was now to discover that once it had strayed into the regulatory quagmire of the US insurance industry, it would lose control of events. The bid was allowed to lapse for 12 months and Patrick Sheehy immediately seized back the initiative by moving to demerge two subsidiaries – papermaker Wiggins Teape and retailer Argos. Shares in the two new quoted companies would be distributed to BAT shareholders, who were also promised a significantly higher dividend.

Hoylake reiterated its intention to bid, but, in the light of adverse decisions in the US courts, the idea was eventually abandoned in April 1990. By this time, BAT had demerged Argos into a £600m company, published details of a £1,200m demerger of Wiggins Teape Appleton, and sold US store chains Marshall Field and Saks Fifth Avenue for £1,500m. These measures had little effect on the share price, but Hoylake was able to withdraw and claim it had won the 'intellectual battle'.

A record year for bids concluded in November 1989 when US motor manufacturer Ford made an agreed bid for Jaguar of 850p or £1,600m. The shares had been offered for sale by the Government in August 1984 at 165p and original subscribers had multiplied their capital 5 times. Following the example of Britoil when taken over by BP, the Government relinquished the protection of its golden share to allow the bid to proceed.

A feature of all these issues and bids is the financial ingenuity displayed by the City and the precedents being set in the form of leveraged buy-outs and management buy-outs or buy-ins, where existing shareholders are bought by the existing management or by new incoming management. Two of the largest have already been described – the £705m buy-out of MFI on the eve of the crash in October 1987 and the £447m buy-in of Harris Queensway by James Gulliver in July 1988. The principles involved came under more scrutiny in January 1989, when Tom Duxbury, Chairman of DIY group Magnet, announced plans for a management buy-out. He believed the company was undervalued and vulnerable to a bid with the shares standing at 205p, although they had recovered to 289p when he indicated a buy-out in the range of 290p to 315p in March.

Opposition to this bid was articulated by Sun Alliance in a statement on 1

June that Magnet was the 'thin end of a wedge', denying shareholders the 'opportunity to invest in sound well-managed companies over the longer term'. There were some genuine conflicts of interest. The management team controls its own information and is even able to fine-tune profits to its advantage, external bidders are discouraged from competing by a fear of lack of cooperation from a frustrated management, and, most critical of all, management is unlikely to fight quite so vigorously on behalf of its shareholders to extract that last penny of value in the price normally demanded from a bidder for control.

In fact, the £630m buy-out was concluded in July, but, ironically, proved to be a financial disaster. Within 3 months, base rates had risen to 15%, raising the cost of servicing the £560m debt mountain used to finance the bid, while at the same time, dampening customer demand in areas of discretionary spending, such as DIY. By December, the financing had been restructured, the management share of the equity scaled down to a nominal amount and Duxbury had resigned. Perhaps the market had been right after all to push the shares down to 205p in January. The same pressures of high interest rates and falling demand forced Harris Queensway and Gateway along the same path of repeated restructuring.

Buy-outs and buy-ins are highly leveraged transactions, enabling existing or incoming management to obtain a significant percentage of the equity of a company at a modest cost by persuading banks and institutions to provide layers of debt financing. There have been many genuine examples over the years of entrepreneurs buying cheaply, or being invited to buy cheaply, into a struggling company to transform its fortunes. Others have bought into the capital of a more or less defunct, or 'shell', company to use it as a vehicle for bringing privately owned businesses to the market. In the 1960s and 1970s spotting the purchase by entrepreneurs of stakes in shell companies was a rewarding policy.

The prospects of an insider transforming the business of a moribund company usually attracted strong shareholder support, but the buy-outs of the late 1980s were rather different. The entrepreneurs mounting these bids had no equity or cash of their own to offer, but could only gain control of their target by making a cash bid. The cash had to be borrowed and the precedent was set in Wall Street with the 'leveraged' bid formed largely of what became known as 'junk bonds'. The consequence was to create a new company with layers of debt capital sitting ahead of a tiny equity.

Financial engineering of this kind created a balance sheet with a gearing bordering on the reckless, although many of the bids from outsiders included the stated intention to dispose of subsidiaries for cash to repay debt. Nevertheless, the new capital structure exposed target companies, which were often very large, to risk and reward on a grand scale. In a very simplified example if profits are divided 90% to the owners of debt and 10% to the equity, it follows that a 10% fall in profits will wipe out the equity, but a 10% rise will double it. If profits double over the longer term, the equity would multiply 11 times.

Two factors are immediately apparent. First, the timing of the bid is crucial, with the examples described above in the retail sector all failing spectacularly because each was mounted at a bad time in the economic cycle. Second, it is self-evident that the rewards are dramatically greater than the risks.

When a quoted company is being bought out by its management, at least the shareholders have a choice whether or not to accept the bid and concede future growth to new owners. The potential for conflict of interest is much greater when the buy-out is by the management of an existing division or subsidiary of a quoted company. If the prospects are good enough to justify the risks of setting up a ludicrously geared company, should those prospects be realised for the current owners of the business or be seized for the personal benefit of its management?

An early startling example was the purchase led by Paul Judge in May 1986 of Premier Brands – the food and beverage division of Cadbury, for £97m, of which £96.7m was debt. When the company was sold in April 1989 for £220m, it had increased in value by around 65% after allowing for movement in the All Share Index, but the management's tiny equity of £330,000 multiplied itself some 500 times, and Judge's personal stake was believed to be worth £45m.

Management buy-outs of this kind usually include a stated intention to seek a stock market quotation within two or three years, but sometimes success is achieved so quickly that the new business is sold to another company with a speed that contradicts the image often cultivated of a suppressed subsidiary desperate to stand on its own feet. This happened with the buy-outs of UK Paper from Bowater and Reedpack from Reed International. The returns generated by the management of Premier were exceptional, but there were many that matched the multiplication of 34 times of the management stake in Reedpack when it was sold to a Scandinavian company for a price some 40% higher, after allowing for a favourable stock market.

Another example of remarkable gearing was Hays plc – a business services group that came to the market in October 1989. The company was the subject of a buy-out from the Kuwait Investment Office at a difficult time in October 1987, and it returned at an equally difficult time in October 1989, just after base rates were increased to 15%. The capital was so highly geared, that the financing of a £255m buy-out was achieved with an equity of only £1.5m, a third subscribed by the directors. If the eventual prospectus for the offer for sale is to be believed, there was little business risk because the company had shown 'significant growth over the last five years', three of which pre-dated the management buy-out, and 'had been highly cash generative'. When the company came to the market two years later, the equity was valued at £393m. In this example, there was no stock market conflict of interest because Hays was bought from a private owner.

Concern about some remarkable changes in fortune after management buy-outs raised the question of whether or not shareholders need protection from possible conflicts of interest when the sale involves the subsidiary of their quoted company. In December 1989, the Takeover Panel tightened the rules by requiring that any bidder competing with the management should have access to any information given to an external provider of finance, and independent directors should receive the same details.

The contrast between success and failure in these buy-outs and buy-ins could hardly have been greater, but while they were happening they joined with the wider bid fever to drive prices higher in 1989. Cash takeover bids were regularly adding to the coffers of the pension funds and life assurance companies, the cash flow into which remained as buoyant as ever at an annual rate of around £30bn, and well able to finance the continuing privatisation programme. Furthermore, there was no pressure to fund Government borrowing, because this was the phase, in 1987/88 and 1988/89, when the Chancellor was repaying debt.

There was a sharp reminder in October that when Wall Street sneezes, the rest of the world catches a cold. The United States was running both high Government and high trade deficits and a severe bout of nerves drove the Dow Jones Index down by 7% on Friday 13 October. With too much time to reflect on this over the weekend, the London market opened with a 9% fall in the FTSE 100, before it recovered to close more than 3% down, while the All Share Index fell by 4.1%. In other volatile markets, the FAZ Index in Germany fell by 13% and dealings in France were suspended. With base rates at 15% the stock market remained fragile in London, and, by the end of the month, the All Share Index stood at 1,052.55 – down by 14 % in 7 weeks.

It then recovered as rapidly as it had fallen, encouraged by the belief that the next move in interest rates would be down, and attracted by reasonable value, with average PE ratios of around 12. The All Share Index recovered and, on 3 January 1990, this particular bull market peaked at 1,226.83. As the year ended, foreign forays into the City had seen Deutsche Bank buy Morgan Grenfell for £950m and Australian Mutual Provident buy Pearl Assurance for £1,240m.

The peaking of the market and the onset of recession brought the 1986–89 takeover cycle to a close, just as the previous 1968–72 cycle closed when the stock market went into serious decline. The total value of successful bids for UK quoted companies into and out of the cycle, based on data published by *Acquisitions Monthly*, is as shown in Table 31.4.

So ended a brilliant decade for the stock market. In precisely 10 years, the All Share Index rose by more than 5 times at a compound annual rate of 18% from 229.79 to 1,204.70 – comfortably exceeding the 95%, or 7% annual increase in inflation. Some of the leading shares produced astonishing performances. Glaxo and Hanson Trust – the fifth and sixth largest companies in the market – multiplied more than 28 and 22 times respectively, and BTR and J. Sainsbury rose more than 14 times.

Table 31.4
Value of acquisitions of
quoted UK companies, 1983–91

Year	Value (£m)
1983	2,343
1984	5,474
1985	6,398
1986	16,550
1987	13,895
1988	19,076
1989	28,372
1990	10,664
1991	6,241

Over the decade, the dividends of companies in the All Share Index increased 3.23 times, or 12½% annually, and the earnings of the FT 500 Industrial Index increased 2.78 times. The yield basis of the All Share Index fell over the decade from 6.87% to 4.24%, adding a further 62% to the rise in the market over and above the growth in dividends. This was a formidable combination of growth and rerating that saw the All Share Index rise 5.2 times, comfortably outperforming, in local terms, the 3.1 times increase in the Dow Jones Index, and only just lagging behind the 5.9 times increase in the Nikkei Index in Tokyo. Even with a 28% sterling depreciation against the dollar, the capital performance exceeds New York, before even taking into account a much higher dividend yield. However, the 57% depreciation against the yen puts the return from Japanese equities in a different light. Ironically, the total return from UK equities proved to have been better than from those overseas equities so avidly sought by the institutions in 1979 after the abolition of exchange controls.

The decade ended with major equity markets worldwide at all-time highs, including the US, Japan and Germany as well as the UK. Most poignant of all was the all-time high of the Nikkei Index in Tokyo of 38,915.87 recorded on 29 December 1989 – the last business day of the decade. It was as if Japan were celebrating the closing of a wondrous decade when, perhaps more so than at any other time in any major market, investors seemed really to believe trees grew to the sky. Leading companies in industries common to all economies were valued at £50bn on PE ratios of 80 in Japan, compared with £10bn and 16 elsewhere.

The decade ended with the FT World indices showing the market value of Japanese stocks at $3,150bn, or 41.5% of the total, and well ahead of the United States at $2,355bn, or 31%. Britain stood in third place in the table at $666bn, or 8.8%. The United States recovered its leadership in 1991, and has since surged ahead to $9,075bn in March 1998, when Britain at $1,930bn moved into second place ahead of Japan at $1,900bn.

That year end high in Tokyo still stands – now more an accusing finger than shining beacon. In New York, it took the Dow Jones Index 25 years to scale its 1929 high. What price Tokyo?

Chapter 32

GULF WAR NERVES
January 1990–September 1990

All Share Index	3 January 1990	1,226.83	
	24 September 1990	962.09	Down 21.6%

No sooner had the market reached a new high in the first week of January than confidence rapidly evaporated. Consensus forecasts for growth of the economy suggested a further slowing down from 5% in 1988 and 2.2% in 1989 to an estimate of 1.4% in 1990. Fears of inflation returned to haunt investors when Ford workers rejected an offer of 10% in 1990, followed by 8% in 1991.

Signs of serious corporate strain emerged from previously glamorous sources. Coloroll – a wallcoverings and home products empire built aggressively in the 1980s by John Ashcroft – was found to be wallowing in debt with customers in retreat. In January, a warning about profits and financing problems caused the shares to halve in price, and a company valued at £300m at its peak was on the path to bankruptcy within 6 months. In February, a leading property developer; Rosehaugh – led by the widely regarded Godfrey Bradman – suddenly announced a rights issue of crisis proportions to raise £125m. Rosehaugh – trapped by high interest rates and falling rentals from Big Bang retrenchment – was also on the path from a market capitalisation of £750m to eventual bankruptcy, but the legacy of its visionary development of the Broadgate complex around Liverpool Street station remains for all to see.

The reporting season of the clearing banks revealed the scale of their continuing problems with Third World debt. Lloyds Bank reported a loss of £715m, caused by writing down the amount of loans outstanding by £1,750m, followed by Barclays adding, a further £1,000m to debt provisions, taking their total to £4,600m. Meanwhile, in Tokyo, the Nikkei Index was in free fall – down 28% in 3 months to 28,002.70 in the first week of April.

This series of gloomy headlines led to a 10% fall in the market in the first 2 months of the year, and a further 5% fall in April. The political and economic background was especially bleak for the Conservative Government. The Chancellor – Nigel Lawson – had resigned after a messy and damaging disagreement with the Prime Minister in October. Labour held opinion poll leads of around 25%, the poll tax was deeply unpopular and house prices were stalling for the first time in a decade. Inflation was heading for double figures, trade deficits persisted and, in a mildly deflationary first Budget on 20 March, the new Chancellor – John Major – forecast growth of only 1% in 1990.

However, the Chancellor encouraged investors by raising the PEP allowance from £4,800 to £6,000, of which 50% could be in unit trusts or investment trusts; by introducing a new savings scheme, TESSA, in which tax-free interest was available on a £9,000 deposit held for 5 years; and by promising to abolish the remaining ½% stamp duty on share transactions when the Stock Exchange's new paperless settlement system, Taurus, went live. Unfortunately, Taurus sank under its own weight to die an early death and this concession never materialised.

Having settled at lower levels, the market took comfort on 17 May from indications that the Government was about to negotiate entry into the Exchange Rate Mechanism (ERM) in the summer, and, on the same day, from the first rise in unemployment in three and a half years, as an indication that the economy was slowing down. The gilt market was particularly strong on implications for the convergence of interest rates at lower levels, putting 3 points on many stocks, and the FTSE 100 rose by almost 3% on the day.

Meanwhile, the list of casualties lengthened. In the first week of June, Coloroll and British & Commonwealth were finally brought down by liabilities well in excess of assets, prompting Lex on 8 June to remind readers of the eternal truth that, when times get difficult, 'assets prove unreliable but liabilities remain unchanged'. They were £400m in the case of Coloroll, and £550m for British & Commonwealth's subsidiary, Atlantic Computers – an acquisition apparently earning healthy profits when acquired two years earlier. British & Commonwealth had been a market leader in the financial sector in 1987, when the shares stood at 565p and capitalised at £1,850m. Dealings had been suspended at 53p earlier in the year in the vain hope of rescue, but Atlantic Computers proved to have been a transaction too far for the restless energies of John Gunn.

A consequence of Big Bang had been to heighten the ambitions of the corporate financiers, who found the perfect outlet for their creative ingenuities in the aggressive corporate ambitions of many chief executives at a time when management fashion was changing. From the 1960s to the late 1980s, the theory of diversification had strongly influenced management thinking and conglomerate empires such as Grand Metropolitan, Hanson Trust and BTR were fashionable leaders in the stock market, while other companies added numerous subsidiaries in vaguely related businesses. Helping to drive this forward in Britain was a punitive and inflexible tax system that made it difficult for companies to hand surplus cash back to their shareholders or float off subsidiaries by distributing shares, and, moreover it positively encouraged companies with large overseas earnings to make acquisitions in Britain to cover the payment of advance corporation tax. These factors directly led Imperial Tobacco and British-American Tobacco to pursue all sorts of contortions to diversify.

In the 1980s, management thinking turned to 'focus' and the identification of 'core' businesses. It was a rebound from the ineffectiveness of diversification and a tendency for the stock market to lower the value of companies lacking a clear identity or, even worse, value diversified companies on the rating of their less glamorous subsidiaries. It became the practice for incoming chief executives to divest their companies of poorly performing or fringe subsidiaries to 'focus' on certain 'core' businesses as the source of future growth. As good an example as any was the ruthlessness with which Ernest Saunders disposed of dozens of peripheral companies when he became Chief Executive of Guinness in 1981.

The Hoylake bid for BAT Industries was an example of the same theme, and it prompted the demerging of Argos and Wiggins Teape in 1990. However, a purer example of demerging was the decision of Christopher Hogg to split Courtaulds in two. There was no particular threat of takeover – and his decision was based on the practical grounds that two different businesses would be better managed independently without a superfluous head office. Furthermore, there was no need to make shareholders pay for something they already owned and, in February 1990, shares in Courtaulds Textiles were distributed free to share-holders in Courtaulds on the basis of one share for four. The chemicals, fibres and coating businesses were now much more dominant than the traditional tex-tiles and, after separation, the businesses were valued at £1,300m and £250m respectively.

It was on equally practical grounds that, in April 1990, the British Coal Board Pension Fund turned predator for the third time in the investment trust market. British Coal – one of the largest of all pension funds, with assets of more than £12bn – had previously acquired British Investment Trust in 1977 for £106m and Industrial & General Trust in 1988 for £560m. It used investment trusts as a vehicle for investing in equities, having cash flows, it claimed, that were too large for the day-to-day stock market. Some troubling conflicts of interest have already been discussed – in particular, the propriety of a monolithic and publicly unaccountable pension fund taking out a decently performing investment trust created for the small, private investor.

This argument surfaced with some force on 21 April when the British Coal Pension Fund bid £1,030m for Globe Investment Trust – the largest in the sector with 40,000 shareholders. The Chairman of the Trust, David Hardy, protested that 'it would be distressing if the premier investment trust for private share-holders should disappear into a nationalised industry pension fund'. The bid price was 191p in cash against a market price of 174p – a trifling 10% premium from the point of view of the long-standing private shareholder about to be pre-sented with a capital gains tax problem. In the event, this successful bid was raised in June to 205p, but only in line with an upward move in the All Share Index.

It may have been a fruitful year for corporate financiers, but the stock market had been no more than treading water by the time of the summer holiday season. Suddenly, there came a rude awakening. In the early hours of 2 August 1990, Iraq invaded Kuwait and seized control. The market had chosen to ignore Iraq's angry confrontation with its oil-producing neighbours in mediation talks that collapsed in the preceding few days, and rumours of troop movements. The invasion occurred with the same suddenness with which Colonel Nasser had nationalised the Suez Canal on 26 July 1956 and Israel invaded Egypt on 6 October 1973.

The intervention in 1956 led to falls in oil shares, but barely a change in markets overall for many weeks. This invasion had the opposite effect, as oil shares rose, but stock markets around the world reacted badly. In 1956, BP shares fell 5% on the day because of threats to shipping deliveries, whereas in 1990 they rose by 5% on the day because of threats to production leading to higher oil prices.

The overnight reaction to the invasion was a fall of around 1½% in all major equity markets, followed by free fall in August and September. There were genuine fears that Saddam Hussein might invade Saudi Arabia and the smaller Gulf States with frightening consequences for oil supplies. There were fears of a serious turndown in global economic activity, with the prospect of sharply higher oil prices bringing back memories of the inflationary consequences of the doubling of oil prices in 1973. Within 3 weeks, the price of North Sea Brent oil had moved steadily up from $20.5 a barrel to $32 a barrel as the probability of further conflict became apparent. Each time the threat of hostilities escalated, markets fell another 2.3%.

By 24 August, markets worldwide were in disarray. The FT Actuaries World Index had fallen by 17½% in 3 weeks, led by falls of 23% and 19% in Japan and Germany – the developed countries most vulnerable to higher oil prices. With the exception of oil-rich Norway, every market in Europe now stood at its low for the year. In London and New York, the All Share Index had fallen by 12% and the Dow Jones by 14%. After a modest recovery, shares began to fall away again in September.

Gold used to be the best refuge in times of international crisis. On this occasion, the price briefly flickered into life, rising from $373 an ounce to $404 in the first 2 weeks of the invasion, but it quickly fell back to its desultory ways. The global battle against the inflation of the 1970s had long since been won and gold has floundered ever since.

There was a strong international will to restore the independence of Kuwait, either by force or negotiation, and share prices fluctuated accordingly in the closing months of 1990. At different moments in September and October, the price of North Sea Brent oil reached $40 a barrel, but, on a later day in October, it fell below $27. Modern stock markets are overloaded with information and forecasts, but, unable on this occasion to assess the outcome, they were confused. And none more so than in oil-dependent Japan when, on 2 October 1990 sudden hopes of a negotiated settlement in Kuwait prompted a 13.2% rise in a single day in the Nikkei Index, from 20,221.86 to 22,898.41.

With hindsight, the low point in the All Share Index proved to be 962.09 on 24 September, but uncertainty continued well beyond that date and, from time to time, other events pushed Kuwait out of the headlines. One in particular was the demise of Polly Peck, the brief corporate history of which encapsulates so much of the fascination of the stock market, but also remains a permanent thorn in the side of theorists about efficient markets.

Polly Peck first came to notice in the annual table of leaders and laggards in 1980. In February, Asil Nadir took control of this tiny textile company at 7p a share and, by the end of the year, the shares had risen to 145p. In February 1983, they reached £35, fuelled by growth and some apparently astonishing profit margins in a business now centred on citrus fruits and cardboard packaging in Cyprus. Within a year, a lack of credibility and a brief suspension had driven the shares down to £10, but, after being split to the equivalent of 50p, the shares gradually returned to favour. The company gained particular respectability with the acquisition of the Del Monte fresh food business in 1989 for £557m.

On 7 June 1990, the shares reached 462p, when the company was firmly established in the FTSE Index with a market capitalisation of £1,850m. It is difficult to understand how it could happen that only 15 weeks later the shares would be worthless. Dealings in the shares were suspended on 20 September at 108p and the company put into administration on 24 October. The collapse began on 12 August when Asil Nadir, surprisingly, and with apparently little consultation, indicated that he may personally bid for the company in which he owned or controlled 26% of the shares, but, within a week, he compounded the mystery by dropping the plan and, on 17 August, the shares fell by 78p to 324p.

A Stock Exchange investigation criticised his behaviour as 'premature and imprudent' and, amid mounting concerns, the shares drifted lower before suddenly collapsing on 20 September from 243p to 108p, then being suspended. It later transpired that some 10m of his personal shares were sold on that day by banks holding them as collateral. Asil Nadir admitted that the company faced a liquidity crisis over £100m of uncommitted loans that are rolled over solely at the discretion of the banks, and he was unable to find alternative financing. A near £2,000m bubble had burst in a matter of weeks. On 16 December, he faced 18 charges of theft and false accounting.

Collapses of this kind usually have in common accounting weaknesses that are obscured by growth and explained away by the personal charm of the incumbent. In simple terms, as long as revenues keep rising, the accounting problem remains hidden, and this charade can last for many years until the growth stops.

Vehicle and General Insurance was an example of this in the early 1970s when its collapse left one motorist in ten uninsured. Doubting shareholders are always put at their ease with soothing words, and Asil Nadir was a man of charm and culture.

One weakness in the Polly Peck accounts concerned the charge to the balance sheet of exchange losses on currency. Polly Peck declared high earnings in the profit and loss account and a high level of retained profits after payment of the dividend. For example, in its last 4 financial years, it reported a total of £292.4m of retained profits after payment of dividends, but in notes to the accounts a total of £356.6m was charged against these retained profits for 'exchange variances'. Another weakness shrugged off at the time was the increase in borrowings revealed in the accounts to December 1989 from £486m to £1,104m. Polly Peck was the sort of share that has enthusiastic supporters or hostile sceptics, with little in between. The enthusiasts usually enjoy a longer ride than the sceptics believe possible, but they eventually lose the race.

The combination of high interest rates and an economy turning into recession can be fatal for companies with stretched balance sheets, and this was the situation in the third quarter of 1990, when base rates were 15%. After the collapse of Polly Peck, it was the turn of others. The shares in advertising agency WPP reached 715p at their peak in 1990, but, in a series of collapses in the last few months of the year, they fell to 50p on fears that its ability to service the mountain of debt incurred in acquisitions would be threatened by the recession in advertising. The share prices of other companies collapsed during the same period. Leading advertisers Saatchi & Saatchi suffered alongside WPP, as did Rupert Murdoch's media empire, News Corporation, but they both survived. Rosehaugh – the property developer led by Godfrey Bradman – eventually failed, and Maxwell Communication Corporation fell victim to the notorious activities of Robert Maxwell. The lesson to be drawn from this fraught period in the stock market is to beware over-borrowed companies.

Sudden unforeseen change is a constant feature of the stock market and this chapter closes with as sudden a change as any. The annual Conservative Party conference had been the backcloth to the momentous announcement at 4 pm on Friday 5 October that Britain was to enter the European Exchange Rate Mechanism. The market responded enthusiastically by turning a 30-point fall in the FTSE Index into a 73.5-point rise by the close, and opened on the Monday morning up another 134.7 points. At that time, Margaret Thatcher was visibly joined on the world stage with President Bush in leadership against the invasion of Kuwait.

However, there was unrest in the Conservative party and a strong lead for Labour in the opinion polls. The Government's unpopularity was evidenced by the result of the Eastbourne by-election on 18 October, when a 17,000 majority was turned into Liberal Democrat majority of 4,500. Nevertheless, few were prepared for the shock of the resignation from the cabinet of Sir Geoffrey Howe, the Deputy Prime Minister, on 1 November, and the damning sentence in his resignation letter, 'I do not believe I can any longer serve with honour as a member of your government'.

This was followed by his devastating resignation speech in the House of Commons on 13 November. His complaint that Margaret Thatcher's attitude to Economic and Monetary Union was 'running increasingly serious risks for the future of our nation' now sounds melodramatic, but his call that 'the time has come for others to consider their own response to the tragic conflicts of loyalty with which I myself have wrestled for perhaps too long', if oddly reminiscent of the Duke of Windsor's abdication speech, was decisive. Margaret Thatcher stood down on 22 November 1990 and resigned six days later.

In the space of three weeks, the Prime Minister was overthrown with no more reference to the electorate than would happen in the crudest *coup d'état* in a distant land. The newspapers produced glowing tributes, as numbing to read as an unexpected obituary. The *Financial Times* on 23 November described her as the 'most remarkable peace-time prime minister since Gladstone'. And the stock market during those three weeks? Glad to see an end to uncertainty, it went up by 5%. As always, it took things exactly as it found them. In a variation on a theme, 'Thatcher has fallen. Long live Thatcherism'.

Chapter 33

REVIEW AND UPDATE
1979–98

For the stock market, the Thatcher years began with a setback and ended on a dull note ahead of the Gulf War, but embedded within them was the most powerful and sustained bull market of the post-war era. It lasted for 7½ years, from 15 November 1979 to 16 July 1987, and multiplied the All Share Index more than 5½ times, from 219.85 to a peak of 1,238.57 – a compound annual growth rate of 25%. As a result of the global crash in October 1987 and the Gulf War in 1991, this peak would remain in place for four years, until exceeded on 29 July 1991.

Margaret Thatcher came into office precisely at the top of a cycle and departed when the economy was well into a cyclical downturn, with sentiment further unsettled by preparations for the Gulf War. Table 33.1 shows a capital return in real terms to investors of 54.8% over her period of office. However the pattern she established continued through the six and a half years of John Major's premiership, and a fairer picture of 'Thatcherism' is conveyed by an overall return of 166.7% over eighteen years to 1 May 1997.

Table 33.1
The All Share Index and inflation, 1979–97

Date	All Share Index	Change (base 100)	Inflation (base 100)	% real return
Thatcher's periods of office				
3 May 1979	280.28	100.0	100.0	
27 Nov 1990	1,038.59	370.6	239.4	54.8
Major's period of office				
27 Nov 1990	1,038.59	100.0	100.0	
1 May 1997	2,138.89	205.9	119.5	72.3
Overall				
3 May 1979	280.28	100.0	100.0	
1 May 1997	2,138.89	763.1	286.1	166.7

The real return of 166.7% over the 18 years from 1979 to 1997 compares with 74.8% over the 13 years from 1951 and 1964.

Just as Clement Attlee led a radical Government that set the political agenda for the next three decades, so also did Margaret Thatcher lead a radical Government that has set a new political agenda for Britain. Attlee's path was paved with good intentions along a journey whose recounting is often coloured by the romantic glow of history. Thatcher drove the country along a forced route march and its memory is so recent that, for many people, a legacy of personal bitterness remains to this day. A Labour minister recently described in graphic terms how in 1979 she took over the great ship of State set on its course by Attlee, threw most of the crew and some of her colleagues overboard, and set the ship on a new course in a direction apparently embraced today by 'New' Labour.

The challenging question is whether or not the Blair Government, by broadly adopting this agenda, has brought to an end the alternating political conflicts that have characterised the chapters of this post-war history. The stock market showed no foreboding about the return of a Labour Government, either during the many months preceding the election when a Labour victory was probable or since the result on 1 May 1997. The All Share Index moved resolutely forward by 35% from 2,138.89 on 1 May 1997 to a peak of 2,885.17 on 20 July 1998, and the FTSE 100 by 39% from 4,445.0 to 6,179.0.

The stock market takes things as it finds them, and its message through to July 1998 has been that the economy is strong and there is little difference between Labour and Conservatives, just as Wall Street accepts Democrats and Republicans alike. Since May 1997, UK equities have benefited from lower long-term interest rates and rising stock markets worldwide, but their prosperity over the long term will depend on the growth of profits, earnings and dividends. Interference in that growth from a combination of politics and economics has been a regular feature of previous Labour governments.

Margaret Thatcher introduced remarkable changes for both the securities markets and the economy. For investors, she lowered taxation on dividends from a maximum of 98% to 40%, on earnings from 83% to 40% and on corporations from 52% to 35%. She abolished exchange and dividend controls, encouraged the pursuit of profit, created millions of new shareholders and introduced tax-free PEPs. Above all, she has deregulated the Stock Exchange, thus creating an environment in which the skills of the City have flourished to give London the leadership of the European leg of the global financial market.

For the economy, she defeated inflation, reduced the powers of the trade unions, reduced the scale of government borrowing, ruthlessly forced industry to become competitive, achieved unheard of productivity gains, allowed profit a far higher proportion of the national cake and brought the growth rate of the economy into line with, or even ahead of, comparable countries rather than lagging well behind. Above all, she pioneered privatisation, turning bloated state

industries into industrial leaders and setting an example that has since been followed by countries around the world of every size and political colour.

She displayed particular courage in challenging and breaking apart that lazy
consensus of government, management and trade unions that had complacently
presided over three decades of economic decline. The legacy of those decades had
been gross overmanning, a symbol of failure that the longer it was allowed to
fester, the greater would be the price to cure it. The eventual price was indeed
high – a brutal and scathing recession in 1981, leading to a level of unemployment of over 3m lasting for five years.

The second recession in 1990 was partly self-inflicted after several years of
unparalleled growth. The instinctive reaction to the October 1987 crash had
been to boost the economy with increased Government expenditure and lower
interest rates. Second, Margaret Thatcher had ruthlessly forced industries and
institutions to stand on their own feet by controlling money, sweeping away subsidies and removing Government support, but she contradicted the essence of
this philosophy by showering privileges on homeowners. The result was an
inflation in house prices that distorted the economy in the late 1980s. Borrowers
in the past had become accustomed to being 'crowded out' by Government borrowing, but now they were crowded out by housebuyers at a time when
Government finances were so strong that the national debt was actually reduced
in 1988 and 1989.

Nevertheless, the outcome of this recession was a second purging of costs and
inefficiencies, and out of much pain has emerged an economy as efficient as any
in Europe. The release of management energy and talent has led to a new generation of businesspeople and entrepreneurs whose formative years were spent
under the influence of Margaret Thatcher.

This transformation of the state of the British economy has been the proud
legacy of Thatcherism, but that native uncertainty about capitalism described in
the Introduction still prevails in many quarters. Will Hutton has condemned the
Thatcher years and pinned on them the label of 'The State We're In' in his book
of the same name (Jonathan Cape, 1995). Any examination of the politics and
economics of the 1970s must surely conclude that today is far better than 'The
State We Were In', and without the Thatcher reforms, the state we would be in
today hardly bears thinking about.

It is for these reasons that the London stock market forged ahead through two
recessions and over 18 Conservative years. Companies were encouraged to build
profits. Shareholders enjoyed sustained earnings and dividend growth. These
years were, without question, the most exciting period of any since the war for
the financial and corporate sectors. However, they have also spawned pockets of
personal wealth in proportions once chronicled in the novels of Galsworthy
and Trollope and financial scandals on an ever greater scale. These are the
prices of capitalism that its extreme critics have never been willing to pay.

The measurement of 'profits' in the economy and an illustration of trends is difficult because there are different definitions and a lack of continuity – the latter distorted by the emergence of many large and profitable privatised industries – but, whatever test is used, profits during the years of Thatcherism have expanded significantly as a percentage of GDP. Datastream figures show that, through most of the 1950s and 1960s the ratio of industrial and commercial profits as a percentage of GDP was typically around 14%, dropping to its post-war low of 8–9% in the recession of the mid-1970s. For several years in the mid-1980s the ratio expanded to 17–19%, and above 20% when the public corporations are included. It fell to around 14% in the 1991 recession, but has since recovered close to 20% in the mid-1990s.

However, a specifically quantifiable measure has been dividend growth in the All Share Index (see Table 33.2).

Table 33.2
Dividend growth in the All Share Index, 1979–97

Date	All Share Index	Gross yield	Gross dividend	Income tax	Net dividend
3 May 1979	280.28	5.27	14.77	33	9.90
9 June 1983	442.80	4.70 (est)	20.90 (est)	30	14.63
11 June 1987	1,119.63	3.11	34.82	27	25.42
27 November 1990	1,038.59	5.12	53.18	25	39.89
1 May 1997	2,138.89	3.58	76.57	23	58.96
3 May 1979 (rebased)	100.0		100.0		100.0
27 November 1990	370.6		360.1		402.9
1 May 1997	763.1		518.4		595.6
Annual compound growth rate %					
1979–90	12.0		12.0		13.0
1979–97	12.0		9.5		10.5

Dividends are declared net of tax and grossed up at the standard rate of income tax to calculate the yield. The reduction in the standard rate from 33% to 23% from 1979 to 1997 caused dividends expressed at the gross level to grow at a slower rate than the underlying net dividends. The slowing of growth from 1990 was caused by the recession in the early 1990s, but whichever period is used, the growth rate of 10–12% has run well ahead of inflation of 6%.

It is not possible to analyse earnings growth in the same way because, until its reconstruction in 1994, the broadest earnings indicator in the All Share Index was the Industrial 500 Index, which excluded the financial sector. Over the Thatcher period, the underlying earnings indicator on the 500 Index rose from the equivalent of 100 in May 1979 to 470 in November 1990. However, at the pre-tax level, profits during those years grew more slowly by the equivalent of 100 to 348 because the rate of corporation tax fell from 52% to 35%, so flattering the growth of the after-tax figure. The All Share Index has since been reconstituted to provide an earnings figure to include the financial sector, but, as with dividends, growth overall has slowed because of the recession in the early 1990s.

The outcome for the equity investor over both the Thatcher years themselves and the total of 18 years of Conservative governments was a sustained bull market with only the briefest of setbacks. This experience was not shared with gilt-edged investors, although the long downward trend in prices since 1945 was halted and reversed. Remarkably, the price of the benchmark Consols 2½% was 23⅛ on the day Margaret Thatcher entered Downing Street and 23¹¹⁄₁₆ on the day she left, and War Loan was, respectively, 33⅝ and 33⁵⁄₁₆. Since then, the fight against inflation was successful enough for Consols to have reached 32⅛ and War Loan 45⁵⁄₁₆ by 1 May 1997.

Margaret Thatcher unashamedly believed that the wealth and strength of the country was created by the private sector, and she brought about a transformation in the competitiveness and success of business and industry from which customers, employees and shareholders have all benefited. In so doing, she influenced three major changes in the securities industry. These are:

- the stock market quotation of new major companies as a consequence of privatisation and greater dynamism in the economy;
- the liberalisation and deregulation of the securities industry, beginning with the abolition of exchange controls and ending with Big Bang;
- the forthright promotion of the 'Anglo-Saxon' system of capitalism and rejection of the 'stakeholder' system of Continental Europe and Japan.

The events leading to Big Bang and privatisation have already been described in Chapters 27 and 29, but their later influence has continued forward. This final review chapter describes these, and other themes, through to the present day.

Privatisation in the 1980s was the corollary of nationalisation in the 1940s. Nationalisation removed from the stock market some 20% of the debenture, preference and equity sectors, then valued at around £9,500m. Privatisation returned the compliment. The list of major companies either created or handed back to the private sector since 1979 is formidable. Five new subsectors have been created in the FT Actuaries Indices specifically to cover the privatisation issues under the headings of 'Telecommunications', 'Electricity', 'Gas Distribution', 'Water' and 'Transport'. They alone accounted for 13.6% of the All Share Index at 31 December 1997.

Many of the privatised companies are today core investments in institutional portfolios. Equally striking is their contribution to the economy. In 1979, the aggregate deficits of the nationalised industries were equivalent to 3p in income tax. In 1997, their combined profits are producing handsome tax revenues for the Government, in addition to the benefit of substantial price reductions in real terms for gas, electricity and telecommunications for both industrial and individual customers.

The privatised companies were launched on the stock market by the Government, but, quite separately, a number of large, privately owned companies were also floated during the Thatcher years. This phenomenon has continued in the 1990s with the flotation of new companies BSkyB and Orange, the demerging of Vodafone and Zeneca, and the demutualisation of some major building societies and life assurance companies.

The emergence of these new companies has transformed the face of the stock market and the shape of the typical institutional portfolio. Their sheer size and marketability in a thriving market has attracted flows of foreign portfolio investment. At 31 December 1997, 34 of the 100 companies in the FTSE 100 Index were new to the stock market since 1981, including 24 companies with a market capitalisation in excess of £4bn, which were:

- **Privatised**   *(£bn)*
  BT   30.1
  BG Group   12.3
  Cable & Wireless   11.9
  British Aerospace   7.5
  National Power   7.2
  Scottish Power   6.2
  PowerGen   5.3
  British Airways   5.3
  BAA   5.0
  National Grid   4.9
  Railtrack   4.8
  United Utilities   4.2
  Centrica   4.0

- **Floated**
  (Glaxo) Wellcome   50.7
  (Lloyds) TSB   42.2
  Reuters   11.1
  BSkyB   7.8

- **Demutualised**

Halifax	19.2
Abbey National	15.4
Norwich Union	7.7
Woolwich	5.1
Alliance & Leicester	4.7

- **Demerged**

Zeneca	20.2
Vodafone	13.4.

The market value of the remaining 32 companies, excluding Glaxo Wellcome and Lloyds TSB, was £246bn at the end of 1997, compared with a total equity market capitalisation of £1,209bn. Their presence on the stock market reflects the scale of change in a revitalised economy.

A particular aspect of the privatisation process has been that it has introduced popular capitalism to the people. Margaret Thatcher wanted to spread the concept of share ownership more widely by encouraging as many people as possible to become shareholders for the first time in their lives. Every incentive was used in the marketing of each privatisation to encourage the individual to apply for shares, culminating in the creation of 'Sid' – a fictional character that no country other than Britain could ever have invented. To encourage 'Sid', privatised shares were offered on an attractive yield basis to ensure a decent premium, in partly paid form to produce a remarkable yield in the first year and with loyalty bonuses to encourage long-term ownership. Furthermore, the egalitarian spirit was encouraged by limiting individual applications to 100 or 200 shares, combined with serious legal penalties for multiple applications.

The privatisation campaigns were highly successful in attracting public subscription, but they appealed as much to the British nose for a bargain as to any wish to become part of a new generation of shareholders with a portfolio of shares spread across the stock market. Nevertheless, privatisation served its purpose of creating millions of first-time shareholders divided broadly between those who retained their 100 or 200 shares and those who took the money and ran. The number of individuals owning shares rose dramatically in the 1980s from an estimated 3m to 9m, and many collected together for the first time a small portfolio of privatised companies. However, there is no evidence that privatisation created a new culture of individuals owning shares in companies across the stock market.

This is understandable given the absence of accessible advice for the small shareholder and the difficulty of selecting individual shares. It is also reflected by the experience of PEPs where investments were originally confined to shares in individual companies. The movement only gathered pace after investment was allowed in unit trusts – a collective form of investment that has generated wide and genuine interest in the stock market as a whole rather than in individual companies.

Some opponents of privatisation argued that State industries belonged to the people and, as has been seen, Harold Macmillan compared privatisation with selling the family silver. Political opponents accused the Government of giving the shares away to their friends in the City, but this was hardly so because applications were limited either to a small number for individuals or to institutions harnessing the savings of millions of people. An alternative would have been simply to give the shares free to the public, but the ground rules would have been difficult to agree and it would have been an administrative nightmare. Furthermore, the Government was intent on raising revenue.

However, a close analogy to this has since happened with the free issue of shares by building societies and mutual life assurance companies to their depositors and policyholders when turning themselves into quoted companies. Millions of risk-averse depositors in building societies have overnight become individual shareholders, but it remains to be seen whether or not an interest in building a portfolio of shares has changed any more than it did with privatisation.

Investors have often been slow to recognise the value offered by shares in industries new to the stock market, and, in particular, the scope for cost-cutting in the privatised industries was seriously underestimated. It is a pity that the popular image of privatisation has been overshadowed by sniping about excess profits and overpaid directors. The real focus should have been on how privatisation revealed the greater scandal – that, for some 30 years, private and industrial customers alike had been overcharged billions of pounds in real terms today to sustain overmanned and inefficient nationalised industries.

Another factor helping the outperformance of the shares of the large new flotations was the need for institutions to match their holdings in line with the size of the company. 'Index tracking' has become fashionable – particularly for large pension funds having a large 'core' portfolio in line with the index – and this creates a natural demand that is not satisfied in the original allocation of shares in new companies. However, negative factors hanging over the privatised companies included an instinctive caution about investing in companies subject to regulation, and the constant threat from Labour to renationalise on penal terms. A particular example of this adverse effect was the vociferous political campaign waged by Labour against the privatisation of British Rail in 1996. Its effect was to lower the price at which privatisation became possible, particularly of Railtrack and, in so doing, deprive the taxpayer of hundreds of millions of pounds.

The second major consequence of the Thatcher years was the liberalisation and deregulation of the securities industry, spurred on by the abolition of exchange controls in 1979 and culminating in October 1986 with Big Bang. The City has always been an aggregation of separate activities – a tradition stemming from historical times when crafts and trades were rigorously defined by the rules set by individual guilds, their memory perpetuated today by many livery companies named after crafts long since abandoned. It was a structure that ensured high standards in each craft or trade, but it also confined activities within well-defined boundaries that smacked of restrictive practice.

It is therefore no surprise that as financial activities developed in the City, they also fell within tightly defined boundaries. Clearing banks, discount houses and merchant banks operated separately, as did stockbrokers and jobbers. They were free to dictate their own rules in the years when Britain was at the height of its imperial powers, but the legacy of inward-looking, separate businesses became outdated.

This was the position in 1979 and, if nothing had changed, the City would have been left behind as a financial centre. The separation of the activities of the merchant bank, stockbroker and jobber looked quaint and uncompetitive from the outside when compared with the integrated structure of the American invest-ment banks and European universal banks. It would never have coped in the late 1980s and 1990s when technology transformed financial markets and turned the world into a global financial village. It was the good fortune of the City that Margaret Thatcher abolished exchange controls and forced through the dereg-ulation of Big Bang. These changes enabled the City to seize its position at the heart of the middle time zone of the 24-hour financial day.

Chapter 27 has described how Big Bang prompted a whole series of acquisi-tions in London – many from American and other foreign sources – but British-owned groups were also formed by putting together the corporate finance, issuing and fund management activities of the traditional merchant bank with the sales, research and market-making activities of the stockbrokers and jobbers to form investment banks. This was broadly the model pursued by merchant banks Hill Samuel, Kleinwort Benson, Morgan Grenfell and S. G. Warburg. At the same time, Barclays Bank formed BZW and National Westminster Bank added two securities firms to its existing County Bank sub-sidiary.

Hopes ran high in the City that these British groups would be successful both in London and on a wider international stage and, during the first year after Big Bang, everybody seemed to be winning on the back of the bull market that eventually collapsed so dramatically in October 1987. Thereafter, many of the alliances fell apart, but, in the context of the ambitions of 1986, the irony of the outcome today, ten years later, could hardly have been predicted. The European universal banks have emerged as the dominant owners of recognisably British businesses.

Among the embryo British investment banks, Hill Samuel and Morgan

Grenfell quickly fell apart and Kleinwort Benson struggled. The most successful integration of the different cultures was achieved by S. G. Warburg under the inspired leadership of Sir David Scholey, and BZW became a powerful force in the British market under the leadership of Sir Martin Jacomb – formerly with Kleinwort Benson, where he had led privatisation campaigns with distinction. S. G. Warburg proceeded to build an international business that enabled its name to be joined briefly in the early 1990s with Goldman Sachs and Morgan Stanley as one of the world's leading international investment banks.

It is sadly apparent with hindsight that S. G. Warburg and the other British groupings were fighting a losing battle on the world stage. International investment banking is dominated by the United States, where a vibrant private-sector generates a volume of issues, bids and stock market turnover on a scale that dwarfs the rest of the world, combined also with a more generous fee structure than available elsewhere. The result is that, in simplified terms, a domestic franchise of, say, 10% of the US market will produce far greater revenues than a 25% share of the British, French and German markets. This domestic base generates the capital and the skills to exploit markets throughout the rest of the world with a competitive advantage not unlike that of Hollywood in the cinema world.

Facing the same need for capital, but without that natural advantage, the likes of S. G. Warburg faced a catch 22 question – that an acquisition in the US, to be worthwhile, would have to be of a size that would compromise its British and European identity. The alternative was to seek shelter under the umbrella of the capital resources of a parent European universal bank, but, in the process, be swamped by size.

In the first phase of Big Bang, the only major European bank to enter at a high level was the Union Bank of Switzerland with its acquisition of Phillips & Drew, but, in November 1989, Deutsche Bank put down a marker of future trends by making an agreed bid for Morgan Grenfell. Thereafter, famous City names were slowly toppled as recorded in Table 33.3.

Table 33.3
The acqusition of City banks by European banks, 1989–95

Date	Bidder	Target	Cost (£m)
November 1989	Deutsche Bank	Morgan Grenfell	950
July 1994	ABN Amro Bank	Hoare Govett	Not known
March 1995	ING	Baring Bros	£1
May 1995	Swiss Bank	S. G. Warburg	860
June 1995	Dresdner Bank	Kleinwort Benson	1,000

These European banks correctly judged that the business skills in financial services lay largely in London, and they used their capital resources to acquire these skills. Ironically, they achieved this with Anglo-Saxon panache, ING pouncing to rescue Barings and Swiss Bank to catch S. G. Warburg in a moment of weakness. Their initial approach has been to learn rather than teach, to own rather than control, and to build in London rather than move to Frankfurt, Paris or Zurich. London is the hub of the European time zone, where the concentration of international banks and investment houses is at its greatest, and where the location, language, communications infrastructure, deregulation and native skills guarantee its future, but its ownership is now heavily Continental.

The involvement of the British clearing banks has been a disappointment. In 1997, both Barclays Bank and NatWest dismantled their investment banking subsidiaries by selling them off in bits and pieces to the best bidders. Both eventually found the ownership of investment banking subsidiaries to be unrewarding, and the remuneration needs of the investment bankers to be disruptive to internal pay scales. The early promise of BZW came to naught. It might have been expected that the British clearing banks would by now have been as well entrenched in the City as their Continental brethren, but they, too, have been carrying the millstone of City history, their historical separation from merchant banks having been an obstacle to change.

The European universal banks are different. They have long been acting as clearing bank, merchant bank, fund manager and securities dealer all in one place, creating a culture apparently better suited to the new financial world. They have been indifferent to the conflicts of interest thrown up by grouping these activities together, and slow to establish rules to prevent insider dealing and ensure fairness for shareholders in acquisitions. In stark contrast, Big Bang in London created the 'compliance officer' and 'Chinese walls'. Employees were issued with individual books of regulations laying down stringent rules for personal dealings and the control of physical access between departments.

The 11 largest European banks measured by market capitalisation in 1997 were HSBC, Lloyds, Barclays and NatWest in the UK; ING and ABN Amro in the Netherlands; Deutsche Bank and Dresdner Bank in Germany; and UBS, Crédit Suisse and Swiss Bank from Switzerland. All seven Continental banks shared in common the ownership of an investment banking subsidiary or division in London.

It is a sobering thought that, with the fall of the Union Bank of Switzerland to its smaller rival Swiss Bank Corporation in 1998, only one of the major alliances put in place at Big Bang has survived – HSBC/James Capel. The leaders today have been those who bided their time and those who stood apart to pursue their traditional specialist roles. Among the latter, Cazenove, Lloyds Bank, Lazards and Schroders have survived and prospered. The leading US houses in Europe have also judged well. Goldman Sachs and Morgan Stanley preferred to grow organically to become formidable competitors in Europe, and Merrill Lynch stood back before acquiring Smith Bros in 1995 and Mercury Asset Management in 1998. In contrast Citicorp, Chase Manhattan, Security Pacific and Shearson Lehman all retired hurt, to varying degrees, from their initial Big Bang purchases.

This European influence has not been confined to the bigger investment banking names. In a series of smaller acquisitions, the Europeans have been shrewd buyers of fund management houses. Between 1988 and 1990, well-established names GT, Touche Remnant, Gartmore and Foreign & Colonial (50%) were taken over by Bank in Liechtenstein, Société Générale, Banque Indo-Suez and Bayerische Hypothenken Bank, and, in 1995, Jupiter was taken over by Commerzbank. It was a similar recognition of the fund management skills existing in the City and a shrewd assessment of their value.

The ultimate irony is that Britain has been at the forefront of the highly successful Anglo-Saxon financial system – with its emphasis on flexibility, competition and power of the shareholder – but the ownership of many of its leading practitioners has passed to those European hands whose social market financial systems are under pressure. Why did this happen, and does it matter?

A prime reason is that it is more rewarding to work in an investment bank than to own it. Highly skilled employees bargain for themselves a proportion of potential profits on a scale that no trade union could ever match, and the unstated threat of walking across the road into the welcoming arms of a competitor puts employers at their mercy. During their existence as a sub-sector of the FT Actuaries All Share Index from 1962, merchant banks were the second worst-performing sub-sector out of 35, and practitioners in the sector were widely outperformed by the companies they advised or invested in. Since Big Bang, a continuing problem on the part of quoted companies or subsidiaries operating in investment banking and securities has been to obtain an acceptable rate of return on capital. These remuneration packages will now squeeze the profit margins of their Continental owners and there are already signs that patience is beginning to be stretched. Should it be tested to breaking point, the brightest talent will further strengthen the dominance of the US investment banks or form niche businesses to start all over again.

Location is far more important than ownership. It is in the British interest that, within the European time zone, the actual location of the securities and investment banking businesses remains in the City of London. This is ever more likely today because corporate ownership in many industries crosses borders in all directions – as also do the nationalities of chief executives. British companies have a long tradition of owning and acquiring foreign subsidiaries, and British investing institutions have an equally long tradition of pursuing investment opportunities overseas. The combined value of these subsidiaries and investments represents a national asset that more than matches the loss of ownership from the occasional well-publicised takeover bid.

The pioneering spirit of the old British Empire is alive and well in the corporate sector and many a Board of directors will recognise those colleagues who are at their happiest taking off from Heathrow to head for foreign lands. However, there are dangers. An ill-judged foreign acquisition is difficult to hide and its consequences can bring a company to its knees – as happened when Midland Bank bought Crocker Bank in California. There have been some successes – such as the Prudential's acquisition of Jackson National Life – but the overall record of acquisitions in the United States by British companies has been mixed.

The third major influence of the Thatcher years has been the promotion of the 'Anglo-Saxon' form of capitalism, a system strongly linked with the English-speaking countries of the United States, Canada, Australia and Hong Kong. The Anglo-Saxon system openly promotes the power of the marketplace where competition is encouraged by deregulation and liberalisation, and legislation prevents the emergence of cartels and monopolies. Its philosophy is to let the market free to meet the wishes and needs of the consumer.

It is in contrast to the 'stakeholder' forms of capitalism that have emerged in Continental Europe and Asia, where companies operate under a structure of regulation, control and restricted ownership, whether it be exercised by the central hand of the banks in Germany or the State in France or government bureaucracy and cross-shareholdings in Japan. The Anglo-Saxon philosophy assumes a structure of freedom that is strengthened by disclosure and no more than tempered by regulation and control. In the stakeholder model, the philosophy assumes there will be a structure of control and regulation, and freedom is measured by the extent to which it can be relaxed. The outcome is a system that protects the company at the expense of its shareholders and the producers at the expense of the consumers. Takeover bids are either discouraged or made impossible by interlocking shareholdings. There is little perceived need to improve disclosure of information to shareholders who lack power to influence events, and there is less imperative to seek earnings growth and raise dividends. In contrast, Anglo-Saxon companies are driven by fear of takeover, encourage their shareholders with maximum disclosure of information and give high priority to the pursuit of earnings and dividend growth.

Until 1979, the instincts of successive governments in Britain probably leaned towards a philosophy of regulation and control, but the well-established structure of the stock market, with its powerful and independent institutional shareholders, acted as an obstacle to any such tendencies. In 1979, Margaret Thatcher moved decisively in favour of Anglo-Saxon thinking, and an unspoken philosophical battle as to which was the better corporate system was joined between the United States and Britain on the one hand, and Germany, France and Japan on the other.

It has been an intriguing encounter. The free market policies endorsed by President Reagan in the United States and Margaret Thatcher in Britain have, become symbols of the 1980s in both countries, but, by the turn of the decade, in 1990, when both had left office, the merits of the two philosophies of capitalism remained open to debate. This was for the good reason that, during the 1970s and 1980s, Germany and Japan were the economic powerhouses of the world, and it was but a simple step to attribute such glowing success to the different financial systems operated by the two countries.

The argument in favour of the stakeholder system was the stability provided by interlocking shareholdings. The German banks form special relationships with their client companies by owning large or controlling equity shareholdings, which gives these companies long-term financing stability and an encouragement to undertake a higher level of investment without fear of short-term pressure on share prices. Major companies in France fall into the network of that famous educational elite that glides seamlessly from government to industry and back again, paranoid about national ownership and fostering strategic shareholdings on the way along. The widespread practice in Japan of companies seeking protection under the umbrella of a powerful conglomerate, or 'keiretsu', in return for interlocking shareholdings, and the practice of companies having close relationships with government departments, together offer the same stability.

Under the stakeholder systems, companies have easier access to bank financing and face less demanding terms. The result is that they are usually more highly geared than in Britain or the United States, place less emphasis on immediate profit and have lower profit margins. Proponents of the German and Japanese systems argue that the Anglo-Saxon system focuses too much on current profits, allows too many takeover bids, encourages short-term thinking on the part of institutional investors and discourages companies from making long-term investment decisions because of the fear of negative short-term price movements.

Proponents of the Anglo-Saxon model, while acknowledging the economic success of Germany and Japan, believe that interlocking shareholdings and an immunity from takeover bids protect companies from the natural sanctions of the capitalist system. A stranglehold of vested interests is put in place, from which complacency and resistance to change will inevitably follow. Protection takes precedence over competition.

The Anglo-Saxon system is confrontational with a paramount role for the shareholder, whereas the German and Japanese systems are consensual and, hence, often referred to as 'social market' or 'stakeholder' forms of capitalism. It can be argued that each strongly reflects the national characteristics of the people of the respective countries, and the post-war success of Germany and Japan has had far more to do with deeper conformist instincts, an acceptance of existing structures and the powerful national incentive of recovering from wartime defeat. Under that argument, the different method of financing companies has been incidental to the outcome.

With the Anglo-Saxon philosophy, companies are owned by the shareholders and serve the consumers. Directors can be removed by the actions of the shareholders in consenting to bids and employees have less certainty of employment. In the stakeholder system, the instinct is to preserve the structure of the company as a producer with stringent employment protection. At this point, the argument extends to include a wider social issue, because the consumer and the employee are one and the same person. Cheaper prices, better customer service and flexible employment run headlong into higher prices, worse service and jobs for life.

The proponents of the stakeholder system believe it provides a fairer division of the interests of shareholders, employees and consumers, and, in an enclosed economy, that may be possible. However, in a global economy where national boundaries have been trampled down by technology, and rapid change demands rapid response, the consumer has the upper hand. This has been the lesson of the 1990s. The stakeholder models are in retreat, their products and services are less competitive and their inflexible employment practices have become obstacles to change.

Companies are being forced to change and, in the face of this, the wisdom of interlocking shareholdings is being called into question. The clearest example of change lies in Germany where companies are restructuring, takeover bids are happening and US pension funds are becoming significant shareholders. A report in *Business Week* on 16 February 1998 showed how the 'Mittelstand' backbone of medium-sized family manufacturing businesses is shedding its dynastic character as the younger generation looks to the Anglo-Saxon ideals of higher profits to generate higher values and displays a willingness to sell its inheritance.

In South-East Asia, the collapse of many economies in 1997/98 has been attributed to the consequences of 'crony' capitalism, where governments deliberately or unwittingly involve themselves so closely with the corporate world that the normal checks and balances no longer operate. 'Crony' is too strong a word for the role played by the banks in Germany or the keiretsu in Japan or the Government in France, but there is a grain of truth in it.

The implication is that the transparency of the Anglo-Saxon model works best, and its influence is gathering pace. The globalisation of markets is playing its part – particularly in Europe, where new external shareholders are vociferous in demanding value. Many of these are foreign investing institutions from the United States, but they will increasingly be joined by domestic institutions following the same pattern. Their combined power and influence will be difficult to resist.

Defenders of the stakeholder system decry 'short-termism' – a particular aspect of the Anglo-Saxon model that became a controversial subject in the City in the late 1980s. Institutional investors were accused of accepting hostile takeover bids too readily, switching in and out of shares for short-term reasons and demanding unnecessary dividend increases. It was claimed that the fear of having shares marked down for short-term reasons forced companies to concentrate so much on current earnings per share that investment decisions were being postponed and longer-term objectives put to one side. Academic and political views claimed that the interests of the economy were not well served by short-termism, and attention was at the same time drawn to the German and Japanese examples of stable shareholders. This complaint emanated not least from a number of industrialists who were frustrated by the volatility of share prices and a perceived lack of shareholder loyalty in the face of hostile bids.

The accusations were primarily aimed at the pension fund movement and there was sufficient concern for the Institutional Fund Managers Association to commission a report in 1990 – *Short-termism on Trial*, by Paul Marsh of the London Business School. Marsh convincingly rebutted these many claims and found a 'paucity of hard evidence' to support the fears expressed. He quoted Paul Samuelson that 'takeovers, like bankruptcy, represent one of nature's methods of eliminating dead wood in the struggle for survival'. On the particular claim that short-termism inhibited investment, he emphasised that 'well-managed firms start from the premise that they should invest in all worthwhile projects', and, in the long term in Britain, any inhibitions had been more influenced by the negative effects of high interest rates and poor productivity.

High dividend payments have, from time to time, been disparaged by academics, commentators, companies and politicians alike, on the grounds that investment opportunities are sacrificed to the demands of greedy institutions, and it is certainly true that equity yields in the UK are high by international comparison. However, there is a purist view that it is better for companies to distribute profits to shareholders and encourage the best companies to compete for capital in the marketplace. There is little point in encouraging inefficient companies to retain cash only to invest it inefficiently or for companies in mature industries to hoard cash before wasting it on unnecessary diversification.

Indeed, a prime function of the stock market is to raise capital for investment, and the amounts raised by rights issues during the Thatcher years rose from a typical £1,000m in 1979 to around £5,000m in the late 1980s, with peaks of £8,500m in 1987 and £10,100m in 1991. Nevertheless, retained earnings have always been much the largest source of capital for investment, but there is little evidence that tax discrimination in their favour will generate higher investment. A natural antipathy of Labour governments towards dividends – once stigmatised as 'unearned' income – will always be an ominous factor for the stock market. In the space of six years, the Attlee Government turned a single rate of profits tax of 5% into a rate of 10% on undistributed profits and 50% on distributed profits. James Callaghan reformed corporation tax in 1965 specifically to discourage dividends, and Gordon Brown is straying down the same path by cutting or removing tax credits to reduce the value of dividends to the shareholder.

The perception of short-termism in the stock market is also enhanced by the violence of price changes taking place on the announcement of unexpected news – particularly when it is negative. A share price will halve in a day if expectations of high profits are suddenly reversed in a warning or the validity of existing profits is questioned. However, this extreme short-term reaction reflects an immediate reassessment of the longer-term prospects. As a general rule, the market will discount as far ahead as it can see – hence, growth companies are occasionally on PE ratios of 60 or 70 – but the factor most closely affecting individual share prices will be forecasts of profits for the current year and next year. As the consensus of forecasts from the analysts is increased or reduced, so share prices are adjusted upwards or downwards.

While the continuing effect on the stock market of privatisation, Big Bang and free markets relates to particular trademarks of the Thatcher era, other noticeable features of the 1990s largely extend existing long-term trends. These include the advancement of technology, a continuing bull market, a fourth post-war takeover cycle, the dominance of the institutional shareholder, the closer alignment of management and ownership and the stretching of the valuation of equities.

Technology first began to influence activities in the stock market in the late nineteenth century when telegraphic communication, by telegram and tape machines, was introduced in the 1870s. As significant an event as any in its day was the introduction of the inland telephone system in 1894 and its extension to Paris and other Continental capitals. In the post-war era, reference has already been made to the automation of contract notes, the invention of electronic calculating machines, the computerisation of research, the availability of direct telephone calling, the introduction of screen information services by the Stock Exchange and Reuters and the creation of global telecommunications systems. All these stages in technology led to the creation of employment, except in settlement, where manual tasks have been computerised.

The mechanisation of settlement continues fitfully – despite the abandonment after six years of development of the ill-fated and over-ambitious Taurus proposal in 1993 – and some mechanisation in trading has been achieved with the introduction of the order-driven SETs system. However, the greatest influence of technology over the stock market in the 1990s has been its application to derivatives. The problem with derivatives is primarily one of understanding. They are difficult to define in layman's language, they are difficult to grasp because their application is essentially mathematical and they are difficult to manage because so few people in any business are capable of understanding them.

A definition of derivatives starts from the premise that the stock market is primarily made up of conventional securities – such as equities or fixed interest investments – which are available for purchase and sale for the payment or receipt of cash. This is known as the 'cash' market, but 'derived' from these securities have emerged new financial instruments, collectively known as derivatives, which are also available to be bought and sold, usually in the form of futures and options. In effect, a derivative allows an investor to avoid the cost of buying an underlying holding in a chosen security by investing, as an alternative, only in its future change in price. As a result, the derivative is highly geared because, in illustrative terms, the same amount of money will buy one share at its full price or the future change in price of ten of the same shares.

The risks and the rewards are hugely magnified. The investor faces an array of choices. In traded options, prices are quoted for the right to buy or sell any of a long list of leading equities at varying prices and varying dates into the future. These options may be exercised, or sold or allowed to lapse, but they tempt the speculator because their price is only a fraction of the underlying security from which it is 'derived'. At least with the traded option the cost is the limit of any loss. More dangerous are the futures where a highly geared commitment is made, as opposed to an option taken, to buy or sell an index of securities at a future date. Transactions in futures in the Tokyo Nikkei Index led to the downfall of Barings.

In their attitude to the use of derivatives, institutions divide into distinctly separate camps of those who do and those who do not. Decisions are driven by mathematical margins between the future and the index, and between different options and the share price. A reasonable example of their use is to achieve an immediate portfolio switch into or out of equities via the futures market in an amount of tens of millions that would take days to complete in the cash market, thus guaranteeing the exposure and allowing the gradual unwinding of the derivative into conventional holdings. However, most fund managers, and the analysts and salesmen who advise them, psychologically think of a security in terms of a conventional cash holding, and only as an afterthought consider the derivative as an alternative means of investing.

Some domestic institutions are active users of derivatives, and there are various hedge funds operating in the fixed interest and currency markets. However, the biggest users are the banks acting as principals and market makers. They build huge positions, short and long, or hedged one against the other in an array of derivatives, and actively seek trading opportunities. Complicated strategies designed to achieve the tiniest of margins on massive exposures are invented by the so-called 'rocket scientists' – often gifted mathematicians who are unable to explain their complicated activities in simple language. They are joined by speculators and traders with gambling instincts who venture into derivatives on a bewildering scale.

The degree of understanding of what is happening outside the immediacy of the derivatives team falls rapidly away, and, at the higher levels of an organisation, it is likely that there will be barely any understanding at all. Most of the multi-million pound losses incurred by banks and companies have emanated from dealings in derivatives, but the textbook example will always be Barings –

brought down by losses of £800m incurred by one employee. It is apparent that nobody of any seniority either knew or understood why a branch office in Singapore required tranches of tens of millions of pounds of additional capital. Barings may have been an unwitting victim of its weak controlling ownership by an in-house charitable foundation. The directors and executives were never exposed to the usual sanctions of being a quoted company, but neither were they in partnership with personal capital. They were more interested in generating cash profits to pay bonuses than guarding the value of a share price.

The flaw in the derivatives market is the assumption made in all illustrations of their usage that those who enter this highly geared arena are assumed to be able to judge correctly the direction in which prices are moving. The rewards for good decisions are huge, but so are the penalties for bad decisions, and there is no reason for the quality of decisions to be any different from those applied to the underlying shares or markets.

Technology has been a decisive factor in the continuation of the long bull market into the 1990s because it has been led by the technology sector and technology has had a decisive effect on raising the profits of companies in so many other industries. From time to time, new phrases have entered the language, such as 'mass production', 'automation' and 'computerisation' – each accompanied by gloomy sentiments about impending unemployment from the replacement of labour. These fears always proved unfounded but the technology of the 1990s has brought about the displacement of people on a major scale, with the convergence of global communications and massive computing power. In a whole range of businesses and industries, the effect of technology has been to reduce employment or shift it to other countries, to lower costs and, in many cases, consign price inflation to history. Its effect on employment in retail banking and insurance has been severe.

The long bull market of the 1990s has shared the same relentless character as that of the 1980s, when the All Share Index reached a new all-time high in every year to 1987. Since reaching its low point ahead of the Gulf War on 24 September 1990 at 962.09, the All Share Index has recorded a new all-time high in each of 8 successive years, to reach 2,885.17 on 20 July. It received a major impetus from the decision to depart from the ERM in September 1992. This released twin benefits to the stock market of a devaluation of around 10% and a fall in base rates from 15% in 1990 to 6% in early 1993. The wall of money so often attributed to one source in many bull markets has this time been widely provided by a combination of personal savings, overseas investors and financial surpluses in the corporate sector.

Three post-war takeover cycles have been identified earlier – 1959–62, 1968–72 and 1986–89. A fourth cycle began in 1995, and has continued through to 1998. The theme of the first cycle was consolidation within domestic industries, but the next two were more concerned with diversification by individual companies or the diverse activities of expanding conglomerates. The latest cycle returns to the theme of consolidation, but is motivated by the need for market leaders to compete across European or global markets, and often involves cross-border bids mounted by foreign companies.

The feast and famine of corporate finance is illustrated by the total value of acquisitions of UK public companies from the peak of the last cycle in 1989 through to 1997, as reported each year by *Acquisitions Monthly* (see Table 33.4).

Table 33.4
Value of acquisitions of quoted
UK companies, 1989–97

Year	Value (£m)
1989	27,999
1990	10,664
1991	6,241
1992	9,890
1993	3,002
1994	5,090
1995	36,209
1996	23,424
1997	31,043

A measure of the scale of the 1989 peak in the cycle is that the value of acquisitions equalled 6.3% of the value of the average All Share Index for the year, but, in the latest peak in the cycle, this ratio had fallen to around 3%. In the fallow years of the early 1990s, the biggest transactions were the £3,700m bid by Hongkong & Shanghai Bank for Midland Bank and the value of £3,100m put on Reed International in its merger with the Dutch company Elsevier, both in 1992. The latest cycle has been dominated by a number of mega-mergers and a series of bids for privatised electricity distribution companies. Giant companies were created in pharmaceuticals and banking when Glaxo bid £9,150m for Wellcome and Lloyds Bank bid £6,075m for TSB in 1995, and in drinks when Grand Metropolitan bid £9,760m for Guinness in 1997.

The cash-generating attractions of the privatised electricity distribution companies prompted bids for 6 electricity distribution companies in 1995 and a further 5 in 1996 and 1997 – all in the £750m to £2,400m range. Seven fell to US utilities, two to water companies in the same region, one to Scottish Power, and one to Hanson Trust for a total consideration of £15,400m. In addition, two successful bids were made for water companies – one by a French conglomerate and the other by Scottish Power.

Demergers have been another corporate theme of the 1990s. In effect, they have been a counter to the leveraged buy-outs of the 1986–89 takeover boom, when bids were financed by debt with the sole intention of breaking up the company and selling off enough individual subsidiaries to repay the debt. This was the principle behind the purchase of Imperial Group by Hanson Trust in 1986 and the failed £13bn bid by the Goldsmith syndicate for BAT Industries in 1989. The unwelcome leveraged buy-out has been finessed by the voluntary demerger, and shareholders have generally prospered as a result. Some early examples have already been described. BAT Industries began the process by demerging Argos and Wiggins Teape in its defence against the Goldsmith bid, Courtaulds voluntarily split itself into separate chemicals and textile subsidiaries, and Racal floated its Vodafone subsidiary partly by selling it to its own shareholders.

However, the prime example was set by ICI, after being threatened in May 1991 by the very public acquisition of a 2.8% stake by Hanson Trust. Shareholders in ICI were not getting proper value for the highly profitable pharmaceuticals division whose contribution was, in effect, being valued at little more than the PE ratio of a cyclical chemical company. Sensing its vulnerability to a bid and anxious to retain control over its own destiny, ICI – together with its advisers S. G. Warburg, boldly pursued the complicated route of demerging its pharmaceutical division. The demerger eventually took place in July 1993 with the creation of the newly named pharmaceutical company Zeneca. When Hanson Trust took its stake, the market capitalisation of ICI was £7.7bn, and, by the date of the demerger, it was £10.5bn. At the end of 1997, ICI was capitalised at £6.9bn and Zeneca at £20.2bn, with the benefit accruing in full to the continuing shareholders of the original ICI. This is the textbook example that has since been followed by three of the largest companies in the stock market – Thorn-EMI, Hanson Trust and British Gas.

The rise in power of the institutional shareholder has been relentless over the whole of the post-war period. In 1945, the life assurance companies and the investment trusts were the only two institutions with an established history. Since then the pension funds have grown from small beginnings to match the size of the insurance companies as the two largest collective institutions, and unit trusts have left the investment trusts far behind. The funds of both have grown because of their ability to attract savings and their wholehearted commitment to equities.

The ownership today of some 30% of the equity market by the pension funds, compared with 3% in the 1950s shows how fundamental their influence has been in the stock market. They are powerful investors with total assets currently estimated at around £600bn and they have an influence relative to the size of the economy matched only in the United States, and, unusually, in a European context, in Holland. In comparable terms, they barely exist in France and Germany.

Their presence owes much to employment policies. For some 25 years after the war, the background to the UK labour market was one of full employment, high personal taxation and frequent controls. To attract labour and soften the effect of taxation, companies resorted to 'perks' of one kind and another, and the offer of participation in a generous pension scheme became an important component of employment packages led not least by the Government in offering index-linked pensions to many of its employees. The commitment to guarantee these pensions required their proper funding in pension funds that were beyond the reach of receivers and other outsiders. Furthermore, the tax treatment of pension funds was highly favourable. The principle was that, because the eventual pension payment was taxable, its build-up in contributions and investment should be tax-free. The principal savings product of the life companies, the endowment policy, was exactly the opposite, with its accumulation taxable, but its final payment to the policyholder tax-free.

Once put in place, the pension funds could only grow. The difference from normal practice in Continental Europe is that these pension commitments are funded in advance by invested assets. In Europe, there is a greater dependence on generous State pensions paid out of current government revenues, and company pensions that are, in effect, a 'pay-as-you-go' cost. As populations live longer, the viability of paying pensions out of current revenues has become a serious matter of concern. Prudence in Britain has been rewarded with the accumulation of assets of some £600bn in pension funds, but the contributions paid by employers and employees to build these assets have been a long-term addition to the cost of goods and services.

The impact of the pension funds on the stock market has been all the greater because of their early commitment to ordinary shares. Figures provided by the WM Company covering three-quarters of the pension fund universe show the percentage of total assets held in UK equities peaking in 1992 at 57.6%, with the inclusion of overseas equities taking the total equity commitment to 79.1%. Estimates for 1997 are approximately 50% in UK equities and 15% in overseas equities.

The life assurance companies form a group of similar size, with assets of around £600bn, but, if measured by their holdings of equities, they fall into second place, currently owning around 22% of all equities compared with 9% in the 1950s. They have always held larger fixed interest holdings than the pension funds, and current estimates are approximately 40% in UK equities and 10% in overseas equities.

Unit trusts have grown at a rapid rate since becoming a prime vehicle for PEPs in 1989, and, in the size of assets under their management, have left the investment trusts far behind. In the 1950s, the unit trusts owned barely more than 1% of the equity market compared with 4% to 5% for the investment trusts. When their funds reached £20.3bn in 1985, they overtook the investment trusts' total of £18.1bn for the first time. By 1997, their total funds of around £155bn compared with £60bn for the investment trusts – boosted by a significant share of the total PEPs of some £40bn. Their funds divide approximately 60% in UK equities and 40% overseas.

The four traditional investing institutions now control nearly 60% of the equity market, but they have been joined over the last two decades by a new category in the form of overseas investors. This amorphous group of institutions, companies and individuals from a variety of countries now owns some 16% of the UK equity market. It has happened for a combination of reasons. Cross-border investing has been made easier by technology, diversification has become fashionable and, because of its economic success in the 1980s and 1990s, Britain has become an attractive country for portfolio investment.

The ownership of equities is notoriously difficult to measure with any certainty. Various organisations have used sampling exercises to extrapolate estimates of the total percentage of the holdings of different categories of investors, and information published by the associations representing the different investors provides a cross-check. The figures most widely quoted are for a series of random years published by the Central Statistical Office. However, its estimates for unit trusts and investment trusts have been adjusted in Table 33.5 to correspond with year end market values of investments published for these two sectors by the DTI.

Table 33.5
Estimated percentage ownership of UK equities, 1957–94

Category	1957	1963	1969	1975	1981	1989	1994
Pension funds	3.4	7.0	9.0	16.8	26.7	30.6	27.8
Insurance companies	8.9	10.6	12.2	15.9	20.5	18.6	21.9
Unit trusts	0.7	1.3	2.9	4.1	3.6	6.0	6.8
Investment trusts	5.0	6.7	6.6	6.8	4.6	2.2	2.0
Totals	18.0	25.6	30.7	43.6	55.4	57.4	58.5
Overseas	n/a	7.0	6.6	5.6	3.6	12.8	16.3
Private individuals	66.0	54.0	47.4	37.5	28.2	20.6	20.3
Miscellaneous	16.0	13.4	15.3	13.3	12.8	9.2	4.9

The long-term decline in the private ownership of equities from around 66% in the 1950s now appears to have stabilised at around 20%, although the number of shareholders has increased from around 3m to some 10m following privatisation in the 1980s and demutualisation of building societies and life assurance companies in the 1990s. A significant element of private ownership has willingly passed from the individual to the collective form of unit trusts, and private interest in the stock market should be measured by adding back the unit trust percentage.

The outcome of these shifting post-war percentages is that domestic institutions effectively control the equity of all quoted British companies and indirectly influence the major corporate financing and acquisition decisions. Much the most fluid segment has been in pension fund management, where there has been intense competition to obtain mandates. Increasingly, however, the business has become concentrated in the hands of the leading five pension fund management groups, a trend accentuated by the tendency of consulting actuaries to play safe in their recommendations. They manage some 35% to 40% of the value of all pension funds and their growing dominance is shown in Table 33.6 of pension funds under management drawn from various FT surveys.

Table 33.6
Pension fund assets under management

Pension fund management	1985 (£m)	1990 (£m)	1997 (£m)
Mercury Asset Management	8,300	22,410	65,780
Schroder	6,250	10,800	54,200
Phillips & Drew (PDFM)	5,160	12,730	50,190
Barclays	4,200	12,140	34,075
Gartmore	–	–	31,000

Mercury Asset Management has headed this table since the early 1970s as a division of S. G. Warburg to the present day, with the mantle of the City's best-known fund manager passing from Leonard Licht to Carol Galley, their names both in turn linked with Stephen Zimmerman.

Within the many institutions, it is often estimated that real power exists in the hands of the largest 40 or 50. However, this power is diluted by the diversity of those larger institutions, drawn from different segments and openly competing with each other, and their voice is only likely to be in collective agreement when the issues are self-evident. The rise of this shareholder power is one notable feature of the post-war era. The major institutional shareholders develop close links with companies at the highest executive levels, but it remains an arm's-length relationship that is perhaps healthier than the 'stakeholder' links described earlier in this chapter.

Companies have responded by setting up investor relations departments to communicate with shareholders and the media or by using the services of the many financial public relations agencies. The typical chief executive is today more sensitive than ever to the significance and importance of his company's share price. This sensitivity exists for a quite separate reason. The probability is that chief executives today have a greater personal financial interest in their companies than ever before, either in the form of shares or options or remuneration based on profits and earnings performance.

Remuneration practices in Britain now closely follow the American model and generate rewards beyond the wildest dreams of occupants of the chief executive's desk of barely a decade ago, and the same effect has trickled down to senior colleagues. In many examples, multi-million-pound remuneration packages are cheap at the price in terms of the value added by the best chief executives to a company's profits and share price, but their credibility is often put at risk in the eyes of the public by a tendency for the rewards of failure to seem to be equally high.

It must be puzzling to the shareholder who purchased WPP shares at over 900p in 1987 to see the chief executive presiding over a collapse in the shares to 30p and then being rewarded with options worth £25m for getting the price back to 304p 10 years later. Outsiders may be puzzled as to why the executives of Barings were paid profit-related bonuses totalling millions of pounds when the bank had collapsed with losses of £700m. They will be constantly puzzled that chief executives are publicly dismissed for failure, only to receive compensation on a scale that assumed success, and, while enjoying that compensation for loss of a job, promptly find another. Perhaps there are some lessons to be learned from the laws of alimony.

Although the price of failure may sometimes seem too high, the far greater personal commitment of the typical chief executive and fellow directors to the share price has been beneficial to the efficiency and competitiveness of the corporate sector. It is an aspect of the capitalist system that has all but turned full circle. Companies at one time were dominantly owned by the founding family and its heirs, with management and ownership in one and the same hands. As and when companies became quoted, so the number of outside shareholders expanded, and management from outside the ranks of the family gradually assumed control. Management and ownership became separated, and visibly so in the early post-war decades when company reports revealed many a Board of directors owning very few shares or none at all. It is no coincidence that the corporate sector was at its least efficient when this separation was at its most marked.

The first signs of change occurred when option schemes for directors and executives were introduced in 1978, but it was not until the taxation reforms of the 1984 Budget that the use of option schemes really developed, and a company managed today by directors with only a negligible number of shares would be regarded with some scepticism. However, just as peaks and troughs are taken to extremes in stock markets, so also the scale of ownership made available to directors and executives under option schemes has moved to a peak. This has certainly become the case in the United States, where the practice of companies using surplus cash to buy in shares for cancellation has been on a multi-billion-dollar scale, only to be more or less cancelled out by the issue of shares in option schemes to directors on a matching scale.

After decades of separation, management has, in effect, recovered or appropriated ownership and the circle has fully turned to bring the two together again in one and the same hands. A result is that management has a common interest with the professional fund manager in maximising shareholder value, and this expresses itself today in many ways. The rise of the equity shareholder since the war has been accompanied by a steady and perceptible stretching of the valuation of the equity share, and the drive for value today by management as personal shareholders is but the latest stage in a continuing process. In simplified form, the pattern has been broadly outlined in Table 33.7.

Table 33.7
Emerging patterns in valuation of equity shares, 1950–95

From Year	Characteristics	Valuation
1950	Restricted dividends. Earnings cover 3 times. Conservative accounting.	Earnings yield 15%+ = PE ratio 5–6
1965	Liberalisation of dividends. Cover 1½ times. Cult of the equity.	Earnings yield 8% = PE ratio 13–14
1970	Corporation tax. Performance cult. Discrimination between PE ratios.	PE ratio 18+
1985	Cost-cutting for productivity gains. Profits high share of GDP. Surge in earnings and dividends.	PE ratio 20+
1995	Focus on core businesses. Mergers and disposals. Demergers. Buy-backs of equity for cancellation. Payment of special dividends.	PE ratio 22+

Based on linking the FT Index from July 1945 into the FT Actuaries All Share Index in October 1964 and through to December 1997, the capital value of equities over 52 years has multiplied 74 times, compared with inflation as measured by the Retail Price Index rising 21 times. Shareholders have benefited from the stretching of valuation set out in the stages in Table 33.7.

The first three stages were influenced by dividend growth, a clearer definition of earnings and the wider use of the PE ratio as a method of valuation. The fourth stage reflected the growth of profits in the 1980s to a new and higher share of GDP. In the fifth stage, in the 1990s, average PE ratios are frequently in the 20–22 range and shareholder value is being created by manipulation and the concentration and disposal of businesses.

Manipulation of the balance sheet involves buying back shares for cancellation. This has been happening on an accelerating scale in 1997 and 1998, primarily for the purpose of raising earnings per share, either by using surplus cash or allowing borrowings to rise. Alternatively, companies have been distributing surplus cash in the form of special dividends. It has already been noted that British companies are modestly geared and many could, in theory, sharply increase borrowings. There have been examples of extreme gearing put in place in management buyouts.

The concentration of business has reflected a change in corporate philosophy from the diversification of the 1970s and 1980s in favour of focus. This involves the ruthless identification of 'core' businesses with a strong market share and sustainable profits, and the disposal of those businesses that are too small or insufficiently profitable. Conglomerates once built up to general acclaim are now being broken up, and companies look for opportunities to demerge to raise shareholder value. Hanson Trust has turned full circle – once one of the largest quoted companies, it has demerged into five. Identifying core businesses has been good for the efficiency of the economy, but once companies have stripped down and completed their disposals, the next stage has been to pursue mergers for the consolidation of core businesses. This policy may legitimately be defended in the context of competitive global markets, but it may also be the only means to bring about any further cutting of costs. But if conglomeration within industries continues, there is the danger of recreating monopolies.

Behind every share price there lurks a bid premium – the extra price an outsider must pay to obtain control. Current practices are almost as though management is capturing and retaining for itself and its shareholders much of the bid premium once obtained only by loss of control to an outside bidder. It is a far cry today from the time 50 years ago when takeover bids never happened, profits were hidden away, and shares stood below asset values on PE ratios of 6.

The Introduction posed the disruptive sequence of six alternating Labour and Conservative governments. The seventh is a Labour Government elected on an economic agenda broadly similar to that of the Conservative Government it replaced. Does this herald an end to disruptive division between the parties? The performance of the stock market since May 1997 would suggest so, as there has been none of the instinctive caution that greeted previous Labour governments.

There is one immediate difference. On each of the previous six occasions, the new government of the left or the right came to power in the midst of actual or impending economic problems or crises. In 1997, the Labour Government inherited an economy at its strongest and most competitive at any time in the post-war period. The Paris-based OECD in its world economic report in December 1996 reported on Britain that its 'prospects for achieving sustained output growth and low inflation are the best in thirty years', and the International Monetary Fund described the state of the economy as 'enviable'. The Swiss-based World Economic Forum placed Britain fourth in its annual global competitiveness report published earlier in 1998, well ahead of any comparable European country. This is the flowering of Thatcherism. At no time in the last 50 years has the British economy received such accolades from independent commentators.

This strength has been reflected in the valuation of the stock market. One measure is to relate stock market capitalisation to the size of GDP as an indicator of the value placed on the total productive resources of the economy or, as occasionally described, the value of UK plc. This ratio moved to all-time highs during the years of Conservative government, much closer to the United States and well ahead of comparable ratios in Continental Europe. Typically, this ratio is around 160% in the United States and Switzerland, 120% in the UK, but only 50% to 55% in France, Germany and Japan. Britain is strongly placed in the growth sectors of the next millennium – airlines, computer software, entertainment, financial services, media, pharmaceuticals, publishing and telecommunications. Furthermore, the inward investment attracted by a skilled and flexible workforce has enabled the 1990s to be a decade of renewal of manufacturing, particularly in motor cars, electrical goods and electronics. The practice of outsourcing has been pioneered in Britain to the benefit of efficiency and the creation of some major specialist service companies.

Since the election, Labour has sustained the value of this inheritance, but, in his history and analysis of the UK economy, *The British Economy at the Crossroads* (Financial Times Pitman Publishing, 1998), Professor James Ball speculates about uncertainties over the future direction of the economy. There is uncertainty about whether or not greater integration into Europe will harm the competitive advantages earned over the last two decades. There is much talk in the Government of a 'third' way between the marketplace and the State. In opposition in one of his set piece performances reminiscent of Harold Macmillan and Harold Wilson – those two great 'actor' prime ministers – Tony Blair propounded with evangelical fervour the concept of the 'stakeholder' society, comparing Britain unfavourably with the Continent. However, it became apparent that the French and German economies were in deep structural trouble, the theme was quickly dropped.

The stock market, as a barometer, reacts to its own prediction of events stretching many months or even a year or two into the future. Under New Labour it has intially acted well in the following wind of a now fading global equity boom. The Chancellor, Gordon Brown, talks resolutely about the control of inflation and the importance of growth, but the cumulative effect of a list of Government measures harmful to profits and dividends augurs less well. The Social Chapter, the minimum wage, the windfall tax, the taxation of pension funds, the threat of tougher regulation as a backdoor method of controlling profits, the strengthening of the legal rights of the individual worker as an alternative to the restoration of trade union rights, examples of knee-jerk indignation about profits and a disdain for dividends will combine slowly to curb competitiveness and eat away some of the profits and dividends on which share prices ultimately depend. The stock market is a reflection of the state of the economy and it faces one crucial question: is the Anglo-Saxon model of capitalism safe in New Labour's hands?

This, though, is a question for the future. The history of most activities over the last 50 years will tell of change, and so it has been for the stock market, although the experience of Big Bang revealed that the Stock Exchange changed only just in time. The daily routine in the 1950s of drifting into a splendidly furnished partners' room just before 10 o'clock has, in the 1990s, become a mass meeting for several hundred at 7.30 am in the amphitheatre of the modern trading floor. A culture once driven by public school values has been replaced by the brashness of New York. Consensus and courtesy have given way to confrontation and competition. The client has become a counterparty to a transaction. The week's work, once an interlude between weekends with fine lunches, has become an exhausting grind refreshed by sandwiches at the desk. A commitment once gladly given by, and to, a firm for life and peaceful retirement at 65 has turned into revolving doors and burned out at 50.

These are the changes that have put London at the hub of the wheel of the European time zone in the middle of the 24-hour day. London has paramount advantages of language, skills, location and technology. Its fund management industry manages more equities than any city in the world. In 1998, its stock market capitalisation once again stands second only to the United States.

Above all, the history of the post-war stock market has been a voyage of discovery by the equity shareholder, beginning with dividends in the 1950s, followed by earnings and PE ratios in the 1960s, inflation in the 1970s, growth in the 1980s and shareholder value in the 1990s. This has been the journey of the stock market over 50 years, the expression of capitalism at work.

Chapter 34

KEY EVENTS
1979–90

GOVERNMENT

Prime Minister

Margaret Thatcher	3 May 1979–28 November 1990	Resigned

Chancellors of the Exchequer

Sir Geoffrey Howe	3 May 1979–12 June 1983	Reshuffle
Nigel Lawson	12 June 1983–26 October 1989	Resigned
John Major	26 October 1989–27 November 1990	Promoted

BUDGETS AND FINANCIAL STATEMENTS

Geoffrey Howe

12 June 1979	Income tax – standard rate reduced from 33% to 30%. Income tax – top rate reduced from 83% to 60%. VAT rate raised from 8–12½% to 15%. MLR raised from 12% to 14%. Dividend controls to end 3 July.
24 October 1979	Exchange controls abolished.
26 March 1980	Medium-term financial strategy introduced. Income tax allowances raised 18% in line with inflation.
10 March 1981	Income tax allowances frozen (inflation 12%). Index-linked Gilt introduced. MLR reduced from 14% to 12%.
9 March 1982	Income tax allowances raised 14% (inflation 11%). National insurance surcharge reduced from 3½% to 2½%. Capital gains to be indexed.

8 November 1982	National insurance surcharge reduced from 2½% to 1½%.
15 March 1983	Income tax allowances raised 14% (inflation 5%). National insurance surcharge reduced 1½% to 1%.

Nigel Lawson

13 March 1984	Corporation tax reduced in phases from 52% to 35% (1984 to 50%, 1985 to 45%, 1986 to 40%, 1987 to 35%). Investment allowances phased out (1985 to 75%, 1986 to 50%, 1987 to nil). Stock allowances abolished. National insurance surcharge abolished. Income tax allowances raised 12% (inflation 5%). Stamp duty on share transactions reduced from 2% to 1%. Tax relief on life assurance policies abolished. Share option schemes liable to CGT instead of income tax. Capital transfer tax maximum rate reduced from 75% to 60%.
19 March 1985	–
18 March 1986	Income tax – standard rate reduced from 30% to 29%. Stamp duty on share transactions reduced from 1% to ½%. Personal Equity Plan (PEP) introduced at £2,400.
17 March 1987	Income tax – standard rate reduced from 29% to 27%.
15 March 1988	Income tax – standard rate reduced from 27% to 25%. Income tax – maximum rate reduced from 60% to 40%. Capital gains to be taxed at marginal rate of income tax. PEP allowance raised from £2,400 to £3,000.
14 March 1989	PEP allowance raised to £4,800, of which £2,400 in unit trusts or investment trusts.

John Major

20 March 1990	TESSA introduced at £9,000 tax-free over 5 years. PEP allowance raised to £6,000. Stamp duty on share transactions to be abolished on the introduction of Taurus.

ALL SHARE INDEX: 1979–90

High: 1,238.57   16 July 1987
Low: 219.85   15 November 1979

Bull and bear markets

Movement	From	To	From	To	Duration
+ 463.4%	219.85	1,238.57	15 November 1979	16 July 1987	7 years 8 months
+ 56.3%	784.81	1,226.83	10 November 1987	3 January 1990	2 years 2 months
− 22.5%	283.82	219.85	4 May 1979	15 November 1979	0 years 6 months
− 36.6%	1,238.57	784.81	16 July 1987	10 November 1987	0 years 4 months
− 21.6%	1,226.83	962.09	3 January 1990	24 September 1990	0 years 8 months

Movements of more than 3% in one day

Date	% Change	From	To	Reason
21 October 1987	+ 5.83	951.95	1,007.47	Crash rebound
29 September 1981	+ 4.83	265.85	278.69	Rebound
11 November 1987	+ 4.21	784.81	817.83	Confidence returns
12 November 1987	+ 3.85	817.83	849.35	Confidence returns
30 October 1987	+ 3.65	856.05	887.33	Rebound
18 August 1982	+ 3.20	333.15	343.80	Interest rates fall
8 October 1990	+ 3.17	1,026.04	1,058.54	Confidence returns
5 October 1990	+ 3.02	995.94	1,026.04	Confidence returns
20 October 1987	− 11.41	1,074.58	951.95	October crash
19 October 1987	− 9.69	1,189.92	1,074.58	October crash
26 October 1987	− 7.16	930.33	863.73	October crash
22 October 1987	− 5.36	1,007.47	953.46	October crash
28 September 1981	− 4.67	278.87	265.85	Global weakness
30 November 1987	− 4.17	831.00	796.31	Weak dollar
16 October 1989	− 4.06	1,124.57	1,078.89	Global weakness
3 November 1987	− 3.64	876.00	844.14	Autumn statement
4 November 1987	− 3.59	844.14	813.85	Autumn statement
9 November 1987	− 3.44	815.68	787.64	Global weakness
23 September 1981	− 3.34	302.28	292.17	Loss of confidence
29 December 1987	− 3.26	905.12	875.62	Dollar weakness

INTEREST RATES

Interest rates	Peaks	Troughs
MLR (MLR ceased 20 August 1981)	17% – 15 November 1979	12% – 10 March 1981
Base rates	16% – 1 October 1981	9% – 4 November 1982
	11% – 11 January 1983	8.5% – 14 March 1984
	12% – 11 July 1984	9.5% – 22 November 1984
	14% – 28 January 1985	10% – 22 May 1986
	11% – 14 October 1986	7.5% – 17 May 1988
	15% – 5 October 1989	

APPENDIX

....

STOCK MARKET INDICES, 1945–98

The table below shows the levels of various stock market indices over successive periods divided by calendar decades. The last column shows the Retail Price Index as a measure of inflation.

Year at 1 January	FT 30 Index	All Share Index	FTSE 100	Dow Jones Index	UK RPI
1945	112.9	–	–	152.58	100.0
1950	106.4	–	–	200.13	113.4
1955	184.0	–	–	404.39	146.7
1960	338.4	–	–	679.36	169.3
1965	335.0	97.95	–	874.13	198.2
1970	407.4	147.34	–	800.36	245.3
1975	161.4	66.89	–	616.24	416.3
1980	414.2	229.79	–	838.74	851.7
1985	952.3	592.94	1,231.2	1,211.57	1,249.2
1990	1,916.6	1,204.70	2,422.7	2,753.20	1,636.8
1995	2,360.9	1,521.44	3,065.5	3,834.44	2,000.0
1998	3,289.3	2,411.00	5,135.5	7,908.25	2,184.9
Formed:	1 July 1935	10 April 1962	3 Jan 1984	26 May 1896.	

Date	Market capitalisation (£m)
10 April 1962	18,170
1 January 1965	18,741
1 January 1970	29,704
1 January 1975	14,840
1 January 1980	64,137
1 January 1985	193,262
1 January 1990	470,126
1 January 1995	709,058
1 January 1998	1,209,030

MARKET VALUE OF INSTITUTIONAL FUNDS, 1945–95

The following table shows, at five-year intervals, the actual or estimated market values of the invested assets owned by the four principal domestic institutions – life assurance companies (book values until 1970), pension funds, investment trusts and unit trusts. Estimates of this kind often vary in the detail, but the figures shown below are largely drawn from totals published in the official annual *Abstract of Statistics.*

The table is completed with indicators of the market value of quoted equities and government stocks in the same years. Stock Exchange figures have been used for the market value of government securities over the whole period, and for equities to 1955, but as at the following end of March. From 1960 onwards, the market value of the All Share Index is shown. When first introduced, it was estimated to include 90% of the capitalisation of the equity market, but, today, it embraces 98%.

Year end	Life assurance companies	Pension funds	Investment trusts	Unit trusts	All Share Index	Government securities
1945	2,370	–	–	–	6,500	12,170
1950	3,370	–	620est	–	9,100	14,370
1955	4,820	–	–	–	13,400est	14,680
1960	7,160	–	1,980	200	18,840	14,900
1965	10,980	5,380	3,120	500	20,000	15,220
1970	15,500	7,850	4,470	1,320	27,620	17,110
1975	23,340	15,880	5,700	2,550	37,400	26,760
1980	53,750	55,790	7,460	4,250	88,740	76,080
1985	131,360	168,060	17,390	19,610	230,900	138,420
1990	234,400	302,710	20,340	44,070	415,440	121,180
1995	499,650	508,580	44,140	107,100	849,370	292,060

TAKEOVER BIDS, 1957–98

The following tables list a selection of takeover bids of quoted British companies, which show the sequential growth in the value of bids. For comparative purposes, the column on the far right shows the value of the original bids in real terms when adjusted for inflation to year-end 1997 prices. The three tables show the successful bids; aggregate value of agreed mergers and bids that either failed, lapsed or were withdrawn.

The values ascribed to takeover bids often vary in the detail, particularly where the consideration is made up of the issue of shares with fluctuating values, or where the bidding company already owns shares in the target company.

Successful takeover bids of UK companies

Date	Bidder and target	Value (£m)	1997 (£m)
April 1957	Courtaulds – British Celanese	20	265
December 1958	Tube Investments – British Aluminium	38	490
November 1960	Ford – (46%) Ford Motors UK	129	1,650
December 1960	Royal Insurance – London & Lancashire	51	645
November 1965	British Shoe Corp – Lewis's Investment Trust	57	610
August 1966	Rolls-Royce – Bristol Aeroplane Co.	63	650
November 1967	General Electric – Associated Electrical	160	1,610
September 1968	General Electric – English Electric	310	2,980
June 1972	Grand Metropolitan Hotels – Watney Mann	405	3,000
July 1980	BP – Selection Trust	410	970
May 1983	BTR – Thomas Tilling	655	1,240
December 1983	BAT – Eagle Star	968	1,780
April 1986	Hanson Trust – Imperial Group	2,660	4,360
April 1986	Guinness – Distillers	2,500	4,100
January 1988	BP – Britoil	2,500	3,870
June 1988	Nestlé – Rowntree	2,550	3,830
June 1989	Hanson Trust – Consolidated Gold Fields	3,200	4,430
March 1992	Hongkong & Shanghai Bank – Midland Bank	3,700	4,330
January 1995	Glaxo – Wellcome	9,150	10,030
October 1995	Lloyds Bank – TSB	6,075	6,490
May 1997	Grand Metropolitan – Guinness	9,760	9,950

Agreed Mergers

Date	Companies	Value (£m)	1997 (£m)
November 1951	Austin – Morris	35	590
May 1961	Bass Ratcliff – Mitchell & Butlers	90	1,125
July 1967	Bass – Charrington United	200	2,030
January 1968	British Motor – Leyland	400	3,980
November 1985	Habitat – British Home Stores	1,520	2,535
May 1989	Smith Kline – Beecham	4,700	6,540

Failed, lapsed or withdrawn takeover bids

Date	Bidder and target	Value (£m)	1997 (£m)
May 1959	J. Sears – Watney Mann	27	350
February 1961	City Centre – City of London Real Property	64	745
January 1962	ICI – Courtaulds	200	2,420
June 1963	BP/Shell – Burmah Oil	290	3,380
February 1965	Barclays – Lloyds – Martins (merger value)	530	5,250
November 1968	Unilever – Allied Breweries (merger value)	610	5,830
January 1972	Beecham – Glaxo	380	2,900
January 1972	Boots – Glaxo	380	2,900
May 1972	Rank Organisation – Watney Mann	430	3,200
April 1981	Hongkong & Shanghai Bank – Royal Bank of Scotland	500	1,080
April 1981	Standard Chartered – Royal Bank of Scotland	500	1,080
June 1984	Thorn EMI – British Aerospace	810	1,460
October 1985	Elders IXL – Allied Lyons	1,800	3,010
June 1986	Dixons – Woolworth Holdings	1,820	2,980
December 1987	Barker & Dobson – Dee Corporation	1,980	3,070
August 1989	Hoylake – BAT Industries	13,400	18,500

EQUITY RIGHTS ISSUES AND FIXED INTEREST ISSUES.

The following tables show the rising sequential value of equity rights issues and fixed interest issues. The fourth column shows the original values in real terms adjusted to year-end 1997 prices.

Rights issues

Date	Company	Amount (£m)	1997 (£m)
July 1948	ICI	20	410
January 1952	ICI	20	335
January 1958	Shell	45	590
January 1966	BP	60	635
September 1971	BP	120	935
May 1976	ICI	204	830
June 1981	BP	624	1,330
April 1985	Barclays Bank	513	865
June 1985	Hanson Trust	519	870
June 1986	NatWest Bank	724	1,180
September 1987	Blue Arrow	837	1,310
April 1988	Barclays Bank	924	1,400
November 1990	Eurotunnel	947	1,165
June 1993	Zeneca	1,350	1,530

Fixed interest issues

Date	Company	Amount (£m)	1997 (£m)
July 1946	Dunlop 3½% debenture	6	130
August 1950	Unilever 3¾% debenture	10	190
October 1950	Imperial Tobacco 4% debenture	20	380
February 1954	ICI 4½% unsecured loan	30	470
November 1956	ICI 5½% convertible	40	550
December 1957	BP 6% convertible	41	540
August 1965	ICI 7¼% unsecured loan	50	535
September 1966	ICI 8% unsecured loan	60	620
September 1980	RTZ convertible	123	285
May 1985	Woolworth convertible ULS	146	245
May 1988	Tate & Lyle convertible Red Pref.	215	325
October 1988	Grand Metropolitan convertible ULS	492	720
March 1992	Thorn EMI convertible ULS	529	620
November 1992	Tomkins convertible ULS	672	770
September 1995	North West Water convertible ULS	849	900

HIGHEST ONE-DAY PERCENTAGE MOVEMENTS

(FT 30 Index to 1962, All Share Index from 1963)

Date	%
24 January 1975	+ 9.36
10 February 1975	+ 8.60
30 January 1975	+ 7.20
4 July 1975	+ 6.24
27 January 1975	+ 6.10
9 October 1959	+ 5.99
30 May 1962	+ 5.86
10 April 1992	+ 5.86
21 October 1987	+ 5.83
29 January 1975	+ 5.53
20 October 1987	− 11.41
19 October 1987	− 9.69
1 March 1974	− 7.28
26 October 1987	− 7.16
29 May 1962	− 6.44
2 January 1975	− 6.41
11 March 1975	− 6.07
6 December 1973	− 5.49
14 December 1973	− 5.39
22 October 1987	− 5.36

INDEX

....